FOURTH EDITION

ACCOUNTING AND INFORMATION SYSTEMS

John Page
Tulane University

Paul Hooper
University of Delaware

D1625459

Prentice-Hall International, Inc.

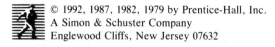 © 1992, 1987, 1982, 1979 by Prentice-Hall, Inc.
A Simon & Schuster Company
Englewood Cliffs, New Jersey 07632

Materials from the Certificate in Management Accounting Examinations, copyright © 1973, 1974, 1975,
1976, 1977, 1978, 1979, 1980, 1982, 1985, 1986, 1987, 1988, 1989, 1990 by the Institute of Management
Accountants are reprinted and/or adapted with permission.

Materials from the Uniform CPA Examination Questions and Unofficial Answers, copyright © 1963,
1964, 1965, 1971, 1972, 1975, 1976, 1978, 1979, 1980, 1981, 1982 by the American Institute of Certified
Public Accountants, Inc., are adapted with permission.

Materials from the Certified Internal Auditor Examinations and Unofficial Answers, copyright © 1976,
1978, 1979, 1982, 1987, 1988, 1989, 1990 by the Institute of Internal Auditors are adapted with
permission.

Printed in the United States of America

10 9 8 7 6 5 4 3 2

ISBN 0-13-006313-4

Prentice-Hall International (UK) Limited, *London*
Prentice-Hall of Australia Pty. Limited, *Sydney*
Prentice-Hall Canada Inc., *Toronto*
Prentice-Hall Hispanoamericana, S.A., *Mexico*
Prentice-Hall of India Private Limited, *New Delhi*
Prentice-Hall of Japan, Inc., *Tokyo*
Simon & Schuster Asia Pte. Ltd., *Singapore*
Editora Prentice-Hall do Brasil, Ltda., *Rio de Janeiro*
Prentice-Hall, Inc., *Englewood Cliffs, New Jersey*

Dedication

*To Maria, James, and David
Pam, Lisa, and Jody*

Acknowledgment

*We wish to thank Gail Lynn Cook for her special
contributions to the preparation of this book.*

Contents

6 Relational Data Bases and the Structured Query Language   186

7 Data Communications and Networks   220

8 Decision Support Systems and Expert Systems   255

Preface

The application of information systems concepts to the accounting process and accounting models is relatively new. However, because of the increasing applications of information systems and computers, these areas have become an essential part of the business curriculum.

Courses in accounting information systems now exist in virtually every business school. Most textbooks written for these courses fall into one of two categories. Books attempting to survey the field are usually so general that the student does not learn how to implement the ideas presented, while books that claim a comprehensive coverage require a technical sophistication beyond the background, interests, and needs of most users. Also, without a firm foothold in basic accounting concepts, books on information systems can serve to isolate accounting information systems from other accounting courses.

Our approach is to integrate information systems concepts into the basic accounting process and extend traditional accounting models to include the systems approach. This integration and extension provides the link that students search for in relating their work in this area to other accounting studies. Without this link, it is difficult for students to appreciate where accounting systems fit into the big picture of accounting study and practice. Our integrative approach works not only for accounting students, but also for business, computer science, and engineering students who are interested in systems work and management consulting but have had only an introductory exposure to accounting.

Overview of the Fourth Edition

The fourth edition of this book offers balanced coverage of technical aspects, computer applications, and systems development. This organization encourages the instructor to decide where to place the emphasis.

Part One establishes the accounting context for the study of information systems. Information systems concepts are introduced only after the student is firmly grounded in the components of accounting systems. Individual chapters discuss the role of accounting, the basic business cycles and documents, system flowcharting, internal control fundamentals, and the additional internal control needed for computer-based business data processing. Such a background is fundamental to understanding and applying the ideas that follow in the text.

Part Two discusses the most important aspects of computer, information system, and communication technology that form the basis for today's and tomorrow's accounting information systems. Individual chapters discuss data files and data bases, relational data bases and structured query language, data communication and networks, and decision support and expert systems.

Part Three synthesizes the concepts of accounting systems and information systems in a computer context. An overview chapter surveys computer-based accounting information systems. Individual chapters discuss the major components of a typical system, including the manufacturing environment. A chapter on microcomputer-based systems applies the large system concepts of the preceding chapters to the personal computer.

Part Four illustrates the system development life cycle by applying system analysis tools to the development of computer-based information systems. Individual chapters provide an overview of system development and a detailed treatment of system analysis and design, system implementation and evaluation, and EDP auditing.

Of special use to the beginning student are two appendices that review the fundamental concepts and relationships underlying financial statements and the processing of accounting transactions. A third appendix presents a sample company with comprehensive supporting documents and demonstrates the application of many of the principles explained throughout this book with a complete system analysis and system development for the company.

New Features of the Fourth Edition

The fourth edition is a major revision that adds important new topics, brings all material completely up to date, and treats many topics in greater depth, while continuing the accounting-based approach of the previous three editions. The new features include:

1. *Compact treatment of introductory material.* Most of the material appearing in Chapters 1 through 8 of the third edition is now presented in the first five chapters of the fourth edition. This allows movement into the core systems material more quickly and facilitates further, in-depth treatment of important topics, particularly relational data bases, the Structured Query Language, data communications and networking, decision support systems, and expert systems.

2. *Incorporation of microcomputer-based systems throughout the book.* Topics covered include connections with a mainframe system, internal control, data base management systems, data communications and networking, decision support systems, accounting information system applications, and system development. This coverage is important because students are likely to use mostly microcomputers during their professional lives.

3. *A new chapter on relational data base management systems (RDBMS) and the Structured Query Language (SQL).* Data of all kinds, including accounting data, are increasingly stored in RDBMS because of the power and flexibility such a system provides. SQL is often used to access these data, both for interactive queries and to draw the data into spreadsheets for further analysis. Eventually, all accountants will become familiar with both RDBMS and SQL. Chapter 6 covers RDBMS operations, data normalization, trends in relational systems, SQL, and Query-by-Example.

4. *A new chapter on data communications and networking.* Accounting data are now being used far from the point where they are accumulated and accounting transactions depend on access to data bases stored far from where the transactions are originated. Data communications and networking are critical components of virtually all new accounting information systems. Chapter 7 includes mainframe, minicomputer, and microcomputer approaches to, and current trends in, data communication and networking.

5. *A new chapter on decision support systems and expert systems.* Decision support systems and, to a lesser extent, expert systems have become important tools for accountants. Chapter 8 contains a discussion of the most important end-user tools, including spreadsheets. These tools allow users to analyze accounting data without having to write special-purpose computer programs. It is these end-user tools that have driven much of the demand for microcomputers.

6. *Overview of computer-based accounting information systems.* Chapter 9 has been reworked to preview the detailed coverage of cash receipts and disbursements, sales and purchases, financial accounting, manufacturing, and microcomputer systems presented in Chapters 10 through 13. This overview chapter can be covered independently of the detailed chapters that follow in Part Three.

7. *Applications update to the IBM AS/400.* Applications Chapters 10, 11, and 12 use the new AS/400 system in place of the System/38 used in the third edition. The AS/400 has been the most successful new system for IBM since the System/360 of the early 1960s.

8. *A new applications chapter on financial and manufacturing information systems.* In recognition of a new awareness of the importance of manufacturing management in the economy, Chapter 12 incorporates manufacturing accounting applications. The treatment of manufacturing is also integrated into the applications overview in Chapter 9 together with the other components of the accounting information system.

9. *A new software package.* Bedford Integrated Accounting is used in Chapter 13 on microcomputer applications to provide an extended treatment of microcomputer-based accounting information systems. Bedford is widely available and well-suited for student and university use. Unlike most accounting packages, Bedford will create a company's data on a floppy disk—an important and convenient feature for the typical university computer laboratory.

10. *Overview of system development.* A new Chapter 14 surveys the role and value of information systems, the management of information systems, and the role of system development. This overview can be covered independently of the detailed chapters on system development that follow in Part Four.

11. *Extended treatment of data flow diagrams and entity-relationship models.* Chapter 15 on system analysis and design presents these important tools for conceptualizing new systems without the necessity for the detail of a complete system flowchart.

12. *Condensed and integrated presentation of system development.* System development material covered in three chapters in the third edition is now covered in Chapters 15 and 16 of the fourth edition.

13. *A new appendix on financial statements.* Appendix A allows optional coverage and review of basic financial statement relationships. The need for this review

usually depends on the placement of the course in the curriculum and the background of the students.

14. *A new appendix presenting a complete basic systems case.* Appendix C can be treated as a chapter (with all necessary end-of-chapter material provided) or used as a reference source, either throughout the course or in conjunction with a term project outside of class. This appendix simulates the reports and correspondence that an analyst would prepare in a system analysis and system development.

15. *Extensive new end-of-chapter problem and case material.* Complete and thoroughly tested solutions to all end-of-chapter material are available in the *Instructor's Manual With Solutions.*

Supplements to the Fourth Edition

- Greatly expanded *Instructor's Manual With Solutions.* This includes suggestions for several alternative paths through the book (each with an appropriate sample syllabus) and transparency masters for coverage of the material in class. Solutions to all end-of-chapter material are also presented. In addition, the Monticello case from the third edition has been moved to the *Instructor's Manual With Solutions* for optional use.

- A new *Test Bank.* The fourth edition *Test Bank* contains both objective and problem material for instructor use.

- *Study Guide.* New with this edition of the text, the *Study Guide,* by Gail L. Cook, contains comprehensive review outlines and self-tests for each chapter with fully explained answers providing immediate student feedback and reinforcement.

- *Paradox®: A Student Tutorial with Cases.* Offered for the first time with this edition of the text, this self-paced tutorial by Eric L. Denna, Michael P. Briggs, and Jeff G. Gibbs teaches full utilization of the number-one rated relational data base management software.

Acknowledgments

This edition has benefited from the many suggestions of reviewers and users of previous editions from around the country, especially Robert Cooper, Keith Martin, Ross Quarles, Anwar Salimi, and Steve Sutton. Critical to the development of this fourth edition has been the work of Gail Lynn Cook. Gail was instrumental in making this edition a significant advance over earlier editions and we are proud to acknowledge her contributions. Also important in the development of this edition were the efforts and talents of Susan Seuling, our Prentice Hall development editor, whose ever-present interest and suggestions had a remarkably positive impact on the book. Finally, special recognition is given to Brian Hatch, our production editor, for his work on this edition; Joe Heider, our acquisition editor; and Frederic Easter, whose experience, guidance, and wisdom helped to turn a set of ideas into a book fifteen years ago.

The authors sincerely welcome comments, suggestions, and tactfully-stated criticisms from the users of this edition and from others who may come into contact with the book.

John Page
New Orleans, Louisiana

Paul Hooper
Newark, Delaware

1 The Accounting System

Overview

Accounting systems and how they relate to the cycles of a business.

Learning Objectives

Thorough study of this chapter will enable you to:

1. Distinguish among transaction processing systems, accounting information systems, management information systems, and computer information systems.
2. Explain why the basic business cycles are the foundation of accounting information systems, and describe each cycle.
3. Describe the functions of the business documents associated with each business cycle.
4. Create an organization chart.
5. Create a system flowchart for each of the basic business cycles.
6. Create a document flowchart for each of the basic business cycles.

Outline

2

Part I
Overview
of Systems
and
Internal
Control

SYSTEMS IN THE REAL WORLD

Uncle Sam's House Sale

We doubt that we can add much to what any rational person would think of the accompanying flow-chart/organization chart. It was provided by the Resolution Trust Corporation, and depicts what it calls the functional relationships among the entities involved in trying to sell the savings-and-loan assets now held by the federal government.

We notice that for the box labeled "Congress," all the lines are flowing in and none are flowing out. Perhaps what this chart is telling us is that Congress is now a black hole from which nothing in America will ever escape.

The S&L Maze

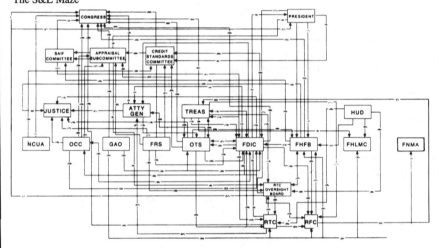

Placement of entities above is not intended to connote relative hierarchy.

Source: *The Wall Street Journal*, Editorial, February 23, 1990.

RELATIONSHIP BETWEEN ACCOUNTING AND INFORMATION SYSTEMS

Accounting is a system for keeping track of the financial events of an organization so that the organization may report its financial activities to any interested parties. From your previous studies in accounting, you will remember that

1. Accounting is concerned with financial events only. This means that the accounting system does not provide all possible information about a business. Information that is not financial in nature, such as the personal qualities of man-

agement, is not reported by accounting and, therefore, must be secured from some other source.

2. Accounting is used not only by businesses but also by individuals and such organizations as governments, hospitals, churches, and universities, which are not businesses in a profit-making sense. Even though the approach to accounting is different in not-for-profit organizations, accounting is, nonetheless, necessary.

3. Even the smallest business has interested parties who are entitled to information on the activities of the business. Interested parties include owners, creditors, governmental taxation and regulatory agencies, and company management. Businesses supply the required information to interested parties by issuing financial statements based on the accounting records.

4. Company management makes the strongest demands on the accounting system because this group must direct the progress of the business. While the accounting system must supply information to interested parties outside the business, it must also supply information to management for decision making, planning, and control of the business.

Although each business is likely to have only one accounting system, the tools, techniques, and output of accounting can be conveniently thought of as falling into one of two categories: financial accounting and managerial accounting. These areas are usually studied separately, although in practice the systems and procedures are seldom completely separate.

Overview of Financial Accounting

Financial accounting supplies information about an organization to outside individuals and groups. Major corporations such as General Motors, Exxon, and IBM have many interested parties outside the business keenly interested in their financial activity. These outsiders include the Securities and Exchange Commission, Internal Revenue Service, creditors such as banks, and the corporate owners (stockholders) themselves. In large corporations, the owners can be viewed as outsiders because they have no direct voice in the day-to-day activities of the business and do not directly participate in business decisions. Even in a small business, however, there is likely to be at least one external group, the IRS, demanding financial information. As a result, some financial accounting activity is carried on by all businesses.

The audiences served by financial accounting are generally outside the management group of the business. These outsiders use the information but do not prepare it. The information that results from financial accounting activity is prepared by the management group, the very group whose successes and failures are documented in the financial accounting reports. This is why outside parties usually want to be assured that the information they receive is objective (that is, fairly depicts what actually happened) and is consistently presented. As a result, **Generally Accepted Accounting Principles** (GAAP) were developed for collecting and reporting financial information to external users. Companies engage certified public accountants (CPAs) to determine and certify that these principles have been fairly and consistently applied in reporting the financial activity of the organization.

Financial accounting operates from an historical perspective. It focuses on the immediate past activities of an organization in order to record and report

4

*PART I
Overview
of Systems
and
Internal
Control*

to outsiders what has happened to that organization since the last financial information was presented to them. Financial accounting reports information on the past and leaves any prediction of the future to the users of the information.

Overview of Managerial Accounting

Managerial accounting supplies the information needs of the management group concerned with decision making and performance evaluation within an organization. Because managerial accounting must meet the needs of only this one group, the reports that result from this process may be tailored specifically to the purposes of that group. In contrast, the reports resulting from financial accounting activity must be of a general nature because many diverse groups use the reports for different purposes.

GAAP are less significant in managerial accounting because management prepares its own information on demand, and externally imposed objectivity

CONCEPT SUMMARY		
The Accounting System		
Overview of the Financial Accounting System		
Purpose	*Output*	*Content*
To provide financial information to individuals, organizations, and governmental agencies outside of the business	Income statement	Revenues − expenses = income
	Balance sheet	Assets = liabilities + capital stock + retained earnings
	Statement of cash flows	Cash inflows and outflows from operations, investment, and financing = net change in cash
Overview of the Managerial Accounting System		
Purpose	*Uses*	*Tools and Techniques*
To provide financial information to company management, ranging from the board of directors and president to supervisors and foremen	Planning and decision making	Cost/volume/profit analysis Differential (incremental) analysis Capital budgeting Budgeting and reporting
	Performance evaluation	Cost accounting systems Standard costs and variances Variable (direct) costing Budgeting and reporting

Characteristics	Financial Accounting	Managerial Accounting
Users	Interested parties outside of management, such as governmental agencies, creditors, and stockholders.	Management groups.
Purpose	To provide information on the past performance of the business.	To provide information that will help managers make decisions, plan for the future, and control the organization's activities.
Guidelines	Generally Accepted Accounting Principles (GAAP), are followed to ensure objectivity and consistency in the financial information transmitted to outsiders.	GAAP are not an important consideration because the information users are also the preparers of the information. Cost versus benefits provides the most significant guidelines in the production of information.
Orientation	Historical. Financial accounting reports what has happened in the immediate past (since the last report) so that outsiders will know what has occurred and can use this information to evaluate the organization's activities and progress.	Future. Management anticipates and predicts the future in order to effectively direct the activities of the organization using information on what is likely to occur in the immediate and distant future.

and consistency are not necessary. The cost of producing information versus the benefits to be obtained by company management from the use of the information provides the guidelines for management reporting.

Managerial accounting is future oriented. Management must be able to plan, make decisions, and then see to it that the decisions are carried out. All these activities require information that helps to anticipate and predict future circumstances. Managerial accounting activity requires past financial information only to the extent that this information is useful in anticipating the future. Prediction is central to the managerial accounting process.

Together, financial and managerial accounting make up an organization's accounting system. Exhibit 1-1 compares these two areas of activity.

Transaction Processing Systems and Information Systems

The function of a **transaction processing accounting system** is to record transactions and report on the operating activities and financial condition of the business. The function of an accounting **information system** is to track the flow

6

PART I
Overview
of Systems
and
Internal
Control

of all accounting-related information (transactions plus nontransactions), and make that information available to those needing it. Sales and purchases represent two of the most important and recurring types of transactions engaged in by most businesses. Exhibit 1-2 presents the flow of sales and purchases transaction data through an accounting information system.

The following important points about this information flow should be gleaned from this diagram:

Transaction Flow. The arrows pointing left to right in Exhibit 1-2 indicate the flow of accounting transaction data. This flow is toward the general ledger, which is the repository for accounting events.

Detail to Summary. Sales and purchases transactions enter the system in the order processing and inventory management areas, respectively, where substantial detail about each of these events is needed in order to process them. As sales and purchase data are passed to the receivables and payables areas, some of these details are summarized because these applications require only total information for each customer and vendor to carry out their processing. As these sales and purchase data are then passed to the general ledger, they are further summarized since breakdowns of this information even by customer

EXHIBIT 1-2   Accounting Transactions and Information Flow

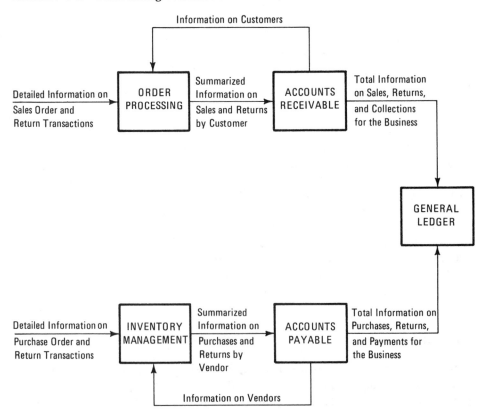

or vendor are not needed for general ledger purposes. Only company totals for these transactions are necessary for general ledger recordkeeping and financial statement reporting.

Audit Trail. As accounting transactions travel through an information system from their point of entry into the system toward the general ledger, they are summarized by each processing and unneeded detail is dropped. Financial statements, then, represent the most summarized information available from the system, while **source documents** like orders for sales and purchases represent the most detailed and least summarized data available. A carefully designed system provides an **audit trail** forward from detail to summary and backward from summary to original detail.

Information Flow. The arrows pointing from right to left in the Exhibit 1-2 indicate the flow of information, but not the flow of accounting transactions. This availability and flow of nontransaction information, which is essentially created by the system, is the distinguishing feature of accounting information systems as compared to transaction processing systems.

Example of Flows in an Accounting Information System

Consider what happens when a company processes a sales order from a customer for several different items. Suppose Seward Auto Parts has an order from Sal's Garage for 3 mufflers, 24 oil filters, and 6 batteries. To process the order, Seward needs a good deal of detail on each of the individual items ordered (price, availability, location) and on the customer (credit rating, shipping address). However, to record the transaction in accounts receivable, all that is needed is the customer's name and the total amount of the sale. Extreme detail on each individual item in the sales order is not necessary for receivables to be processed and collections controlled. As a by-product of this receivables processing, however, credit information on this customer is generated and passed back through the system for future decision-making purposes. Even less detail is needed for general ledger and financial statement purposes. The amount sold to Sal's Garage is not necessary, but rather the total amount sold to all customers is required so that revenue can be reported on the income statement and accounts receivable can be reported on the balance sheet. This same kind of summary activity takes place as all accounting transactions are processed in the information system. At the same time, new nontransaction information, created and stored by the system as a by-product of the processing, becomes available for decision-making purposes.

Thus, when accounting-related information is added to a transaction processing system, an **accounting information system (AIS)** is created. When the accounting information system is coupled with the other information systems of a business (i.e., marketing, production, personnel), a **management information system (MIS)** is created. When an information system of any type (AIS, MIS) is computer based, it is frequently called a **computer information system (CIS).**

8

Part I
Overview
of Systems
and
Internal
Control

THE BASIC BUSINESS CYCLES

Although all businesses are unique, most engage primarily in four major kinds of activities:

1. Selling goods to customers
2. Purchasing goods from suppliers
3. Receiving cash
4. Disbursing cash

This section will review the basic ways that businesses accomplish each of these types of activities. The set of procedures for each activity is called a **business cycle.** A typical merchandising business will have a sales cycle, a purchases cycle, a cash receipts cycle, and a cash disbursement cycle. Service businesses may not engage in all of these cycles, and manufacturing businesses may have additional cycles.

The process of collecting accounting data for each of the business cycles has the same basic logic:

1. As business activity occurs, business documents are filled out; thus, the documents track the operations of the business.
2. These business documents then provide most of the raw data for the accounting system (the detail of this process is discussed in Appendix A and Appendix B).
3. These business documents also play a role in controlling operations (preventing and detecting errors and theft), as will be discussed in Chapter 2.

This section will first present the basic types of business documents that are necessary parts of each of the cycles of business activity and then discuss the cycles.

Business Documents

Most business activities are supported by some type of written evidence. This written evidence signals that a business event has occurred and provides the data for recording any accounting transactions that result. Whenever a business engages in such an activity, the record of that activity will take the form of a business document. Business documents, then, are the raw material of accounting systems, and all the data processed by accounting systems should be traceable to one or more of these documents. Most data entering the system come directly from business documents, and these documents are usually kept and stored as support for financial statement information. Although the form and design of individual documents can vary and any given business may handle many different documents, five types are common and support most business activity. These are the sales slip, credit memorandum, purchase order, debit memorandum, and invoice.

Sales Slip. This document may take many forms, but all **sales slips** are created to verify sales transactions. The sales slip may simply be a copy of a cash register tape (in the case of a cash sale), it may be a credit slip for credit sales, or it may be a standard credit card form. Sales slips identify the goods being sold, give the quantity and price of the goods, and supply information about the customer to whom the sale is made. The salesperson will also usually be identified on a sales slip so that commissions on sales can be calculated and other information gathered.

Like most business documents, the sales slip has several copies. The original may be kept by the seller and sent to accounting, a copy would necessarily go to the customer as a receipt, and the salesperson may retain a copy to verify commission calculations. The type and amount of detailed information on a sales slip can vary with the size of the business, the type of sale being made, and the information needs of the business.

Credit Memorandum. If a customer returns goods bought on credit, the amount owed by the customer to the business is decreased. The business prepares a document verifying that the goods have been returned and that the amount owed by the customer should be reduced. This document, the **credit memorandum,** also serves as the customer's verification that the bill should reflect the return of these goods. The credit memo is so named because it results in a credit to accounts receivable by the business preparing the document and receiving the returned goods.

Purchase Order. Most businesses prepare a **purchase order** as a formal offer to purchase inventory or other materials from a supplier. This document is an order for goods or supplies from a specific vendor under specifically requested terms. Purchase orders provide evidence as to what was ordered, who was responsible for the order, and desired terms. The original of the document may go to the supplier, with copies going to the person ordering the goods, the accounting system, and the group that will receive the goods when they are delivered. Additional copies may be prepared and forwarded to others as well.

Although the purchase order indicates that an important event has occurred, the event is only an offer to purchase goods. Until the offer is accepted by a supplier and title to the goods is passed from seller to buyer, no accounting transaction has taken place.

Debit Memorandum. When goods purchased on credit are not suitable and are returned to the supplier, the amount owed to the supplier by the business is decreased. The business prepares a document that authorizes and explains the appropriate decrease in its accounts payable. This document also provides notification to the supplier that goods are being returned and that the amount owed is being reduced by the purchase cost of the returned goods. The **debit memorandum** does these things, and is so named because it results in a debit to accounts payable by the business preparing the document and returning the goods.

The debit memo is usually a multicopy document, with the original serving as notification to the supplier, a copy staying with the goods to be returned, and a copy going to the accounting system. The information on a typical debit memo includes the original purchase order number so that the returned goods can be traced to the original order and the signature of the person returning the goods.

10

PART I
Overview
of Systems
and
Internal
Control

Invoice. This document is simply a billing statement for goods purchased or sold on credit. Businesses receive **invoices** from suppliers of goods for amounts owed to them and send invoices to customers for amounts owed to the business by customers. Invoices notify the purchaser of the terms of the purchase, the total amount owed, and the due date and trigger the inflow or outflow of cash for a business. When returned with payment, invoices also help the seller to record the buyer's payment correctly in the accounting system. Invoices vary considerably in the type and amount of information they contain, as well as in the format in which the information is presented.

Sales Cycle

Since every business is unique, it is impossible to go through all cycles for all types of businesses. However, it is possible to go through the basic cycles for a typical business, and this knowledge can be adapted to the differences found in other firms. This discussion will assume the use of a manual accounting system in order to concentrate on understanding the basic business activities involved. The text will later (beginning with Chapter 3) shift focus to computer-based systems.

The sale of goods for cash or credit is often the most frequent event for any merchandising business. Sales reflect the continuing operations of the business and are the major source of revenues. A **sales cycle** begins with a customer order, which is either mailed to or obtained by telephone in the sales order department. The sales order department typically prepares a multipart copy of an invoice. One copy of the invoice goes to the credit department for approval of credit terms. The credit department then accepts or rejects (perhaps for poor credit or other reasons) this customer request for goods.

Once credit is approved and an order is accepted, the company must make the appropriate arrangements to ship the goods to the customer. This is accomplished by distributing copies of the invoice to those who require them:

1. The billing department, to let them know that a customer billing is imminent.
2. The shipping department, to let them know that a shipment is imminent.
3. The warehouse, as a request to issue the goods.

Another copy goes to the customer to confirm the order. The sales order department thus originates the invoice, but does not have custody or control of the goods and does not record the transaction.

The warehouse releases the goods upon receipt of the stock request copy of the invoice. Thus, the goods leave only after the warehouse receives an appropriate request. The goods go with the stock request copy to shipping, where the stock request is matched with the copy of the invoice received earlier. The invoice copy then doubles as a packing slip, which accompanies the shipment to describe its contents. The goods then go to the customer with the packing slip included. The stock request copy goes to the billing department to indicate that the goods have been shipped and it is now time to bill the customer.

Only after the goods are shipped is the customer billed for the goods. The billing department matches the copies of the invoice received earlier with the stock request copy, checks the prices and extensions (individual quantities multiplied by price), and completes the invoice. The invoice copies in the billing department thus act as a control on orders that have not yet been shipped. One copy of the completed invoice goes to the customer as a bill, and the stock request copy is filed permanently by customer name. Daily, the billing department runs a calculator tape of all invoices and sends it to accounting for entry in the sales control account and the accounts receivable control account.

Another copy of the invoice goes from the billing department to the accounts receivable department, where it is posted to the accounts receivable subsidiary ledger on a daily basis. Accounts receivable prepares monthly statements of account, which are sent to the customers, that incorporate the invoices, the credit memos, and other paperwork generated in the cash receipts cycle.

Purchases Cycle

The **purchases cycle** deals with events related to buying goods from suppliers (often called vendors), since most businesses purchase at least some goods from other companies. The cycle begins when either a user or a purchasing department recognizes a need for goods and places an order with a supplier. The purchasing group prepares a three-part purchase order and sends the first two copies to the vendor. The vendor acknowledges the order by returning a copy of the purchase order, perhaps with a notation that the order is being processed and some indication of when it might be shipped. This returned copy is kept by the purchasing group, and the other copy is sent to the accounts payable department as notification that a payment will be made in the near future.

Next, the vendor must ship the goods. The vendor sends the goods accompanied by a packing slip to the business' receiving department and, at the same time, sends a two-part invoice to the purchasing group. The receiving department verifies the goods received and the accuracy of the packing slip and forwards it to the accounts payable department. The purchasing group determines that the invoice accurately reflects the order and sends the received invoice to the accounts payable department, which compares it to the verified packing slip. Thus, receiving and purchasing are kept separate and each provides a check on the other.

Accounts payable compares the information on the invoice to the information on the verified packing slip and the information on the original purchase order, checks the extensions and totals, and approves the invoice for payment either by initialing or signing it. Accounts payable then records the purchase in the purchases journal and sends the purchase order, verified packing slip, and approved invoice to the cash disbursements clerk, who initiates the payment of the invoice. Each week, accounts payable posts from the purchases journal to the accounts payable subsidiary ledger. Each month, the accounts payable clerk prepares summary total information on purchases, which goes to the general ledger for entry to control accounts.

12

Part I
Overview
of Systems
and
Internal
Control

Cash Disbursements Cycle

Cash disbursements result primarily from the payments for goods purchased; these payments may occur either immediately at the time of purchase or after a specified period of time. Cash outflows also occur as payment for services rendered, such as employee wages, rent of assets, or other items necessary to the continued operation of the business. Thus, the **cash disbursements cycle** is initiated as a result of some other documented business activity.

In most cases, the cash disbursements group receives the supporting documents from accounts payable and prepares checks, which are sent to and signed by the secretary-treasurer (or other appropriate company official). This official then cancels the supporting documents by marking them paid and signs the check. Canceling the supporting documents prevents them from being submitted for payment more than once. The check is sent directly to the vendor. The supporting documents are sent by the signing official back to the cash disbursements group, which uses the information to record each check in the cash disbursements journal. The supporting documents are filed permanently by date. On a weekly basis, the information in the cash disbursements journal is posted to the accounts payable subsidiary ledger. Monthly, the cash disbursements group prepares summary total information on cash disbursements, which is sent to the general ledger group for control account updating.

Cash Receipts Cycle

The **cash receipts cycle** usually begins with sales, either cash sales or the collection of accounts receivable, although it may also arise from other business activities, such as bank loans or sales of assets.

When the customer mails in a check, it is received by the mailroom. Some customer checks will come with a remittance advice (often, the detachable portion at the top or bottom of a customer statement); if so, the remittance advice is detached by the mailroom. If payment is sent without a remittance advice, the mailroom usually prepares one. The remittance advice is sent to accounts receivable for posting to the accounts receivable subsidiary ledger. The check itself goes to cash receipts, which records the transaction in the cash receipts journal and prepares two copies of a deposit slip. One copy is kept to keep track of deposits in transit, and the check and a copy of the deposit slip go to the bank. A total of all cash receipts goes to general ledger to post the control accounts. After the bank processes the deposit, it returns a copy of the deposit slip to cash receipts, where it is filed by date.

After a sale, the customer will sometimes return goods. When the returned goods arrive, receiving prepares a sales return receiving slip. This slip goes to the credit department, which approves sales returns. The sales return receiving slip then goes to the billing department, which prepares a three-part credit memo. One copy of the credit memo goes to the customer, and one to accounts receivable, where it is posted (credited) to the accounts receivable subsidiary ledger. The third copy is filed in billing by credit memo number to provide physical control over credit memos; any missing credit memos should be apparent from the gap in the number sequence. On a daily basis, the total of all credit memos goes to general ledger for recording in the control accounts.

Thus, accounts receivable gets (1) a copy of each invoice from billing, (2) the remittance advices from the mailroom, and (3) a copy of each credit memo from billing—all of which are posted to the accounts receivable subsidiary ledger. On a monthly basis, accounts receivable prepares statements of account that are sent to customers.

As an additional control over cash receipts, the bank statement may be sent directly to the controller or other responsible company official. The official compares the information on the bank statement to that contained in the cash receipts journal, cash disbursements journal, and general ledger. When these records are reconciled, the bank statement can be filed permanently by date.

FLOWCHARTING THE BUSINESS CYCLES

The business cycles described in the preceding section are representative of a moderately sized merchandising business. Procedures will typically become even more complex in a larger business or a manufacturing firm. As a result, there is a need to organize and present complicated business cycle activities in a comprehensible way. The most widely used method for accomplishing this task is the system flowchart.

A **system flowchart** is a diagram depicting the procedures and document flows of a system—a picture of how the system actually works. A computerized system may also have program flowcharts, which are flowcharts of the steps of individual computer programs, as well as system flowcharts, which are the flowcharts of the entire system (including manual processing steps and document flows.)

All flowcharts should be developed in as standard a way as possible for three reasons:

1. Every person drawing a flowchart should not have to create a new method.
2. Different flowcharts developed by different people should be roughly comparable.
3. If a person can understand one flowchart, that person should be able to understand all flowcharts.

Standard Flowchart Symbols

This section will introduce 13 standard flowchart symbols and illustrate their application in a simplified sales system. The next section will apply this material to the business cycles discussed earlier. Exhibit 1-3 presents the standard flowchart symbols.

The simplified sales system begins with the customer, who sends in a written order. The sales department takes the order, prepares a six-part invoice, and files the order by customer name. The invoice set then goes to the credit department for a credit check comparing the customer's present balance and proposed sale with his credit limit and history. If the credit is rejected, the customer is informed, the invoice is filed by customer name, and the processing is completed. If the credit is approved, the six copies of the invoice are distributed this way: the first copy goes to the customer as a bill, the second is

14

Part I
Overview
of Systems
and
Internal
Control

EXHIBIT 1-3   Standard Flowchart Symbols

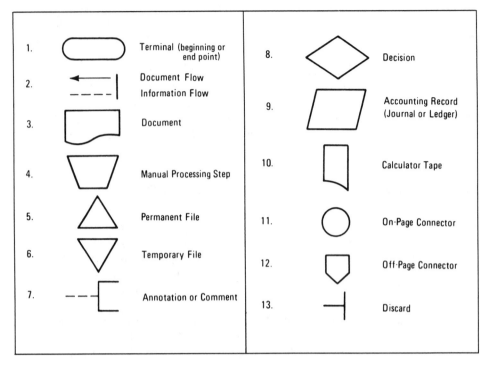

filed by invoice number, the third is filed by customer name, the fourth goes with the goods as a packing slip, the fifth is filed by billing date, and the sixth goes to the customer as an acknowledgment of the order. Although many possible additional steps of an actual sales system have been omitted here, this simplified system will serve to illustrate standard flowchart symbols and concepts. This system is flowcharted in Exhibit 1-4.

Terminal. The first symbol is the oval, which stands for a **terminal** in the system—either a beginning or an end. The terminal generally shows something coming from outside the system in or shows something going from inside the system out. If a sale begins with a customer, as it does in Exhibit 1-4, the flowchart begins at an oval labeled *customer.* In Exhibit 1-4, the beginning oval is at the top of the chart; a well-drawn flowchart reads from top to bottom.

Flow line. The second symbol is the **flow line.** The solid line indicates a document flow, and the broken line indicates an information flow without a document. If a person prepares a form or mails in a form, the flowchart would have the solid line. An example would be the customer who writes out an order. This is illustrated in Exhibit 1-4, with the order essentially flowing from the customer. The broken line shows which parts of the information flow are conducted orally.

Since English reads from top to bottom and left to right, a flowchart should flow in the same manner to make it as easy to read as possible. The

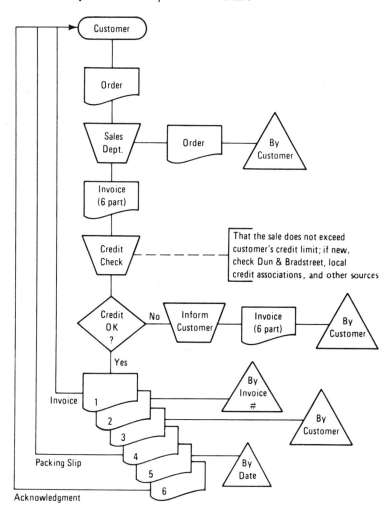

flow lines should also indicate the direction of the flow. However, an arrow is not always necessary to indicate direction, because the assumption is that, unless otherwise indicated, the flow lines go from top to bottom and left to right. Sometimes a flow must go the other way, and, in those cases, an arrow indicates the direction. Exhibit 1-4 illustrates several types of flows.

Document. The third symbol is the document—any document, form, or report used in the system. Exhibit 1-4 illustrates the use of this symbol in a number of ways. The first use illustrated is to show that the customer generates an order. Since this is a written order, the solid (document) flow line connects the terminal symbol representing the customer to the document symbol representing the order.

Manual processing. The fourth symbol represents a manual processing step. This symbol, a trapezoid, indicates any filling out of forms, adding up of

16

*PART I
Overview
of Systems
and
Internal
Control*

numbers, or other manual activity. In Exhibit 1-4, the customer order goes to the sales department, which prepares a six-part invoice. The next processing step is a credit check. Thus, the processing step box indicates the standard steps to be performed at any point in the system.

△ *Permanent file.* The fifth symbol, the triangle, stands for a **permanent file.** Exhibit 1-4 shows that after preparing the six-part invoice, the sales department still has the customer order, which then disappears into a permanent file. However, it is not enough just to know that something is filed; it is also necessary to know how the document is filed. The notation within the file triangle indicates that the order has been filed by customer.

▽ *Temporary file.* The sixth symbol is a downward-pointing triangle representing the **temporary file,** where documents reside only for an interim period or until a specific event occurs. The file itself may always exist, but if individual documents remain in the file only for a short period, it is a temporary file. For example, a file in the shipping department may contain a copy of an invoice that serves as a control on open (unfilled) orders that have not yet been shipped. The document will be removed from the file when the goods are shipped. Representing its transient nature, the temporary file triangle is on its point, whereas the permanent file triangle rests on its base.

--⊏ *Comment.* The seventh symbol represents the annotation or comment. This symbol is used to provide further explanation as necessary. For example, in Exhibit 1-4, the space within the symbol for the credit check is insufficient to explain the complete processing step. To provide a better explanation, the symbol for comment is used to provide further details.

◇ *Decision.* The eighth symbol is a diamond shape and represents a decision. This symbol is used for steps in the flowchart where alternative paths may be taken based on the result of some decision. An example appears in Exhibit 1-4, where the decision is whether or not to approve the customer's credit. There are two possible results (yes or no) and the processing path taken depends on the result. If the result is no, the customer is informed, the invoice is filed, and the system is complete. If the result is yes, the credit is approved, and the six parts of the invoice are then processed in designated ways.

▱ *Record.* The ninth symbol represents an accounting record, usually either a journal or a ledger. The accounting record has a symbol separate from other documents because it is not necessary to show the filing of an accounting record. The flowchart simply assumes that the accounting records exist as permanent documents in and of themselves. You will see this symbol used when you reach Exhibits 1-9 and 1-10. (Note: Worksheets and financial statements are not considered part of the formal accounting records and should be represented by the document symbol.)

⊔ *Tape.* The tenth symbol represents a calculator or adding machine tape. This symbol is used when compiling a total, for example, from a batch of sales slips. Exhibit 1-5 depicts the preparation of a tape of the accounts receivable

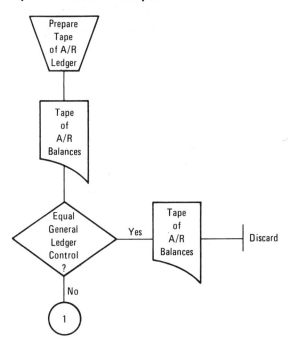

subsidiary ledger. The tape symbol is used in essentially the same way as the document symbol.

○ *On-page connector.* The eleventh symbol is a circle representing the **on-page connector.** It is sometimes impossible to connect all parts of a flowchart with flow lines without making the chart look like a maze. The on-page connector is keyed with a number that indicates the point where the flow is being interrupted. Another connector keyed with the same number indicates where the flow is being picked up again. Exhibit 1-5 shows the use of an on-page connector; another connector would be placed elsewhere on the page to continue the process of what happens when the tape total equals the general ledger control.

▽ *Off-page connector.* The twelfth symbol represents the **off-page connector.** Often, the flowcharts of different cycles are on different pages, and these cycles must ultimately be tied together. The off-page connector is used to show where and how the flowcharts fit together.

⊣ *Discard.* The thirteenth and last symbol is the discard symbol. Exhibit 1-5 shows how to indicate the discard of a tape after it is no longer required.

Information Flow and Document flow

The broken flow line represents information flow, rather than the document flow illustrated by a solid flow line. Exhibit 1-6 illustrates these concepts. The

18

PART I
Overview
of Systems
and
Internal
Control

EXHIBIT 1-6   Information Flow and Document Flow:
(a) Oral and (b) Written Requisitions

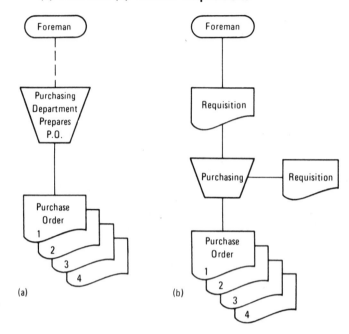

left side of the exhibit depicts an oral request by the foreman for some product or products. Upon receiving this oral request, the purchasing department prepares a four-part purchase order, and the system will continue from there. The right side depicts a written requisition prepared by the foreman and given to the purchasing department. Upon receiving this written request, the purchasing department prepares a four-part purchase order and continues the processing by filing or otherwise disposing of the requisition.

Business systems commonly use multipart forms or generate multiple copies of reports for the various company departments and other users. There are three basic ways to show this in a flowchart, as presented in Exhibit 1-7.

EXHIBIT 1-7   Alternative Flowchart Presentations for Multipart Forms

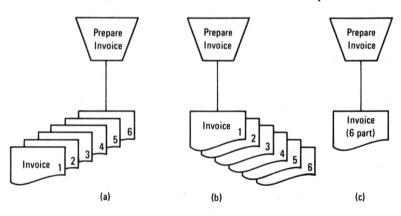

Flowcharts (a) and (b) are similar in that they show the six copies so as to make it visually apparent (even without reading) that there are multiple copies of the form. This presentation has the advantage that lines can be drawn from each copy of the form to show where each goes. The difference between (a) and (b) is simply the direction in which the documents fan out, so the choice is strictly a matter of taste or the direction of the flow. Flowchart (c), however, is a more compact presentation, which is useful when the set of forms is transported or used as a group rather than individually. Judgment is required concerning the most appropriate presentation for any particular flowchart.

Disposition of Documents

Every flowchart must show the final disposition of every document, form, or report used by the system. Consider the flowchart in Exhibit 1-4 of the simplified sales system. The order is filed by customer name; copies 1, 4, and 6 of the invoice go out of the system and back to the customer; copy 2 is filed by invoice number; copy 3 is filed by customer name; and copy 5 is filed by date. Thus, all copies of all documents are accounted for. Ultimately, every document in every flowchart should be

1. Sent out of the system to a terminal destination, which is represented by an oval, or
2. Stored in a permanent file, which is represented by a stable triangle (on its base), or
3. Discarded, which is represented by the vertical line and the word discard.

ANALYZING ORGANIZATIONS AND BUSINESS CYCLES

Given a specific system, it is important to understand how the system accomplishes its objectives. There are several techniques for describing different aspects of a system in a comprehensible way: system flowcharts, organization charts, and document flowcharts. This section will illustrate the organization chart and the system flowchart, and their relationship for a hypothetical firm, French Quarter Company, Inc., and will discuss and illustrate document flowcharts.

Organization Chart

The **organization chart** portrays the structure of responsibility and authority in a company, that is, who is in charge of what and who reports to whom.

Exhibit 1-8, the organization chart of the French Quarter Company, shows the lines of authority and areas of responsibility in the corporation. The highest level of authority is the board of directors, which is represented by the top box. The board of directors hires the president, who in turn reports to the board. For this reason, the box representing the president lies below that of

20

*Part I
Overview
of Systems
and
Internal
Control*

EXHIBIT 1-8   Organization Chart

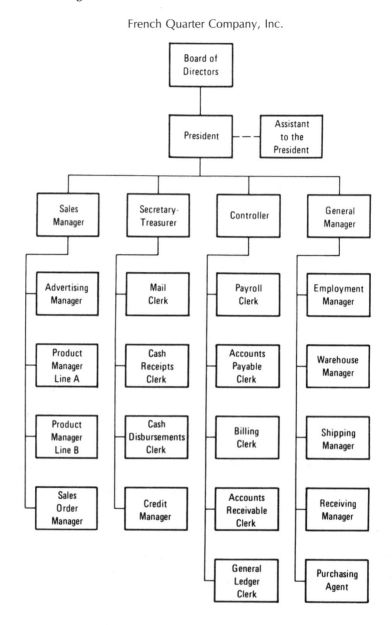

French Quarter Company, Inc.

the board of directors and a vertical line connects them. Similarly, a number of people report to the president. In this company they are the sales manager, the secretary-treasurer, the controller, and the general manager. All these people have comparable areas of responsibility, and all report to the president; therefore, their relationship to the president is represented by vertical lines. Note that the chart is easier to read if the lines flow either horizontally or vertically and not at an angle.

There are a number of people who are not strictly within the organizational chain of command. These people are called staff, such as executive assistants, administrative assistants, and various advisors. People in these positions are placed on the same "level" as the person to whom they report and are connected to that person with horizontal, broken lines. One such example is the assistant to the president in Exhibit 1-8. People within the organizational chain of command who comprise most of the organization chart are called line.

The way the president is connected to the sales manager, the secretary-treasurer, the controller, and the general manager is the preferred method; however, this approach is not always practical because the chart can become too cumbersome and difficult to condense. Exhibit 1-8 shows that the advertising manager, the product manager of line A, the product manager of line B, and the sales order manager all report to the sales manager. Similarly, four people report to the secretary-treasurer and five people each to the controller and to the general manager. If continued in a pyramid fashion, the chart would rapidly become huge. An alternative approach, then, would be to put each subpyramid on a separate chart; thus, there would be an individual organization chart for the sales manager, the secretary-treasurer, the controller, and the general manager. In Exhibit 1-8, the goal is to put the whole chart in one picture, so the entire organization structure can be comprehended at a glance. Therefore, everyone reporting to each of these four people is placed under them in the chart. The connecting lines show the levels of authority. To return to the sales manager, the chart shows that the advertising manager, the managers of product lines A and B, and the sales order manager are all on the same level of authority and all report to the sales manager.

System Flowchart for the Sales Cycle

To tie together information concerning the different business cycles, business documents, flowchart symbols, and the organization chart, this section will flowchart a sales system. This sales system will be for the French Quarter Company, Inc., whose organization structure is shown in Exhibit 1-8.

The sales system flowchart in Exhibit 1-9 is divided into departmental columns for ease of comprehension. Thus, the sales system has separate columns for customer, sales order, credit, billing, accounts receivable, general ledger, warehouse, and shipping. The flowchart then shows everything that occurs within a specific department in that department's column. This arrangement makes it easier to see where documents come from and where they go. When steps of the cycle are inside of the business, that column of the flowchart should correspond to a position on the organization chart.

The flowchart begins in the top left-hand corner with a customer order. Since the flowchart is in columns, it is only necessary to write *Order* on the document symbol to indicate that it is a customer order. The order goes to the sales order column, indicating a document flow to this department. There is a processing step for invoice preparation, which shows that copy 2 of the invoice (the credit copy) goes to the credit department for approval and then is returned. (For the sake of clarity, it may not be possible for a flowchart to show every small step in the process; judgment as to detail versus readability is required.)

EXHIBIT 1-9 Sales Cycle System Flowchart

French Quarter Company, Inc.

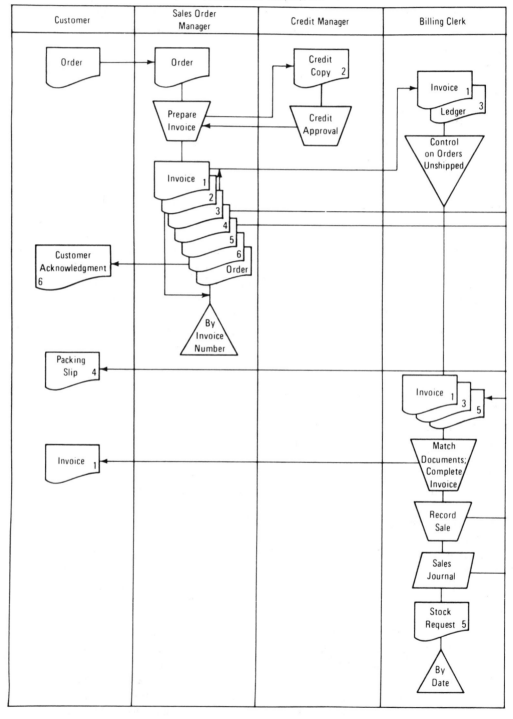

EXHIBIT 1-9 (continued)

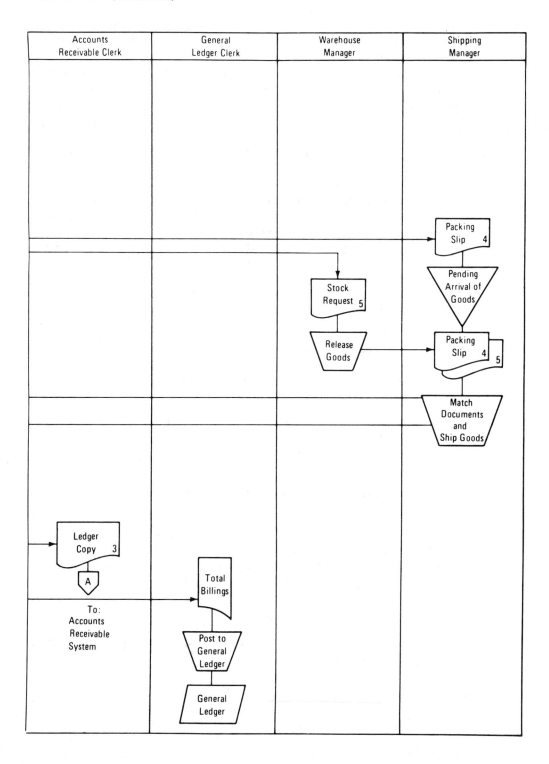

24

*PART I
Overview
of Systems
and
Internal
Control*

After the invoice is prepared, there are seven documents—six invoice copies and the customer order. The invoice (copy 1) and the ledger copy (copy 3) go together to billing, where they are placed in a temporary file that provides a control on orders not yet shipped. The credit copy (copy 2) and the customer order are filed together by invoice number in a permanent file. This provides physical control over invoices; any gap in the number sequencing indicates that an invoice is missing. The packing slip (copy 4) is sent to shipping, where it goes into a temporary file awaiting arrival of the goods from the warehouse. The stock request (copy 5) goes to the warehouse, where it triggers another action, the release of goods. The stock request (copy 5) then goes to shipping along with the goods, and the related packing slip (copy 4) is removed from the temporary file.

Then the next processing steps occur. The documents are matched and the goods are shipped. The packing slip (copy 4) goes with the goods to the customer to show what should be in the shipment. The stock request (copy 5) goes to billing to trigger the billing process, at which time the invoice (copy 1) and ledger copy (copy 3) are removed from the temporary file. Billing then performs the following processing steps:

1. The three copies of the invoice (1, 3, and 5) are matched.
2. The invoice (copy 1) is sent to the customer.
3. The ledger copy (copy 3) goes to accounts receivable, which is continued on a later flowchart.
4. The sale is recorded in the sales journal.
5. The stock request (copy 5) is placed into a permanent file of invoice copies sequenced by date.
6. A daily total of all billings is sent to the general ledger.

Because there is often a delay in shipping orders, the sales department may mail an acknowledgment copy of the invoice (copy 6) to the customer at the same time that copies of the invoice are distributed to the different departments.

System Flowcharts for the Cash Receipts Cycle

The sales cycle is not a closed system, but instead connects to and interacts with other cycles in the business. The cycle with the closest connection to sales is the cash receipts cycle. The cash receipts cycle for the French Quarter Company is flowcharted in two parts in Exhibits 1-10 and 1-11 because it connects to and extends the earlier sales cycle flowchart. The purchases cycle and the cash disbursements cycle also fit together; Problems 1-18 and 1-19 offer the opportunity to prepare these flowcharts.

The Notes columns in Exhibits 1-10 and 1-11 further explain the material in the flowcharts. In this case, two flowcharts were used because one would have become overly complex.

Need for Multiple Copies of Documents

Passively flowcharting a system is not enough. We must also understand why the system is the way it is in order to see whether or not it is operating effectively and efficiently. Consider the sales system for the French Quarter Company.

The system uses a six-part invoice, but is that the proper number of copies? Too few to be effective? Too many to be efficient? To understand why this system uses six copies, review where each one goes and what purpose it serves:

#1   goes to the customer as an invoice.

#2   is filed by invoice number in the sales order department to maintain physical control over invoices and to make sure no invoices are missing.

#3   goes to accounts receivable to update the customer account with the sale, where it is filed by customer name.

#4   goes to the customer as a packing slip accompanying the goods to show what items the shipment should contain.

#5   is filed by date in the billing department to support the total billings for the day that is forwarded to the general ledger.

#6   goes to the customer as an acknowledgment of the receipt of the order.

Only by referring to the specific situation is it possible to determine whether the document preparation and flow is appropriate. There is no one perfect approach to apply in all situations, so each copy of each document should be scrutinized to determine whether it is actually necessary. As an example, consider the acknowledgment copy, #6. Some companies take a long time to fill a customer's order. Furniture companies often take several months to deliver, and some computer companies take a similar amount of time to deliver on certain models. In situations such as these, it is essential that the customer receive an acknowledgment to indicate that the order has been received and is being processed. Suppose, however, the firm can generally ship goods to customers very soon after orders are received, perhaps because of an extensive or just-in-time inventory. In that case, an acknowledgment (copy 6) would not be necessary because it would reach the customer at essentially the same time as the merchandise. Every situation demands its own assessment of what is necessary or desirable in document preparation and flow.

The French Quarter Company prepares six copies of the invoice. The customer gets three—an acknowledgment, a packing slip, and an invoice— and the company retains three. But all three copies retained by the company have the very same information on them, so the question arises: Is it not wasteful to keep three copies of the same thing? The answer is that all three copies would probably be necessary in a manual system because the firm must be able to access the same information in three different ways:

1. One copy must be filed by invoice number to provide physical control over invoices and quick access to the invoice by its identifying number.

2. One copy must be filed by customer name to provide support for the customer statement of account (bill). Thus, if a customer calls or writes about a bill, all relevant documents should be grouped together for convenient access.

3. One copy must be filed by date of billing. The total is entered in the sales journal as sales for the day. To maintain a proper audit trail, the firm must be able to go to the source documents supporting this journal entry. In this case, the source documents are the invoices; therefore to back up a daily journal entry, the firm need only go to the filed batch of invoices for that day.

Thus, there are good reasons for keeping multiple copies of the same information in a manual system. However, the computer and the concept of

26

PART I
Overview
of Systems
and
Internal
Control

data bases have had a considerable impact on this necessity. Computers can store information only once but then allow access to the information in many different ways. These topics will be discussed extensively in Chapter 3 and beyond.

Advantages of System Flowcharts

There are tremendous advantages of flowcharts and their use, primarily in ensuring completeness and displaying clearly the essence of a complex situation. When there is a narrative description of a system or cycle and how it

EXHIBIT 1-10   Accounts Receivable Cycle System Flowchart

French Quarter Company, Inc.

Notes	Mail Clerk	Credit Manager	Billing Clerk
A — when post to A/R subsidiary ledger, file document by customer name *B* — file sales return receiving slip by date *C* — file totals by date; compare totals in control accounts with subsidiary ledger; use filed totals in case of difference	From: Cash Collection System B Remittance Advice	Approval of Sales Accounts Sales Return Receiving Slip	By No. Credit Memo 2 Total Credit Memos Prepare Credit Memo (B) Sales Return Receiving Slip

works, it may be impossible to tell whether the description is complete just by reading it. However, flowcharting the system from the narrative quickly identifies any gaps or omissions while at the same time illustrating the separation of activities and how the system actually works.

Convenience of Document Flowcharts

This chapter has introduced and illustrated system flowcharts, which include not only the documents used by the system but also the procedures and processing steps involved in the system. However, in many situations a complete

EXHIBIT 1-10 (continued)

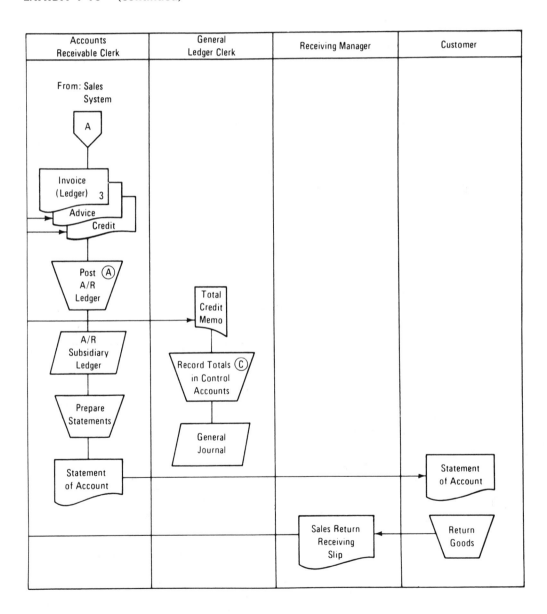

EXHIBIT 1-11   Collection of Receivables Cycle System Flowchart

French Quarter Company, Inc.

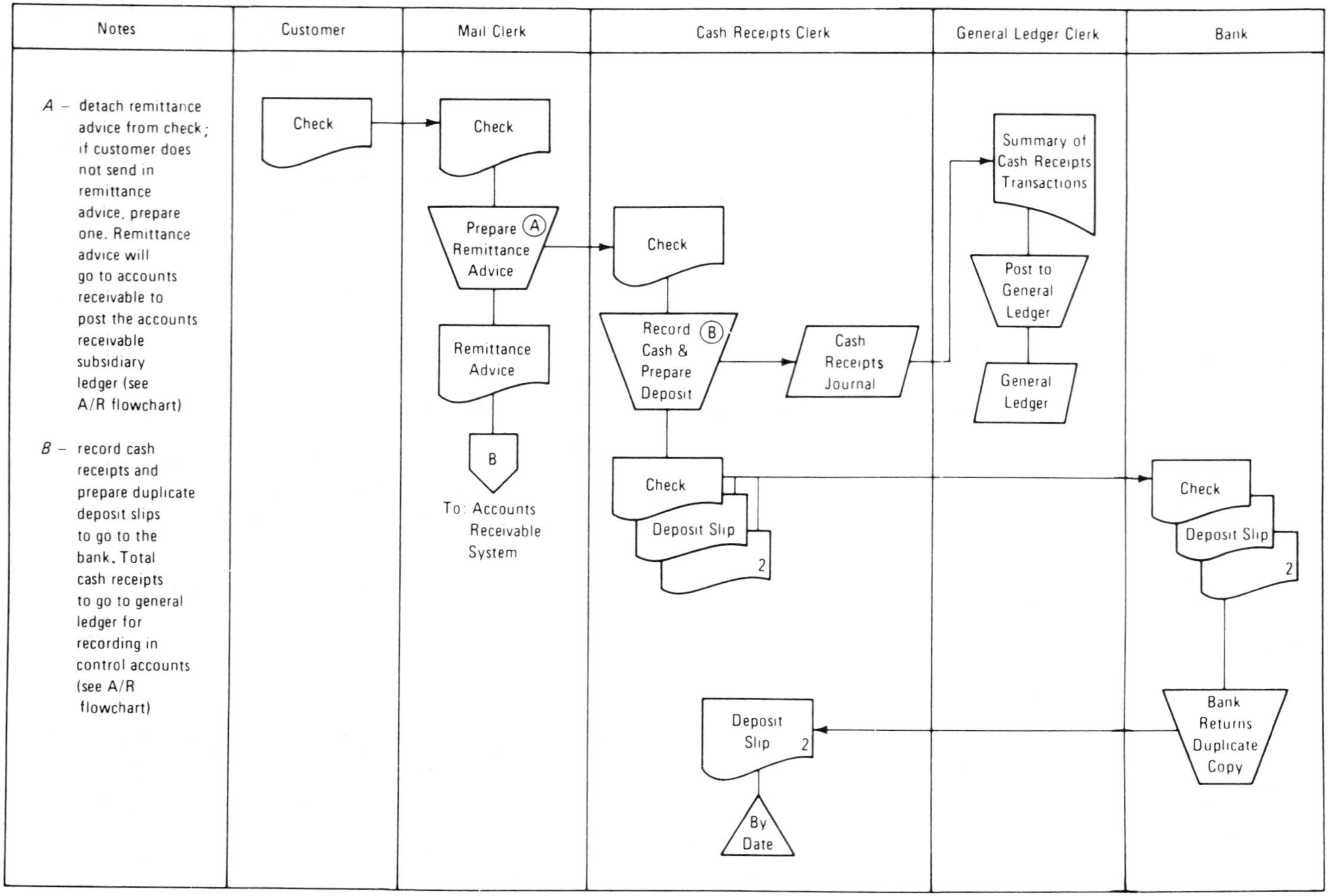

system flowchart may not be necessary or even desirable. For a general overview of the system, some processing detail may be an unnecessary distraction when reading the flowchart.

A **document flowchart** is often the answer to circumstances such as these. In a document flowchart, all processing steps are omitted and only the flow of documents is shown. It is therefore important to understand the distinction and level of detail between the document flowchart and the system flowchart. Exhibit 1-12 is a document flowchart for the familiar accounts receivable system of the French Quarter Company, Inc. A great deal of detail has been left out, namely, what is actually done with each of the forms in each department. However, the document flowchart gives a good overview of the information processing in a cycle, uncluttered by a lot of detail. Often, by using experience and common sense, it is fairly easy to see what must occur at each stage of the system.

CHAPTER SUMMARY

Accounting systems provide financial information about a business to interested parties outside the business and to management groups within the business. A transaction processing system with the addition of accounting-related nontransaction information creates an accounting information system. When the AIS is coupled with other information systems, a management information system is created. Any of these systems might be called a computer information system if it is computer based.

The typical business has a sales cycle, a purchases cycle, a cash receipts cycle, and a cash disbursements cycle. Business documents such as sales slips, invoices, debit and credit memos, and purchase orders provide the raw data for each cycle's information system.

Flowcharts should be prepared with standard symbols for universal understanding. System flowcharts must show the origin, flow, and ultimate destination of every document that passes through the system. They also show information flow, that is, nondocumented events, such as an oral request for supplies, which occur within the system. Document flow is represented by a solid line, information flow by a broken line.

Businesses can be analyzed according to their authority structure and business cycles. Authority structure can be diagrammed in an organization chart, which shows who is in charge of what and who reports to whom. Each business cycle can be diagrammed with a system flowchart. Sales and cash receipts are related cycles. Purchases and cash disbursements are related cycles. The sales cycle system flowchart begins with the customer's order and shows the disposition of the order and all copies of the invoice. The cash receipts cycle system flowchart shows the disposition of the remittance advice, credit memo, stock request, check, deposit slip, and all other documents that pass through the system.

Multiple copies of documents are essential in a manual system because the affected departments in both the selling company and the purchasing com-

EXHIBIT 1-12 Accounts Recivable Cycle Document Flowchart

French Quarter Company, Inc.

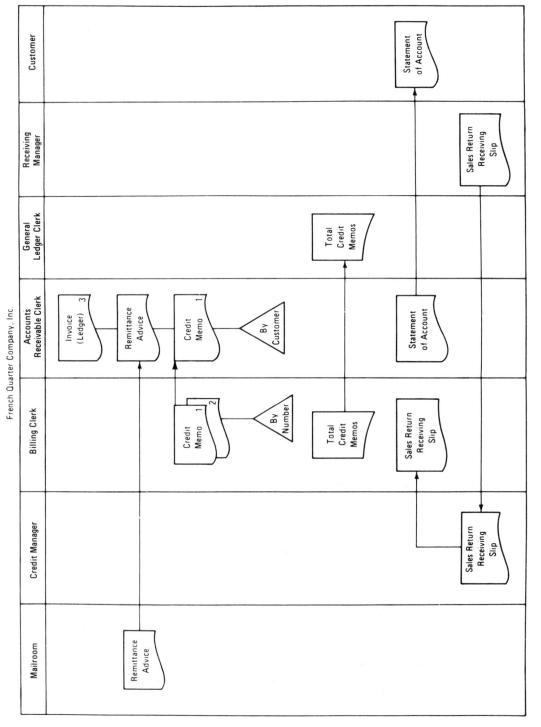

pany require physical access to much of the same information in different ways. Computers and data bases make information systems more efficient by eliminating most of the need for multiple copies.

There may be occasions when an abbreviated overview of an information system is required. A document flowchart provides this abbreviated overview by showing the flow and disposition of all system documents but omitting the details of processing provided in a system flowchart.

KEY TERMS

Accounting (*p. 2*)
AIS (*p. 7*)
Audit trail (*p. 7*)
Business cycle (*p. 8*)
Cash disbursements cycle (*p. 12*)
Cash receipts cycle (*p. 12*)
CIS (*p. 7*)
Credit memorandum (*p. 9*)
Debit memorandum (*p. 9*)
Document flowchart (*p. 29*)
Financial accounting (*p. 3*)
Flow line (*p. 14*)
Generally accepted accounting
    principles (GAAP) (*p. 3*)
Information system (*p. 5*)
Invoice (*p. 10*)

Managerial accounting (*p. 4*)
MIS (*p. 7*)
Off-page connector (*p. 17*)
On-page connector (*p. 17*)
Organization chart (*p. 19*)
Permanent file (*p. 16*)
Purchase order (*p. 9*)
Purchases cycle (*p. 11*)
Sales cycle (*p. 10*)
Sales slip (*p. 8*)
Source document (*p. 7*)
System flowchart (*p. 13*)
Temporary file (*p. 16*)
Terminal (*p. 14*)
Transaction processing accounting
    system (*p. 5*)

QUESTIONS

1-1. Distinguish between financial and managerial accounting.

1-2. Describe the processing that might occur in a transaction processing system and in an accounting information system using an order for the purchase of inventory to illustrate the difference.

1-3. Discuss four basic cycles that a business goes through in its normal operations.

1-4. For each of the cycles given in Question 1-3, identify its basic steps.

1-5. What is the purpose of an organization chart? What kinds of problems may be pointed out by an organization chart?

1-6. Distinguish among a program flowchart, a system flowchart, and a document flowchart.

1-7. Draw and identify the 13 standard flowchart symbols. Why are standard symbols used in flowcharting?

1-8. The flowchart of a well-designed system should show a final destination for all documents. What are the three possible final destinations for documents?

1-9. Explain the advantages of a flowchart over a narrative description of a system.

1-10. Describe what happens to copy 5 of the invoice in the sales system flowchart of Exhibit 1-9.

32

*PART I
Overview
of Systems
and
Internal
Control*

PROBLEMS _____

1-11. Accounting financial statements are commonly used by at least the following groups: (a) management; (b) creditors, such as banks; and (c) owners. For what specific purpose would each of these groups use financial statements? What kind of information from financial statements would be most important to each of these groups?

1-12. Distinguish transaction processing systems, accounting information systems, and management information systems. Could any of these be computer information systems? What would be required? Which of these terms is broader?

1-13. The following is a narrative description of the lines of authority and responsibility for data processing and accounting matters in a medium-sized firm. From this material, prepare an organization chart in good form.

Both the data processing manager and the controller report to the president. The data processing manager is in charge of operating the already existing systems and developing new systems as necessary. The controller is in charge of the accounting for the company. The data processing manager has five people reporting to him: (a) the data control supervisor, who is in charge of detecting and correcting errors in the computer's input data; (b) a systems programmer, who is responsible for the computer system software; (c) an applications programming manager, who is in charge of developing programs for new systems and maintaining old programs; (d) a data librarian, who is responsible for physical control over the tapes and disks used in the system; and (e) an operations supervisor, who is in charge of the computer's operations. The data control supervisor has three clerks who work for her. The applications programming manager supervises four programmers. The data librarian has one assistant. The operations supervisor has two operators who work for him.

Four people report to the controller: (a) a systems accountant, who is responsible for developing new accounting-related systems; (b) the chief accountant, who is responsible for accounting records; (c) the budget manager, who develops budgets and monitors performance relative to the budget; and (d) the internal auditor, who provides an independent verification of performance. Five clerks report to the chief accountant, one for each of the following areas: general ledger, accounts payable, accounts receivable, billing, and payroll.

1-14. This problem refers to the organization chart of Tulane University pictured in Exhibit 1-13. Answer each of the following specific questions concerning the organization chart:

1. How many people report to the president?
2. What is the relationship between the board of visitors and the board of administrators?
3. What is the relationship between the board of administrators and the board of governors of Tulane Medical Center?
4. To whom does the Vice-President of Health Affairs report?
5. Briefly describe the areas of responsibility of the dean of students.
6. To whom does the director of administrative services (Medical Center) report?

EXHIBIT 1-13 Organization Chart

Tulane University

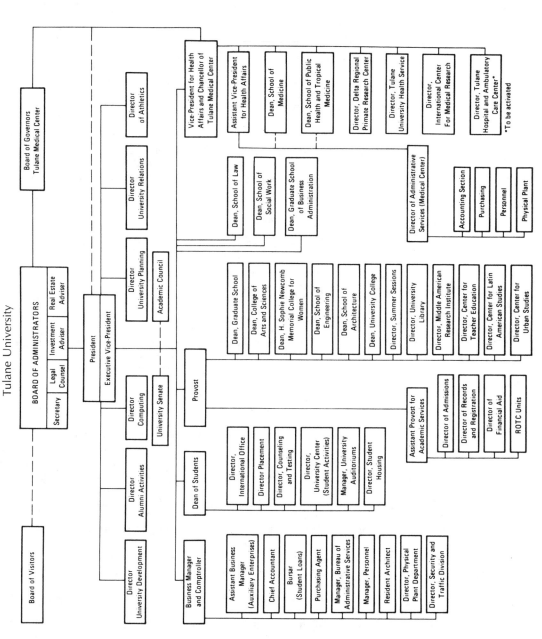

34

PART I
Overview
of Systems
and
Internal
Control

7. Why might there be an accounting section under the director of administrative services (Medical Center) as well as a chief accountant under the business manager?

8. Do the activities and responsibilities of the director of admissions make it more desirable for him to be under the provost rather than the dean of students?

9. What is the role of the university senate?

10. It is unusual for the director of computing to report directly to the president. Where might the head of the computer center be placed?

1-15. For this exercise, use the information given in Problem 1-14:

1. One of the primary activities of university administrators is academic administration. These administrators do not primarily teach or do research, but they hire, supervise, and dismiss those who do. From the chart, give a narrative description of the lines of authority and responsibility in the academic administration of the university.

2. Another important area of university administration is the management of business affairs. Give a narrative description of the lines of authority and responsibility in the business administration of the university.

1-16. (*AICPA, adapted*) Charting, Inc., processes its sales and cash receipts documents in the following manner:

a. *Receipts on account.* The mail is opened each morning by a mail clerk in the sales department. The mail clerk prepares a remittance advice (showing customer and amount paid) if one is not received. The checks and remittance advices are then forwarded to the sales department supervisor, who reviews each check and forwards the checks and remittance advices to the accounting department supervisor

    The accounting department supervisor, who also functions as credit manager in approving new credit and all credit limits, reviews all checks for receipts on past due accounts and then forwards the checks and remittance advices to the accounts receivable clerk, who arranges the advices in alphabetical order. The remittance advices are posted directly to the accounts receivable subsidiary ledger cards. The checks are endorsed by stamp and totaled. The total is posted to the cash receipts journal. The remittance advices are filed chronologically.

    After receiving the cash from the previous day's cash sales, the accounts receivable clerk prepares the daily deposit slip in triplicate. The third copy of the deposit slip is filed by date, and the second copy and the original accompany the bank deposit.

b. *Sales.* Salesclerks prepare sales invoices in triplicate. The original and second copy are presented to the cashier. The third copy is retained by the salesclerk in the sales book. When the sale is for cash, the customer pays the salesclerk, who presents the money to the cashier with the invoice copies.

    A credit sale is approved by the cashier from a credit list after the salesclerk prepares the three-part invoice. After receiving the cash or approving the invoice, the cashier validates the original copy of the sales invoice and gives it to the customer. At the end of each day the cashier recaps the sales and cash received and forwards the cash and the second copy of all sales invoices to the accounts receivable clerk.

The accounts receivable clerk balances the cash received with cash sales invoices and prepares a daily sales summary. The credit sales invoices are posted to the accounts receivable subsidiary ledger, and then all invoices are sent to the inventory control clerk in the sales department for posting to the inventory control cards. After posting, the inventory control clerk files all invoices numerically. The accounts receivable clerk posts the daily sales summary to the cash receipts journal and sales journal and files the sales summaries by date.

The cash from cash sales is combined with the cash received on account to comprise the daily bank deposit.

c. *Bank deposits.* The bank validates the deposit slip and returns the second copy to the accounting department, where it is filed by date by the accounts receivable clerk. Monthly bank statements are reconciled promptly by the accounting department supervisor and are filed by date.

You recognize that there are weaknesses in the existing system and believe a diagram of information and documentation flows would be beneficial. Complete the flowchart for sales and cash receipts of Charting, Inc. (Exhibit 1-14), by labeling the appropriate symbols and indicating information flows. The chart is complete as to symbols and document flows.

1-17. The organization chart given in Exhibit 1-8 and the flowcharts in Exhibits 1-9, 1-10, 1-11, and 1-12 all pertain to the French Quarter Company, Inc. Flowchart the payroll system for this company given in the narrative that follows.

When a person is hired, the employment manager prepares an employment and wage rate authorization form and deductions slip, which are forwarded to the payroll clerk. Each week employees turn in time cards showing hours worked to the payroll clerk. Every two weeks the payroll clerk computes earnings and deductions for each employee and payroll taxes for the company. This detailed information is then forwarded to the cash disbursements clerk, who (a) prepares paychecks, (b) enters the payroll transactions in the cash disbursements journal, and (c) sends paychecks back to the payroll clerk. Employee year-to-date earnings and deductions are then updated by the payroll clerk, and checks are distributed to employees.

1-18. Flowchart the purchases system for the French Quarter Company, Inc., given in the narrative that follows.

The purchasing agent prepares a three-part purchase order and sends the first two copies to the vendor. Acknowledgment of the order by the vendor is obtained when the vendor returns copy 2 to the purchasing agent. Copy 2 is kept by the purchasing agent, and copy 3 is sent to the accounts payable clerk. The vendor sends the goods accompanied by a packing slip to the receiving manager and a two-part invoice to the purchasing agent. The receiving manager verifies the accuracy of the packing slip and forwards it to the accounts payable clerk. The purchasing agent determines that the invoice accurately reflects the order and sends the received invoice to the accounts payable clerk, who compares it to the verified packing slip. The accounts payable clerk approves the invoice for payment and sends the purchase order, verified packing slip, and approved invoice to the cash disbursements clerk and records the purchase in the purchases journal. Each week, the accounts payable clerk posts from the purchases journal to the accounts payable subsidiary ledger. Each month, the accounts payable clerk prepares summary total information on purchases, which goes to the general ledger clerk.

EXHIBIT 1-14   Flowchart for Sales and Cash Receipts

Charting, Inc.

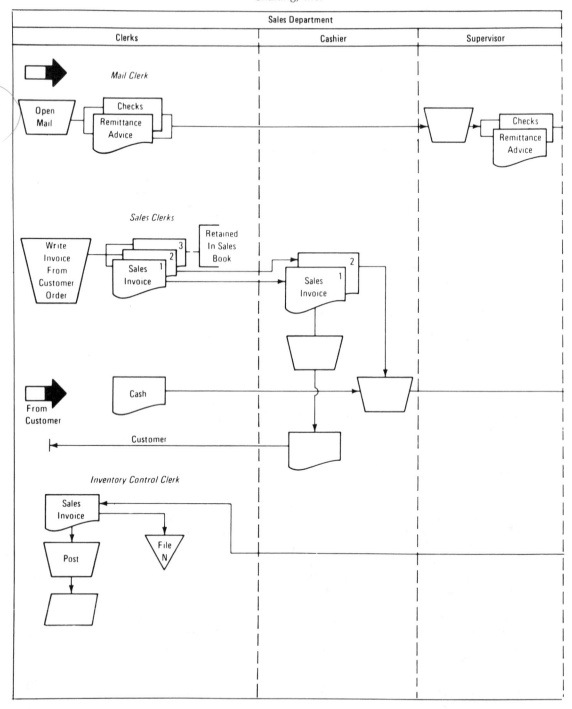

EXHIBIT 1-14 **(continued)**

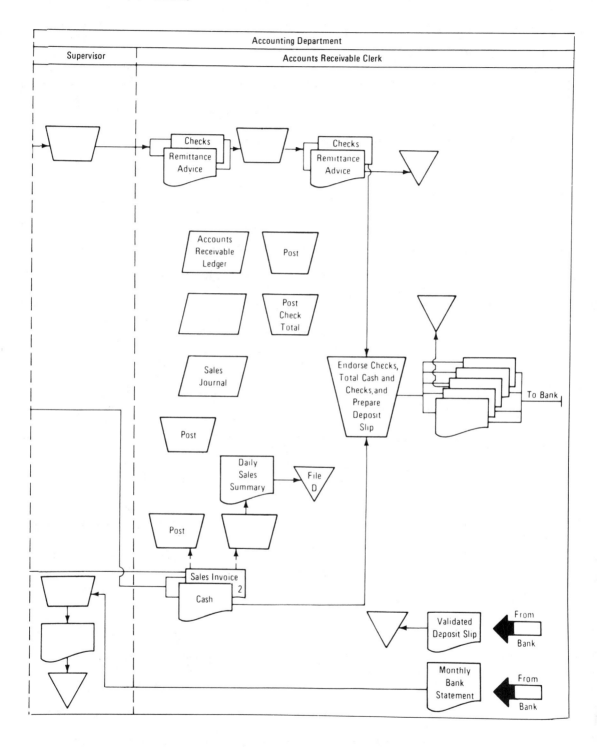

38

PART I
Overview
of Systems
and
Internal
Control

1-19. Flowchart the cash disbursements system (for purchases) for the French Quarter Company, Inc., given in the narrative that follows.

The cash disbursements clerk receives the supporting documents from the accounts payable clerk and prepares checks for vendors, which are signed by the secretary-treasurer. These checks are entered in the cash disbursements journal and sent directly to the vendor. Each week, the accounts payable clerk posts from the cash disbursements journal to the accounts payable subsidiary ledger. Each month, the cash disbursements clerk prepares summary total information on cash disbursements that goes to the general ledger clerk. The bank statement goes to the controller, who compares it to the cash receipts journal, cash disbursements journal, and general ledger.

1-20. For each of the systems given in Problems 1-17, 1-18, and 1-19, prepare a document flowchart.

1-21. (*CMA, adapted*) Wooster Company is a beauty and barber supplies and equipment distributorship servicing a five-state area. Management has generally been pleased with the company's overall operations to date. However, the present purchasing system has evolved through practice rather than having been formally designed. Consequently, it is inadequate and needs to be overhauled.

The present purchasing system can be described as follows. Whenever the quantity of an item is low, the inventory supervisor phones the purchasing department and gives the item description and quantity to be ordered. A purchase order is prepared in duplicate in the purchasing department. The original is sent to the vendor and the copy is retained in the purchasing department and filed in numerical order. When the shipment arrives, the inventory supervisor sees that each item received is checked off on the packing slip that accompanies the shipment. The packing slip is then forwarded to the accounts payable department. When the invoice arrives, the packing slip is compared with the invoice in the accounts payable department. Once any differences between the packing slip and the invoice have been reconciled, a check is drawn for the appropriate amount and is mailed to the vendor with a copy of the invoice; a copy is filed alphabetically in the paid invoice file.

Wooster Company intends to redesign its purchasing system from the time when an item needs to be ordered until payment is made.

1. Identify the internally and externally generated documents that would be necessary to satisfy the minimum requirements of a basic system and indicate the number of copies of each document that would be needed.

2. Explain how all these documents should flow among Wooster's various departments, including the final destination or file of each copy.

1-22. (*CMA, adapted*) Special Alloys Corporation is a production firm that manufactures a variety of metal products for industrial sale. Most of the revenues are generated by large contracts with companies that have government defense contracts. The company also develops and markets parts to major automobile companies. The company employs many metallurgists and skilled technicians because most of its products are made from highly sophisticated alloys.

The company recently signed two large contracts. As a result, the work load of Wayne Washburn, the general manager, has become overwhelming. To relieve some of this overload, Mark Johnson was transferred from the research planning department to the general manager's office. Johnson, who had been a senior metallurgist and supervisor in the research planning department, was given the title "Assistant to the General Manager."

Washburn assigned several responsibilities to Johnson in their first meeting. Johnson will oversee the testing of new alloys in the product planning department and be given the authority to make decisions as to the use of these alloys in product development; he will also be responsible for maintaining the production schedules for one of the new contracts. In addition to these duties, he will be required to meet with the supervisors of the production departments regularly to consult with them about production problems they may be experiencing. Washburn is expecting that he will be able to manage the company much more efficiently with Johnson's help.

1. Positions within organizations are often described as being line or staff. Describe what is meant by these two terms.
2. Of the responsibilities assigned to Mark Johnson as assistant to the general manager, which ones are considered line and which are staff?
3. Identify and discuss the conflicts Mark Johnson may experience in the production departments as a result of his new responsibilities.

1-23. (*CMA, adapted*)   Centronics, Inc., is a large electronics component manufacturer in Fort Wayne, Indiana. It has grown substantially during the past four years. As the company has expanded its operations, the duties and responsibilities of the accounting department have increased. Both the size of the controller's staff and the number of the department's responsibility centers have also increased. Each responsibility center manager reports directly to William Smart, the company controller. An organization structure in which all subordinates report directly to a single supervisor is referred to as a flat organization. The organization chart in Exhibit 1-15 represents the controllership function of Centronics, Inc.

EXHIBIT 1-15   Controllership Function

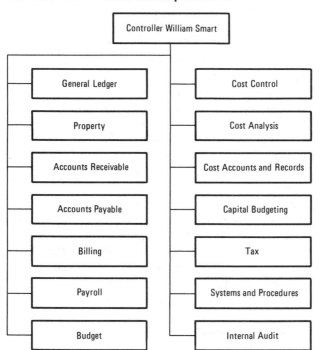

40

PART I
*Overview
of Systems
and
Internal
Control*

Each manager of a responsibility center supervises a moderate-sized staff and is responsible for undertaking the tasks to accomplish the designated objectives of the individual responsibility center. The managers depend on William Smart for direction in coordinating their separate activities.

Redraw the organization chart of the controllership function to reflect sound organizational standards; add one or more staff units that should facilitate the communication process of Centronics, Inc.'s controllership function.

DECISION CASE

Well-body Drug Co. is a small wholesale distributor of drugs to independent drugstores in the southwest United States. The sales manager, purchasing and inventory control manager, and chief accountant report directly to the president, who is also the owner of the firm. The sales manager supervises five out-of-town sales representatives. Both the warehouse manager and the purchasing agent report directly to the purchasing and inventory control manager. The chief accountant supervises a bookkeeper, an order clerk, and a billing clerk.

Customer orders are processed as follows:

Customer orders are received by the order clerk. All orders must be approved by the president before the order clerk prepares a four-part sales order. Copy 1 is filed by the customer's name. Copy 4 is sent to the customer as confirmation of receipt of the order. Copy 2 is sent to the warehouse manager, and copy 3 is sent to the billing clerk with the customer order.

The warehouse manager prepares a four-part bill of lading to accompany the shipment of goods. Copy 1 is filed by sales order number, copy 2 is sent to the customer as a notice of shipment, copy 3 is turned over to the carrier when the goods are shipped, and copy 4 is sent to the billing clerk with the sales order.

The billing clerk prepares a four-part sales invoice when the bill of lading matches the previously received customer order and sales order. Copies 1 and 2 of the invoice are mailed to the customer. Copies 3 and 4 of the sales invoice are sent to the bookkeeper with copy 4 of the bill of lading, copy 2 of the sales order, and the customer order. Copy 3 of the sales order is filed by customer name.

The bookkeeper records the sales in the sales journal and the accounts receivable subsidiary ledger. One copy of the invoice is filed by customer name, and one copy is filed with the bill of lading, customer order, and sales order by the invoice number.

All bill of lading numbers are accounted for weekly by the accountant and traced to the sale invoices. Statements are sent to customers monthly. The accountant reconciles the accounts receivable subsidiary ledger and accounts receivable control on a monthly basis. Sales invoices are recorded individually in the journal as they are received by the bookkeeper. There are no cash sales.

Procedures for cash receipts are as follows:

The receptionist receives all checks and immediately stamps them with a restrictive endorsement. The checks are sent with a listing prepared by the receptionist to the bookkeeper, who updates the accounts receivable subsidiary ledger and records the checks in the cash receipts journal. The checks and list are returned to the receptionist, who prepares a two-part deposit slip, of which one copy is sent to the bank with the checks and one copy is filed with the list by date. Deposits are made weekly, and the accountant reconciles the bank account monthly. The accountant also initiates all write-offs of unpaid accounts, which must be approved by the president.

Required:

1. Draw an organization chart.
2. Prepare a complete system flowchart.
3. Give the steps taken in this system to identify errors as they may occur.
4. Give the areas of this system where errors could occur without being identified and suggest changes in the system that would help to identify these errors.

2 Internal Control in Manual Accounting Systems

Overview

Concept of controls to prevent error and theft in a noncomputerized accounting system; how those controls impact and alter the way the system is designed and used.

Learning Objectives

Thorough study of this chapter will enable you to:

1. Distinguish between the accounting objectives and administrative objectives of internal control.
2. Use the checks built into the manual accounting system, and other techniques, to detect error.
3. Design systems that guard against defalcations of cash and inventory.
4. List the internal controls necessary in all accounting systems.
5. Understand controls over cash disbursements, cash receipts, accounting records, and inventory.
6. Analyze a flowchart for evidence of weakness in internal control.

Outline

Elements of Internal Control

Internal Control Features of Accounting Systems

Deliberate Errors in Accounting (Irregularities)

Internal Control of Cash

Prevention and Detection of System Errors

Illustration of Internal Control: The Purchasing Function

SYSTEMS IN THE REAL WORLD

43

CHAPTER 2
*Internal
Control in
Manual
Accounting
Systems*

Shop Till You Drop (Without Paying)!

A supervisor at a big retailer devised what he considered a foolproof plan for ripping off his employer: He bought a cash register, placed it among three others in the store—and kept each day's proceeds.

His take reached a total of more than $10,000, but the scam was undone when an alert co-worker noticed it and phoned an employee-theft hot line to report it.

U.S. retailers are stepping up efforts to fight employee theft. Their concern is understandable. One Justice Department study estimates that employee theft accounts for almost 70 percent of retailers' losses to all kinds of crime, which amounted to $11.77 billion in 1980, the last year for which the agency has made an estimate. Other studies suggest that three in four retail employees know at least one colleague who is stealing.

Where Thefts Occur
A survey of 113 retail companies found their employee thefts occurred at:

Point of sale — 39%
Sales floor — 17%
Stock area — 16%
Receiving area — 10%
Warehouse — 10%
Trash — 5%
Other — 3%

Source: Arthur Young & Co.

SOURCE: David J. Solomon, *The Wall Street Journal*, September 17, 1987. "Hotlines and Hefty Rewards: Retailers Step Up Efforts to Curb Employee Theft."

ELEMENTS OF INTERNAL CONTROL

The best designed accounting system will not result in accurate records and reports if the transactions the system is designed to handle are not properly processed. Improper processing of transactions divides neatly into two categories: accidental errors and intentional errors. The group of techniques and procedures used to discover errors and correct them, as well as prevent or at least detect theft, is called collectively, **internal control.**

All internal control procedures have two major objectives:

1. To protect assets (especially cash and inventory) from being lost or stolen.
2. To ensure that the accounting records are accurate and complete.

It is not sufficient for an accounting system to be simple and efficient, and provide management with the information it requires. The system must also

44

*Part I
Overview
of Systems
and
Internal
Control*

1. Help protect the assets with which it deals.
2. Protect itself against errors and ensure the accuracy of its records.

Internal control is the total collection of measures taken to secure the company's assets and the accounting system itself. The name internal control makes a good deal of sense; it refers to control techniques that are internal to and part of the system.

A system can have external controls as well as internal controls. External controls would include outside auditors, the police, or the FBI. The goals of these **external controls** are the prevention of misleading financial statements, in the case of auditors, or the prevention or discovery of theft, in the case of the police and FBI. These external controls cannot be counted on to be constantly effective; in fact, they tend to work only in special situations. There are so many transactions in even a small business that they can never all be checked to determine that they were processed correctly. If a system is to be protected from errors, it must protect itself from errors. Internal control is the way a system protects itself from all types of errors.

Accounting Controls and Administrative Controls

Large companies, such as General Motors, have hundreds of thousands of employees located all over the world. The chairman of the board of Textron claimed at his confirmation hearing as head of the Federal Reserve System that he was a small businessman; his company had sales less than the profit of IBM and his company had "only" 65,000 employees.

The problem with such a vast number of employees is that top management cannot supervise (in any direct sense) all the workers. As a result, controls must be developed to ensure that top management's policies and directives are carried out. Thus, in addition to asset protection and accounting accuracy, internal control has the following further objectives:

3. To promote efficient operations by reducing waste and duplication of effort.
4. To encourage the following of company policies and procedures.

The first two objectives of asset protection and records accuracy are called **accounting controls.** The latter two objectives, efficient operations and compliance with company policies and procedures, are called **administrative controls.** This breakdown is illustrated in Exhibit 2-1.

EXHIBIT 2-1   Objectives of Internal Control

Objectives of accounting controls	1. Protect assets from being lost or stolen. 2. Ensure that the accounting records are accurate.
Objectives of administrative controls	3. Promote efficient operations. 4. Encourage the following of company policies and procedures.

Administrative controls include

45

CHAPTER 2
*Internal
Control in
Manual
Accounting
Systems*

1. Personnel procedures designed for hiring, training, and retaining employees.
2. Quality standards to help guarantee that only high-quality merchandise will be sold to customers.
3. Guidelines for determining whether salespersons are visiting an appropriate number of customers per day.
4. Ratios and other statistics (such as inventory turnover) developed by operating departments to check if operations are running properly.

These controls are administrative controls because they promote efficient operations. They do not protect assets or ensure records accuracy, at least not directly.

Components of Internal Control

It is impossible to memorize enough lists of internal control procedures and techniques to handle every situation. The only successful approach is to keep the general concepts of internal control in mind and to apply these concepts in particular situations. The following elements of internal control should be part of all accounting systems. If any are missing, the system is deficient to some extent in internal control.

Honest and Capable Employees. Any system is critically dependent on the people who use it. If the people are dishonest or incompetent, even the finest system cannot perform properly. In contrast, honest and capable employees can function even in a situation where the other five elements of internal control are lacking. However, to deter employee dishonesty, a firm should require

1. *Annual vacations* to make sure employees are aware that any fraud requiring their constant attention will be discovered.
2. *Bonding of employees* to protect the company from loss resulting from employee dishonesty. If the company suffers a loss from employee dishonesty, a fidelity bond issued by an insurance company will cover the loss. A firm should bond employees in positions of trust in order to provide an outside check (by the bonding company) on the employees and to protect itself against loss.
3. *A stated conflict of interest policy* to prevent misunderstanding and potential abuse.

Clear Delegation and Separation of Duties. For a system to work properly, the employees must know what they are to do and what others are to do. This can be partly accomplished by an organization chart, but that is not always sufficient. Job descriptions may be necessary for proper delegation.

Even more important is the clear separation of duties. Custody of assets must be separated from the recordkeeping for those assets. For example, if the person in charge of inventory also keeps the inventory records, it is easy to conceal any theft of inventory by manipulating the accounting records. Such a person may cover stealing even though not the thief in order to conceal failure to protect the assets.

46

*PART I
Overview
of Systems
and
Internal
Control*

Authorization of transactions must also be separated from recording the transactions in the journals, and both must be separated from posting the transactions to the ledgers. The discussion later in this chapter about cash defalcations gives a number of potential abuses if this rule is not followed.

Finally, for inventory the purchasing function should be separate from the receiving function. This is discussed at greater length later in the chapter.

Proper Procedures. Proper procedures must start with proper authorization. Although a corporation's board of directors has ultimate authority for the business, day-to-day operating authority is given to company management with specific guidelines to follow (for example, the maximum amount that may be borrowed without authorization by the directors). In turn, management might allow others to give the authorization for credit sales to customers as long as a credit limit is not exceeded. This delegation of authority is necessary, but it must be appropriate under the circumstances, and there should be a check that the proper guidelines are followed.

Some examples of other specific procedures are: (1) to ensure proper document support before signing any checks; (2) to approve all noncash accounting entries on returns, discounts, and write-offs; and (3) to review all past due or uncollectible accounts as a check to see if they are properly accounted for.

Suitable Documents. Documents should be

1. As simple and easy to use as possible to help cut down on error.
2. Prenumbered to make it easier to keep physical control over the documents.
3. As few in number as possible to minimize confusion and form cost.
4. Designed to ensure that they will be properly filled out, by providing for necessary approval signatures.
5. Canceled after their proper use.

Additionally, the financial statements should be comparative. The following accounting documents help provide a basis of substantiation for the present period's accounting results.

1. The **chart of accounts** should always be used to encourage consistency. It should contain a list of all account numbers and names used by the business. It should also contain a description of each account and guidance on when each should and should not be used.
2. The **procedures manual** should explain the accounting and other procedures to be followed. This manual is necessary to train new employees in the operation of the system, and to ensure that the same types of transactions will always be handled in the same way no matter who is involved.
3. The **budget** gives the expected results of operations and financial position. Comparing actual results with the budgeted amounts will point out possible areas of concern or potential problems.

Adequate Physical Control. What constitutes adequate physical control over assets and accounting records varies with the circumstance—diamonds are treated differently from nails. Inventory should be kept in a stockroom under the custody of one person to allow the assignment of responsibility.

Additionally, critical paper such as cash, certificates of deposit, marketable securities, accounting journals, and accounting ledgers should be stored in secure fireproof safes. An important factor in the physical control of paperwork is the cost and time to reconstruct documents or accounting records. If the risk of their loss is great enough, backup copies may be justified. A related

47

CHAPTER 2
Internal
Control in
Manual
Accounting
Systems

CONCEPT SUMMARY	
Elements of Internal Control	
Honest and capable employees	1. Hire qualified people with good references. 2. Require annual vacations. 3. Bond employees in positions of trust. 4. State conflict of interest policy.
Clear delegation and separation of duties	1. Develop organization chart and job descriptions. 2. Separate recordkeeping from custody of assets. 3. Separate authorization from recordkeeping and records from each other. 4. Separate purchasing from receiving and receiving from custody.
Proper procedures for processing of transactions	1. Ensure proper authorization of transactions. 2. Sign checks only with proper support. 3. Approve all general journal entries. 4. Review past due and uncollectible accounts. 5. Develop procedures manual.
Suitable documents and accounting records	1. Prenumber important documents. 2. Develop comparative financial statements. 3. Describe accounting methods in manuals. 4. Prepare budget of anticipated results. 5. Cancel all documents after use.
Adequate physical control over assets and records	1. Limit access to inventory. 2. Safeguard all important records, have backup and retention policies. 3. Deposit cash receipts intact daily. 4. Keep all voided checks. 5. Document all stock movements.
Independent verification of performance	1. Reconcile bank statement independently. 2. Prelist cash receipts. 3. Take complete inventory regularly and use perpetual system for comparison. 4. Have an annual audit by a CPA firm.

48

*P*ART *I*
Overview
of Systems
and
Internal
Control

problem is the need for reasonable records retention and storage. Important considerations in this area are the needs of the firm, the volume of the records to store, and the relevant state and federal rules on records retention and availability.

Independent Verification.   There should be an independent verification of performance. No one is able to verify or evaluate their own performance very objectively. Thus, verification must be done by someone independent of the subject and the system, such as an outside auditor or other person.

As time passes, employees tend to become sloppy and careless about procedures. Additionally, there is always the potential for accidental and deliberate errors. Thus, periodic independent verification of performance is necessary to help ensure that the system still works properly. Independent verification includes

1.   The bank reconciliation if done by a person other than the one who controls cash or the related accounting records.
2.   A list of cash receipts prepared immediately when the mail is opened.
3.   A frequent physical count of inventory to compare with perpetual inventory records.
4.   Two separate groups to count inventory (an independent verification of an independent verification, so to speak). Perhaps the most common and best known independent verification is an **audit** by an outside certified public accounting firm at periodic intervals.

INTERNAL CONTROL FEATURES OF ACCOUNTING SYSTEMS

Accidental improper processings of transactions are simply mistakes. People will always make some errors, and no system can possibly prevent them all. However, the system should be designed to point out the existence of an error as soon as possible. All accounting systems contain a number of inherent features that help to detect errors, and these features should be understood and used in internal control.

Double-Entry Method

The most important error-detecting feature of accounting systems is the double-entry method itself. The constant requirement that debits equal credits will point out numerous mistakes, since it is likely that an error on either the debit half or the credit half of an entry would not be compensated by an equivalent error on the other half. The balancing of the special journals prior to posting, the taking of the trial balance, and the taking of the adjusted trial balance are all examples of attempts to catch errors as soon as possible. However, the fact that debits equal credits does not always mean there are no mistakes in the records.

Audit Trail

49

*Chapter 2
Internal
Control in
Manual
Accounting
Systems*

The second most important error-detecting feature is the **audit trail,** which ties the figures in the financial statements and records to their supporting documents. The figures in the financial statements come from ledger balances. The ledger accounts indicate by their posting reference the journal source of all the amounts. The journals give the original entries and hence identify both the supporting source documents and the ledger accounts to be posted. Similarly, the source documents point figures forward through the journal and ledger to their appearance on the financial statements.

This audit trail is absolutely essential for error detection. Whenever an error is discovered in an accounting number, it must be possible to see the origin of the number in order to determine the source of the mistake. Suppose the amount in an asset account, such as inventory, does not balance with the result of a physical check of the inventory. The accounting records will show where the balance in the records came from and why the records went wrong. (Note: The assmption here is that the count of inventory is correct and the accounting records are wrong. Possibly, the records are correct and some inventory is missing; the chapter will discuss this possibility later.) Even if an error is small in amount, it may be a symptom of a larger problem, the start of a growing problem, or the result of several major (but offsetting) errors. Because of this, the audit trail must always exist in order to be able to get to the origin of a number or amount.

Bank Reconciliation

The **bank reconciliation** aids in error detection because the cash in the bank is compared against the cash on the books. Accounting depends a great deal on judgment and two different accountants could derive two somewhat different figures for net income for the same firm for the same period. Cash, however, is objective. What the bank states is the cash balance should reconcile with what the books indicate is the cash balance; any discrepancy should be explainable as timing differences in the recording of cash transactions. An accurate bank reconciliation is an effective test that

1. All outgoing checks were recorded properly.
2. All deposits were recorded properly.
3. Miscellaneous charges, such as bank service charges and checks returned NSF (not sufficient funds), were properly incorporated into the accounts.

Subsidiary Ledgers

The control accounts in the general ledger for accounts receivable and accounts payable should always equal the total of the individual accounts in the respective subsidiary ledgers. If the control does not agree with (or in accounting terminology, balance to) the total of the subsidiary ledger accounts, there is an error somewhere. It is quite possible for these totals not to agree. If a cash receipt from the collection of accounts receivable is entered properly in the

50

Part I
Overview
of Systems
and
Internal
Control

cash receipts journal, but is not posted to the individual account in the subsidiary ledger, the accounts receivable control account will be correct while the subsidiary ledger will not be correct. Also, if a sales return is recorded in the general journal, it may be that only one of the two necessary postings (to the control account *and* to the subsidiary ledger) will be made, causing the other to be incorrect.

Billing Statements

It is possible (in fact, it often happens) for a cash receipt on account or a credit sale to be posted to the wrong individual account. Both the control total and the total of the subsidiary ledger will be correct. It is the individual accounts that will be incorrect; one account will be overstated by some amount, while another will be understated by the same amount. Since these two errors cancel each other out when totaling the subsidiary ledger, balancing to the control account does not detect this error. However, if statements of account go to customers, the customer whose balance due is higher than it should be is likely to complain, pointing out the existence of an error in the records.

Communication with Vendors

Companies do not send statements to vendors as they do to customers; nevertheless, vendors will complain if they are not paid in full. Suppose, for example, a payment to Fireplaces Unlimited was debited to the account payable of Fireworks Unlimited. The total of the subsidiary ledger will be correct: one balance

CONCEPT SUMMARY	
Basic Error-Detecting Features of a Manual Accounting System	
Double-Entry Method	Points up errors, since rarely will an error in one-half of an entry be exactly offset by an equivalent error in the other half.
Audit Trail	Allows the accountant to track backwards through the accounting records to the source of an error.
Bank Reconciliation	Provides an independent check that all checks, deposits, and miscellaneous charges were recorded properly.
Subsidiary Ledgers	Provides cross checks of the general ledger control account with the subsidiary ledger totals.
Billing Statements	Provides independent check of accounts receivable subsidiary ledger account balances.
Communication with Vendors	Provides an independent check of accounts payable subsidiary ledger account balances.

will be understated, but another will be overstated by an equivalent amount. However, Fireworks will eventually complain that it has not been paid (their account was debited, but no check was sent to them). If Fireplaces receives another payment, it is at least possible that it will send a refund check. Thus, communication with vendors helps to point out mistakes that may have been made.

51

CHAPTER 2
*Internal
Control in
Manual
Accounting
Systems*

DELIBERATE ERRORS IN ACCOUNTING (IRREGULARITIES)

Deliberate accounting errors or irregularities constitute theft. Stealing through the manipulation of accounting records does not usually involve physical violence, but it does involve the betrayal of trust. Two words are commonly used for theft through accounting manipulation—**embezzlement** and **defalcation.** Both these words mean the fraudulent appropriation to one's own use of property of another entrusted to one's care. It can happen anywhere. An international CPA firm learned that a bookkeeper in the main office had been stealing large sums from travel and expense money over a period of years. This fraud at the very heart of the CPA's own business was discovered only when the bookkeeper confessed and gave herself up.

It is impossible to determine the total amount of embezzlement precisely—much is never discovered. Estimates place this type of white-collar crime at multiple billions of dollars per year, truly an astonishing figure. Understandably, cash and inventory are the primary targets of dishonest employees.

The embezzler is seldom an inveterate thief. Often, the embezzler is a trusted employee who has been with the firm a long time. In one group of embezzlers studied, the people were employed an average of six and a half years before they started to steal. Embezzlers usually believe that it is impossible to live on their salary or that, for some reason, their salary is otherwise inadequate. This may be due to several factors such as: (1) associating with people wealthier than they, (2) feeling that they are being treated unfairly by the company, or (3) addiction to drugs, alcohol, or gambling. Such employees eventually convince themselves that they either need the money or at least deserve it.

Embezzlers often believe that the stealing is only temporary; they will repay the money when things turn around. However, they often become trapped in a never-ending cycle to avoid detection. Exhibit 2-2 provides a summary of red flags that point to the possible existence of fraud and embezzlement.

INTERNAL CONTROL OF CASH

Like cash and inventory, prepaid expense is also an asset, but there really is nothing to steal. Cash and inventory are the main targets of theft for all businesses. A CPA firm study bears this out: 88 percent of their client's defalcations that were uncovered involved cash (including petty cash), and virtually all of

52

PART I
Overview
of Systems
and
Internal
Control

EXHIBIT 2-2   Seven Red Flags for Fraud and Embezzlement

Red Flags	Examples of Problems That May Result
1. An employee who exceeds scope of responsibilities	1. Individual negotiates contracts and assumes responsibility for approving invoices in order to negotiate kickbacks.
2. An unusual reduction in, or loss of, a regular customer's business	2. Key employee has silent partnership in new competitor.
3. Absentee ownership of a small business	3. Manager pays personal debts with company funds.
4. A property appraiser also approves a mortgage loan	4. Appraisals are inflated and loans are given in exchange for kickbacks.
5. An employee who appears to be living beyond his means	5. Employee is embezzling to support high life of gambling debts.
6. Open-ended contracts with suppliers	6. With no measure of amount delivered, purchaser must take supplier's word.
7. An ususual increase in purchases by a customer during a brief period	7. Customer is making large credit purchases just prior to planned bankruptcy.

the remainder involved inventory. For cash embezzlements, the majority of individual incidents involve cash receipts, but by far the greater of the dollar amounts embezzled (80 percent) involve cash disbursements.

Defalcations of Cash Disbursements

Cash disbursements is usually the area of greatest dollar loss for businesses. Consider the following general techniques for embezzling from cash disbursements.

Preparing Checks Payable to Real or Fictitious Vendors. A bookkeeper might prepare checks payable to other firms, so that the checks appear to be normal payments on account. After the checks are signed, the bookkeeper can divert the funds by either: (1) forging the endorsement of the check and then cashing it, or (2) depositing it to a bank account created to receive the funds. Techniques for doing this depend on whether the embezzler created the payee vendor or used an existing and real vendor. If the vendor is fictitious, the embezzler must also create false invoices from it as well as any supporting documents that might be required for signature. If the payee firm is a real vendor, the embezzler simply resubmits invoices that have already been paid. The problem of having two checks tied to the same invoice is then solved by intercepting the second, fraudulent check when it is returned from the bank and destroying it. The number and date of the original check are changed, and the altered original is substituted for the fraudulent check.

Padding the Payroll. **Padding** the payroll is another method of issuing checks to others and then appropriating them. In this method, an employee might either continue the issuing of checks for people after they have quit or been fired or add fake employees to the payroll. Padding can be accomplished by a number of people in addition to the bookkeeper. If the foreman distributes paychecks, he might "forget" to inform the office that an employee has quit and appropriate the check. Similarly, the person who adds employees to the payroll might add a brother-in-law or cousin.

53

CHAPTER 2
*Internal
Control in
Manual
Accounting
Systems*

Preparing Checks Payable to Oneself. Employees could prepare checks to themselves by using either a check that was not prenumbered or a prenumbered check from the rear of the checkbook. They can get the check signed by either forging an authorized signature or by using checks that have been signed in blank (that is, with the date, payee, and amount not yet filled in). Then they must intercept or control the bank statement so that the checks can be destroyed when the bank returns them. The cash balance per bank would be reduced by the cleared checks, but the general ledger balance would not have been reduced. Part of the process of balancing special journals prior to posting involves adding up the totals of the various columns (called **footing**). Underfooting is the misadding of a column to arrive at too small a total, and overfooting is the opposite. A person could overfoot the cash column of the cash disbursements journal to reduce the general ledger cash balance. However, credits would then exceed debits in the journal. Therefore, the employee must either decrease credits by underfooting purchase discounts or increase debits by overfooting expenses.

Overpaying Vendors. At first glance, overpaying the amount due a vendor does not seem to help the embezzler much, but some vendors will automatically send the firm a refund check for the amount overpaid. The embezzler can then appropriate this refund check. The books are perfectly in balance: An asset or expense is simply overstated. This technique, however, may not always work since many vendors will carry a credit balance in the company's account rather than refund the money.

Defalcations of Petty Cash

Although disbursements should generally be made by check, almost all companies use cash when a check would be inconvenient, such as to pay for items like postage due. For this reason, most firms keep a small amount of cash on hand. This amount is called **petty cash.** Defalcations of petty cash are particularly easy to accomplish since they involve no more than removing cash from the petty cash fund. In most systems, there can be little effective detection of these thefts.

Because of this risk of loss, many companies use an **imprest petty cash system.** In such a system, a certain amount (say, $100) is set up as the amount for petty cash. The petty cash fund begins with a $100 check written to petty cash; petty cash is thus set up as an asset account. After the check is cashed, the petty cash fund is established. To remove cash from the fund, a voucher is prepared, stating the reason for and the amount of the cash needed. After approval by a responsible official, the voucher is placed with the petty cash fund and the cash is withdrawn. Thus, the total of all the vouchers plus the cash still on hand should always total $100. When the cash in the fund becomes too low, another check is drawn to petty cash in the amount of the total of all

54

PART I
Overview
of Systems
and
Internal
Control

vouchers. The vouchers are then removed from the petty cash fund and the cash should again total $100. The journal entry to record this activity will debit the expenses (or possibly assets) affected by the cash payments evidenced by the vouchers. Thus, the petty cash account in the general ledger will always remain $100, and the journal entries will occur only when the petty cash fund is replenished and vouchers removed.

An employee may still steal from an imprest system by preparing false vouchers. This can be done by

1. Increasing the amount of a voucher that has already been approved,
2. Creating vouchers and forging the necessary signatures, or
3. Submitting vouchers twice by changing the date of the voucher.

However, the amounts would necessarily be small.

Defalcations of Cash Receipts

Cash Sales. An embezzler who takes cash from cash sales can keep the books in balance by simply not recording the transaction or by recording an amount smaller than the actual sale. If a cash register or sales slip is part of the system, either can be used improperly. In a situation such as a bar or small restaurant, the cash register need not be used at all. Consider, for example, the case of a movie theater where tickets are serially prenumbered. The cashier can get around the system by getting used tickets back from the ticket taker, selling the same ticket twice, and pocketing the amount of the second sale. If the tickets must be torn and half returned to each customer, the ticket taker may take a couple's two tickets, tear one, give the two halves of the same ticket back to the people, and keep the second complete ticket for reuse. Obviously collusion between the cashier and the ticket taker would be necessary for this to work.

Cash Collections on Accounts Receivable. A major technique for stealing collections on accounts receivable is called **lapping.** Lapping consists essentially of stealing Paul's payment, but then paying Paul's account by using the next receipt, say, that of Peter. Peter's account is then paid by the next receipt, and the process continues indefinitely. Some people cannot believe this is a prevalent practice because it is a process that never ends. However, many embezzlers feel that their theft is only temporary; they will eventually put the money back and everything will be covered.

Another possibility is to bill a sale at the total amount due, while recording the sale at some lower amount. The embezzler can then appropriate the difference when the customer pays the bill. Also, if a collection is not discounted because the discount period has passed, the embezzler can still record the receipt incorporating the discount, and then pocket the discount amount.

A bolder method involves taking the cash, but then recording the collection as usual in the cash receipts journal. The bank balance and the general ledger balance will not agree because the books have "too much cash." This shortage in the bank balance can be covered by manipulating the bank reconciliation so the books and bank statement appear to balance. Alternatively, the embezzler can improperly use the cash receipts journal by underfooting the cash column but keep debits equal to credits by overfooting the sales discount column.

Finally, the embezzler may not record the cash receipt at all. Since the customer involved will complain of an incorrect bill if the balance is left in the account, the embezzler must then intercept the statement of account and any dunning letters that might follow. To reduce the customer's balance, a credit must be obtained. The embezzler can get this desired credit by either creating a sales return credit memo or by writing off the debt as an uncollectible account.

55

CHAPTER 2
Internal
Control in
Manual
Accounting
Systems

CONCEPT SUMMARY

Internal Control of Cash

Area of Defalcation	How to Obtain Cash	How to Cover in Accounting Records
Cash disbursements	Issue checks to others, appropriate the checks.	1. Create false invoices. 2. Use invoices twice for support. 3. "Pad" the payroll. 4. Pocket unclaimed wages.
	Issue check to yourself.	1. Incorrectly foot the cash disbursements journal. 2. Increase recorded amount of another check.
	Overpay vendor, appropriate refund.	1. Allow asset or expense to remain overstated.
Petty cash	Remove cash from petty cash fund.	1. Increase amount on vouchers. 2. Create false vouchers. 3. Submit vouchers twice. 4. Allow fund to remain short.
Cash receipts	Take cash from cash sales.	1. Record no amount. 2. Record less than was received.
	Take cash payments on accounts receivable.	1. Engage in lapping. 2. Bill for full amount, but record sale at lower amount. 3. Record cash receipt, but manipulate bank reconciliation. 4. Record cash receipt, but incorrectly foot the cash receipts journal. 5. Do not record cash receipt, but intercept statements of account. 6. Do not record cash receipt, but create credit memo to write off the amount. 7. Pocket payment on an account that has been written off.

56

PART I
Overview
of Systems
and
Internal
Control

PREVENTION AND DETECTION
OF SYSTEM ERRORS

When considering how to detect and prevent mistakes in the processing of accounting transactions, it is important to distinguish the orientation of management from that of outside independent auditors. Management is concerned with the operations of the firm. Management would like a system to detect and correct any errors, accidental or deliberate, and do so immediately and in an inexpensive manner. The auditor is concerned with the operation of the accounting system.

Role of the Auditor in Detecting Errors

The independent auditor attests only to the representativeness of a company's financial statements and cannot be relied upon to detect all errors in the processing of transactions. The financial statements are prepared by the company, not the auditor, and the responsibility for the financial statements ultimately lies with management. The auditor's purpose is to provide an independent check that the financial statements are presented fairly in accordance with generally accepted accounting principles.

Error Detection Concerns of Management
Versus Those of the Auditor

Company management has the following specific differences in perspective from outside auditors:

1. *Speed.* Management wishes to detect errors as soon as possible in order to minimize the potential for making bad decisions based on incorrect information. The auditor is also interested in detecting errors, but is concerned more with whether or not they are ultimately detected than when.

2. *Accuracy.* Management is interested in errors because they have the potential to grow and may indicate a system out of control. The auditor is concerned with whether the financial statements are presented fairly, but fair statements may still contain a certain amount of error; it is enough that the amounts are roughly correct.

3. *Fraud Detection.* Management is interested in detecting fraud in order to protect the assets and profitable operation of the company. The auditor may assert that the necessary audit procedures to detect fraud would be too expensive for any possible financial statement benefit that might result. The auditor is concerned only with fraud if it is so gross that it makes the financial statements materially misstated as a result.

4. *Costs and Benefits of Controls.* Management is concerned with the trade-off between the costs of increased controls and their benefits. Management must consider what additional procedures will cost in terms of dollars, irritation, and increased time and justify these costs with the potential benefits that result. Auditors will generally be pleased with any additional procedures that will provide further assurance of accuracy.

5. *Time Spent on the Audit.* Management is more jealous of its own time than are the auditors. The auditor may make more demands on the time of management than management feels is justified. No internal control system can or should elimi-

nate the role of management in maintaining accuracy and reliability. Nonetheless, auditors' demands on management time should be kept to a minimum.

57
CHAPTER 2
Internal
Control in
Manual
Accounting
Systems

General Techniques to Prevent or Detect Errors in Cash

What should be done in particular business situations to detect mistakes and to help prevent their occurrence? Effective error detection and prevention is possible even in the smallest businesses. The system should consist of controls over cash disbursements, cash receipts, accounting records, and inventory.

Cash Disbursements. All cash disbursements except petty cash should be made with prenumbered checks. Using checks ensures that the disbursement is authorized and there is a permanent receipt. Checks should be prenumbered to ensure that they are accounted for properly. This procedure helps to prevent the issuance of a check that is not recorded in the cash disbursements journal or makes it clear when that happens.

Checks should be drawn only if there is proper support for them. This support should consist of

1. A proper invoice.
2. Evidence that the goods or services were received.
3. Evidence that the goods or services were ordered.
4. Evidence that the purchase transaction was properly authorized.

A company should pay only properly authorized and justified expenditures. Any supporting documents should be canceled once a disbursement is made in order to guard against paying the same invoice twice.

Check signing should be the responsibility of management who have no access to the accounting records. This step is necessary to ensure that the accounting records accurately reflect the checks written. In a small company, this rule may be relaxed for the owner.

If someone makes a mistake in preparing a check and the check must be redrawn, the check should be voided before preparing a new one. The voided check should then be

1. Altered to prevent reuse.
2. Kept to make sure all prenumbered checks are accounted for.
3. Filed with other checks as a part of a permanent record of check activity.

All checks should be mailed promptly and directly to the payee. This step helps ensure that the payee and only the payee receives the disbursement. Otherwise, an employee may appropriate the check.

The system should use an imprest petty cash fund with one custodian in charge of and accountable for the fund. The imprest fund is only reimbursed when properly approved vouchers justifying all expenditures are presented.

Cash Receipts. The system should utilize a cash register to record any cash transactions which occur over the counter. The cash register makes two records of all transactions; one is kept internally and one is given to the cus-

58

*Part I
Overview
of Systems
and
Internal
Control*

tomer. Thus, in order to make a receipt for the customer, the operator must make a record which the machine retains. Daily checks should be made of the cash register totals to ensure that all cash receipts according to the register equal those recorded in the cash receipts journal and deposited in the bank. In businesses such as bars, where no receipt is given to the customer and no receipt is expected, it is not uncommon for cash to be pocketed and no record made.

Daily cash receipts should be deposited intact. This is essential to ensure that cash receipts are not being taken. If disbursements are made directly from cash receipts, the system will lose accountability; it will be difficult or impossible to distinguish proper from improper disbursements.

Someone other than the person controlling the checkbook should reconcile the bank statement and the accounting records on a monthly basis. This is essential to determine if any unauthorized checks were issued or receipts stolen. To make this process effective, the bank statement must be unopened when the person responsible for the reconciliation receives it. Even in the smallest business, this division of labor is possible; the owner can and should personally reconcile the bank statement.

Accounting Records.   There should be physical control over documents so that they cannot be improperly reused or falsified. In addition, prenumbered documents help ensure that all paperwork will be accounted for.

As the mail is opened, a list of collections should be made immediately. A responsible official should then compare the list with the cash receipts journal and the bank deposit information. This procedure helps ensure that all mail collections are retained by the firm.

Management (in a small company, the owner) should review monthly comparative financial statements. These statements ought to be sufficiently detailed to allow detection of any unusual revenue, expense, asset, or liability account movements.

All general journal entries should be properly approved by a responsible person. Since these entries can affect all ledger accounts, they must be adequately supervised and controlled.

Even though these are basic control techniques, they are certainly not all that could, or even should be used in any particular situation. Judgment is required to determine exactly what a particular system should contain. The important point is not the memorization of long lists of procedures, but rather to understand the basic concepts and needs of a control system and design it accordingly.

Special Problems of Inventory

Many businesses, such as real estate firms and doctors' offices, are service oriented and thus do not have significant amounts of inventory. However, merchandising firms, such as retail stores and wholesalers, that do have significant amounts of inventory must have procedures to protect these assets. Theft losses by supermarkets from employees and customers average 2 percent of sales; conscientious use of internal control techniques can cut this to $\frac{1}{2}$ per-

59

CHAPTER 2
*Internal
Control in
Manual
Accounting
Systems*

CONCEPT SUMMARY

General Control Techniques

Techniques	Reason for Techniques
Cash disbursements	
1. Use only prenumbered checks for disbursements.	Ensure that all checks are accounted for.
2. Have proper support for checks.	Pay only properly authorized and justified expenditures.
3. Cancel supporting documents when paid.	Pay only once, even for proper expenditures.
4. Check signing by management with no access to records.	Ensure that accounting records accurately reflect checks written.
5. Alter but keep voided checks.	Ensure voided checks are not used.
6. Mail check directly to payee.	Ensure that payee and only payee receives disbursement.
7. Use imprest petty cash fund with one custodian	Establish responsibility for petty cash and review periodically.
Cash receipts	
1. Use cash register, check register daily.	Ensure that all cash receipts are recorded.
2. Deposit cash receipts intact.	Ensure that all cash reciepts are desposited and retained.
3. Reconcile bank statements monthly.	Ensure that all checks are recorded and receipts deposited.
Accounting records	
1. Use prenumbered invoices.	Ensure that all invoices are accounted for.
2. List mail collections, compare with journal.	Ensure that all mail collections are retained by firm.
3. Review monthly comparative financial statements.	Check any unusual revenue, expense, asset, or liability amounts.
4. Approve all entries to general journal.	Ensure that only authorized and proper journal entries are made.

cent. In this regard, there are three basic areas of concern with respect to inventory: purchasing, custody, and recordkeeping.

Purchasing. Purchasing is acquiring the inventory at the best price possible. This area of responsibility should be centralized under a responsible official, usually called the purchasing agent. Since inventory purchasing is one of the primary areas of a firm's operations, proper support for checks and the cancellation of support documents after payment is critically important. Purchase returns are often a major concern and the system should ensure that proper credit is obtained for the returned merchandise. Finally, if an individual operating department requests that inventory be purchased, the department should fill out a requisition form (called a purchase requisition) and have it

60

*Part I
Overview
of Systems
and
Internal
Control*

approved to ensure that all purchases are properly authorized and traced to the source.

Custody. Custody of the inventory involves receiving, storing, and eventually transferring the merchandise. Purchasing and receiving should be performed by different employees, so that each can provide a check upon the other. Similarly, receiving and custody should be independent operations to provide additional checks. Further, there should be a **physical inventory** count taken on a regular basis by employees who are not in charge of the inventory; it is essential that the firm periodically check its inventory to make sure that the records are accurate and the amount is reasonable given the levels of purchases and sales. Finally, there should be physical control of the inventory. The value of the inventory should dictate the amount of physical control—locks, guards, and authorization for access and withdrawal may be used as appropriate.

Recordkeeping. Recordkeeping is the task of keeping track of the amount in inventory. The person in charge of inventory should not also maintain the accounting records; if the same person does both, then a loss of merchandise could be covered in the books. Additionally, when merchandise is moved, for example, from the storeroom to the sales department, vouchers should be prepared to assign responsibility for the transferred goods, and the receiving person should sign them to indicate receipt of the goods. As in the case of checks, all inventory documents should be prenumbered to ensure their physical control. If practicable, a perpetual inventory system should also be used. A perpetual system keeps constant track directly in the accounting records of the receipts and withdrawals of items of inventory as they occur. If a perpetual

CONCEPT SUMMARY	
Inventory Control Techniques	
Purchasing	1. Centralize under a responsible official. 2. Attach purchase invoices and other support to checks for payment. 3. Cancel support when check is paid. 4. Supervise all returned purchases. 5. Use requisitions to initiate purchases.
Custody	1. Separate purchasing from receiving. 2. Separate receiving from custody. 3. Take physical inventory regularly. 4. Use independent employees for physical inventory. 5. Physically control access to inventory.
Recordkeeping	1. Separate recordkeeping from custody. 2. Use vouchers on merchandise moved. 3. Require all documents to be prenumbered. 4. Use a perpetual system, if possible. 5. Compare results of physical inventory to records.

inventory system is operated properly, the accounting records will always be up to date and should agree with the physical realities of inventory.

61

CHAPTER 2
Internal
Control in
Manual
Accounting
Systems

ILLUSTRATION OF INTERNAL CONTROL: THE PURCHASING FUNCTION

The flowchart in Exhibit 2-3 portrays the purchasing function of a medium-sized company, from the preparation of initial documents through the approval of invoices for payment of accounts payable. Assume that all documents are prenumbered.

Use the flowchart to identify and explain the evident internal control weaknesses in the purchasing function. Include in your analysis the internal control weaknesses resulting both from activities performed and activities not performed. Then review the analysis that follows.

Inventory (or Stores) Department

The purchasing flowchart indicates that the purchase requisition does not require approval. This is a practice that invites abuses. The purchase requisition should be approved by a responsible person in the stores department. The approval should be indicated on the purchase requisition after the approver is satisfied that the purchase order was properly prepared based on a need to replace goods or on the proper request from a user department.

Purchase requisition number two is not necessary. Sending purchase requisitions from the stores department to the receiving room serves no purpose. The receiving room does not make any use of the purchase requisitions. It would make more sense to send a copy of the requisition directly to accounts payable in the controller's division where it could be compared to the purchase order to verify that the merchandise requisitioned has been properly ordered.

Purchase requisitions and purchase orders are not compared in the stores department. Although purchase orders are attached to purchase requisitions, there is no indication that any comparison is made of the two documents. Before attaching the purchase order to the purchase requisition, a check should be made that

1. Prices are reasonable and correct.
2. The quality of the goods ordered is proper.
3. Delivery dates are in accordance with company needs.
4. All pertinent data on the purchase order and purchase requisition (such as quantities, specifications, and delivery dates) are in agreement.

Since the requisitioner will ultimately be charged for the materials ordered, this is the logical person to perform these steps.

Purchase orders and purchase requisitions should not be combined and filed in the stores department with the unmatched purchase requisitions. A separate file should be maintained for the combined and matched documents. The unmatched purchase requisitions file can serve as a control over merchandise requisitioned but not yet ordered.

EXHIBIT 2-3   Purchasing Function Flowchart   *(AICPA, adapted)*

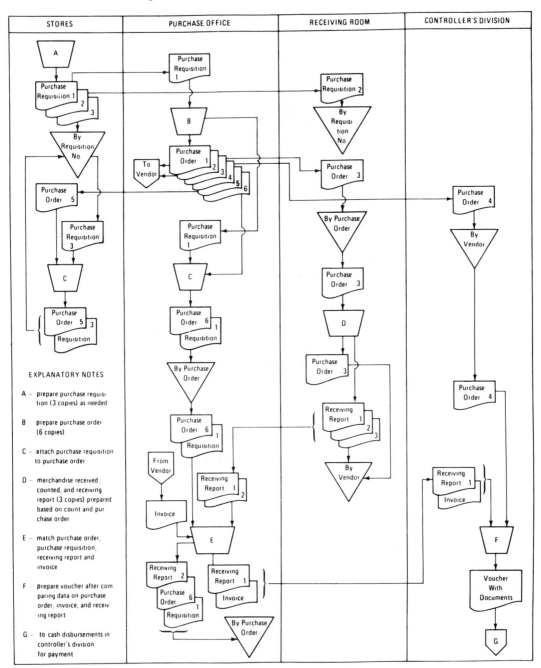

EXPLANATORY NOTES

A – prepare purchase requisition (3 copies) as needed

B – prepare purchase order (6 copies)

C – attach purchase requisition to purchase order

D – merchandise received, counted, and receiving report (3 copies) prepared based on count and purchase order

E – match purchase order, purchase requisition, receiving report and invoice

F – prepare voucher after comparing data on purchase order, invoice, and receiving report

G – to cash disbursements in controller's division for payment

Purchasing Department (or Purchase Office)

63

CHAPTER 2
*Internal
Control in
Manual
Accounting
Systems*

Before preparing the purchase order, the company's purchase office should review the need for the specific merchandise requisitioned and approve the request.

The purchase office should attempt to obtain the highest-quality merchandise at the lowest possible price, and the procedures to achieve this should be included on the flowchart. There is no indication that the purchase office submits purchase orders to competitive bidding when appropriate. This office should be directly involved with vendors in determining the cost of merchandise ordered and should be primarily responsible for deciding the appropriate price and specific vendor to be used.

The purchase office does not review the purchase invoice prior to processing approval. The purchase office should review the vendor's invoice for overall accuracy and completeness and verify details such as quantities, prices, specifications, terms, and dates. If the invoice is in agreement with (1) the purchase requisition, (2) the purchase order, and (3) the receiving report, then the purchase office should clearly indicate on the invoice that it is approved for payment processing. The approved invoice should then be sent to the accounts payable department.

Receiving Department (or Room)

The copy of the purchase order sent to the receiving room should not show quantities ordered. Without this information, receiving will be forced to count goods received carefully. In addition to counting the merchandise received from the vendor, the receiving department personnel should examine the condition and quality of the merchandise upon receipt.

There is no indication of the procedures to follow when the quantity of merchandise received differs from what was ordered. Procedures for handling overshipments and short shipments should be clearly outlined and included on the flowchart.

The receiving report is not sent to the stores department. A copy of the receiving report should be sent from the receiving room directly to the stores department with the goods received. The stores department, after verifying the accuracy of the receiving report, should indicate approval on that copy and send it to the accounts payable department. The copy sent to accounts payable will serve as proof that the merchandise ordered was received by the company and is in the proper department.

Accounts Payable (in the Controller's Division)

There is no indication that any procedures exist for control over vouchers in the accounts payable department. In the accounts payable department, a record of all vouchers submitted to cash disbursements should be maintained, and a copy of the vouchers should be filed in an alphabetical vendor reference file.

There is no indication of control over dollar amounts on vouchers. Accounts payable personnel should prepare and maintain control sheets on the

64

*P*ART *I*
Overview
of Systems
and
Internal
Control

dollar amounts of vouchers. Such sheets should be sent to departments posting transactions to both the general and subsidiary ledgers.

There is no examination of documents prior to voucher preparation. In addition to the matching procedure, the mathematical accuracy of all documents should be verified prior to preparation of vouchers.

The controller should not be responsible for cash disbursements. The cash disbursement function should be the responsibility of the treasurer, so as to provide proper division of responsibility between the custody of assets and the recording of transactions.

There is no indication of procedures for handling purchase returns. Although separate return procedures may be in effect and given on a separate flowchart, some indication of this should be included as part of the purchases flowchart.

Discrepancy procedures are not indicated. The flowchart should indicate what procedures are followed whenever matching reveals a difference of information on the various documents being compared.

There is no indication of any control over prenumbered forms. All prenumbered documents should be accounted for and appropriately filed.

CHAPTER SUMMARY

Internal control should satisfy the accounting objectives of asset protection and financial records accuracy and the administrative objectives of efficiency and compliance with company policies. An effective system of internal control provides for honest and capable employees, separation of duties, establishment of proper procedures, suitable documents, physical control over assets and records, and independent verification by an outside auditor.

Accounting systems contain such built-in safeguards as double-entry bookkeeping, an audit trail, reconciliation of bank statements with company books, and comparison of subsidiary ledger totals with control account balances. In addition, mistakes will be pointed out by customers inquiring about incorrect bills and by vendors inquiring about incorrect or unreceived payments.

Honest, capable employees will on occasion make unintentional accounting errors. These cause minimal damage because they are usually detected and corrected quickly. Embezzlers make deliberate accounting errors (often called irregularities) in order to hide defalcations of cash and inventory. These errors are difficult to find and cost employers billions each year. Embezzlement schemes are often elaborate frauds that involve cash sales, accounts receivable collections, payments to vendors, payroll, and inventory.

The auditor is concerned with finding errors only insofar as they affect the fair presentation of financial statements. Management wants immediate notice of all errors because they may affect the profitability of the business.

To protect cash, management must exercise controls over cash disbursements, cash receipts, and the accounting records. To protect inventory, management must exercise controls over purchasing, custody, and record-keeping.

Analysis of a flowchart can reveal weaknesses in internal control. The flowchart will reveal whether proper reviews and approvals are required, whether documents are processed properly and efficiently, and whether contingency procedures are in place.

65

CHAPTER 2
*Internal
Control in
Manual
Accounting
Systems*

KEY TERMS

Accounting controls *(p. 44)*
Administrative controls *(p. 44)*
Audit *(p. 48)*
Audit trail *(p. 49)*
Authorization *(p. 46)*
Bank reconciliation *(p. 49)*
Budget *(p. 46)*
Chart of accounts *(p. 46)*
Defalcation *(p. 51)*
Embezzlement *(p. 51)*

External controls *(p. 44)*
Footing *(p. 53)*
Imprest petty cash system *(p. 53)*
Internal control *(p. 43)*
Lapping *(p. 54)*
Padding *(p. 52)*
Petty cash *(p. 53)*
Physical inventory *(p. 60)*
Procedures manual *(p. 46)*

QUESTIONS

2-1. What are the four major goals of a system of internal control? Distinguish between accounting and administrative controls.

2-2. The double-entry system and subsidiary ledgers are two important characteristics of accounting systems that help detect errors. Describe how they accomplish this purpose.

2-3. Discuss two techniques for the embezzlement of cash receipts and specify how these embezzlements could be prevented.

2-4. Discuss two techniques for the embezzlement of cash disbursements and specify how these embezzlements could be prevented.

2-5. Discuss two techniques for the theft of inventory and specify how these thefts could be prevented.

2-6. How can the use of prenumbered documents improve internal control? If checks were not prenumbered, what might happen?

2-7. Why is the separation of record keeping from physical custody of assets an important internal control feature? Give three examples of areas where separation would be essential.

2-8. Explain why access to the general journal should be limited and all general journal entries properly authorized.

2-9. List and briefly describe the basic areas of internal control concern with respect to inventory.

2-10. Identify the different individuals and groups involved in the processing of the purchasing system given in Exhibit 2-3.

2-11. Identify the documents used in the purchasing system shown in Exhibit 2-3, and briefly explain the use of each document.

2-12. Rank the deficiencies of the purchasing system which were identified in the chapter in descending order of significance, with the most important deficiency identified as number 1, and on from there.

PART I
Overview
of Systems
and
Internal
Control

2-13. (*AICPA, adapted*)   The Galliano Company has come to you with the following problem. It has three clerical employees who must perform the following functions:

   a.   Maintain general ledger.
   b.   Maintain accounts payable ledger.
   c.   Maintain accounts receivable ledger.
   d.   Prepare checks for signature.
   e.   Maintain cash disbursements journal.
   f.   Issue credit memos on returns and allowances.
   g.   Reconcile the bank account.
   h.   Handle and deposit cash receipts.

The employees are all equally capable. The company requests that you assign the above functions to the three employees so as to achieve the highest degree of internal control. These employees will perform no accounting functions other than the ones listed. Any accounting functions not listed will be performed by persons other than these three employees.

   1.   State how you would distribute the preceding functions among the three employees. Assume that, with the exception of the tasks of the bank reconciliation and the issuance of credit memos on returns and allowances, all functions require an equal amount of time.
   2.   List four possible unsatisfactory combinations of the functions listed.

2-14. (*CMA, adapted*)   Well-managed organizations prepare, use, and maintain policy and procedure manuals covering all important functions. However, because the first-time development of a procedures manual may appear to be a formidable task, an organization may procrastinate in developing the manual in spite of the numerous long-term benefits.

   1.   Explain how a procedures manual benefits an organization.
   2.   Identify and discuss the important attributes that a procedures manual should have as a communication device.
   3.   Identify several important communication weaknesses in a procedures manual that should be avoided in its preparation.

2-15. (*AICPA, adapted*)   Give the purposes or functions of each of the following procedures or techniques that may be included in a system of internal control, and explain how each purpose or function is helpful in strengthening accounting and administrative internal control.

   a.   Fidelity bonding of employees.
   b.   Budgeting of capital expenditures.
   c.   Listing of mail remittances by the mail department when the mail is opened.
   d.   Maintaining a plant ledger for fixed assets.

2-16. (*AICPA, adapted*) Jones is about to commence a study and evaluation of Ajax's system of internal control and is aware of the inherent limitations that should be considered.

67

CHAPTER 2
*Internal
Control in
Manual
Accounting
Systems*

1. What are the objectives of a system of internal accounting control?
2. What are the reasonable assurances that are intended to be provided by a system of internal accounting control?
3. When considering the potential effectiveness of any system of internal accounting control, what do you think might be the inherent limitations that should be recognized?

2-17. (*AICPA, adapted*) Jerome Paper Company engaged you to revise its internal control system. Jerome does not prelist cash receipts before they are recorded and has other weaknesses in processing collections of trade receivables, the company's single largest asset. In discussing the matter with the controller, you find he is chiefly interested in economy when he assigns duties to his 15 office employees. He feels the main considerations are that the work should be done by people who are most familiar with it, capable of doing it, and available when it has to be done.

  The controller believes he has excellent control over trade receivables because receivables are pledged as security for a continually renewable bank loan, and the bank sends out positive confirmation requests occasionally, based on a list of pledged receivables furnished by the company each week. You learn that the bank's internal auditor is satisfied if he gets a rate of response of 70 percent on his requests.

1. Explain how the prelisting of cash receipts as received strengthens internal control over cash.
2. Assume that an employee handles cash receipts from trade customers before they are recorded. List the other duties that this employee should not do, to minimize the opportunity to conceal embezzlement of cash receipts.
3. What do you think are the implications to the bank (if any) if, during the bank auditor's examination of accounts receivable, some of the client's trade customers do not respond to his request for positive confirmation of their accounts?

2-18. (*AICPA, adapted*) The Cook Company had poor internal control over its cash transactions. Facts about its cash position at November 30 were as follows:

a. The cash on the books showed a balance of $18,901.62, which included undeposited receipts.
b. A credit of $100 on the bank's records did not appear on the company's books.
c. The balance per bank statement was $15,550.
d. Outstanding checks were No. 62 for $116.25, No. 183 for $150.00, No. 284 for $253.25, No. 8621 for $190.71, No. 8623 for $206.80, and No. 8632 for $145.28.

The cashier embezzled all undeposited receipts in excess of $3,794.41 and prepared the following reconciliation:

68

PART I
Overview
of Systems
and
Internal
Control

Balance, per books, November 30		$18,901.62
Add: Outstanding checks		
No. 8621	$ 190.71	
No. 8623	206.80	
No. 8632	145.28	442.79
		19,344.41
Less: Undeposited receipts	3,794.41	
Balance per bank, November 30		15,550.00
Deduct: Unrecorded credit		100.00
True cash, November 30		$15,450.00

1. Prepare a supporting schedule showing how much the cashier embezzled.
2. How did the cashier attempt to conceal the theft?

2-19. (*AICPA, adapted*)   Discuss briefly what you regard as the more important deficiencies in the system of internal control in the following situation; in addition, include what you consider to be a proper remedy for each deficiency.

The cashier of the Easy Company intercepted customer A's check payable to the company in the amount of $500 and deposited it in a bank account which was part of the company petty cash fund, of which he was custodian. He then drew a $500 check on the petty cash fund bank account payable to himself, signed it, and cashed it. At the end of the month, while processing the monthly statements to customers, he was able to change the statement to customer A so as to show that A had received credit for the $500 check that had been intercepted. Ten days later he made an entry in the cash received book which purported to record receipt of a collection of $500 from customer A, thus stating A's account at its proper balance, but overstating cash in bank. He covered the overstatement by omitting from the list of outstanding checks in the bank reconcilement, two checks, the aggregate amount of which was $500.

2-20. (*AICPA, adapted*)   Henry Brown is a large independent contractor. All employees are paid in cash because Brown believes this arrangement reduces clerical expenses and is preferred by his employees. You find in the petty cash fund approximately $200, of which $185 is stated to be unclaimed wages. Further investigation reveals that Brown puts unclaimed wages in the petty cash fund so that the cash can be used for disbursements. When the claimant to the wages appears, he is paid from the petty cash fund. Brown contends than this procedure reduces the number of checks drawn to replenish the fund and centers the responsibility for all cash on hand on one person because the petty cash custodian also distributes the pay envelopes.

1. Does Brown's system provide proper internal control of unclaimed wages? Explain fully.
2. Because Brown insists on paying wages in cash, what procedures would you recommend to provide better internal control over unclaimed wages?

2-21. (*AICPA, adapted*)   The Billon Company has an employee bond subscription plan under which employees subscribe to bonds and pay in installments by deductions from their salaries. The cashier keeps the supply of unissued bonds in a safe together with the records showing each employee's subscription and payments to date. The amounts of unissued bonds in the hands of the cashier and the balances due from employees are controlled in the general ledger, which is located in another department. However, the employees may, if they desire, pay any remaining balance to the cashier and receive their bonds.

69

CHAPTER 2
*Internal
Control in
Manual
Accounting
Systems*

When an employee makes a prepayment, the cashier notes the amount on the employee's account, delivers the bond, and receives a receipt from the employee for the bond. The cashier deposits bond cash received in a bond bank account and submits a report showing the transaction to the general ledger department; this report is used as a basis for the necessary adjustments to the bond-related control accounts. Periodic surprise counts of bonds on hand are made by independent employees, who check the amounts of unissued bonds and employees' unpaid balances against the control accounts.

During the cashier's lunch hour or at other times when absent, another employee, with keys to the safe in which unissued bonds and employee bond payment records are kept, comes in and carries out the cashier's procedures as described.

1. Point out the deficiencies in internal control and describe the errors of manipulations that might occur because of each weakness.
2. Recommend changes in the system procedures to eliminate those weaknesses.

2-22. Accounting systems often contain methods, procedures, or divisions of duties which may appear wasteful to an outsider. For each of the following, explain its importance to internal control.

a. Having two financial officers, a treasurer and a controller.
b. Budgeting expenses and capital expenditures.
c. Requiring that every customer be given a cash register tape of his or her purchase.
d. Requiring cash disbursements to be made by check when cash receipts for the day could be used.
e. Not allowing the bank to cash checks payable to the company, even when the company needs cash on hand.
f. Keeping voided checks even though they cannot be used and they take up space.
g. Reconciling the bank statement, even though the bank almost never makes a mistake.
h. Making a separate list of mail collections, even though the bank deposit slip will contain a breakdown of the cash received and deposited.
i. Approving all general journal entries, even though they are almost always routine.
j. Requiring prenumbered checks and sales invoices rather than simply using stacks of available forms.

2-23. (*AICPA, adapted*)   You have been recently engaged by the Alaska Branch of Far Distributing Company. This branch has substantial annual sales which are billed and collected locally. As a part of your review you find that the procedures for handling cash receipts are as follows:

a. Cash collections on over-the-counter sales and C.O.D. sales are received from the customer or delivery service by the cashier. Upon receipt of cash, the cashier stamps the sales ticket "paid" and files a copy for future reference. The only record of C.O.D. sales is a copy of the sales ticket which is given to the cashier to hold until the cash is received from the delivery service.

70

PART I

*Overview
of Systems
and
Internal
Control*

b. Mail is opened by the credit manager's secretary and collections are given to the credit manager for his review. The credit manager then places the collections in a tray on the cashier's desk. At the daily deposit cutoff time, the cashier delivers the checks and cash on hand to the assistant credit manager who prepares collections lists and makes up the bank deposit slip which he takes to the bank. The assistant credit manager also posts collections to the accounts receivable ledger cards and verifies the cash discount allowable.

c. You ascertain that the credit manager obtains approval from the executive office of Far Distributing Company, located in Chicago, to write off uncollectible accounts and that he has retained in his custody as of the end of the fiscal year some collections that were received on various days during last month.

1. Describe the irregularities that might occur under the procedures now in effect for handling cash collections.

2. Give procedures that you would recommend to strengthen internal control over cash collections.

2-24. (*AICPA, adapted*) The Generous Loan Company has 100 branch offices. Each office has a manager and four or five subordinates who are employed by the manager. Branch managers prepare the weekly payroll, including their own salaries, and pay employees from cash on hand. The employee signs the payroll sheet signifying receipt of his salary. Hours worked by hourly personnel are inserted in the payroll sheet from time cards prepared by the employees and approved by the manager.

The weekly payroll sheets are sent to the home office along with the other accounting statements and reports. The home office compiles employee earning records and prepares all federal and state salary reports from weekly payroll sheets. Salaries are established by home office job evaluation schedules. Salary adjustments, promotions, and transfers of full-time employees are approved by a home office salary committee based upon the recommendations of branch managers. Branch managers advise the salary committee of new full-time employees and terminations. Part-time and temporary employees are hired without referral to the salary committee.

Based upon your review of the payroll system, explain several ways that funds for payroll could be diverted.

2-25. (*AICPA, adapted*) The town of Commuter Park operates a private parking lot near the railroad station for the benefit of town residents. The guard on duty issues prenumbered parking stickers to residents who submit an application form and show evidence of residency. The sticker is affixed to the auto and allows the resident to park anywhere in the lot for 12 hours if four quarters are placed in the parking meter. Applications are maintained in the guard office at the lot. The guard checks to see that only residents are using the lot and that no resident has parked without paying the required meter fee.

Once a week the guard on duty, who has a master key for all meters, takes the coins from the meters and places them in a locked steel box. The guard delivers the box to the town storage building where it is opened, and the coins are manually counted by a storage department clerk, who records the total cash counted on a "Weekly Cash Report." This report is sent to the town accounting department. The storage department clerk puts the cash in a safe, and on the following day the cash is picked up by the town's treasurer who manually recounts the cash, prepares the bank deposit slip, and delivers the deposit to the

71

CHAPTER 2
*Internal
Control in
Manual
Accounting
Systems*

bank. The deposit slip, authenticated by the bank teller, is sent to the accounting department where it is filed with the "Weekly Cash Report."

Describe weaknesses in the existing system and recommend one or more improvements for each of the weaknesses to strengthen the internal control over the parking lot cash receipts.

2-26. (*AICPA, adapted*) You have been asked by the board of trustees of a local church to review its accounting procedures. As a part of this review, you have prepared the following comments relating to the collections made at weekly services and recordkeeping for members' pledges and contributions.

The church's board of trustees has delegated responsibility for financial management and audit of the financial records to the finance committee. This group prepares the annual budget and approves major disbursements but is not involved in collections or recordkeeping. No audit has been considered necessary in recent years because the same trusted employee has kept church records and has served as financial secretary for 15 years.

The collection at the weekly service is taken by a team of ushers. The head usher counts the collection in the church office following each service. He then places the collection and a notation of the amount counted in the church safe. Next morning, the financial secretary opens the safe and recounts the collection. She withholds about $100 to meet cash expenditures during the coming week and deposits the remainder of the collection intact. In order to facilitate the deposit, members who contribute by check are asked to draw their checks to "cash."

At their request, a few members are furnished prenumbered predated envelopes in which to insert their weekly contributions. The head usher removes the cash from the envelopes, includes it with the loose cash included in the collection and discards the envelopes. No record is maintained of issuance or return of the envelopes, and the envelope system is not encouraged.

Each member is asked to prepare a contribution pledge card annually. The pledge is regarded as a moral commitment by the member to contribute the stated weekly amount. Based upon the amounts shown on the pledge cards, the financial secretary furnishes a letter to members that supports the tax deductibility of their contributions.

Describe the weaknesses and recommend improvements in procedures for

    a.   Collections made at weekly services.
    b.   Recordkeeping for members' pledges and contributions.

2-27. (*AICPA, adapted*) Trapan Retailing, Inc., has decided to diversify operations by selling through vending machines. Trapan's plans call for the purchase of 312 vending machines which will be situated at 78 different locations within one city and also the rental of a warehouse to store merchandise. Trapan intends to sell only canned beverages in its machines at a standard price. Management has hired an inventory control clerk to oversee the warehousing functions and two truck drivers who will periodically fill the machines with merchandise and deposit cash collected at a designated bank. Drivers will be required to report to the warehouse daily. What internal control will be required in order to assure the integrity of the cash receipts and warehousing functions?

2-28. (*AICPA, adapted*) The Kowal Manufacturing Company employs about 50 production workers and has the following payroll procedures.

The factory supervisor interviews applicants and on the basis of the in-

72

*PART I
Overview
of Systems
and
Internal
Control*

terview either hires or rejects the applicants. The applicant who is hired prepares a W-4 form (Employee's Withholding Exemption Certificate) and gives it to the supervisor. The supervisor writes the hourly rate of pay for the new employee in the corner of the W-4 form and then gives the form to a payroll clerk as notice that the worker has been employed. The supervisor orally advises the payroll department of rate adjustments.

A supply of blank time cards is kept in a box near the entrance to the factory. All workers take a time card on Monday morning, fill in their names, and note in pencil on the time card their daily arrival and departure times. At the end of the week the workers drop the time cards in a box near the door to the factory. The completed time cards are taken from the box on Monday morning by a payroll clerk. Two payroll clerks divide the cards alphabetically between them, one taking the A to L section of the payroll and the other taking the M to Z section. Each clerk is fully responsible for a section of the payroll. The clerk computes the gross pay, deductions, and net pay; posts the details to the employee's earnings records; and prepares and numbers the payroll checks. Employees are automatically removed from the payroll when they fail to turn in a time card.

The payroll checks are manually signed by the chief accountant and given to the supervisor. The supervisor distributes the checks to the workers in the factory and arranges for the delivery of checks to the workers who are absent. The payroll bank account is reconciled by the chief accountant who also prepares the various quarterly and annual payroll tax reports.

List your suggestions for improving the Kowal Manufacturing Company's system of internal control for the factory hiring practices and payroll procedures.

2-29. The following are descriptions of systems of internal control for three companies:

a. When Mr. Clark orders goods for his wholesale business, he sends a duplicate purchase order to the receiving department. When inventory is delivered, Mr. Smith, the receiving clerk, records the receipt of the shipment on this purchase order. Mr. Smith sends the purchase order to the accounting department where it is used to record inventory purchased and accounts payable. The inventory is transported to the storage area, and the purchased quantities are entered on storage records.

b. Every day hundreds of employees clock in using time cards. The timekeepers collect these cards once a week and deliver them to the payroll department. There the time cards are used in the preparation of the payroll checks. The treasurer, Mrs. Webber, signs the checks and returns them to Mr. Strode, the supervisor of the payroll department. The payroll checks are distributed to the employees by Mr. Strode.

c. The smallest branch of Connor Cosmetics in South Bend employs Mary Cooper, the branch manager, and her sales assistant, Janet Hendrix. The branch uses a bank account in South Bend to pay expenses. The account is kept in the name of "Connor Cosmetics—Special Account." To pay expenses, checks must be signed by Mary Cooper or by the treasurer of Connor Cosmetics, John Winters. Ms. Cooper receives the canceled checks and bank statements. She reconciles the branch account herself and files canceled checks and bank statements in her records. She also periodically prepares reports of disbursements and sends them to the home office.

1. List the weaknesses in internal control for each of the above three systems.

2. For each weakness, state the type of error(s) that is (are) likely to result. Be as specific as possible.

3. How would you improve each of the three systems?

73

CHAPTER 2
*Internal
Control in
Manual
Accounting
Systems*

2-30. (*CMA, adapted*) The Jameson Company produces a variety of chemical products for use by plastics manufacturers. The plant operates on two shifts, five days per week, with maintenance work performed on the third shift and on Saturdays as required.

An audit conducted by the staff of the new corporate internal audit department has recently been completed, and the comments on inventory control were not favorable. Audit comments were particularly directed to the control of raw material ingredients and maintenance materials.

Raw material ingredients are received at the back of the plant, signed for by one of the employees of the batching department, and stored near the location of the initial batching process. Receiving tallies are given to the supervisor during the day, and he forwards the tallies to the inventory control department at the end of the day. The inventory control department calculates ingredient usage from weekly reports of actual production and standard formulas. Physical inventory counts are taken quarterly. Purchase requisitions are prepared by the inventory control department, and rush orders are frequent. In spite of the need for rush orders, the production superintendent regularly gets memos from the controller stating that there must be excess inventory because the raw material ingredient inventory dollar value is too high.

Maintenance parts and supplies are received and stored in a storeroom. There is a storeroom clerk on each of the operating shifts. Storeroom requisitions are to be filled out for everything taken from the storeroom; however, this practice is not always followed. The storeroom is not locked when the clerk is out because of the need to get parts quickly. The storeroom is also open during the third shift for the maintenance crews to get parts as needed. Purchase requisitions are prepared by the storeroom clerk, and physical inventory is taken on a cycle count basis. Rush orders are frequent.

1. Identify the weaknesses in Jameson Company's internal control procedures used for
   a. Raw materials ingredients inventory.
   b. Maintenance materials inventory.
2. Recommended improvements that should be instituted for each of these areas.

2-31. (*CMA, adapted*) The Pioneer Sporting Goods Company is a publicly held corporation producing a complete line of sporting goods. The corporate headquarters are located at the major producing location. PSG has a policy that employees may purchase products for their own personal use at the regular wholesale prices. With the exception of normal seasonal activity, sales transactions with employees are neither large nor frequent.

The employee purchase procedure requires that the employee fill out an employee purchase form and have it signed by the warehouse supervisor to verify that the merchandise is available. The form is then taken to the cashier's department where payment is made and the form is stamped "PAID" and initialed. The employee then returns to the warehouse with the form to pick up the merchandise. The warehouse supervisor records the sale for inventory control purposes and files the form in alphabetical order; the alphabetic file is maintained to monitor employee purchases to assure that no employee abuses the purchase privilege. In the cashier's department the cash is received by the custodian of the cash drawer which also is used to meet petty cash needs. All cash receipts and disbursements are recorded on a daily cash activity sheet. The sheet is totaled daily by the cash drawer custodian and is given to the custodian's

74

*PART I
Overview
of Systems
and
Internal
Control*

supervisor, the assistant cashier. Cash activity takes no more than 25 percent of the cash drawer custodian's time; this person's main function is opening mail and sorting and photocopying incoming checks in payment of accounts.

The assistant cashier's primary duties are supervision of two clerks (including the cash drawer custodian) and the daily preparation of the bank deposit. In addition, if the cash drawer custodian is busy or absent, the assistant cashier fills in handling cash disbursements and receipts. The assistant cashier uses the daily cash activity sheets to monitor the fund. On the basis of this analysis, the assistant cashier requests additional cash or deposits excess cash, whichever is required. The fund is counted and balanced to the daily cash activity sheets on a weekly basis.

The internal audit manager recently was hired after the retirement of the previous audit manager. The internal audit manager is currently completing the first audit of the cashier department, and, while there is no evidence of the misuse of cash, the manager feels some recommendations concerning cash handling should be made.

The internal audit manager reports directly to the treasurer. The treasurer and controller of Pioneer Sporting Goods both report to the company president.

Identify and explain briefly the changes you would recommend regarding the cash handling procedures of Pioneer Sporting Goods Company if you were the internal audit manager.

2-32. (*CMA, adapted*) Beccan Company is a discount tire dealer that operates 25 retail stores in the metropolitan area. Both private-brand and name-brand tires are sold by Beccan. The company operates a centralized purchasing and warehousing facility and employs a perpetual inventory system. All purchases of tires and related supplies are placed through the company's central purchasing department to take advantage of quantity discounts. The tires and supplies are received at the warehouse and distributed to the retail stores as needed. The perpetual inventory system at the central facility maintains current inventory records, designated reorder points, optimum order quantities, and continuous counts for each type and size of tire and other related supplies.

The documents employed by Beccan in its inventory control system and their use are as follows.

a. *Retail stores requisition.* This document is submitted by the retail stores to the central warehouse whenever tires or supplies are needed at the stores. The shipping clerks in the warehouse department fill the orders from inventory and have them delivered to the stores.

b. *Purchase requisition.* The clerk in the inventory control department prepares this document when the quantity on hand for an item falls below the designated reorder point. The document is forwarded to the purchasing department.

c. *Purchase order.* The purchasing department prepares this document when items need to be ordered. The document is submitted to an authorized vendor.

d. *Receiving report.* The warehouse department prepares this document when ordered items are received from vendors. The receiving clerk completes the document by indicating the vendor's name, the date the shipment is received, and the quantity of each item received.

e. *Invoice.* The invoice is received from vendors specifying the amount owed by Beccan.

The departments involved in Beccan's inventory control system are as follows.

75

CHAPTER 2
*Internal
Control in
Manual
Accounting
Systems*

a. *Inventory control department.* This department is responsible for the maintenance of all perpetual inventory records for all items carried in inventory. This includes current quantity on hand, reorder point, optimum order quantity, and quantity on order for each item carried.

b. *Warehouse department.* This department maintains the physical inventory of all items carried in inventory. All orders from vendors are received (receiving clerk) and all distributions to retail stores are filled (shipping clerks) in this department.

c. *Purchasing department.* The purchasing department places all orders for items needed by the company.

d. *Accounts payable department.* Accounts payable maintains all open accounts with vendors and other creditors. All payments are processed in this department.

Prepare a flowchart to show how these documents should be coordinated and used among the departments at the central facility of Beccan Company in order to provide adequate internal control over the receipt, issuance, replenishment, and payment of tires and supplies. You may assume that the documents have a sufficient number of copies to assure that the perpetual inventory system can achieve the necessary internal controls.

2-33. (*CICA, adapted*)   After completing the interim examination of the accounts of B. Ltd., a Canadian company, CA sent a letter to the controller, commenting on several matters which she felt required improvement. The controller discussed the comments with his staff and then sent a reply rejecting all of CA's suggested improvements.

Excerpts from CA's letter are marked (L), and exerpts from the controller's reply are marked (R).

a. Petty cash:
   (L)   The positions of petty cash custodian and cashier should be filled by different people. At present, the cashier controls the $500 petty cash fund; this situation results in weak internal control because of the possibility of cash being temporarily transferred between petty cash and cash receipts.
   (R)   A $500 fund is too small to warrant segregation of duties. If the cashier, for example, were involved in a lapping operation of cash receipts, and was using the petty cash fund to cover the shortage, $500 would not go very far. Similarly, if part of the $500 were borrowed by the cashier, the amount would not be significant. The cashier is covered by our blanket employee bond.

b. Bank reconciliation:
   (L)   The bank reconciliation should be prepared by an employee who takes no part in the regular cash receipts or disbursement functions. The reconciliation is now prepared by the bookkeeper, who also prepares the checks and is a signing officer for the company.
   (R)   We do not wish to segregate duties with respect to the bank reconciliation and cash disbursements because the payroll checks are included with the returned checks. The confidential nature of the payroll amounts must be preserved.

76

Part I
Overview
of Systems
and
Internal
Control

c. Purchase orders:

  (L) A purchase order when accepted by the supplier is a binding agreement to purchase the merchandise or services ordered and should therefore include unit prices. Approximately 75 percent of the purchase orders presently issued do not show unit prices.

  (R) As we deal with a limited number of suppliers, and as all of their prices are published in catalogs (against which the accounts payable department checks invoice prices), entering the unit price on the purchase order is an unnecessary clerical step.

d. Cancellation of documents:

  (L) Suppliers' invoices and supporting documents should be canceled by, or under the direct supervision of, a second check-signing officer. At present, vouchers are not canceled; this could lead to a fraudulent or accidental duplicate payment of an invoice.

  (R) Our cash disbursement policy is that all invoices are paid within 15 days of receipt. The chance of a duplicate payment is minimal because a signing officer would notice an old invoice at the time the check was signed. The clerical effort to cancel the vouchers is therefore not warranted.

e. Sales invoices:

  (L) Sales invoices should be prenumbered by the printing company. Without the control provided by prenumbering, the company has no assurance that employees are not suppressing invoices and misappropriating sales proceeds.

  (R) We gave up prenumbering sales invoices because we found that the time spent controlling them was quite significant. Sales invoices in our organization can originate in a number of places; accordingly, the clerk charged with the responsibility of accounting for the numbers had a very difficult time with the many numerical sequences. This problem was further aggravated when we switched to the present prebilling system. The invoices are prepared before the merchandise is shipped, so the shipping department sometimes will hold an invoice for a considerable period of time awaiting receipt of the items from production or from an outside supplier.

f. Vouchers payable:

  (L) The trial balance of vouchers payable should be reconciled monthly with the general ledger control account, by someone other than the accounts payable clerk. At the time of my examination there was a substantial difference between the total of the accounts payable detail listing prepared by the accounts payable clerk and the control account in the general ledger.

  (R) We have a new clerk in the accounts payable department; unfortunately, your examination was conducted after she had been in the position for only two weeks. Our usual practice is to have the accounts payable clerk prepare a listing of unpaid vouchers at the month end and pass this listing to the general ledger clerk, who reconciles it to the general ledger control account. At the time of your examination, the listing had been returned to the accounts payable clerk as a large number of errors had become apparent—she was instructed to locate the errors in her listing as a training exercise.

For each of the six matters described, suggest what CA's position should be in her reply to the controller, supporting the position you suggest by listing factors CA would consider in drafting her reply.

DECISION CASE

77

CHAPTER 2
*Internal
Control in
Manual
Accounting
Systems*

(*CMA, adapted*) Dragano, Inc., a regional distributor of building products with headquarters in New York, has been operating on the East Coast for a number of years. By the end of 1992, there were 15 local sales branches and annual sales totaled $15 million.

In an effort to expand its area of sales coverage, Dragano acquired Gruendo, Inc., in 1993 and operated the company as a wholly owned subsidiary. Gruendo, also a distributor of building products, with ten branches and annual sales of $10 million, is located in the Midwest with headquarters in Chicago.

Both companies sell to individuals as well as to contractors. Terms of sale to individuals are cash; sales to contractors are made on 30-day open account, provided the contractor's credit is cleared by the headquarters office. The bulk of the company's dollar sales volume is to contractors on account.

Dragano customers are billed from the New York office, and Gruendo customers are billed from the Chicago office, on a cycle basis. The billings are completed on the basis of daily sales listings, along with prenumbered charge slips, rendered by the branches to headquarters. The listings identify cash and charge sales separately. All cash receipts are deposited daily and intact by the branches in local depositories. Charge account payments are remitted directly to the office from which the account was billed.

Early in 1994, Dragano management became concerned about the apparent excess of accounts receivable on the books of Gruendo relative to Dragano. Both companies utilize the same credit policy and had approximately the same mix of cash and credit sales. Gruendo's accounts receivable, however, represented 50 days' sales, while Dragano's represented 30 days' sales.

This concern prompted the management of Dragano to ask the corporate accounting staff to investigate the situation. In confirming the accounts of Gruendo, the accountants conducting the audit discovered that

   a. Ten percent of account balances represented invoices already paid by customers, and
   b. An additional 20 percent of the account balances represented underpayments by customers on specific invoices.

The audit disclosed that the Gruendo cashier opened the mail and deposited some checks to a company-named account for which his signature was the only authorized one. He was responsible for preparation of monthly billing statements and thus was able to remove from the statement invoices already paid by customers.

The underpayment of accounts was the result of arrangements made by branch salespersons with the knowledge of the credit manager, a long-time employee of Gruendo, whereby favored customers were quoted lower than list prices. The granting of discounts in this fashion had been a practice of long standing. The Chicago office billed at list prices, but the customers paid at the quoted rates, resulting in the apparent underpayments. The amount of the difference totaled $600,000.

78

PART I
Overview
of Systems
and
Internal
Control

Required:

1. Comment critically on the accounting, internal control, and other procedures of Gruendo, Inc., described above.

2. Recommend any changes that you think should be made in Gruendo's procedures. Explain your answer fully.

3 Approaches to Business Data Processing

Overview

The different ways in which business data processing systems can be organized to trade off timeliness, flexibility, complexity, and cost; approaches to acquiring computer systems.

Learning Objectives

Thorough study of this chapter will enable you to:

1. Select appropriate hardware for the needs of a business.
2. Describe the role of software in a computer system.
3. Determine the type of batch (sequential) or interactive (on-line) processing best suited to a business application.
4. Flowchart a computer-based system for business data processing.
5. Suggest solutions to problems of data communication among collection and processing locations.
6. Explain the roles of hardware, software, maintenance, and operation in a computer system.
7. Choose the type of computer system vendor best suited to the requirements of a business.
8. Know what to look for in a computer acquisition specification sheet, a vendor proposal, and a contract with a vendor.

Outline

Computer-Based Data Processing

The Batch and Interactive System Approaches

Centralized Versus Decentralized Approaches

Computer System Acquisition

80

*PART I
Overview
of Systems
and
Internal
Control*

SYSTEMS IN THE REAL WORLD

Hard Disk Basics

Building a workable hard disk drive requires a variety of engineering disciplines, a little luck, and some black magic.

For example, consider the drive's read/write heads. In a garden-variety hard disk drive, a read/write head "flies" approximately 4 microns (10 millionths of an inch) above the surface of a data platter rotating at 3,600 rpm. Near the edge of a 5.1-inch platter, that's equivalent to a linear velocity of 55 mph. On the platter, data consists of patterns of magnetization squeezed 10,000 or more to the inch. Each track holds approximately 10,000 bytes, and adjacent data tracks lie barely a few thousandths of an inch apart. Under these demanding conditions, the read/write head must reliably extract a weak electrical signal, while ignoring the influence of data stored on adjacent tracks.

To visualize what happens in a hard disk failure scenario, imagine that you're riding in a hovercraft traveling at 55 mph along a glassy-smooth road. You're holding your hand a fraction of an inch above the road surface. Now, imagine your hand encountering some spilled gravel. As your hand passes over the gravel, air pressure forces your hand up. The muscles in your arm (analogous to the read/write head's support structure) attempt to compensate by forcing your hand downward into the road surface. You can picture the results.

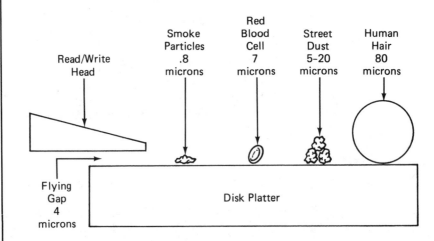

SOURCE: *Computer Shopper, 7/90,* reprinted by permission.

COMPUTER-BASED DATA PROCESSING

Chapters 1 and 2 discussed the basic business cycles, their related processing, and their internal control aspects. Chapters 3 and 4 extend this discussion to computer-based systems. Chapter 3 discusses the basic advantages and characteristics of computer-based systems, including their flowcharting. The use of a computer in business systems is often called electronic data processing (EDP). Chapter 4 presents the internal control aspects of these systems.

Characteristics of Business Processing

All business processing systems, such as those discussed in Chapters 1 and 2, whether completely manual or totally automated, exhibit the following characteristics.

Large amounts of data. All businesses create significant amounts of data in the course of their operation, which must be processed accurately. Some of these data must be retained for long periods of time, while other data must be digested into some form of usable output (such as statements and reports).

Repetitive events. Businesses tend to experience the same common transactions repeatedly. Most business processing time is spent on a few (perhaps a dozen or so) basic events, and the calculations and decisions required to process these events are very simple. Each event is called a transaction, and this is then called **transaction processing.**

Advantages of the Computer in Business Data Processing

There are three distinct advantages to processing data through a computer system:

Speed. In the speed of calculations, decisions, and input/output, no processing alternative can match a computer system.

Memory. Storage devices and the processor are able to keep extremely large amounts of data accessible in very small spaces without ever forgetting any of it.

Reliability. Computer hardware does exactly what it is told to do. Since they follow instructions without deviation and without complaint, **computer systems** do not make mistakes in their own right. The drawbacks are that hardware devices must be given instructions in minute detail; will do everything they are told to do (no matter how silly it may seem to a human being); and apply no perception, reasoning, initiative, or common sense to their activities.

Thus, the advantages of computer systems could not be better suited to the needs of business processing. Business systems must have the capacity to receive, store, and output very large amounts of data quickly and accurately, and do very simple (for a computer) and repetitive processing of these data. Since processor speed, even for complex calculations and decisions, is well in excess of the speed of other hardware, the emphasis in the design of a business computer system must be on the input/output and data storage components of the system. Here is where bottlenecks and inefficiencies can occur in business processing systems. Contrast this situation to scientific processing, where comparatively small amounts of data input and output might be required in a processing problem, relatively little or no permanent storage is necessary, and calculations are complex. In scientific systems, the emphasis must be placed on the processor.

PART I
Overview
of Systems
and
Internal
Control

Scale of Equipment for Business Data Processing

The speed and memory of any computer are far greater than the speed and memory of people, but there is a wide range of equipment used in business data processing, with a wide range of speed and memory. This range is almost continuous in every measure of speed, capacity, capabilities, and cost. However, to make this vast array of computer equipment intelligible, most people break this range down into three groups:

1. Mainframe computers, the largest ones.
2. Minicomputers in the midrange.
3. Microcomputers, the smallest ones.

A number of characteristics are used to distinguish among mainframes, minicomputers, and microcomputers: number of users, processing speed, main memory, and disk storage. Each level of computer was introduced at a different stage in the history of computer development. Today all three are widely used each with its own market niche.

Mainframes. Mainframes were introduced in the mid-1950s by UNIVAC. Other manufacturers, especially IBM, soon entered the market. Technological advances have increased both the speed and size of the main memory of mainframes. Mainframes are used for the largest-scale data processing, such as airline reservation systems, the largest banks, and the largest insurance companies.

Minicomputers. Minicomputers entered the market in 1965 with the introduction of the DEC PDP-8. These computers were smaller than the then available mainframes and cost less. Software and input/output devices were adapted or developed for use on minicomputers for business data processing. Minicomputers are typically used in business for medium-scale processing, for either a department or a modest-sized company.

Microcomputers. As technology advanced, the components of computers became smaller in size while retaining some of the power of the bigger machines. The term microcomputer was used to indicate a desktop, single-user computer. By 1975 microcomputers became available; this led to the first marketable microcomputer, the Apple. IBM entered the microcomputer (sometimes called the personal computer) market in 1981, and the market has exploded since then, with over 40 million microcomputers sold and tremendous gains made in speed, memory, reliability, and cost.

These different types of computers are rapidly changing and each is taking on the best characteristics of the others. In addition, there is a major movement toward data communication between computers of all sizes to form networks of computers. Chapter 7 discusses these issues in greater depth.

Computer Software

83

CHAPTER 3
*Approaches
to Business
Data
Processing*

Regardless of the size of the computer system, the system has the same basic components. Computer **software** refers to the entire set of instructions that direct and control the activities of the hardware. Without software the hardware would sit unused; together hardware and software make up the computer system. At a minimum, computer systems software always require an operating system and an application program.

Operating System. This is a set of internally stored general instructions that control and coordinate the activities of the various hardware devices (input, storage, processing, and output). These instructions are called the master program, the control program, or the **operating system** and are, generally speaking, supplied by the hardware vendor. Thus, at a minimum, this software comes with the hardware as a combined package from the vendor. The most common operating systems are MVS for mainframe computers, UNIX for minicomputers, and DOS for microcomputers; again, these are discussed further in Chapter 7.

Application Program. This is a set of specific instructions to the processor to perform certain actions on certain specific data and the location of these relevant data. It is these instructions, usually called the **application program** because they do a specific set of processing toward a desired result or solution, that people normally think of when programming or computer programs are discussed. These instructions (the application program) may be written by the user or purchased from companies called software vendors. Many different programming languages can be used to write these application programs and writing such an application program is generally called programming the computer. The person who writes the program is called a **programmer.** The end-user tools, such as spreadsheets and word processing programs, are the most common application programs; Chapter 8 discusses these application programs in greater depth. Other important application programs are data base management systems (discussed in Chapters 5 and 6) and accounting applications (discussed in Chapters 9–13).

Relationship Between Software and Hardware: The Translation Process

System users have a processing need or problem and want to use computer hardware to fill the need or solve the problem. However, computers only understand their own language, called machine language, which is a series of 0's and 1's used in various combinations. Initially, people wrote computer software in machine language. The difficulties of doing this, however, are overwhelming in all but the most straightforward instances. For effective and efficient human-to-computer communication to take place, computers themselves must assist the translation of human language instructions into machine language instructions to be carried out by the hardware. This translation process involves three steps.

84

PART I
Overview
of Systems
and
Internal
Control

Programming Language. The use of a programming language rather than a natural language is the first step in the translation process. All natural languages contain ambiguities that require inference and contextual translation and thus would be impossible for a machine to translate in an exact manner. Programming languages require people to issue instructions in a precise format using commands, syntax, and structure in a rigidly fixed manner. Although programming languages may be based on natural language, the ambiguities are removed and a precise structure is substituted, to provide for unambiguous translation. An application program written in a programming language is called a **source program,** and the programming language is often called a **source language.** The most common programming languages now in use are COBOL, FORTRAN, and C. End-user tools such as spreadsheets and word processors, for which speed of response to the user is critical are sometimes written in Assembler.

Compiler. Even programming languages, however, are not understood by computers, so they must undergo a further translation into machine language. The rigid syntax and structure of programming languages makes them susceptible to translation by a special software component called a **compiler.** The compiler is itself a program designed to accept a source program as input and convert it instruction by instruction into machine language. Each programming language must have its own unique compiler based on the structure of the language. Compilers are often acquired, along with the operating system, from the computer vendor as a package with the hardware system, but can be also acquired from other software publishers.

Object Program. The original set of instructions translated into machine language is called the **object program.** It is the object program that is understood by the processor. The processor interprets each machine language instruction and issues directions to other hardware components of the system to carry out the processing. A purchaser of an application program, such as programs for word processing, spreadsheets, data bases, or accounting, will get the object program.

Computer Hardware

Computer **hardware** refers to the machines that make up the system. Most people mean hardware when they use the terms computer or computer system.

Processor. The **processor** (sometimes called the **central processing unit** or CPU) is the computer in a computer system. The processor directs the activities of the entire system. The processor gets its instructions from humans via a computer program, which details the processing steps necessary to solve a problem. In effect, users communicate through computer programs to the processor, which, in turn, issues directions to the other components of the system to carry out the processing task.

Processors have their own storage capacity, usually called **main memory** or **primary storage.** The information stored here is accessible to the processor without intervention by humans. This primary storage is less than other types of storage and is usually reserved for the operating system that exercises overall control of the system and the program and data for the particular processing application currently being "run" on the system. One of the commonly accepted measures of processor capacity and sophistication (and consequently price) is the size of primary storage.

Input/Output Devices. Before any of the advantages of computer processing can be realized, a link must be provided between the computer (processor) and the person with a problem to be solved. Input/output devices provide this link by transferring instructions (programs) and data (names, numbers, symbols) efficiently from people to machines and then returning the results of this processing to the users. Some machines, such as a bar code reader at a supermarket checkout counter, are exclusively input, and some machines, such as a printer, are exclusively output. However, most can serve both the input function, which provides for the entry of instructions and data to the computer and the output function, which provides for results. In addition, many input/output devices also serve a data storage function for processed information. These are sometimes called **file devices** because their storage capacity makes possible the long-term retention of large files of data within the system on magnetic tapes or disks. Any equipment attached to the processor is called a **peripheral.**

Characteristics of Data Access

Despite the tremendous range of equipment suitable for business data processing, there are certain basic characteristics of data access. These characteristics are the basis for topics later in the chapter regarding the basic orientation of the processing system.

On-Line Versus Off-Line. Since the processor is the focal point of any computer hardware system, the relationships of the other hardware components to the processor are important in hardware system designs. Some hardware devices remain in direct, two-way contact with the processor at all times without human assistance; others have only one-way and intermittent contact with the processor. The same distinction can be made with respect to data transmitted or stored by these devices. The terms **on-line** and **off-line** are used to describe the relationship of computer hardware devices to the processor as well as the accessibility of data to the processor. On-line and off-line, then, may be applied to hardware components or to data in a computer system. A hardware device is said to be on-line if the device is in constant contact with the processor and interchange is possible. Data are said to be on-line if they are input from or stored in a system that is accessible to the processor at all times without intervention. Hardware devices and data whose accessibility to the processor is intermittent and requires some human action are described as off-line.

On-line and off-line distinctions are most important in system design when applied to data storage in a computer system. Large amounts of information

86

*Part I
Overview
of Systems
and
Internal
Control*

CONCEPT SUMMARY		
Characteristics of Data Access		
	Availability	*Accessibility*
Primary storage	On-line	Direct access
Disk storage	On-line or off-line	Direct access
Magnetic tape storage	Off-line	Sequential access

(files) must be stored, processed, and then stored again, so business processing systems must be able to provide for extensive storage capacity beyond the processor. This storage is often called **external, secondary,** or **peripheral storage** and almost always takes the form of magnetic tape or disks. Secondary storage may be on-line or off-line. Generally, magnetic tape storage is off-line because there may be only a relatively few tape drives compared to the number of reels of tape on which information is stored, and these reels must be placed on the tape drive to be within the reach of the processor. Disk storage is usually on-line; however, with removable disk packs this type of storage may also be off-line.

Direct Versus Sequential Access. Another important distinction for hardware system design is between direct access and sequential access to data. **Direct access** (sometimes referred to as **random access**) means that the time it takes for the computer to retrieve instructions or data is not affected by the exact storage location of the information on the media. On direct access storage devices like disks, each piece of information is equally accessible regardless of its position on the disk. All disks are necessarily direct access by their design. In **sequential access** storage, the location of the information affects the time it takes for the processor to retrieve it since all instructions and data on the beginning of the media must be passed through in order to get to information stored at the end. Magnetic tape is sequential access.

Flowcharting of Computer-Based Systems

The computer is well suited to business data processing, and virtually all new systems will involve computer processing as part of the system. Thus, we need to extend the flowchart symbols for manual processing, summarized in Exhibit 1-3, to include the flowchart symbols necessary for systems involving a computer. Exhibit 3-1 shows the additional symbols needed for a computer-based system. The manual flowchart symbols will continue to be required in the flowcharting of all systems because virtually all business systems have manual components. The computer-oriented symbols have numbers to connect to the following discussion.

EXHIBIT 3-1   Standard Flowchart Symbols for Computer-Based Processing   *87*

CHAPTER 3
Approaches
to Business
Data
Processing

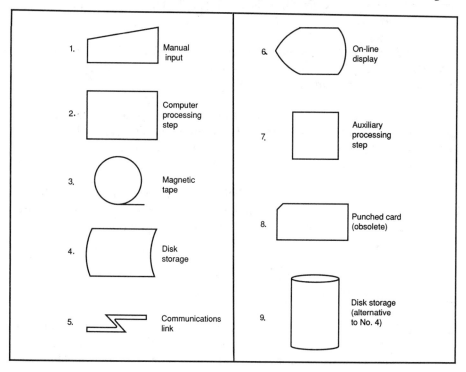

Note: Refer to Exhibit 1-3 to review the standard flowchart symbols for manual processing.

Manual input. The first computer-based symbol is that for manual input, typically through a keyboard. This keyboard may be attached to an off-line device that will accumulate data until the time for processing. Alternatively, the keyboard may be attached to a terminal, with both input and output capability. Often, typing data into a computer is called keyboarding.

Computer processing. The second symbol is that for a computer processing step, usually a computer program or group of related programs.

Magnetic tape. The third symbol is for magnetic tape storage. These magnetic tapes will function as either input or output from a processing run, so there will be a flow line either from the magnetic tape symbol to the processing step (for input) or from the processing step (for output).

Disk storage. The fourth symbol is for disk storage. Disks can function as both input and output, so there may be double-headed flow lines both from and to disk storage from the processing step.

Communications link. The fifth symbol is for communications links over data lines or the telephone system. Chapter 7 will discuss data communications and networks in greater depth. Most discussion of these topics is deferred to that chapter.

88

*Part I
Overview
of Systems
and
Internal
Control*

On-line display. The sixth symbol is for a on-line display, usually the screen attached to a terminal. This will typically be used for output or both input and output.

Auxiliary processing step. The seventh symbol is for an auxiliary processing step. This is a processing step not involving the computer, such as an off-line device to prepare input to the system.

Punched card (obsolete). The eighth symbol is for a punched card. The punched card is now obsolete, and the flowcharts in this book will not include them. But other flowcharts you may deal with could still have them.

Alternative disk storage. The ninth symbol is an alternative symbol for disk storage and thus serves the same function as the fourth symbol. The flowcharts in this book and elsewhere use these symbols interchangeably.

THE BATCH AND INTERACTIVE SYSTEM APPROACHES

The actual design of a computer system to take full advantage of this suitability depends on the particular information needs of a business, its most repetitive and important processing problems, and many other factors, including cost. But the first decision to be made in establishing a hardware configuration is the basic orientation of the system. Two such basic orientations—batch and interactive—will be discussed in this section.

Batch Processing Systems

In **batch processing systems,** data are stored and processed in a specified order and at specified discrete times. Generally, data are accumulated and stored for a certain period of time or until a certain quantity of data is accumulated. Then, processing of all data accumulated, called a batch of transactions, takes place at once, and output is generated from the complete data. This approach, called batch processing, is ideal if information needs are predictable, and timely, immediate processing results are not necessary. Data, however, must be organized on some numerical (sequential) basis for batch processing to be efficient. Data storage in batch systems may be off-line since processing takes place only at predetermined times and data needs are known well in advance. Most batch systems are built around magnetic tapes, although data may be processed sequentially from disk storage. Either batch or interactive processing is possible with disk, while magnetic tape is purely sequential.

Refinements of the batch processing approach can be made in the process of conversion of source documents data to machine input form and in the methods of transmission of these converted data to the computer for processing. Consider the brief descriptions of two sequential batch approaches in Exhibit 3-2, and note the differences in data conversion and transmission.

EXHIBIT 3-2 Two Approaches to Batch Processing   89

CHAPTER 3
Approaches
to Business
Data
Processing

Basic Batch	Batch with Remote Data Transmission
Source documents are gathered and manually transferred to the computer site.	Documents are converted to machine input form at various remote data collection points.
All data are converted to machine input form at the computer site.	At certain predetermined times, the data are electronically transferred to the computer site to be stored for processing.
Processing takes place in batches at predetermined times.	Processing takes place in batches at predetermined times.
Output is generated at the computer site and then manually transferred to users.	Output is generated at the computer site and may be electronically transferred to remote points to users.
Keyboard for input and printers for output is usual in such a system.	Input and output devices are probably a combination of those used in basic batch plus some remote devices such as terminals and printers.
Data storage is likely magnetic tape for files of permanent or semipermanent data.	Data storage is likely magnetic tape for files of permanent or semipermanent data.
This is the simplest and least expensive large system to operate.	Better turnaround and accuracy often result as compared to basic batch, since some manual functions are eliminated. Costs of this system are generally higher than basic batch.
Example applications include payroll processing and financial statement preparation.	Example applications include remote collection of sales data from stores for sales analysis and remote transmission of sales orders by traveling sales representatives.

Both approaches to batch processing require that

1. Data be susceptible to sequential organization and processing.
2. Data be processed at discrete times in groups of similar transactions or events.
3. Management does not require immediate information on individual transactions.

The second approach to batch processing, with remote data transmission, is often called **remote job entry (or RJE).** Sequential orientation and batch processing represent the oldest approach to computer hardware system design and is still a widely used approach in business. On computers specifically designed for batch processing, it is the simplest and least expensive approach to processing business data. Also, batch processing is the most efficient method of processing from the point of view of machine efficiency.

90

PART I
*Overview
of Systems
and
Internal
Control*

How Batch Processing Works

Exhibit 3-3 is a schematic of how basic batch processing works in the processing of customer orders. The exhibit is not a complete flowchart because it does not show the final disposition of all the input used and output generated. But it is enough to illustrate the basic concepts without distraction by excessive detail.

Receive Orders. The company receives customer orders, either through the mail already filled out or over the phone where a salesperson fills out the appropriate form. In both cases there is a source document, the customer order. Other copies will trigger shipment of the goods and update various manual files, but one copy of each customer order will eventually go to data processing. Every day, a copy of the customer order for each order shipped that day will be accumulated into a batch. The batch of that day's shipped customer orders will then go to data processing.

Enter Data. Data processing will then enter at a terminal each item on the order. There will be one line of input per item rather than one line per order because this transaction must update both the customer balance and the amount on hand of each of the inventory items. The input data go to the data control clerk, who processes the data through an edit program that generates

1. An edit listing of all input data, with any errors identified.
2. A file of order transactions, with one record for each item on each order.

If there are any errors, the data control clerk corrects the data in error and reruns the edit program, creating another edit listing and another order transaction file. The data control clerk repeats this process until there are no errors in the data. No further processing occurs until all errors are corrected. When there are no longer errors, the order transaction file is sorted into inventory item number sequence. This sort is required: The transaction file must be in the same order as the master file because both are accessed sequentially.

Process Transactions. The inventory processing program then reads in both the sorted order transaction file and the inventory master file. For every set of information on inventory items read from the inventory master file, a similar set is written to the updated inventory master file. If one or more transactions affect an inventory item, the program reduces the amount of inventory on hand. The updated information is then written to the updated inventory master file. If no transaction affects an inventory item, then unchanged information is written to the updated inventory master file. The output master file will then always have information on exactly the same number of inventory items as the input master file, whether it is 1,000 inventory items or 10,000 inventory items.

The same order transaction file is then sorted into customer number sequence. The reason for this sort is the same: The transaction file must be in the same order as the master file it will update. Processing the transactions against the customer master file uses the same logic as that given for the in-

EXHIBIT 3-3 **Flowchart of Batch Processing**

91

CHAPTER 3
*Approaches
to Business
Data
Processing*

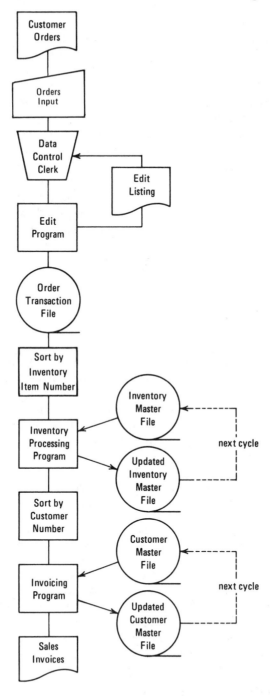

ventory master file. Any customer records with transactions are updated to reflect the new balance owed before writing the customer information to the updated customer master file. In addition, the invoicing program prints a sales invoice for each customer with transactions. The master file is in sequential

92

*PART I
Overview
of Systems
and
Internal
Control*

order, and as a result, it is necessary to put transactions in sequential order for processing.

Tape Rotation. The physical tapes used are rotated in a grandfather-father-son system. Because the input file (called the father) and the output file (called the son) could be destroyed while the computer is processing them, there is a third, earlier copy of the master file called the grandfather. The advantage of this approach is that there is always a copy of each master file (the grandfather) that is not on the computer. This copy can then re-create the current master file (the father) if that master copy is destroyed.

The batch approach does not require all data to be on-line. If, for example, a bank had a demand deposit (checking account) application and a savings accounts application, the bank could load the appropriate tapes for the demand deposit application, process the entire day's transactions for that application, and then, only after that application is completely finished, move on to the tapes and transactions of the next application. Normally, the transactions were accumulated during the day and then processed over night. When the staff arrived the next morning, the printout of the updated master file would be available for use.

Interactive Processing Systems

Interactive processing systems are characterized by data storage in direct access, easily accessible media, and by processing that can take place immediately as transactions occur. Since processing in interactive systems takes place in any order as events occur or as information is needed, data storage must be in on-line, direct access form. Disks are the most widely used on-line, direct access storage, and most interactive systems are built around this media. Often, interactive processing is also called on-line processing.

The interactive approach to processing requires that

1. Data always be available in direct access storage.
2. Some processing be initiated from remote locations away from the computer system.
3. Management needs for timely information make it impossible for processing to wait while significant data accumulation takes place or for specific points in time.

In summary, interactive processing makes up-to-date information constantly available. Basic approaches to interactive systems can differ in the extent to which processing can be initiated from remote locations as transactions occur. Exhibit 3-4 describes two interactive systems that differ in the degree that continuous transaction processing is allowed. Sometimes on-line transaction processing is called **real-time processing.**

How Interactive Processing Works

Exhibit 3-5 gives a schematic of how interactive processing works in the processing of customer orders. As in the schematic for batch processing, it is not a complete flowchart, but it does illustrate the basic concepts.

EXHIBIT 3-4   Two Approaches to Interactive (On-Line) Processing   *93*

CHAPTER 3
*Approaches
to Business
Data
Processing*

Inquiry/Response Only	*On-Line Transaction Processing (OLTP)*
Direct interaction with the computer is possible through remote terminals for questions and answers.	Direct interaction with the computer is possible through remote terminals for questions and answers and for the processing of data.
Normal processing is interrupted as questions come in and the processor searches data stored in on-line, direct access disks to answer questions.	Normal processing is initiated from remote terminals as transactions occur with data stored in on-line, direct access disks.
No processing is done from remote terminals; only a question-and-answer diaglogue is possible and questions are answered using the data available.	Since normal processing is continuous, there is no time lag between the occurrence of a transaction and the reflection of that transaction in the the stored data of the computer system. This is sometimes called a real-time system.
Normal processing is accomplished at the computer site at fixed times using input/output devices similar to that used in batch processing systems.	Unless errors occur, information is constantly accurate and up to date because the computer system data instantly reflect events as they occur.
This approach provides much more timely information than batch processing at greater cost. The information is still not precisely up to date because processing is not continuous and some time lag is necessary between the occurrence of an event and its reflection in the data files of the system.	This is very costly and complex system to implement and operate. However, the movement in computer systems has been toward this design.
Example applications are utilities and department stores, where payments and purchases are processed at night, but where inquiry on the status of an account is possible during the day.	Example applications are airline reservation systems and some banks where reservations and banking transactions would be processed immediately on-line.

The company could receive customer orders in the mail or fill out customer order forms from phone calls; in those cases there would be a source document. A clerk would then take the information from the customer order forms and key it into the terminal. For orders received over the phone, it would also be possible to key the information directly into the terminal, eliminating the need for a source document. This approach is more efficient because it eliminates a time-consuming step. But this approach also increases the difficulty of ensuring the proper authorization of all transactions, since all transactions would no longer tie back to a source document.

The computer will immediately perform all program checks, such as reasonableness, completeness, and validity, as the information is keyed into the terminal. In addition, as the customer order is entered, the computer checks

94

PART I
Overview
of Systems
and
Internal
Control

EXHIBIT 3-5   Flowchart of Interactive (On-Line) Processing

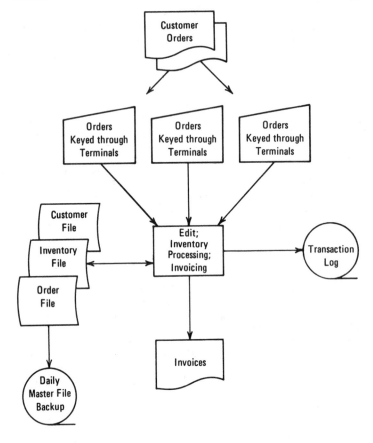

available inventory quantities and checks the customer's credit. If the order is accepted, the computer allocates the inventory quantities to that order. When the goods are shipped, the computer invoices the customer and updates the on-hand inventory balances.

Advantages and Disadvantages of the Batch and Interactive Approaches

The particular system orientation a company chooses will depend on its overall processing problems and applications and its information needs. Generally, however, the necessity for up-to-date accurate information must be balanced against the extra cost and complexity of interactive systems. Also important in basic hardware design is the level of flexibility in the system. The capacity of the system for change and growth as business processing needs and circumstances change is a critical dimension of any hardware configuration. Business data processing systems exhibit a strong general trend toward quick response (interactive) systems as competition and customer demands accelerate and hardware and system costs decrease.

CONCEPT SUMMARY

Comparison of Processing Alternatives

	Batch	*Interactive (On-line)*
Data entry	Data are keyboarded off-line prior to processing.	Data are typed in on-line through the terminals or read in from bar code scanners.
Input validation	Data are processed with separate edit run to validate input.	Program checks input for errors as the data are typed in.
Error correction	Data control clerk corrects errors and reruns edit; no further processing occurs until there are no errors.	Terminal operator corrects errors as they occur.
Transaction order	Because of sequential access, transactions must be sorted and are processed in master file order.	Because of direct access, transactions need not be sorted and are processed in the order they occur.
Master file backup	Reflecting the grandfather-father-son concept, father tapes are saved for backup, and son tapes become father tapes in the next cycle.	Entire contents of all master files are dumped to tape on a daily basis.
Transaction backup	Transaction files are saved even after they have been processed to re-create father and son master files.	Transaction log tape is created containing every processed transaction.

CENTRALIZED VERSUS DECENTRALIZED APPROACHES

Centralized Processing

One stand-alone computer that processes every transaction and that maintains all data files for the system is still the standard approach to business data processing. This centralized approach can work with either a batch system or an interactive system. With a batch system, all source documents are transmitted to the computer center, while with an interactive system, all terminals are connected to the central computer. This centralized system, which is often referred to as the **host computer,** makes it easier to establish and maintain control standards. These stand-alone computers can be quite large and arrayed with numerous tape drives, disk drives, printers, and other equipment to do the general accounting for a large business or they can be quite small (such as a single microcomputer system to prepare a departmental budget). Eventually,

96

Part I
Overview
of Systems
and
Internal
Control

however, the following circumstances create the need for the stand-alone computer to communicate with other computers.

Nonresponsive. The host computer is often not responsive to the needs of users. As a result, people out in the organization buy microcomputers to help them with their tasks. Eventually, however, the user will find it necessary to get information from the host computer down into the microcomputer. This requires that the host computer and the microcomputer communicate to transfer data from the host to the microcomputer.

Local Data Needs. Most of the detailed data processed by a centralized system are of interest only to local management, while higher management is concerned only with summary information. As a result, local management seeks its own processing capability, but the local and central computers then need to communicate to send data from the local computer to the host.

Dispersed Operations. A business often has several computers in various locations across the country. If a company has several branch operations or different areas of the business in different locations, coordination of overall company operations requires communication between the computers.

Multiple Computers. A business can have several computers in the same office, such as one computer for accounts receivable, one for payroll, and one for general ledger accounting. The need then arises for sharing disk files, since all the computers may require information from the same set of transactions to be processed differently.

Distributed Processing

Because of situations like those just described, there has been a trend to **distributed data processing.** The concept of distributed data processing is to place computing power in the organization at the appropriate level so that data entry, inquiry, and initial processing can occur where the data originate and where the data are most used. For most firms, distributed data processing amounts to a hierarchy of computers, with local machines sending summary information to the central, host computer system.

In the case of giant retailer Sears, each cash register/terminal at a store is connected to the store's minicomputer, which performs local processing tasks, such as checking credit status of customers and keeping track of the store's inventory levels. Each night, the regional computer center dials the store's minicomputer and receives a summary of transactions for the day; this information is then used for such tasks as analysis of regional sales trends. The information is then summarized still further before it is transmitted to the national computer center.

This distribution of processing can also increase the efficiency of the host computer. Before the development of microcomputers and their use as "intelligent" terminals, the central mainframe was burdened by having to control the terminal device through every step of processing. This greatly restricted the level of sophistication that could be achieved. Intelligent terminals relieve the host of processing each entry at the terminal, since the microcomputer can efficiently perform edit checks and prepare data for transmittal to the central computer. However, certain required functions cannot normally be duplicated at each terminal due to equipment limitations and economic considerations. For example, an order entry system will require looking up a customer's balance and credit limit to check if an order should be accepted. As applications become more sophisticated, the need to perform such functions centrally may actually increase.

Thus, with distributed processing, computing activity is decentralized among a network of interconnected units. Typically, this approach may involve placing one or more computer systems at user locations. Each computer performs applications oriented to the particular user, with data communications facilities employed to communicate with a central computer or other computers in the network. Unfortunately, distributed data processing also makes it difficult to maintain control standards and consistency when processing occurs at many different sites.

Role of the Mainframe

As a result of the difficulties associated with distributed processing, for most firms the maximum benefits of computer use involve cooperative processing between a mainframe or host computer (and the related central data processing staff) and microcomputers supporting the users. The central data processing staff is often called the management information systems (MIS) department; however, if the central staff supports interactive computing for users, the current trend is to call it the information center. Regardless of terms, the host mainframe computer and the related MIS department have several advantages over distributed smaller computers and end-user computing.

Timeliness. A microcomputer can perform many of the functions of a mainframe, but processing time for the mainframe is faster; output takes less time; and programming, service, maintenance, and technical problems are handled by professionals rather than the user. Unfortunately, a manager may sometimes receive information faster with a microcomputer than by waiting for the data processing department to generate it. Such a situation may indicate that the MIS department's priorities are set not by management but by the MIS department itself.

Cost-Effectiveness. Most applications can be done for less cost in a centralized MIS department. However, because many MIS departments may be inefficient and charge users accordingly, efficient use of microcomputers can often cost less than inefficient use of mainframes. When this is true, management has probably failed to control its MIS resource economically.

Individual Data Bases. Individual managers may have special needs for data that are not shared by the corporation as a whole. If so, a microcomputer re-creates the problems of corporate data management on a smaller scale, including (1) input with verification and (2) update, as telephone numbers change, people move, or sales and inventory figures become obsolete. Although it is

98

*PART I
Overview
of Systems
and
Internal
Control*

possible to create data bases more easily with a microcomputer, one mainframe data base is usually less costly in total and more accurate than 40 to 50 individual ones on microcomputers.

Security. There always is some concern with the security of mainframe computer files. However, because microcomputers tend to be in environments that are not secure, mainframes are less accessible to unauthorized personnel than are microcomputers. In a microcomputer environment, disks are easier to copy, steal, or lose, and hard copy output may be more casually disposed of or lost.

Software Support. Lack of proper documentation and the inflexibility of corporate programming capabilities have long been headaches to user managers. At first glance, the microcomputer should free managers to buy or develop whatever software suits their needs. But the problem then arises of who will modify the software if it does not directly do the job. Also, a common problem is the inefficiency of different managers all using different software, which makes communication between their computers impossible.

Role of the Microcomputer

With the microcomputer, local managers can often concentrate on major business decisions with factual, current, and accurate data. Countless cost/benefit and "what if" analyses can be run before committing resources to a decision. The corporate data processing hierarchy can be cut through or circumvented to access what is needed when it is needed. The benefits of microcomputers are not the features that allow a manager to create his or her own "mini" data processing department. The microcomputer should not be used as a substitute for an unresponsive central computer function, but it does offer the following advantages:

Communication. One of the most underused capabilities of the microcomputer is for communication. This is also the area in which managers spend much of their time and frequently experience the greatest frustrations. Microcomputers can communicate machine to machine on a selective, intracompany basis without delays and with nothing lost in the mail. Microcomputers can function as word processors to generate external correspondence or internal proposals and can store and quickly retrieve historical data that might otherwise be accessible, if at all, only through the work of an assistant. As these types of activities occur, the microcomputer evolves from a "disassociated" unit into a critical integrated component in the "automated office."

Budgeting and Business Planning. When a budget is approved or a business plan accepted, it becomes part of the business's public domain. At this point, any quantitative data developed by the process should be entered into all financial planning and reporting systems. During the budget preparation process, which can frequently last three to four months, large amounts of data, which have been gathered by local managers, are analyzed. The microcomputer is well suited for such a task—analyzing and manipulating special-purpose data with a limited life expectancy. But this should not supplant the companywide mainframe activity of overall financial reporting.

However, with these benefits, there are also problems of duplication of effort, uncontrolled costs, and lack of equipment compatibility. There is an additional possible problem in the loss of centralized control.

The Use of a Mainframe-to-Microcomputer Link

Moving data from the mainframe to the microcomputer is called **downloading** the data. This allows the user to access different pieces of information (for example, data from the sales and inventory files) for further processing. However, because the downloaded data will be used by the employee to form a decision that will affect the company, the data must be accurate, valid, and relevant.

The following scenario highlights the importance of the meaning and validity of downloaded data. An employee in a company has been assigned the task of preparing a report that answers the question: "How is the company doing in real growth when compared to its competitors?" The employee goes to the MIS department and meets with a systems analyst who has a great technical understanding of the system but does not understand the employee's task. The employee explains to the analyst the scope of the project and the information that is needed. The analyst suggests that the MIS department prepare the report, but the employee declines, saying he or she would rather have the raw data to manipulate with spreadsheet and graphics packages on a microcomputer. There is an abundance of sales information on the mainframe system: There are sales forecasts for planning production, another set for sales and marketing, and a third for sales commissions. The production sales forecast captures data that are used to keep the company's inventory lean, the sales and marketing forecast is presented to the parent company to show how well things are going, and the sales commissions forecast is used to motivate the company's sales force. To complicate the matter, the information is stored in a data base that is accessed by, for example, COBOL programs with identifiers that only the systems analyst can understand. The employee must then decide how he or she wants the information. By quarter? With smoothing factors? Have error-checking procedures been run on the data?

Because the analyst does not understand the employee's task, the employee may inadvertently end up with data that are not valid for the project but base the answer to the question on that data. What started out as a seemingly straightforward project to be completed with the help of modern technology has turned into a "data nightmare," in part, because of that technology.

Solutions to the Problems of Downloaded Data

Data Dictionary. Software vendors and companies are trying to solve this data problem. One approach is the concept of an on-line data dictionary that can be viewed as "data about data." The dictionary typically defines each piece of data used in a system with the functional meaning of that data, values

100

*PART I
Overview
of Systems
and
Internal
Control*

that the data can have, and its physical characteristics. Unfortunately, data dictionaries are very costly and time consuming to implement. First, the information must be acquired, then carefully defined, and finally coded into the system. Dictionaries for large systems could take years to complete. Not only is the dictionary time consuming to implement, but it is also time consuming for an employee to use. Instead of the employee working with a person, the on-line dictionary is used to select all the data needed for a project or report. To select the correct data needed, the employee must learn how to use the on-line dictionary and then read through all the possibly relevant data in order to complete the report or project.

New Information Set. The second solution is to create a new "information" set that is designed using data from the mainframe. This set of data would contain the specific information needed to complete an employee's task. Unfortunately, it may take a technical analyst in the MIS department or information center one day or more to collect all of the relevant information and test the data for the end user.

Once the link from a microcomputer to a mainframe is established, there are still many issues that need to be addressed to get the fullest benefit of the technology and from employees using the technology. The link provides the path to the data, but it takes good management to see that all of the components needed to realize the correct, accurate data in the least amount of time are actually present.

COMPUTER SYSTEM ACQUISITION

When a company wishes to incorporate a computer into a system, it needs the hardware and software discussed earlier, but also maintenance and operations. Providing for all four elements of a computer system requires an investment of time, funds, and expertise which some companies find cost effective and convenient, and other companies find unaffordable or burdensome. Vendors exist to supply the computer needs of both. They range from firms that supply a complete line of hardware and software products and maintenance and operations services, to firms that supply a single type of product or service.

For many users, **computer system acquisition** means the purchase of a microcomputer. Chapter 13 discusses the use of a microcomputer for accounting purposes. Also, Appendix C has a section on computer system acquisition which illustrates this process with a specific company that will likely buy a microcomputer system.

Maintenance

Computer maintenance is the continuing process of keeping the equipment working. This includes the necessary spare parts and the technician(s) capable of keeping the equipment in operation. Maintenance is important for all computer systems, since virtually all equipment (no matter how advanced) will sometimes break. However, different users will place differing emphasis on maintenance. In the case of an on-line system such as airline reservations, computer failure puts the entire system (and, at least briefly, the company) out of operation; thus, maintenance is critical. In the case of a small business computer used for accounting purposes, a delay of one day in fixing the equipment might not be excessive or even troublesome.

101

CHAPTER 3
Approaches
to Business
Data
Processing

Operations

Computer operations involves the actual turning on of the machine, paying electricity bills, mounting tape drives, buying paper and other supplies, and replacing disk drives. Simple computers can be operated by their users—their operation is relatively straightforward. Large computer systems, on the other hand, require a separate operations staff to handle all the tape drives, printers, and other input/output functions.

A summary of these four elements is given in Exhibit 3-6.

Computer System Vendor Alternatives

Acquiring a computer system requires that all four necessary elements—hardware, software, maintenance, and operations—be obtained. These four elements are not, however, necessarily available from one or even from four neat, separate sets of vendors. Some vendors offer only one element, whereas some offer a combination of elements. The following are the primary computer system vendor possibilities.

Mainframe Computer Manufacturers. These companies, primarily IBM, make the most powerful computers available for business data processing. These machines are most useful for airlines, banks, insurance companies, and others who have to maintain records and information for vast numbers of customers or policyholders. The manufacturers of mainframe computers also provide supervisory software and perform the necessary maintenance for their equipment. This equipment is so expensive and important to the company using it that the maintenance is very good. Operation of these machines is difficult and usually requires a large separate operations staff.

Mainframe Replacement Companies. These companies, primarily NAS and Amdahl, make equipment that substitutes for the computers made by IBM. Because they use advanced technology and because they are in large measure

EXHIBIT 3-6   Elements of a Computer System Package

Hardware	The physical computer equipment
Software	The instructions to tell the equipment what to do
Maintenance	The process of keeping the equipment working
Operations	The operating of the tapes, disks, and printers

102

PART I
Overview
of Systems
and
Internal
Control

copying rather than developing, these replacement machines are much smaller and less expensive than the IBM equivalent. These companies then use IBM software for their machines, but they must provide maintenance. Operation is essentially the same level of difficulty as that of the replaced equipment.

Minicomputer Manufacturers. These companies make computers that are primarily used for small- to medium-scale transaction processing, such as an inventory system which must be continually updated by sale and purchase transactions as they occur. The main minicomputer manufacturers are Digital Equipment Corporation (DEC is its common acronym) and IBM. These companies also provide software and maintenance, as do the mainframe manufacturers. Operation is not as complex, and a separate operations staff is generally not required.

Microcomputer Manufacturers. These companies make complete, but small, data processing systems that are designed under the philosophy of a one-person system. The microcomputer can be important in business applications, especially for individual-level data processing, such as calculations of budgets, time scheduling, and word processing. The microcomputer is also effective for small, stand-alone transaction processing, such as in a small business accounting system. Primary microcomputer manufacturers are IBM and Apple. They provide software available for separate purchase, and maintenance is usually handled by maintenance contract similar to that for typewriters and other office equipment. Microcomputers are sold through retailers, directly to the purchaser by the manufacturer, and through mail order.

Value-Added Resellers (VARs). These systems packagers buy different components directly from factories and then put together a complete computer system. Many microcomputers and minicomputers for business uses are purchased from a VAR. The packager generally provides three services for the customer:

1. The assembly of a compatible collection of equipment that functions together.
2. A package of software to help accomplish the user's goals.
3. One entity where the user can go for assistance in case of hardware or software problems.

If a business is in a specialized field, such as an insurance agency or dentist's office, but is not technically expert in computer systems, the VAR can be a useful resource. Operation is the responsibility of the user, but the packager helps keep the operation as simple as possible.

Service Bureaus. These companies take input from their customers, process the data, and then return the results. Thus, the **service bureau** buys the equipment (hardware), develops the software, and has the burden of maintenance and operation of the computer. The user need only prepare the data for input. Generally, the service bureau receives the data, processes it overnight, and then returns the resulting output. Service bureaus are used most often for applications like payroll, where the service bureau will pick up time cards and then return payroll checks, a payroll register, and the necessary government forms like W-2s. The user is relieved of the burdens of computer ownership and operation, at the cost of reduced flexibility and timeliness of information. Most communities have several local service bureaus available.

103

CHAPTER 3
Approaches
to Business
Data
Processing

Computer Leasing Companies. Many computer users want a large system but do not wish to (or cannot) purchase a system. The manufacturer will lease the computer system to the user, but the charges are high. Instead, the computer leasing company buys the computer system from the manufacturer and then leases it to the user at a charge reduced from the manufacturer's charge. The leasing company can reduce the price by requiring a lower return on equity than the manufacturer and by locking the user into a longer-term lease and reducing his flexibility in changing machines.

Used Computer Brokers. These firms, such as American Used Computer Corporation, buy used computers from companies getting new equipment and then resell the used equipment to others. Computer manufacturers help their customers contact potential purchasers of the equipment they have when they acquire new equipment. However, manufacturers generally do not accept old equipment as a "trade in." The used computer broker thus provides an important service in buying surplus equipment. Used computers are most important as a backup for other equipment a company already has. Purchase of used equipment should not be attempted by the novice computer user because parts and service are often hard to find.

Peripheral Equipment Manufacturers. Peripheral equipment manufacturers make substitutes for the peripherals available from the computer manufacturers that simply plug in as replacements. Because of lower overhead and less needed development, these companies can offer peripherals which are less expensive and give as good or better performance. The primary difficulty with these products is that, in a mixed vendor environment, if anything goes wrong, the "fingerpointing" starts and each vendor points to another as the source of difficulty.

Facilities Management Firms. The operation of a large-scale computer installation can be a complicated and often tedious task. Employees of widely varying capabilities must be hired and fired, supplies must be purchased, and deadlines must be met. Additionally, in organizations like city and state governments with fixed salary scales, it may be almost impossible to attract qualified people. As a result, **facilities management** firms operate the computer installation for their customer. The customer owns the equipment; the facilities management firm operates it. Also, in situations with detailed and specialized programming requirements, such as hospitals, the facility management firm provides appropriate software.

Computer Consultants. Computer systems are so new to many users that computer consultants are often valuable. Consulting firms range from small independent consultants to international CPA firms employing several thou-

104

*PART I
Overview
of Systems
and
Internal
Control*

sand professionals. Consultants provide a wide range of services, from advice in computer acquisition, to system design, to programming. Unfortunately, consultants are often not called in until a disaster has occurred, and they are then asked to straighten out the situation. Consultants are best used in the beginning of an acquisition or project to make sure everything is planned properly, not after the fact when the mistakes have been made.

Software Vendors.   Programming is a large and growing aspect of computer systems. However, there is often a sufficient similarity in the needs of different users that the same software can be used by many different people or firms. The software vendor puts together a complete software package to

CONCEPT SUMMARY
Computer System Vendor Alternatives

Type of Company	*Product or Service Activity*
Mainframe computer manufacturers	Build large-scale systems for large-scale processing, such as airline reservations.
Mainframe replacement copies	Offer substitutes for IBM mainframe computers at lower cost.
Minicomputer manufacturers	Offer smaller computers for small number of terminals for transaction processing.
Microcomputer manufacturers	Offer desktop computer for personal productivity tasks, such as word processing and spreadsheets, and small business systems.
Value-added resellers	Offer complete package of hardware and software for the end user.
Service bureaus	Receive input from customer, does all processing off-site, and returns results.
Computer leasing companies	Purchase computer from manufacturer and leases to the end user.
Used computer brokers	Buy surplus hardware and then resells to others.
Peripheral equipment manufacturers	Make "plug-compatible" replacements for the peripherals of the computer manufacturers.
Facilities management firms	Operate computer system for customer, hires employees, often provides software.
EDP consultants	Provide advice, guidance, system design, and programming for clients.
Software vendors	Offer programming packages to satisfy the common goals of many users.

accomplish certain objectives and then sells the package to users with those needs. For example, there are now over 500 firms selling accounting software packages for microcomputer systems.

105

CHAPTER 3
Approaches
to Business
Data
Processing

Computer Acquisition Specification Sheet

The simple economics of computer technology imply that most new companies and all major companies will include a computer as part of their accounting and information system in some fashion. Often, a company will decide it needs a computer and then go to several vendors. The company asks the vendors for advice, and then proceeds to become overwhelmed by vastly differing proposals and suggestions. The proper approach to computer system acquisition, then, is not to go to the vendors and ask, "What should I do?" Instead, the firm should develop the objectives that it hopes to achieve and then go to the vendors and ask, "How can you best help me to accomplish my objectives?" This difference in approach can make the difference between confusion and clarity, failure and success.

The best approach to computer acquisition is to prepare a specification sheet for the vendors. The specification sheet should concentrate on what the user wants the system to accomplish; material backing up those goals and detailing why the user wants and needs them accomplished can be omitted from the specification sheet. The vendor is not primarily concerned with the origin and reasons for the user's problems; the vendor is primarily concerned with selling equipment.

The computer acquisition specification sheet should contain the following basic components:

Background. This section gives the vendor a description of the company, its present situation, future prospects, the present accounting system, and present automated equipment.

Automated applications. This section gives the vendor a description of the areas and activities for automation in roughly the order of priority. The section should discuss for each area the volume of transactions, the report requirements, and any necessary potential for future growth.

Proposal format. This section gives the vendor a description of the type of proposal required, including a detailed list of all specific items needed. A standard proposal response format is absolutely essential to compare proposals from different vendors.

Contract

After analyzing the vendor proposals and selecting one, the company signs a contract with the chosen vendor. The contract should include a description of the exact system to be purchased, with all of the peripheral components, such as disk drives, and all incidental materials, such as cables. In addition, the contract should be clear on a specific date for delivery and the purchaser's ownership rights to software or software licenses. There should be no tricky language that forgives breaches of system descriptions or delivery promises or that makes the purchased product or service unmarketable or unusable. Ex-

106

Part I
Overview
of Systems
and
Internal
Control

CONCEPT SUMMARY

Computer Acquisition Specification Sheet

Background	1. Description of company
	2. Future prospects for company
	3. Present accounting system
	4. Present equipment, if any
	5. Company's timetable for action
Automated applications	1. Areas of potential automation
	2. Priorities set between areas
	3. Volume of transactions processed
	4. Report requirements
	5. Potential for future growth
Proposal format	1. Place and deadline for proposal
	2. Detailed description and cost breakdown of all proposed equipment
	3. Physical planning considerations, such as additional airconditioning and raised floors
	4. Systems and programming assistance
	5. Service facilities, including the time required to get a service call and the availability of any service packages

amples include clauses limiting liability, requiring consent to resell, or permitting spare parts and maintenance to be withheld from original or later owners.

CHAPTER SUMMARY

Business data processing is characterized by large amounts of data and repetitive events, while computer systems are characterized by great speed, large memory capabilities, and reliability. Thus, computer systems are well suited for business data processing and come in a vast range of equipment, usually grouped as mainframe computers, minicomputers, and microcomputers.

Computer hardware refers to the machines in a computer system, including the processor and input/output devices. Computer software refers to the programs of instructions that control the hardware. These programs include

107

CHAPTER 3
*Approaches
to Business
Data
Processing*

the operating system and application programs written in a programming language. Input/output devices allow users to put instructions and data into the system and get the results of processing out of the system. Sequential access to data requires batch processing, which provides the greatest machine efficiencies. On-line, interactive access to data allows for processing of transactions as they occur; this is most efficient for those who use the system or its output. Data can be stored on magnetic tape for sequential access or on disks for direct access.

Centralized processing has the advantage of controlling all information within one system. The disadvantage is that the system becomes too overburdened with details to serve all its purposes efficiently. Distributed processing decentralizes computing activity among a network of interconnected units so that each unit processes only the amount of detail that the user requires. The advantage is efficiency. The disadvantage is difficulty in maintaining control. With cooperative processing, a mainframe provides the advantages of centralized data, while local microcomputers provide the efficency of individual applications. Data within the centralized system can be downloaded to local microcomputers.

Vendors range from firms that provide hardware, software, maintenance, and operations to firms that provide only a single computer product or service. Instead of acquiring a complete system, some companies choose to contract out for maintenance and operations, while others send their data out to service bureaus for processing. The most efficient way to acquire a computer system is to present appropriate vendors with a computer acquisition specification sheet describing the user, prioritizing areas for automation, and requesting a proposal in a specified format for ease of comparison.

KEY TERMS

Application program *(p. 83)*
Batch processing systems *(p. 88)*
Central processing unit (CPU) *(p. 84)*
Compiler *(p. 84)*
Computer maintenance *(p. 100)*
Computer operations *(p. 101)*
Computer system *(p. 81)*
Computer system acquisition *(p. 100)*
Direct access *(p. 86)*
Distributed data processing *(p. 96)*
Downloading *(p. 99)*
External/secondary/peripheral storage *(p. 86)*
Facilities management *(p. 103)*
File device *(p. 85)*
Hardware *(p. 84)*
Host computer *(p. 95)*
Inquiry/response *(p. 93)*
Interactive processing systems *(p. 92)*

Main memory/primary storage *(p. 84)*
Object program *(p. 84)*
Off-line *(p. 85)*
On-line *(p. 85)*
On-line transaction processing (OLTP) *(p. 93)*
Operating system *(p. 83)*
Peripheral *(p. 85)*
Processor *(p. 84)*
Programmer *(p. 83)*
Random access *(p. 86)*
Real-time processing *(p. 92)*
RJE (remote job entry) *(p. 89)*
Sequential access *(p. 86)*
Service bureau *(p. 102)*
Software *(p. 83)*
Source language *(p. 84)*
Source program *(p. 84)*
Transaction processing *(p. 81)*

108

PART I
Overview
of Systems
and
Internal
Control

QUESTIONS

3-1. Give the basic characteristics of business data processing and the advantages of computer systems. Are computer systems suited for business data processing?

3-2. Where are inefficiencies in a business processing system likely to occur? What characteristics of business systems contribute to this problem?

3-3. Distinguish among a mainframe computer system, a minicomputer system, and a microcomputer system and give examples of when each might be used.

3-4. Give two basic types of software, with examples of each.

3-5. Describe the process of going from a person's conception of a problem to the computer output with the solution of the problem.

3-6. Describe the four functions performed by computer hardware and give an example of a specific hardware component for each.

3-7. Identify four basic input devices and briefly describe their function.

3-8. Identify four basic output devices and briefly describe their function.

3-9. Contrast magnetic tape and disk storage media. Under what circumstances would magnetic tape be preferable? Under what circumstances would disk be preferable?

3-10. When is a hardware device considered on-line? Off-line? What types of devices are primarily on-line? Off-line?

3-11. Describe a basic batch processing system and specify when this type of system is appropriate.

3-12. Describe a batch with remote data transmission processing system and specify when this type of system is most appropriate.

3-13. Describe an interactive with inquiry/response processing system and specify when this type of system is most appropriate.

3-14. Describe an on-line transaction processing system and specify when this type of system is most appropriate.

3-15. Give the advantages and disadvantages of a centralized data processing system. Specify the circumstances where this choice would be preferred.

3-16. Give the advantages and disadvantages of a distributed data processing system. Specify the circumstances where this approach would be preferred.

3-17. Why has there been a trend toward distributed data processing? What is the problem with using this type of approach?

3-18. Discuss the relationship of the batch versus interactive distinction to the centralized versus distributed distinction.

3-19. What are the four basic elements of a computer system? Describe the function of each element and give the possible sources for that product or service.

3-20. What information should the prospective purchaser provide the vendor in a system specification sheet? What information should the vendor provide in a system proposal?

PROBLEMS

3-21. Consider the system used by the Internal Revenue Service to process annual income tax returns. The taxpayer mails his return, supporting documents, and check to a regional office where the information is converted and input to a computer system for basic accuracy checks. Computer-sensible data on what each taxpayer has filed is then manually forwarded to the national computer center in Maryland for further analysis and comparison with previous years' returns. From this analysis and comparison, the computer generates lists by region of returns with high probabilities of negligence or fraud; these lists go back to the regional offices for audit purposes. As a by-product of this processing, data are generated and stored in the central computer system. These data are used immediately to answer general statistical and policy questions about income and taxes for all taxpayers.

109

CHAPTER 3
Approaches
to Business
Data
Processing

1. Specify the input, file, and output hardware devices that would likely be used in each regional computer system.

2. Explain the data flow through each of these devices in the regional computer systems.

3-22. Using the data presented in Problem 3-21, specify the input, file, and output hardware devices that would likely be used in the national computer system. Explain the data flow through each of these devices in the national computer system.

3-23. Following is a list of information that might be input to, stored by, or generated from a computer system. For each item, specify the hardware device(s) that would process or transmit it in a batch system:

   a. Data on year-to-date earnings for each employee
   b. Current pay period hours worked for one employee
   c. Monthly department store billing statement
   d. Amounts of inventory on hand for immediate response to customer questions
   e. Payroll check
   f. Customer payment of account
   g. Invoice for credit sale
   h. General journal entry

3-24. For each item listed in Problem 3-23, specify the hardware device(s) that would process or transmit it in an interactive system.

3-25. One important consideration in computer hardware is whether the system will have a sequential, batch orientation or a direct access, interactive orientation. For each of the following processing areas, state whether a batch or an interactive orientation would be most appropriate and why.

   a. Airline reservations
   b. Banking generation of monthly statement
   c. Payroll
   d. Telephone company generation of monthly bills
   e. Motel chain reservation
   f. Inventory in a retail store
   g. Financial statements
   h. Student registration at a university

3-26. Suppose a medium-sized retail firm wants to computerize the billing of its customers as well as the payment of bills from suppliers.

110

*Part I
Overview
of Systems
and
Internal
Control*

1. Describe a hardware configuration that could accomplish this processing in batches at specific predetermined times. Give the flow of data through these devices.

2. Describe a hardware configuration that could accomplish this processing if up-to-date information on customers and suppliers is desired at all times. Give the flow of data through these devices.

3-27. Suppose a wholesale firm wants to computerize its processing of sales orders from retailers and purchases of inventory from manufacturers.

1. Describe a hardware configuration that could accomplish this processing in batches at specific predetermined times. Give the flow of data through these devices.

2. Describe a hardware configuration that could accomplish this processing, if up-to-date information on inventory levels is desired at all times. Give the flow of data through these devices.

3-28. A typical retail firm is characterized by a large number of relatively small sales that take place within the store. A wholesale firm, on the other hand, usually engages in relatively few but large sales that may originate long distances from the business. How would input devices for these types of businesses differ as a result of these different sales patterns? Would there be any differences in file or output devices as a result of these patterns?

3-29. Computer services can be required from any of several alternative sources. Each source has its own advantages and disadvantages. For each of the following computer vendor alternatives, discuss a situation where that alternative would be most appropriate.

    a. Mainframe computer manufacturer
    b. Minicomputer manufacturer
    c. Programmable calculator manufacturer
    d. Service bureau
    e. Facilities management firm

3-30. If a company wants computer capability, it can be obtained by buying the equipment, leasing the equipment, or using a service bureau. For each of the following, state whether it is most characteristic of buying, leasing, or service bureau use.

    a. High salary cost
    b. No in-house systems capability
    c. Data processing staff
    d. Large initial cost
    e. No maintenance cost
    f. Software development
    g. Necessarily batch oriented
    h. Long-term commitment to specific hardware

3-31. Contrast minicomputers and microcomputers. For which situations would each be better suited? Contrast a service bureau and buying computer hardware. For which situations would each be better suited? How do the activities of facilities management firms differ from those of computer consultants?

111

CHAPTER 3
*Approaches
to Business
Data
Processing*

3-32. *(AICPA, adapted)*   Time Corporation's employee payroll system is in part as follows. Factory employees punch daily time clock cards when entering or leaving the shop. At the end of each week the timekeeping department collects the cards and prepares duplicate batch-control slips by department showing total hours and numbers of employees. The time cards and original batch-control slips are sent to the payroll accounting section. The second copies are filed by date.

In payroll accounting, payroll transactions are keyboarded from the time card information, and a batch total for each batch is keyboarded from the batch-control slip. The time cards and batch-control slips are filed by batch for possible reference. The payroll transactions and batch totals are sent to data processing where they are sorted by employee number within each batch. Each batch is edited by a computer program that checks the employee number against a master employee tape file and the total hours and number of employees against the batch total. A detailed printout by batch and employee number is produced, which indicates batches that do not balance and invalid employee numbers. The printout is sent to payroll accounting, which reconciles the differences. Batch totals and transactions are discarded.

1. Prepare a system flowchart of the payroll system.
2. Cite five strengths of the payroll internal control procedures.

3-33. *(IIA, adapted)*   The management of Cross Country Company is currently considering a change from centralized data processing to either decentralized or distributed data processing. Briefly define each of the following:

a. Centralized data processing.
b. Decentralized data processing.
c. Distributed data processing.

3-34. *(IIA, adapted)*   Each data processing approach referred to in Problem 3-33 has advantages and disadvantages as compared to one or both of the other two approaches. List the numbers 1 through 6 on your answer sheet, representing the processing approaches in Column I in the table that follows. Select one advantage or disadvantage from Column II that would be the most appropriate for each item in Column I. Each item in Column II can be used only once. Place the appropriate letter from Column II beside each number from Column I.

I	*II*
1. Centralized	a. Reduces the risk of loss, destruction to hardware and critical data
2. Decentralized	b. No opportunity for distributed network
3. Distributed	c. Dependence on one computer
4. Both centralized and distributed	d. Permits the use of the data base approach and minimizes duplication of common data
5. Both decentralized and distributed	e. Most difficult to maintain the overall security of data
6. Both centralized and decentralized	f. No method for coordinating or exchanging data during processing

3-35. *(CMA, adapted)*   Saxon Company manufactures and sells several product lines. It has a batch processing EDP system. All sales orders received during regular

112

*PART I
Overview
of Systems
and
Internal
Control*

working hours are immediately typed on Saxon's own sales order form. This typed form is the source document for the keyboarding of a shipment or back-order for each item ordered. An order received one day is to be processed that day and night and shipped the next day. The daily processing that has to be accomplished at night includes the following activities:

a. Preparing the invoice to be sent to the customer at the time of shipment. Input data are sorted by customer number.

b. Updating the accounts receivable file.

c. Updating the finished goods inventory. Data must be sorted by stock number for this and the next process.

d. Listing of all items back-ordered and short.

Each month the sales department would like to have a sales summary and analysis. At the end of the month, the monthly statements are prepared and mailed to customers. Management also wants an aging of accounts receivable each month.

Prepare a system flowchart to reflect the processing just described.

3-36. (*CMA, adapted*) The controller of Kensler Company has been working with the data processing department to revise part of the company's financial reporting system. A study is under way on how to develop and implement a data entry and data retention system for key computer files used by the various departments responsible to the controller. The departments involved and details on their data-processing-related activities are as follows:

General Accounting

a. Daily processing of journal entries submitted by various departments

b. Weekly updating of file balances with data from areas such as payroll, accounts receivable, and accounts payable

c. Sporadic requests for account balances during the month, with increased activity at month end

Accounts Receivable

a. Daily processing of receipts for payments on account

b. Daily processing of sales to customers

c. Daily checks to be sure that the credit limit of $200,000 maximum per customer is not exceeded and identification of orders in excess of $20,000 per customer

d. Daily requests for customer credit status regarding payments and account balances

e. Weekly reporting to general accounting

Accounts Payable

a. Processing of payments to vendors three times a week

b. Weekly expense distribution reporting to general accounting

Budget, Planning and Control

a. Updating of flexible budgets on a monthly basis

b. Quarterly rebudgeting based on sales forecast and production schedule changes

c. Monthly inquiry requests for budget balances

113

CHAPTER 3
*Approaches
to Business
Data
Processing*

The manager of data processing has explained the concepts of the following processing approaches to the controller's staff and the appropriate staff members of the departments affected:

a. Batch processing
b. On-line transaction processing
c. On-line inquiry/response

The data processing manager has also indicated to the controller that batch processing is the least expensive processing approach and that a rough estimate of the cost of each of the other approaches relative to batch would be as follows:

a. On-line transaction processing—2.5 times the cost of batch processing
b. On-line inquiry/response—1.5 times the cost of batch processing

1. Identify and explain the type of input techniques and type of file inquiry that probably should be employed by Kensler Company for each of the four departments responsible to the controller.
2. Suggest relevant information that should be captured concerning accounts receivable.

DECISION CASE

Weekender Corporation owns and operates 15 large retail hardware stores in major metropolitan areas of the southwest United States. The stores carry a wide variety of merchandise, but the major thrust is toward the weekend "do-it-yourselfer." The company has been successful in this field, and the number of stores in the chain has almost doubled since 1970. Each retail store acquires its merchandise from the company's centrally located warehouse. Consequently, the warehouse must maintain an up-to-date, well-stocked inventory ready to meet the demands of the individual stores.

The company wishes to hold its competitive position with similar types of stores in its marketing area. Therefore, Weekender Corporation feels it must improve its purchasing and inventory procedures. The company's stores must have the proper goods to meet the customer demand, and the warehouse in turn must have the goods available. The number of company stores, the number of inventory items carried, and the volume of business are providing pressures to change from basically manual data processing routines to electronic data processing procedures. Recently, the company has been investigating two different approaches to computerization—batch processing and on-line processing. No decision has yet been reached on the approach that will be followed. Top management has determined that the following items should have high priority in designing the new system:

a. Rapid ordering to replenish warehouse inventory stocks with as little delay as possible
b. Quick filing and shipping of merchandise to the stores (this involves immediately determining on request if sufficient stocks exist)

114

PART I
Overview
of Systems
and
Internal
Control

c. An indication of inventory activity

d. Perpetual records in order to determine inventory level by item number quickly

A description of the current warehousing and purchasing procedures follows:

Warehouse Procedures. Stock is stored in bins and is located by an inventory number. The numbers generally are listed sequentially on the bins to facilitate locating items that are difficult to find. Whenever a retail store needs merchandise, a three-part merchandise request form is completed—one copy is kept by the store and two copies are mailed to the warehouse the next day. If the merchandise requested is on hand, the goods are delivered to the store accompanied by the third copy of the request. The second copy is filed at the warehouse. If the quantity of goods on hand is not sufficient to fill the order, the warehouse sends the quantity available and notes the quantity shipped on the request form. Then a purchase memorandum for the shortage is prepared by the warehouse. At the end of each day, all of the purchase memos are sent to the purchasing department. When the ordered goods are received by the warehouse, they are checked at the receiving area and a receiving report is prepared. One copy of the receiving report is retained at the receiving area, one is forwarded to accounts payable, and one is filed at the warehouse with the purchase memorandum.

Purchase Department Procedures. When the purchase memos are received from the warehouse, purchase orders are prepared. Vendor catalogs are used to select the best source for the requested goods, and the purchase order is completed and mailed. Copies of the order are sent to accounts payable and the receiving area; one copy is retained in the purchasing department. When the receiving report arrives in the purchasing department, it is compared with the purchase order on file. The receiving report is also checked with the invoice before forwarding the invoice to accounts payable for payment. The purchasing department strives periodically to evaluate the vendors for financial soundness, reliability, and trade relationships. However, because the volume of requests received from the warehouse is so great, this activity currently does not have a high priority. Each week a report of the open purchase orders is prepared to determine if any action should be taken on overdue deliveries. This report is prepared manually from scanning the file of outstanding purchase orders.

Required:

1. Weekender Corporation is considering two possible computerized data processing systems: a batch system and an on-line transaction processing system. Which of these systems would best meet the needs of Weekender Corporation? Explain your answer. Briefly describe the basic hardware components that Weekender would need for the system you recommend to meet the company's goals.

2. Regardless of the system selected by Weekender Corporation, the same basic data will have to be processed. Identify the type of information that would be kept and updated on the computer.

4 Internal Control in a Computer Environment

Overview

Concept of controls to prevent errors and theft in a computerized environment; how those controls impact and alter the way the system is designed and used.

Learning Objectives

Thorough study of this chapter will enable you to:

1. Identify the sources of potential internal control problems in computer-based systems.
2. Guard against internal control problems of data input, processing, storage, output, and communications.
3. Guard against internal control problems unique to microcomputers.
4. Implement procedures to meet the internal control requirements of a computerized accounting system.

Outline

Internal Control Concerns in Computer-Based Systems

Elements of Internal Control in a Computer Environment

116

*PART I
Overview
of Systems
and
Internal
Control*

SYSTEMS IN THE REAL WORLD

Hackers, Bandits, and Disasters

VIRUSES AND OTHER MALICIOUS SOFTWARE

These potentially devastating programs are usually planted by means of a "Trojan Horse"—a seemingly normal package hiding a destructive program that can wipe out a computer's data files. Use antiviral programs to detect viruses. Prohibit employees from loading untested software into the system.

FIRES, FLOODS, POWER FAILURES, EARTHQUAKES

A few precautions can prevent acts of God from becoming data disasters. Store copies of data at another site. Set up a backup computer. Disaster recovery services guarantee restoration of normal data processing within hours of a crisis.

SNEAK ATTACKS BY OUTSIDE HACKERS

Simple passwords won't stop these techno-terrorists from breaking in by phone. Encrypt data and program the computer to accept calls only from authorized phones. At night, shut down disk drives containing sensitive data.

WIRETAPS AND ELECTRONIC EAVESDROPPING

It's easier than most companies think for outsiders to tap the telecommunications lines that connect their computers. Advanced cryptographic techniques can scramble messages, and special enclosures can contain the emissions that electronic eavesdroppers intercept and decode.

THE ENEMY WITHIN: EMPLOYEE TAMPERING

The No. 1 security threat is employees, whose theft, sabotage, or ineptitude can cause havoc. Employees should have access only to the systems and data needed to do their jobs. Lock up machines that do critical tasks. Change passwords frequently.

SOURCE: *Business Week,* 8/1/88, reprinted by permission.

Chapters 1–3 presented the fundamental concepts of business information systems and showed the advantages of creating a computer system to provide the necessary processing and storage of business systems. In addition, building a computer-based business data processing system eliminates some major internal control concerns associated with manual systems:

> *Accuracy.* The computer is immeasurably more accurate than any person performing the same calculations. Unlike the human clerk, the computer will not extend invoices incorrectly or foot journals improperly. Additionally, the computer will not accept a journal entry that does not balance or post an entry to the wrong account.

117

CHAPTER 4
*Internal
Control in
a Computer
Environment*

Consistency. Once the computer is programmed, it will be consistent in its treatment of transactions. For example, if the program instructs the computer to check the customer's credit limit before the sale, the computer will always consistently check the credit limit.

Motivation. The computer will not have any dishonest or disloyal motivations, since the machine cannot profit from any misstatement. The employee, on the other hand, may place his or her own interests before those of the company.

However, there are important internal control problems associated with computer-based systems. The same basic internal control concepts are useful for all application areas and will be used throughout later chapters. The internal control benefits just cited will be used to show how the internal control deficiencies of computer systems can be overcome. A focus on the internal control problems of computer systems is crucial because of the enormous importance of computer systems to business. A recent study showed the reliance of most businesses surveyed on their computer system:

Totally dependent	19.6%
Heavily dependent	65.8
Moderately dependent	13.9
Slightly dependent	0.7

Seventy-five percent said they would have a critical or total loss of functioning within 14 days if they lost their computer support.

INTERNAL CONTROL CONCERNS IN COMPUTER-BASED SYSTEMS

Internal control problems inherent in computer use include input, processing, storage, output, and communications. In addition, there are some that are specifically microcomputer related.

Input and Its Preparation

Source Documents Are Eliminated. In a computer-based system, a terminal operator often makes an entry directly into the computer using the terminal, without a source document. An example is order entry, where an order is received over the phone and is entered directly into the system. Another, more familiar example occurs at the airline reservation desk, where the operator receives phone calls and makes reservations without a source document. The problem is that there is no source document that indicates proper authorization, and the audit trail can be lost. The solution to this problem has two aspects. The first aspect is physical control over the terminals (including a lockable keyboard, terminal, or both) to ensure that only those who are properly authorized have access to the terminals that would allow them to initiate transactions. The second aspect is to tie each transaction back to the operator, terminal, and time where it was initiated. This process should include user authorization requirements for a specific terminal, program, file, or record in

118

PART I
Overview
of Systems
and
Internal
Control

order to assign responsibility and provide a check on the authorization of transactions.

Sophisticated Tampering Can Cause Unauthorized Actions. A standard approach to data processing is to have various physical, organizational, and other internal controls on the entry of data to the computer system. Then, when the information is in the computer, the assumption is made that the transaction has been authorized. Note that if someone can surreptitiously enter information into the system by bypassing the various controls, he or she can, in effect, get his or her transactions authorized. If someone can enter information into the system that appears to be an authorized transaction, then the system assumes that it is an authorized transaction. For example, a California man became very familiar with the system of Pacific Telephone. He used the telephone to place orders for telephone equipment in excess of $100,000. The company delivered the goods to various sites, where he picked them up and then resold them. In order to combat this problem, the system must ensure that proper authorization is required for all transactions. Additionally, the system must allow the check of all authorizations—another example of the importance of a proper audit trail. Thus, if a person avoids the various controls and manipulates data on the computer, he or she will still not have the proper authorization.

New Sources and Potentials for Error. A user of a program is generally not intimately familiar with it and will often put in erroneous data or respond incorrectly. All programs should be written assuming that the user will try to use the wrong disk or tape and that all data are possibly incorrect. Some people frankly enjoy getting the computer to make mistakes. Others will simply make mistakes through inexperience or inadvertence. The computer programs must contain extensive edit checks to detect and help correct errors.

Processing

The Machine Lacks Judgment. There are many stories about computer systems that wrote payroll checks for $20,000 instead of $200 or sent a truckload of magazines to a startled subscriber. In a manual system, the people doing the work will not do something completely ridiculous; they will realize that something is wrong. The machine, on the other hand, has no judgment of its own and will do strange things if told to do them. However, even though the machine lacks judgment, the computer system can exercise judgment by having it built into the computer programs. The programs should contain the programmed controls discussed later in this chapter.

Duties Are Concentrated Within the Computer. The separation of duties is absolutely critical for effective internal control. As a particular example, in a manual system the duty of journalizing transactions should be separate from the duty of posting the transaction to the ledger accounts. However, in a computer-based system, these duties and many others are done by the computer. As an additional example, in a payroll system, a computer might keep payroll and personnel records, make the labor distribution, and prepare the payroll

119

CHAPTER 4
*Internal
Control in
a Computer
Environment*

checks. In and of themselves, these facts are no particular cause for alarm. Unlike the human employee, the computer (since it is only a machine) cannot ever desire to divert funds or assets to itself. (Computers with a will of their own, like HAL in *2001, A Space Odyssey*, are purely science fiction and will remain so.) The problem is that, although the computer will not abuse its concentrated duties, others can.

If a person has unauthorized control of the computer, the standard protection of separated duties will no longer be effective. Examples of this sort of problem abound in computing. In one instance, a programmer modified a bank program that printed out a list of overdrawn accounts. He had the program omit his account from the list and was thus able to overdraw his account without being detected. He was finally caught when a machine breakdown required the list to be prepared manually. The general solution to this problem, as discussed later in this chapter, is the separation of knowledge and access. Those with knowledge of how the system works (such as programmers) should not have access to the computer. Those with access to the computer (such as operators) should not learn how the system works.

Great Speed Extends One Person's Capabilities. One of the protections in manual systems is the human limitation of speed: one person is capable of doing only so much. Thus, one person can alter only so many checks or change only so many records. With the use of the computer, this limitation no longer exists. An example of this problem is the computation of interest for banks. When the bank computes the appropriate interest to credit the accounts of its depositors, the computation is made to only a fixed, limited number of decimal places. Thus, there is a small difference between the interest an individual actually receives and the exact interest. Programmers have taken advantage of this and have modified the interest calculation program to credit this difference to their account. Notice the difficulty of detecting this technique: the accounts all balance, and nobody is in a position to detect an error. As a result, to protect against this type of problem, the system must provide for a review of all programs by a supervisor, and physical protection of programs from unauthorized modification.

New Sources and Potentials for Error. Manual systems are susceptible to numerous types of error, such as incorrect calculations and mispostings. With computer-based systems, the potential for error is generally reduced; however, new and different sources of errors are created. Least important are vendor-supplied errors. These errors include faulty hardware or errors in the system software, such as operating systems and compilers. These errors are usually quickly apparent and are corrected by the vendor.

There are also errors in application programs. A satellite launch went out of control and had to be destroyed (at a cost of many millions of dollars) when a programmer omitted a minus sign from the control program. When the computer does something major wrong, there is generally an error in an application program. The solution is extensive and effective testing of programs prior to their use in production. Unfortunately, this is easier to suggest than to accomplish because of the insidious nature of many errors; they often do not become apparent until weeks, months, or even years have passed.

120

PART I
Overview
of Systems
and
Internal
Control

Another source of error is a poor design of either the program or the system. A standard problem in a computer-based system is excessive rigidity in the system; it is too difficult or impossible to handle special circumstances or situations. There have been a number of articles in newspapers and magazines about people's problems with computerized billing. The person writes concerning an error with his or her bill and fights for some months with the system, all the while receiving increasingly abusive letters concerning non-payment. The solution is proper system design in the first place; the system should be designed to handle unusual situations and circumstances.

Extreme Complexity Results in the Impossibility of Complete Testing. Some software systems become so complex that it is impossible to test every possibility; for example, software defects have been known to kill a patient through excessive radiation, maim other patients, kill sailors, compromise corporations, and threaten a collapse of the government securities market. A computerized banking system may consist of millions of lines of computer code, written by hundreds of people, who each work on small segments of the program. There is no way to know with certainty that all the segments will work together. A computer error at the Bank of New York blocked the bank from delivering government securities to customers and accepting payment; the bank had to borrow $23.6 billion from the Federal Reserve and pay $5 million in interest on the one-day loan.

The Operating System May Not Be Secure. According to an association of French insurers, companies in France suffered at least 15,000 breaches of computer security, 70 percent by the companies' own employees. Coopers & Lybrand found only 1 out of a sample of 20 large European companies was adequately secure. The U.S. government grades the security of operating systems from A to D (the worst). Few commercial systems score better than a poor C. The problem with a class C operating system is that once a user has given his or her password, the system does not distinguish between different types of information he or she might be using. For example, a class C operating system lets the user decide whether a file transfer to another computer system is allowed. In addition to the password identification of the class C system, a class B system actively checks the movement and access of data. For a file transfer, even after the user has given the password, the operating system will determine if such a transfer is allowed. Each file can be flagged by its owner that it can only be accessed at certain times, such as office hours, or that it cannot be transferred from one department to another; the operating system will ensure that these restrictions are followed. In addition, as each file is accessed in a B operating system, that fact is noted so that systems managers know who is doing what, and when. Unfortunately, there is a trade-off between security and productivity. In a secure system, only 70 percent of the traffic is genuine data; the rest are the tags, passwords, and protocols of security. Only the class A operating system has an unfriendly reputation for being more preoccupied with security than productivity. Most commercial systems are moving to class B.

Storage

121

CHAPTER 4
*Internal
Control in
a Computer
Environment*

Records and the Audit Trail Are Invisible. Some writers like to say that with a computer system the audit trail vanishes. This is misleading, however, for even though it is not possible to see the audit trail, it does exist, but only in machine-readable form. This invisibility of records and the audit trail means that checking accuracy, cross-checking, and the analysis of support for figures on financial statements are made more difficult. The checking and analysis cannot be done manually. The computer must be used to analyze its own record and audit trail. Because of this, the system has to be designed to incorporate the data for all necessary analysis.

Information Can Be Changed Without Physical Traces. One of the great protections of manual systems is that the records are in ink. If someone tries to change any information in the records, the erasures and smudge marks will make this immediately apparent. If someone replaces a page with a new one, appropriately doctored, then the different tint of the new paper will show up. There is no similar protection for computer records: electronic information can be changed without a trace. Viewed in another light, this is a tremendous advantage, since it allows the same storage media to be used over and over again. However, from an internal control viewpoint, this computer capability is a serious difficulty. In addition to the potential problems resulting from the changing of data, another serious problem is the possibility of changing programs. If done properly, a program becomes operational and is used on a regular, production basis only after it has been approved, reviewed, and tested. A sophisticated embezzler could get around this either by modifying the production program directly or by replacing the production program with a new version. Protection against this problem of change without traces is difficult, but it should be concentrated in two areas:

1. Physical controls to reduce access to the computer (in order to prevent manipulation).
2. Cross-checks to make sure that all data file changes are backed up by properly authorized transactions.

Concentrated Information Is Easier to Steal. Manual records are often so bulky that stealing them would present serious logistical problems in just moving the vast quantity of material. Additionally, the loss of vast records would be immediately apparent. This same problem no longer exists with computer-readable information: Vast quantities of information are stored in a small volume and can easily be copied or physically stolen. Investigators of the General Accounting Office (the investigative arm of the U.S. Congress) walked out of the Social Security System's national computer complex with a case containing names, addresses, and other information for more than 1 million beneficiaries. Only good physical controls for the records in electronic form will prevent such raiding. Only authorized people should have access to the records, and an audit trail should be available to determine who used what, when.

122

PART I
Overview
of Systems
and
Internal
Control

Electronic Information Is Easy to Lose.   In a manual system, the records are written in ink on substantial paper. The only way to lose the information is to lose the physical records or to have them burn up in a business fire. The written information essentially cannot be erased—it is permanent. The situation is completely different with electronic information. As discussed earlier, the information on the computer can be easily changed, leaving no trace of the earlier content. This change often happens inadvertently, and huge amounts of information can be quickly lost. An example of this problem occurred during a fund-raising campaign. The pledges were recorded on a computer tape as they were phoned in; the names, addresses, and amounts were kept so that follow-up efforts would then collect the money. The information on that tape was accidentally wiped out, so a great deal of money was never collected. The international CPA firm in charge of the system paid several million dollars to the charity to cover the loss. Since electronic information can be lost so quickly and easily, it is essential to provide backup capabilities for all data.

Output and Its Use

The User Is in Awe of the Computer.   The earlier discussions of internal control stressed the importance of outside checks on the system's accuracy. For example, the statements of account sent to customers were relied upon to check that the accounting records were correct. It is common, however, for people to neglect checking the computer and to assume simply that the computer is correct. One potential computer thief took advantage of that attitude by modifying the payroll deductions for the employees at his organization. He reduced everyone else's deductions by a small amount in each case and then added the total amount (large) to his deductions. Thus, the total of all deductions was correct, but he was going to get an extra-large refund from the IRS at the expense of the other employees. He was caught only when a janitor added up his weekly paychecks for the year and noticed the discrepancy between his totals and the amounts on his W-2 form. However, very few people add up the totals from their paychecks, completely check their bank statement, or completely check their credit card bill (comparing it to a file of receipts). A similar problem occurs within companies, where often the user departments do not check the output of the computer. The general solution is to try to provide control totals and other information to user departments to help them check the computer output. It may even be necessary to require active checks by users of the output rather than to assume that, if no one complains, it must be all right.

Vast Capabilities Can Create a Different Reality.   In some companies, the information stored in the computer no longer reflects reality: it becomes the reality. Originally, the computer record simply reflected the operations of the firm. In extremely sophisticated applications, however, the computer record is the operations of the firm. For example, a bank balance is the electronic information stored in the bank's computer; in the life insurance business, an individual policy is essentially the information stored on the computer. Equity Funding took the final step and created life insurance policies without policyholders; Equity Funding created a different reality, one that only existed on its computers. The solution to problems of this scale is effective testing of account balances. The amounts in the account balances have to be constantly checked to determine if the computer system (even if it is internally consistent) is consistent with the world outside of the computer center.

123

CHAPTER 4
*Internal
Control in
a Computer
Environment*

Communications

The internal control of a computer system using communication links to remote locations is much more complex than in centralized environments with no communication. A particular concern must be "hackers," data communications experts who delight in unauthorized break-ins into computers. Exhibit 4-1 gives a case history of the problems of one installation using data communications.

The Company's System Becomes Dependent on the Phone System. An online transaction processing system may have terminals and multiusers just like a communications system, but there is no use of the telephone system. But a communications system often uses the phone system for critical links. In general, the telephone system is reliable for low-speed communications, such as the connection to terminals. However, the phone system can and does have problems, sometimes severe ones. For example, a fire gutted a telephone-switching station outside Chicago. Banks could not process checks, order cash, or wire money through the Federal Reserve System. The Federal Reserve bank

EXHIBIT 4-1 Case History of Network Security Compromise (*Datamation*)

> The Department of Agriculture (DOA) leased in Las Vegas four nationwide IN WATS 800 phone numbers to access data bases maintained on DOA mainframes in Kansas City, Missouri. In addition, however, unknown unauthorized users from over 40 different area codes used these lines for free computer usage after they learned the 800 numbers. These toll-free numbers gained access to the Telenet system, which provides long-distance calling through a local phone call. Next, these hackers placed a collect call to a host in New Jersey through the Telenet system. The New Jersey host regarded these as routine collect calls and accepted them. Once the hackers accessed this host, they immediately executed another prepaid call to an additional target host. The New Jersey facility was paying for the communication from Las Vegas to New Jersey and from New Jersey to the target host. During one three-month period, 247 different corporate, educational, medical, and government hosts were improperly accessed by this method. Both the New Jersey host and the target hosts were accessed by using the protocols embedded in the systems when they were manufactured to allow remote systems maintenance. Since maintenance personnel need to be able to bypass any and all security features, the potential exists for a serious breach of security and system integrity.
>
> When hackers completed their activities, they did not log-off the system. They just hung up and broke the circuit. The result was that no log-in/log-out history record was created. The only internal record that would show that the New Jersey host had been used as an intermediate switch was the console log, a document not normally subjected to detailed review. Monthly bills were not examined for indications of unauthorized use. The way the billing tapes were formatted makes detection very difficult. Very few organizations conduct a detailed review of their monthly communications costs or would know what to look for if they did.

124

PART I
Overview
of Systems
and
Internal
Control

sent an employee for two weeks to a designated parking lot, where he used a car phone to help bankers order cash and conduct wire transfers. Tellers at banks were forced to check accounts, update balances, and process loan payments by hand; this tripled transaction times and increased exposure to fraud because the tellers could only check transactions over $500. Air traffic controllers could not transmit data to other airports. Bekins Co.'s dispatchers were cut off from the company's moving vans and from its mainframe computer in Glendale, California. Executives with portable computers set up shop at the nearest working pay phones they could find, some along the Northwest Tollway. United Stationers, a $730-million-a-year office products wholesaler, was better prepared. The company lost its links between its company's offices and customers and its central computer in Forest Park, Illinois. Without those links, customers could not place orders, salespeople could not check inventory, and clerks could not find pencils and other supplies in the company's 12 warehouses. Fortunately, the company had an extensive disaster plan. By the next day, the company had reconstructed its entire computer network around a borrowed mainframe in New Jersey. Cost: $600,000 over two weeks. Benefit $30,000,000 in sales that would otherwise have been lost.

Use of Phone System Allows Access by Outside Hackers. For fun or malice, some people like to "hack" into corporate data bases. Every evening, hackers on electronic bulletin boards swap tales and techniques of computer break-ins. They trade passwords, debate fine points of stealing long-distance calls, give tutorials on how to find and eliminate "Feds," provide primers for rookie "hacklings," post phone numbers such as Citibank's checking and credit card records, and provide instructions for tapping into the systems of Dun & Bradstreet. Going through printouts found in garbage bins can result in the discovery of passwords. In at least one patent infringement suit, the company believes a rival stole secrets by hacking into its computer system. The result: Ernst & Young estimates computer fraud losses, corporate espionage, and hassle at more than $3 billion per year.

Errors Can Be Introduced During Communications. In addition to the other possible errors in any computer system, the data being transmitted can become corrupted during communication due to power surges, noise from electrical equipment, and device failures. Fundamental to internal control in a communication environment is the detection of transmission errors, that is, detection of errors in the messages sent over the communications links. There are a number of ways to detect and sometime correct transmission errors. These are discussed in greater length in Chapter 7 on data communications. Further complicating this problem is that in most communication environments, the company is critically dependent on access to the computer system. Thus, reliability of the equipment is as important as the need to control communication errors. As discussed in the next section, the system must be robust and continue to function despite equipment failure.

Data Are Spread Over Multiple Locations. Because many users are all accessing the same data, two users may attempt to update the same record concurrently. To prevent this, application programs should lock records before they are updated. This works easily for centralized data. Where multiple copies

125

CHAPTER 4
*Internal
Control in
a Computer
Environment*

of the same data are kept in different locations, the lock must be placed on at least two computers. But if locks are applied simultaneously at two different computers by two different users, then one user has the record locked on one computer, while another user has the same record locked on the other computer. Then neither user has complete control over the record. One of the locks will have to be released and control given to the other user. Any type of partitioned data contributes to this type of problem. If a user seeks to update several records with the same transaction, and two of the records are located on different computers, there is again the need for locks on separate machines and the possibility of two users locking each other out.

Terminals Are More Prevalent and More Difficult to Control. Terminals provide easy access to the computer by users, and this opens the door for dishonest or incompetent users to access the system and its data. The communication facilities should be lockable so they cannot be used. Typically, a front-end communications processor attached to the host computer calls (or polls) each terminal to determine if there are any messages to be transmitted. When a terminal is inoperative, the polling list should exclude that terminal. Polling a terminal that is out of service offers the opportunity for illegal entry into the data communications network by unauthorized persons. Moreover, line protocols should be present to ensure the appropriate connections between a terminal and its computer. These protocols should include verification that the devices are correct and that each type of terminal identifies itself to the host computer so that no other terminal can be masquerading.

Microcomputers

All computer systems have roughly the same internal control advantages and disadvantages, and the same principles should be followed in providing proper internal control in any computer environment. However, internal control problems are specific to microcomputers, largely as a result of microcomputers' design for ease of use and availability. These characteristics can mitigate against good internal control. Microcomputer users should realize that along with the benefits of having their own computers comes new responsibilities for performing internal control tasks. In large-scale systems, most internal control tasks are taken care of by the system and the information systems professionals. Even those using the system are unaware of the control, backup, and so on performed "behind the scenes." When users have microcomputers, however, they have to perform these tasks themselves.

The User Is Responsible for Data Processing Tasks. The typical computer user is an expert in his or her area, not in data processing. Yet it is important for the user of a microcomputer to accomplish the microcomputer equivalent of data processing tasks to be properly protected against errors and problems. Backup is the most important and least accomplished data processing task. The hard disk containing extremely valuable information accumulated over months or years of work is a mechanical device subject to failure at any time. Loss of all accumulated information can be devastating. The rarity of hard disk

126

PART I
Overview
of Systems
and
Internal
Control

failure should not make one complacent about its importance. The microcomputer is virtually an open book to anyone who walks up to it and turns it on. Most microcomputers designed for business now have a lock, which should be used if confidential data are on the computer. In case the data are particularly sensitive, the data can be encrypted so that they are not readable by other programs used by the curious or the intruder. Microcomputers are typically designed for the normal office environment, where the most common physical threats are cigarette smoke, spilled coffee, and magnetic fields from heavy electrical equipment. In more demanding environments, such as an auto garage or a manufacturing plant, the keyboard must be covered or a "ruggedized" version of the microcomputer used. Theft is always a problem, because microcomputers are easily sold. The user should have a plan for how to continue working in case of fire, theft, or other loss of equipment and/or the data on the computer. In addition to the backup of the data mentioned earlier, there must be access to other computing equipment and the possibility of continuing work after restoring the backed-up data. Often, the user does not comply with all software licensing agreements, and thus does not get access to "bug reports" documenting errors in the software and information regarding upgrades to make work more efficient.

The User Is Responsible for System Development Tasks. With the microcomputer, most users can develop systems to meet their own needs. The tools available are constantly changing, but include the capability of linking data from one application to another and the ability to write "batch files" and "macros" that automate repetitive tasks. These applications can be very powerful and useful, but typically they are not tested thoroughly. The most frequent problem is that the application is developed and even checked with one set of data and later, when revised or updated data is incorporated, the new results are incorrect because the application only worked on the original data. Also, because the application is developed by the person who uses it, there is typically insufficient documentation. The person knows what he or she is trying to do, but the next person to use the application is normally not so lucky.

The User Is Responsible for Communications Control. One of the great advantages of the microcomputer is the sharing of information among users. Unfortunately, that important benefit has some negative aspects now. Some people who enjoy discomforting others have developed computer "viruses" that spread and cause problems for others. A programmer may write a small piece of code that can attach itself to other programs and alter them or destroy data kept on a computer disk. The virus can also reproduce by copying itself to other programs stored in the same computer. Typically, the virus is attached to a normal program and is then spread as the owner of the tainted program exchanges software with others via electronic bulletin boards or by trading floppy disks. The more the tainted program is swapped, the more the virus replicates itself. Often, however, the spread of the virus is unknown because the virus remains dormant for several months. At a predetermined time, such as January 1 or December 25, the virus seizes control of the computer and either simply gives a message to the user on the screen or deletes the files from the disk. When severe damage is inflicted, the virus will then taunt the victim with some message such as "Gotcha!" Every microcomputer user has to be sensitive to these problems and be careful about the source and type of program used. A user's microcomputer can be a very useful tool even when the user is away from the computer. It is possible to access your microcomputer from a remote location to check mail, send and receive faxes, and connect to the mainframe data bases. The user must also be aware, however, that others may connect to the computer also and that the microcomputer typically does not protect itself from prying or data deletion by its users.

127

CHAPTER 4
*Internal
Control in
a Computer
Environment*

CONCEPT SUMMARY

Internal Control Problems Specific to Computer Systems

	Control Problem	Typical Result	General Solution
Input and its preparation	Source documents are eliminated.	Audit trail is lost.	Physically control access to terminals.
	Sophisticated tampering can cause unauthorized actions.	Name is added to pension rolls when person is fired.	Ensure proper authorization.
	There are new sources and potentials for error.	Incorrect data are input into the system.	Institute extensive program checks.
Processing	The machine lacks judgment.	Spectacular errors occur.	Build in judgment with reasonableness tests.
	Duties are concentrated within the computer.	Person in charge of computer can circumvent controls.	Segregate duties within data processing.
	Great speed extends one person's capabilities.	Round-off error in one account accumulates.	Review programs limit access to programs.
	There are new sources and potentials for error.	System is used incorrectly.	Complete debugging and proper system design.
	Records and the audit trail are invisible.	Audit trail is hard to use, if it is there.	Use the computer to analyze records and audit trail.
Storage	Information can be changed without physical traces.	Account balances change without a trace.	Use physical controls and cross-checks.
	Concentrated information is easier to steal.	Social Security gets over 1 million records stolen.	Institute physical controls and proper authorization.
	Electronic information is easy to lose.	Fund raising loses millions in pledges.	Institute proper backup.
Output and its use	The user is in awe of the computer.	User does not check computer output.	Use control totals to check computer results.
	Vast capabilities can create a different reality.	Equity Funding creates fictitious policyholders.	Make independent checks with 'real world.'

128

PART I
Overview
of Systems
and
Internal
Control

ELEMENTS OF INTERNAL CONTROL
IN A COMPUTER ENVIRONMENT

Internal control should be of concern to all computer users, not just those charged with that responsibility in the data processing, management information system, or information technology group. To make this clear, Exhibit 4-2 gives a checklist of internal control guidelines for those who have their own microcomputer.

Characteristics of Internal Control
in Computer-Based Systems

Controls for computer-based systems have the same goals as controls for manual systems. These goals are to help ensure that

1. All transactions that should be processed are processed.
2. Only transactions that should be processed are processed.
3. All processing is done correctly.

Good controls will

1. Identify errors at the earliest possible point in the cycle of transaction processing.
2. Prevent unauthorized use of the system and its related data files and records.
3. Be as simple as possible while still being logical, comprehensive, and standardized.

EXHIBIT 4-2   Internal Control Checklist for Microcomputer Users

Data processing tasks	1. Comply with all software licensing agreements, including proper registration.
	2. Guard all data and applications from unauthorized use and access.
	3. Regularly backup data and store them in secure locations.
	4. Protect microcomputer equipment from damage and theft.
	5. Arrange for disaster recovery.
System development tasks	1. Test applications thoroughly to be sure they perform as intended.
	2. Document applications for future users.
Communications control tasks	1. Guard against viruses when using public domain software.
	2. Apply security measures when communicating with other systems.

These are ambitious goals, and there is no magic group of controls that will always work in all situations. You will have to use your judgment concerning what is applicable in each particular case. There will be a number of differences between internal control in a computer environment and in a manual environment. However, it will be most useful to use the same elemental breakdown as given in Chapter 2. The elements of internal control are the same; the computer just changes the methods by which these elements are implemented.

129

CHAPTER 4
*Internal
Control in
a Computer
Environment*

Honest and Capable Employees

Honest and able employees are more important in a computer environment than in a manual system. The dishonest or incompetent employee can use the vast speed and electronic nature of the computer to create far more difficulties than would be possible with a manual system, with related human limitations.

Establish a Climate Where Security Is Taken Seriously. Many, if not most, computer centers simply do not consider the problem of security to be a serious one. As a result, the employees will share this lack of concern and will not be sensitive to potential problems or weaknesses in internal control.

Ensure Proper Training on the Computer. Many of the people using the computer will be unfamiliar with the machine, its capabilities, and its limitations. It is essential that these people be properly introduced to the computer, so they will be capable of using it well. Even if the people were capable in the manual environment, they will not necessarily be capable in the computer environment.

Exclude Disgruntled Employees from the Computer Area. Fired employees have been known to manipulate the computer records or add errors to the system because of anger and resentment at their firing. At the termination interview, the employee should be asked to surrender keys or other means of access to the computer.

Reduce Temptation. The reduction of temptation will help ensure that the basically honest employees will remain so. Attempts to reduce temptation should include:

1. A policy of having two people present when the computer is in use, so that one person will not be alone with his or her temptations.
2. Control of overtime, to reduce the likelihood of an employee engaging in illicit activities in addition to his or her regular job.
3. A mandatory vacation policy, to ensure that people will not be able to keep up a consistent fraud.
4. A policy of rotating jobs, so the possibility of personal manipulation of the system will be more difficult.

Clear Delegation and Separation of Duties

Just as in the manual system, there should be a written plan of organization, with clear assignments of authority and responsibility. The separation of duties in a computer environment, however, will not be the same as the separation

130

PART I
Overview
of Systems
and
Internal
Control

of duties in a manual system. Exhibit 4-3 gives the basic job descriptions in data processing. Only those with knowledge and access can compromise the system, so the goal must be to separate those with knowledge of how the system works from those with access to the computer. Exhibit 4-4 gives an organization chart for a typical data processing installation, illustrating this separation of duties.

EXHIBIT 4-3   Basic Job Positions in Data Processing

		Title	*Description of Duties*
Those with KNOWLEDGE of how the system works		**Data processing (DP) manager**	The top executive in data processing; sets long- and short-range goals; supervises the data processing staff.
		System analyst	Works with users to define data processing projects; formulates problems; defines solutions; develops specifications for programmers.
		Application programmer	Develops effective, efficient, well-documented programs meeting the specifications set by systems analysts.
		System programmer	Maintains the operating system of the computer and adapts its capabilities to the particular company needs; this position is only necessary in large computer installations.
must be separate from		**Computer operator**	Runs the programs according to the operating instructions; mounts tapes and disks; loads paper into printers.
		Data entry clerk	Puts information into computer-readable form by typing into a terminal; sometimes called a terminal operator.
Those with ACCESS to the computer, documentation, and files		**Data control clerk**	Compares control totals from the computer with manually prepared control totals to ensure accurate processing; corrects transactions in error.
		Librarian	Maintains the library of documentation, magnetic tapes, and disks (containing both programs and data).

131

CHAPTER 4
*Internal
Control in
a Computer
Environment*

Separate Those Who Might Collude. It is important to separate people who might collude. Thus, the EDP department must be separate from operating departments. Additionally, no one in EDP should have custody of assets or should be able to authorize transactions, initiate master file changes, or reconcile output controls. Also, to the extent possible, programmers and accountants should be separated, as a combination of the two skills could be disastrous for internal control.

Limit Programmer Scope. It is also important to limit the scope of individual programmers. Programmers and systems analysts should not be allowed to use programs they wrote or designed, and they should not be allowed to operate the computer. Their detailed knowledge of the program and application would allow them to circumvent controls. Also, the users (with guidance and assistance) should specify the functions or programs; the programmer should not work independently. The programmer's supervisor should review each program the programmer writes, and some other qualified employee should conduct the final testing of the program. Also, one programmer should not write all programs for a sensitive application.

Proper Procedures for Processing Transactions

Proper procedures in the computer environment are different from those in a manual environment because the computer is used for multiple procedures and does many of the procedures itself.

EXHIBIT 4-4   Organization Chart for Data Processing

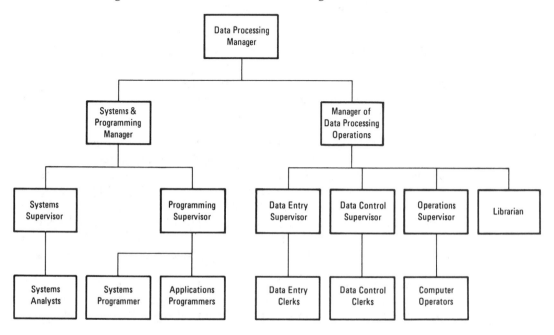

132

*PART I
Overview
of Systems
and
Internal
Control*

Authorization of Transactions. As in a manual system, proper procedures begin with proper authorization of transactions. Even in a computer system, transactions often begin with **hard copy**, such as a check copy or an invoice. Thus, the authorization can consist of the written initials of the person authorizing the transaction. Also, special authorization for large items (such as large checks) should probably require two managers to approve the transaction. More sophisticated systems often originate transactions in machine-readable form only, eliminating hard copy. Examples of this include point-of-sale recorders and remote terminals. In these cases, proper authorization can only be assured by restricting access to the terminals to those responsible for authorizing and initiating transactions.

Terminal Dialogue. **Terminal dialogue** is the "conversation" between the computer system and the operator, as the system prompts for information and the operator gives a response. This dialogue should be designed to make incorrect data entry, whether accidental or deliberate, impossible. Exhibit 4-5 provides a summary of these **programmed controls**.

Tape File Handling. Even a moderately sized data processing operation can have hundreds of tapes and disks, all physically almost identical. Each tape will have an external label that identifies it, including the date the file was created. But even with this external label, it is easy to use the wrong tape, destroy a valuable tape, or update the wrong version of a master file. For these reasons, most tapes have an internal header label at the front of the tape that contains the same information as the external label. The application program uses the header label to ensure that the proper tape is being used. In addition, a trailer label at the end of the file contains a count of the number of records in the file and control totals of the entire file, such as a total balance owed by all customers. Checking the trailer label can help ensure that no information is added to or deleted from the file inappropriately. Labels can also be used with disk files. Exhibit 4-6 gives a description of tape and disk labels.

Protection from Loss. As discussed in Chapter 3, for batch data processing systems there is a standard backup method called the grandfather-father-son concept, where there is always a copy of each master file that is not on the computer. This copy can then re-create the current master file if that master copy is destroyed.

Authorization of New Systems and Programs. In addition to requiring proper authorization of transactions, it is also important to require proper authorization of new systems and programs. Any new systems need approval by the user department, an executive independent of EDP, and the systems and programming management. Additionally, each new program must be completely tested and authorized. After the programmer writes the program and signs off on it, his supervisor checks the program and approves it, the control group tests it, the users test it, and only then does it come into production.

Computer Breakdown. The procedures just discussed assume that the computer will keep working, but it does not always do so. A fire in Boston short-circuited the Putnam Company's money management computers. Floods in Chicago left the data center of A. M. Castle, a metals distributor, underwater. An earthquake in Los Angeles knocked out computer equipment at the California Federal Savings and Loan Association. The system must have alternatives to employ when the computer breaks down, even if it breaks down in the middle of processing. System restart and recovery in case of computer breakdown is difficult, but it must include recovery of programs, data being processed at the time, and data bases. Because of the varying levels of possible

133

CHAPTER 4
*Internal
Control in
a Computer
Environment*

EXHIBIT 4-5   Programmed Controls

Control Group	Control	Description	Example
Check input wholly within program.	Reasonableness	Test whether the amounts are within reason.	Invoice should not exceed $10,000,000.
	Validity	Check whether numbers or codes are valid.	Month should be between 1 and 12.
	Completeness	Determine that all elements of the transaction are included.	Date must be included.
	Self-checking number	Add digit to item numbers to catch transposition errors.	32876 is valid and 38276 is not.
Compare input totals to manually prepared totals.	**Control total**	Program sums an item for all transactions.	Independent sum of dollar amounts compared to computer totals given on an edit listing.
	Hash total	Program sums an item with a meaningless total.	Similar to control total, except a sum of part numbers or quantities rather than dollar amounts.
	Record count	Program counts the number of transactions.	Similar to control total except a count of transactions rather than a sum.
Compare input to information on the file.	Redundancy	Input information about the item in addition to its number to make sure the number is correct.	Input the first five characters of a customer's name as well as the customer number.
	Existence	Ensure item is on the file and active before processing transaction.	Customer number should refer to an active customer on the file.
	Descriptive feedback	Get name or description from master file when primary key is input to check correctness before continuing.	Program prints out customer name when customer number is input.

134

PART I
Overview
of Systems
and
Internal
Control

EXHIBIT 4-6   Tape and Disk Labels

Type		*Description*
External label		Label on the outside of the file to ensure the operator and librarian can identify it.
Internal labels	Header label	Label at the beginning of the file to ensure the correct file is processed.
	Trailer label	Label at the end of the file to ensure that file totals and record counts stay correct.

failure, applications must be subjected to stringent testing. A primary concern is to ensure that no double updates (where two users make changes at the same time to the same data) occur and to avoid the situation where a user thinks an update occurred when in reality it did not. A second concern is that the system be capable of recovering data lost because of power loss or hardware failure.

One method of disk recovery is to write dual copies of all information to dual disk drives. This allows disk rebuilding on-line once the secondary disk data has been corrected. This technique provides extremely higher availability and reliability. Another method of disk recovery is to write two records on tape every time a transaction is processed. These two records would be the status of the updated data record before the transaction was processed and then again after the transaction was processed.

Software Provisions for Breakdowns.   Software must provide message accountability by ensuring that no inputs or outputs are lost. This means that messages must be logged (by a dump of a copy of each message to a tape) and time tagged as they are received. It is also desirable to check format and content for error, and there should be immediate diagnosis and action on errors. Suppose, for example, that a message received from a particular node (computer or terminal in the network) is garbled. The software should respond by requesting that the message be retransmitted. If customer accounts are involved, typically limits on dollar amounts for such attributes as order amount, credit, and withdrawals are also involved. If transactions that exceed the limits by only a small amount are received, the software should place the transaction data in a temporary file to await modification of the transaction amount. A message should be transmitted to the sender that the amount exceeds the specified limit. If an appropriate response is not received within a few minutes, the transaction should be deleted from the temporary file, and all further processing should be prohibited. If transactions are received that exceed the limits by very large amounts, an error message should be transmitted to the sender, requesting reentry of the transaction details. The transaction details should be logged for later examination and not held in a temporary file. A **store-and-forward system** stores incoming messages by copying them to a storage medium and later transmitting them to their destinations. Good practice requires that a copy of all incoming and outgoing messages be kept. Then, in case of computer failure, the log containing these copies can be scanned, recording each incoming message in memory. Each message should be subsequently erased if a corresponding outgoing message is found on the log. When the entire log has been scanned, the remaining messages are those not yet processed at the time of failure.

135

CHAPTER *4*
Internal
Control in
a Computer
Environment

Suitable Documents and Accounting Records

Just as in the manual system, the computer files must contain all necessary information and an effective audit trail. In addition, there are a number of requirements specific to a computer system. These requirements basically arise from the ease of losing electronic information and from the increased importance of proper documentation.

Backup. Because the information on the computer is so easily lost, there must be proper backup files that are tested. No important information should ever exist in the computer system in only one place; for safety, it should always be duplicated somewhere else. To ensure that they can be relied upon, these duplicate or backup files must be periodically tested to assure that they can restore lost files. Recovery for failures in transaction processing involves periodically filing on tape the balances of valid transactions received. Each of these periodic filings of balances is called a checkpoint. The balances at the time of failure can be reconstructed by processing the transactions in the audit trail tapes or disks after restart of the transaction processing system from the status at the time of the last checkpoint.

Documentation. A critical requirement is for **documentation** on three levels: systems documentation, program documentation, and operator instructions. The **system documentation** provides an overall view of the system, how it works, and its control features. The **program documentation** provides the information necessary for understanding and modifying each program. The **operator instructions** provide information necessary to use the program. Documentation that explains the system and how it works is far more important in a computer environment than it is in a manual system. In a manual system, the records and their contents can be seen, and it is possible to follow the flow of information through the system—in a sense the manual system is self-documenting. This is not true in a computer system: documentation is necessary to understand the system and how it works.

Procedures and Standards. The next required documents are written procedures and standards of performance. These documents should include standards for:

1. Documentation, so that documentation prepared by different people at different times will be uniform and easier to understand and maintain.
2. Security measures over data files, program libraries, and the computer room, so that policy will be consistent.
3. The authorization of requests for data processing, whether it is a new program, a new system, or a routine run, to ensure that order is maintained and that priorities are established in an orderly way.
4. Operation of the computer and maintenance of the files.

136

PART I
Overview
of Systems
and
Internal
Control

Adequate Physical Control over Assets and Records

Manual records are, in a way, protected against manipulation—the erasures, changes, or substitutions will generally be visually apparent unless done in an unusually expert way. Changes in computer systems can be invisible, so physical control over access to the system and records is even more important. The proper controls on access to the computer itself, the terminals, and computer records depend on the particular situation, but the following are basic elements of physical control.

Access Control. It is important to protect programs as well as data. There should be a library of tapes and disks with one person accountable for them. Inventory records should be maintained and checked periodically in order to account for all file movement. The systems and program documentation should be locked to protect them from the operation. The computer room should be locked (with emergency exits for safety's sake) to restrict the access of programmers to the computer. It is often important to change keys, passwords, and combinations regularly to ensure that access is available only to those authorized at that time rather than to everyone who has been authorized in the past. There should be controls on access to sensitive input and output. While the input data are waiting for processing or after it is processed, the information should be protected from unauthorized access. Also, after the computer output is generated, it should be protected. It is often a good idea to log the distribution of reports to help check that everyone who should get the reports does get them and that only those who should get them do so.

Physical Protection. The next item of importance is physical protection and insurance coverage against loss from catastrophic accidents, such as a fire or flood. For example, fire protection should include a fire extinguisher. Decisions on the use of further techniques should trade off convenience and safety. In different situations, all of the following are useful:

1. Store data in fireproof cabinets.
2. Use vaults for on-site data storage.
3. Use off-site storage.
4. Divide key data processing operations between two sites.
5. Build backup centers that could be used in an emergency.
6. Sign on with a disaster recovery firm.

For a monthly fee, a company will arrange a disaster contingency plan, including copying computer data frequently, usually every night, and storing the backups at an off-site location. The backup plan is then tested every six months. In all these considerations, there are two costs to keep in mind. The first is the physical loss of equipment, such as computer hardware and physical tapes and disks. The second, and often more important, cost is that of reconstructing the programs and data files.

137

CHAPTER 4
*Internal
Control in
a Computer
Environment*

Physical Care.   Computer equipment requires proper physical care in order to function properly. First, the equipment billings from the vendor should match the computer equipment present; it is possible for equipment to "walk," and it is possible for the vendor to overbill. The temperature and humidity should be kept at the proper levels for the particular equipment. Also, there should be proper preventive maintenance by qualified technicians on a regular basis. Do not wait until something breaks, but have everything reviewed on a scheduled basis.

Independent Verification of Performance

It is possible for a computer-based system to paint a balanced and consistent picture of reality that is nonetheless completely false. As a result, it is absolutely essential to have independent verification of the system picture. The basic independent verification is to check asset balances periodically: Determine if the system balances of cash and inventory match with the actual amounts. Another important independent verification is for the system's users to maintain independent control totals of input and review the output of the system. Additionally, the system should periodically develop summaries for users to check. For example, the gross margin should appear reasonable based on past performance.

Verification That Procedures Are Followed.   Written procedures and standards of performance should be checked to see if they are, in fact, being followed. It does little good to have procedures and standards if they are widely ignored. Physical controls and security measures must be checked and lax security must be disciplined if there is to be effective internal control.

System Logs.   System logs of both transactions and operator actions will allow an independent check of transactions using the audit trail. System logs will also allow a check if errors become excessive for any particular system, terminal, or operator. Excessive errors could indicate faulty system design, poor forms, poor terminal dialogue, untrained operators, or attempts at unauthorized access. In a communications environment, logical errors should be immediately detected and corrected or corrections requested. Audit trails should be designed using a standard format for all data transmissions. all substantive information is recorded for any transaction, record update, inquiry/ response, message switching action, or data entry operation. This trail can then be used for billing, activity analysis, error analysis, security evaluation, and data base activity analysis.

Independent Audit.   Finally, there should be an independent audit. This is an excellent means of checking compliance with established standards and of identifying internal control deficiencies. This topic is discussed in greater length in Chapter 17.

138

*PART I
Overview
of Systems
and
Internal
Control*

CONCEPT SUMMARY	
Elements of Internal Control in Computer-Based Systems	
Honest and capable employees	1. Create climate where security is taken seriously. 2. Provide proper training in use of computer. 3. Check background and bond employees. 4. Promptly exclude fired employees from computer.
Clear delegation and separation of duties	1. Develop written plan of organization. 2. Do not allow any employees to be essential. 3. Assign responsibility for data, systems, and programs. 4. Separate people who might collude.
Proper procedures for processing of transactions	1. Ensure transactions are properly authorized. 2. Check entered data for accuracy. 3. Use only authorized and tested programs. 4. Develop and test procedures for computer breakdown.
Suitable documents and account records	1. Provide backup files of data and programs. 2. Have written procedures and standards of performance. 3. Develop documentation of systems and programs. 4. Use prenumbered documents and forms.
Adequate physical control over assets and records	1. Control access to computer and terminals. 2. Protect equipment and data against loss. 3. Control access to sensitive input and output. 4. Maintain equipment on a regular basis.
Independent verification of performance	1. Develop overall system controls. 2. Check adherence to policies and procedures. 3. Check security and discipline lax security. 4. Have audit by independent CPA firm.

CHAPTER SUMMARY

Computers are always accurate, consistent, and disinterested. However, computer-based systems can have weaknesses in internal control. Problems with data input stem from lack of documentation, susceptibility to tampering, and human error. Processing problems result from

1. The machine's inability to reason.
2. Performance of multiple of tasks that in a manual system would be performed by separate employees.
3. The speed with which both unintentional mistakes and deliberate fraud can spread systemwide.

139

CHAPTER 4
*Internal
Control in
a Computer
Environment*

CONCEPT SUMMARY

Elements of Internal Control in a Communications Environment

Know the limits for all authorized users, including (1) whether they are authorized to access the system from remote locations, (2) where they are, (3) what their user identifications are, (4) what system facilities they are authorized to employ, and (5) what files they can access.

Use a communications **front-end processor** that breaks the circuit with the calling user, verifies the particular user for authorized access, and dials the user's telephone number or network address.

Require the use of passwords that are unique to the user and secret (no initials, predictable passwords, or passwords taped to the terminal). These passwords should be changed regularly and have a minimum of six characters. Allow only three attempts to type in a password.

Remove all hardware manufacturer-intalled systems access protocols. Change the maintenance access protocol on a scheduled basis.

Accept only prepaid calls from network users. Hackers are notoriously reluctant to spend their own money.

Review data communications billings from both the telephone company and any networks used. Verify every host-to-host connection. Conduct a detailed review of dial-up terminal users and determine if you have authorized users in that area.

Use only unlisted phone numbers and change them at least once a year.

Revoke systems access authority for terminated employees.

Encrypt sensitive information. An encryption device can scramble the original data before transmission, so that it cannot be understood until the receiver decodes it.

---

4. Faulty hardware, software, application programs, or system design.
5. The impossibility of completely testing complex software.
6. The trade-offs between security and productivity.

Storage problems arise because computerized information can easily be changed, stolen, or lost with no visible traces. Output may not be controlled properly because people tend not to question it. Communication of data may cause problems if the telephone system crashes, is invaded by hackers, or causes transmission errors, and if there is multiple access to the data. The user of a microcomputer must take responsibility for internal control because the user typically processes data, develops systems, and controls communications. The system is small and easy to use, so safety measures must be in place to guard against theft, unauthorized access to data, and infection by a computer virus.

The elements of accounting control in a computer environment are the same as in a manual environment, but implementation is different. Employees

140

PART I
Overview
of Systems
and
Internal
Control

must operate the computer properly. System analysts and programmers must not work with operators and clerks. Access to terminals should be restricted to those responsible for authorizing and initiating transactions, terminal dialogue should check for error, the system should log and detect errors in messages, and new systems and programs should be properly authorized. In addition, procedures should be in place to provide hardware and software backups in the event of system failure. The system must back up information and test the backups periodically; it must have adequate documentation to explain systems, programs, and operator instructions; and it must have standards for documentation, security measures, authorization of requests for data processing, and computer operation and file maintenance. Data must be protected and equipment protected and maintained. Finally, independent checks on procedures and performance can be provided by an audit.

KEY TERMS

Application programmer *(p. 130)*
Computer operator *(p. 130)*
Control total *(p. 133)*
Data control clerk *(p. 130)*
Data entry clerk *(p. 130)*
Data processing (DP) manager
  (p. 130)
Documentation *(p. 135)*
Front-end processor *(p. 139)*
Hard copy *(p. 132)*
Hash total *(p. 133)*

Operator instructions *(p. 135)*
Program documentation *(p. 135)*
Programmed controls *(p. 132)*
Record count *(p. 133)*
Self-checking number *(p. 133)*
Store-and-forward system *(p. 134)*
System analyst *(p. 130)*
System documentation *(p. 135)*
System programmer *(p. 130)*
Terminal dialogue *(p. 132)*

QUESTIONS

4-1. What are the major internal control concerns that are eliminated by the introduction of a computer?

4-2. Describe the new internal control problems created by computerized data input and those associated with computer output and its use.

4-3. Describe the new internal control problems associated with the processing and storage of data in a computer environment.

4-4. Give the basic causes of failures in a network and how the system can protect itself from these failures.

4-5. What are the internal control responsibilities of microcomputer users? Why are they greater than users of larger systems?

4-6. Explain why the separation of duties is a different sort of problem in a computer system than in a manual system. What can be done to provide a proper separation of duties in a computer environment?

4-7. How can a company ensure that transactions are properly authorized? That input data are accurate? That a new program is properly authorized?

4-8. Is documentation more important in a computer system than in a manual system? If so, why? Give the basic types of computer system documentation and a brief description of each.

141

CHAPTER 4
*Internal
Control in
a Computer
Environment*

4-9. Discuss the means by which a company can control access to the computer, terminals, and sensitive input and output.

4-10 What are the basic independent checks useful in a computer system? Why is an audit important?

4-11. Identify the basic elements of internal control in a communication environment.

PROBLEMS

4-12. Internal control is an important consideration in computer-based systems. In fact, internal control may be more significant in computer-based systems than in manual systems. Give three specific internal control problems of computer systems that are not significant problems in manual systems.

4-13. The concept summary of the elements of internal control also gives the specific steps that must be taken to make the element effective. For an accounts receivable system in a company with only one accounts receivable clerk and an accountant, give a specific example of each of these steps and how each step might be accomplished.

4-14. This chapter has stressed the internal control problems that may be part of computer-based systems. However, there are a number of internal control benefits that result from using the computer. List ten accidental or deliberate mistakes that are entirely possible in a manual system but that are unlikely in a computer-based system.

4-15. The concept summary that presents the internal control problems that are specific to computer systems also gives the typical result from such control problems and a general solution for each problem. For an accounts receivable system in a small organization with an accountant and a bookkeeper, give a specific example of each type of control problem and how it might arise.

4-16. For best internal control, the responsibilities for system development, program maintenance, and data accuracy should be separated since processing is concentrated within the computer. However, many small businesses have only one person directly responsible for all data processing activities. Discuss five specific internal control techniques that could be used where data processing duties and responsibilities cannot be separated.

4-17. *(AICPA, adapted)* A savings and loan association installed an on-line, real-time computer system. Each teller in the association's main office and seven branch offices has an on-line, input/output terminal. Customers' mortgage payments and savings account deposits and withdrawals are recorded in the accounts by the computer from data input by the teller at the time of the transaction. The teller keys the proper account by account number and enters the information in the terminal keyboard to record the transaction. The accounting department at the main office has both punched card and terminal input/output devices. The computer is housed at the main office. List the internal controls which should be in effect in such a system, classifying them as (a) controls pertaining to the input of information and (b) all other types of controls.

4-18. *(AICPA, adapted)* Your client, Lakesedge Wholesale Company, is installing an electronic data processing system. You have been asked to recommend con-

142

PART I
Overview
of Systems
and
Internal
Control

trols for the new system. Discuss recommended controls over (a) program documentation, (b) program testing, (c) EDP hardware, and (d) data files and software.

4-19. (*CMA, adapted*)   The Department of Taxation of one state is developing a new computer system for processing state income tax returns of individuals and corporations. The new system features direct data input and inquiry capabilities. Identification of taxpayers is provided by using the Social Security number for individuals and federal identification number for corporations. The new system should be fully implemented in time for the next tax season. The new system will serve three primary purposes:

a. Data will be input into the system directly from tax returns through terminals located at the central headquarters of the Department of Taxation.

b. The returns will be processed using the main computer facilities at central headquarters. The processing includes (1) verifying mathematical accuracy, (2) auditing the reasonableness of deductions, tax due, and so on through the use of edit routines (these routines also include a comparison of the current year's data with prior years' data), (3) identifying returns that should be considered for audit by revenue agents of the department, and (4) issuing refund checks to taxpayers.

c. Inquiry service will be provided to taxpayers upon request through the assistance of tax department personnel at five regional offices. A total of 50 terminals will be placed at the regional offices. A taxpayer will be allowed to determine the status of his or her return or get information from the last three years' returns by calling or visiting one of the department's regional offices.

The state commissioner of taxation is concerned about data security during input and processing over and above protection against natural hazards such as fire and floods. This includes protection against the loss or damage of data during data input or processing, or improper input or processing of data. In addition, the tax commissioner and the state attorney general have discussed the general problem of data confidentiality which may arise from the nature and operation of the new system. Both individuals want to have all potential problems identified before the system is fully developed and implemented so that the proper controls can be incorporated into the new system.

1. Describe the potential confidentiality problems that could arise in each of the following three areas of processing: (a) data input, (b) processing of returns, and (c) data inquiry. Recommend corrective action(s) to solve the problems.

2. The State Tax Commission wants to incorporate controls to provide data security against the loss, damage, or improper input or use of data during data input and processing. Identify the potential problems (outside of natural hazards such as fire and floods) for which the Department of Taxation should develop controls, and recommend the possible controls for each problem identified.

4-20. (*IIA, adapted*)   Currently, your company is experiencing a rapid increase in the use of microcomputers for stand-alone application processing in both its central and branch locations. Management is becoming increasingly concerned about the following conditions:

143

CHAPTER 4
*Internal
Control in
a Computer
Environment*

a. *Lack of segregation of duties.* In the offices where microcomputers are used, sometimes only one person is responsible for the programming, operating, and training in the use of the microcomputer.

b. *Limited knowledge of data processing.* Personnel in the various company offices lack sufficient knowledge and skills in data processing. Supervisors have not been trained to oversee and control the microcomputer operations.

c. *Utility programs.* The microcomputer vendor has supplied utility programs that can access data files to change, delete, and report data.

d. *Diskettes.* Because of the limited amount of storage capacity on diskettes, each location requires a large number of diskettes for application processing.

e. *Software packages.* At the time the microcomputers were purchased, several software packages were acquired for common business functions. In addition, each location has the discretion to purchase software packages for its specific needs.

f. *Documentation.* Documentation is neither required nor uniform for the microcomputer-based systems.

For each of the previously stated conditions,

1. Identify the risks.
2. Specify control techniques relative to the exposures that exist.

4-21. (*IIA, adapted*) The following policies or procedures exist in XYZ Corporation's electronic data processing department:

a. Access to the computer room is limited to the company's employees.

b. The vault door of the tape library is locked at night and opened each morning by the data processing manager or his assistant. The combination is known only to EDP personnel.

c. The grandfather-father-son retention cycle is used for files, with ancestors stored in the vault.

d. The department has an administrative manager who authorizes the development of applications, runs schedules, and supervises the work of programmers, analysts, and operators. Another of his responsibilities is to review all program modifications.

e. The programmers and analysts have flexible work requirements and frequently work into the evening or come in at night to debug and test programs on the computer.

f. All systems development is initiated by the EDP manager. An informal mechanism exists to assess users' needs and to set priorities for application requests. Priorities are determined by the data processing manager according to a long-range master plan initiated last year by the data processing department. The EDP department absorbs all the cost of development work.

g. Each program is assigned exclusively to a programmer who is responsible for coding, testing, and documenting that program.

Each of these policies or procedures represents one or more strengths and/or weaknesses. For each policy or procedure, identify the strengths and/or weaknesses present. For each strength, indicate why it is a strength; for each weakness, suggest a procedure to correct the deficiency. Restrict your comments to the policies or procedures identified.

4-22. (*CMA, adapted*) Simmons Corporation is a multilocation retailing concern with stores and warehouses throughout the United States. The company is in the process of designing a new integrated computer-based information system.

144

*Part I
Overview
of Systems
and
Internal
Control*

In conjunction with the design of the new system, the management of the company is reviewing the data processing security to determine what new control features should be incorporated. Two areas of specific concern are (a) confidentiality of company and customer records and (b) safekeeping of computer equipment, files, and EDP facilities.

The new information system will be employed to process all company records, which include sale, purchase, financial, budget, customer, creditor, and personnel information. The stores and warehouses will be linked to the main computer at corporate headquarters or to any other location from each location through the terminal network. At the present time, certain reports have restricted distribution because not all levels of management need to receive them or because they contain confidential information. The introduction of remote terminals in the new system may provide access to this restricted data by unauthorized personnel. Simmons' top management is concerned that confidential information may become accessible and may be used improperly. The company is also concerned with potential physical threats to the system, such as sabotage, fire damage, water damage, power failure, or magnetic radiation. Should any of these events occur in the present system and cause a computer shutdown, adequate backup records are available so that the company could reconstruct necessary information at a reasonable cost on a timely basis. However, with the new system, a computer shutdown would severely limit company activities until the system could become operational again.

1. Identify and briefly explain the problems Simmons Corporation could experience with respect to the confidentiality of information and records in the new system.
2. Recommend measures Simmons Corporation could incorporate into the new system that would ensure the confidentiality of information and records in the new system.
3. What safeguards can Simmons Corporation develop to provide physical security for its (a) computer equipment, (b) files, and (c) EDP facilities?

4-23. (*CMA, adapted*) The documentation of data processing applications is an important step in the design and implementation of any computer-based system. Documentation provides a complete record of data processing applications. However, documentation is a phase of systems development that often is neglected. While documentation can be tedious and time consuming, the lack of proper documentation can be very costly to an organization.

1. Identify and explain briefly the purposes proper documentation can serve.
2. Discuss briefly the basic types of information that should be included in the documentation of a data processing application.
3. What policies should be established to regulate access to documentation data for purposes of information or modification for the following four groups of company employees: (a) computer operators, (b) internal auditors, (c) production planning analysts, and (d) systems analysts.

4-24. (*CMA, adapted*) Peacock Company, a wholesaler of soft goods, has an inventory composed of approximately 3,500 different items. The company employs a computerized batch processing system to maintain its perpetual inventory records. The system is run each weekend so that the inventory reports will be available on Monday morning for management's use. The system has been func-

145

CHAPTER 4
*Internal
Control in
a Computer
Environment*

tioning satisfactorily for the past 15 months and has provided the company with accurate records and timely reports. The preparation of purchase orders has been automatic as a part of the inventory system to ensure that the company will maintain enough inventory to meet customer demand. When an item of inventory falls below a predetermined level, a written record is made of the inventory item. This record is used in conjunction with the vendor file to prepare the purchase orders. Exception reports are prepared during the update of the inventory and the preparation of the purchase orders. These reports identify any errors or exceptions identified during the processing. In addition, the system provides for management approval of all purchase orders exceeding a specified amount. Any exceptions of items requiring management approval are handled by supplemental runs on Monday morning and are combined with the weekend results. A system flowchart of Peacock Company's inventory and purchase order procedure is shown in Exhibit 4-7.

The illustrated system flowchart of Peacock Company's inventory and purchase order system was prepared before the system was fully operational. Several steps important to the successful operation of the system were inadvertently omitted. Indicate in narrative terms where the omissions have occurred. The flowchart does not need to be redrawn.

4-25. It is estimated that several hundred million dollars are lost annually through computer crime. The first conviction of a computer "hacker" under the Computer Fraud and Abuse Act of 1986 occurred in 1988. There have been other cases of computer break-ins reported in the news, as well as stories of viruses spreading throughout vital networks. While these cases make the headlines, most experts maintain that the number of computer crimes publicly revealed represent only the tip of the iceberg. Companies have been victims of crimes but have not acknowledged them in order to avoid adverse publicity and not advertise their vulnerability. Although the threat to security is seen as external, through outside penetration, the more dangerous threats are of internal origin. Management must recognize these problems and commit to the development and enforcement of security programs to deal with the many types of fraud that computer systems are susceptible to on a daily basis. The primary types of computer systems fraud are (a) input manipulation, (b) program alternation, (c) file alteration, (d) data theft, (e) sabotage, and (f) theft of computer time.

For the six types of fraud identified, explain how each is committed. Also, identify a different method of protection for each type of fraud, describing how the protection method operates. The same protection method should not be used for more than one type of fraud.

EXHIBIT 4-7   Peacock Company System Flowchart

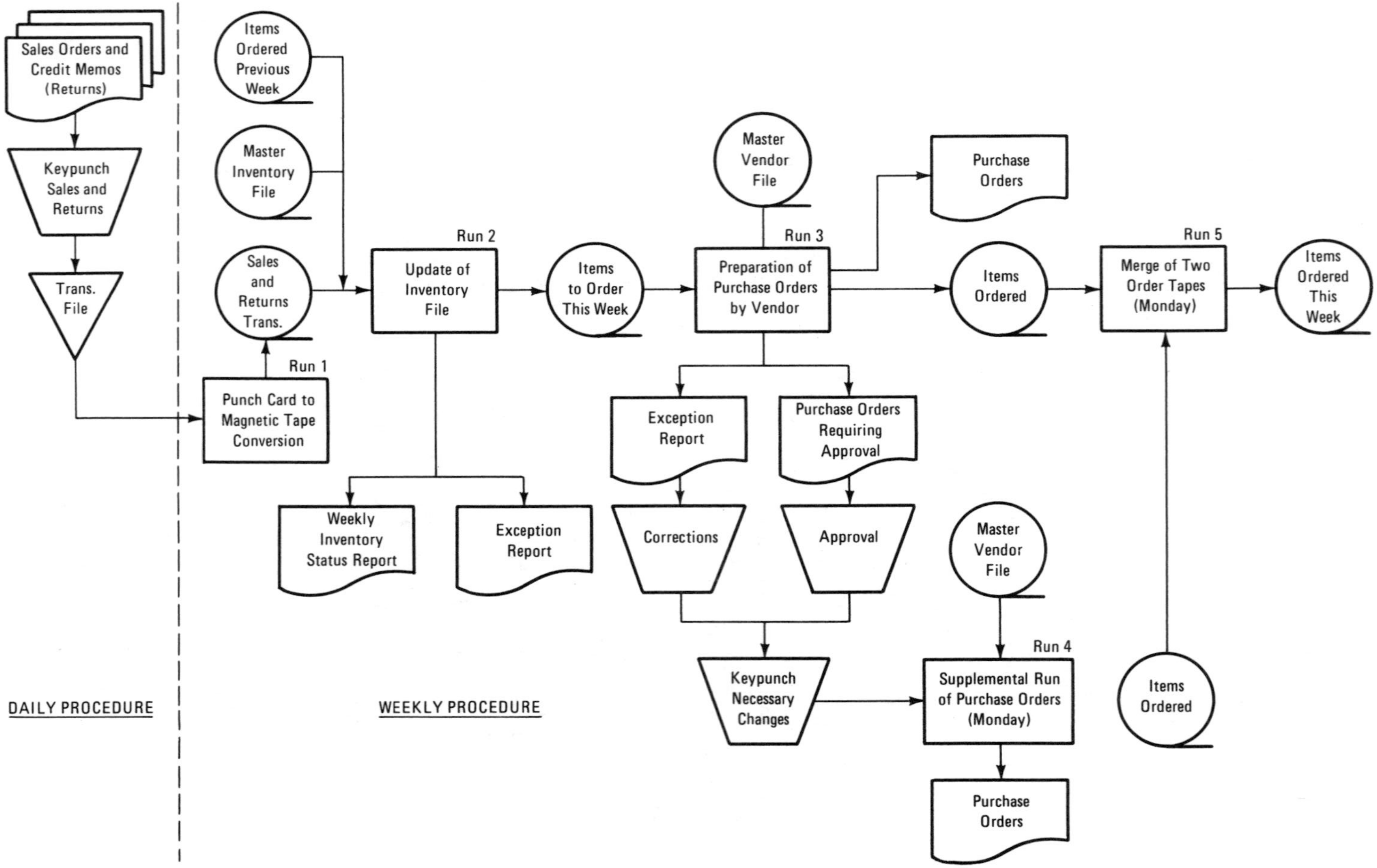

DAILY PROCEDURE

WEEKLY PROCEDURE

146

DECISION CASE

147

CHAPTER 4
*Internal
Control in
a Computer
Environment*

Bank Holding Corporation (BHC) of Cleveland, Ohio, has 25 affiliate banks scattered over several counties. Local banks generally manage themselves, but on-line processing has been centralized at the BHC data center. A number of the vice presidents of operations of affiliate banks have recently expressed concern over the use of centralized data processing. They worry about the cost and competitive disadvantage of an interruption in business activity that might be caused by the loss of data or the ability to process it. The centralized processing makes them especially sensitive since they no longer have control over their own data. In response to this concern, BHC's internal audit staff visited the computer operations facility to review control policy. The on-site visit proceeded as follows:

Mr. Heckman, the manager of computer operations, assured the auditors it was not necessary to sign the visitors' log since they were with him. When they approached the computer room door, Mr. Heckman remembered that he had forgotten his magnetic card used to gain access to the room, but luck was with them and the door was unlocked. Inside the computer room, five operators were gathered in a group. Mr. Heckman explained that they were deciding who would run which jobs that day. The computer room seemed drafty, and Mr. Heckman pointed out that this was caused by opening the back door on cool days to help reduce the load placed on the air conditioners.

In the back of the computer room, where the magnetic tape drives were located, the operator loading a tape accidentally dropped it. He assured the auditors that no damage had been done and proceeded to load the tape. He was asked what tape he was holding, but he said all he knew was that he was to load it on drive #612. There was a large computer printout proclaiming "HAPPY BIRTHDAY, HARRY" hanging from a fire detector. Mr. Heckman explained that the computer has a program that can create these large printouts, and operators and programmers create the signs when the work gets slow. "It adds a personal touch and helps boost morale," he said. The computer room was very clean and well organized. Mr. Heckman explained that the cleaning crew scrubbed the room on Sundays when there were no employees around to bother them. Sunday was also the day when technicians performed preventive maintenance on the computer.

Backup tapes are stored off-site at Murphy's Supply. The librarian was waiting for the pickup person from Murphy's, but he was late. The librarian had only been on the job for two weeks and said she had been told during training time that sometimes he did not show up at all. There was a large volume of tapes stacked on the librarian's desk. Mr. Heckman said that many of the tapes were past the date when they should be destroyed, but the librarian had been busy lately. Mr. Roll, a programmer, walked into the library, picked up a tape, and was greeted cordially by Mr. Heckman. Mr. Roll was Mr. Heckman's first programmer and, since his wife died five years ago, had become so devoted to his work that he rarely took a vacation. The Murphy's pickup man finally arrived. He left the old storage tapes and packed up the box of tapes to be sent to the computer center and briefly counted nine of them. He

148

PART I
Overview
of Systems
and
Internal
Control

asked the librarian why there were not the usual ten tapes. She replied that one was temporarily misplaced, but she was too busy to look for it.

The auditors decided to visit the off-site storage facility located on the outskirts of Cleveland. The off-site storage building was very hot inside, and the receptionist said it got even hotter in the summer because the building was right next to a restaurant kitchen. The list provided of tapes stored at the site was out of date, and a more current set of tapes was actually stored there. There was only a partial inventory list for the most recent set of tapes. The physical storage of the tapes was in locked closets labeled only by letters. There was no fire detection device in the storage site, but Mr. Heckman assured the auditors there had never been a fire in the building in the 60 years since it had been built.

Required:

1. Identify internal control weaknesses that exist in the (a) computer operations facility, (b) tape library, and (c) storage site.
2. Specify protective and control measures that should be used by the data center to (a) control access to files and (b) protect the facility from environmental hazards or disasters.

5 Data Files and Data Bases

Overview

Different available methods of data storage and access available to process large volumes of business data.

Learning Objectives

Thorough study of this chapter will enable you to:

1. Distinguish between programs and data.
2. Explain the advantages of the file approach over the list approach.
3. Define terms essential to file technology.
4. Distinguish between master files and transaction files.
5. Describe the structure and uses of the four types of file organization.
6. List the advantages and costs of the data base approach.
7. Diagram a file structure.
8. Distinguish between the hierarchical (tree), network (plex), and relational approaches.
9. Describe the nature and purpose of data base management systems.
10. Explain why many businesses are shifting toward distributed data processing.

Outline

Basic File Concepts

Master File/Transaction File Data Structure

Data Base Approach

Distributed Data Base Systems

150

PART II
Technical
Aspects of
Accounting
Information
Systems

SYSTEMS IN THE REAL WORLD

The IRS Has Your Number

At the Internal Revenue Service (IRS) computer center in Martinsburg, W. Va., vast data files on taxpayers are stored on magnetic tape in a massive data base. But critics say the data are often filed and forgotten and almost never actually used.

Can you find your tax returns among the thousands of reels of magnetic tape in this picture?

SOURCE: *George Tames NYT Pictures,* 3/16/80, reprinted by permission.

The business data processing systems discussed in Chapters 3 and 4 process a tremendous volume of transactions. Every day at General Motors 1,183 mainframes process 17,000,000 transactions and using accounts at 700 banks make $1.7 billion of daily borrowings. The IRS receives over 500,000,000 information returns each year. VISA has 77,200,000 cards generating $60.6 billion in charges; 25 million card users access 1,564 automated teller machines (ATMs) in 25 states. MasterCard has 60,000,000 cards generating $49.7 billion in billings; 9 million cards get cash at 3,000 ATMs in 28 states. American Express has 15,000,000 cards generating $36.6 billion in billings; 3 million cards get cash at 2,000 ATMs in 31 states.

This chapter introduces the means of handling today's tremendous volume of business activity. The basic concepts discussed are widely applicable to business data processing.

BASIC FILE CONCEPTS

Files are essential for business data processing because they provide an efficient means to store and retrieve data.

Program Versus Data

A computer program is a series of instructions for the computer, while the data are the pieces of information with which the program operates. Consider a program that computes the square of a given number. The program consists of instructions that tell the computer to

1. Print out a question asking for a number to square.
2. Accept a number from the keyboard.
3. Print out words of explanation, the input value, and the result.

The data on which these instructions operate consist, in this case, of the number input from the keyboard. The instructions of the program are the same no matter what number is input from the keyboard. In the program, a symbol stands for whatever number the instructions are carried out upon. Thus, the program is separate from the data. The user writes the program and checks it for correct form without regard to the particular data to be used. The program can then apply to whatever data are appropriate. When the computer executes the program, it brings the data and the program together and the instructions are carried out on the data. Thus, the data are not incorporated into the program until execution.

Program Flowcharts

This chapter discusses programs that may be difficult to visualize. To make the concepts more concrete and the discussion more easily comprehensible, flowcharts will often accompany the programs. The concepts are independent of any particular programming language, so the discussion is not tied to any one language. Exhibit 5-1 provides the basic program flowchart symbols; earlier chapters presented system flowcharting. Here the flowcharting concept is extended to the preparation of diagrams showing the structure of the program.

The Need for Files

Consider a program to

1. Read from the keyboard the number of numbers to follow.
2. Read in the numbers.
3. Add up their total.
4. Calculate the average.
5. Read the data from the keyboard again.

152

PART II
Technical
Aspects of
Accounting
Information
Systems

EXHIBIT 5-1   Program Flowchart Symbols

	Symbol	*Name*	*Description*
1.		Processing	Processing steps such as calculations or variable assignments
2.		Terminal	The start or end of a program
3.		Decision	Choice of path based on a particular condition
4.		Input/Output	Accept input or generate output, such as printing
5.	---	Annotation	Comments on the program flow or further explanation
6.		On-page Connector	Ties flowchart together on the same page
7.		Off-page Connector	Ties flowchart together on separate pages

6. Count the number above the average.
7. Calculate the percentage above the average.
8. Print out the average and the percentage above the average.

(The program flowchart is illustrated in Exhibit 5-2).

This approach is very inefficient because the user inputs the same data twice, which doubles the work and the opportunity for error. The program would be more efficient if the data were input and stored in a **list** (sometimes called a vector or one-dimensional array) for future use. The data are input only once, thus cutting the input work in half and eliminating the chance of putting different numbers in the second time.

Disadvantages of Lists.   A list to store the data for future use cannot be used in general for two major reasons:

1. The data can only be used by this one program. When the program is finished, the user can no longer access the data—they are lost.
2. There is not enough computer memory to use this approach in real-world programs to process a bank's customer accounts or an airline's ticket reservations.

EXHIBIT 5-2   Program for Percent Calculation

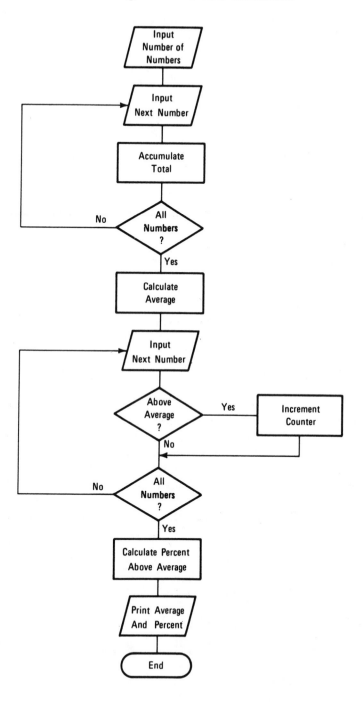

154

PART II
Technical
Aspects of
Accounting
Information
Systems

Criteria for Data Storage. There must be a way to store data separately from the program(s) that use them, but such storage must meet two criteria:

1. The method must allow the data to be used by several different programs.
2. The method must allow for the storage of vast quantities of data.

Files. The use of **files** is a way to store data that satisfies these criteria. A file (as defined in computer science) is a collection of data stored on a secondary storage device, such as disk or tape, rather than stored in main computer memory (primary storage). A file in the computer science sense is thus very similar to a manual file, except that the computer file is only machine readable.

Record/File/List Relationship. A file resembles a list in that both lists and files are collections of building blocks of a similar nature. For example, the list P is built up from the individual elements P(1), P(2), P(3), and so on. In the case of a file, the file is built up from individual records. A record is then the basic building block of the file, and each building block or record is similar to every other.

Exhibit 5-3 illustrates these relationships. The file is the collection of all the records and is built up of many similar building blocks; in this way the file is like the list. The main differences between the file and the list are

1. The file will exist on the disk (or other secondary storage device) while the list will exist in the computer's main memory.
2. The file will continue to exist after the program is over while the list will no longer be available.

File Terminology

Data-Item. Records can contain more than one piece of information. The **data-item** is the smallest unit of information that has meaning to users. In this sense, the term "users" means the ultimate users of the data processing output, such as managers, rather than the actual machine users, such as programmers. Examples of data-items are a customer name or a price for an item of inventory. To the programmer, every letter of the name may have meaning. However, since only the whole name has meaning to the ultimate user, the name is the data-item.

EXHIBIT 5-3   Record/File Relationship

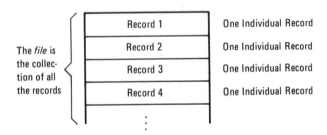

Record. Related data-items are grouped to form records. A **record** is a set (collection) of related data-items. An example is a customer record: The record would contain a data-item for name, another for the account balance, and perhaps several for the address. The concept of a record is particularly important because computer programs usually read and write records. The computer reads in a record from storage, processes it, and then writes it back out onto storage once it has been updated. Suppose a person in a company's personnel department wanted to change an employee name, either due to an earlier error or to marriage. The person would run a program that would then read in the entire record for that employee, not just the particular data-item for update (the employee name). The person would then give the program the new employee name, the program would then update the record, and then the program would write the entire employee record out onto storage.

Entity. The **entity** of a file is the type of person or object about which the file has data. In an accounts receivable master file, the entity is a customer. For a general ledger master file, the entity would be general ledger accounts; for an accounts payable master file, the entity would be vendors; for a student record master file, the entity would be students at a university. In all cases, the file is storing information about something; this "something" is called the entity. This is a convenient term for all discussions about files; it is possible to discuss files in general by using the term "entity" without tying the discussion to any specific type of file.

Primary Key. Each record in a file is distinct. Thus, in one file, different records might contain information about different customers. This creates the problem of indicating to the computer exactly which record is sought in a particular situation. In ordinary conversation the reference may be to a customer's name. However, when dealing with the computer, this is not adequate—there must be a unique identifier that unmistakably picks out one and only one record in the file. Such an identifier is called a key, or more precisely a **primary key**. In most situations, this key will be an identifying number, such as the customer number, the general ledger account number, or the vendor number.

It is possible, however, to have an alphabetic key, such as a name, to identify the record uniquely. The main difficulty of an alphabetic key is that it must generally be spelled exactly right for the computer to find the proper record. Sophisticated systems can get around this problem by providing a dialogue with the terminal operator: The computer provides the user with a list of keys "closest" to the key the operator used and gives the operator a "menu" of possible choices from which the operator can select the exact entity required.

Coding. The task of assigning a primary key is often referred to as **coding**. Appendix B of this book briefly discusses the chart of accounts and the assignment of account numbers to the various general ledger accounts. This assignment of account numbers is only one example of the problem of assigning the primary key; other examples of coding include assigning inventory item numbers, vendor numbers, customer numbers, and employee numbers. There is a trade-off between the complexity of the code (primary key) and the com-

156

*Part II
Technical
Aspects of
Accounting
Information
Systems*

plexity of the file. In some cases it is useful to have a complex code that conveys information in the code itself. An example is the coding of general ledger accounts: The 100 accounts might be assets, the 200 accounts might be liabilities, and so on. This type of coding will probably result in fewer errors in the use of the code, as well as make financial statements and other reports from the general ledger file easier to generate. In a customer file all records are basically equivalent and their information is manipulated in the same way. In the general ledger file, however, the various types of records (asset, liability, owners' equity, revenue, and expense) all get processed in different ways and are printed out quite differently in the financial statements.

Coding Versus Data-Items. Another example of complex coding is the assignment of an inventory item number where one digit indicates color, another part of the number indicates size, and so on. However, the information (such as color or size) that could be conveyed in the item number would be better stored as a data-item in the record. If the information is stored in the record, there are two advantages:

1. The code is shortened and simplified.
2. A conversion process is not needed in the programs to convert from the code to the information it is trying to convey.

Generally speaking, therefore, it is better to make the code or primary key as simple as possible and store all information in the record as separate data-items. Thus, the code will only uniquely identify the record and will convey no information by itself. Codes can then be assigned in a sequential manner; every time a new entity is added to the file, it is simply assigned the next higher code number.

Attribute. For each entity, the file stores various **attributes** of that entity, such as name, address, or current balance. A specific accounts receivable file may have entities that are customers. The attributes stored for each entity might be the customer number, name, address, and credit limit, among others. The data-items then represent the attribute. The specific information stored in the record for an entity would be the specific values of those attributes.

Secondary Keys. Often, a master file record contains data-items that identify the record but do not uniquely identify the record. These data-items are called **secondary keys**. For example, consider a customer file. The primary key would probably be a customer number, which would allow the computer to answer the question: What is the information stored on customer number X? A possible secondary key would be the zip code. Generally, there will be more than one customer for any one zip code, and thus the zip code could not be used to uniquely identify a customer record. The zip code, however, could be used to answer the following question: What customers have their address in a particular zip code? Despite the fact that the question will, in general, have multiple answers, the zip code still identifies the record (though not uniquely) and thus is a secondary key. In a university's student file, the primary key would almost certainly be a student number. Secondary keys would then prob-

CONCEPT SUMMARY

Basic File Concepts

Structure of Payroll File

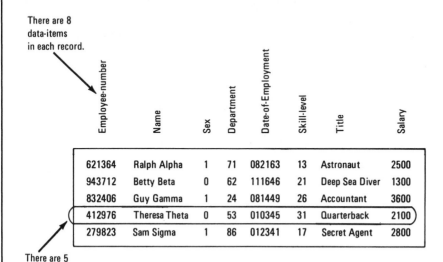

There are 8 data-items in each record.

Employee-number	Name	Sex	Department	Date-of-Employment	Skill-level	Title	Salary
621364	Ralph Alpha	1	71	082163	13	Astronaut	2500
943712	Betty Beta	0	62	111646	21	Deep Sea Diver	1300
832406	Guy Gamma	1	24	081449	26	Accountant	3600
412976	Theresa Theta	0	53	010345	31	Quarterback	2100
279823	Sam Sigma	1	86	012341	17	Secret Agent	2800

There are 5 records in the file.

Entity/Attribute/Key Concepts

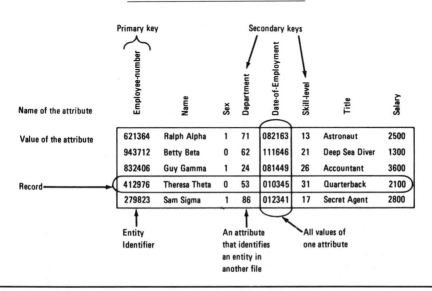

Primary key

Secondary keys

Name of the attribute

Value of the attribute

Employee-number	Name	Sex	Department	Date-of-Employment	Skill-level	Title	Salary
621364	Ralph Alpha	1	71	082163	13	Astronaut	2500
943712	Betty Beta	0	62	111646	21	Deep Sea Diver	1300
832406	Guy Gamma	1	24	081449	26	Accountant	3600
412976	Theresa Theta	0	53	010345	31	Quarterback	2100
279823	Sam Sigma	1	86	012341	17	Secret Agent	2800

Record

Entity
Identifier

An attribute
that identifies
an entity in
another file

All values of
one attribute

158

*Part II
Technical
Aspects of
Accounting
Information
Systems*

ably include year in school and declared major. These secondary keys could be used to access data by a means other than through the primary key and thus answer questions such as: How many junior accounting majors are enrolled at the university?

Data Dictionary. In any organization, the number of data-items necessary for all the myriad accounting, recordkeeping, and analysis functions is quite large. For the data to be consistent, organized, and accessible, the organization should compile a dictionary to specify each of the different data-items. The **data dictionary** includes all variables used by all of the programs.

Simple (Flat) File Systems

Many programming applications utilize simple, flat file systems, with one record for each item of interest. These applications are typically personal data processing applications, such as mailing lists, employees who must be supervised and evaluated, and customers to see. Microcomputers are particularly well suited to these applications. Programs designed for flat file systems make these applications straightforward for end users to set up and process by themselves. More sophisticated applications, however, require a more sophisticated approach and more sophisticated (and complex) programs.

MASTER FILE/TRANSACTION FILE DATA STRUCTURE

The basic file concepts in the preceding section are the foundation for developing the basic programs and files for a business data processing system.

Basic Tasks of Business Data Processing

There are four fundamental tasks for business data processing:

File Creation. A **file creation program** initially loads information onto the file so it can be used by other programs. As an example, a file creation program would initially load a customer's name and address and establish a customer's record when the company adds a new customer's account.

File Maintenance. A **file maintenance program** keeps the master file current, except for transactions. If a customer changes names (due to marriage, for example), a file maintenance program would update the customer record.

Transaction Processing. A **transaction processing program** does all computer-related steps with each transaction as it occurs, such as a customer payment on account or a credit sale. These transaction processing programs are the building blocks of business data processing.

Report Writing. A **report writing program** reads the information from the data files (created and updated by the file creation, maintenance, and transaction processing programs) and then generates a printout analyzing the information. For example, an aged trial balance is a report that is a printout and analysis of the information on file about customers and the amount each owes.

Master File/Transaction File Relationship

159

CHAPTER 5
*Data Files
and Data
Bases*

Creating a program that can update a file to reflect a completed transaction requires new concepts—the master file and the transaction file. The **master file** contains the name, address, phone number, and other data-items that are relatively permanent. The **transaction file**, on the other hand, contains the transactions that have developed the ending balance. Thus, the transaction file can provide an audit trail—it will always be possible to determine from this file where the balance came from. The approach will be to process the transaction (updating the master file) and then to store the transaction in the transaction file. In a sense, the master file in a computer system is similar to the top part of each ledger account in a manual accounts receivable subsidiary ledger. The transaction file is the collection of the individual lines of the ledger account.

Master File.   The master file contains the information occurring once per entity. For example, in an accounts receivable system, the master file would contain the customer number, customer name, customer address, Dun & Bradstreet credit reporting number (DUNS number), the contact person to call about the status of the account, and the phone number.

Transaction File.   The transaction file contains the information about the transactions, which could occur zero times for a particular entity or many times. For example, in an accounts receivable system, the transaction file would include customer number (to tie to the master file), date, amount, and transaction code (payment, charge, return, credit, and so on).

Transaction Processing Programs

Sequential, Batch Approach.   A flowchart of a sequential, batch transaction processing program appears in Exhibit 5-4. Typically, the reading from and writing to files will be tape files, but disk files are possible. Its structure is

1. Open both the master file and the transaction file.
2. Check if there are more entities in the master file by checking if there are any more valid primary keys. If not, then end the program. For example, if customer number is the primary key, then the program ends when there are no more customer numbers.
3. Get the record for the next entity from the master file. For example, this could be the master file record for the next customer in the file.
4. Check the next transaction to see if it applies to the current entity. If it does not, go to step 6. For example, this could be a check that the transaction applies to the current customer.
5. Update the information about the entity. For example, this could mean updating the customer's balance based upon purchases or payments.
6. Write the updated master file record to the new master file. For example, this could be the creation of an updated customer file.
7. Go to step 2.

160

*Part II
Technical
Aspects of
Accounting
Information
Systems*

EXHIBIT 5-4   File Transaction Program

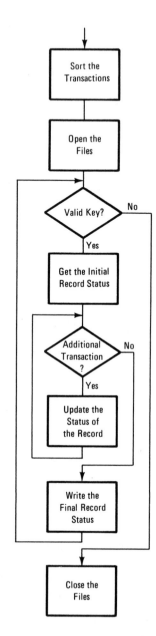

Interactive, On-Line Approach.   The basic approach of an interactive, on-line file maintenance and transaction program is very similar. Its structure is

1. Input the transaction and identify the master file record to which it applies.
2. Read the information from the appropriate master file record into the computer's main memory.

3. Update this information in the main memory with the maintenance and/or file balance transaction.
4. Write the updated information back to the master file. Because the updated information takes exactly the same amount of storage space, the updated record goes back in the same location in the file.
5. Go to step 1.

When the information is read off the master file, the information on the master file is not lost or changed in any way. A copy of the information is simply transferred into the computer's main memory. Therefore, if updating does not occur, the information on the master file will remain as it was. This is important because the updating will often not occur (for example, the transaction is rejected because it is invalid or does not match the information on the master file). As a further example, suppose the transaction was for an inactive customer; the transaction could be rejected when the master file record was read in, but not before, because the information necessary for rejection was not available. Some transactions can be rejected offhand (such as a credit sale of $1,000,000,000), but others must be checked with information on the master files.

Notice that this interactive, on-line approach does not have a defined end. The program runs continuously, always available for processing of transactions. The program ends only when the computer is shut down or when operations cease, such as overnight or on weekends and holidays.

Reasons for Separate Files

At this point the following question may arise: Why not have the information in the master file and the transaction file all in the same file? Basically, there must be separate files because different master file records will have differing numbers of transactions, and it is not usually possible to know the maximum number of transactions per master file record. Some data-items occur a fixed number of times per master file record, such as monthly financial statement figures for a general ledger master file. Because each master file record will have 12 months in each year, those 12 data-items would go in the master file record and not in a separate file. These facts lead to the following conclusions:

Wasted Space.   Since different master file records have differing numbers of transactions, the file layout will have to leave room for the maximum number in every record, thus leading to tremendous wasted space in those records not having the maximum number of transactions.

Unknown Transaction Volumes.   Even if wasted space is not a problem, it is not possible to know how much space to leave since there is no maximum number of transactions. If a guess leaves too little room, a record might fill up, making it impossible to process another transaction for that record without reorganizing the entire file, making every record that much bigger.

For these reasons, it is far better to design files so that each record has the same number of data-items and each record has the same length. It is true

162

PART II
Technical
Aspects of
Accounting
Information
Systems

that some languages (such as COBOL) will allow variable-length records; however, the variable-length record is best used to handle data-items of variable length (such as names and addresses) rather than a variable number of data-items. Thus, with a separate master file and transaction file, the master file record can contain the information that will always be kept for every master file record (such as name and current balance), while the transaction file will contain every transaction for every master file record. In this way, additional transactions merely add to the length of the transaction file by adding a record to the transaction file for each transaction, which is easily handled.

Types of File Organization

The primary key uniquely identifies the record. A related concern is determining how to find the record corresponding to a given primary key. The method by which the system orders the records in the file and provides access to those records is called the **file organization**. There are four basic types of file organization:

Serial Organization. With **serial organization**, the records are placed in the file in no particular order. Access to a particular record is provided by reading through the file until the value on a record matches the given primary key. An example of this approach is a mailing list, where people or organizations are added to a file of names and addresses. The mailing list need not be in any particular order because the entire file will normally be searched each time it is used, and the computer will print out either all items or all items that satisfy some given criterion. This method of access is extremely slow, but it is easy to program.

Sequential Organization. With **sequential organization**, the records in the file are sequenced by the primary key. Similarly to the serial organization, access is provided by reading through the file until a match is found for the primary key. Because the file is sequenced, however, multiple accesses to the file can be made much more efficiently than in the case of serial organization. Each program begins at the beginning of the file accessed and reads or writes the first record, then the second, and so on until it reaches the end of the file. The program either writes all the way through the file, or it reads all the way through the file—it does not mix reading records with writing records. This is the standard file organization for batch processing systems, which, as discussed in Chapter 3, are frequently used in business data processing. For example, a reasonable approach to writing payroll checks is to access the file sequentially, thus checking everyone on the file and paying all employees who should be paid.

Direct Organization. With **direct organization**, the primary key for the record is the storage address on the disk drive or other direct access device on which the file is stored. Access is then provided by reading the storage area given by the primary key. This approach is usually difficult to program.

Indexed Sequential Organization. With **indexed sequential organization,** records are stored sequentially by primary key. In addition, a separate index file stores all of the primary keys for all records on the file; this index file also contains the location on the file for the record matching that primary key. Access is then provided by searching the index file for a match of the primary key and then accessing the master file at the given location. Indexed sequential is a hybrid of sequential and direct access to allow both access methods; it provides the machine efficiencies of sequential processing with the user efficiencies of random information retrieval. Indexed sequential is the most widely used approach for the interactive, on-line systems discussed in Chapter 3.

Indexed Sequential Storage and Interactive (On-Line) Processing

Indexed sequential was the first disk-oriented file organization for the large files necessary for business data processing. This approach, usually referred to as indexed sequential access method (ISAM) or virtual indexed sequential access method (VSAM), was built into COBOL, the most widely used business data processing language. In addition to the master file, ISAM stores an index file which gives the order of master file records. This index file allows interrogation of the current balance and the status of accounts. To find a particular record, the system first finds its location in the index file and then accesses the record in the master file. The index file is a tiny fraction of the size of the master file and is thus much faster to search.

Binary Search. Since the index file is in sequential order, search is possible without having to read the index file sequentially. Typically, the desired record is found through a binary search. This involves comparing the key of the desired record to the value in the middle of the index file. The computer can then determine in which half of the file the record is located. That half of the file is then split into two, and the process of comparison and elimination is repeated. The index file keeps getting subdivided in half in this manner until the desired record is located.

Logical Versus Physical Sequence. With sequential files, the logical and physical sequence of the files are the same. In other words, the file is physically created of records in order by primary key. To make access more efficient, the ISAM approach tries to keep the physical sequence of master file records in the same order as the logical sequence, so that, for example, employees in the personnel master file would physically be in employee number sequence. But with indexed sequential, logical and physical sequence need no longer be the same. Suppose a company adds an employee to the personnel master file in an on-line system, where the employee's Social Security number would be in the middle of the file. The new employee record cannot be added to the middle of the file because that would involve moving data that are already there. Thus, additions to the master file must go to an overflow file. As this overflow file grows, processing becomes less efficient. As a result, files require a periodic reorganization in which the master file and the contents of the overflow file are combined and put into proper sequence.

164

*PART II
Technical
Aspects of
Accounting
Information
Systems*

CONCEPT SUMMARY		
Master and Transaction Files for Accounts Receivable		
	Master File	*Transaction File*
One record for	Each customer	Each transaction for each customer
Contents	Many data-items, including 1. Customer number 2. Total amount owed by the customer	Many data-items, including 1. Customer number 2. Amount and date of purchase or payment
Update	File maintenance	Transaction processing

DATA BASE APPROACH

Appendix B of this book goes through the processing of the accounting transactions of a firm where one clerk handles all the books. This bookkeeper takes each transaction from the initial recording in the books of original entry all the way to the preparation of the financial statements. This mode of operation has the significant advantage that the information is up to date and the files and balances are current. Thus, if a customer or supplier had to know the status of his account, the information would be available and current.

Batch Processing and Its Disadvantages

The one-bookkeeper approach is impossible to implement manually for large volumes of transactions because one person is not capable of doing that much work. Historically, this has led to the division of the work into batches of transactions. Thus, transactions were not processed as they occurred but, rather, were divided into separate batches, such as a cash receipt batch, credit sale batch, and so on. Then, after a certain size batch had been accumulated or a certain time limit exceeded, the system would process all the transactions in the batch. This processing of all the transactions by groups (i.e., batch processing) adapts directly to punched card equipment and the earliest sorts of computers. As a result of its economy, batch processing is the standard means of processing accounting transactions even to the present day. Unfortunately, batch processing has tremendous drawbacks.

Data Are Not Current. The information kept by the system is no longer current. The time between occurrence of a transaction, its accumulation in a sufficient batch, and its subsequent processing can be quite substantial. During that time lag the balances in the accounts affected by these transactions are no longer current. This leads to the now common frustration of dealing with credit departments of hospitals, department stores, and the like which do not know current balances of accounts.

Separate Files Are Required for Each Application. The generation of separate files for each batch processing application seems to be an inevitable result of this approach. Each batch application, such as accounts payable or accounts receivable, receives machine assistance when it reaches a certain size. This machine assistance usually includes setting up computer files and computer programs. However, each application is developed independently of other applications, so the files and programs of separate applications are unrelated to one another. Thus, even though it does not have to be true, batch processing generally results in separate files for each application.

Error Correction Is Difficult. Correction of errors is a problem with batch processing. A lag exists between the time the source document is recorded and the time the batch is processed. As a result, if a transaction is rejected by the computer, it becomes necessary to go back several days to try to determine the source of the error. For example, suppose a hospital records a patient charge that includes a doctor code of 35. If the computer processes the charge a day or so later and determines that doctor code 35 is invalid, the computer will reject the transaction. Then the user will have to go back and decide whether the code should have been 55, 33, 53, or some other number.

The Disadvantage of the Traditional File Approach

Because of the problems with batch processing, many files have been converted to the use of interactive processing. This approach helps correct errors and keep the information in the files current. However, in addition to the basic tasks of (1) getting the files organized initially and (2) keeping the files current as new documents are generated, there is the additional problem of (3) accessing the same information in new and different ways, even after the information has been recorded in the files. Management often needs information that spans departments, which means data from several different files. For example, when analyzing the introduction of a new product line, information would be needed from both sales and distribution. In these circumstances, the data are not simply needed for the processing of specific applications; the data are an important resource in their own right and are necessary for many decisions. With the file approach, only previously anticipated queries of the data can be permitted because the programs are, in essence, attached to the files they process. But there is no way to anticipate completely all of the possible questions that the manager might want answered. Traditionally, the solution to a request like this is (1) to forget it, (2) to assign a clerk(s) or analyst to go through all the source data and accumulate the information, or (3) to assign a programmer to write a program to answer this specific request. Unfortunately, with the last alternative, the decision for which the data are to be used usually must be made before the program can be written.

166

PART II
Technical
Aspects of
Accounting
Information
Systems

The Benefits of the Data Base Approach

Fortunately, in addition to being quite a help in the filing of information, the computer can be absolutely crucial in the accessing of information once it has been filed. The problems with retrieving data in batch processing and interactive processing systems using the file approach led to the basic concept behind the **data base** approach. This is to have one set of uniquely defined data-items and require all computer applications use the same data-items that are therefore separate from the applications that use them. This, then, allows analysis of data across applications. But it also means that the applications and the data can be changed independently of one another, so data-items can be added to, modified, or deleted from the data base without affecting the programs using them.

For example, for materials, a company has one set of prices that is used by inventory control for costing issues, another set of prices in the engineering department used for design of new or revised products, and still another set of prices used by the purchasing department for determining from whom to purchase. These different sets of prices are all updated at different times by different people from different information. Needless to say, these prices are never in agreement, even though they presumably represent the same thing. Rather than this, the data base approach is to have one set of prices for materials and then have each application use the same information. Another example of one set of uniquely defined data-items would be the data-item, supplier number. Every company must have a way of uniquely identifying its suppliers, but often different groups within the company use different numbers for the same supplier. With the data base approach, each supplier would have a supplier number that would be used by each application, such as ordering, accounts payable, and inventory.

This data base approach also made applications easier to develop. All file systems have the same basic components of file creation, maintenance, transaction processing, and report writing. Once the applications were separated from the data, these programs could be developed once for all application data. There had been much duplication of effort in the development of these programs because they were tied to the files they used.

Relationship with Manual Accounting. In a sense, data processing has come full circle. In the simplest manual accounting systems, one person handled all the books and kept files and balances up to date. The data base approach then implies that the computer will become superbookkeeper and, with its incredible speed, keep unimaginably vast files current for all users. Importantly, however, the computer's function as superbookkeeper is not its most valuable contribution to the firm. Its most valuable contribution is the analysis it can perform once the data are in machine-readable form; it is a small task to access the data to obtain desired reports. This sort of analysis and the improved management and control it can provide are the real promise and use of a computer system. Chapter 8 discusses these topics further.

Costs of the Data Base Approach

The main cost of the data base approach is the necessity of coordination and cooperation. If the same number will uniquely identify a particular supplier in the ordering system, the accounts payable system, and the inventory system, someone or some group must coordinate the design of these systems. Thus, the corporation cannot allow separate groups to develop systems independently of everyone else. However, the price of coordination and cooperation is higher than many firms will pay. There is another, less significant cost. Since each system is not designed by itself, certain compromises must be accepted in each individual system design so that the systems will fit together. Thus, each system will not be optimal for that particular task. However, this should only disturb those who are more interested in optimizing one specific subsystem, such as inventory, than in optimizing the overall company's operations.

Depicting the Data Base Approach

The next step is to try to picture a tree structure of the data. The first example will be the file structure of the customer master file and the related invoices for that customer. There is one master file record for each customer, but there will usually be multiple invoices for each customer.

Schema. The diagram in Exhibit 5-5 includes this file structure. Such a representation of file structure is called a **schema**. However, the file structure can be much more sophisticated than this (relatively) simple customer/invoice relationship. Thus, Exhibit 5-5 provides a more complex schema, which includes the customer and invoice. Each invoice has a separate line for each item ordered and usually more than one item is ordered. Thus, in a manner similar to the customer/invoice relationship, there is one record for each invoice in the invoice master file and separate records in the line-item file for each line of each invoice. Further, each inventory part number ordered on each line will correspond to an inventory part in the inventory part master file. The part number in the line item file will allow the retrieval of any desired part information from the part master file.

Subschema. In the schema of Exhibit 5-5, there is not only a multiple set of invoices for each customer, but also a multiple set of line items for each invoice. Thus, the file will keep track of the individual items in the invoice, not just the total amount as in less sophisticated systems. Each line item will contain the part number of that item, and that item number will give the system a cross-reference to the inventory master file record for that item. But every programmer and every program that uses this set of files need not be interested in all the data in all the files; they may be only interested in a small portion of the data. For this reason, they may be only interested in a **subschema**, as illustrated in Exhibit 5-6. The subschema extracts a small part of the overall data that might be of interest in one particular program-printing invoices, for example.

168

*PART II
Technical
Aspects of
Accounting
Information
Systems*

EXHIBIT 5-5   Sample Schema

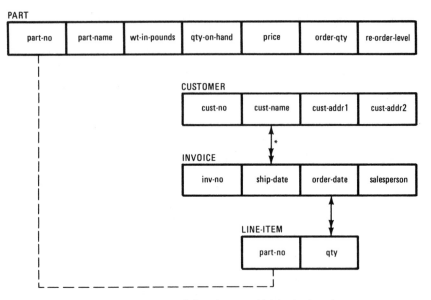

*This is the customary way to indicate there are multiple invoices for each customer.
There is no special connection between cust-name and ship-data.

Flat File or Normalized Representation of this schema:
CUSTOMER (cust-no, cust-name, cust-addr1, cust-addr2)
INVOICE (inv-no, cust-no, ship-date, order-date, salesperson)
LINE-ITEM (part-no, inv-no, qty)
PART (part-no, part-name, wt-in-pounds, qty-on-hand, price,
      order-qty, re-order-level)

EXHIBIT 5-6   Sample Subschema

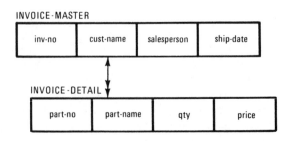

Flat File or Normalized Representation of this Subschema:
INVOICE-MASTER (inv-no, cust-name, salesperson, ship-date)
INVOICE-DETAIL (part-no, inv-no, part-name, qty, price)

Types of Data Bases

There has been a great deal of experimentation with different ways to accomplish this data base approach. Three turned out to be the most commonly used. These are the hierarchical or tree structure, the network or plex structure, and the relational or table structure.

Hierarchical or Tree Structures. The first major data base was developed at Rockwell International for the purpose of tracking the development of the Apollo space program. The resulting computer program later became known as information management system (IMS) when it was sold by IBM. This data base had a hierarchical focus: The product (spacecraft) is composed of parts and subassemblies, and each subassembly can be composed of parts and further subassemblies. This process continues, but eventually all subassemblies are broken down into their component parts. A complete breakdown of a product into its components parts is often called a bill of materials.

A hierarchical file, such as a bill of materials detailing the components of a manufactured product, has a **tree structure** relationship between the records of the file. Exhibit 5-7 shows a tree structure. A tree is composed of a hierarchy of elements, called nodes. The uppermost level of the hierarchy has only one node, called the root. This root would correspond to the finished spacecraft. With the exception of the root, every node has one node related to it at a higher level, called its parent. No element can have more than one parent. Each element can have one or more elements related to it at a lower level, called children; these would be the parts and subassemblies that compose it. Elements with no nodes in the next level down are called leaves, which would be parts with no assembly. Therefore, each node (component) has only one parent (the component it goes into), the root has no parent (because it is complete), and leaves have no children (because they are not assembled). Note that if you

EXHIBIT 5-7   Example of Tree or Hierarchical Structure

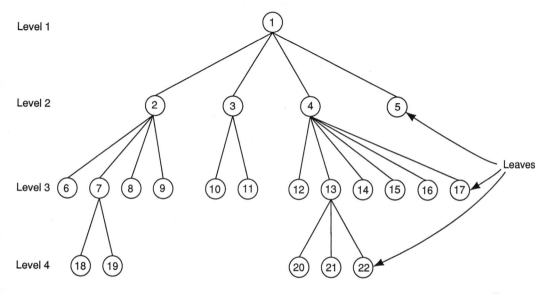

170

*PART II
Technical
Aspects of
Accounting
Information
Systems*

look at each element in level 2 of Exhibit 5-7 and think of it as a root, then its children and descendants form a tree. A master file/transaction file structure can also be thought of as a hierarchical or tree file structure.

The hierarchical approach has the advantage of extremely fast transaction processing. Transactions are processed even faster than the standard (for the time) indexed sequential file organization. The disadvantages of this approach are

1. It is extremely complex to set up, often requiring 18 months for the initial project.
2. It is very difficult to maintain and change as circumstances and data change.

Thus, the hierarchical approach and the IMS program are suitable only for highly structured, extremely high-volume, transaction processing environments.

Network or Plex Structures. If a child in a data relationship has more than one parent, the structure is not hierarchical, but a network or plex structure. As with a tree structure, a **plex structure** can be described in terms of children and parents; the only difference is that in a network or plex structure a child can have more than one parent. Also, as in tree structures, plex structures may have levels. Exhibit 5-8 shows the network structure of a purchasing system with five record types. Each relationship is a parent-child relationship. The Purchase Order record type is a child of the Part (that is, inventory item) record type and a parent of the Purchase Item record type. A more complex structure is the one-to-many relationship in both directions between Part and Purchase Order. Each part (inventory item) can be purchased on many different purchase orders and each purchase order can be for many different parts.

The network or plex structure approach is easier to use (though slower) than the rigid tree or hierarchical approach, and is the basis for the market

EXHIBIT 5-8   Example of Plex or Network Structure

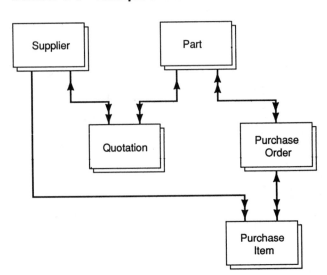

success of non-IBM systems such as IDMS. The major difficulty with the network approach is that the questions or queries that the system can answer efficiently have to be designed into the system. Queries, however, often arise that have not been planned for; these are not efficiently handled with the network approach.

Relational Data Bases. The basic notions of data-items, records, and files are in constant use by businesses of all sizes in keeping track of their operations and accounting records. After years of analysis and experimentation, both theoretical and practical, most people agree that, except in special situations, the most useful way to visualize data-items and records is as a table of information, called a flat file or **table**. These terms are used because the information can be looked at in two dimensions; the file consists of rows (records) and columns (data-items) like tables of data in a book. Exhibit 5-9 has a row for each (customer) record in the file and a column for each of the four data-items. For convenience, the name of each data-item, such as cust-no, is at the top of the appropriate column.

For a flat file to work as a way of storing and analyzing data, it must have the following characteristics:

1. All items in each column must be the same kind of data-item, such as a customer number, a customer name, or a customer address.
2. Each column must have its own unique name, separate from all others. In this case, the names are cust-no, cust-name, cust-addrl, and cust-addr2.
3. All rows must be different in at least one data-item from every other row; in other words, there cannot be two rows that are exactly alike. If two rows are exactly alike, either they refer to the same customer, so the duplicate can be eliminated, or they refer to two separate customers, in which case there must be more data items to distinguish between those customers.
4. Every "cell," the intersection of a row and a column in the table, has only one data-item in it. Thus, in Exhibit 5-9 every customer has exactly one cust-no, one cust-name, and so on.

Having one and only one data-item per cell is significant to the design and resulting number of flat files. Suppose a manager is interested in all of the

EXHIBIT 5-9   Flat File or Table

CUSTOMER

cust-no	cust-name	cust-addr1	cust-addr2
4000	SURF CITY	100 Ocean Blvd.	Santa Monica, CA
3000	MOUNTAIN HIGH	1250 Capitol Hill	Denver, CO
2000	SOUTHERN FRIED	943 Front Street	Mobile, AL
1000	AMERICAN WIDGET	1400 Midwest Ave.	Racine, WI
5000	YANKEE CLIPPER	3450 Charles St.	Boston, MA

Key

A Shortened Representation of the Contents of the Same File:
   CUSTOMER(cust-no,cust-name,cust-addr1,cust-addr2)
   Note: The primary key is underlined to identify it.

172

PART II
Technical
Aspects of
Accounting
Information
Systems

EXHIBIT 5-10   Example of Normalization

A Repeating Group:

CUSTOMER

cust-no	cust-name	cust-addr1	cust-addr2				
				inv-no	ship-date	order-date	salesperson

Is Represented by Two Flat Files (Two Tables):

CUSTOMER

cust-no	cust-name	cust-addr1	cust-addr2
4000	SURF CITY	1000 Ocean Blvd.	Santa Monica, CA
3000	MOUNTAIN HIGH	1250 Capital Hill	Denver, CO
2000	SOUTHERN FRIED	943 Front Street	Mobile, AL
1000	AMERICAN WIDGET	1400 Midwest Ave.	Racine, WI
5000	YANKEE CLIPPER	3450 Charles St.	Boston, MA

INVOICE

inv-no	cust-no	ship-date	order-date	salesperson
1001	1000	780930	780825	Ralph Flax
2002	2000	860210	860115	Susie Que
5001	5000	861015	860819	John Randolph
1002	1000	860814	860726	James Garcia
4001	4000	860320	860310	Janet Daly
3001	3000	781001	780915	Vahe Baladouni
5002	5000	861112	861019	David Older
2001	2000	861210	861110	Maria Gomez
4002	4000	861126	861025	Vincent Pica

A Shortened Representation of the Contents of the Same Files:
   CUSTOMER (cust-no, cust-name, cust-addr1, cust-addr2)
   INVOICE (inv-no, cust-no, ship-date, order-date, salesperson)

invoices for a particular customer. Some of the customers will have 1 invoice while others will have 2, 3, 4, or more invoices. These invoices would, therefore, not fit into a flat file without some modification since each "cell" must contain exactly one item. A situation like invoices for a customer is called a repeating group because there is potentially more than one invoice for a given customer. Fortunately, repeating groups can be dealt with by forming two flat files. The process of forming flat files from the repeating groups is called normalization.

Another name for a flat file is a relation because it represents a relationship between the various data-items. In Exhibit 5-9, the relation is that all the data items in one record represent one customer. There are two relations shown in Exhibit 5-10, one of customers (similar to Exhibit 5-9) and one of invoices. In this second (invoice) relation, there is one record for each invoice. Thus, if there are three invoices for each of six customers, there would be 18 invoices and thus 18 records in the invoice file and 18 rows in the table. However, there would still be only six customer records in the customer relation.

With the normalization technique of creating a second relation, all repeating groups can be transformed into two flat files. Most data base software can only process flat files, but since it is possible to transform any repeating group into flat files, this is not a great restriction. Data bases that are based on flat files and relations are called **relational data bases**. This concept of transforming repeating groups into flat files implies that there is duplication of data. In the invoice example, the customer number is repeated in both the customer file and the invoice file. However, relational data bases are easy to use and provide flexibility in the use of the data, which in most applications outweighs this repetition of data. Because of the importance of relational data bases, and a language created specifically for their use, Chapter 6 will discuss these topics in greater depth.

Logical and Physical Data

The way a company's data are viewed by users is not necessarily the way the data are stored on a storage device such as tape or disk. The user's view of the data is much simpler than the actual manner in which data are stored. A user's view of the data, how they are used and understood, is called the logical structure or logical view. Since the logical view is not necessarily the most efficient way to store the data on a storage device, the data are rearranged for storage purposes. The way the data are stored is called the physical structure or physical view. Internal linkages allow the data to be connected in the order needed by the user. The appropriate set of linkages is activated by the data base program. Therefore, the user is not concerned with the physical storage of his or her data and is often unaware of the physical view of the data.

    The difference between physical and logical view began as an economic measure. When records are stored on tape, a gap called an interrecord gap is left between consecutive records. The gap was long compared to the length of the record, and therefore, wasted a lot of storage area on the tape. In order to conserve storage space, logical records were grouped together on the tape, thereby eliminating some of the interrecord gaps. The records were separated by the application program, processed as necessary, and stored together. Later, as discussed in the previous section of this chapter, in the indexed sequential approach to file organization, the logical and physical sequence of the data on the disk were not the same. Since data bases allow for multiple uses of data, there is not necessarily only one logical view of the data. Therefore, physical views are no longer necessarily just groups of logical data.

Data Base Management Systems

There are two important conclusions to be drawn from the earlier discussions in this chapter:

1. The programming to handle these very complicated file structures will itself be very complicated.
2. The same file structure will be useful in many apparently different situations.

Very complicated, generalized software packages have been developed by many different organizations to allow the user to specify the file structure, while the software package handles much of the attendant programming. These

174

PART II
Technical
Aspects of
Accounting
Information
Systems

software packages are called **data base management systems** because they handle the task of managing the data base. All major computer equipment vendors as well as independent firms provide data base management systems (often abbreviated DBMS). Three popular data base products for mainframes are IMS (tree or hierarchical structure) and DB2 (relational) from IBM, and IDMS (network or plex structure) from Cullinet, another firm. The most popular data bases for minicomputers are Ingres and Oracle, while for microcomputers the most popular DBMS are Paradox and dBASE. All of these DBMSs for minicomputers and microcomputers use the relational approach.

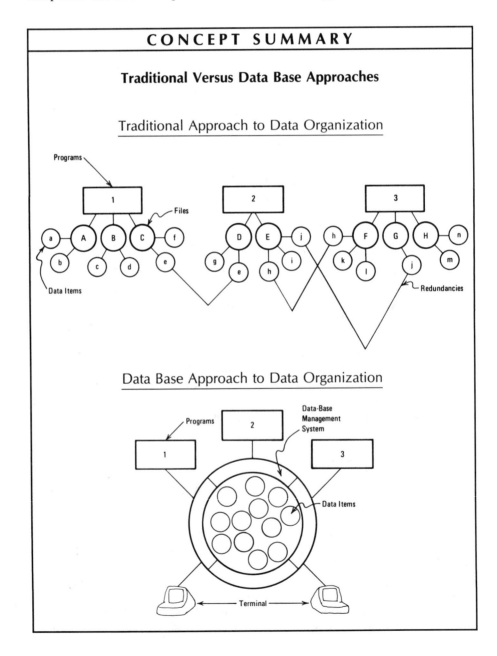

CONCEPT SUMMARY

Traditional Versus Data Base Approaches

Traditional Approach to Data Organization

Data Base Approach to Data Organization

A typical application for a merchandiser's data base would be to display an invoice on a terminal. With a DBMS, the person who wanted to review an invoice could simply enter the invoice number and the data-item of importance. The values of the items named in the query would then be displayed. The DBMS gets the user the information when it is wanted. The DBMS analyzes the queries and compares them to what it knows about the data base. It determines the best way to find the answer to the request and then displays the answer. The DBMS makes it easy for users to get information without knowing complex data base structures. The user does not need to know that some of the requested information is in one file and the rest is in another file. The DBMS analyzes the query and displays the requested data. If the user wants a different format than the DBMS supplies, it is possible to create a report format and ask the DBMS to use that format. The DBMS produces reports in such a way that they can be viewed at a terminal or printed onto paper (hard copy). The report need only be defined once to the computer. After the definition, the user can generate the report at any time simply by using the report name.

It is possible to ask the DBMS for some information that it cannot find. This will often happen when a query has more than one meaning. For example, in a university data base, any query asking about students associated with a particular professor could have three interpretations if faculty teach, employ, and advise students. Is the query asking for the number of the professor's pupils, advisees, or employees? The DBMS will note when an ambiguous situation occurs. In some cases, it will help select the desired query. In other cases, it will not be able to accept the command.

DISTRIBUTED DATA BASE SYSTEMS

In business data processing there is a movement of processing power away from the central mainframe as the power of the microcomputer increases and the end user assumes a far more active role. Much more difficult to achieve, but also inevitable, is the movement of data away from the cental mainframe out to where it is created and used. For example, one branch of a company in one location may have primary contact and virtually all transactions with some of the firm's customers, while other branches work with other customers. It is more efficient from the standpoint of data storage, transaction processing, and data communications if each branch maintains the data files for its customers, while allowing access from other branches. This approach is called distributed data processing because the data bases are distributed around the operational locations of the firm. If the data bases in different branches or divisions are not connected and are kept totally separate, the firm is operating with a decentralized data processing system.

Distributed data processing and distributed data bases pose one of the biggest challenges for business data processing today because they present major technical challenges as well as major internal control challenges. Because of the necessity of frequent changes to the structure of the data, distributed DBMS of any kind are virtually always a relational DBMS. There are no complete distributed data processing systems and data bases in operation today. The goals of a distributed data base system are

176

*PART II
Technical
Aspects of
Accounting
Information
Systems*

1. To each user, a distributed system should look like a single, nondistributed system, so that queries and transactions that affect distributed data should appear no different from purely local queries and transactions.
2. Each location should have local autonomy and not require the approval of some centralized group for local changes.
3. A central site is not required for data storage or processing.
4. Operation is continuous.

To achieve these goals, there are several features of a distributed DBMS which should be transparent; that is, the user need not concern himself or herself with these items. The concept summary gives these ten basic features. The subject of networks and their relationship to distributed data will be dealt with at greater length in Chapter 7.

CONCEPT SUMMARY	
Features of Distributed Data Base Management Systems That Should Be Invisible (Transparent) to the End User	
Location	A user can submit a query that accesses distributed data without having to know where the data are.
Performance	A query can be submitted from any location, and it will run with comparable performance.
Copy	The system supports the optional existence of multiple copies of data by obtaining copies from another site.
Transaction	A user can run a transaction that updates data at a number of sites. The transaction behaves exactly like a local one.
Fragment	The disributed DBMS allows a user to cut up a relation into multiple pieces and place the pieces at multiple sites.
Schema change	Users who add or delete data-items or tables from a distributed data base need only make the change once to the distributed dictionary.
Local DBMS	The distributed DBMS provides its service without regard for the local data base systems that are actually managing local data.
Hardware	Equipment from different manufacturers can be mixed and matched without affecting the distributed DBMS.
Operating system	Different computers using the DBMS can use different operating systems.
Network	The distributed DBMS can function over different network types and configurations.

CHAPTER SUMMARY

A file allows access to data by multiple programs and accommodates large amounts of data. A file is built of records. Records contain related data-items (or fields) about an entity. Each entity is coded with a unique identifier called the primary key. Records provide a data-item for each of the attributes of an entity, such as customer number, customer name, and credit limit. A nonunique identifier called a secondary key allows records to be accessed without using the primary key. For example, a primary key could call up an individual customer's record, and a secondary key could call up all customer records of customers in the northeast region. A master file contains the information that occurs once per entity, while a transaction file contains a separate record for each transaction.

Files can be arranged serially, sequentially, or directly or with an indexed sequential organization. Serial organization is easiest to program, but it offers slow access to data because the program must read through the file until it finds the desired record. Serial organization can be useful for simple applications such as mailing lists. Sequential organization sequences records by the primary key and reads or writes through them in this sequence. Sequential organization is standard for batch processing. Direct organization provides the fastest access to data, but is the most difficult to program. Indexed sequential organization allows both sequential processing and random access because it has additionally an index file of primary keys. Indexed sequential organization is used for interactive, on-line systems.

The traditional file approach makes it difficult to put data together from more than one application. Data base processing provides for one set of uniquely identified data-items that can be accessed by all applications and makes possible the integration of all company systems. Data bases are structured logically from the user's point of view either hierarchically (tree structure), as a network (plex structure), or as a relational data base containing related tables (called flat files). Data base management systems are software packages that take care of the programming chores once the user has specified the desired file structure. Data processing is moving away from centralized mainframe processing toward either decentralized processing, with totally separate data bases, or distributed data base systems, which move data to their source where they are primarily used, while allowing access from other locations.

KEY TERMS ━━━━━━━━━━━━━━━━

Attribute (*p. 156*)

Coding (*p. 155*)

Data base (*p. 166*)

Data base management system
  (*p. 174*)

Data dictionary (*p. 158*)

Data-item (*p. 154*)

Direct organization (*p. 162*)

Entity (*p. 155*)

File (*p. 154*)

File creation program (*p. 158*)

File maintenance program (*p. 158*)

File organization (*p. 162*)

Indexed sequential organization
  (*p. 163*)

List (*p. 152*)

178

PART II
Technical
Aspects of
Accounting
Information
Systems

Master file (*p. 159*)
Plex structure (*p. 170*)
Primary key (*p. 155*)
Record (*p. 155*)
Relational data base (*p. 173*)
Report writing program (*p. 158*)
Schema (*p. 167*)
Secondary key (*p. 156*)

Sequential organization (*p. 162*)
Serial organization (*p. 162*)
Subschema (*p. 167*)
Table (*p. 171*)
Transaction file (*p. 159*)
Transaction processing program
   (*p. 158*)
Tree structure (*p. 169*)

QUESTIONS

5-1. Explain the relationship among data-items, records, and files.

5-2. Distinguish between a primary key and a secondary key and give an example of each for an accounts receivable application.

5-3. Explain the trade-off between more complex coding and more data-items.

5-4. List the four types of business data processing programs and give an example of each.

5-5. Explain why both a master file and a transaction file are necessary for efficient storage and processing.

5-6. Why is batch processing the standard approach to the processing of accounting transactions? Discuss four of its drawbacks.

5-7. When is the direct access of data more effective than the sequential access of data? Name two applications in which the direct access of data would be necessary. Name two applications in which direct access would not be necessary.

5-8. Discuss the data base approach and state its major purposes.

5-9. What is a schema? Why is it useful in a data base management system?

5-10. Define a flat file and give four examples from business data processing.

5-11. Identify the three basic data base approaches. Give their advantages and disadvantages.

5-12. Describe the process by which a file with a repeating group is transformed into two flat files. What is the purpose of this transformation?

5-13. Give the basic features of a distributed data base management system.

PROBLEMS

5-14. Widespread use of computers in business data processing has led many observers to predict that computers will ultimately replace accountants. Based on your knowledge of computers and accounting, do you believe this is true? Why or why not? How does your answer here compare to your opinion prior to the start of this course?

5-15. The distinction between programs and data is fundamental to understanding the use of computers in data processing. This distinction is important because programs are not necessarily tied to one particular file and data are not necessarily processed by only one program.

   1. Give three specific examples from business data processing of one file being used by more than one program.

2. Give three specific examples from business data processing of one program using both a master file and a transaction file.

3. Can you think of a program that might use more than one master file?

5-16. In Chapter 3 there was an extended problem on the IRS and its method for processing taxpayer income tax returns. Review this material and give the files that would likely be used in the regional offices and the files that would likely be used in the national office in Maryland. (Be sure to include the files used to answer the inquiries.) Also, for each file, give the organization of files into records and the data-items to be included in each record.

5-17. The St. Charles Company is in the midst of converting to a new computer-based information system. A critical step in the conversion process is the design and specification of each necessary file. One of the areas to be included in the new system is accounts payable. Processing accounts payable requires that information on each vendor be kept and that purchase invoices, payments to vendors, and debit memos be handled. Determine the files required, the organization of the files into records, and the data-items to be included in each record.

5-18. Suppose the St. Charles Company is interested in including in the new system the processing of payroll. Processing payroll requires that information on each employee be kept and that earnings and all related payroll deductions, as well as all necessary government reports, be handled. Determine the files required, the organization of the files into records, and the data-items to be included in each record.

5-19. Suppose the St. Charles Company is interested in including in the new system the processing of accounts receivable. Processing accounts receivable requires that information on each customer be kept and that sales invoices, collections from customers, and credit memos be handled. Determine the files required, the organization of the files into records, and the data-items to be included in each record.

5-20. Suppose the St. Charles Company is interested in including the processing of inventory in the new system. Processing of inventory requires that information on each inventory item be kept and that purchase orders, sales orders, inventory receipts, inventory shipments, and adjustments be handled. Determine the files required, the organization of the files into records, and the data-items to be included in each record.

5-21. Suppose the St. Charles Company is interested in including in the new system general ledger recordkeeping and financial statement preparation. These activities require that information on each general ledger account be kept and that all debits and credits for the period be handled. Determine the files required, the organization of the files into records, and the data-items to be included in each record.

5-22. For each of the applications described in Problems 5-17 through 5-21, identify the entity, the primary key, and any secondary keys.

5-23. (*IIA, adapted*) The Ultimate Life Insurance Company recently established a data base management system. The company is now planning to provide its

180

Part II
Technical
Aspects of
Accounting
Information
Systems

branch offices with terminals that have on-line access to the central computer facility.

1. Define a "data base."
2. Give one fundamental advantage of a data base.
3. Briefly describe three security steps to safeguard the data base from improper access through the terminals.
4. Briefly describe four steps to control the completeness and accuracy of data transmitted through the terminals to the data base.

5-24. (*CMA, adapted*) Forward Corporation is a progressive and fast-growing company. The company's executive committee consists of the president and the four vice presidents who report to the president—marketing, manufacturing, finance, and systems. The company has ordered a new computer for use in processing its financial information. Because the computer acquisition required a substantial investment, the president wants to make certain that the computer is employed effectively. The new computer will enable Forward to revise its financial information system so that the several departments will get more useful information. This should be especially helpful in marketing because its personnel are distributed widely throughout the country. The marketing department is organized into 9 territories and 25 sales offices. The vice president of marketing wants the monthly reports to reflect those items for which the department is responsible and can control. The marketing department also wants information that identifies the most profitable products; this information is used to establish a discount policy that will enable the company to meet competition effectively. Monthly reports showing performance by territory and sales office also would be useful.

The vice president of finance has recommended that the accounting system be revised so that reports would be prepared on a contribution margin basis. Further, only those items controlled by the respective departments would appear on their report. The monthly report for the manufacturing department would compare actual production costs with a budget containing the standard costs for the actual volume of production. The marketing department would be provided with the standard variable manufacturing cost of each product so that it could calculate the variable contribution margin of each product. The monthly reports to the marketing department would reflect the variable contribution approach; the reports would present the net contribution of the department calculated by deducting standard variable manufacturing costs and marketing expenses (both variable and fixed) from sales. The company wants to retain the basic structure of the chart of accounts to minimize the number of changes in the system. However, the numbering system will have to be expanded in order to provide the additional information that is desired. A portion of Forward Corporation's chart of accounts is shown here:

Account number	Description
2000	Sales
2500	Cost of sales
3000	Manufacturing expenses
4000	Engineering expenses
5000	Marketing expenses
6000	Administrative expenses

The coding structure now in effect must be modified to satisfy the needs of Forward Corporation's management. Using the marketing areas as the example, devise an account number coding system that will permit the preparation of the contribution reports for the marketing department. In the presentation of the account number coding system, be sure to

1. Add additional accounts to the chart of accounts as needed.
2. Provide flexibility in the coding structure so that it would not have to be revised completely if Forward Corporation expands or restructures its sales area.
3. Explain and justify the coding structure presented.

5-25. (*CMA, adapted*) Ollie Mace has recently been appointed controller of a family-owned manufacturing enterprise. The firm, S. Dilley & Co., which was founded by Mr. Dilley about 20 years ago, is 78 percent owned by Mr. Dilley and has served the major automotive companies as a parts supplier. The firm's major operating divisions are heat treating, extruding, small parts stamping, and specialized machining. Sales last year from the several divisions ranged from $150,000 to over $3,000,000. The divisions are physically and managerially independent, except for Mr. Dilley's constant surveillance. The accounting system for each division has evolved according to the division's own needs and the abilities of individual accountants or bookkeepers. Mr. Mace is the first controller in the firm's history to have responsibility for overall financial management. Mr. Dilley expects to retire within six years and has hired Mr. Mace to improve the firm's financial system. Mr. Mace soon decides that he will need to design a new financial reporting system that will

a. Give managers uniform, timely, and accurate reports on business activity. Monthly divisional reports should be uniform and available by the tenth of the following month. Companywide financial reports also should be prepared by the tenth.

b. Provide a basis for measuring return on investment by division. Divisional reports should show assets assigned each division, and revenue and expense measurement in each division.

c. Generate meaningful budget data for planning and decision-making purposes. The accounting system should provide for the preparation of budgets that recognize managerial responsibility, controllability of costs, and major product groups.

d. Provide a uniform basis for evaluating performance and quick access to underlying data. Cost center variances should be measured and reported for operating and nonoperating units, including headquarters. Also, questions about levels of specific cost factors or product cost should be quickly answerable.

A new chart of accounts, as it appears to Mr. Mace, is essential to getting started on other critical financial problems. The present account codes used by divisions are not standard. Mr. Mace sees a need to divide asset accounts into six major categories (current assets, plant and equipment, etc.). Within each of these categories, he sees a need for no more than 10 control accounts. On the basis of his observations to date, 100 subsidiary accounts are more than adequate for each control account. No division now has more than five major product groups. The maximum number of cost centers Mr. Mace foresees within any product group is six, including operating and nonoperating groups. He views general divisional costs as a non-revenue-producing product group. Altogether, Mr. Mace estimates that 44 natural expense accounts plus 12 specific variance

182

Part II
Technical
Aspects of
Accounting
Information
Systems

accounts would be adequate. Mr. Mace is planning to implement the new chart of accounts in an environment that, at present, includes manual records systems and a computer-based system (used by one division). Mr. Mace expects that, in the near future, most accounting and reporting for all units will be automated. Therefore, the chart of accounts should facilitate the processing of transactions manually or by machine. Efforts should be made, he believes, to restrict the length of the code for economy in processing and convenience in use.

1. Design a chart of accounts coding system that will meet Mr. Mace's requirements. Your answer should begin with a digital layout of the coding system. Explain the coding method you have chosen and the reason for the size of your code elements. Explain your code as it would apply to asset and expense accounts.

2. In the small parts stamping division, Bill Shaw, supervisor in the polishing department of the door lever group, spent $100 on cleaning supplies. Code the expense item using the code you developed.

3. A new motorized sweeper has been purchased for the maintenance department of the extruding division for $3,450. Code this asset item using the code you developed.

5-26. Exhibit 5-5 has both an example schema and the normalized representation of the same file structure. Explain why the following are true:

a. The INVOICE file has only the inv-no as the primary key and not a combination of both the inv-no and cust-no.

b. The LINE-ITEM file has both the part-no and the inv-no together as the primary key.

In other words, explain why the inv-no is sufficient in the first case while the part-no is not sufficient in the second.

5-27. For each of the following, identify whether it is a data-item, a record, or a file:

a. Information on one customer
b. Customer name
c. Information on all customers
d. The customer's first name
e. Date of a customer payment
f. Amount owed on a particular purchase
g. All information stored about one customer purchase
h. Zip code for particular customer
i. Customer address
j. Total purchases to date this month

5-28. A bank may have transactions with customers in each of the following application areas:

a. Checking accounts
b. Savings accounts
c. Installment loans
d. Signature loans
e. Certificates of deposit
f. Travel agency functions

1. Suppose you developed systems for all of these application areas separately and in sequence. Design a file or set of files for each of the application areas to keep track of the bank's transactions with its customers.
2. Suppose you developed a system that would integrate all information about customers in all of these application areas so the bank would be able to find the status of all its dealings with a particular customer, regardless of the area. Design a file or set of files for this approach.
3. Discuss the advantages and disadvantages of sequential and direct access to the data files for both parts (1) and (2) of this problem.

5-29. (*CMA, adapted*) Imtex Corporation is a multinational company with approximately 100 subsidiaries and divisions, referred to as reporting units. Each reporting unit operates autonomously and maintains its own accounting information system. Each month, the reporting units prepare the basic financial statements and other key financial data on prescribed forms. These statements and related data are either mailed or telexed to corporate headquarters in New York City for entry into the corporate data base. Top and middle management at corporate headquarters utilize the data base to plan and direct corporate operations and objectives. Under the current system, the statements and data are to be received at corporate headquarters by the twelfth working day following the end of the month. The reports are logged, batched, and taken to the data processing department for coding and entry into the data base. Approximately 15 percent of the reporting units are delinquent in submitting their data, and three to four days are required to receive all of the data. After the data are loaded into the system, data verification programs are run to check footings, cross-statement consistency, and dollar range limits. Any errors in the data are traced and corrected, and reporting units are notified of all errors by form letters.

Imtex Corporation has decided to upgrade its computer communication network. The new system would allow data to be received on a more timely basis at corporate headquarters and provide numerous benefits to each of the reporting units. The systems department at corporate headquarters is responsible for the overall design and implementation of the new system. The systems department will utilize current computer communications technology by installing smart computer terminals at all reporting units. These terminals will provide two-way computer communications and also serve as microcomputers that can utilize spreadsheet and other applications software. As part of the initial use of the system, the data collection for the corporate data base would be performed by using these terminals. The financial statements and other financial data currently mailed or telexed would be entered by terminals. The required forms would initially be transmitted (downloaded) from the headquarters computer to the terminals of each reporting unit and stored permanently on disk. Data would be entered on the forms appearing on the reporting unit's terminal and stored under a separate file for transmission after the data are checked.

The data edit program would also be downloaded to the reporting units so the data could be verified at the unit location. All corrections would be made before transmitting the data to headquarters. The data would be stored on disk in proper format to maintain a unit file. Data would either be transmitted to corporate headquarters immediately or retrieved by the computer at corporate headquarters as needed. Therefore, data arriving at corporate headquarters would be free from errors and ready to be used in reports.

Charles Edwards, Imtex's controller, is very pleased with the prospects of the new system. He believes that data will be received from the reporting units two to three days faster and that the accuracy of the data will be much

184

*PART II
Technical
Aspects of
Accounting
Information
Systems*

improved. However, Edwards is concerned about data security and integrity during the transmission of data between the reporting units and corporate headquarters. He has scheduled a meeting with key personnel from the systems department to discuss these concerns.

1. Imtex could experience data security and integrity problems when transmitting data between the reporting units and corporate headquarters. Identify and explain the data security and integrity problems that could occur.

2. For each problem noted, identify and explain a control procedure that could be employed to minimize or eliminate the problem.

5-30. (*IIA, adapted*) An accountant should have a sound understanding of basic data processing concepts such as data organization and storage in order to evaluate systems adequately and make use of retrieval software.

1. Define the following terms: (a) Field (b) File (c) Record.

2. Define a data base. List two advantages and two disadvantages of a data base system.

3. Describe how serial (sequential) access differs from random access.

4. Differentiate between a transaction file and master file.

5-31. (*IIA, adapted*) The president of a small midwestern university has requested that you investigate and report on the growth of the university computer system. "When we purchased our central computer our studies indicated that we would not need additional hardware for at least ten years. Only five years later we are swamped with requests for local capabilities and peripheral equipment by the business school, engineering college, and social sciences. All of the requests indicate that our decision to develop a 'centralized' EDP facility five years ago was a mistake. Apparently, we need to develop a less 'centralized' system."

1. Prepare a statement contrasting the university's 'centralized' system and a distributed system.

2. Specify three advantages and three disadvantages of the university's 'centralized' system.

3. Specify three advantages and three disadvantages of a distributed system.

DECISION CASE

Lawn Cutters, Inc., is a medium-sized manufacturer of electric- and gasoline-powered lawn and garden equipment. The company needs a file system to record its purchases of raw materials, accounts payable, and items in raw materials inventory. The system would store and access such information as

a. Vendors' names, addresses, and sales terms.

b. Items purchased on each purchase order, the vendor from whom the items were obtained, quantity ordered, and total cost.

c. Accounts payable by vendor.

d. Descriptions of every item in the raw materials inventory, the quantity in inventory, units in which the quantity is measured (feet or pounds) and unit price.

Required:

185

CHAPTER 5
Data Files
and Data
Bases

1. Prepare a list of files needed.
2. What should be the data-items in each file?
3. Give a primary key for each file.
4. Describe this file structure as a series of flat files.
5. Draw a schema of the file structure.
6. Lawn Cutters wants a list of all vendors from whom a purchase order greater than $1,000 has been made for the purchase of steel bars.

   a. What files would be needed to find this information?
   b. What secondary keys would be required?
   c. Describe the process a computer would follow to answer this question from the file data.

6 Relational Data Bases and the Structured Query Language

Overview

More advanced and most popular current techniques for data storage (relational data bases) and data access (structured query language).

Learning Objectives

Thorough study of this chapter will enable you to:

1. Choose among the hierarchical, relational, and network approaches to data bases.
2. Prove that relational data base management systems have advantages over nonrelational systems.
3. Normalize data.
4. Predict future trends in relational systems.
5. Show how Structured Query Language (SQL) and Query-by-Example (QBE) support the relational approach.
6. Compare Structured Query Language to other data base languages.

Outline

Accounting Data in Data Bases

Relational Data Base Management Systems

Data Normalization

Future Trends in RDBMS

Structured Query Language and Its Alternatives

SYSTEMS IN THE REAL WORLD

187

*CHAPTER 6
Relational
Data Bases
and the
Structured
Query
Language*

Trading the Street for the Keyboard

Ralph D. Thomas peered at the little computer perched on a desk in a corner of his cluttered office, while his wife, Barbara, typed in the Social Security number of two men who had skipped out of Killington, Vt., leaving a stack of unpaid bills. After a short pause, up popped new addresses for the deadbeats—one in Salt Lake City, the other in Palm Beach. In about 90 seconds, without leaving Texas, Thomas had followed an electronic trail of computerized data bases winding from Vermont through half a dozen other states to Utah and Florida.

Move over, Sam Spade, Jim Rockford, and Magnum P.I., you're being outgunned by computer jocks. Private detectives these days are working with new kinds of clients, new targets and new technologies.

A DETECTIVE'S ELECTRONIC SLEUTHING

How a Texas private detective tracks two suspects across the country without ever leaving the office.

SOURCE: Datafax Information Services

1. In Vermont, two men skip town leaving many unpaid bills

2. Private investigator hired in Austin, Texas enters debtors' social security numbers into a computer in Ohio.

3. National Credit Information Network taps into data base in California

4. TRW credit data base pops up the debtors' new addresses.

5. Debtors found in Salt Lake City and Palm Beach.

SOURCE: *The Sun Herald*, 8/26/90, reprinted by permission.

188

*PART II
Technical
Aspects of
Accounting
Information
Systems*

ACCOUNTING DATA IN DATA BASES

Accounting data are the heart of any company's information system, regardless of its level of computer sophistication. Computer-based accounting systems have traditionally been written in a programming language, such as COBOL. As a result, only highly trained computer professionals could access computerized data. This meant that accountants could not access the data directly, so the data were not as useful as they could have been.

Often, the company needs the answer to questions that its system is not programmed to answer, but that could be answered from the accounting data. These questions are called **queries** or sometimes ad hoc queries because of their specific, nonprogrammed nature. These queries are easily formulated, for example, "Who were the top five salespeople in each region last month?" Unfortunately, such a query typically requires laborious steps to answer, including committee approval and the writing of a separate computer program. With the traditional approach, a separate computer program is required for every type of analysis, and it is hard to get access to data for purposes other than those planned for originally and thus preprogrammed into the accounting system.

There is now a major movement in the computer industry toward making new data available directly to the user, so that the data can become more responsive. This means putting the accounting system data in a data base. The accounting programs, such as transaction processing and financial reporting, would remain much as they are. But the data base is accessible directly with data base tools that the end user can handle. Almost anyone can query the data base. The user does not have to go through the preprogrammed accounting system or learn programming to get to the data.

The relational data base approach is superior to other approaches in the answering of these queries. Relational data bases usually have two powerful tools, **Structured Query Language (SQL)** and **Query-by-Example (QBE)**, that allow the accountant (and other users) to get the answers they need quickly and easily.

RELATIONAL DATA BASE MANAGEMENT SYSTEMS

Comparison and Contrast with the Other Primary Approaches

Many people and many companies in the computer industry have experimented with different approaches to the development of data bases and data base management systems (DBMS). This experimentation has led to the following conclusions.

Hierarchical Approach. The hierarchical data base approach (or tree structure) is the fastest in processing transactions, that is, the fastest in updating the files with events as they occur. However, the hierarchical approach is the most difficult to use, primarily because it is so difficult to change its structure

189

CHAPTER 6
*Relational
Data Bases
and the
Structured
Query
Language*

as the situation or environment changes. As a result, the hierarchical approach is used only when absolutely necessary for performance reasons. Most hierarchical applications are therefore already written; there is very little growth in the number of these applications. If a system is large enough to require the hierarchical approach, then it must already use the computer. And if it uses the computer, it must use a hierarchical DBMS. Most IMS (the leading hierarchical) data bases have now been developed; there is little growth in the number of these data bases.

Relational Approach. The relational data base approach is the easiest to query and to modify the structure of, but is the slowest in processing transactions. Because ease of use is so important to most computer users, virtually all new DBMS applications are in relational data bases. However, most current work in the computer science side of DBMS is to make **relational DBMS (RDBMS)** more efficient and faster in transaction processing. These systems continue to improve.

Network Approach. The network approach (or plex structure) is somewhere between the hierarchical and relational approaches in both speed and ease of use. Thus, it has fallen out of favor. Users requiring speed choose the hierarchical approach, while those desiring ease of use choose the relational approach. As a result, there is virtually no new development of network DBMS or new applications using a network DBMS.

Characteristics of a Relational Data Base Management System

In 1969, mathematician E. F. Codd, while at IBM, developed the relational theory of data which he proposed as a universal foundation for data base systems. Codd's theory has formed the basis for all further work in this area. A relational DBMS satisfies the following conditions.

Information. All information in the RDBMS is represented in only one way: as values in tables. This allows users to more easily access, understand, and manipulate data. All data values should be guaranteed to be accessible by the combination of the name of the table in which the data are stored, the name of the column under which they are stored, and the primary key that identifies the row in which they are stored.

Relational Language. An RDBMS does not force the use of procedural application code. This will require that the RDBMS offer a data language to

1. Define data.
2. Define views.
3. Manipulate data.
4. Establish rules to prevent errors, such as acceptable values for codes or a required connection between a master file and a transaction file.
5. Maintain authorization of which users can access which data.

190

PART II
Technical
Aspects of
Accounting
Information
Systems

This language must be able to process entire tables (not row by row) not only for queries, but also for data modification, insertion, and deletion. These capabilities should be available both interactively and embedded in other programming languages, such as C, COBOL, and FORTRAN. However, the RDBMS must not permit procedural languages to bypass the rules designed to prevent errors as defined by the relational language. The market standard is Structured Query Language, discussed later in the chapter.

Catalog.   A description of the data base is represented as tables that are maintained by the RDBMS. This allows users to use the same relational language with both catalog and user data.

Independence.   Users must not be required to modify queries or application programs if the data base has been reorganized and there is no loss of information in the tables. This would include moving data from one computer to another to be closer to the source or the location where they are used more often. Business policy changes can be implemented with a single change to the catalog. Integrity management, that is, the maintenance of required links between tables and validity of values for the data-items should not be duplicated in each application, but are implemented by the DBMS.

Views.   Tables with data physically in them are called **base tables**. The RDBMS must also be able to create logical tables (called **views**) from the base tables. For example, the information about an individual's personnel file that the payroll clerk is authorized to look at could be put into a view that the payroll clerk would use. The view could be queried and processed just as a base table would be, even though the original data are not repeated in the view and are only stored once in the base table. Information about the connection of the view and the base tables from which it is formed are stored in the catalog. Views are illustrated later in this chapter.

Advantages of the Relational Approach

The relational approach is based on tables of data in rows and columns, with operations defined on those tables, but these tables must obey the characteristics of the relational approach given. The RDBMS (not the user) must ensure that all data base tables comply with these requirements. When they do, the RDBMS can apply mathematical operations and strict logic to them. This eliminates traditional deficiencies of DBMS and offers significant practical benefits.

Traditional Deficiencies of DBMS.   Most DBMS leave most of the job of managing data bases to their users, and usually require programming skills. Except for the simplest tasks in accessing and manipulating data, the user typically cannot ask for the desired results directly. Frequently, someone must create procedures (that is, detailed sets of steps) that the system must follow to obtain the desired results. Moreover, where the user wants to perform a

191

CHAPTER 6
*Relational
Data Bases
and the
Structured
Query
Language*

data operation—retrieval, update, or deletion—on multiple data records, the procedure must loop over the records one at a time, until the task is complete. Often, technical personnel need to help users to process their own data because the tools that traditional DBMS products provide are unfamiliar to users.

A great deal of this procedural detail consists of explicit references to how the data are stored, which are irrelevant to the user. Thus, traditional systems involve the user in machine complexities and performance considerations, which most people are ill-equipped to handle and should not have to deal with anyway.

Another major concern is sharing data among computers at different locations. This typically requires moving entire files from computer to computer, which is quite inefficient when the applications that require access to the data need only a few records. Also, when moving files between computers and applications, an additional step is often necessary to convert the data from one format to another.

Traditional data base systems lack a theoretical foundation, and therefore DBMS products were developed ad hoc. Despite some similarities, each (proprietary) DBMS approaches the same data processing tasks in its own unique way. Also, without theory, consistent product comparisons are difficult, and thus scarce. DBMS are often evaluated either against each other or against (arbitrary) lists of features.

Practical Advantages of an RDBMS. The table structure of an RDBMS is simple and familiar. It is general enough to represent most types of data; it is independent of any internal computer mechanisms; and it is flexible, because the user can restructure tables.

With RDBMS, transaction processing is slower than with other approaches, but modifying the structure of files and adding data-items (columns) is easier. Also, the relational approach allows structure or relationships between tables to be added later, after the data tables have been developed and the data entered. In the hierarchical and network approaches, allowable queries about the data all have to be identified before the data base is developed so that the pointers between files and records will be created along with the data base.

Data manipulation by an RDBMS consists of a well-defined, complete set of mathematical operations, which always yield tables as results. With relational operations, data access need no longer be procedural.

The user can specify a data request by giving the operations that must be performed on other tables to derive it. The system then translates these requests into efficient processing steps. A relational DBMS can accumulate information about the data base (such as statistics) in its catalog to optimize these operations.

The relational approach requires the system to enforce in the data base strict and comprehensive rules to ensure data accuracy and consistency. Thus, a relational DBMS relieves the user of the task of developing in each application procedures to enforce validity of codes and required links between tables. Therefore, the RDBMS offers productivity and reliability superior to that of traditional systems.

192

PART II
Technical
Aspects of
Accounting
Information
Systems

Operations in RDBMS

To translate from file terminology to relational terminology, we have the following:

1. A **relational table** is a file.
2. A **row** in a relational data base corresponds to a record.
3. A **column** in a relational data base corresponds to a field or data-item.

Tables (files) are tied together by keys. A primary key in any table uniquely identifies that row (or record). For example, the primary key in an accounts receivable system would likely be a customer number, although it could be the customer name. In the master file table, the primary key would uniquely identify the customer's master file record or row. In the transaction file table, each transaction would have the customer number appropriate for that transaction. The customer number key in another file like the transaction file is not unique, because one customer could have several transactions. However, this key ties to the master file.

The primary operations on tables in the relational approach are projections and joins.

Projections. **Projections** take one table and create others by identifying the name of the desired table and the data-items that should be in that table. Exhibit 6-1 gives an example of a projection for an employee application. Notice that in the original table, the location of each employee's department is given in the employee table. However, several employees are in the same department. Thus, while there are six employee records, there are only three unique departments. This repetition of departmental location can be eliminated by creating two tables as shown in the middle of the exhibit.

Joins. To store data most efficiently, it is necessary to eliminate duplicate data. However, data from many different tables must then be brought together to answer routine queries by users. The **join** operation puts tables together to form a new table. The bottom of Exhibit 6-1 gives an example of a join operation on the tables split in the projection in the middle of the exhibit. In this example, the school name, which is common to both tables, can be used to tie the tables together.

Current Relational Data Base Management Systems

This relational approach is now standard with IBM and the rest of the computer industry. Because relational data bases are an important area commercially, virtually all DBMS claim that they are relational. The leading programs for mainframes are DB2 for the MVS operating system and SQL/DS for the VM/CMS operating system. An SQL/DS application, for example, can have up to 70 million rows, hundreds of tables, and thousands of columns. SQL/DS is installed on over 7,500 mainframes and costs over $100,000 per installation. Other leading, somewhat relational data bases are, for minicomputers, Oracle and INGRES, and, for microcomputers, dBASE and Paradox.

EXHIBIT 6-1 Examples of Projection and Join Operations

Original Table

EMPLOYEE

Employee-#	Employee-Name	School	Phone	Building
23981	Hendrickson G H	Liberal Arts	5233	Dixon Hall
54912	Woodruff C J	Engineering	5631	Boggs
34519	Ochsner M A	Medicine	581-2354	Richardson
56120	Lee C J	Business	5422	Goldring
74311	Law V J	Engineering	5347	Boggs
98443	Petry G W	Engineering	5882	Boggs

Example of Projection to Eliminate Duplicate Building Locations

EMPLOYEE

Employee-#	Employee-Name	School	Phone
23981	Hendrickson G H	Liberal Arts	5233
54912	Woodruff C J	Engineering	5631
34519	Ochsner M A	Medicine	581-2354
56120	Lee C J	Business	5422
74311	Law V J	Engineering	5347
98443	Petry G W	Engineering	5882

SCHOOL

School	Building
Liberal Arts	Dixon Hall
Engineering	Boggs
Medicine	Richardson
Business	Goldring

Example of a Join to Get Building Location for All Employees

LOCATION

Employee-Name	School	Building
Hendrickson G H	Liberal Arts	Dixon Hall
Woodruff C J	Engineering	Boggs
Ochsner M A	Medicine	Richardson
Lee C J	Business	Goldring
Law V J	Engineering	Boggs
Petry G W	Engineering	Boggs

194

*Part II
Technical
Aspects of
Accounting
Information
Systems*

No existing DBMS completely satisfies all of the foregoing conditions of the relational approach. The features of an RDBMS are highly dependent, and the lack of any one feature affects the support of the others. It is not possible to provide all benefits by implementing only some of the features or by adding a relational-type interface to a nonrelational DBMS. DBMS range from close to these rules (DB2) to very far away (dBASE). As a result, some people call DBMS such as dBASE pseudorelational. But as all DBMS are upgraded and new versions released, they move toward the satisfaction of all the rules of a relational data base. As a practical matter, most people call any DBMS allowing projections and joins (as does dBASE) relational.

DATA NORMALIZATION

To use relational data bases it is necessary to represent data in the form of tables, with rows and columns of data. However, it is typically the case that

1. When first looking at the data, it will often not seem to fit into row and column form.
2. When putting data into row and column form, the data can be represented by tables in several different ways.

Normalization is an orderly process for organizing data into tabular form, and typically results in several tables. The normalization process has two goals:

1. To ensure that in every table, each row/column cell position has only one item. This means that all repeating groups are eliminated. When this goal is achieved, the data are in first normal form.
2. To minimize redundant data. There are two primary advantages to minimizing redundant data. One is that less storage will be required for the same amount of useful data. The other is that if any data need to be changed, that data need only be changed in one place. As redundancies in the first normal form are removed, then the data moves into second and third normal form and occasionally into fourth and fifth normal form.

First Normal Form

A basic concept of the relational approach is that a table has a fixed number of columns, but the number of rows is limited only by the physical storage of the computer system. Any repeating groups are eliminated in order to store data in tabular form. After these repeating groups are eliminated, the data are in **first normal form**. Exhibit 5-10 gave an example of eliminating a repeating group to put the data into normal form. Exhibit 6-2 gives an example of data on employees and projects in first normal form.

Second Normal Form

As discussed earlier under projections, data in a table can be repeated. When these data are split into further tables so that data depending on components of the primary key are not repeated, then the data are in **second normal form**.

EXHIBIT 6-2   Example of First Normal Form

EMPLOYEE

Employee-Number	Dept-Number	Employee-Name	Job-Code	Job-Title	Location	Hours-Worked
120	01	Abriel	1	Accountant	New Orleans	37
120	08	Abriel	1	Accountant	Los Angeles	12
121	01	Bayer	1	Accountant	New Orleans	45
121	08	Bayer	1	Accountant	Los Angeles	21
121	12	Bayer	1	Accountant	New York	107
270	08	Boudreaux	2	Supervisor	Los Angeles	10
270	12	Boudreaux	2	Supervisor	New York	78
273	01	Wolbrette	3	Manager	New Orleans	22
274	12	Scanlon	2	Supervisor	New York	41
279	01	Richards	1	Accountant	New Orleans	27
279	08	Richards	1	Accountant	Los Angeles	20
279	12	Richards	1	Accountant	New York	51
301	01	Daly	1	Accountant	New Orleans	16
301	12	Daly	1	Accountant	New York	85
306	12	Magrew	3	Manager	New York	67

196

PART II
Technical
Aspects of
Accounting
Information
Systems

In Exhibit 6-2, the employee's name, job code, and job title are uniquely identified by the employee number. Similarly, the completion date of a project is uniquely identified by the project number. Thus, it is possible to split the EMPLOYEE table into three tables and eliminate these redundancies. Exhibit 6-3 gives the data from Exhibit 6-2 put into second normal form.

Second normal form has three major advantages:

1. Less disk space is needed to store the data because the data are not repeated. For example, the name RICHARDS appears three times in the EMPLOYEE table in first normal form but only once in the EMPLOYEE table in second normal form.

2. The information is easier than first normal form to update. If, for example, the location of a department changed, the new name would only have to change in one location in one table.

3. No information is lost in the movement from first normal form to second normal form because the data can be put back into first normal form by joins if necessary in order to answer a question about the data.

Third Normal Form

Once all data are in second normal form, further data redundancies not involving the primary key can sometimes be eliminated. Once this is accomplished, the data are then in **third normal form**. In Exhibit 6-3, the JOB-TITLE is dependent on the JOB-CODE, so it is not necessary to store the JOB-TITLE more than once. Thus, it is possible to eliminate the JOB-TITLE redundancies by creating a new JOB table. Exhibit 6-4 gives the data from the previous two exhibits in third normal form. Note that it would be possible to join the EMPLOYEE and JOB tables in third normal form to get back to the EMPLOYEE table in second normal form.

Fourth and Fifth Normal Forms

Fourth and **fifth normal forms** are only occasionally necessary. They are concerned with multivalue dependencies, where one data-item is associated with multiple values of another data-item. See, for example, Exhibit 6-5 on page 199. The EMPLOYEE-DEPT-TASK table is in third normal form, but the same three tasks are needed by each employee on each project. This is a redundancy. Splitting EMPLOYEE-DEPT-TASK into the two tables EMPLOYEE-DEPT and EMPLOYEE-TASK eliminates this redundancy. Note that the EMPLOYEE-DEPT and EMPLOYEE-TASK tables can be joined to return to the table EMPLOYEE-DEPT-TASK table.

Fifth normal form involves a multivalued dependency that does not have a fixed number of values for the second data item. In the last example of fourth normal form, there were always three values of skill for every project. The first table in Exhibit 6-6 on page 200 gives an example in third normal form in which the number of values of skill varies by employee and by project. The middle of Exhibit 6-6 then shows this table split into fourth normal form as

EXHIBIT 6-3   Example of Second Normal Form

197

CHAPTER 6
Relational
Data Bases
and the
Structured
Query
Language

EMPLOYEE

Employee-Number	Employee-Name	Job-Code	Job-Title
120	Abriel	1	Accountant
121	Bayer	1	Accountant
270	Boudreaux	2	Supervisor
273	Wolbrette	3	Manager
274	Scanlon	2	Supervisor
279	Richards	1	Accountant
301	Daly	1	Accountant
306	Magrew	3	Manager

DEPT

Dept-Number	Location
01	New Orleans
08	Los Angeles
12	New York

HOURS

Employee-Number	Dept-Number	Hours-Worked
120	01	37
120	08	12
121	01	45
121	08	21
121	12	107
270	08	10
270	12	78
273	01	22
274	12	41
279	01	27
279	08	20
279	12	51
301	01	16
301	12	85
306	12	67

198

PART II
Technical
Aspects of
Accounting
Information
Systems

EXHIBIT 6-4   Example of Third Normal Form

EMPLOYEE

Employee-Number	Employee-Name	Job-Code
120	Abriel	1
121	Bayer	1
270	Boudreaux	2
273	Wolbrette	3
274	Scanlon	2
279	Richards	1
301	Daly	1
306	Magrew	3

JOBS

Job-Code	Job-Title
1	Accountant
2	Supervisor
3	Manager

DEPT

Dept-Number	Location
01	New Orleans
08	Los Angeles
12	New York

HOURS

Employee-Number	Dept-Number	Hours-Worked
120	01	37
120	08	12
121	01	45
121	08	21
121	12	107
270	08	10
270	12	78
273	01	22
274	12	41
279	01	27
279	08	20
279	12	51
301	01	16
301	12	85
306	12	67

EXHIBIT 6-5   Example of Fourth Normal Form

199

CHAPTER 6
*Relational
Data Bases
and the
Structured
Query
Language*

Given the Following Table in Third Normal Form

EMPLOYEE-DEPT-TASK

Employee-Number	Dept-Number	Task
120	01	Analyze
120	01	Process
120	01	Document
120	08	Analyze
120	08	Process
120	08	Document

The Following Pair of Tables Are in Fourth Normal Form

EMPLOYEE-DEPT

Employee-Number	Dept-Number
120	01
120	08

EMPLOYEE-TASK

Employee-Number	Task
120	Analyze
120	Process
120	Document

before. Note, however, that if these two tables in fourth normal form are joined, they do not go back to the table in third normal form. Such a joint would add a row with EMPLOYEE-NUMBER = 120, DEPT-NUMBER = 08, and TASK = 'ANALYZE'. As a result, it is necessary to split the table in third normal form into three tables, which are then in fifth normal form. These three tables in fifth normal form are at the bottom of Exhibit 6-6. Joining these three tables together would get back to the original table in third normal form.

Data Base Design and Performance Considerations

It is possible to put all data tables in third normal form. However, virtually all applications have data in second or even first normal form. The purpose of this is to make access faster. If all data are in third normal form and only stored once, then accessing the data can often be difficult because of requirements for too many joins for all the relevant data to be put together. Because joins are so time consuming, some of the data are usually left with the joins already done in second (or first) normal form. For example, if the EMPLOYEE-NAME is always wanted when the EMPLOYEE-NUMBER is used, then the EM-PLOYEE-NAME might be stored along with EMPLOYEE-NUMBER wherever the latter is used in a file.

200

Part II
Technical
Aspects of
Accounting
Information
Systems

EXHIBIT 6-6   Example of Fifth Normal Form

Given the Following Table in Third Normal Form

EMPLOYEE-DEPT-TASK

Employee-Number	Dept-Number	Task
120	01	Analyze
120	01	Process
120	08	Process
205	01	Process

The Following Pair of Tables Are in Fourth Normal Form

EMPLOYEE-DEPT

Employee-Number	Dept-Number
120	01
120	08
205	01

EMPLOYEE-TASK

Employee-Number	Task
120	Analyze
120	Process
205	Process

The Following Three Tables Are in Fifth Normal Form

EMPLOYEE-DEPT

Employee-Number	Dept-Number
120	01
120	08
205	01

EMPLOYEE-TASK

Employee-Number	Task
120	Analyze
120	Process
205	Process

DEPT-TASK

Dept-Number	Task
01	Analyze
01	Process
08	Process

However, the best way to deal with a frequently needed join is to put the data first into completely normalized form. Then, views (data tables themselves) can be created from these base tables which have the necessary joins defined. The joins are then performed when the data are accessed. Thus, it is not a good idea to store partially normalized tables, that is, tables where further normalization is possible but not done. For performance reasons, though, it is often necessary to have normal form views that include columns which come from other tables. Both partially normalized tables and views with columns from other tables reduce the cost of some retrieval operations, but only the use of views allows a clean way to store the facts represented in normal form tables.

Thus, as a general rule, redundantly stored or defined data simplifies and speeds up retrieval, but complicates and slows down updates. Design of a high-performance data base therefore requires measuring or estimating the volume and rate of each type of access. The trade-off is not between relational purity and real-world performance; the trade-off is between the two different types of access.

201

CHAPTER 6
*Relational
Data Bases
and the
Structured
Query
Language*

CONCEPT SUMMARY

Data Normalization

Status of Data	Meaning	Example
Unnormalized	Repeating groups appear in the data.	Customer file has multiple invoices per customer.
First normal form	There are no repeating groups; all data are in tabular (row/column) form.	Customer file is expanded to include all customer-invoice combinations.
Second normal form	There are no data redundancies involving the primary key.	Two tables exist for customers and invoices so information on customers is not repeated for each invoice.
Third normal form	There are no data redundancies involving other (secondary) keys in the table.	Two tables exist for sales representatives and invoices so representative name is not repeated for each invoice.
Fourth normal form (only occasionally necessary)	There are no multivalued dependencies, where a value in one column identifies multiple values in another column.	Two tables exist for sales tasks and invoices if the tasks should all be done for each invoice.
Fifth normal form (only occasionally necessary)	There are no join dependencies, where it is impossible to split the table into two projections without losing data.	Three tables exist for tasks possible, tasks done, and invoices if different tasks are done for different invoices.

202

PART II
Technical
Aspects of
Accounting
Information
Systems

FUTURE TRENDS IN RDBMS

Standards

The mathematical and logical basis of the relational approach makes it a natural candidate for a data base standard. A standard based on the relational model would yield the best of both worlds: The products that complied would offer both relational features and compatibility with a defined standard. The underlying data base functions would be the same for all products, regardless of whether they are designed for a single user on a microcomputer or multiple users in more sophisticated systems. In addition, tools such as spreadsheets and word processors could all operate on data bases, not on different types of files. The American National Standards Institute (ANSI) and the International Standards Organization (ISO) have developed standards for SQL, and all DBMS are moving toward those standards, but this movement is still in process. Unfortunately, few DBMS reliably work with any others. No existing DBMS satisfies all of the characteristics of the relational approach, including the ANSI Standard.

Distributed Data

RDBMS are moving toward support of distributed data bases, that is the ability to access data at multiple locations, including locally, without the user needing to know where the data are located. One benefit of a distributed data base is that local data can be retrieved without any network activity, thus reducing communications costs when compared with a centralized data base at a remote site. Another potential advantage is that each data base can be made the size appropriate for its amount of data, the complexity of user requirements, and the number of users. As the system grows, added demand can be met more easily than with a centralized system, by making smaller changes to existing data bases or by adding new data bases to the network. Current RDBMS deliver these benefits by allowing a collection of data base operations (called a unit of work) to retrieve and update data at a remote site. Future capabilities will add support for a distributed unit of work, which allows a single unit of work to access data at multiple locations simultaneously.

Data Base Servers

RDBMS are moving toward the function of providing access to the data for applications running on remote computers. This style of distributed computing is called the client/server applications, where the computer providing access to the data is called the data base server, and the remote computer requesting the data is called the client. Data base servers can be mainframes, but more and more they are microcomputers. Microcomputer RDBMS are evolving in two directions:

1. To acquire access to data base servers running on mainframe computers.
2. To become data base servers themselves for other (remote) microcomputers.

Chapter 7 discusses these trends as part of the larger discussion of data communications and networks.

203

CHAPTER 6
Relational
Data Bases
and the
Structured
Query
Language

STRUCTURED QUERY LANGUAGE AND ITS ALTERNATIVES

Even after the computer industry moved to the relational approach, there were still extensive differences between the various implementations of the relational approach. Each developer of an RDBMS found it necessary to develop a new language and method of access to the data. Thus, to use a new RDBMS, the user generally had to learn a new language. In addition, all the applications had to be rewritten in the new language. In essence, users felt stuck with their initial choice of RDBMS.

The Structured Query Language is the only means of supporting relational data bases and the relational approach that has gained industry acceptance. SQL can be used on a stand-alone basis, but it can also be embedded in other (host) languages, such as COBOL. SQL is a language for interacting with relational data bases. It is not a full application development language, such as C, COBOL, and FORTRAN. This has the following advantages:

1. The well-defined, set-oriented data base foundation is kept distinct from the less precise, procedural character of existing programming languages.
2. It avoids creating yet another general-purpose language that, by trying to be everything to everybody, becomes too complex to master and invites compromises.
3. It avoids the long process that would be required to extend standard procedural languages such as COBOL and FORTRAN with relational data base functions.

SQL Concepts

What SQL does is provide standard methods of performing relational data base tasks. The previous section on relational DBMS discussed all the operations necessary for a complete RDBMS. SQL can perform all of these operations. SQL can be used in two primary ways, interactively and invoked from an application program. In both cases, the structure is the same:

SELECT	this is a list of data-items of interest
FROM	this is a list of tables where these data-items exist
WHERE	this is the condition(s) the data-items must satisfy

The result of a SELECT/FROM/WHERE is itself another table, which can then be used like any other table.

204

Part II
Technical
Aspects of
Accounting
Information
Systems

Following are some illustrations of a relational data base being queried using SQL. This will illustrate the basic concepts. There will be three tables as illustrated in Exhibit 6-7, S (suppliers), P (parts), and SP (shipments of parts by suppliers).

An example of an interactive invocation of SQL is the following:

```
SELECT      S.LOCATION
FROM        S
WHERE       S.SUPPNUM = 'S4'
```

Result: LOCATION
             Chicago

The following are important items to be noted about this example:

1. The result is a table with one data-item (LOCATION) with only one row (Chicago). This is because only one city satisfied the condition. In general, however, there can be multiple data-items and multiple rows resulting from an SQL command.
2. The same data-item name can be used in different tables. In this case, to identify the data-item uniquely, you need to identify the data-item by both its table and name. As an example, in this case, LOCATION is a data-item in both the S table and the P table. To identify that data-item uniquely, it was referred to as S.LOCATION to distinguish it from P.LOCATION in the P table.
3. S4 could be the name of a data-item or variable. To make it clear that we wanted to match on the value S4 instead of the data-item or variable S4, we put single quotes around the 'S4'.

SQL Capabilities

The following are examples of a relational data base created and updated using SQL with the data given in Exhibit 6-7. Each of these examples is independent of the other, so the statements are not meant to be executed sequentially. Exhibit 6-8 summarizes these examples. The third column of Exhibit 6-8 gives the result of the task as given in column 1 and the SQL statement in column 2. Try to determine the result before examining column 3.

Create Table Structure. The first step in the use of any DBMS is to create the structure of the data tables. Note that a data-item or pair of data-items is identified as unique. Unique is basically the same thing as a primary key. The DBMS will check that this uniqueness is maintained, so a user will not be allowed to add another item to the file that matches an item already on the file.

These three tables are base tables because they are the only tables that are created and the only tables that physically exist. Other tables generated by joins or other operations can be used just like base tables, but do not exist separately. There will be no data in these tables after the **CREATE statement** is executed. The data have to be added separately.

EXHIBIT 6-7 Supplier/Parts/Shipments Data Base

205

CHAPTER 6
Relational
Data Bases
and the
Structured
Query
Language

S—Suppliers

Suppnum	Suppname	Status	Location
S1	Seuling	20	Chicago
S2	Heider	10	Seattle
S3	Albelli	30	Seattle
S4	Page	20	Chicago
S5	Hooper	30	Houston

P—Parts

Partnum	Partname	Metal	Weight	Location
P1	Lever	Steel	12	Chicago
P2	Knob	Alum	17	Seattle
P3	Cover	Alloy	17	Dallas
P4	Cover	Steel	14	Chicago
P5	Base	Alloy	12	Seattle
P6	Brace	Steel	19	Chicago

SP—Shipments

Suppnum	Partnum	Qty
S1	P1	300
S1	P2	200
S1	P3	400
S1	P4	200
S1	P5	100
S1	P6	100
S2	P1	300
S2	P2	400
S3	P2	200
S4	P2	200
S4	P4	300
S4	P6	400

EXHIBIT 6-8 Structured Query Language

Function	SQL Statements	Result

Create table structure.	CREATE TABLE S (SUPPNUM CHAR(5) NOT NULL,
	  SUPPNAME CHAR(20),
	  STATUS DECIMAL(3),
	  LOCATION CHAR(15)
	  UNIQUE (SUPPNUM))
		S for Suppliers, P for Parts, and SP for Shipments.

Insert a row.	INSERT INTO SP (SUPPNUM, PARTNUM, QTY) VALUES ('S5', 'P1', 100)	Adds row to table SP.
Delete rows.	DELETE FROM P WHERE P.WEIGHT > 15	Delete rows in table P for P2, P3, and P6.
Join two tables.	SELECT SP.PARTNUM, S.LOCATION FROM SP, S WHERE SP.SUPPNUM = S.SUPPNUM	PARTNUM LOCATION P1 Chicago P2 Chicago ... ... P1 Seattle
Sum the total quantity of part P2.	SELECT SUM (SP.QTY) FROM SP WHERE SP.PARTNUM = 'P2'	Total quantity of P2 is 1000.
Create view.	CREATE VIEW CS (SUPPNUM, SUPPNAME, STATUS) AS SELECT S.SUPPNUM, S.SUPPNAME, S.STATUS FROM S WHERE S.LOCATION = 'Chicago'	"File" of Chicago suppliers, view CS, does not exist separately.
Use view.	SELECT CS.SUPPNUM FROM CS WHERE CS.STATUS < 50	SUPPNUM S1 S4
Translate query using view.	SELECT S.SUPPNUM FROM S WHERE S.STATUS < 50 AND S.LOCATON = 'Chicago'	SUPPNUM S1 S4

207

CHAPTER 6
*Relational
Data Bases
and the
Structured
Query
Language*

Modify Table Values. The three primary means to update table values are insert, update, and delete. The **INSERT statement** in Exhibit 6-8 shows an insertion subsequent to loading the initial values into the tables. But the initial values would all have been loaded with INSERT statements. All table values are subject to change and the **UPDATE statement** allows this capability, though this statement is not illustrated here. It is sometimes necessary to remove items from the data base once they have outlived their usefulness and this is accomplished by the **DELETE statement.**

Query Tables. Perhaps the most powerful capability of SQL is in querying the data base. In response, the DBMS does the difficult task of performing the necessary joins. As discussed earlier in the chapter, joins put the data in different tables back together in order to answer queries. In addition, functions, such as COUNT and SUM, are also useful for answering queries about the data base.

Views. Views are an extremely powerful capability of the relational approach. They create logical views of the data in addition to the base tables. These views are then logical tables, though they are often not stored separately. However, for performance reasons, as discussed earlier, the RDBMS may store a view redundantly for faster retrieval. The views can then be used as tables in any SQL statement. It is also possible to update a view by adding data to it and having that data update the base tables. An example of a use of a view would be to create a restricted view of a payroll file and give certain clerks permission to only use a particular view, rather than the base tables.

The example here is to create a view of the suppliers in Chicago. View CS is then a table which can be used like any other. The RDBMS will translate any use of the view into the appropriate use of the original base tables.

Embedded SQL Statements

Relational DBMS that use SQL also allow application programs that are written in programming languages such as C, COBOL, and FORTRAN to access the data base with SQL statements. Exhibit 6-9 gives examples of embedded SQL in each of those languages. At least in theory, it is possible to access the same data with the same commands from different languages. Also, it is possible to change the RDBMS without changing programs or the commands in the programs.

SQL statements embedded in a programming language always begin with the keywords EXEC SQL to separate the SQL statements from the regular language. The end of the statement differs somewhat among the different languages. In between, however, the SQL statements follow the same format illustrated earlier in Exhibit 6-8.

SQL statements can refer to data-items in tables of the relational DBMS, or they can refer to variables in the programming language defined by the

EXHIBIT 6-9   Comparison of Embedded SQL Statements in Different Host Languages

Language	SQL Statements	Comments
C	EXEC SQL SELECT S.LOCATION INTO :SL FROM S WHERE S.SUPPNUM = 'S4';	Statement ends with semicolon ;
COBOL	EXEC SQL SELECT S.LOCATION INTO :SL FROM S WHERE S.SUPPNUM = 'S4' END-EXEC.	Statement ends with END-EXEC.
FORTRAN	EXEC SQL SELECT S.LOCATION * INTO :SL * FROM S * WHERE S.SUPPNUM = 'S4'	* is the continuation character in column 6 of the next line

application program. Names of data-items and tables are used as discussed before. Names of variables defined by the application program (called host variables) have a colon (:) at the beginning of the variable's name.

Host variables can provide input to the SQL statement as well as receive the results of the SQL statement. One of these capabilities is illustrated in Exhibit 6-9. The host variable :SL receives the results of the query. The program can then use this variable for any desired processing.

The examples in Exhibit 6-9 return a single value for the host variable, so the value can be placed directly into the host variable. Application programs often issue SQL queries that return multiple rows, and in this case, the programming becomes more complicated. There must be a loop in the program that reads and processes a row at a time until all rows are processed. SQL retrieves sets of rows from the data base and maintains a cursor. Then SQL steps the cursor through the rows one at a time and passes each to the host variables for further processing.

The attraction of these approaches is that you can use SQL within familiar, standard languages. However, the interface between the procedural row-at-a-time approach of the programming language is cumbersome and defeats many of the relational intentions of performing operations on entire sets of rows.

Query-by-Example

In addition to being incorporated into programming languages, SQL can be incorporated into end-user tools such as spreadsheets. The system can include menus or prompts that guide the user in specifying the table operations underlying SQL. The system generates and executes the appropriate SQL statements without the user specifying them in detail. This is the direction for the future.

209

CHAPTER 6
*Relational
Data Bases
and the
Structured
Query
Language*

Of these alternative uses of SQL, the one used most is Query-by-Example, and most relational DBMS also support QBE. QBE displays table structures on the screen and allows the user to choose interactively the data needed and the operations to be performed. QBE thus uses a graphical approach to query formulation. QBE displays a table structure, and the user forms the query by entering operators and data into the skeleton structure. Conditions can use comparison operators, such as greater than or less than; expressions, such as computations based on data-item values; and lists and ranges of values.

The user has enormous control over the query and can

1. Add columns to the table to display values calculated from other columns.
2. Specify a sequence for displaying the results.
3. Join two or more tables by specifying example elements.
4. Specify built-in functions for an entire table or for groups of rows.
5. Link multiple queries using example elements to determine values to be used in a condition. The linked queries can be for different tables or the same table.
6. Merge the results of two or more queries.
7. Insert, update, and delete data.

As a result of these capabilities, QBE can perform most of the functions of SQL. Each RDBMS has its own implementation of QBE and, as a result, QBE has different limitations. However, QBE cannot perform the following functions:

1. Create, alter, or drop a table.
2. Create or drop a view.
3. Grant or revoke authorization.

Paradox is the microcomputer DBMS which is most effective in implementing QBE. The next section will show the Paradox QBE approach to answering the same queries that are also answered using SQL, the dBASE language, and the SAS language.

Comparison of SQL with dBASE, Paradox, and SAS

This section will compare SQL to other popular data base languages, including dBASE, Paradox, and SAS. The aim is not to teach dBASE, Paradox, or SAS in one section of a chapter. An industry of data base programmers-consultants exists because these data base languages are difficult to learn and to use in a practical application. Rather, the aim is to illustrate data bases, tables, projections, and joins and to provide an introduction to packages that are frequently found in business applications.

Refer to Exhibit 6-7, the Supplier/Parts/Shipments data base used earlier to illustrate SQL. Exhibit 6-10 provides the alternative commands for each of the data base languages discussed here. Paradox is illustrated here by using its Query-by-Example capability. Paradox also has a programming language, PAL,

EXHIBIT 6-10 Comparison of SQL, dBASE, Paradox, and SAS

Projection: Get supplier numbers for suppliers who supply part P1.

SQL	SELECT SP.SUPPNUM FROM SP WHERE SP.PARTNUM = 'P1'
dBASE	USE SP DISPLAY SUPPNUM FOR PARTNUM = 'P1'
Paradox	SHIPMENT ═══SUPPNUM═══╤═══PARTNUM═══╤═══QTY═══ | √ | | P1 |

SAS	DATA PROJECT;
	       SET SP;
	       IF PARTNUM = 'P1';
	       KEEP SUPPNUM;

Join: Get all shipments (part number, part name, and supplier number columns only) that are
    supplied by supplier S3 or use part P1.

SQL	SELECT P.PARTNUM, P.PARTNAME, SP.SUPPNUM FROM P, SP WHERE P.PARTNUM = SP.PARTNUM AND (SP.SUPPNUM = 'S3' or SP.PARTNUM = 'P1')
dBASE	SELECT 1 USE SP COPY TO S3P1 FOR SUPPNUM = 'S3' .OR. PARTNUM = 'P1' USE S3P1 SELECT 2 USE P JOIN WITH A TO PN FOR PARTNUM = A—>PARTNUM FIELDS PARTNUM, PARTNAME, SUPPNUM USE PN DISPLAY ALL

Paradox	SHIPMENT ═══SUPPNUM═══╤═══PARTNUM═══╤═══QTY═══
	  | √ S3 | | / P1 |
	                          abc
	
	PARTS ═PARTNUM═╤═PARTNAME═╤═METAL═╤═WEIGHT═╤═LOCATION═
	  | abc | √ |

SAS	PROC SORT DATA = SP; BY PARTNUM;
	PROC SORT DATA = P; BY PARTNUM;
	DATA JOIN;
	       MERGE SP P;
	       BY PARTNUM;
	       IF SUPPNUM = 'S3' OR PARTNUM = 'P1';
	       KEEP PARTNUM PARTNAME SUPPNUM;

which could be used to write programs to answer the questions. QBE, however, is more direct.

211

CHAPTER 6
Relational
Data Bases
and the
Structured
Query
Language

Projection.   As discussed earlier in the chapter, the most important operations are projections and joins. Consider the projection necessary to get the supplier numbers for suppliers who supply part P1. The result is S1 and S2.

Join.   Create a view consisting of all projects (part number, part name, and supplier number columns only) that are supplied by supplier S3 or use part P1. The result of this join would be

Partnum	Partname	Suppnum
P1	Lever	S1
P1	Lever	S2
P2	Knob	S3

Advantages of SQL

SQL has several advantages over its alternatives:

Connection to Easier-to-Use Tools.   Because SQL can directly manipulate data as sets, there is no need for the one row at a time approach of procedural tools.

Reduced Training Costs.   Rather than teach everyone who needs to access a data base the procedural tools of traditional data base systems, the user can apply SQL directly, or indirectly through QBE, much more easily.

Application Portability.   SQL applications move between different DBMS, different operating systems, and different computer hardware much more easily than traditional data base languages.

Application Longevity.   As the RDBMS technology improves and computer hardware gets faster, the results of transaction processing and querying capability will also improve and get faster. But the queries themselves and the data language for them will not need to be changed.

Cross-System Communication.   The relational nature of SQL has propelled it as the language for connections between different computers because of its support of data independence. Distributed data bases among many different types of computers become possible because

1. Computers can now communicate in a standard language with different remote data base servers.
2. Data base functions, including integrity and security, are now centrally, relationally, effectively, and efficiently managed by those servers.
3. Only the data required are moved between computers. This improves performance, preserves data reliability, distributes the processing load, and eliminates conversions between different data base formats.

212

Part II
Technical
Aspects of
Accounting
Information
Systems

4. Distributed DBMS will decide which DBMS on which computer should perform an operation on distributed data in order to optimize overall performance.
5. Tools and applications running on microcomputers will be able to operate on data bases that exist on any computer. This reduces the importance of portability of applications between computers.

Disadvantages of SQL

The forces behind SQL are so strong at this point that any alternative will be a long time in coming. Nonetheless, there are several problems with SQL:

Lack of Referential Integrity. If a key should exist in a related table, but does not exist, then the data base lacks referential integrity. For example, in Exhibit 6-8, there is an example of the INSERT statement to add a row to the table SP with the value of 'S5' for SUPPNUM, 'P1' for PARTNUM, and 1000 for QTY. How is it possible to ensure that 'S5' is in the S table and that 'P1' is in the P table? Without this assurance, the relational connections between the tables do not exist. SQL does not now ensure that the connections exist and that referential integrity is maintained.

Redundancy. All but the most trivial of problems can be expressed in SQL in a variety of different ways. For example, suppose a user wants the names for suppliers who supply part P2. One approach would be the following:

```
SELECT    S.SUPPNAME
FROM      S, SP
WHERE     S.SUPPNUM = SP.SUPPNUM
          AND SP.SUPPNUM = 'P2'
```

However, another approach to the same query would be:

```
SELECT    S.SUPPNAME
FROM      S
WHERE     SUPPNUM IN
          (SELECT SUPPNUM FROM SP
          WHERE PARTNUM = 'P2')
```

These differences would not be important if all formulations worked equally well, but that is unlikely. As a result, users are forced to search for the version that performs best, which is one of the things the relational model was trying to avoid in the first place. Actually, the entire "IN subquery" construct could be deleted from SQL with no loss of function, though with some loss of compatibility with existing applications.

Lack of Orthogonality. In English, this means that the rules are not consistent. Different language concepts are not cleanly separated, and there are a number of seemingly arbitrary restrictions, exceptions, and rules.

Lack of a Complete Standard. The ANSI standard, while an advance, is still not complete. It has the three problems just discussed (referential integrity,

213

CHAPTER 6
*Relational
Data Bases
and the
Structured
Query
Language*

redundancy, and lack of orthogonality) and does not even satisfy all of the characteristics of the relational approach discussed earlier. In these important matters the standard lags behind some commercial implementations, especially DB2. Also, the standard concentrates on the proper form of SQL statements and leaves important aspects to the developers, such as how to store data. Thus, it is possible for two SQL implementations to conform to the standard and yet be incompatible with each other. Most SQL developers extend their dialects beyond the standard and exploit the laxity of the standard by claiming compatibility for products that are not genuine SQL implementations. This creates significant difficulties for those who want to use SQL DBMS and for those who must decide which products to choose—one problem the relational approach was intended to solve.

Different Data Types for Each Host Language and Architecture. The SQL standard defines different data base data types for each host language. There is no guarantee, for example, that a data base created by a COBOL program will be accessible by a program in another language. Further, important matters are left as implementation defined, with the result that a standard application that runs on a Digital Equipment Corporation VAX computer may not run on an IBM mainframe.

Difficult Changes and New Challenges. Issues such as simultaneous users, security, and data administration are complex and were ignored in early microcomputer data base systems. These issues must now be addressed by data base software and managed by microcomputer users. Also, the trend toward SQL pushes progress in both hardware and software because of SQL's processing demands as well as the new capabilities it makes possible. SQL pushes for:

1. Hardware progress on the central processor, on disk storage, and on the connection between them.
2. Software progress toward more sophisticated operating systems which can handle multiple requests simultaneously and which can use large amounts of memory.
3. Software progress toward connections between microcomputers.

SQL is a relational data language whose dialects are different in many ways. Nonetheless, these dialects have more advantages and more in common with each other than do the proprietary, procedural data languages in existence.

REFERENCES

AMERICAN NATIONAL STANDARDS INSTITUTE, *Database Language SQL,* Document ANSI X3.135-1986. Also available as International Standards Organization Document ISO/TC97/SC21/WG3 N117.

D. D. CHAMBERLAIN et al., "A History and Evaluation of System R," *Communications of the ACM*, Vol. 24, No. 10 (October 1981).

214

PART II
Technical
Aspects of
Accounting
Information
Systems

E. F. CODD, "A Relational Model of Data for Large Shared Data Banks," *Communications of the ACM*, Vol. 13, No. 6 (June 1970); reprinted in *Communications of the ACM*, Vol. 26, No. 1 (January 1983).

C. J. DATE, *An Introduction to Database Systems*, Volume I, 4th ed. (Reading, MA: Addison-Wesley, 1985); Volume II, 1st ed. (Reading, MA: Addison-Wesley, 1983).

C. J. DATE, *A Guide to DB2* (Reading, MA: Addison-Wesley, 1984); *A Guide to INGRES* (Reading, MA: Addison-Wesley, 1987).

CHAPTER SUMMARY

Accounting data are more and more in relational data bases, so that in addition to traditional analysis and reporting, the data can also answer the ad hoc queries that arise in the course of business. Relational data bases have proved to be the easiest to query. Hierarchical (or tree) approaches are the fastest in transaction processing but are too rigid and difficult to modify. Network (or plex) approaches fall between these two in both flexibility and speed and are falling out of favor.

Relational data bases keep their data in a series of related flat files called tables. These tables hold data in a row and column format, with the rows corresponding to records and the columns corresponding to fields or data-items. Logical tables called views can be formed from other tables by combining them or extracting from them to let some users see only part of the full data base. The two most widely used operations in relational data bases are the projection, which restricts data from the tables, and the join, which combines different tables based upon a matching key.

Data in a relational data base must be put into row and column format; this is called first normal form. Second normal form eliminates redundancies based upon the primary key. Third normal form eliminates redundancies based on any secondary keys. Fourth normal form eliminates any multivalue dependencies. Fifth normal form eliminates join dependencies. Data should be completely normalized and views used to join data which are often put together in answering queries.

Structured Query Language is the primary language for manipulating relational data bases. SQL uses the structure SELECT/FROM/WHERE to perform most of its operations. The user SELECTS data-items, identifies FROM which tables these data-items are drawn, and gives the conditions they must satisfy in the WHERE clause. SQL has the capability of creating table structures, modifying table values, querying tables, and establishing views. SQL can be used interactively or embedded in a more complete programming language like C, COBOL, or FORTRAN. Query-by-Example is an alternative to SQL which displays table structures on the screen and allows the user to choose interactively the data needed and the operations to be performed. There are other popular data base languages, including dBASE, Paradox, and SAS, but the trend is to standardize on SQL and QBE, rather than learn many different proprietary languages.

KEY TERMS

215

CHAPTER 6
*Relational
Data Bases
and the
Structured
Query
Language*

Base table (*p. 190*)
Column (*p. 192*)
Create statement (*p. 204*)
Delete statement (*p. 207*)
Fifth normal form (*p. 196*)
First normal form (*p. 194*)
Fourth normal form (*p. 196*)
Insert statement (*p. 207*)
Joins (*p. 192*)
Projections (*p. 192*)
Queries (*p. 188*)

Query-by-Example (QBE) (*p. 188*)
Relational DBMS (RDBMS) (*p. 189*)
Relational table (*p. 192*)
Row (*p. 192*)
Second normal form (*p. 194*)
Structured Query Language (SQL)
   (*p. 188*)
Third normal form (*p. 196*)
Unnormalized (*p. 201*)
Update statement (*p. 207*)
Views (*p. 190*)

QUESTIONS

6-1. Why is the development of the relational data base approach and SQL important to accountants?

6-2. Describe the advantages and disadvantages of the three approaches to data base management.

6-3. Give the characteristics of a relational data base management system.

6-4. Identify the traditional deficiencies of other data base approaches.

6-5. List three practical advantages of the relational approach.

6-6. Define projections and joins and explain the usefulness of each.

6-7. Explain the purposes of normalization.

6-8. Distinguish between first, second, third, fourth, and fifth normal forms.

6-9. Explain the performance considerations involved in deciding whether to store redundant data.

6-10. Identify the main trends involving relational data bases.

6-11. Give the main purpose of the Structured Query Language.

6-12. Describe the structure of a query using SQL, including the purpose of each of its three parts.

6-13. Identify the capabilities of SQL in addition to answering queries.

6-14. How is SQL used in more traditional programming languages?

6-15. Contrast SQL and QBE.

6-16. Compare and contrast SQL with dBASE, Paradox, and SAS.

6-17. Give the advantages and disadvantages of SQL.

PROBLEMS

6-18. Respond to each of the following statements:

a. A relational DBMS is one that handles multiple files at a time.

b. The relational approach is theoretical, and, therefore, it has no practical relevance for users.

c. New technologies, such as object-oriented or semantic data bases, are making the relational approach obsolete.

216

PART II
Technical
Aspects of
Accounting
Information
Systems

    d. SQL is useful only for connecting microcomputers to minicomputer or mainframe data.

    e. An SQL interface can offer full relational benefits while preserving compatibility with existing applications.

    f. Relational DBMS require the user to learn and use SQL directly. This is more difficult than using traditional data bases.

    g. If a DBMS provides easy-to-use icons, menus, and screens, then the user need not care about the underlying data base technology.

    h. The same relational benefits can come from any combination of front-end tool on the client computer and SQL back-end on the server computer.

    i. To retrieve 100 records from a data base requires issuing 100 separate SQL statements, each retrieving one row.

    j. DBMS enforcement of integrity is not important because the user does that anyway.

    k. The relational approach shifts the burden of managing the data base from the users to the DBMS.

6-19. In the section on disadvantages of SQL, there is an example of its redundancy with two alternative ways of expressing the same query. There are five more superficially different alternatives. Identify them.

6-20. Join the two tables in fourth normal form in the middle of Exhibit 6-6. How does this compare to the table in third normal form in the same exhibit?

6-21. Show the process of joining the three tables at the bottom of Exhibit 6-6 that are in fifth normal form. How does this compare to the table in third normal form in the same exhibit?

THE NEXT TEN PROBLEMS WILL USE THE FOUR TABLES
IN EXHIBIT 6-11.
In each case, give the SQL statement(s) required as well as the resulting table.

6-22. Identify all projects (project number and city columns only) that are supplied by supplier S1 or use part P1.

6-23. Identify supplier numbers and part numbers for suppliers and parts that are not located in the same city.

6-24. Get supplier numbers for suppliers who supply project R1.

6-25. Get all shipments where the quantity is in the range 300 to 750.

6-26. Get all supplier number/part number/project number triples such that the indicated supplier, part, and project are all located in the same city.

6-27. Get the total number of projects supplied by supplier S1.

6-28. Get the total quantity of part P1 supplied by supplier S1.

6-29. Change the color of all red parts to orange.

EXHIBIT 6-11   Supplier/Parts/Projects/Shipments Data Base

217

CHAPTER 6
*Relational
Data Bases
and the
Structured
Query
Language*

S—Suppliers

Suppnum	Suppname	Status	Location
S1	Seuling	20	Chicago
S2	Heider	10	Seattle
S3	Albelli	30	Seattle
S4	Page	20	Chicago
S5	Hooper	30	Houston

P—Parts

Partnum	Partname	Metal	Weight	Location
P1	Lever	Steel	12	Chicago
P2	Knob	Alum	17	Seattle
P3	Cover	Alloy	17	Dallas
P4	Cover	Steel	14	Chicago
P5	Base	Alloy	12	Seattle
P6	Brace	Steel	19	Chicago

R—Projects

Projnum	Projname	Location
R1	Disk	Seattle
R2	DotPrinter	Dallas
R3	Monitor	Houston
R4	Keyboard	Houston
R5	LaserPrinter	Chicago
R6	Terminal	Atlanta
R7	Tape	Chicago

(Exhibit continues on next page.)

218

PART II
Technical
Aspects of
Accounting
Information
Systems

EXHIBIT 6-11 Supplier/Parts/Projects/Shipments Data Base (continued)

SPR—Shipments

Suppnum	Partnum	Projnum	Qty
S1	P1	R1	200
S1	P1	R4	700
S2	P3	R1	400
S2	P3	R2	200
S2	P3	R3	200
S2	P3	R4	500
S2	P3	R5	600
S2	P3	R6	400
S2	P3	R7	800
S2	P5	R2	100
S3	P3	R1	200
S3	P4	R2	500
S4	P6	R3	300
S4	P6	R7	300
S5	P2	R2	200
S5	P2	R4	100
S5	P5	R5	500
S5	P5	R7	100
S5	P6	R2	200
S5	P1	R4	100
S5	P3	R4	200
S5	P4	R4	800
S5	P5	R4	400
S5	P6	R4	500

219

CHAPTER 6
*Relational
Data Bases
and the
Structured
Query
Language*

6-30. Delete all projects for which there are no shipments.

6-31. Get supplier numbers for suppliers supplying some project with part P1 in a quantity greater than the average in which part P1 is supplied to that project.

6-32. Using the data base software available to you:

1. Split the EMPLOYEE table in Exhibit 6-2 into its second normal form.
2. Demonstrate that no information was lost in this step in the normalization process (requirement 1) by creating a table that lists Richards's employee number, job code, job title, all projects Richards is assigned to, the completion date on the projects, and the hours worked on each project (include Richards's name in the final table).

6-33. Using the data base software available to you, split the EMPLOYEE table in Exhibit 6-3 into the third normal form presented in Exhibit 6-4.

6-34. Using the data base software available to you, split the EMPLOYEE-DEPT-TASK table in Exhibit 6-6 into

a. The fourth normal form
b. The fifth normal form

DECISION CASE

Using the data base software available to you:

1. Create the three tables in Exhibit 6-7.
2. Get supplier numbers for suppliers who supply part P2.
3. Get all shipments (part number, part name, and supplier number columns) that are supplied by supplier S2 or use part P2.
4. Get supplier number, part number, quantity, and average quantity for all shipments of part P2.
5. Using the table created in part (4), list all supplier numbers and names for all suppliers that supply part P2 in quantities greater than the average.
6. Add supplier S6, whose name is Stone with a status of 20, located in Toronto.
7. Add a new field in each supplier record for the COUNTRY where the supplier is located.
8. Add the country to each record.
9. Increase the STATUS for all suppliers by 10.
10. Supplier S3 is no longer an approved vendor; delete Albelli's record.

7 Data Communications and Networks

Overview

How the hardware, software, management, and internal control aspects of business data processing systems change when operations occur at widely different locations.

Learning Objectives

Thorough study of this chapter will enable you to:

1. Explain why data communications are important to an accounting information system.
2. Describe the IBM mainframe approach to data communications.
3. List the advantages and disadvantages of IBM's System Network Architecture (SNA).
4. Describe the capabilities of the minicomputer.
5. Differentiate among the options for networking minicomputers.
6. Describe the microcomputer approach to data communications and networking.
7. Give examples of how mainframes, minicomputers, and microcomputers are beginning to take on the characteristics of one another.
8. List current trends in communications involving electronic data processing.
9. Show how network management affects internal control.

Outline

SYSTEMS IN THE REAL WORLD

221

CHAPTER 7
Data
Communi-
cations and
Networks

The Trail of an Electronic Transaction

1 Customer buys diamond earrings for $895 in Detroit. The clerk passes the Visa card through a credit-verification terminal and punches in purchase data.

2 The data travel by satellite, land lines, or microwave to National Data Corp.'s computers in Cherry Hill, N.J.

3 From Cherry Hill the credit query goes to NDC headquarters in Atlanta for processing.

The transaction tops $50, so it needs a second opinion. The request is turned over to Visa USA minicomputers at NDC.

4 The Visa minis shoot the query to mainframes in McLean, Va., or San Mateo, Calif.

5 The Visa mainframe determines that the card is from a San Francisco bank and sends the transaction to the bank's computer, which checks to see if there is $895 in available credit.

The bank's O.K. retraces the path of the authorization request: From the bank to Visa USA to NDC in Atlanta to NDC in Cherry Hill to the merchant in Detroit.

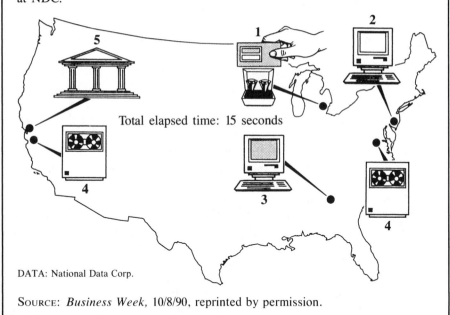

Total elapsed time: 15 seconds

DATA: National Data Corp.

SOURCE: *Business Week*, 10/8/90, reprinted by permission.

ACCOUNTING AND DATA COMMUNICATIONS

Accounting Need for Data Communications

In the first years of business data processing, data communications were not critical to accounting information systems because the transactions were first recorded on paper before they were made machine readable. The transactions

222

PART II
Technical
Aspects of
Accounting
Information
Systems

could then be processed either locally or centrally, but the system was not dependent on data communications because the physical document was sent to the location of the data processing. Now, however, data communications are becoming critically important components of an accounting information system. The reasons are that

1. *Transactions are first recorded electronically, rather than physically.* An example is the electronic cash register with bar code scanner that reads the item and quantity being purchased and gets the price from computer storage and captures the entire transaction electronically.

2. *Transactions occur far from where their significance is assessed.* An example is the accumulation of information from branch stores on which items are selling and which are not. The totals for each store and combinations by region, line of product, and so on need to be seen at regional or national headquarters for efficient and timely restocking or repricing.

3. *Transactions depend on data that are located far away.* An example is a credit card sale that requires a credit check from the credit card computer. This central computer will often be hundreds or thousands of miles from the transaction.

Data Communication Through Networks

Thus, the proper processing of accounting transactions now requires major investments in the communication between the computers processing transactions, those analyzing information, and those maintaining data files. For all of these communications to take place, a number of physical and logical connections are needed. The aggregate of those connections is called a **network,** and each entity that communicates on the network is said to be a user of the network. This network can be either a **local area network (LAN)** for microcomputers, or a user-defined custom network to connect virtually any type of device. In the past, there have been separate voice and data communications networks. Some companies have now integrated these functions into the same network, while others still keep the two separate.

Networks are getting very large: There are private networks with over 60,000 separate users. The city of New York leases 6,000 telephone lines for computer communications supporting services such as police, fire, and ambulance dispatch. Merrill Lynch & Co. links over 600 brokerage locations in the United States, Canada, and overseas; this network runs 24 hours a day, 7 days a week. DuPont has a network in the United States connecting 108,000 phones and computer terminals. The Health and Welfare Agency Data Center of California, which requires that 90 percent of on-line transactions be completed within 4 seconds, processes 6 million transactions per week with over 350 simultaneous users.

The reason for the rapid growth of networks is that they reduce costs, provide better customer service, and improve managerial decision making. Exhibit 7-1 provides some examples of these uses of data communication and networking. These applications are in virtually every industry, including airlines, banks, broadcasting, education, health care, insurance, manufacturing and retailing. The importance of such systems was illustrated by the Chairman of the Board of American Airlines; he stated that if he had to choose between selling the reservation system and selling the airline, he would sell the airline.

EXHIBIT 7-1 **Networks as a Competitive Edge—Industry Examples**

223

CHAPTER 7
*Data
Communi-
cations and
Networks*

Industry	Example Applications	Benefits
Airlines	Reservation system for airlines, lodging, and rental cars; automatic ticketing; computerized flight information	Market differentiation from competitors; fee from participating hotels and car agencies; better customer service; fewer airline personnel
Banks	Communications between remote branches; network allowing customers to use another bank's automated teller machine (ATM) to perform routine transactions; access to bank's data base for loan application information	Better coordination and decision making; customer reponsiveness; fewer personnel needed; faster transfer of funds (less float); faster loan decisions; enhanced productivity of loan officers
Broadcasting	Satellites and movable receivers on trucks for news coverage; links to sophisticated graphics for creation of art, headlines, etc.	Exclusive coverage potential of news or special events drawing high viewership; better image and viewer interest
Education	Microcomputer access between students and faculty; on-line registration for courses	Better student/faculty relations due to timely information and feedback; faster response to student needs
Health care	Image transmission to doctors for diagnosis; at-home patient monitoring; emergency communications to patients needing organ transplants	Better decision making; saving lives while reducing in-hospital costs
Insurance	Network links to agents in remote locations; on-line access to applictions for risk and policy analysis	More timely communications of policies and new products; faster and improved decision making
Manufacturing	Standard methods for suppliers of information systems hardware and software; links between manufacturing, quality control, accounting, and management	Reduced costs of development; higher productivity; better management control
Retailing	Access to data base of store sales and purchases; automatic bar codes reading, check and charge card authorization feeding into customer billing information system; information transferred to remote billing and collections site; networked inventory at all locations; automated reordering	Better buying decisions; enhanced productivity and better input/access to functions at remote sites; better deployment of inventory; reduced staff; better reordering

224

PART II
Technical
Aspects of
Accounting
Information
Systems

Obstacles to Understanding Data Communications

The computer user of data communications capabilities must know a great deal about the technical aspects of data communication. The computer industry is far from the happy state of the consumer audio industry, where equipment such as tuners, amplifiers, and compact disc (CD) players from different manufacturers and different countries all connect and can be used together. This interconnection of communications hardware, communications software, and various computers is still a distant goal.

Data communications and networks are difficult topics to master for several reasons:

Different terminology. Different names exist for the same thing. For example, IBM often uses terms that are different from those used elsewhere in the industry.

Different approaches. Often, different alternatives exist, with neither approach having advantages over the other. Conceivably, while Ford puts the steering wheel on the left of the car, Chevrolet could put it on the right. However, the automobile industry recognized the value of standardization. Standardization is now impossible in the computer industry because of the installed base of equipment using each of the approaches. For example, the connection to IBM's midrange computers has different wiring, keyboard, screen, and control software from the connection to the IBM mainframes.

Obsolete technology still in use. Obsolete technology is still being used, even though it is no longer manufactured or sold. It must therefore still be understood. For example, although IBM replaced its former data transmission method with a superior one, the former method, now obsolete, remains in widespread use.

Exhibit 7-2 gives an overview of some of the basic choices that must be made in the use of data communications. In most data communications choices,

EXHIBIT 7-2 Choices in Data Communications

Issue	Choices	Explanation	Advantages/Disadvantages
Communications between computers	Telephone line	Modem converts from digital to analog at the transmitting end and another modem at the receiving end converts from analog back to digital	Hardwiring often not available, such as remote communications with limited volume
	Direct line	Hardwire with direct digital communication	Fastest transfer of information with the least interference from noise
Telephone line	POTS	Plain old telephone service; regular dial-up telephone service	Noise on the telephone line; not dedicated to data transmission
	Leased line	Users have own line	More expensive; error rate is much lower

Exhibit continues on next page

EXHIBIT 7-2   Choices in Data Communications (continued)

Issue	Choices	Explanation	Advantages/Disadvantages
Direct line	Twisted pair	Media involving a pair of copper wires; unshielded twisted pair is the same as phone wire	Lines susceptible to noise and cannot be run past any heavy equipment; can be shielded to extend these limits somewhat
	Coaxial cable	Central core of conducting material surrounded by an insulated sheath	More expensive than twisted pair; data transmission speed is increased and the usable distance is increased
	Fiber optic cable	Lasers transmit information along a fiber optic (glass) wire	Allows high-speed transmission of data; transmissions are not susceptible to noise
Transmission methods	Asynchronous	Sends or receives one character at a time; beginning (start) and end (stop) of each character is identified	Slower; equipment is less expensive
	Synchronous	Continuous transmissions; start and stop of each character is not marked	Faster; when the timing gets out of synchronization, data are lost and must be retransmitted
Coding standard	**ASCII**	**American Standard Code for Information Interchange;** eight bits per byte coding system where the rightmost seven bits represent letters, numbers and characters	Used for all equipment except IBM mainframes
	EBCDIC	**Extended Binary Coded Decimal Interchange Code;** eight-bit code with two four-bit portions	Used only on IBM mainframes
Network configurations	Star	Central computer (the host computer) connected to terminals or other computers	Better control; network depends on central computer, which must grow as terminals or computers are connected to it
	Ring	Connects computers (not terminals) in a circle	More difficult to set up; if one computer goes down, network continues to operate and identifies which computer is down
	Bus	Connection of computers to a core wire, which can be either twisted pair or coaxial cable	Easy to add new computers; when there is a problem on the line, the system cannot tell which computer is down

226

PART II
Technical
Aspects of
Accounting
Information
Systems

there is a tradeoff between speed and price. A direct line connecting computers is faster, but using a telephone line is less expensive over moderate to long distances. Among direct lines, twisted pair is the slowest but least expensive, while fiber optic cable is the fastest but most expensive, with coaxial cable in the middle of both speed and price. The regular telephone lines are slower but less expensive, while a leased line is faster and more expensive. Asynchronous transmission of information is slower but less expensive, while synchronous transmission is faster and more expensive. In any particular situation, the choice among these various alternatives would depend upon the business need for speed.

However, there are tradeoffs other than that between speed and price in other communications choices. In the case of the choice between the ASCII and EBCDIC coding standards, both are equivalent; they are just different ways of doing the same thing. Network configurations tradeoff control for ease of use; the star provides more control but is harder to use, while the bus provides less control while being easier to use; the ring is in the middle of both control and ease of use.

THE IBM MAINFRAME APPROACH

The first, mainframe-oriented IBM approach to data communications and networks was developed for on-line transaction processing (OLTP). (OLTP was discussed in Chapter 3 as the most sophisticated approach to business data processing.) IBM developed this approach before the emergence of the microcomputer and has subsequently responded to this development; later, this chapter will discuss these responses. However, understanding data communications and networking and its usefulness for business data processing begins with the IBM mainframe-oriented approach to OLTP because it dominates the current market, with over 80 percent of high-end systems. There are now over 4,000,000 terminals connected to over 10,000 mainframes using this IBM mainframe-oriented approach.

This approach had two primary goals:

1. Have the mainframe do all processing of data, including all accesses of data from data bases and all computations.
2. Move everything else off of the mainframe, because even the largest mainframe could not do everything. What this meant in practice was that all communications-related tasks were delegated to other devices.

Hardware Components

The IBM mainframe-oriented approach includes the following components:

Mainframe. From the user's standpoint, the mainframe does have advantages, primarily the centralization of control. The central mainframe in a communications environment is called the host. Current mainframes are the successors to the System/370; the latest versions are called the System/390.

Communications Controller. Directly connected to the mainframe is a communications controller, which is in essence a smaller, special-purpose computer of its own. The communications controller accepts information from a wide range of sources (discussed shortly) and then channels it into a single stream of information for the mainframe to process. Several communications controllers can be attached to one mainframe.

Cluster Controller. Communicating with the communications controller are typically several cluster controllers. The purpose of the cluster controller is to control several terminals.

Terminals. A terminal consists primarily of a screen and keyboard connected directly and synchronously to a cluster controller. This terminal does little more than transfer keystrokes to the cluster controller and display information sent to it from the cluster controller.

Exhibit 7-3 provides a schematic of the IBM mainframe approach.

Operating System Software

Multiple Virtual System (MVS) is the primary IBM operating system, the one on which the large-scale transaction processing mainframes depend. All extremely large-scale programming applications, such as the data base management systems IMS and DB2 (see Chapters 5 and 6), are designed for MVS. MVS is extremely complex, now with over 20 million lines of programming code, and is one of the most difficult-to-use operating systems in existence. Effective use of MVS requires a large, extremely skilled data processing staff. However, if the application demands it, this operating system is the only alternative.

EXHIBIT 7-3   Schematic of the IBM Mainframe Approach

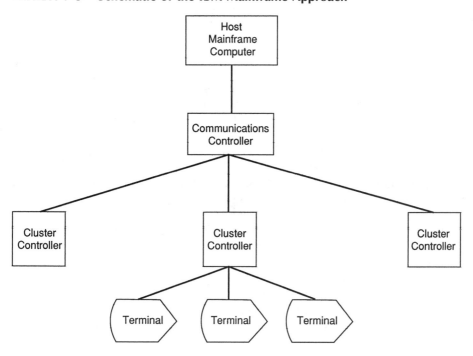

227

CHAPTER 7
Data
Communi-
cations and
Networks

228

PART II
Technical
Aspects of
Accounting
Information
Systems

A software layer on MVS does most of the detailed work necessary for an application program (typically written in COBOL) to use terminals for input and output. This makes using terminals about as difficult as using files. A large-scale application program can easily have hundreds of simultaneous users; each user shares the same program, so a single program can have hundreds of sessions (each terminal/user/application program is one session).

There will typically be hundreds of terminals connected to an IBM mainframe. Each of these terminals will be sending information to and receiving information from one or more application programs it is using. In order to share communication lines efficiently, the information from the terminals is split up into and sent as packets. These packets of information arrive at random times as the user at the terminal enters the information. The packets from these hundreds of different sources go into a stream of data for each application session which then passes the information to the application program.

MVS was designed as a transaction processing operating system. However, there are other on-line applications for a shared user system, such as electronic mail, engineering applications, text processing, and software development. Designers of MVS sacrificed these other on-line applications in order to achieve maximum efficiency for transaction processing. Later, IBM added a software module on top of MVS for these other on-line applications. Unfortunately, this module is extremely inefficient and consumes major quantities of mainframe resources, so the module is used only when absolutely necessary. IBM has two separate operating systems, VM/CMS and MUSIC, which are less resource-intensive alternatives to MVS.

IBM uses the same basic approach with its midrange AS/400 series computers. However, the entire process is greatly simplified. The cost, both initially and in support staff, is greatly reduced. However, the capacity of these systems is limited in comparison with the System/390 mainframes.

Network Design: System Network Architecture

Virtually every network application requires a custom network tailored to the individual situation. Exhibit 7-4 gives a "simple" schematic of an IBM mainframe network with connections to other networks; the network controller provides any necessary conversions, such as between ASCII and EBCDIC (see Exhibit 7-2). Unfortunately, designing, building, and operating such a network is extraordinarily difficult. Only firms such as airlines, which absolutely require a complete network to tie together worldwide reservations, have more than a few pieces of a fully functioning network.

The most complete network design is IBM's **System Network Architecture (SNA).** SNA is very flexible and it works. Also, it is comforting to know that the vendor is likely to be around in the future. The disadvantages of SNA are that it is extremely complex and enormously expensive. These disadvantages make SNA too difficult and costly for routine setup of large-scale networks. Additionally, some important areas of SNA are still in the planning stages, even though IBM introduced SNA in 1974. The slowness of its development underscores the complexity of data communications and networking.

EXHIBIT 7-4   A Schematic of a Network

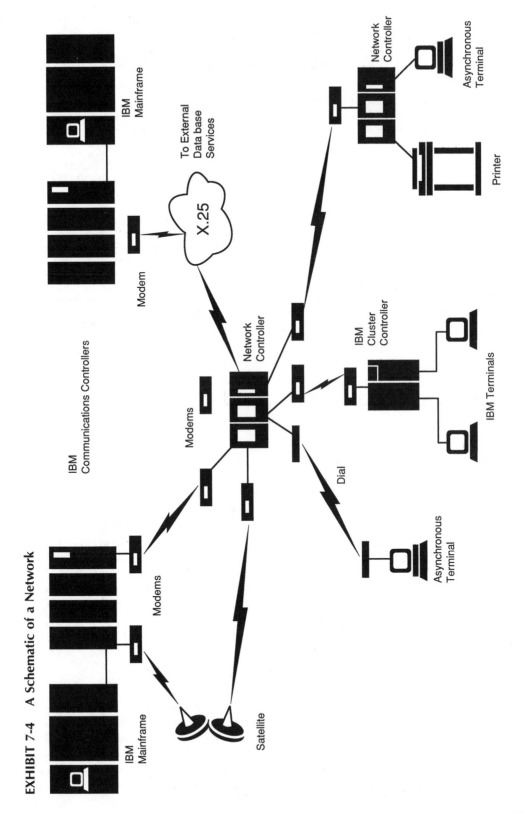

230

*PART II
Technical
Aspects of
Accounting
Information
Systems*

	C O N C E P T S U M M A R Y		
	Initial IBM Approach to On-Line Transaction Processing		
	Device	*Functions*	
Hardware	Mainframe	All processing; centralized data storage; all control of the network	
	Communications controller	Concentration of streams of data from various cluster controllers	
	Cluster controller	Control of terminals; set up data to transfer to communications controller	
	Terminal	Transmit screen of information to cluster controller and display screen of information from cluster controller	
Software	Multiple Virtual System	Operating system; controls terminals for application program so that terminals appear like external files; takes packets of information as it comes in from the communications controller and separates into the communication sessions	

Advantages and Disadvantages of the Initial IBM Approach

IBM mainframe on-line processing is very efficient at transaction processing because other functions that could slow down the processor are moved to other devices. Also, by providing centralized control over the data, this approach helps to ensure security, accuracy, and privacy. However, this approach is extremely expensive and very difficult to set up. Also, as changes occur, it is difficult to modify the network with new devices and the movement of devices. Finally, this approach, since it was developed before the introduction of the microcomputer, does not take advantage of the capabilities of the microcomputer.

THE MINICOMPUTER APPROACH

IBM mainframes were designed for transaction processing. On-line but non-transaction-processing applications, such as electronic mail, engineering computations, text processing, and system development, were extremely inefficient and extremely expensive on IBM systems. Digital Equipment Corporation (DEC) designed a machine, which it called a minicomputer, especially for these other on-line applications. Because of its on-line orientation and low cost, the minicomputer could do transaction processing on a smaller scale than the IBM mainframes. DEC was enormously successful with the minicomputer approach and is now the second largest computer company in the world, though still about one-fourth the size of IBM.

The minicomputer supports a number of (inexpensive) terminals, so each minicomputer user has a terminal and a share of the central processor and its resources, such as tapes, disks, and printers. Minicomputer users can communicate easily, since they are all connected to the same machine. They can easily share data and programs, as is necessary in inventory, programming, or engineering applications. Huge programs and data files do not have to have multiple copies for multiple users.

231

CHAPTER 7
*Data
Communi-
cations and
Networks*

Terminal Control

Exhibit 7-5 illustrates the minicomputer arrangement. It is a **star network** configuration (see Exhibit 7-2 for network configurations). The simplest, most straightforward method of controlling the terminals is called **polling.** In polling,

EXHIBIT 7-5 Polling of Terminals

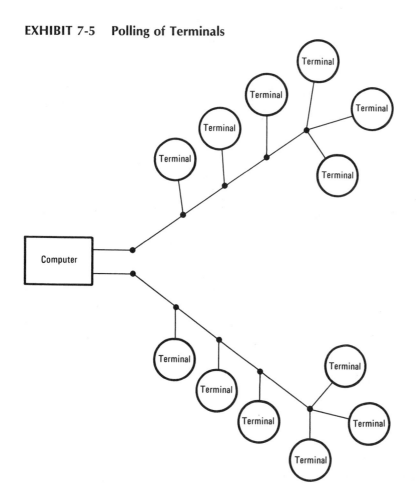

232

PART II
Technical
Aspects of
Accounting
Information
Systems

the computer checks each terminal in sequence until it finds a terminal that needs to use the line. After the terminal transmits its message, the computer continues its sequential search of terminals.

UNIX

Many other firms followed DEC into the minicomputer market. They also followed DEC in producing their own proprietary operating systems for their computers. As a result, if a user wanted to change hardware from one company to another, it was also necessary to change software because the operating system changed. Eventually, with the rapidity of changes in hardware, this situation became intolerable to minicomputer users.

UNIX is the only alternative operating system to the proprietary operating systems of computer vendors. UNIX was designed at Bell Laboratories as a portable, efficient operating system for minicomputers (at first, a DEC computer), especially suited for the on-line, non-transaction-processing applications. UNIX is now the dominant operating system for minicomputers, with only the DEC proprietary operating system still being upgraded and sold. All other minicomputer vendors have committed to UNIX.

UNIX is addressing its deficiencies, without getting away from its portability among vendors.

Transaction Processing. UNIX was not designed for transaction processing and is relatively inefficient at it. A UNIX system polls its terminals, until it comes to one that has a transaction. The IBM mainframe approach is more efficient processing transactions because it responds to a terminal only when the terminal signals that it has a transaction.

Security. As discussed in Chapter 4, different operating systems have different security levels. Because UNIX was designed for a trusting, productivity-oriented environment, its security procedures are rudimentary. Unauthorized log-ons and access of data are much easier in UNIX than in other, commercially oriented operating systems, such as MVS.

Multiple Processors. UNIX is not designed to work with multiple processors. This means that the one central processor must do all the processing chores. The IBM approach allows for as many as eight processors to be coupled so that they can all share the work. It is more efficient to increase throughput of the computer system by adding additional processors than to require that a larger processor or an entire additional computer be acquired.

Network Design

There is no established network standard for minicomputers as SNA is for IBM. However, there are different methods of communication that provide needed services in different areas.

233

CHAPTER 7
Data
Communi-
cations and
Networks

CONCEPT SUMMARY

Comparison of IBM and Minicomputer Approaches to On-Line Processing

	IBM Approach	Minicomputer Approach
Transaction processing	Primary focus of initial development	Secondary focus of initial development
Information and file sharing	Difficult for security, privacy, and control purposes	Easy for efficiency and productivity purposes
Advantages	Most efficient transaction processing; able to handle largest volumes	Easy to set up and use; lower cost; good peer-to-peer networking
Disadvantages	Extremely expensive, both in initial cost and in need for highly qualified computing staff	Less controlled and relatively inefficient transaction processing
Hardware focus	Mainframe	Minicomputer
Operating system	MVS	UNIX
Relationship between computers	Hierarchical	Peer-to-peer
Response to competitors	Developed a new operating system, VM/CMS, for information and file sharing	Transaction processing is an important focus of current development
Primary vendors	IBM, Amdahl (Fujitsu), and NAS (Hitachi)	DEC and various UNIX suppliers
Terminal connection	Synchronous	Asynchronous
Terminal control	Wait for interrupt from terminal	Poll terminals continuously for new keystrokes
Transmission of data	Screen at a time	Character at a time
Coding of data	EBCDIC	ASCII
Network approach	SNA	Open systems interconnect when possible; TCP/IP as necessary

234

PART II
Technical
Aspects of
Accounting
Information
Systems

TCP/IP. **Transmission Control Protocol/Internet Protocol (TCP/IP)** was developed for the Department of Defense (DoD) to create a network of DoD computers and the computers at major research institutions which do DoD contract research. The initial DoD network was called ARPAnet; its successor, called Internet, connects 40,000 computers at universities, government installations, military installations, and companies. Traffic on the Internet is now growing at 20 percent *per month.* TCP/IP has been widely used in commercial applications because it is the only practical way for computers of different manufacturers to communicate.

TCP/IP allows people to use a remote computer as if it were local. This is far more sophisticated than just sending messages between machines. TCP/IP is based on packet switching to efficiently control an interactive session with a remote computer. In **packet switching,** the message is grouped into packets of approximately 2,000 characters, which are then transmitted. If an error occurs, only the packet that was erroneously transmitted needs to be retransmitted. The packets are smaller pieces of information. For example, you might think of a single line in a letter as a packet of information; the line makes little sense by itself, but makes complete sense when it is properly placed with all the other packets (lines) in the message (letter).

X.25. X.25 is an international standard that allows the widespread use of **value-added networks (VANs),** such as Telenet. A VAN is a publicly available, packet-switched network that extends nationally and internationally to allow long-distance data communication through the network rather than through phone lines. For example, if a computer user in one city needed to access a computer in another city, a local X.25 connection over phone lines to Telenet would allow Telenet to connect the two computers. The alternatives would be to use the dial-up lines for a long-distance call or to lease a line between the two cities. X.25 provides a more reliable connection than a long-distance call and is less expensive than a leased line in all but the most high-volume applications.

THE MICROCOMPUTER APPROACH— LOCAL AREA NETWORKS

The microcomputer initially was designed as a personal computer. It is particularly good for personal, interactive applications such as spreadsheets and budgeting, for personal data files such as mailing lists and evaluation information concerning employees, and for word processing. Most microcomputers in business are initially justified as personal computers for stand-alone applications.

Need for Communication

However, after people are comfortable with their microcomputers, they want to communicate with other computers.

235

Chapter 7
*Data
Communi-
cations and
Networks*

Electronic Mail. Rather than print a memo out, copy it, and physically distribute it, the microcomputer can send the message electronically. Electronic mail saves time, work, and paper.

File Transfer. Files important to a microcomputer user may exist on another computer. File transfer capability allows the user to get an electronic copy of the file so it can be incorporated into a spreadsheet or report. For example, a microcomputer could access mainframe information, and the mainframe could process data collected or developed on the microcomputer.

Shared Peripherals. Expensive peripherals, such as laser printers, fax machines, and color plotters, are rarely used full time by individual users and are too expensive to issue to everyone. Multiple microcomputer users can share the use of these expensive peripherals.

Terminal Emulation. Often specific programs and data (usually large and expensive) only exist on certain minicomputers and mainframe computers. To assess those programs and data, the microcomputer can log-on to that computer as a terminal.

Shared Data Base. Often the microcomputer user connected to a LAN needs access to only part of a very large file. With only file transfer capability, the microcomputer user must transfer (download) the entire file to get at the needed data. Users sometimes make copies of files as large as 60,000 records. This causes a tremendous waste of processor time and data storage.

With the **file server approach,** the shared data base appears to the microcomputer software as another disk drive. Access to this disk is then over the network rather than directly to a disk inside the microcomputer. This file server approach is easier to program, but access to the data can be slow, especially if the query requires extensive data base processing.

The **client/server approach** tries to solve this problem by having the individual microcomputer (the client) make requests of the computer where the large files reside (the server or file server). Then the server processes the request and sends the client only the requested information. SQL (as discussed in Chapter 6) is typically used to make these data base requests. The client/server approach tries to give the LAN the most valuable characteristics of the microcomputer approach, namely, the ability to share large files efficiently.

Components of a Local Area Network (LAN)

A local area network (LAN) is a direct, high-speed connection of microcomputers that allows all of the communication needs just presented. LANs are typically formed from a group of stand-alone microcomputers whose users need to communicate. In addition to the microcomputers, a LAN typically requires the following:

Network Interface Cards. The **network interface card (NIC)** plugs into an expansion slot on the microcomputer and gives the microcomputer a "window"

236

Part II
Technical
Aspects of
Accounting
Information
Systems

to the network. The major types of network interface cards are token ring and Ethernet.

1. **Token ring** is a **ring** configuration. A token or message stating that the channel is clear is passed between microcomputers in sequence until someone wants to use the network. Then the microcomputer takes the token and changes the message to "the channel is busy" and the busy message is then transmitted. When the transmission is completed, the token message is changed back to "channel is clear" and is passed along. This token ring approach is part of the SNA approach of IBM.

2. **Ethernet** is a **bus** configuration that allows each microcomputer on the network to look at the line and see if it is busy. If it is not busy, then the computer is free to transmit its message. It is possible that two computers could try to transmit at the same time, thus causing a collision problem. The network design may solve this problem by using a collision detection device. If the device detects another message on the line, it will retransmit the message after a random interval of time. Ethernet is the primary non-IBM approach.

Connection Between NICs. There is then a connection between these network interface cards. This connection is usually twisted pair or coaxial cable. See Exhibit 7-2 for these alternatives.

Network-Aware Software. To access the LAN, each microcomputer must run network-aware software that enables the microcomputer to access files or printer services on another computer on the network.

File Server. The file server is a computer that contains the program and data files that all microcomputers on the network will share. This is typically the largest microcomputer on the network, or it could be a minicomputer or mainframe.

Network Operating System. The network operating system allows the file server to be utilized by many different microcomputers simultaneously. A network operating system only runs on the network's file server. Most often, the network operating system is Netware, from Novell.

These different components can generally be changed without changing the other components. For example, both token ring and Ethernet can work with Netware because the choice of network interface card is separate from the choice of network operating system.

Advantages and Disadvantages of LANs

The microcomputer is growing in capability at the same time as the workstation is decreasing in cost. As a result, there is now considerable blurring between the low end of workstations and the high end of microcomputers. Microcomputers on a LAN are trying to replace minicomputers. With a large file server, perhaps even a minicomputer itself, the LAN is beginning to provide small-scale transaction processing.

There are applications for minicomputers and applications for LANs. The trade-off depends primarily on how much of the data and information on the system is shared. The more the information is shared, the more attractive a minicomputer, while the more the data are distributed, with each user having his or her own data, the more attractive a LAN. For example, an inventory system is best done on a minicomputer because every user will share the same information on parts and their availability. On the other extreme, for faculty members who each have information on students in their classes, connectivity is best served by a LAN.

Exhibit 7-6 on page 238 provides a schematic of the connection of a microcomputer to an IBM mainframe in various possible ways.

237

CHAPTER 7
*Data
Communi-
cations and
Networks*

Blurring of Distinctions

The distinctions between mainframes, minicomputers, and microcomputers are blurring as they take on the best characteristics of each other.

Workstations. The leader in the workstation market is SUN Microsystems, with its SPARC architecture. The workstation is essentially a minicomputer for one user, and therefore typically uses UNIX for its operating system. The primary users of workstations are now scientists and engineers, people who have traditionally shared minicomputers for their work. The cost of providing a given amount of computing power to each user is often now less if each user has his or her own processor. Workstations are almost always connected to an Ethernet LAN with a large file server for the traditional other purposes of minicomputers, such as electronic mail and file sharing.

Cash Registers. Cash registers are helping to drive the movement to OLTP because they can change a periodic inventory system to a perpetual inventory system. With bar code scanning, the store gets transaction by transaction information, often for the first time. The cash register can function as a microcomputer on a LAN or as a terminal to a minicomputer. This can provide information on what items are selling. The cash register can also provide control by checking on the claims of the deliverer for sales of milk, bread, and other perishables because prior to the electronic cash register, the store had to accept the statement of the vendor concerning the amount delivered.

Microcomputers and SNA. There is no need for a user even in an IBM mainframe environment to have both a microcomputer and a terminal. The microcomputer can do stand-alone processing, such as budgeting, word processing, and personal data bases, but it can also emulate the terminal. An emulation board converts between the EBCDIC of the IBM mainframe to the ASCII of the microcomputer, so typically the microcomputer displays the same screen as the mainframe terminal. However, using the microcomputer as simply a terminal is quite wasteful—the microcomputer can do more. As discussed earlier, the microcomputer can be connected with other microcomputers in a token ring LAN (the IBM approach), and then the LAN can be connected to the mainframe in order to replace the cluster controller.

EXHIBIT 7-6 Connection of Microcomputers & Local Area Network to Mainframe

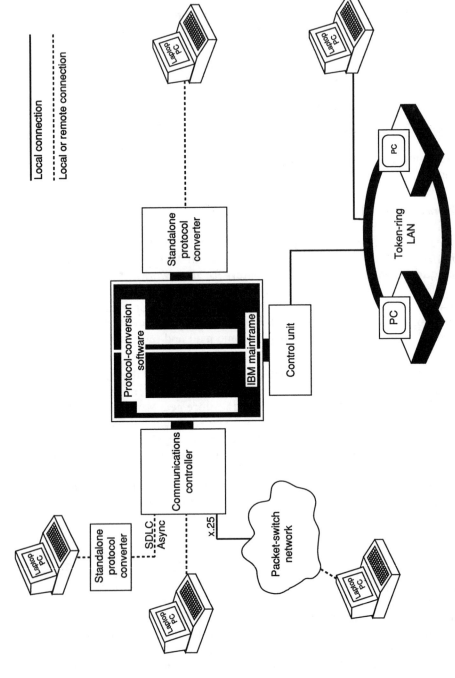

CONCEPT SUMMARY

Data Communication Options

	Microcomputer	Minicomputer	Mainframe
Primary focus	Stand-alone applications such as budgeting, word processing, and establishing personal data bases such as mailing lists	On-line, but not transaction processing applications such as electronic mail, text processing, and software development	Transaction processing
Operating system	DOS	UNIX	MVS
Advantages	Easiest to use; least expensive to start; easiest to grow incrementally	Easiest controlled access to large files by multiple users; less expensive than mainframes	Highest-volume transaction processing; fastest disks and tapes
Disadvantages	Can easily have insufficient controls; software for multiple users is least developed	Does not have the high-end capabilities of the mainframe; low-end capabilities are being supplanted by microcomputers	Most expensive to buy; most expensive support staff; most difficult to use
Response to competition and future trends	LANs combining the microcomputers together for minicomputer and eventually mainframe replacement	Transaction processing enhancements to operating system to allow OLTP applications for small and medium-sized businesses	Larger networks to control more aspects of the company and integrate larger quantities of information that minicomputers and LANs cannot match
Interactions	Minicomputers and mainframes performing as file servers on microcomputer LAN	Microcomputers functioning as terminal to minicomputer	Mirocomputer becoming peer with mainframe in the most sophisticated networks

CURRENT TRENDS IN DATA COMMUNICATION

Electronic Data Interchange

Many companies have realized that there is a great deal of wasted effort if both the company and its supplier or the company and its customer have computer systems and those systems are operated without data communications. For example, a company may print out (from the computer) a purchase order and then send it to a supplier. The supplier will then have to enter that information

240

*Part II
Technical
Aspects of
Accounting
Information
Systems*

into its computer system. Similar reentry of data into the computer system will be done when the supplier sends an invoice to the company, when the company receives a purchase order from its customer, and when the company sends an invoice to its customer. The strong incentive is to send the data to and from the supplier, the company, and the customer electronically, without printout, without reentry, without mail delays, and without mailing expense. The term used for this electronic process is **electronic data interchange (EDI).**

Initial EDI systems developed by K-Mart and American Hospital Supply Corporation (AHSC) were very successful and widely publicized. The AHSC operation will be discussed in greater depth in Chapter 14. Many firms, such as Haggar, followed their lead. Retailers of Haggar clothes now read in bar code information and transmit sales data to the Haggar mainframe. Haggar is also linked to its fabric suppliers. Volvo dealers were connected to the factory, so they could sell what was being produced. Cars now sit 3 days in New Jersey instead of 20 days. Many firms, such as Sears, now require that their suppliers use EDI.

Because EDI systems were developed independently, the result was a wide variety of formats which did not communicate. This situation would be similar to having AT&T voice customers not be able to call MCI or Sprint customers. Eventually, a standard was developed by the American National Standards Institute (ANSI). Firms such as Procter & Gamble led the move toward standards because they deal with so many different firms.

X.400

None of the EDI standards were complete solutions because special EDI connections were required between all of the affected companies, and they were difficult to arrange. Business needed a standard way to use public or private networks for EDI and other forms of communication, so the same network could have multiple uses. The result of this need is the X.400 standard. Any network that corresponds to the X.400 standard can communicate with other X.400 systems and can transmit all of the following: telex, electronic mail, formatted documents, electronic data interchange, videotex, and voice. Vendors over whose networks you can send X.400 messages include General Electric Information Services, IBM, and Control Data.

Electronic Mail

The movement to X.400 has had a major push from the users of electronic mail. The major electronic mail service providers, such as MCI mail and Western Union's EasyLink do not have compatible systems. If you signed on to one provider, you could not send an electronic mail message to the subscriber to another system. Gradually, LANs, corporate networks, and electronic mail service providers are adding X.400 capabilities.

Just-in-Time Inventory

241

CHAPTER 7
Data
Communi-
cations and
Networks

EDI allows communication between suppliers' and customers' computers. This may facilitate communication and the selling/buying process. One goal of many companies is to have a **just-in-time (JIT) inventory.** Long-term arrangements can be made with the supplier, with the supplier delivering the items only as necessary for production. As a result, there is no need to store weeks or even days of raw materials and supplies. This can eventually reduce raw material inventories from several months to as few as two hours in some cases, depending on the distance of a supplier.

Electronic Funds Transfer

Funds can also be transferred electronically. The Federal Reserve System has a wire transfer capability for banks. However, a similar process can be used by all types of organizations. Employees' pay can be deposited directly into their bank accounts. In addition, funds to pay suppliers can be transferred electronically to the supplier's account. This approach eliminates the internal control problems of printing and mailing checks, but it adds the internal control problem of limiting access to the **electronic funds transfer (EFT)** capability.

Systems Application Architecture

The future direction of the IBM approach is away from the centralized control of the mainframe toward a network of mainframes and microcomputers as peers. This peer-to-peer networking is growing, but it requires a more powerful microcomputer than is typically available to microcomputer users. Part of the IBM movement to peer-to-peer networking is **Systems Application Architecture (SAA).** The purpose of SAA is to make consistent the different computers that IBM sells. SAA has defined standard ways for all systems to communicate with users, software developers, and other systems. For example, each program is consistent; each program will use F1 as the Help Key, and each menu bar will begin with File as the first choice. SAA began life as a mainframe-dominated specification. The focus was on program portability, so programs could be written on one type of computer and moved to another. Future versions of SAA will rely more on microcomputer networks to better distribute the needed processing.

Movement to the OSI Model

When a network spreads over a large geographic area, it is often called a **wide area network (WAN).** Many WANs consist of several types of computers connected worldwide. There are three network standards that can provide the backbone to sustain such a diverse network. Each of these backbone candidates defines how data are formatted, transferred, routed, and retransmitted if errors

242

PART II
Technical
Aspects of
Accounting
Information
Systems

occur. These definitions, in turn, are implemented by connectivity software products, incorporated into operating systems, and built into communications hardware.

Systems Network Architecture. SNA has become a de facto industry standard by virtue of IBM's control of 80 percent of the mainframe market.

Transmission Control Protocol/Internet Protocol. TCP/IP is a series of specifications originally developed to ensure interoperability among U.S. Defense Department networks. It has since found widespread commercial applications. Unfortunately, TCP/IP is incompatible with SNA and is only a partial network solution.

Open Systems Interconnect. **Open Systems Interconnect (OSI)** is a model developed by the International Standards Organization (ISO) for use in designing multivendor networks. Although the OSI model has not yet been completely implemented, parts of it have. Probably the most important parts yet implemented are X.25 and X.400. As OSI becomes more complete, TCP/IP will become less significant. However, because TCP/IP works now and is inexpensive, it is indispensable for the near term.

The network model most suitable for the communication of products from different vendors is OSI. The OSI model divides communications into seven layers and has specifications for each. These specifications are functional only; the tasks to be performed are defined exactly, but the methods to be used are left to the designer. Any method is acceptable as long as the same method is used at both ends of the communications link. OSI products have been very slow in coming—although those products that do appear are open, so anyone can use them and therefore connect to all other users of OSI products.

In addition, most currently installed networks were developed before the OSI model and are inconsistent with it. However, if data communications and networks are to achieve their potential, products incorporating all levels of the OSI model will probably have to be completed. Exhibit 7-7 gives the layers of the OSI model and the location in that model of some of the network products discussed earlier in the chapter.

EXHIBIT 7-7   Layered Approach to Data Communications

Open Systems Interconnect			Network Products	Local Area Network Products
Layer	Name	Function	Name	Name
7	Application	Formatted data are delivered to the user; responsible for getting the appropriate screens, menus, and headers to the user; provides standard user requests and connections to networks	X.400	

Exhibit continues on next page

EXHIBIT 7-7   Layered Approach to Data Communications (continued)

Open Systems Interconnect			Network Products	Local Area Network Products
Layer	Name	Function	Name	Name
6	Presentation	Prepares information for application; converts files from one format to another; ensures that all devices can understand each other at the application layer; can include additional services, such as message compression and data encryption.		DOS 3.1 and later
5	Session	Establishes links between computers; enables users to access programs and data on other machines; organizes and coordinates the dialogue between the two computers; validates identity and authorization for communication.		Netware covers layers 3, 4 and 5
4	Transport	Keeps message components in sequence and controls data flow; detects and corrects errors; expedites priority messages; provides a logical connection from a process on one machine to a process on another.	TCP	
3	Network	Routes information through network (set up once in LAN); specifies how communications within and between networks should occur; defines all possible routes that a message could take to its destination.	IP, OSI Internet protocols, X.25 packet level	
2	Data link	Detects and corrects transmission errors; transfers units of information to other end of physical link; foreman in railroad yard—puts information in right place and checks it; establishes, maintains, and releases communication connections.	X.25 link level	
1	Physical	Specifies physical and electrical connections; transmission onto network; electrical and physical layer; transmits data across physical links; defines physical signal characteristics	X.25 physical level	Ethernet, token ring

244

Part II
Technical
Aspects of
Accounting
Information
Systems

NETWORK MANAGEMENT
AND INTERNAL CONTROL

Network problems, such as leased-line outages or terminal failures, are easy to solve in a small network: Users call a help desk when their terminals go down. In a large network, however, problems can be magnified to the point of chaos, such as 100 simultaneous outages. Most program failures are related to a network failure. But these two areas are often under separate service organizations. Thus, the first step in network management is assigning responsibility to one group for keeping the network running and looking at the network as a whole.

Exhibit 7-8 shows the growing importance of network management. As discussed earlier in the chapter, data communications and networks are increasingly important components of virtually all accounting information systems. But spending on network management is increasing even faster than the total spending (itself rapidly increasing) on networks. This added focus on network management is due to growing network complexity, which requires better management; the new availability of needed, but sophisticated and expensive, tools to help control the networks; and the increasing dependence of business operations on networks, which requires constant availability of the network.

Responsibilities of Network Management

The network management group should have the following responsibilities:

Control Operation of Nodes.   Each network consists of **nodes,** such as computers connected by lines. It is essential that an organization be able to manipulate what happens in its network. Certain parts of the network might need to be brought down at night, others might require remote booting, while others need to be turned off after a power failure. In addition, it is necessary to monitor each network element; improve the interface with human operators; compile, analyze, and present statistical and general performance data; and

EXHIBIT 7-8   Recent Spending of *Fortune* 1000 Firms on Network Management

Year	Total Budget (in billions)	Network Management (in billions)	Percentage
1987	$50	$0.5	1.00%
1988	55	0.7	1.27
1989	60	1.1	1.83
1990	66	1.7	2.57
1991	76	2.8	3.68

monitor systems software, communications software, applications software operation, and hardware.

245

CHAPTER 7
Data
Communi-
cations and
Networks

Maintain Equipment. The heart of network management is making sure the underlying media, whether twisted pair, coaxial cable, or fiber optics, is working properly. Networks are perpetually adding, deleting, and moving nodes, and adding software and equipment to nodes. It is essential that change be planned, organized, and controlled so that outages due to poor coordination are avoided.

Report Equipment Failures. When a node goes out of service, a central site operator is notified of the failure, and he or she can dispatch service personnel. In many organizations, users shop for results; three people may work on the same problem, because the user felt that the more people asked to resolve the problem, the better. In advanced applications, the network management processor telephones a vendor and specifies the specific failing component and what parts to bring. When a unit has encountered a predetermined level of temporary errors, or a telephone line encounters an unacceptable level of degradation, then alarms should direct repairs.

Track Function Breakdowns. The one thing that all the machines thus far invented have in common is that they fail occasionally. Software has bugs, hardware breaks down, and operations procedures are discovered not to work. A method must be devised to track these problems in order to measure availability or unavailability equipment in the network.

Reduce Costs. Asset management helps corporations model networks and find the cheapest way to run operations. A continuing goal should be to reduce the number of technicians required for network operation and eliminate network management system duplication.

Exhibit 7-9 provides the areas of most concern in maintaining a network.

EXHIBIT 7-9   Reasons for Network Failure

The following are typical statistics on the reasons for network failures:

Host hardware and software	10%
Communications controllers	13
Modem	6
Cluster controller	4
Terminal or microcomputer	10
Data lines	57
Total	100%

246

Part II
Technical
Aspects of
Accounting
Information
Systems

Vendors of Network Management Systems and Services

Network management systems and services are sold by computer firms, such as DEC; vendors of data communications equipment, such as Codex and Racal-Vadic; vendors of voice communications products which can control both voice and data networks; the Regional Bell operating companies, sometimes called Baby Bells; AT&T; and IBM. IBM is the current leader in network management systems, but IBM is focused on its own SNA networks. AT&T is developing network management systems for the OSI-based systems it hopes will be the wave of the future.

Detection of Transmission Errors

Loop Check. One approach to detecting transmission errors is using a loop check. The receiving device echoes the message it gets, so the sender can check the message received. If there is an error, the correct message is transmitted again, or a correction is transmitted. This method of error detection is wasteful of transmission capacity since it halves the throughput on communications lines. Moreover, the original transmission may be correct, but an error may occur in the return transmission. As a result, loop checking is best suited for low-speed terminals using short, direct lines.

Redundancy. The alternative approach is to try to detect errors by building redundancy into the transmitted message and then retransmitting only those messages in error. This approach takes three forms:

1. The parity check incorporates an extra parity bit in each character sent in addition to the data. This parity bit is set to 0 or 1 so that the sum of the bits in a transmitted character is always odd (odd parity) or even (even parity). The receiving device can check each character for the agreed-upon even or odd parity and detect a character with an incorrectly changed bit. The simple parity check needs to be backed up by additional error detection characters, since noise bursts on communication lines often result in the corruption of two or more adjacent bits.
2. Constant ratio codes detect errors by checking the ratio of 1 bits to 0 bits. A common method is the 4-8 code in which four 1 bits and four 0 bits are expected in the character bit configuration. The absence of the correct ratio signals an error. This method of error detection is somewhat inefficient since it allows only 70 valid character combinations—as opposed to 128 possibilities with the single parity bit.
3. Cyclic codes (or cyclic redundancy checks) are the most powerful form of the redundancy approach yet devised. Cyclic codes check all bits using a mathematical algorithm. The sending and receiving units perform the same algorithm. If the results are the same, the message is judged correct. From an internal control point of view, the cyclic code is the best protection against data error during transmission.

Audit Trail

In the distributed data processing environment, logical errors should be immediately detected and corrected or corrections requested. However, immediate processing can create problems with the audit trail, backup, and recovery,

247

CHAPTER 7
*Data
Communi-
cations and
Networks*

when direct entry of transactions is involved. Audit trails should be designed using a standard format for all data transmission. An example is shown in Exhibit 7-10, in which certain control fields are described. Others of interest are

> *SOH (start of header).* This character identifies the beginning of the message header.
>
> *STX (start of text).* STX indicates termination of a header and start of the text characters.
>
> *ETX (end of text).* ETX terminates a block of characters that started with STX or SOH. A block is an entity that is transmitted together without any intervening control characters.
>
> *EOT (end of transmission).* This character identifies termination of a transmission consisting of one or more blocks. It is also used as a response to polling when a terminal or computer has no data to transmit.
>
> *ETB (end of transmission block).* ETB indicates the end of the block of characters that started with SOH or STX.

All information from SOH to STX and ETX to EOT is recorded for any transaction, record update, inquiry/response, message switching action, or data entry operation. This resulting trail can be used for billing, activity analysis, error analysis, security evaluation, and data base activity analysis.

EXHIBIT 7-10 Format for Data Transmission

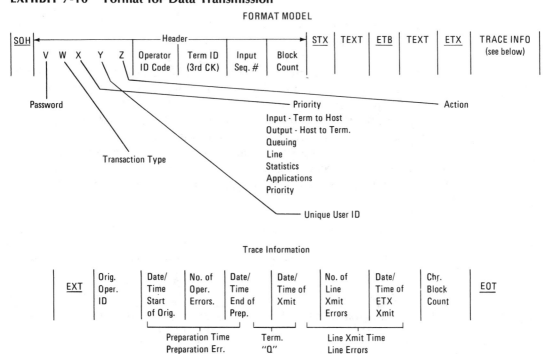

248

Part II
Technical
Aspects of
Accounting
Information
Systems

CHAPTER SUMMARY

Accounting information systems increasingly require data communications and networking because transactions

1. Are recorded electronically.
2. Occur far from where they are analyzed.
3. Depend on data that are located far away.

Networks can provide a company with comparative advantages in increased speed of processing, better customer service, reduced costs, and more complete analysis.

IBM first used data communications for transaction processing before the availability of microcomputers and developed a mainframe-oriented approach. This approach has major control advantages, as the processing takes place in the mainframe (host) and data communications are moved out to other devices. The minicomputer allows for slower but lower-cost transaction processing for medium-scale firms and departments of larger firms. The microcomputer was originally developed as a stand-alone computer, but increasingly, microcomputers are being connected into local area networks to provide electronic mail, file transfer, shared peripherals, and shared data bases. All of these types of computers are changing rapidly and each is taking on the best characteristics of the others.

Current trends in data communications include a movement to the Open Systems Interconnect model, which hopes to allow computers and communications devices of all manufacturers to work together. This movement to OSI is being driven in part by the increased need for electronic data interchange, electronic funds transfer, and just-in-time inventory. The X.25 standard allows the interconnection of packet-switched networks, while the X.400 allows the interconnection of electronic mail systems. The major alternative to the OSI model is IBM's System Network Architecture. In addition, however, the Transmission Control Protocol/Interconnect Protocol, developed for the Department of Defense and used in the Internet, is also an important part of the networks of many companies.

Network management involves maintaining the network to keep it running, along with tracking errors and breakdowns. As networks become part of the accounting information system, network management becomes an important part of internal accounting control. Of particular concern is the detection of transmission errors and the maintenance of the audit trail even when there are errors.

KEY TERMS

ASCII (*p. 225*)
Bus network (*p. 236*)
Client/server approach (*p. 235*)
EBCDIC (*p. 225*)
EDI (*p. 240*)

EFT (*p. 241*)
Ethernet (*p. 236*)
File server approach (*p. 235*)
JIT (*p. 241*)
LAN (*p. 222*)

249

CHAPTER 7
Data
Communi-
cations and
Networks

MVS (p. 227)
Network (p. 222)
Network interface card (p. 235)
Node (p. 244)
OSI (p. 242)
Packet switching (p. 234)
Polling (p. 231)
Ring network (p. 236)

SAA (p. 241)
SNA (p. 228)
Star network (p. 231)
TCP/IP (p. 234)
Token ring (p. 236)
UNIX (p. 232)
VAN (p. 234)
WAN (p. 241)

QUESTIONS

7-1. Explain why the development of data communications is crucial to accountants and accounting systems.

7-2. Why is the area of data communications and networks so difficult to understand?

7-3. Give the types of lines used today in data communication.

7-4. Identify the basic configurations of computer networks and briefly explain their advantages and disadvantages.

7-5. Describe the IBM mainframe approach to data communications, including its advantages and disadvantages.

7-6. Give the advantages of an SNA network. Why do not all computer users use SNA networks?

7-7. Describe the minicomputer approach to data communications, including its advantages and disadvantages.

7-8. Describe the microcomputer local area network approach to data communications, including its advantages and disadvantages.

7-9. What is the likely effect of electronic data interchange?

7-10. Define the terms X.400, EFT, JIT, X.25, and TCP/IP. Why are they important in accounting data communications?

7-11. Give the advantages of an OSI network. Why do not all computer users use OSI networks?

7-12. Give the basic causes of failures in a network and how the system can protect itself from these failures.

7-13. Explain how the audit trail can be maintained, even if there are equipment failures in the network.

PROBLEMS

7-14. Discuss the evolution of communications, starting with the telephone system. What do you feel are the most likely developments over the next five years?

7-15. If you were going to redesign the telephone system from scratch, what changes would you make to the current system?

7-16. For the following choices regarding data communications, give the advantages and disadvantages of each option and give a situation where each option might be used:

    a. ASCII versus EBCDIC

    b. Asynchronous versus synchronous

250

Part II
Technical
Aspects of
Accounting
Information
Systems

    c.   Telephone line versus hardwired

    d.   Star versus ring versus bus

    e.   LAN versus minicomputer

    f.   Collision detection versus retransmission

    g.   Twisted pair versus coaxial cable versus fiber optic

    h.   Regular telephone line versus dedicated line

7-17. The following techniques and characteristics tend to group together:

    a.   Microcomputer, ASCII, modem, asynchronous

    b.   Terminal, EBCDIC, hardwired, synchronous

Explain why this is so and how each forms a "package."

7-18. For the three main sizes of computers (that is, mainframes, minicomputers, and microcomputers) discuss the following:

    a.   The advantages and disadvantages of each in data communications.

    b.   Situations where each would likely be used.

7-19. For each of the following situations, describe the data communication option that you would recommend and briefly defend your choice:

    a.   University mainframe with 1,000 microcomputers owned by faculty, staff, and students.

    b.   Accounting department where one person handles accounts payable and payroll, another handles accounts receivable, and another handles the general ledger.

    c.   Accounting department where 40 people process accounts receivable transactions and another 3 people handle customer service telephone calls which include answering questions about the customer's account.

    d.   Company with traveling salespersons who want access on the road to inventory information and the ability to check credit and submit orders electronically.

    e.   Company where microcomputers are used by employees for work such as budgets, but where those same people would like to access data on the mainframe.

    f.   International company, such as a large brokerage firm, where transactions occur at any of over 100 branch offices, but where the central computer in New York should summarize the results of all transactions.

    g.   University mainframe on one campus with a minicomputer on the separate medical school campus for data processing of the medical center's accounting records; faculty on the medical school campus need access to the statistical packages on the mainframe computer; microcomputers are also available on each campus.

    h.   Decentralized corporation with five divisions in five states; the firm was enlarged by acquisition, and each division has a different mainframe computer; corporate headquarters has an IBM mainframe; employees on their own purchased microcomputers and now there are over 100 microcomputers representing 12 different types, including some discontinued models and some firms which have gone out of business.

    i.   State highway police department which keeps track of current car registration, new registrations are required every two years; traffic tickets are given locally and by the state police; the state's policy is to not give a new registration if any traffic tickets are outstanding; new registrations can be obtained from any of 14 state police locations throughout the state.

j. Company where people can work at home on a microcomputer and wish to transmit the results of their work to the company.

7-20. (*CMA, adapted*) Vincent Maloy, director of special projects and analysis for Milok Company, is responsible for preparing corporate financial analyses and projections monthly and for reviewing and presenting to upper management the financial impacts of proposed strategies. Data for these financial analyses and projections are obtained from reports developed by Milok's systems department and generated from its mainframe computer. Additional data are obtained through terminals via a data inquiry system. Reports and charts for presentations are then prepared by hand and typed. Maloy has tried to have final presentations generated by the computer but has not always been successful.

The systems department has developed a package utilizing a terminal emulator to link a microcomputer to the mainframe computer. This allows the microcomputer to become part of the current data inquiry system and enables data to be downloaded to the microcomputer's disk. The data are in a format that allows printing or further manipulation and analyses using commercial software packages, for example, spreadsheet analysis. The special projects and analysis department has been chosen to be the first users of this new computer terminal system. Maloy questioned whether the new system could do more for his department than implementing the program modification requests that he has submitted to the systems department. He also believed that his people would have to become programmers. Lisa Brandt, a supervisor in Maloy's department, has decided to prepare a briefing for Maloy on the benefits of integrating microcomputers with the mainframe computer. She has used the terminal inquiry extensively and has learned to use spreadsheet software to prepare special analyses, sometimes with multiple alternatives. She also tried the new package while it was being tested.

1. Identify five enhancements to current information and reporting that Milok Company should be able to realize by integrating microcomputers with the company's mainframe computer.

2. Explain how the utilization of computer resources would be altered as a result of integrating microcomputers with the company's mainframe computer.

3. Discuss what security of the data is gained or lost by integrating microcomputers with the company's mainframe computer.

7-21. (*IIA, adapted*) As a result of recent advances in information processing and communications technology, a large manufacturing firm is proposing the following changes in its field sales operation:

a. All salespersons will be issued personal computers equipped with a modem. They will be trained to use an integrated software package which will give them data base, word processing, spreadsheet, graphics, and communications capabilities.

b. Regional sales managers will be housed at the home office. Teleconferencing will be used for communications between the sales managers and the members of the sales force should a group conference be required.

c. Regional sales offices will be closed and sales personnel will work out of

252

*Part II
Technical
Aspects of
Accounting
Information
Systems*

their homes. All "office" work will be conducted using the concept of "telecommuting."

The company is concerned about making such drastic changes in its operations and has asked you to evaluate the advantages and disadvantages of the changes. Identify three advantages and three disadvantages of the changes noted above in terms of the following concepts:

a. End user computing
b. Teleconferencing
c. Telecommuting

7-22. (*IIA, adapted*) On a monthly basis, a planning analyst computes several profitability indices for the company's divisions and product lines. For the last six months, the analyst has used a microcomputer spreadsheet program for this purpose, manually entering data into the spreadsheet from printed listings of financial data. To improve the accuracy and decrease the preparation time of the indices, the analyst suggested a micro-to-mainframe link (MML) for obtaining financial report data from the financial reporting data base system. The data base is maintained on the mainframe computer at the company's headquarters. The planning analyst works at a regional headquarters location in another city.

For the MML application described, explain considerations for selecting designing, implementing, and using:

a. Hardware
b. Software
c. Controls

7-23. (*CMA, adapted*) Gorman Corporation is a manufacturing firm that is organized along product lines. Each product line has a vice president of operations who reports directly to the president and is responsible for all aspects of design and manufacture as well as sales, costs, and profits for the product line. The vice president of finance and administration is responsible for the functions common to all product lines such as human resource management and general accounting.

The accounts payable department of Gorman has a supervisor and five clerks. Each clerk is assigned to a specific product line and is responsible for matching invoices with the proper documentation for payment and for maintaining files of check copies and supporting paperwork. The supervisor is responsible for actual check preparation from a supply of prenumbered checks. Checks are prepared daily for all invoices ready for payment; check numbers are assigned without regard to the product line payment being made. Gorman's external auditing firm has generated a random listing of check numbers to be reviewed for proper documentation. The supervisor has instructed the clerks to work together in gathering the documents for presentation to the auditors in the same number sequence as shown on the random listing provided.

In an unrelated situation, Gorman has discovered a defect in one of its products and must develop a program for the recall and repair/replacement of the items sold. The vice president of operations for the affected product line has established a task force to troubleshoot this problem. Those selected to serve on the task force are the product line supervisor, a representative of the quality control department, the engineer most familiar with the product, the appropriate cost accountant, and the product line sales manager. The group has been instructed to present its recommendations to management within one week.

The two circumstances described at Gorman Corporation present problem-solving situations. Studies have found that, in most cases, a communication network emerges in a group that is appropriate to the assigned task. Exhibit 7-11 presents diagrams of common communication networks.

1. For each of the four communication networks presented in Exhibit 7-11, describe the implied behavior of the participants in the group.
2. Identify the communication network that is likely to develop among the accounts payable clerks at Gorman Corporation, and explain the reasons for its formation.
3. For the troubleshooting task force established at Gorman Corporation, identify the communication network that would be most appropriate, and explain why.

253

CHAPTER 7
Data
Communi-
cations and
Networks

EXHIBIT 7-11   Four Communications Networks

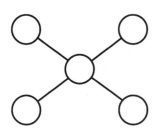

Wheel

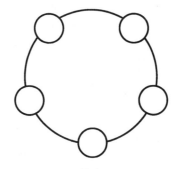

Circle

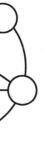

All Channel

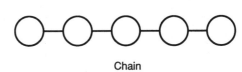

Chain

254

Part II
Technical
Aspects of
Accounting
Information
Systems

DECISION CASE

(*CMA, adapted*) In the last two decades, there has been a transition from a centralized mainframe computer environment to a distributed network where an organization has the ability to share computer processing. One of the fastest-growing segments of the computer industry is the local area network which is said to be the "wave of the future." LANs permit the transfer of information between microcomputers, word processors, data storage devices, printers, voice devices, and the telecommunication devices. Current opinion states that the flow of organizational communications has been enhanced by the transition from the optimization of computers experienced in the traditional distributed network to the optimization of human resources in the LAN environment.

Required:

1. Describe the reasons why an organization would choose a distributed network over the traditional centralized computer environment.
2. Compare and contrast the characteristics of a traditional distributed computer network with those of a local area network as they relate to the
   a. utilization of computer hardware.
   b. user interaction and the sharing of electronic information.
3. Identify and explain three problems that can result from the use of local area networks.
4. Explain the hardware characteristics associated with a computer modem as it relates to distributed information processing.

8 Decision Support Systems and Expert Systems

Overview

Introduction to basic decision-making concepts and the use of advanced computerized software to support decision making.

Learning Objectives

Thorough study of this chapter will enable you to:

1. Describe the components of decision support systems.
2. Suggest guidelines for the development of decision support systems.
3. Identify the basic types of decision support systems.
4. Recognize opportunities for the successful use of decision support systems.
5. Use the PERT/CPM network to manage projects.
6. Give the types of software available for decision support systems and their uses.
7. Explain the relationship of expert systems and artificial intelligence.
8. Discuss the components of an expert system and the accounting applications of expert systems.

Outline

Decision-Making Process

Decision Support Systems

Software for Decision Support

Expert Systems

256

*PART II
Technical
Aspects of
Accounting
Information
Systems*

SYSTEMS IN THE REAL WORLD

Experts on a Disk

Picture in your mind's eye (because American Express wouldn't let us photograph it) a giant computer room with row upon row of big blue IBM machines. The room is a storage bank whose treasure is account information about millions of American Express card users. In the center of this vast array two microcomputers perch on a pair of little wooden tables. Programmers have arranged it so that the microcomputers can rummage through the files of their mainframe cousins, selecting the odd bits of data they need and translating them into a language they can understand and put to use.

The small intruders are part of an expert system, a down-to-earth incarnation of artificial intelligence—the technology that tries to get computers to think the way people do. At their heart is an innovative software program that embodies the rules specialists use to make decisions, in this case whether someone using an American Express card for a purchase is likely to be a fraud or a deadbeat. The accuracy of these decisions is crucial to the company, which loses money not only from fraud but also by denying credit to good risks. It

is enthusiastic about the improvements its new system will make by enabling less-experienced employees to arrive at credit judgments that are as sound as an expert's.

However, very probably the most homey application of expert system technology is Campbell Soup's Aldo on a Disk. That's Aldo Cimino, who retired in May as Campbell's resident expert on the hydrostatic and rotary cookers that kill bacteria so a customer's next cup of Crispy Gazpacho won't be his last. Aldo was getting on in years and being run ragged, flying from plant to plant whenever a cooker went on the blink. Over eight months in 1984 and 1985, Aldo spent about 30 days telling his secrets to so-called knowledge engineers from Texas Instruments. Now employees enter the symptoms of a balky machine into a computer and answer a series of questions that lead to the diagnosis Aldo would have made. "Here was a storehouse of knowledge about to leave the company," says Reuben Tyson, the project manager, "We basically retained an asset."

SOURCE: *Fortune,* 10/2/87, reprinted by permission.

DECISION-MAKING PROCESS

The objective of accounting information systems is to provide users with information that is useful in making business decisions. Typically, in addition to processing accounting transactions, information systems process other kinds of information (such as physical quantities) that help management make decisions. Information systems can improve the decision-making process by providing more useful information, educating the user about decision methods, and automating the decision-making process. Decision support systems and expert systems are designed to make one or more of these improvements.

Decision support systems (DSS) and expert systems (ES) are interrelated with accounting information systems in the following ways:

257

CHAPTER 8
*Decision
Support
Systems
and Expert
Systems*

1. Both DSS and ES use the data recorded in the accounting information system and thus must have access directly to that data base.
2. The processing and calculations necessary in a DSS and ES are usually so great that computer assistance is required, usually the same computer systems used in the accounting information system.
3. The decisions must often be made as a part of entering a transaction into the accounting information system.
4. The decisions reached may then need to be recorded and incorporated into the accounting information system.

Types of Decisions

Management decisions can be classified as structured, semistructured, and unstructured. This classification of decisions ranges from the most repetitive, easily specified decisions to individual, highly complex decisions. The term *programmed* is often used to describe structured decisions; the term *nonprogrammed* is used to describe unstructured decisions.

Structured Decisions. **Structured** or programmed **decisions** are repetitive and use a predetermined series of steps to reach a conclusion. Little judgment is required to make a structured decision. Classification of accounting transactions into the proper accounts when recording them is an example of this type of decision. Structured decisions are easily automated through the use of **algorithms**, which provide standard, unambiguous procedures for arriving at solutions. Typically, structured decisions are handled by transaction processing systems that automate manual procedures.

Semistructured Decisions. **Semistructured decisions** are partially structured. The final decision requires the judgment of the decision maker. These decisions are best suited to decision support system models. The structured portion of the decision can be automated to take advantage of the speed and accuracy of the computer and encourage more timely, better informed decisions. The decision maker applies business judgment to the information provided by the computer and makes the final decision. An example of a semistructured decision is financial budgeting. The budget will depend not only on the accounting relationship between revenues, expenses, and income, but also on relationships that exist between units sold and related expenses. All relationships can be automated so that a manager can pose hypothetical, "what if" type questions (what if we increase sales volume; what if we decrease sales volume of product A and increase the volume of product B) and quickly see the various effects. In the end, the manager must choose the most likely alternative based on judgment and other nonprogrammable factors. The use of the computer for budgeting purposes helps alleviate some of the problems of the time and cost of budget preparation.

Unstructured Decisions. **Unstructured**, ill-structured, nonprogrammed, or "wicked" **decisions** rely heavily on the judgment of decision makers. Unstruc-

258

*Part II
Technical
Aspects of
Accounting
Information
Systems*

tured decisions include complex decisions for which an established method of solution does not exist, extremely important decisions that require individualized attention, and decisions that have not previously been addressed. Research and development planning requires unstructured decisions.

Steps in Decision Making

To use a computerized decision support tool successfully, a problem must exist and be recognized. Individuals each have their own methods of attacking and solving problems. However, the basic steps of the decision making process should include

1. Defining the problem to be solved or choice to be made.
2. Establishing alternative solutions or courses of action.
3. Analyzing the alternatives.
4. Selecting the most advantageous alternative.
5. Implementing the chosen alternative.
6. Evaluating the results and providing feedback to the decision maker.

DECISION SUPPORT SYSTEMS

Decision support systems (DSS) are computerized systems that help managers at all levels of an organization to make structured and semistructured decisions. The objective of DSS is to provide support for the decision-making process and to improve the effectiveness of the process, not to make a final decision. The DSS automates the structured part of the problem. DSS provide better information than the decision maker otherwise would have and allow the manager to be more thorough in considering options before making a decision.

Once the manager has identified and understood the structured or semistructured decision, the manager can enter the relevant data into the appropriate computerized model. The model allows managers to change the assumptions on which the decision is based and evaluate alternative solutions. The manager judges the alternatives, selects the best, implements it, and evaluates it under operating conditions. Relying on data bases for the inputs to automated decision models, DSS automate the programmable part of the decision. The objective of providing support and guidance for the decision making process necessitates that DSS be flexible, provide inquiry and response capabilities, and consider both the present and the future. These characteristics of decision support systems make them extremely useful for planning and control purposes.

Components of Decision Support Systems

A DSS consists of a data base, a model base, and a user interface. The components may be owned by an individual or shared among users.

259

CHAPTER 8
*Decision
Support
Systems
and Expert
Systems*

Data Base. Organizations may have one or more data bases available for management decision making. These data bases may contain data from internal and external sources. Analysis of the information required to make management decisions or fulfill reporting obligations identifies the specific pieces of data collected in an organization's data base(s). An internal source of data is the accounting information system. The data collected in the processing of accounting transactions are a necessary part of the DSS data base. The data base will also contain nonfinancial data about the events in the life of a business. External sources of data are publicly available data bases. On-line information services provide access to over 1,700 data bases. An organization may subscribe to one or more of the many data bases available. Data bases can supply stock prices, market share, line of business data, five-year summaries of operating data, earnings data, names of officers and directors, management letters, and other financial accounting information for publicly traded companies. For example, the American Institute of Certified Public Accountants (AICPA) offers on-line data bases like Total On-Line Tax and Accounting Library (TOTAL), NEXIS, and National Automated Accounting Research System (NAARS).

Model Base. The **model base** is a collection of decision models. Each decision model is independent from all other decision models. The decision model specifies the required data, which is then accessed from the data base. Models range from very simple, straightforward mathematical models (such as the aging of accounts receivable) to more sophisticated programs (such as project management).

User Interface. The **user interface** provides a user-friendly mechanism such as menus for the accountant/manager to interact with the DSS. The interface allows the user to choose the decision model needed to support the identified problem and to change the assumptions of the model (what if or goal-seeking analysis). Some data base applications also include a programming language (for example, Paradox includes PAL). These languages allow the user to develop applications based on the data base (e.g., accounts receivable processing) and to query the data base in ways not possible by using the available menuing system. Exhibit 8-1 on page 260 illustrates the components of a DSS for sales forecasting.

Development Guidelines for Decision Support Systems

Top Management Support. When developing a DSS, as with any information system, it is critical to have upper-level management support. The participating managers should include representatives from both the decision area and the MIS support group. This type of involvement will help the system developer in structuring the DSS within the organization.

Ease of Use and Flexibility. A DSS must be easy to use. It should be flexible enough so the user can analyze the problem in a variety of ways.

EXHIBIT 8-1   Components of a DSS for Sales Forecasting

DATA

1111		Order Number	Due Date	Forecast	Sales Quantity	Unit Price
		Viewing 1111 table:				
	1	10001	1/27/92	5186	4952	12.00
	2	10002	2/24/92	4826	4926	12.00
	3	10003	3/24/92	5111	5191	12.00
	4	10004	4/21/92	4827	5002	12.00
	5	10005	5/19/92	4976	4824	12.00
	6	10006	6/16/92	5044	4876	12.00
	7	10007	7/14/92	5414	5290	12.00
	8	10008	8/11/92	4832	4941	12.00
	9	10009	9/08/92	5194	4967	12.00
	10	10010	10/06/92	5050	4883	12.00
	11	10011	11/03/92	4979	5157	12.00
	12	10012	12/01/92	5290	5228	12.00
	13	10013	12/29/92	4734	4906	12.00
	14	10101	1/26/93	5297		

INTERFACE

Marketing Models

0. Main Menu

Forecasting

1. Simple Average
2. Weighted Moving Average

Selling Price

3. Contribution Margin Analysis

Please enter your selection:

Simple Average Forecasting Model

Enter the product to forecast:

0. Marketing Models

1. 1111
2. 1112
3. 1113

Selection:

Simple Average

The number of past time periods is: 13
The sum of prior sales is: 65143
The simple average is: 5011
The forecast for next period is: 5011

Forecast another product? (Y/N)

MODEL

```
IF c10 = "0" THEN QUITLOOP ENDIF

IF c10 = "1" THEN tbl = "1111"
                   fld = "Sales Quantity"
ENDIF

IF c10 = "2" THEN tbl = "1112"
                   fld = "Sales Quantity"
ENDIF

IF c10 = "3" THEN tbl = "1113"
                   fld = "Sales Quantity"
ENDIF

CLEAR
@3,30 ?? "PLEASE WAIT"
?
@5,15 ?? "- calculating the forecast for next
period -"
CANVAS OFF
CLEAR
        sum__sales = csum(tbl,fld)
        avg__sales = caverage(tbl,fld)
        cnt__sales = ccount(tbl,fld)
        avg__sales = ROUND(avg__sales,0)
CANVAS ON
CLEAR
```

Model Bases and Data Bases.   An appropriate type of problem must be identified in order to establish the need for a DSS. The problem will indicate the models to include in the model base. Decision models, although simplified representations of the problem, should represent realistically the decision environment. The decision models will specify the relevant data that must be available in the data base. Some organizations employ dedicated model builders and data base management supervisors.

261

CHAPTER 8
*Decision
Support
Systems
and Expert
Systems*

Documentation.   Throughout the development process it is very important to document accurately all aspects of the DSS. This documentation will help in the development process and in any future updating. A set of documentation should also be available to users to help them understand how to use the DSS.

Types of Decision Support Systems

Decision support systems can be divided into seven types ordered by the ability of the DSS to determine directly the decision to be made or the outcome to be selected.

File Drawer.   File drawer systems are simply highly automated filing systems. They are on-line to allow for inquiry and response so the user can get immediate answers to questions. An example of this type of system is the typical airline reservation system.

Data Analysis.   Data analysis systems provide on-line access to data files for the purpose of data analysis and manipulation, inquiry and response, and data input. Systems that allow the comparison of actual results with any budget or standard figure fall into this category of DSS.

Information Analysis.   Information analysis systems provide a wider range of capabilities than data analysis systems. Information analysis systems provide for the use of data from files to be combined with external data from other models. An example is a sales analysis system (discussed later in Chapter 11) that routinely provides breakdowns of sales by customer, product, sales representative, or any other basis for management analysis.

Accounting Models.   Accounting models, as the name implies, are based on accounting relationships. Typical output is in the form of financial statements that depict the result of the financial data and accounting relationships and assumptions input to the model. A common accounting model is the budgeting system discussed earlier in this chapter.

Representation Models.   Representation models are state-of-the-art simulation models. They incorporate accounting relationships as well as nonaccounting equations. The nonaccounting equations may represent cause and effect relationships and may contain the probabilities of certain events occurring, as in risk analysis. These decision support systems are oriented toward giving the estimated consequences of possible actions by management.

262

*PART II
Technical
Aspects of
Accounting
Information
Systems*

Optimization Models. Optimization models provide the "optimal" solution to complex quantitative problems having specific objectives. The constraints affecting the problem must be expressible in mathematical terms and then combined in a mathematical equation that will ultimately result in the optimal solution to the problem. The models are designed based on these equations and provide guidance for the optimal use of resources, such as inventory or materials. While the precise assumptions of these models are rarely satisfied in real life, the resultant solutions turn out to be very useful approximations for many practical situations.

One frequently used optimization model is linear programming (LP). This involves the optimization of a linear function (usually either a cost function to be minimized or a profit function to be maximized) subject to the satisfaction of related linear constraints. For example, a firm may wish to determine the optimal level of productive activities. This would involve maximizing a profit function, but would then also require explicit treatment of any constraints on production facilities, such as limited availability of labor or a limit on the amount of a needed raw material.

Suggestion Models. Suggestion models determine a solution to a specific problem when provided with the necessary input data. These models are mostly used for more structured, repetitive problems. Unlike optimization models, the suggested solution requires no interpretation because the DSS itself provides the answer to the problem or the proper alternative to follow.

Exhibit 8-2 illustrates one type of a typical DSS model. This financial model is based on a series of equations which link the input variables provided by company management to output predictions. For example, the predicted success of decisions such as pricing, advertising, and new product introductions or old product terminations can be quickly surveyed with this "what if" decision support system model.

This accounting model is more sophisticated than the normal budget because many components of the budget are not simply given, but are instead derived from other parameters of the model. For example, in the usual budget the amount of total sales is given, with the rest of the budget derived from this figure. But in this model, sales are derived from employment levels, demographic trends, competition, interest rates, disposable income levels, and other economic indicators. Making these connections between the larger economy and the firm's sales is quite challenging.

Benefits of Decision Support Systems

The DSS offers help with formulating and understanding problems, in-depth analysis, and time savings.

Problem Formulation and Understanding. Developing and using a DSS helps the manager to formulate the problem to be solved. To develop the decision model and identify the correct data to include in the data base requires that the manager fully work through the problem. This process focuses the manager's thinking by forcing the manager to structure and organize the problem.

EXHIBIT 8-2   A Financial Decision Support System (DSS) Model

263

CHAPTER 8
Decision
Support
Systems
and Expert
Systems

Component	Input Variables		Output Predictions
	External to Firm	Internal to Firm	
Sales	Employment levels Demographic trends Competition Interest rates Disposable income levels Other economic indicators	Product or service prices Amount of advertising Types of marketing Types of products or services Size of sales force	Total sales Returns and allowances Sales backlog Net sales Units sold or services rendered
Cost of goods or services	Raw material prices Salary and wage rates Cost accounting data Fuel costs General inflation rate Government regulations	Location of facilities Personnel policies Union contract terms Product mix Raw materials Production processes Equipment and facilities Employee benefits policies Inventory management	Cost of goods sold Costs by product or service line Raw material costs Labor costs
Selling, general, and administrative (SGA) expenses	Prevailing salary and wage rates Government inflation rate Government regulations	Company organization Location of facilities Size of sales force Sales commission rates Administrative support functions Amount of advertising Salary and employee benefits policies	Total SGA expense Expenses by category
Investment borrowing	Current interest rates Riskiness of investments Credit ratings	Maturities of investments Maturities of borrowings Types of investments Sources of borrowed funds Cash management policies	Yield on investments Interest expense
Income taxes	Federal, state, and local tax regulations	Accounting policies Capital expenditures Locations of operations	Income tax expenses Income tax credits

264

PART II
Technical
Aspects of
Accounting
Information
Systems

In-Depth Analyses. The "what if," goal-seeking, and data analysis capabilities of DSS allow more in-depth analyses and understanding of a decision than would otherwise be possible. These capabilities allow a manager to change the values of the assumptions in the decision and see the new outcome. In this way, managers can evaluate the uncertainty associated with a specific decision.

Time Savings. With the structured aspects of the problem automated, managers have more time to address other problems or to analyze more thoroughly the current problem. This improves the effectiveness of the manager.

Limitations of Decision Support Systems

DSS are not appropriate if the problem is not suitable to the use of algorithms (that is, the problem is based on heuristics or "rules of thumb"). DSS are also not appropriate if an optimal solution cannot be determined because the mathematics are too complicated, there are numerous objectives, or the mathematics are not yet programmable. Finally, when the uncertainty associated with the decision is so variable that it causes difficulty in forecasting values or ranges of values for the assumptions of the problem, a DSS is inappropriate.

Individual Versus Group Decision Support Systems

One or more of the components, or the entire DSS, may be owned by an individual. That person has sole access to the DSS either through security measures like password protection or because the DSS is developed on a stand-alone microcomputer. Complete ownership of a DSS minimizes the advantages of a data base approach to information systems design. Alternatively, some of the components may be shared in a **group decision support system (GDSS)**. A shared DSS or a group DSS (GDSS) may facilitate group decision making. A typical group decision is budget preparation. A group of managers representing the different segments of an organization meet to develop a budget for the organization. Each manager is intimately familiar with his or her area, but probably not familiar with another manager's area. The budgeting process requires the meshing of all areas to form a cohesive plan for the larger group. The use of a GDSS may assist managers in understanding the larger picture of budget preparation.

Group Data Base. It is most likely that the data base will be the shared component of the DSS. Individual users will then access the data necessary to run their models and support their decisions. A shared data base necessitates the additional component of a data base management system (DBMS).

Group Decision Models. Just as the data base may be available to numerous users, so may decision models. This minimizes the computer facilities needed to store decision models and adds an element of consistency to the available models. Everyone using a PERT/CPM model will use the same PERT/CPM model. When the model base is shared, a model base management system

(MBMS) is also needed. This component is similar to the DBMS except it manages the access and use of the models.

265

CHAPTER 8
*Decision
Support
Systems
and Expert
Systems*

Other Components. Existing GDSS have additional components to achieve the objective of group support. A mechanism for displaying information to the group is an integral part of a GDSS. Since group consensus is often the goal, voting mechanisms are also embedded in GDSS.

Facility Layout. To date, GDSS research and development have concentrated on providing assistance when a group of managers come together in a single location to make one decision. Various layouts of the physical facilities (e.g., tables and chairs, computer terminals, display screens) have been tried. The horseshoe-shaped room, now often seen in classrooms used for case discussions, is one effective design. Often, off of the main meeting room are a number of small, individual offices with computers for the managers to use to develop their part of the group decision.

Some Real-Life Examples of Decision Support Systems

A Big Six public accounting firm designed and implemented a micro-mainframe DSS for the Department of Commerce. This system extracts key data from several dissimilar accounting systems, transforms the data to a standard chart of accounts, and downloads the data to microcomputers for spreadsheet analysis and graphical display. The system has proven so successful at Commerce that the Treasury has expressed interest in a similar system.

Clover Club Foods, a subsidiary of Borden, Inc., contracted the design and installation of an integrated, distributed DSS using microcomputers and a minicomputer. The system provides managers in marketing, finance, and production with the ability to perform "what if" analyses of different business scenarios and to generate sales forecasts, production schedules, and financial projections.

A financial services firm had developed for it a microcomputer-based DSS to analyze the amount and sources of float income (the income generated by funds invested while the funds are waiting to be paid out). The system also allows the client's money managers to assess the potential impact of mix changes in investment transactions.

A defendant firm involved in a major antitrust litigation constructed a DSS to aid in its defense against damage claims by the plaintiff. The model simulates the operations of the plaintiff's firm that would have occurred over the past 25 years but for the alleged illegal actions of the defendant. Sensitivity to economic, environmental, and competitive factors can be analyzed to identify issues critical to the formation of the defense and strategies the defense could pursue in arguments against models of the damages presented by the plaintiff.

PLEXSYS is a GDSS project at the University of Arizona that has been tested in academic and business settings. PLEXSYS is currently in place and used by a major multinational electronics firm.

266

PART II
Technical
Aspects of
Accounting
Information
Systems

CONCEPT SUMMARY

Examples of Decision Support System (DSS) Problems

Type of Problem	Data	Model	Explanation
Overhead rate calculation	Values of costs and cost drivers	Regression	Generates overhead cost per cost driver—user assesses "reliability" of results
Reorder point and quantity	Demand, ordering costs, carrying costs, cost of capital, lead time	Reorder point and EOQ, L4L, POQ, PPB	Generates a quantity to order and an inventory level when order should be placed—user applies judgment in implementing results
Project scheduling	Due dates, steps in project, timing of steps, order of steps	CPM/PERT, GANTT charts	Generates a schedule of events, may indicate available slack time—user applies judgment in implementing schedule
Sales forecasting	Historical demand, seasonality information	Moving average, autoregressive models, multiple parameter models, combination models	Generates a forecast of sales—user assesses the "reliability" of the forecast
Cash budgeting	Cash inflows, cash outflows, timing of flows, interest rates, credit terms	Simultaneous equations	Generates a cash budget and indicates cash needs—user assesses reasonableness
Resource allocation	Selling price, costs, units of resource needed	Linear programming	Generates a priority of use for resources—user applies judgment in following priority

Project Management: An Example

267

CHAPTER 8
*Decision
Support
Systems
and Expert
Systems*

An example of a semistructured decision that is amenable to a DSS environment is project management. PERT/CPM or GANTT charts are models that are used to help managers deal with the many aspects of completing a major project on schedule in an orderly way. When any variable is changed after a project has begun, the DSS can see to it that the effect on other steps of the project becomes immediately observable. Management can then make any necessary adjustments to schedules, shipments, or orders to accommodate the change.

GANTT Charts

GANTT charts are very straightforward, which is one of their great advantages. Exhibit 8-3 gives an example of a GANTT chart for a ten-week implementation schedule in a small business. Every implementation will be different, and, in the implementation of many large systems, each of these steps might take several months.

EXHIBIT 8-3   Ten-Week Implementation Schedule

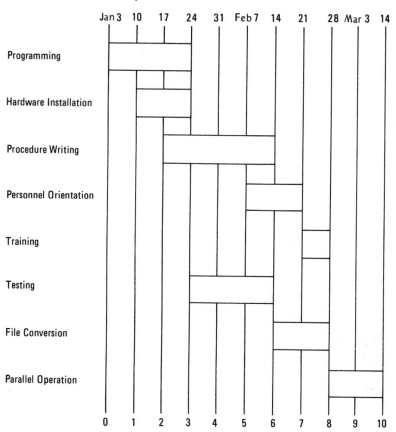

268

PART II
Technical
Aspects of
Accounting
Information
Systems

The chart breaks down into two basic parts: On the left are the required steps, and on the right is the time frame in which the steps will be performed. In Exhibit 8-3, there are eight steps, ranging from programming to parallel operation, with each step represented by a different line. The time frame in the exhibit is ten weeks, but the chart could have any number of appropriate time units (such as years, months, days, hours, or even minutes).

Since the exhibit shows ten weeks, there are 11 vertical lines, from 0 (the beginning of the first week) to 10 (the end of the tenth week). Each line is numbered twice; the actual date is at the top of the line and the relative date is at the bottom of the line. For example, the middle line is marked February 7 at the top and 5 at the bottom, meaning that the end of the fifth week occurs on February 7. For each step, a mark is made in the time frame showing the time units in which a particular step is to be performed. The exhibit shows that programming should take three weeks, and will be done in the first three weeks, while parallel operation will occur during weeks 9 and 10.

One important piece of information that the GANTT chart does not give is the interrelationships between tasks. In Exhibit 8-3, both training and testing begin after programming is completed, but the chart does not indicate whether programming has to be finished before training can begin, before testing can begin, before both can begin, or even whether any such relationship exists. The exhibit also has file conversion beginning just after procedure writing ends, but does not indicate whether there is a connection, that is, whether procedure writing must be finished before file conversion can begin.

In some cases, these interrelationships are not particularly important or are so few in number that they can be handled using the experience of the project manager. However, in more complicated situations, these interrelationships can be extremely important, primarily because they imply that delay in completing one task may have far-reaching consequences. In other words, some tasks are critically important to the entire project because later tasks depend upon their completion, while other tasks essentially stand alone. What is often needed is a method to show these relationships in a clear and easily used fashion. Such a method is available in the PERT/CPM network.

PERT/CPM Network

The PERT/CPM network will work with any project that meets two conditions:

1. It must consist of a well-defined collection of tasks, that, when completed, mean that the project is completed.
2. It must have tasks that have to be performed in sequence (for example, the file conversion must be complete before parallel operation can begin).

The **PERT (or Project Evaluation Review Technique) network** approach was developed originally to manage the construction of the *Polaris* submarine for the U. S. Navy. The **CPM (or Critical Path Method)** network approach was independently developed for building construction projects. There are slight differences in the two approaches. PERT is oriented to the uncertainty associated with the time estimate given for each task (for example, the programming

269

CHAPTER 8
*Decision
Support
Systems
and Expert
Systems*

may take more or less time than the three weeks estimated). CPM is oriented to the trade-off between cost of completion and time of completion for each task (for example, it may be possible to complete the file conversion in one week rather than two weeks by spending more money). However, for the purposes of this text, the two approaches are identical because we do not get into the complexities that distinguish them. Those who wish to read further on this topic will find the literature on these techniques is vast and widely available.

PERT and CPM have been used for the construction of a multistory office building, a maintenance overhaul of large-scale equipment, a research and development program for a new weapons system, and the market introduction of a new product. In all of these cases, PERT/CPM helps with the enormous task of managing a process that involves numerous steps, many dependent on other steps, often done by different people, and many which require different amounts of time. As discussed later in this book (in Chapters 14, 15, and 16), system development is a similar process with a similar management challenge.

Using PERT/CPM

PERT/CPM is one model, in the model base, that can be used to support project management. The PERT/CPM network approach begins by drawing a picture. The network is a picture of the implementation schedule where activities are represented by arrows and events are represented by nodes. The top diagram in Exhibit 8-4 gives a first sketch of the implementation schedule in a network form. The node on the far left represents the event of starting the implementation schedule. Four activities begin from that point—programming, hardware installation, personnel orientation, and procedure writing. The uncircled number next to each activity represents the number of weeks necessary to complete that activity. The next event is the completion of both programming and hardware installation; when that event occurs, the activity testing can begin. Similarly, when both personnel orientation and procedure writing are complete, the training activity begins. After testing is complete, file conversion can begin, and, finally, after both file conversion and training are complete, parallel operation can begin. Parallel operation is the final activity, and hence, when it is complete, the entire project is finished.

This network representation is not particularly appropriate for future analysis. It will be more convenient if there is only one arrow (activity) going between any two nodes (events). For this reason, a dummy activity taking zero time is used just so this format requirement can be met. The middle diagram in Exhibit 8-4 shows the network after these dummy activities have been added. There are now eight events and ten activities—the regular eight activities and the two added dummy activities. Node 1 (or event 1) represents the start of the implementation schedule, and node 8 (or event 8) represents the end of the implementation schedule. Hardware installation is now the activity between events 1 and 2, programming is now the activity between events 2 and 3, and the dummy activity between events 2 and 3 indicates that hardware installation must be completed before event 3 has occurred. A similar process was carried out for personnel orientation and procedure writing. Personnel orientation is

EXHIBIT 8-4   Network Diagrams

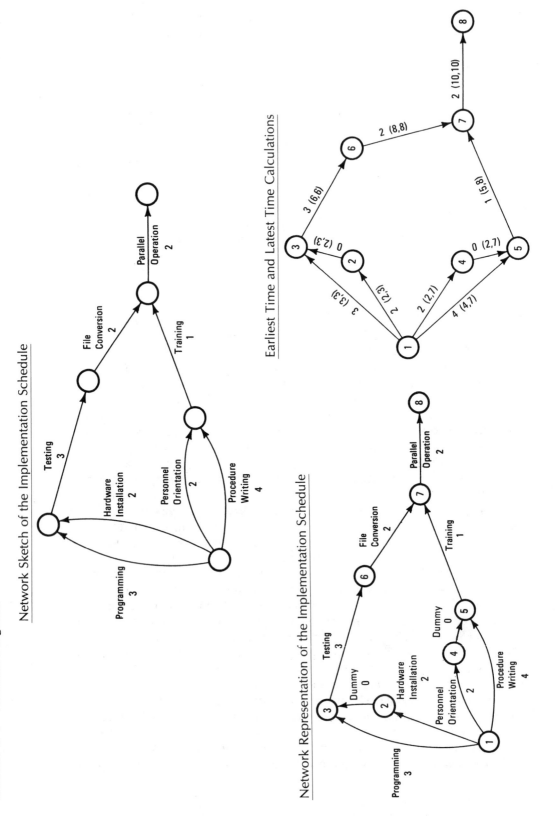

Network Sketch of the Implementation Schedule

Earliest Time and Latest Time Calculations

Network Representation of the Implementation Schedule

the activity between events 1 and 4, while procedure writing is the activity between events 1 and 5. Again, a dummy activity was added between events 4 and 5 to indicate personnel orientation must be completed before training can begin.

271

CHAPTER 8
*Decision
Support
Systems
and Expert
Systems*

Network Path

The next step is to introduce the concept of a path. A path is a string of events and activities stretching from the start, node 1, to the end, node 8. In the example problem there are four paths through the network. One path is from node 1 to node 3 to node 6 to node 7 to node 8. The four paths through the network are

Path	Nodes
1	1—3—6—7—8
2	1—2—3—6—7—8
3	1—4—5—7—8
4	1—5—7—8

Suppose path 1 were the entire network; that is, assume that the network did not contain any nodes or arrows not on path 1. How much time would it take to go from node 1, the start, to node 8, the end? For path 1 it would take three weeks to go from node 1 to node 3 (programming takes three weeks), three weeks to go from node 3 to node 6 (testing), two weeks to go from node 6 to node 7 (file conversion), and two weeks to go from node 7 to node 8 (parallel operation). Thus, path 1 would take ten weeks. Repeating this process for each of the other three paths finds that path 2 would take nine weeks, path 3 would take five weeks, and path 4 would take seven weeks.

Critical Path. Path 1 is thus the longest path and is therefore called the **critical path**. The critical path is so named because if any activity on the critical path is delayed, then the entire project is delayed. The entire implementation schedule is supposed to take ten weeks, but if any activity on the critical path (programming, testing, file conversion, or parallel operation) takes longer than expected, the entire project will be correspondingly delayed. But the same is not true of all activities in the network. If training took two weeks instead of one, then path 3 would take six weeks rather than five, and path 4 would take eight weeks rather that seven, but the overall project would still be completed within ten weeks.

Earliest Time/Latest Time. In a complicated situation, the network sketch may contain hundreds of nodes and thousands of paths, so there needs to be an algorithm for determining the critical path. The bottom diagram in Exhibit 8-4 illustrates the standard algorithm. This algorithm is based on two concepts for each activity, the earliest time and the latest time. The earliest time is the soonest that activity could be completed, while the latest time is the latest that activity could be completed without delaying the entire project. Those activities which have no difference between these two different times are the activities

272

Part II
Technical
Aspects of
Accounting
Information
Systems

on the critical path. In other words, if the activity on the critical path is delayed, then that will delay the entire project. Exhibit 8-4, therefore, has three numbers for each activity:

1. The time necessary for completion
2. The earliest time
3. The latest time

Time for Completion (Earliest Time). The earliest times are computed by going through the network forward, and the latest times are computed by going through the network backward. The earliest time calculations begin with node 1. Programming, hardware installation, procedure writing, and personnel orientation all have no activities before them, and thus the earliest any of them can be completed is the time necessary for their completion. The dummy activities take no time, so their earliest time is the same as that of their predecessor activity. Testing and training are more complicated because they both require that two activities be completed before they can even begin. Thus, the earliest testing can even begin is the maximum of the two earliest times of its predecessor activities. Testing cannot begin for three weeks, and it then takes three weeks to complete, thus making the earliest time for completion for that activity six weeks. Similarly, the earliest time for training is five weeks. It is then straightforward to determine that the earliest time for file conversion is eight weeks and the earliest time for parallel operation is ten weeks. All these figures for earliest time appear in Exhibit 8-4.

Time for Completion (Latest Time). The latest time calculations begin with node 8, the end. The earliest completion for the project is ten weeks. The procedure is to go back through the network to determine how late an activity can be completed without delaying the entire project. Parallel operation must be completed by ten weeks to keep from delaying the project. The next step is to file conversion and training; since parallel operation takes two weeks, they must both be completed before eight weeks and thus their latest times are both eight. Since file conversion takes two weeks, the latest time for testing is six. Then, the latest time for both activities going to node 3 is three because testing takes three weeks. Similarly, the latest time for both activities going into node 5 is seven because training takes one week. Since both dummy activities take no time, the latest time for hardware installation is then three, while the latest time for personnel orientation is then seven.

Slack Time. **Slack time** is the difference between the earliest time and the latest time that an activity will be completed. This difference is the amount of time that the activity could be delayed without delaying the entire project. The activities on the critical path are, then, those activities with zero slack time. These computations are summarized in Exhibit 8-5.

Advantages of the Network Approach. The network representation of the project has the advantage of picking out the critical path—those activities which must be most closely watched because the project most directly depends on them. Another advantage is the picture that the network provides of the entire

EXHIBIT 8-5 Network Calculations

273

CHAPTER 8
Decision
Support
Systems
and Expert
Systems

| Activity | Nodes | | Times | | |
	Begin	End	Earliest	Latest	Slack
Programming	1	3	3	3	0
Hardware installation	1	2	2	3	1
Dummy	2	3	2	3	1
Procedure writing	1	5	4	7	3
Personnel orientation	1	4	2	7	5
Dummy	4	5	2	7	5
Training	5	7	5	8	3
Testing	3	6	6	6	0
File conversion	6	7	8	8	0
Parallel operation	7	8	10	10	0

project and the interrelationships between the activities that make up the project. The network makes clear the overall picture and how the various activities fit together.

SOFTWARE FOR DECISION SUPPORT

Types of software that support DSS include spreadsheets, financial modeling packages, and data analysis packages. A wide variety of software is provided by different vendors. The choice of software that best suits the problem situation will maximize the benefits of developing a DSS.

Spreadsheets

Budgeting.   The original use in business of spreadsheet software was the budgeting application. A manager can usually prepare the first budget faster by hand. However, preparation of each subsequent budget is faster and easier on the computer using a spreadsheet. The overall spreadsheet should be segmented into discrete subparts. The first, and very critical, subsection includes the assumptions and parameters of the problem (for example, the expected sales growth used in developing budgeted financial statements). The remaining subsections capture well-defined parts of the problem (for example, the income statement, cash flow statement, and balance sheet). Each subsection is related to the assumptions, parameters, and other subsections through cell formulas. However, each subsection should allow for addition and deletion of rows and columns within a part without affecting other blocks.

"What If" Analysis.   The "what if" feature of spreadsheets allows users to change the parameters of the decision and see what will happen. For example, a budgeting DSS would allow a manager to ask, "If sales volume increases by 10 percent, what will happen to the required production levels and raw material purchase requirements, and what is the impact on income?"

274

Part II
Technical
Aspects of
Accounting
Information
Systems

Exhibit 8-6 is an extended example of the "what if" capabilities in Borland International's spreadsheet, QUATTRO. The first spreadsheet shows a very simple forecast of gross income, business expenses and net income. Gross income is expected to grow 10% annually, while the business expenses are expected to grow at 6.5% annually. Net income is defined as gross income less business expenses. This first spreadsheet also shows that spreadsheet programs allow copying cells so that relationships like a 10% growth rate are maintained.

The second spreadsheet explores the effect of different assumptions about inflation rates on forecasted business expenses and forecasted net income. In the "What If" table, the net income and business expenses figures are given for different possible inflation rates, from 5% to 10% in steps of 0.5%. Note that the figures for gross income and business expenses in the spreadsheet match the figures in the "What If" table for an inflation assumption of 6.5%.

Data Analysis. Spreadsheets are also valuable for data analysis. Built-in functions perform some types of data analysis, such as calculating sums, averages, standard deviations, and regressions. There are also simple data base sorting and lookup facilities available. In addition, current spreadsheets are capable of using accounting numbers from accounting applications as the basis for further data analysis. For accounting data in printouts, the data parse function can be used to separate the data into columns. Exhibit 8-7 on pages 276–77 illustrates the data parse capability in an accounts receivable setting. The first half of the exhibit gives a sample output from a standard accounts receivable subsidiary ledger. This printout can be captured as a disk file and then imported into a spreadsheet. The numbers, labels, and dates can then be converted into spreadsheet cells, and computations can be performed on them. The second half of Exhibit 8-7 then shows calculations of days past due, a sorting of individual invoices (breaking them into groups of those due and those not yet due), and a cumulative total of amounts owed. Thus, the analyst can use the spreadsheet to do an analysis on an invoice basis even though the output was generated on a customer basis. This means the user can generate different types of analyses without changing the data processing application.

A spreadsheet application can also become part of the company's routine data processing when calculations are structured and determined. For example, a complicated management compensation plan based on overall company performance may be extremely complex, with no straightforward calculations derivable from the financial accounting system. The necessary accounting data could be exported from the financial accounting system to the spreadsheet. Using built-in functions and the programming available with the spreadsheet application, a manager could perform the computations to calculate compensation. In this example, the spreadsheet becomes part of the data processing since the computations are predetermined. Each spreadsheet has a programming language (usually called the macro language) in a spreadsheet that facilitates standard, routine computations. A macro can be built to execute a sequence of commands and automate the analysis. This process could save users time since they would not need to sit at the terminal and enter each step in the computation. While the computer is processing the steps in the macro, the user could attend to other duties. However, in general, spreadsheets are not good for normal, day-to-day data processing. Spreadsheet software is a data analysis

EXHIBIT 8-6   Example of "What If" Analysis Using a Spreadsheet Application   *275*

CHAPTER 8
Decision
Support
Systems
and Expert
Systems

A Database Projecting Yearly Income

	A	B	C	D	E	F	G
1		1992	1993	1994	1995	1996	1997
2	Gross Income	$45,000	$49,500	$54,450	$59,895	$65,884	$72,473
3	Bus. Expenses	$10,016	$10,667	$11,360	$12,099	$12,885	$13,723
4	Net Income	$34,984	$38,833	$43,090	$47,796	$52,999	$58,750
5							
6	Sales Increase:	10.00%					
7	Inflation Rate:	6.50%					

+B3*(1 + B7)   copied to D3..G3

+C2−C3   copied to D4..G4

+B2*(1 + B6)   copied to D2..G2

A1: [W16]

12-Oct-92 03:44 PM   READY

A Table Showing Net Income at Different Inflation Rates

	A	B	C	D	E	F	G
1		1992	1993	1994	1995	1996	1997
2	Gross Income	$45,000	$49,500	$54,450	$59,895	$65,884	$72,473
3	Bus. Expenses	$10,016	$10,667	$11,360	$12,099	$12,885	$13,723
4	Net Income	$34,984	$38,833	$43,090	$47,796	$52,999	$58,750
5							
6	Sales Increase:	10.00%					
7	Inflation Rate:	6.50%			The "What If" Table		
8			+G4	+G3			
9		5.00%	$59,690	$12,783			
10		5.50%	$59,382	$13,091			
11		6.00%	$59,069	$13,404			
12		6.50%	$58,750	$13,723			
13		7.00%	$58,425	$14,048			
14		7.50%	$58,094	$14,379			
15		8.00%	$57,756·	$14,717			
16		8.50%	$57,412	$15,061			
17		9.00%	$57,062	$15,411			
18		9.50%	$56,705	$15,768			
19		10.00%	$56,342	$16,131			
20							

Inflation Rates   Net Income   Business Expenses

A1: [W16]

12-Oct-92 03:44 PM   READY

Source: QUATTRO ®, Copyright © 1987, Borland International, Inc. Used by permission.

EXHIBIT 8-7   Data PARSE Capability

06/01/92

DOME HOMES, INC.
AGED TRIAL BALANCE

ID	CUSTOMER NAME	INVOICE NO	STAT TYPE	INVOICE DATE	AMOUNT	CURRENT	AGED BALANCE OVER 30	OVER 60	OVER 90	OVER 120
TOL001	TOLEDO DOME HOMES	00010584	IN	11/14/91	7723.00					7723.00
		00011349	IN	01/12/92	3045.29					3045.29
		00012718	IN	03/15/92	345.00			345.00		
		00013294	IN	04/13/92	4840.00		4840.00			
		00013293	IN	05/29/92	2390.00	2390.00				
	CUSTOMER TOTAL				18343.29	2390.00	4840.00	345.00	0.00	10768.29
LOS001	LOS ANGELES CONSTRUCTION	00012583	IN	03/15/92	20000.00			20000.00		
		00013777	IN	04/13/92	10000.00		10000.00			
		00013760	IN	05/19/92	5800.00	5800.00				
	CUSTOMER TOTAL				35800.00	5800.00	10000.00	20000.00	0.00	0.00
SUN001	SUNSHINE HOMES, INC.	00011753	IN	02/13/92	8105.06				8105.06	
		00013594	IN	05/14/92	1470.22	1470.22				
		00013584	IN	05/24/92	1210.58	1210.58				
	CUSTOMER TOTAL				10785.86	2680.80	0.00	0.00	8105.06	0.00
TEN001	TENNESSEE SHELTERS, INC	00010992	IN	02/13/92	2216.66				2216.66	
		00013246	IN	05/14/92	5571.18	5571.18				
		00013245	IN	05/14/92	340.25	340.25				
	CUSTOMER TOTAL				8128.09	5911.43	0.00	0.00	2216.66	0.00
	GRAND TOTALS				73057.24	16782.23	14840.00	20345.00	10321.72	10768.29

EXHIBIT 8-7 Data PARSE Capability (continued)

	A 3	B 7	C 25	D 9	E 10	F 6	G 5	H 6	I 5	J 8	K 9	L 10	M 10	N 10

1 A/R Analysis
2 ***********

Report Date	06/15/92
Calc W/ Terms? (1=T, 0=N)	1
Interest % Rate	11%

Numerical Avg Days Outstanding (NADO)
Dollar Avg Days Outstanding (DADO)
Interest Cost @ 11%

	Within Terms	Over Terms	Total
	46	31	77
	46	45	91
	$1,015	$986	$2,001

	ID	CUSTOMER NAME	INVOICE NO	INVOICE DATE	DAYS OLD	TERMS	DAYS PAST DUE	DUE?	$-DAYS W/IN TERMS	$-DAYS OVER TERMS	TOTAL $-DAYS	INVOICE AMOUNT	CUMULATIVE
13	7 LOS001	LOS ANGELES CONSTRUCTION	00012583	03/15/92	92	30	62	1	600000	1240000	1840000	20000.00	20,000
14	8 LOS001	LOS ANGELES CONSTRUCTION	00013777	04/13/92	63	30	33	1	300000	330000	630000	10000.00	30,000
15	11 SUN001	SUNSHINE HOMES, INC.	00011753	02/13/92	122	60	62	1	486304	502514	988817	8105.06	38,105
16	1 TOL001	TOLEDO DOME HOMES	00010584	11/14/91	213	120	93	1	926760	718239	1644999	7723.00	45,828
17	16 TEN001	TENNESSEE SHELTERS, INC	00013246	05/14/92	32	10	22	1	55712	122566	178278	5571.18	51,399
18	2 TOL001	TOLEDO DOME HOMES	00011349	01/12/92	154	120	34	1	365435	103540	468975	3045.29	54,445
19	15 TEN001	TENNESSEE SHELTERS, INC	00010992	02/13/92	122	10	112	1	22167	248266	270433	2216.66	56,661
20	17 TEN001	TENNESSEE SHELTERS, INC	00013245	05/14/92	32	10	22	1	3403	7486	10888	340.25	57,001
21	9 LOS001	LOS ANGELES CONSTRUCTION	00013760	05/19/92	27	30	0	0	156600	0	156600	5800.00	62,801
22	4 TOL001	TOLEDO DOME HOMES	00013294	04/13/92	63	120	0	0	304920	0	304920	4840.00	67,641
23	5 TOL001	TOLEDO DOME HOMES	00013293	05/29/92	17	120	0	0	40630	0	40630	2390.00	70,031
24	12 SUN001	SUNSHINE HOMES, INC.	00013594	05/14/92	32	60	0	0	47047	0	47047	1470.22	71,502
25	13 SUN001	SUNSHINE HOMES, INC.	00013584	05/24/92	22	60	0	0	26633	0	26633	1210.58	72,712
26	3 TOL001	TOLEDO DOME HOMES	00012718	03/15/92	92	120	0	0	31740	0	31740	345.00	73,057
27													
28									3367349	3272610	6639959	73057.24	

278

Part II
*Technical
Aspects of
Accounting
Information
Systems*

tool, not a data processing tool. To develop data processing applications, software like Paradox or dBase or a full programming language like COBOL or C are more appropriate. These applications were discussed in Chapters 5 and 6.

Financial Modeling Languages

Financial modeling languages are also available for building the models of the DSS. The Interactive Financial Planning System (Execucom Systems Corporation's IFPS) is an example of model building software. These packages can be used as spreadsheets for data analysis even on normal budgeting applications. But the advantage of financial modeling language is in the area of long-range planning and modeling of the firm. Financial modeling languages allow simulations of uncertain estimates, which allows a better suited model in complex decisions than would be possible with a standard spreadsheet, though this capability is becoming part of some spreadsheets. Also, because financial models are written in English-like statements, the resultant models are more likely to be correct. Models developed with a financial modeling language are easier to share and consolidate (for example, the model of a subsidiary can be incorporated into the models of the organization as a whole).

Financial modeling languages include a goal-seeking option. Goal-seeking options allow the user to ask what needs to be done to achieve a desired goal. The user specifies a desired goal and the variables that should be changed in achieving the goal. The software application determines the necessary value of the variables needed to achieve the goal. For example, a manager may want to know what level of sales is necessary to achieve a target net income. Using a cost/volume/profit model, the target net income would be entered as the goal. Fixed costs, variable cost per unit, and selling price per unit would be held constant, while sales volume would be allowed to vary to achieve the goal. This goal-seeking capability is now becoming part of advanced spreadsheets.

The disadvantage of financial modeling languages is the time it takes to develop the model. Exhibit 8-8 on pages 279–80 is an example of an IFPS session.

Data Analysis Packages

Data analysis packages (SAS, SPSS, SYSTAT, MYSTAT) compensate for the statistical limitations of spreadsheet software. These limitations include the number of statistics that spreadsheets are programmed to calculate, the level of complication in preprogrammed spreadsheet statistics, and the number of observations includable in the data set. The data handling capabilities of data analysis packages are also better than spreadsheet software. For example, SAS reads data from a file, not memory as in spreadsheets, which permits more complicated graphs and more sophisticated statistical analyses. Data analysis packages also include specialty programs. For example, SAS has modules that perform quality control calculations and advanced forecasting techniques.

EXHIBIT 8-8   IFPS Session

279

CHAPTER 8
*Decision
Support
Systems
and Expert
Systems*

Sample Model

This user's guide will use a simple income statement model to illustrate the entry and solution of a model with IFPS. The Example Corporation is currently evaluating the feasibility of introducing a new product by looking at after-tax profits projected over the next five years. The following data have been collected:

(1) Initial volume will be 100,000 units with an expected growth rate of 4.5% per year.
(2) Initial sales price will be $2.25, with annual growth of 6%.
(3) Unit costs will be $.85 throughout the five-year period.
(4) Operating expenses will be 2% of sales. Division overhead will be 15% of variable cost.
(5) Scheduled expenses will be:

	1992	1993	1994	1995	1996
Interest expense	$ 15,742	21,522	21,147	24,905	21,311
Capital investment	$225,000	0	0	0	0

All new investments are depreciated using double declining balance depreciation over a life of 10 years, assuming no salvage value.

(6) Tax rate is 46%.

Sample IFPS File

```
EXAMPLE
MODEL
EXAMPLE
 1   COLUMNS 1-5
 2   *
 3   *   INCOME STATEMENT
 4   *
 5   VOLUME = VOLUME ESTIMATE, PREVIOUS VOLUME * 1.045
 6   SELLING PRICE = PRICE ESTIMATE, PREVIOUS SELLING PRICE * 1.06
 7      SALES = VOLUME * SELLING PRICE
 8   UNIT COST = .85
 9   VARIABLE COST = VOLUME * UNIT COST
10   DIVISION OVERHEAD = 15% * VARIABLE COST
11   DECBAL DEPR (INVESTMENT, SALVAGE, LIFE,'
12      DEPRECIATION FACTOR, 0, DEPRECIATION)
13   COST OF GOODS SOLD = VARIABLE COST +'
14      DIVISION OVERHEAD + DEPRECIATION
15   GROSS MARGIN = SALES − COST OF GOODS SOLD
16   OPERATING EXPENSE = .02 * SALES
17   INTEREST EXPENSE = 15742, 21522, 21147, 24905, 21311
18   *
19   NET BEFORE TAX = GROSS MARGIN − OPERATING EXPENSE −'
20      INTEREST EXPENSE
21   TAXES = TAX RATE * NET BEFORE TAX
22      NET AFTER TAX = NET BEFORE TAX − TAXES
23   *
24   INVESTMENT = 225000, 0
25   *
26   RATE OF RETURN = IRR(NET AFTER TAX + DEPRECIATION, INVESTMENT)
27   *
28   * DATA ESTIMATES
29   TAX RATE = 46%
30   VOLUME ESTIMATE = 100000
31   PRICE ESTIMATE = 2.25
32   SALVAGE = 0
33   LIFE = 10
34   DEPRECIATION FACTOR = 2
SOLVE
ALL
```

280

Part II
Technical
Aspects of
Accounting
Information
Systems

EXHIBIT 8-8 IFPS Session (continued)

Output

Income Statement	1	2	3	4	5
VOLUME	100000	104500	109203	114117	119252
SELLING PRICE	2.250	2.385	2.528	2.680	2.841
SALES	225000	249233	276075	305808	338744
UNIT COST	.8500	.8500	.8500	.8500	.8500
VARIABLE COST	85000	88825	92822	96999	101364
DIVISION OVERHEAD	12750	13324	13923	14550	15205
DEPRECIATION	45000	36000	28800	23040	18432
COST OF GOODS SOLD	142750	138149	135545	134589	135001
GROSS MARGIN	82250	111084	140529	171219	203743
OPERATING EXPENSE	4500	4985	5521	6116	6775
INTEREST EXPENSE	15742	21522	21147	24905	21311
NET BEFORE TAX	62008	84577	113861	140198	175657
TAXES	28524	38905	52376	64491	80802
NET AFTER TAX	33484	45672	61485	75707	94855
INVESTMENT	225000	0	0	0	0
RATE OF RETURN			.0542	.1932	.2778
DATA ESTIMATES					
TAX RATE	.4600	.4600	.4600	.4600	.4600
VOLUME ESTIMATE	100000	100000	100000	100000	100000
PRICE ESTIMATE	2.250	2.250	2.250	2.250	2.250
SALVAGE	0	0	0	0	0
LIFE	10	10	10	10	10
DEPRECIATION FACTOR	2	2	2	2	2

Extensions to Sample IFPS File

```
VOLUME THRU SALES

ANALYZE COST OF GOODS SOLD

WHAT IF
VOLUME ESTIMATE = 105000
PRICE ESTIMATE = 2.30
SOLVE
NET AFTER TAX, VOLUME, SELLING PRICE

WHAT IF
UNIT COST = .85, PREVIOUS UNIT COST * 1.065
SOLVE
NET AFTER TAX, VOLUME, SELLING PRICE

WHAT IF CONTINUE
VOLUME ESTIMATE = 105000
PRICE ESTIMATE = 2.30
SOLVE
NET AFTER TAX, VOLUME, SELLING PRICE

WHAT IF

SENSITIVITY TO PRICE ESTIMATE
−10, 5, 5
NET AFTER TAX

IMPACT ON NET AFTER TAX, BY 10
PRICE ESTIMATE
NONE

GOAL SEEKING
VOLUME
NET AFTER TAX = 60000, PREVIOUS NET AFTER TAX * 1.10
NET AFTER TAX
NONE
```

281

CHAPTER 8
Decision
Support
Systems
and Expert
Systems

CONCEPT SUMMARY			
Software Support for Decision Support			
Application Type	*Examples*	*Uses*	*Limitations*
Spreadsheets	QUATTRO, Lotus 1-2-3, Excel	Budgeting, data analysis, sensitivity analysis, graphics	Size of data set; types of statistics; sophistication of graphics; not a data processing tool
Financial modeling	IFPS, SLAM	Long-range planning, modeling, decision simulation	Time to develop; not a data processing tool
Data analysis	SAS, SPSS, SYSTAT, MYSTAT	Sophisticated data analysis, graphics, specialty modules	Less user friendly; documentation is often more technical; requires some programming skills

EXPERT SYSTEMS

Expert systems are growing in importance to accountants. Expert systems are best understood in the context of artificial intelligence.

Artificial Intelligence

Artificial Intelligence (AI), a broad area within computer science, attempts to develop computer software that achieves the same results as human intelligence and behavior. Originally, researchers in AI were involved in both hardware and software development. These pioneers set their goal at developing a computer that mimicked human intelligence and behavior. As AI developed, specialties emerged. Natural language programs, voice recognition, visual recognition, robotics, and expert systems are all included within the area of AI.

Natural Language Programs and Voice Recognition. Natural language programs allow communication with the computer in spoken languages. Applications now support computerized output in a natural language, for example, supermarket checkout registers that announce the price of a product as it is scanned. Using natural language as an input mechanism (voice recognition) is much more difficult because of the personal nuances in speech patterns. A few software vendors (ECCO Industries is a principal developer) are developing programs that recognize voice patterns as part of security systems. Cognitive

282

Part II
Technical
Aspects of
Accounting
Information
Systems

Systems has developed natural language programs that assist clients with insurance and investment decisions. Natural language programs are also being used to interface with data bases.

Visual Recognition. Visual recognition software relies on the recognition of programmed patterns. Programs of this type are used, for example, to inspect products visually for compliance to standards and as security devices (e.g., retinal scans or fingerprint images).

Robotics. Robotics is the area of AI that attempts to reproduce human movements. The most popular applications of robotics are in manufacturing of products and in research and development (R & D) of new products. Robots are often used to perform repetitive, tedious tasks that are boring to human workers. Since the robot does not tire or grow disinterested, it offers minimal chance of error. Robots are also used to perform hazardous procedures. For example, the R & D departments of chemical companies use robots to add dangerous catalysts to chemical mixtures in explosionproof rooms. If the mixture explodes, a robot is damaged, but a person is not injured. Automobile manufacturers use robots for painting applications to protect employees from inhaling the paint particles, which can be hazardous.

Expert Systems. Expert systems are computerized programs that address problems requiring the knowledge, experience, and judgment of an expert in the specific area. Expert systems may improve the decision-making process by providing better (expert) knowledge than the manager alone could provide, educating the user through its explanations, and automating decision making by providing a final decision. Within AI, the development and use of expert systems is of particular interest to accountants.

Characteristics of Expert Systems

Expert system applications are developed according to the rules that an expert would use to solve a specific problem. These rules include algorithms for any structured aspect of the decision and heuristics to capture the expert's judgment. Algorithms are those quantifiable statements used in making decisions (for example, the production of one unit of finished product requires 3 pounds of raw material A and 5 pounds of raw material B). **Heuristics** are rules of thumb that an expert has internalized through repeated experience with the decision (for example, a certain sound of an engine is associated with a particular problem). The rules can be weighted through the use of certainty factors to consider uncertainty. This process is similar to the process of assigning probabilities to outcomes in decision theory. For example, in analyzing the collectability of accounts receivable to determine the reasonableness of the allowance for doubtful accounts, the accountant may be 95 percent certain that the 30-day-old accounts are collectible but only 65 percent certain that the 60-day-old accounts are collectible. Certainty factors are equivalent to the probability of collection (95 percent and 65 percent) in this scenario. Many expert systems have the ability to provide an explanation of the logic used in making the resultant decision. A future goal, in the study and design of expert systems, is to develop a system that learns from its experiences. Exhibit 8-9 is an example of the explanation capability of an expert system.

283

CHAPTER 8
Decision
Support
Systems
and Expert
Systems

Components of Expert Systems

A typical expert system consists of a data base, a collection of rules, an inference engine, a user interface, and some type of knowledge acquisition mechanism.

Data Base.   The data base contains the facts pertinent to the specific problem. The combination of the data base and the collection of rules that an expert would use to solve the problem is known as the knowledge base.

Knowledge Base.   **Knowledge bases** are typically one of two types: rule based or frame based. Rule-based systems, the most common form, represent the accumulated knowledge in a series of IF-THEN rules. These IF-THEN rules are known as the production rules. Frame-based systems represent knowl-

EXHIBIT 8-9   Explanations from an Audit Consultation

The following dialogue illustrates how the normal series of questions that AUDIT-PLANNER asks can be interrupted to find out *why* a particular question was being asked. As before, the capitalized entries following the double asterisks represent the user's responses. The other statements are AUDITPLANNER's responses to the questions.

   3. Is this the first time that we have audited Example?
   **WHY
   [i.e., WHY is it important to determine whether this is the first time that we have audited Example?]
[1.0] Whether this is the first time that we have audited a client is one of the five standard parameters that identify a client. This may be useful later in the consultation. For example, it is relevant in determining whether there is a need to reduce the calculated materiality level due to the increased risk associated with an initial audit of the client and is relevant in determining the percentage rate used to determine the materiality level.
[back to question 3 . . .]
  ** YES

(note: several questions asked by AUDITPLANNER are skipped until the next time the user asks "WHY.")

  10. Is Example filing with a regulatory agency in preparation for the sale of its securities in a public market?
  ** WHY
  [i.e., WHY is it important to determine whether Example is filing with a regulatory agency in preparation for the sale of its securities in a public market?]

Source: Steinbart, P. J. "The Construction of a Rule-Based Expert System as a Method for Studying Materiality Judgments," *The Accounting Review* (January 1987), p. 112. Reprinted by permission of The American Accounting Association.

284

Part II
Technical
Aspects of
Accounting
Information
Systems

edge as slots and frames. Slots are specific pieces of information associated with frames, which are representations of a concept.

Inference Engine. An **inference engine** contains the logic and reasoning necessary to apply the rules. In a rule-based system, inference engines predominantly use either forward-chaining or backward-chaining methods to execute (fire) rules. Forward-chaining is data driven and relies on deductive logic (general to specific). The process begins by looking at the IF portion of the IF-THEN rule and matches the IF requirements to the data base. Backward-chaining is goal oriented and relies on inductive logic (specific to general). The process looks for the path of logic that might have achieved the desired goal.

Knowledge Acquisition Mechanism. A **knowledge acquisition mechanism** is a tool used by the experts and knowledge engineers to capture the rules, heuristics, and knowledge of the expert. The process of documenting the steps that an expert takes and the knowledge used in making a decision is probably the most difficult and time consuming in the development process. The development of tools to assist in this process is an ongoing challenge.

User Interface. The user interface provides a user friendly way for the human user, either an expert or novice, to interact with the expert system. The user must input the specific data that pertain to the situation and respond to follow-up queries posed by the expert system. The user should also have a mechanism to query easily the expert system for explanations as to why a path of reasoning was followed or how a conclusion was reached. Exhibit 8-10 is a schematic of the components of an expert system.

Development of an Expert System

Identify the Problem. The first step in expert system development is to identify an appropriate problem. The problem should be very specific and narrow in scope and should require the accumulated experience and judgment of an expert. Such a problem might be internal control evaluation, materiality evaluation, or investment decisions. Problems involving rules that change frequently or on a large scale (such as filing an income tax return) are not suited to expert systems. Problems that require common sense, rely on historical information about the organization, or involve complex models are also unsuitable.

Develop a Prototype. Next a prototype is developed. This step involves capturing the knowledge of the expert(s) in the form of IF-THEN rules, choosing software for use in building the expert system, and developing a working model of the expert system. The process of capturing the knowledge of the expert is an extremely time consuming, difficult, and tedious task. An expert system can be created by using a programming language or a commercially available shell. Lisp, Interlisp, and Prolog are the three common artificial intelligence programming languages used to develop expert systems. Shells are commercially available applications that contain an inference engine and a

EXHIBIT 8-10   Components of Expert Systems

285

CHAPTER 8
*Decision
Support
Systems
and Expert
Systems*

DATA BASE

Customer File
Item File
Open Orders

INFERENCE ENGINE

forward chaining or
backward chaining determined
by software

KNOWLEDGE BASE

IF credit card number is valid
THEN check balance in account

IF balance in account after
    transaction will be below
    authorized credit limit
THEN authorize credit

IF order is accepted
THEN check availability of item

IF item is in stock
THEN tell customer that the item
    may be picked up in three days

USER INTERFACE

What is the customer's phone number?

_____-_____-_____

What is the customer's name?
    Last:
    First:
    Middle Initial:
What is the customer's address?
    Street:
    Apt. #:
    City:
    State:
    Zip Code:
What is the item number?

_____-_____ ____

Quantity ordered:

_____

What is the credit card number?

____ ____ ____ ____ __

fourth generation language (4GL). The inference engine determines the type of logic used in making decisions and the 4GL is used by a knowledge engineer to build the knowledge base. Commonly available shells include VPEXPERT, M.1 from Teknowledge, Guru from MDBS, and KEE from Intellicorp. The development of the prototype should include the expert(s), knowledge engineer(s), and potential users. The knowledge engineer and the expert should work to capture accurately and completely the rules necessary to solve the problem. The involvement of the user is necessary to be sure that the expert system is understandable and user-friendly to those who will actually be using the program. Based on this interactive, iterative process the prototype is updated and modified.

Build a Model. A critical step is to validate the expert system; that is, Are the decisions made by the program equal to or better than those made by the expert(s)? It is also important that the decisions made by the expert system be consistent from situation to situation. Validation of an expert system is a time-consuming and ongoing process. The difficulties with validation of an expert system can be compared to those encountered in using a test deck approach in auditing an accounting information system.

286

*PART II
Technical
Aspects of
Accounting
Information
Systems*

Complete the Commercial System. The remaining steps of development involve building a production model and building a commercially usable system. The production model is the expert system that is actually used by a small group of users. During its use the validation process continues. After a period of testing, a commercially available expert system is built, which incorporates all of the accumulated knowledge from the testing phases. To keep the expert system current, ongoing maintenance is performed to update the data base, knowledge base, and user interface.

Benefits of Expert Systems

The benefits of expert systems include time savings, provision of a second opinion, the quantity of information that can be considered, consistency, and training capabilities.

Time Savings. Once the knowledge of the expert is captured, the expert system can be used to streamline the decision process and save time. In some cases, the expert system can be used instead of the expert to free up the expert's time for other decisions.

Second Opinion. Expert systems may be used as a source of a second opinion. The expert system provides a decision and an explanation as to how the decision was made. This result and logic process may be considered the equivalent of bringing in another expert to consult on the decision.

Quantity of Information Considered. The computer is capable of evaluating more information than a human decision maker since the quantity of information that the computer can process is limited only by the size of the computer memory. The computer will not forget any information that is programmed into memory and will always consider all possible scenarios related to the decision. A human decision maker is limited in the quantity of information that can be processed at any one time and may forget to consider some piece of information.

Consistency. This ability of the computer always to consider all relevant information also makes the computer a consistent decision maker. Every time the computer must make the same decision, it will follow the same rules.

Training. Computers do not tire of performing the same procedure over and over again. This attribute makes them a very patient teacher. As such, expert systems are used as training tools for novices, such as beginning auditors in Big Six accounting firms. Through the use of the explanation features novices can learn the thought processes of experts.

Limitations of Expert Systems

Expert systems are not without their limitations. Costs are high, knowledge acquisition may be time consuming and difficult, the computer lacks common sense, and validation is difficult.

Costs.   Although the cost of computer hardware is decreasing, the cost of developing an expert system is very high. In addition to hardware and software costs, expert system development requires a great deal of time from, at minimum, one expert and a knowledge engineer.

287

CHAPTER 8
*Decision
Support
Systems
and Expert
Systems*

Knowledge Acquisition.   The process of capturing expert knowledge is not easy. The expert must carefully verbalize all the steps used to make a decision and the knowledge engineer must record each step. This process is time consuming, and difficult, and often takes numerous iterations to complete.

Lack of Common Sense.   The computer will consider only those rules that are programmed into the knowledge base. To date, no computer is capable of using common sense.

Validation.   After a prototype is developed it must be validated, verified for completeness and correctness. For the difficulty of the problems addressed by expert systems, validation is not a trivial task.

Real-World Examples

Probably the most frequently cited expert system is MYCIN, a medical application. MYCIN, developed at Stanford University during the mid-1970s, diagnoses infectious diseases and recommends a drug treatment program. Other disciplines that have embraced the expert system technology include the sciences (for example, Dendral analyzes molecular structure of unidentified compounds; Prospector helps geologists interpret oil well logs; MUDMAN helps the mud engineer determine the composition of the drilling mud to use when drilling an oil or gas well; Delta, developed by General Electric, identifies malfunctions in diesel locomotives) and business (for example, DEC's R1 helps build computer systems and ISIS, developed by Westinghouse Electric Corporation and Carnegie Mellon, develops job shop schedules).

In the area of accounting, expert systems are currently used in auditing and tax preparation and for internal investment decisions. Examples include EDP-Expert, TICOM, TAXADVISOR, ExperTAX, Loan Probe, Arthur D. Little's variance analysis program, and BUCKS. EDP-Expert provides advice on the adequacy of internal computer controls. This expert system is intended to assist computer audit specialists by solving problems that arise in an EDP audit. TICOM, developed at the University of Minnesota, was seen as a first step in developing an auditing expert system. TICOM is an audit aid for the evaluation of internal controls. TAXADVISOR, built in 1982, provides individual estate planning advice. ExperTAX makes tax accrual and tax planning decisions. The knowledge base was constructed using the knowledge of over twenty experts. KPMG's Loan Probe analyzes bank loans to determine an appropriate level of loan loss reserves. Arthur D. Little's expert system analyzes cost variances for manufacturing operations. This expert system is linked with the organization's accounting information system and Lotus 1-2-3 spreadsheets. DEC's BUsiness Control Knowledge System (BUCKS) is also integrated with an organization's accounting information system. BUCKS, used in European countries since 1986, analyzes division performance and regional

288

PART II
Technical
Aspects of
Accounting
Information
Systems

CONCEPT SUMMARY

Comparison of Decision Support Systems and Expert Systems

	Decision Support Systems	*Expert Systems*
Task structure	Structured to semistructured	Unstructured or requiring an expert
Model	Optimization/algorithm	Heuristics
Domain	Broad, complex problems	Narrow, specific problems
Explanatory power	Little to none	Available
Capabilities	"What if" and goal seeking	Reasoning
System structure	Data base contains facts; model base contains decision models	Knowledge base contains facts and decision rules
Cost	Less expensive	Very expensive
Training	On-line training	On-line training
Decision support	Provides optimal solution; user must use judgment to make decision	Provides a decision
Sharability	Data and model may be shared among users	Shares the expertise of the expert with all users
Flexibility	Easy if only parameters of the model change; difficult if there is a structural change	Easy if only extension to existing rules is needed; difficult if new approach required

consulting activities; its output includes recommendations and an explanation of the reasoning used in the analysis.

The Future of Decision Support Systems and Expert Systems

There is a possible synergy in the combination of decision support systems and expert systems. One way of combining these computerized support systems is to integrate an expert system into a DSS. Another is to use an expert system as a separate component of a DSS. In the first method, an expert system could be integrated into each component of a DSS to support that component. Or an expert system could be integrated into a DSS as a whole. For example, integrating an expert system into a DSS might allow the user to interact with an

289

CHAPTER 8
*Decision
Support
Systems
and Expert
Systems*

expert system to choose the best decision model for the problem. In the second method, adding an expert system as a separate component of a DSS would mean that the output of an expert system is a direct input to a DSS or the output of the DSS is a direct input to the expert system. For example, an expert system could be used to identify the problem and the alternatives to be considered, a DSS could be used to analyze the alternatives, and the results of the analyses could be returned to the expert system for a decision. Rapid advances in information technology are presenting vast opportunities for development in the area of computerized support for decision making. These two alternatives are just the beginning of what may be possible.

REFERENCES

M. J. ABDOLMOHAMMADI, "Decision Support and Expert Systems in Auditing: A Review and Research Directions," *Accounting and Business Research* (Spring 1987), pp. 173–185.

S. ALTER, *Decision Support Systems: Current Practice and Continuing Changes* (Reading, MA: Addison-Wesley, 1980), Chapter 2.

S. ALTER, "How Effective Managers Use Information Systems," *Harvard Business Review* (November/December 1976), pp. 97–104.

C. E. BROWN, AND M. E. PHILLIPS, "Expert Systems for Management Accountants," *Management Accounting* (January 1990), pp. 18–23.

N. A. D. CONNELL, "Expert Systems in Accountancy: A Review of Some Recent Applications," *Accounting and Business Research* (1987), Vol. 17, No. 67, pp. 221–233.

A. R. DENNIS, J. F. GEORGE, L. M. JESSUP, J. F. NUNAMAKER, JR., AND D. R. VOGEL, "Information Technology to Support Electronic Meetings," *MIS Quarterly* (December 1988), pp. 591–624.

K. G. KING, AND R. W. ELLIOT, "In Plain English, Please," *Journal of Accountancy* (March 1990), pp. 43–48.

R. LIBBY, *Accounting and Human Information Processing: Theory and Applications* (Englewood Cliffs, NJ: Prentice-Hall, 1981).

D. C. MELTON, "Information at Your Fingertips," *Journal of Accountancy* (December 1990), pp. 42–48.

E. TURBAN, AND P. WATKINS, "Integrating Expert Systems and DSS," *MIS Quarterly* (June 1986), pp. 121–136.

CHAPTER SUMMARY

Accounting information systems generate information useful in making managerial decisions that may be structured, semistructured, or unstructured. The computer does not replace the decision maker in any of these cases, but computer-based decision support systems can use the information from the accounting information system to help improve the speed and quality of decisions. Examples of decision support systems include overhead rate calculation, reorder point and quantity, project scheduling, sales forecasting, cash budgeting,

290

PART II
Technical
Aspects of
Accounting
Information
Systems

and resource allocation. There are many different types of DSS, but all require a data base, a model base, a user interface, and a programming language. When developing these systems, top management support is crucial. The usefulness of the resulting DSS depends on its ease of use and flexibility. DSS can help in problem formulation and understanding, provide in-depth analysis, and deliver time savings. Particularly useful in system development is the project scheduling techniques of PERT/CPM networks and GANTT charts. These techniques help manage complex tasks involving many subtasks, all of which must be completed. The PERT/CPM approach has the further advantage of showing the interrelationships of the various subtasks.

Software is available which is useful in developing DSS. Spreadsheets support budgeting, "what if" analysis, and some data analysis including regression. Financial modeling languages support financial models of the company and its operations and allow the incorporation of uncertainty into the model. Data analysis packages provide powerful statistical and graphical tools for use with large amounts of data or very sophisticated analyses.

Expert systems are the most useful accounting-related tool of artificial intelligence. By following explicitly stated rules, in many cases expert systems can make decisions similar to the decisions that would be made by a human expert in the area. Expert systems include a data base, a knowledge base, an inference engine, a knowledge acquisition mechanism, and a user interface. These expert systems can provide time savings, a second opinion, consistency in decision making, and training. Limitations of expert systems involve the costs of development, knowledge acquisition, a lack of common sense, and difficulty in validation. In the future, expert systems will be more integrated with DSS.

KEY TERMS

Algorithm (*p. 257*)
Artificial intelligence (AI) (*p. 281*)
Critical path (*p. 271*)
Decision support systems (DSS) (*p. 258*)
Expert system (*p. 281*)
GANTT chart (*p. 267*)
Group decision support system (GDSS) (*p. 264*)
Heuristics (*p. 282*)
Inference engine (*p. 284*)

Knowledge acquisition mechanism (*p. 284*)
Knowledge base (*p. 283*)
Model base (*p. 259*)
PERT/CPM network (*p. 268*)
Semistructured decision (*p. 257*)
Slack time (*p. 272*)
Structured decision (*p. 257*)
Unstructured decision (*p. 257*)
User interface (*p. 259*)

QUESTIONS

8-1. Distinguish between structured, semistructured, and unstructured decisions and give two examples of each.

8-2. Describe each of the components of a decision support system.

8-3. File drawer, data analysis, and information analysis are three types of decision

291

CHAPTER 8
Decision
Support
Systems
and Expert
Systems

support systems. Give an example of each of these types of DSS other than the ones discussed in the chapter.

8-4. Classify each of the four real-life examples of decision support systems given in the chapter as one of the seven DSS types discussed.

8-5. Describe a GANTT chart and how it might be used in system implementation.

8-6. Explain the advantages of PERT/CPM analysis over GANTT charts in system implementation.

8-7. Give the three basic types of software that support DSS and explain how each would be used.

8-8. Describe each of the components of an expert system.

8-9. Describe a problem that would be an appropriate application for an expert system.

8-10. Distinguish between expert systems and decision support systems.

PROBLEMS

8-11. The cost formulas for Devils, Inc., are given as follows. The formulas apply to a range of 4,000 to 6,000 direct labor hours. The Devils can produce two units per direct labor hour.

Cost	Cost Formula
Direct material	$3.00 per unit
Direct labor	$5.00 per labor hour
Supplies	$0.30 per unit
Indirect labor	$2,500 plus $0.25 per direct labor hour
Utilities	$0.50 per direct labor hour
Maintenance	$1,000 plus $0.10 per direct labor hour
Depreciation	$3,000

1. Using a spreadsheet application, prepare a flexible budget in increments of 1,000 direct labor hours. Include all of the costs shown.

2. "What if" the union negotiates a pay raise and direct labor is increased to $5.35 per hour; show the change to the flexible budget.

3. "What if" an expansion program results in an increase of $500 in fixed maintenance costs and an increase of $0.05 per direct labor hour; show the effect on the flexible budget. (Refer to the original data.)

4. "What if" the Devils attained a level of 5,500 direct labor hours? Using the model developed in (1), prepare the budget needed to calculate variances.

8-12. FMS Interior/Exteriors, Inc., has asked you to prepare a cash budget for the firm for the month of January. The cash balance on January 1 is $4,000, and FMS must maintain a minimum cash balance of $5,000. In January, dividends of $0.25 per share (500 shares outstanding) will be paid, a ladder costing $300 will be purchased for cash, and salaries and wages of $600 will be paid.

Sales for November, December, and January are:

	November	December	January
Cash	$2,000	$1,500	$1,500
Credit	1,000	3,000	2,000

292

*PART II
Technical
Aspects of
Accounting
Information
Systems*

Credit sales are collected over a two-month period, 25 percent in the month of the sale and 75 percent in the following month. Inventory purchases for January will total $2,500. December's purchases were $2,000. Accounts payable are paid 50 percent in the month of the purchase and 50 percent in the following month. (Assume that all inventory purchases are made on account.) Selling and administrative expenses are budgeted at $2,000, of which $500 is for depreciation. Using a spreadsheet application,

1. Prepare a schedule of expected cash collections, a schedule of payments to suppliers, and a cash budget based on the information given.
2. "What if" credit collections are improved to 35 percent in the month of sale and 65 percent in the following month; show the effect on the cash balance for each month.
3. "What if" accounts payable are paid 75 percent in the month of purchase and 25 percent in the following month; show the effect on the cash balance each month.

8-13. (*CMA, adapted*) The Dreyfus Company specializes in large construction projects. The company management regularly employs the Program Evaluation and Review Technique in planning and coordinating its construction projects. A schedule of activities and their expected completion times (in Exhibit 8-11) has been developed for an office building which is to be constructed by Dreyfus Company. Identify the critical path for this project and determine the expected project completion time in weeks.

**EXHIBIT 8-11   Schedule of Activities for the
Dreyfus Company**

		Expected Activity	
Activity Description	Predecessor Activity	Completion Time (in Weeks)	
a. Excavation	—	2	
b. Foundation	a	3	
c. Underground utilities	a	7	
d. Rough plumbing	b	4	
e. Framing	b	5	
f. Roofing	e	3	
g. Electrical work	f	3	
h. Interior walls	d, g	4	
i. Finish plumbing	h	2	
j. Exterior finishing	f	6	
k. Landscaping	c, i, j	2	

8-14. (*CMA, adapted*) Edward Jones is responsible for finding a suitable building and establishing a new convenience grocery store for Thrift-Mart, Inc. Jones enumerated the specific activities that had to be completed and the estimated

EXHIBIT 8-12   Network Diagram for Thrift-Mart, Inc.

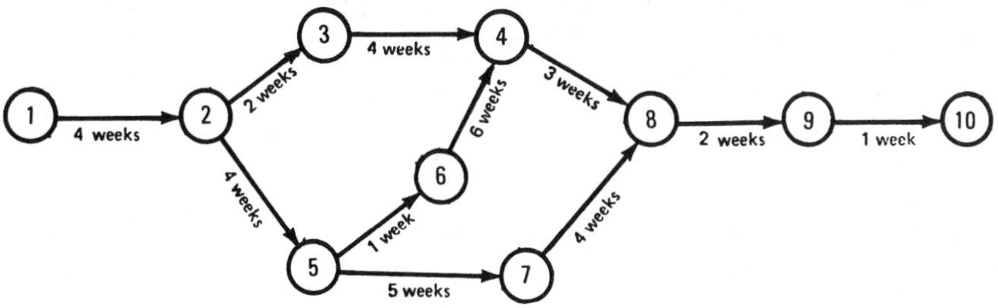

293

CHAPTER 8
Decision
Support
Systems
and Expert
Systems

time to establish each activity. In addition, he prepared a network diagram, which appears in Exhibit 8-12, to aid in the coordination of the activities. The list of activities to locate a building and establish a new store is as follows:

Activity Number	Description of Activity	Estimated Time Required
3-4	Draft lease	4 weeks
2-5	Prepare store plans	4 weeks
5-6	Select and order fixtures	1 week
6-4	Deliver fixtures	6 weeks
4-8	Install fixtures	3 weeks
5-7	Hire staff	5 weeks
7-8	Train staff	4 weeks
8-9	Receive inventory	2 weeks
9-10	Stock shelves	1 week

1. Identify the critical path for finding and establishing the new convenience store.

2. Edward Jones would like to finish the store two weeks earlier than indicated by the schedule, and as a result, he is considering several alternatives. One such alternative is to convince the fixture manufacturer to deliver the fixtures in four weeks rather than in six weeks. Should Jones arrange for the manufacturer to deliver the fixtures in four weeks if the sole advantage of this schedule change is to open the store two weeks early? Justify your answer.

8-15. Trevor Kennedy, the cost analyst at a can manufacturing plant of United Packaging, used a regression model to examine the relationship between total engineering support costs reported in the plant records and machine hours. After further discussion with the operating manager, Kennedy discovered that the materials and parts numbers reported in the monthly records are on an as purchased basis and not on an as-used basis. By examining materials and parts usage records, Kennedy is able to restate the materials and parts costs to an "as-used" or accrual accounting basis. No restatement of the labor costs was necessary. The reported and restated costs are:

294

PART II
Technical
Aspects of
Accounting
Information
Systems

Month	Labor: Reported Costs	Materials and Parts: Reported Costs	Materials and Parts: Restated Costs	Total Engineering Support: Reported Costs	Total Engineering Support: Restated Costs	Machine Hours
March	$347	$847	$182	$1,194	$529	30
April	521	0	411	521	932	63
May	398	0	268	398	666	49
June	355	961	228	1,316	583	38
July	473	0	348	473	821	57
August	617	0	349	617	966	73
Sept.	245	821	125	1,066	370	19
Oct.	487	0	364	487	851	53
Nov.	431	0	290	431	721	42

1. Identify the data items to be stored in the data base. What is the decision model to be stored in the model base?

2. Using the available spreadsheet software, present plots of the data relating the (a) total engineering support reported costs to machine hours and (b) total engineering support restated costs to machine hours. Calculate the regression analysis using your spreadsheet and determine a cost function for both sets of data.[1]

8-16. Teri Bush, executive assistant to the president of Western University, has been hearing many complaints from university administrators that the nonacademic overhead costs of the business school are out of control. The business school has grown from 14 full-time faculty to 61 full-time faculty in the last 12 years. The nonacademic overhead costs include the salaries of numerous individual supply items such as photocopying paper. Bush decides that some data analysis is warranted. She collects the following information pertaining to the business school:

Year	Nonacademic Overhead Costs (000s)	Number of Nonacademic Staff	Number of Student Applications	Number of Enrolled Students
1	$2,200	29	1,010	342
2	4,120	36	1,217	496
3	3,310	49	927	256
4	4,410	53	1,050	467
5	4,210	54	1,563	387
6	5,440	58	1,127	492
7	5,600	88	1,892	513
8	4,380	72	1,362	387
9	5,270	83	1,623	346
10	7,610	73	1,646	487
11	8,070	101	1,870	564
12	10,388	103	1,253	764

1. Identify the data items to be stored in the data base. What is the decision model to be stored in the model base?

[1] Adapted from *Cost Accounting: A Managerial Emphasis,* 7th Edition, by Horngren and Foster, p. 810. Copyright © 1991, reprinted by permission of Prentice Hall.

295

CHAPTER 8
*Decision
Support
Systems
and Expert
Systems*

2. Using spreadsheet software, plot the relationship between nonacademic overhead costs and each of the following three variables: (a) number of nonacademic staff, (b) number of student applications, and (c) number of enrolled students. Calculate the regression analysis using your spreadsheet and determine a cost function for each set of data.[2]

8-17. (*CMA, adapted*) Alice Williams, the manager of the financial analysis department, has been asked to forecast the cash position for the third quarter for the Linden Corporation. Williams will use the pro forma income statement presented in Exhibit 8-13 (page 296) that was prepared by Jerry Miller, a financial analyst who recently left the company. Miller prepared the pro forma income statement by using a common spreadsheet package on a microcomputer.

All sales are on account, and the accounts receivable have historically been paid, and are forecasted to be paid, 30 days after the sale. All other revenues are presumed to be paid as they occur. Cost of goods sold relate to raw materials which are purchased on account. Accounts payable are settled in 30 days. All other cash expenses are paid as incurred. Accrued taxes are equal to the tax liability and are paid 45 days after the end of the quarter. The second quarter's total tax liability was $95,000. Linden is purchasing a $25,000 microcomputer network to be delivered, installed, and paid in September. Depreciation on this equipment will be straight line, over five years, with no salvage value at the end of five years. The depreciation expense for this equipment is not currently reflected in the projected expenses. In July, Linden will be receiving $500,000 from a public stock offering of 100,000 shares sold in June. On June 10, 1992, the board of directors declared dividends of $75,000 to be distributed on August 15 to the shareholders of record as of June 30. The ending cash balance at June 30, 1992 is projected to be $250,000. For forecasting purposes, Linden Corporation assumes that all cash flows and transactions consistently occur at the end of each month.

Williams is preparing a projected internal cash flow report by referencing the amounts given in the pro forma income statement prepared by Miller and the financial transactions presented previously. Before Miller left Linden, he gave Williams a brief lesson on forecasting the cash flows by using the spreadsheet package and referencing income statement values. Although Miller had not developed any specific directions on using this spreadsheet model, he believed that Williams was proficient enough to prepare the cash flow projection. It should be noted that the pro forma income statement is correct. In reviewing the first draft of the cash flow report presented in Exhibit 8-13, Williams observed six errors that are indicated by numbers 1 through 6.

1. The six errors identified on Linden Corporation's third quarter 1992 projected cash flow report were caused by either incorrect reasoning or spreadsheet logic. Describe the six errors and explain how specifically to correct each error by providing the correct spreadsheet formula.

2. List at least three problems inherent in the use of spreadsheet models developed by users who are not trained in the procedural controls of systems design and development.

8-18. (*CMA, adapted*) Barker Systems, founded by Janice Barker in 1984, manufactures a highly sophisticated tracking system, FasTrac, which is used in con-

---

[2] Adapted from *Cost Accounting: A Managerial Emphasis,* 7th Edition, by Horngren and Foster, p. 812. Copyright © 1991, reprinted by permission of Prentice Hall.

296

PART II
Technical
Aspects of
Accounting
Information
Systems

EXHIBIT 8-13   Pro Forma Income Statement and Projected Cash Flow Report

A	B	C	D	E
1				
2	Linden Corporation			
3	1992 Partial Pro Forma Income Statement			
4	($000 omitted)			
5				
6	June	July	Aug	Sept
7 Revenues				
8 Sales	$230	$250	$260	$290
9 Other revenues	20	10	30	20
10 Total revenue	250	260	290	310
11 Expenses				
12 Cost of goods sold	80	90	120	110
13 Salaries	50	50	50	50
14 Depreciation	40	40	40	40
15 Other	0	10	10	20
16 Total expenses	170	190	220	220
17 Income before taxes	80	70	70	90
18 Taxes (40 percent)	32	28	28	36
19 Net Income	$ 48	$ 42	$ 42	$ 54

AA	BB	CC	DD
51	Linden Corporation		
52	Third Quarter 1992 Projected Cash Flow Report		
53	($000 omitted)		
54			
55	July	Aug	Sept
56 Beginning cash balance	$250	$735	$735 #1
57 Cash receipts			
58 Sales receipts	250	260	290 #2
59 Other revenue	10	30	20
60 Equity	500	0	0
61 Total cash receipts	760	290	310
62			
63 Cash disbursements			
64 Purchases and expenses	180	190	230 #3
65 Tax payments #4	95	0	0
66 Dividends	0	75	0
67 Other (capital purchases)	0	0	25
68 Total cash disbursements	275	265	230 #5
69 Net cash contribution	485	25	80
70 Ending cash balance	$735	$760	$1,045 #6

junction with the Navy's PDQ^2 water-to-water, antisubmarine missile guidance system. FasTrac is largely hand assembled from component parts in seven distinct steps at a manufacturing cost of $200,000 per unit. Barker systems uses PERT to schedule and keep track of all projects. Exhibit 8-14 includes a PERT chart showing the normal number of days required to complete a FasTrac unit.

One Monday evening, Barker received a telephone call at her home from the PDQ^2 missile staging base. Commander Grecon, procurement officer, requested delivery of a FasTrac unit ten days earlier than the normal delivery time, indicating the government would pay the additional costs associated with this accelerated delivery. Barker called Howard Green, the company's production manager and asked him to have a plan for meeting this delivery date, along with the incremental crash costs, ready for her review in the morning. Using the crash cost listing presented in Exhibit 8-14, Green prepared his plan for the accelerated delivery of a FasTrac unit, keeping in mind the need to minimize the cost impact. Shown in Exhibit 8-14 is the accelerated delivery schedule Green presented to Barker for her evaluation. He was pleased that the necessary ten days could be eliminated at the cost of only $25,000.

297

CHAPTER 8
Decision
Support
Systems
and Expert
Systems

EXHIBIT 8-14   PERT Chart with Alternatives

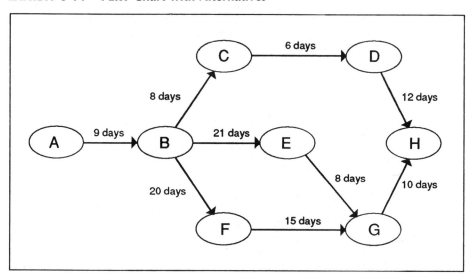

Crash Cost Listing

Activity	Normal Time	Crash Time	Crash Cost per Reduced Day
A–B	9 days	6 days	$10,500
B–C	8 days	6 days	1,000
C–D	6 days	5 days	1,000
D–H	12 days	8 days	6,000
B–E	21 days	20 days	3,000
E–G	8 days	6 days	4,500
G–H	10 days	9 days	4,000
B–F	20 days	16 days	5,000
F–G	15 days	12 days	2,000

Accelerated Delivery Schedule

Activity Crashed	Days Crashed	Total Crash Cost
B–C	2	$ 2,000
C–D	1	1,000
F–G	3	6,000
B–E	1	3,000
G–H	1	4,000
E–G	2	9,000
Total	10	25,000

298

Part II
Technical
Aspects of
Accounting
Information
Systems

1. By preparing a schedule of paths, from nodes A to H and their total days, from the PERT network for the normal production of Barker Systems' FasTrac unit, identify the critical path and explain why it is the critical path.

2. Janice Barker has found Howard Green's plan for the accelerated delivery to be unsatisfactory. Explain why it is unsatisfactory.

3. Revise the accelerated delivery schedule so that the delivery time of the FasTrac unit can be ten days ahead of the normal schedule at the least incremental cost.

8-19. (*CMA, adapted*) During the early 1980s, ProSoft Corporation developed and marketed business applications software for minicomputers, achieving a significant market share and a secure position in the industry. After maturing at this level of success, the company's mission became less clear. Further software development for minicomputers was seen as costly with little value to the company, as the market for major business applications was saturated and the minor applications had limited markets. In order to maintain ProSoft's market share, management decided to enter the growing personal computer field. While major programming would be required to make the company's existing software compatible with personal computers (PCs), management viewed the commitment of all personnel to this project as critical to the continued growth of ProSoft. The emphasis was to be placed on product development, with minimal effort directed toward market analysis. After weeks of executive strategy sessions regarding product specifications, management imposed the task deadlines and set the date for the introduction of its first PC product, an accounting package for general ledger, accounts payable, and accounts receivable applications. Three months prior to the introduction date, ProSoft began an advertising and dealer promotion campaign announcing the new product and setting the introduction date. Several technical problems arose during development, but the staff believed that a few time-saving measures would enable them to complete the package in time to meet the announced date. Management felt considerable pressure to meet this date as ProSoft had previously missed an announced date and suffered the consequences.

Two weeks before the announced date, ProSoft's marketing personnel learned that an updated version of the PC operating software that ProSoft's new package was designed to interact with was to be released shortly. The marketing staff knew that features could quickly be added to ProSoft's new product to take advantage of the new features in the operating software; however, there would not be time to field test the program changes. The technical personnel warned the marketing staff of the dangers of releasing a product without proper field testing; however, these warnings were not heeded. Management, with encouragement from the marketing staff, made the decision to incorporate the features necessary to take advantage of the new operating software and introduce the product on the scheduled date. Not long after ProSoft made the first shipments of its new software, complaints were received from customers about processing problems in the accounts payable and accounts receivable modules. Very quickly, it was determined that portions of ProSoft's new package were not compatible with the updated operating software. To correct the problem, the company had to rewrite the software and manuals and replace all existing product. The technical personnel were now dedicated to the development of the next PC product, and this problem fragmented their efforts. The revised product was not available for three months causing a loss of sales. The financial impact of the $1.7 million error on a company with annual profits of $1.1 million was devastating.

299

CHAPTER 8
*Decision
Support
Systems
and Expert
Systems*

1. Identify the steps in the general decision-making process.
2. Using the steps identified in (1), describe the weaknesses in ProSoft's decision-making process.
3. Recommend changes to correct the weaknesses identified in (2).

8-20. (*CMA, adapted*) Home Cooking Company offers monthly service plans providing prepared meals that are delivered to the customers' homes and that need only to be heated in a microwave or conventional oven. The target market for these meal plans includes double-income families with no children and retired couples in the upper-income brackets. Home Cooking offers two monthly plans—Premier Cuisine and Haute Cuisine. The Premier Cuisine plan provides frozen meals that are delivered twice each month; this plan generates a profit of $120 for each monthly plan sold. The Haute Cuisine plan provides freshly prepared meals delivered on a daily basis and generates a profit of $90 for each monthly plan sold. Home Cooking's reputation provides the company with a market that will purchase all the meals that can be prepared. All meals go through food preparation and cooking steps in the company's kitchens. After these steps, the Premier Cuisine meals are flash frozen. The time requirements per monthly meal plan and hours available per month are as follows:

	Preparation	*Cooking*	*Freezing*
Hours required			
Premier Cuisine	2	2	1
Haute Cuisine	1	3	0
Hours available	60	120	45

For planning purposes, Home Cooking uses linear programming to determine the most profitable number of Premier Cuisine and Haute Cuisine monthly meal plans to produce.

1. Using the notations P = Premier Cuisine and H = Haute Cuisine, state the objective function and the constraints that Home Cooking should use to maximize profits generated by the monthly meal plans.
2. Graph the constraints on Home Cooking's meal preparation process. Be sure to label your graph clearly.
3. By using the graph prepared in (2) or by making the necessary calculations, determine the optimal solution to Home Cooking's objective function in terms of the number of (a) Premier Cuisine meal plans to produce and (b) Haute Cuisine meal plans to produce.
4. Calculate the optimal value of Home Cooking's objective function.
5. If the constraint on preparation time could be eliminated, determine the revised optimal solution in terms of the (a) number of Premier Cuisine meal plans to produce, (b) number of Haute Cuisine meal plans to produce, and (c) resulting profit.

8-21. (*CMA, adapted*) Brian Haggerty, manager of budgeting and analysis for Fiber Products, Inc., is preparing to issue the first quarter's income statement in spreadsheet format. Haggerty has used the reporting format already developed in the spreadsheet software on his microcomputer and is reviewing the spreadsheet report shown in Exhibit 8-15 with Fiber Products' controller before presentation at the quarterly management meeting. Upon careful review, Haggerty

300

Part II
Technical
Aspects of
Accounting
Information
Systems

EXHIBIT 8-15   Fiber Products Inc. Spreadsheet Report

MANAGEMENT REPORT PRODUCED

April 10, 1992

Fiber Products Inc.
Income Statement Compared
to the Revised Budget
March 31, 1992
($000)

Desired contribution   60%
  (as a percentage of sales revenue)
Effective tax rate   40%

	JAN	FEB	MAR	First Quarter Actual	First Quarter Revised Budget	Actual Better/ (Worse) Revised Budget
Revenues						
Sales	$25	$26	$29	$80	$79	$ 1
Other revenue	1	3	2	6	0	6
Total revenue	$26	$29	$31	$86	$79	$ 7
Cost of goods sold	9	12	11	(21) ← #2	32	(11)
Bad debt expense	2	2	2	6	6	—
Total direct expenses	11	14	13	38	38	—
Contribution	15	15	18	48 #3	41	7
Contribution %	60%	58%	(58%	56%)	52%	#6
Fixed expenses	5	6	5	16	15	(1)
Income before income taxes	$10	$ 9	$13	$32 #4	$26	$ 6
Income tax (calculated and rounded)	4	4	(8)	16	10	6
Net income	$ 6	$ 5	$ 5	16	$16	$ —

#5
(the
whole
column)

and the controller have found errors in the printed report. These errors were highlighted by the fact that the actual income before income taxes for March was $10,000, while the income before income taxes reported on the spreadsheet report is $13,000.

This is the first time that Haggerty has prepared and issued these reports. Joan Michaels, the financial analyst who previously prepared these management reports for the quarterly meeting, terminated her employment on March 25. Prior to leaving, she gave Haggerty a brief lesson on issuing this report from the spreadsheet package. Although Michaels had not developed any specific directions on using this spreadsheet model, she believed that Haggerty was proficient enough to produce the report. The quarterly report is formatted by compiling information from a budget spreadsheet file and an actual spreadsheet file onto a third new spreadsheet. The saved budget spreadsheet file is called BUDG92, shown in Exhibit 8-16, and has provisions for both the original budget and the revised budget. The saved actual spreadsheet file is named ACT92 and is shown in Exhibit 8-16. This was initially developed by copying the revised budget file

EXHIBIT 8-16 Saved Spreadsheet Files

BUDGET FILE

301

CHAPTER 8
*Decision
Support
Systems
and Expert
Systems*

BUDG92	4/10/92	JAN	FEB	MAR
BUDGET				
Revenues				
Sales		24	27	28
Other revenue		0	0	0
Total revenue		24	27	28
Cost of goods sold		10	11	11
Bad debt expense		2	2	2
Total direct expenses		12	13	13
Fixed expenses		5	5	5
Income before income taxes		7	9	10

* * * * * * *

REVISED BUDGET				
Revenues				
Sales		25	27	29
Other revenue		2	2	2
Total revenue		27	29	31
Cost of goods sold		10	11	11
Bad debt expense		2	2	2
Total direct expenses		12	13	13
Fixed expenses		5	5	5
Income before income taxes		10	11	13

ACTUAL FILE

ACT92	4/10/92	JAN	FEB	MAR	← #1
Revenues					
Sales		25	26	29	
Other revenue		1	3	2	
Total revenue		26	29	31	
Cost of goods sold		9	12	11	
Bad debt expense		2	2	2	
Total direct expenses		11	14	13	
Fixed expenses		5	6	5	
Income before income taxes		10	9	13	

ACTUAL FILE (printed when Haggerty updated the March actuals)

ACT92	4/4/92	JAN	FEB	MAR	← #1
Revenues					
Sales		25	26	30	
Other revenue		1	3	1	
Total revenue		26	29	31	
Cost of goods sold		9	12	12	
Bad debt expense		2	2	3	
Total direct expenses		11	14	15	
Fixed expenses		5	6	6	
Income before income taxes		10	9	10	

302

*PART II
Technical
Aspects of
Accounting
Information
Systems*

and is updated monthly with actual information. Before merging the information from BUDG92 and ACT92 into the quarterly report, Haggerty had entered the March actuals into ACT92 on April 4, 1992 and printed the updated actual file for the first quarter, shown in Exhibit 8-16. It should be noted that the reported actuals for both January and February were correctly reported.

The first quarter's management report comparing the first quarter's actuals to the revised budget is presented in Exhibit 8-15. Six of the errors that the controller and Haggerty observed are indicated #1 to #6 in both Exhibit 8-15 and Exhibit 8-16.

1. Describe the six errors identified on Fiber Products, Inc.'s spreadsheets and explain why each of these computer spreadsheet errors occurred.

2. List the problems inherent in the use, by others, of spreadsheet models developed by users who are not trained in the procedural controls of system design and development.

8-22. (*CMA, adapted*)   The firm of Miller, Lombardi and York was recently formed by the merger of two companies providing accounting services. York's business was providing personal financial planning, while Miller and Lombardi conducted audits of small governmental units and provided tax planning and preparation for several commercial firms. The combined firm has leased new offices and acquired several microcomputers that are used by the professional staff in each area of service. However, in the short run, the firm does not have the financial resources to acquire computers for all of the professional staff. The expertise of the professional staff can be divided into three distinct areas that match the services provided by the firm: tax preparation and planning, insurance and investments, and auditing. However, since the merger, the new firm has had to turn away business in all three areas of service. One of the problems is that while the total number of staff seems adequate, the staff members are not completely interchangeable. Limited financial resources do not permit hiring any new staff in the near future, and therefore, the supply of staff is restricted in each area. Rich Oliva has been assigned the responsibility of allocating staff and computers to the various engagements. The management has given Oliva the objective of maximizing revenues in a manner consistent with maintaining a high level of professional service in each of the areas of service. Management's time is billed at $100 per hour, and the staff's time is billed at $70 per hour for those with experience and $50 per hour for inexperienced staff. Pam Wren, a member of the staff, recently completed a course in quantitative methods at the local university. She suggested to Oliva that he use linear programming to assign the appropriate staff and computers to the various engagements.

1. Identify and discuss the data that would be needed to develop a linear programming model for Miller, Lombardi and York.

2. Discuss objectives other than revenue maximization that Rich Oliva should consider before making staff allocations.

8-23. (*CMA, adapted*)   Belmont Company is a temporary employment firm that has offices throughout the United States. Belmont is a well-established company in a highly competitive industry. It provides both clerical and professional workers to a broad range of customers. The temporary workers are hired for the day, a week, or a month at rates commensurate with each worker's skill level. Belmont's top management wants to develop a forecasting system in order to es-

303

CHAPTER 8
Decision
Support
Systems
and Expert
Systems

timate revenues and to plan work force levels. Management wants to forecast its revenues for each quarter during the current year as well as the annual revenue for each of the next five years.

Kathy Gregsen, budget analyst in Belmont's accounting department, has been given the responsibility for this project. She has determined that Belmont has historical data by month for at least the last ten years. Her cursory review of the monthly revenue history indicates that Belmont's business may have a pronounced seasonal pattern. She also suspects that the business may be cyclical in nature. Gregsen has concluded that she would like to develop a statistically based sales forecasting system. She is considering the applicability of simple linear regression analysis and/or time series analysis. One of the things she would like to do is compare Belmont's revenue to the index of industrial production and to gross national product (GNP).

1. Identify the typical things Gregsen needs in order to develop a forecasting decision support system.

2. For both simple linear regression analysis and time series analysis, (a) describe the technique, being sure to include the purpose of the technique, (b) identify the variables and/or data required to use the technique, and (c) explain how Gregsen will be able to evaluate the results of the analysis.

DECISION CASE

(*CMA, adapted*) Silver Aviation assembles small aircraft for commercial use. The majority of Silver's business is with small freight airlines serving those areas where the airport size does not accommodate larger planes. The remainder of Silver's customers are commuter airlines and individuals who use planes in their businesses such as the owners of large ranches. Silver recently expanded its market into Central and South America, and the company expects to double its sales over the next three years. In order to schedule work and keep track of all projects, Silver uses the Program Evaluation and Review Technique. The PERT diagram for the construction of a single cargo plane is shown in Exhibit 8-17. The PERT diagram shows that there are four alternative paths with the critical path being ABGEFJK.

Bob Peterson, president of Coastal Airlines, has recently placed an order with Silver Aviation for five cargo planes. At the time of contract negotiations, Peterson agreed to a delivery time of 13 weeks (five working days per week) for the first plane, with the balance of the planes being delivered at the rate of one every 4 weeks. Because of problems with some of the aircraft Coastal is currently using, Peterson has contacted Grace Vander, sales manager for Silver Aviation, to ask about improving the delivery date of the first cargo plane. Vander replied that she believed the schedule could be shortened by as much as 10 working days or two weeks, but the cost of construction would increase as a result. Peterson said he would be willing to consider the increased costs, and they agreed to meet the following day to review a revised schedule that Vander would prepare. Because Silver Aviation has assembled aircraft on an accelerated basis previously, the company has compiled a list of crash costs for this purpose. Vander used the data shown on the Crash Cost Listing in

EXHIBIT 8-17   Single Cargo Plane PERT Diagram and Alternatives

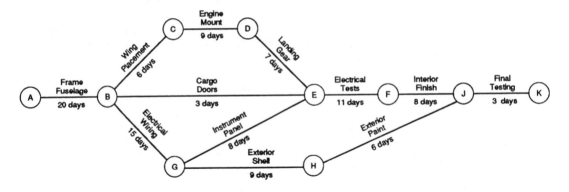

Crash Cost Listing

		Expected Activity Times		Direct Cost		Added Crash Cost per Reduced Day
	Activity	Regular	Crash	Regular	Crash	Day
AB	Frame fuselage	20 days	16 days	$12,000	$16,800	$1,200
BC	Wing placement	6	5	3,600	5,000	1,400
CD	Engine mount	9	7	6,600	8,000	700
DE	Landing gear	7	5	5,100	6,700	800
BE	Cargo doors	3	3	1,400	1,400	—
BG	Electrical wiring	15	13	9,000	11,000	1,000
GE	Instrument panel	8	6	5,700	8,300	1,300
EF	Electrical tests	11	10	6,800	7,600	800
GH	Exterior shell	9	7	4,200	5,200	500
FJ	Interior finish	8	7	3,600	4,000	400
HJ	Exterior paint	6	5	3,600	4,000	400
JK	Final testing	3	2	3,500	4,400	900
				$65,100	$82,400	

Accelerated Delivery Schedule

Completion Time	Activity Crashed	Additional Cost per Day	Total Direct Cost
65 days			$65,100
64	HJ by one day	$ 400	65,500
63	FJ by one day	400	65,500
61	GH by two days	500	66,900
59	CD by two days	700	68,300
58	EF by one day	800	69,100
56	DE by two days	800	70,700
55	BG by one day	1,000	71,700

305

CHAPTER 8
Decision
Support
Systems
and Expert
Systems

Exhibit 8-17 to develop a plan to cut 10 working days from the schedule at a minimum increase in cost to Coastal Airlines. Upon completing her plan, Vander was pleased that she could report to Peterson that Silver would be able to cut 10 working days from the schedule. The associated increase in cost would be $6,600. Presented in Exhibit 8-17 is Vander's plan for the accelerated delivery of the cargo plane starting from the regularly scheduled days and cost.

Required:

1. Explain how the expected regular times for each activity are derived in using PERT.

2. Define the term "critical path" and explain why path ABGEFJK is the critical path here.

3. Explain why the accelerated delivery schedule plan as prepared by Grace Vander is unsatisfactory.

4. Revise the accelerated delivery schedule so that Coastal Airlines will take delivery of the first plane two weeks (10 working days) ahead of schedule at the least incremental cost to Coastal.

5. Calculate the incremental costs Bob Peterson will have to pay for this revised accelerated delivery.

9 Overview of Computer-Based Accounting Information Systems

Overview

How accounting functions are accomplished in a computer-based system, the components that comprise the system, and the interactions necessary to make the system work.

Learning Objectives

Thorough study of this chapter will enable you to:

1. Differentiate between computer-based transaction processing systems and accounting information systems.
2. Describe the components and capabilities of a computer-based information system.
3. Chart the information flow to and from the cash receipts and disbursements subsystem.
4. Chart the information flow to and from the sales and purchases subsystem.
5. Chart the information flow to and from the financial accounting subsystem.
6. Chart the information flow to and from the manufacturing subsystem.
7. List the characteristics common to all subsystems and modules within a computer-based information system.

Outline

Computer-Based Information Systems

The Cash Receipts and Disbursements Subsystem

The Sales and Purchases Subsystem

The Financial Accounting Subsystem

The Manufacturing Subsystem

Similarities Among Computer-Based Information System Components

SYSTEMS IN THE REAL WORLD

307

CHAPTER 9
*Overview of
Computer-
Based
Accounting
Information
Systems*

Computer Trauma for Top Executives

While top executives have spent billions on computers to run their businesses, they have often been reluctant to use such machines personally. That has sometimes meant drowning in paper reports from middle managers. But that's changing. Today many corporations are discovering the benefits of Executive Information Systems (EIS), designed around easy-to-use personal computers. As a result, top executives are slowly entering the computer age. Executive information systems, however, often look different from other computers. They typically have very high-quality monitors with bigger screens that can display lots of splashy colors and a variety of detailed charts and graphs. Senior executives also rarely touch any keyboards. They control their computers by touching the screen or by using a "mouse."

For companies that can't justify—or don't want to pay—the cost of custom-designed, easy-to-use computers systems for top executives, ordinary personal computers and software can be useful. Such technology, however, summons up more of executives' resistance to computers because using it requires more knowledge of the machines than does using the special executive systems. Changing executives' attitudes and training them effectively can prove to be difficult.

For instance, many executives consider keyboards degrading; they either don't know how to type or think it's for secretaries. Or they may be technophobic and don't want to mess up in front of their subordinates, who are typically younger and, they feel, more comfortable with computers. They may be right. Trainers tell of executives who, when asked to remove a floppy disk from its jacket, not only remove the disk from the paper holder that is called the jacket but also tear off the permanent paper housing. Or, when told, "Hit the enter key, the one with the arrow on it in the shape of an elbow," executives will sometimes ask, "Which key do I hit with my elbow?"

There are successes, however. Consider what has happened at Kraft. Keeping track of business at Kraft, Inc.'s Grocery Products Group was a nightmare. The division sells 500 products under 15 separate brands to 33,000 grocery stores. Until last September the group's president and six vice-presidents received stacks of paper with the previous day's sales results each afternoon at 3 P.M. But now, with computers, they get the same information as early as 8:30 A.M.—organized geographically and by product line. Executives can spot and solve problems faster. And at meetings, there's no dispute anymore about whose numbers are current or correct. Not only does the system increase white-collar productivity, says Vice-President Jack A. Peterson, "we conduct our works lives differently."

SOURCE: *Business Week,* June 27, 1988, p. 84 and *The Wall Street Journal,* June 20, 1988, p. 13.

308

Part III
Computer-
Based
Accounting
Applications

COMPUTER-BASED
INFORMATION SYSTEMS

A business information system is the sum of all the tools, techniques, and procedures used by the business to process data. Such a system accepts input data about a business and generates required or desired output information. These tools, techniques, and procedures may be carried out manually or by a computer. The chapters that make up this section of the book present the fundamental data inputs, processing requirements, and outputs produced by computer-based accounting-oriented systems. This chapter and Chapters 10, 11, and 12 discuss and illustrate moderate and large-scale computerized accounting information systems, and Chapter 13 presents microcomputer-based AIS.

Like all systems, accounting information systems are made up of component systems and modules that are designed to process data in specific areas of business activity. Thus, any business information system can be divided into processing systems and modules of narrower scope which accept input data, process it, and interact with each other to produce output information and new files of data.

Components of an Information System

The same fundamental ideas apply to both computer-based systems and to manual systems. Indeed, the component parts of computer-based systems generally parallel those of manual systems since the goals of both are fundamentally the same. The activities and data of most businesses fall into four major categories: cash inflows and outflows, sales and purchases, financial accounting, and manufacturing (cost) accounting. A computer-based information system can then be logically viewed as consisting of four component subsystems which are identifiable and distinguishable, but not isolated from one another. Each of these subsystems processes data from a certain area of business activity; however, each depends on the other, and information must flow between them for the computer-based system to work.

Exhibit 9-1 illustrates the conceptual relationships and the logical flow of information between component subsystems and their **application modules**. It deserves careful study because it represents the "big picture" on which this chapter and the following three are based. As you examine this figure, consider the following significant points:

1. The entire figure represents a computer-based business information system composed of four distinct, but interrelated, component subsystems (represented by the four broken lines, each enclosing a set of rectangles).
2. The four component subsystems are
   a. A cash receipts and disbursements system.
   b. A sales and purchases system.
   c. A financial accounting system.
   d. A manufacturing system.
3. Each subsystem consists of specific processing applications or modules which are represented by labeled rectangles. These application modules are the building blocks of an information system.

EXHIBIT 9-1   Information Flow in a Computer-Based Information System

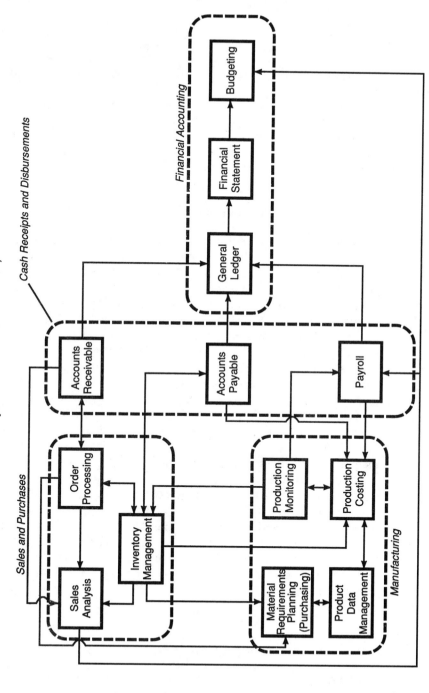

310

Part III
Computer-
Based
Accounting
Applications

4. Information and data flow between modules is absolutely necessary in a computer-based information system. Arrows indicating such flow intersect the subsystems. This demonstrates that all subsystems interact with each other through the modules that make up the systems.

5. Accounting systems process only certain kinds of events, called transactions. Information systems, however, are capable of processing any data and information (not just accounting transactions) that is useful to management or any other user of the system. Notice how transaction data from the other three subsystems flows left to right into the financial accounting subsystem.

Information systems, then, process accounting transactions plus many other kinds of data and information that ordinarily are beyond the scope of accounting systems. Many of the arrows indicating flow in Exhibit 9-1 represent information or data that are not accounting transactions and thus would not be available in an accounting system.

Interdependence of Components

The necessary flow of information between applications areas makes it unlikely that any individual module, or even any component subsystem, can efficiently stand alone or operate independently. Each of these modules provides at least part of the necessary environment for the other. Many processing modules use the same data, but require that the data be organized or accessed differently. In addition, the output of some modules may be required as input for other modules. This commonality of data needs makes it possible for a computer-based system to create a basic set of data that is available to all processing applications and flexible enough to be referenced by these modules in many different ways. Such a set of data within reach of all processing modules is, of course, a data base. Instead of each module organizing and storing all of its own data (which would result in redundancy throughout the system), the data base concept extracts data that are common to many application modules and makes them accessible to all. Only with the aid of a computer's speed and memory is this possible; implementation of the data base idea in a manual system is not feasible.

Consider, for example, the Accounts Receivable and Order Processing modules appearing at the top center of Exhibit 9-1. These modules belong to separate subsystems but the processing carried out by each intersects with the other and both require some of the same data. Order processing requires data on customers in order to make order acceptance decisions and process orders, and accounts receivable uses data on processed orders to update customer accounts and produce customer bills. All of this information can be supplied by the system data base.

Characteristics of an Information System

Most processing modules of computer-based information systems have five important characteristics in common. They produce output reports, exchange information with other modules, provide information on request, update master and transaction files, and use terminals to promote interactive processing.

Output Reports. From each application module some output will be generated to provide information on which decisions can be based or statements to meet the business' reporting requirements. Although it is conceivable for a package to produce no printed output, this is not likely to occur in business processing. The ability of computer-based systems to provide information not available from a manual system is one of the primary reasons for their existence. Timely and useful management reports are one of the significant advantages of an information system.

311

CHAPTER 9
Overview of
Computer-
Based
Accounting
Information
Systems

Interaction with Other Modules. **Interface** capability, that is, the ability to transfer data between modules exists to reduce duplication in an information system. With computer systems, this kind of interchange between modules is relatively easy to carry out as compared to manual systems. It is unusual to find an individual computer-based module that is not made more efficient by accepting some organized and (at least) partially processed data from another application. By the same token, almost all modules generate some data which can be used by other applications in the system.

Inquiry and Response Capability. The immediate availability of up-to-date information by direct **inquiry and response** to the system is one of the most valuable advantages of computer systems.

Data Organization into Files. The concepts of file, record, and data-item introduced earlier are essential to every computer-based application. Since the computer does not have intuition, judgment, or reasoning powers, the organization of input data must follow a known logical design. This logical design most often results in each module having access to at least one permanent master file which is updated with each processing run by a file of current activity. Although other types of files are sometimes necessary, the basic master and transaction files are common to all modules.

Use of Terminals. In addition to their inquiry and response capability, **terminals** (sometimes called workstations) are increasingly being used in business processing to input data, initiate processing, and receive output from processed data. This use is part of a general move toward more interactive business information systems.

Data Organization and Input

To generate output reports and information, the computer system must have access to certain input data, and this data must be organized so that processing can be done efficiently. The input data to a system can be thought of as falling into three categories: report files, master files, and transactions files.

Constant or Report Files. Relatively permanent data may be used over and over as input to an application module. These data are not altered by the processing that takes place and are changed externally only occasionally. The data may consist of constants, such as tax rates and limits, exemption amounts,

312

Part III
Computer-
Based
Accounting
Applications

deduction percentages, and so on, or headings and titles to be used in output reports, such as financial statements.

There are two ways to input constant data. The simple way is to maintain a different computer program for each set of constants to be used, and to make headings, titles, subtotal, and total format a part of the program. This method does, however, require that the program be changed if a change in permanent data or report format is desired. Given that program debugging is often a major step in system development, this method has some significant potential problems.

An alternative way to input permanent data allows the user to change the data without the necessity for altering the computer programs of a system. A permanent input file specifies the constant data to be used or the headings, titles, subtotal, and total format for each output report. Such a file is often called a **constant** data or **report** format or report writer **file**. In the first approach, data and format are part of the program which generates the output; in the second, they are a part of the input data on which the program operates. Most business processing applications use one or more of these types of input organized into permanent files.

Master Files. Semipermanent data of a cumulative nature may be input, then processed and changed by the processing (this is usually called **updating**), and then become output that will be updated again in later processing. An example of semipermanent input data are the balances in general ledger accounts. General ledger data are kept in a file, and at the end of each period the account balances are updated for all of the transactions (debits and credits) that occurred during the period. The ending balances in each account are stored and become input to the next period's transaction processing. All business processing modules require at least one file of this kind of data. Files of this type are called **master files**.

Transaction Files. Current data pertaining to activity of the present period must be processed and then may or may not be stored in its raw form. Master files are updated with this current data. For example, accounting transactions that take place during an accounting period will update the balances in the general ledger master file. All business processing involves this type of data input because without current activity no processing would be necessary. Files of current activity data are called **transaction files**.

Now that we have an overview of the important characteristics and relationships in a computer-based information system, the remaining sections of this chapter will discuss the component subsystems that make-up the total system.

THE CASH RECEIPTS AND DISBURSEMENTS SUBSYSTEM

This subsystem consist of the accounts receivable, accounts payable, and payroll applications. These processing applications are probably the best-known computer-based modules. They are usually the first areas to be computerized

313

CHAPTER 9
*Overview of
Computer-
Based
Accounting
Information
Systems*

by a business because they are relatively easy to convert and represent highly visible and active areas of activity. Exhibit 9-2 illustrates the information flow between a cash receipts and disbursements system and other subsystems. In this figure we are focusing on the centermost set in the total information system depicted in Exhibit 9-1.

Accounts Receivable and Accounts Payable

The **cash receipts and disbursements subsystem** stands between (in an information flow sense) the other major component subsystems. The accounts receivable and accounts payable applications receive input from the sales and purchases subsystem and provide output to that system. Since accounts receivable are a factor in both sales and cash receipts, and accounts payable are a factor in purchases and cash disbursements, this interaction is not surprising. In addition, the receivables and payables modules produce essential transaction processing information for the general ledger of the financial accounting subsystem.

Payroll

The payroll application is interesting because it represents the closest thing to a stand-alone module in computer-based systems. Payroll applications can and sometimes do exist as the sole computerized area of business activity, since no input from other areas may be necessary for the module to work. However, as sales or other activity-related variables become important factors in the determination of compensation, data from the sales and purchases subsystem

**EXHIBIT 9-2   Information Flow in a Cash Receipts
and Disbursements Subsystem**

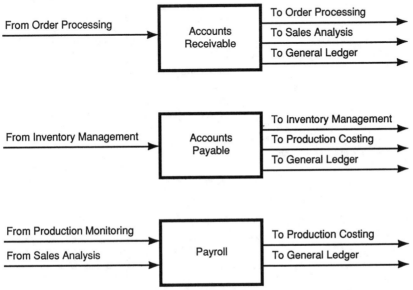

314

PART III
Computer-
Based
Accounting
Applications

becomes either very desirable or absolutely necessary input to the payroll area. The most common example of this type of situation is a company with a large sales payroll where sales pay is based primarily on commissions. Here, input from a sales analysis module is essential to payroll since, at the very least, a breakdown of sales by salesperson is needed for the payroll calculation. Also, payroll processing does generate important transaction-based output to be included in the general ledger.

Note from Exhibit 9-2 that the cash receipts and disbursements subsystem is very active in terms of information interchange with other systems. These interfaces are an important distinguishing characteristics of this subsystem.

THE SALES AND PURCHASES SUBSYSTEM

The **sales and purchases subsystem** consists of the order processing, inventory management, and sales analysis applications. These modules represent the point of original data entry into the information system for many transactions and events. Therefore, there is significant information flow among the individual modules which make up the sales and purchases subsystem, as well as between these modules and those of the cash receipts and disbursements subsystem and manufacturing subsystem. In addition, there is limited one-way information flow from this system to the financial accounting subsystem. Exhibit 9-3 illustrates these flows, and in doing so focuses on the upper left set in the total information system depicted in Exhibit 9-1.

EXHIBIT 9-3   Information Flow in a Sales and Purchases Subsystem

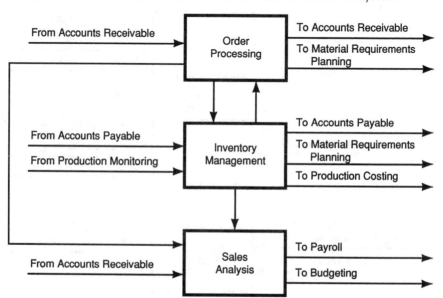

Order Processing and Inventory Management

315

CHAPTER 9
*Overview of
Computer-
Based
Accounting
Information
Systems*

The sales and purchases subsystem interacts significantly with the cash receipts and disbursements subsystem. There is an important pairing of packages between these component systems. Order processing and accounts receivable combine to process data on sales and cash receipts, while inventory management and accounts payable combine to process data on purchases and cash disbursements. For example, sales invoice summary information is passed from order processing, where these invoices are created, to accounts receivable, so that the customer master file can be updated. At the same time, information on the status of individual customer accounts can be returned to order processing to aid in sales order processing and credit decision making. Similarly, accounts payable receives purchase invoice summaries from inventory management, where they are created, in order to update the vendor master file, and returns vendor activity breakdowns which aid in making purchasing timing and vendor selection decisions.

Sales Analysis

Sales analysis is the only application of the sales and purchases subsystem that directly interacts with the financial accounting subsystem. Data from order processing and inventory management are ultimately included in the general ledger, but only after being processed and summarized by the modules of the cash receipts and disbursements subsystem. Output from sales analysis, however, is incorporated into the budgeting module directly, so that detailed comparisons of sales and profit performance by product, territory, salesperson, customer, or other basis can be readily made. Also, this sales analysis output provides a sound basis for the preparation or revision of future financial budgets. Sales analysis by salesperson can also be used in the calculation of payroll where compensation is based on commissions. Because most detailed data on customers is processed and stored in accounts receivable, necessary information flow also takes place between sales analysis and accounts receivable.

Exhibit 9-3 shows that the information flow among modules within the sales and purchases subsystem is the heaviest of all the subsystems and that the sales and purchases subsystem interacts less with other systems than does cash receipts and disbursements.

THE FINANCIAL ACCOUNTING SUBSYSTEM

In many ways, the **financial accounting subsystem** is the most basic of the processing systems. It handles the bookkeeping and accounting cycle events for a business, from journalizing and posting transactions, to producing the period-end financial statements, to comparing of results with budgeted (expected) figures. Exhibit 9-4 illustrates the information flow in a financial accounting subsystem. In this figure, we are focusing on the extreme right set in Exhibit 9-1 and examining the flow within this system.

316

*Part III
Computer-
Based
Accounting
Applications*

EXHIBIT 9-4   Information Flow in a Financial Accounting Subsystem

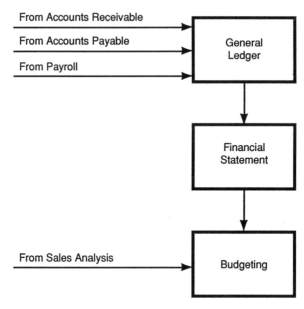

General Ledger and Financial Statements

The cash receipts and disbursements system provides much of the input to the general ledger module of the financial accounting subsystem. The accounts receivable, accounts payable, and payroll areas provide the transaction data necessary for the cash receipts and cash disbursements journals and the sales and purchases journals. Then, transactions not handled by the other processing applications are input directly into the general ledger module. Such transactions are usually those found in the company's general journal (for example, adjusting entries).

Periodically, the module produces a listing of all general ledger accounts, together with beginning balances, a summary of the debit and credit activity in each account, and the resultant ending balances. The general ledger produced by a computer system is not the familiar T-account, but a running balance form, consisting of a series of lines representing debits, credits, and balances on a printed sheet. A trial balance is then produced proving the equality of debits and credits in the system. Finally, at the end of each period, the traditional accounting financial statements can be provided by the financial statement module according to any format specified by the system user.

In addition, the general ledger module can produce detailed listings of all transactions, together with posting references, so that an audit trail of all transaction activity through the accounting information system in either direction is established.

Budgeting and the Master Budget

Managers are constantly engaged in planning (decision making) and control (monitoring and evaluating performance). The managerial tool that connects these two functions is called financial **budgeting**. A financial budget for a busi-

317

CHAPTER 9
*Overview of
Computer-
Based
Accounting
Information
Systems*

ness brings together and integrates all management decisions and shows the expected cumulative impact of these decisions on the business future. This cumulative impact is expressed in the form of projected (budgeted) financial statements. Taken together, the projected financial statements are called the **master budget** of the business and become the standard or benchmark against which future performance will be measured and evaluated.

The budgeting module can produce budgeted statements in the same format as actual period-end financial statements so that departures (or variances) from expected results in any important revenue, expense, or other category can be disclosed and highlighted for management analysis and action. The analysis of variances and the subsequent corrective action decisions that result from the analysis is called management control. Of course, the computer cannot perform management control functions, but the computer-based budgeting module can, as a matter of course, provide the information that makes these actions possible. Simultaneously, a master budget of **pro forma statements** can be generated that will serve as the benchmark for the following period.

The particular components of a master budget may vary from business to business because of differing circumstances and needs for information on the part of management. However, a master budget usually consists of at least three distinct statements about a firm's future.

1. Profit plan (projected income statement)
2. Cash budget (projected cash flow)
3. Budgeted balance sheet (projected financial position)

Profit Plan. The **profit plan** is an income statement projected over a future period. This projected income statement details the revenues, expenses, and resulting income or profit that the firm expects to achieve. The most critical figure in the profit plan is budgeted sales volume for the upcoming period. Virtually all figures, not only in the profit plan but in the entire master budget, are tied to projected sales volume. This projection is usually accomplished by combining past data on sales with known or expected changes for the budget period, such as new economic conditions, new products, new outlets, new competing products, and so on. Once a budgeted sales volume figure has been derived, budgeted sales revenue and the remainder of the profit plan can be determined.

Profit plans are typically prepared in one of two formats: accrual accounting or contribution margin. The accrual accounting approach is used for external reporting purposes. Businesses often choose to present a profit plan in the same format in which external income statements have been prepared. It is more useful to management, however, for the profit plan to emphasize decision-oriented variable and fixed cost breakdowns and contribution margin ideas. The contribution margin approach is frequently used for internal budgeting purposes because it provides management with more information for revenue and expense control and decision making. In a multiproduct company, this format can be used to break down revenues and expenses further by product, which provides additional insight into operations. Exhibit 9-5 illustrates both the accrual and contribution margin approaches to a profit plan.

318

PART III
Computer-
Based
Accounting
Applications

EXHIBIT 9-5   Profit Plan Approaches

Accrual	*Contribution Margin*
Sales revenue − Cost of goods sold = Gross profit − Selling expenses − Administrative expenses − Interest expense = Income before taxes − Income taxes = Net income	Sales revenue − Variable cost of goods sold = Contribution margin from production − Variable selling expenses − Variable administrative expenses = Contribution margin of the firm − Fixed cost of goods sold − Fixed selling expenses − Fixed administrative expenses − Interest expense = Income before taxes − Income taxes = Net income

Cash Budget.   The revenues, expenses, and income projected by the profit plan are needed for budgeting cash flows. Most firms budget cash on a monthly basis to make sure sufficient cash is available to meet short-term needs, such as payroll and disbursements to suppliers. These short-term **cash budgets** show the individual receipts and disbursements of cash expected and point up expected short-term excess cash balances or shortfalls and their probable duration. In addition to projected short-term cash flows, however, every business needs a cash budget that provides the ''big picture'' of the firm's cash flows over a longer period of time. The long-term cash budget highlights excess cash balances or deficiencies for perhaps, six months to one year, and helps company management plan the amounts and timing of any new financing (external funds) that may be needed to keep the business running smoothly.

Budgeted Balance Sheet.   The **budgeted balance sheet** requires the projected income information from the profit plan and the information on projected cash balances and financing needs from the cash budget. The statement summarizes all planned business activities in that it depicts the final effects on the business of all decisions, assumptions, and projections. If decisions made are implemented and have the planned effect, and the assumptions on which they are based prove realistic, the budgeted balance sheet discloses where the business will be as of the end of the upcoming planning period. This type of information is obviously necessary for both short-term and long-term planning.

Budgets and Decision Support Systems

Since budgeting necessarily involves committing future expectations to numbers, management must make some assumptions about the firm and its expected future environment. A budget is only as good as the assumptions on which it is based. If the assumptions are realistic, the master budget will be a useful tool. If not, the budget will not be useful (its effect may even be negative) and the time spent in its development wasted.

The master budget produced by the budgeting module of the financial accounting subsystem can be thought of as an accounting model that depicts the results of data, relationships, and assumptions. The budget model illustrates how a decision support system (discussed in Chapter 8) can be integrated with a processing subsystem in order to produce decision support information as a by-product of the processing of business data. Chapter 8 illustrated a financial DSS profit plan model which links, by a series of equations, the input variables provided by management to the financial accounting subsystem to generate output predictions.

319

CHAPTER 9
*Overview of
Computer-
Based
Accounting
Information
Systems*

THE MANUFACTURING SUBSYSTEM

Up to this point we have discussed computer-based information systems suitable for service, merchandising, or other nonmanufacturing environments. However, manufacturing operations have some additional information needs. These needs can be met by supplementing the computer-based information system with a specialized **manufacturing subsystem**. A computer-based manufacturing subsystem provides internal, management-oriented information, and its addition adds significantly to the size and complexity of the information system.

Exhibit 9-6 illustrates the information flow into and from the manufacturing subsystem of a total information system, which is given in the lower left

EXHIBIT 9-6   Information Flow in a Manufacturing Subsystem

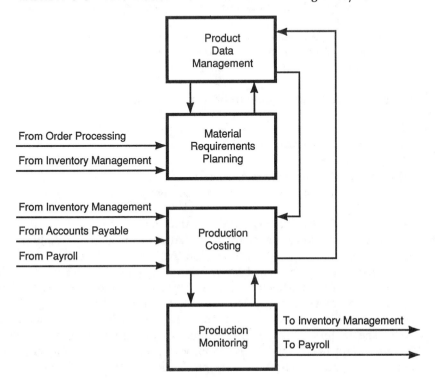

320

*PART III
Computer-
Based
Accounting
Applications*

set of Exhibit 9-1. This subsystem connects to the total information system primarily at the sales and purchases subsystem. The manufacturing subsystem is made up of four processing applications: product data management, material requirements planning (purchasing), production costing, and production monitoring. With computerized manufacturing modules, management hopes to accomplish at least the following:

- Reduce raw materials and component parts inventory on hand as well as work in process inventory.
- Increase productivity.
- Reduce late and incorrect shipments.
- Decrease indirect labor costs that result from poor routing and scheduling.

Product Data Management

The **product data management (PDM) module** accumulates semipermanent data about the various products manufactured by a company. The data collected are produced by and used by a number of departments including accounting, production, engineering, quality control, and others. As the number of departments collecting and using product information increases, so does the potential for errors. By accumulating this information in one place and making it accessible to all departments, the accuracy and consistency of the information is improved and the costs of maintaining it are reduced. The data stored for each product by PDM might consist of

1. A description of each of the raw materials and component parts used in the manufacturing process.
2. The sequence of operations necessary for the manufacturing process.
3. A description of the equipment and facilities used in the manufacturing process.
4. Certain master file product or item information.

Managers want the PDM module to provide on demand information on

1. What materials and components are used in each product.
2. Any special product features available to customers.
3. The projected cost to manufacture the product.
4. Historical deviations from projected costs.
5. In which departments the deviations have occurred.

Information Exchange. The product data management application provides critical information about required materials to the material requirements planning (purchasing) application. Based on the bills of materials generated in PDM, material requirements will be updated and orders placed when the inventory quantity of a particular item falls below a stated level. The bill of materials information also notifies material requirements planning of any changes in required materials, materials no longer needed, or new materials required. The material requirements planning application, in turn, provides information about raw materials availability to product data management for routing and scheduling purposes. The production costing application makes

321

CHAPTER 9
Overview of
Computer-
Based
Accounting
Information
Systems

use of the information on these routing reports to schedule production runs and provides cost information to product data management as the products are manufactured.

Inquiry and Response. Because a number of products may each offer a variety of features and options, it is desirable to have a list of the available choices on a product-by-product basis. The product features/options response display available from PDM lists all available features, whether or not the feature is required, any special options within the feature, and cost information about each option. This information is useful for order processing because it allows the customer or salesperson to select from the available options easily. It is also useful to management for planning material purchases and determining product costing.

Material Requirements Planning

The **material requirements planning (MRP),** sometimes called the purchasing, **module** produces a master production schedule based on actual sales as accumulated by the order processing module and on forecasted sales from the budgeting module. Based on bills of materials from product data management, MRP determines the quantity of materials, subassemblies, and other component items needed to meet the forecasted demand. This calculated amount is then compared to inventory on hand and inventory on order to determine necessary management actions. The MRP module advises management whether to reorder certain items, cancel orders for items no longer needed, or make no changes to the ordering plans. The objective of this module is to increase efficiency and customer service, while keeping materials inventory levels at the minimum necessary to meet demand.

Typically, the MRP process begins by reviewing the master production schedule. Any changes needed to reflect current forecasts are made at this point. After the master production schedule is approved, the module determines the actions necessary to meet the planned needs for material, subassemblies, and parts. Management may then view or print out any of a number of planning reports. Based on this information, management then chooses a course of action and enters it.

Information Exchange. In order for MRP to operate, it must have access to up-to-date information from product data management in the form of bills of materials. The information on the bills of materials is used by MRP, together with information provided by order processing on actual sales, budgeting on expected sales, and inventory management on inventory levels and open purchase orders, to calculate the quantity of materials, subassemblies, and other component items needed to produce a particular product.

Inquiry and Response. MRP is designed around inquiry and response capabilities. The purpose of the module is to assist management in planning inventory levels; as such, management must be able to access current production schedules, make actual or ''what if'' type changes, and immediately see the result.

322

PART III
Computer-
Based
Accounting
Applications

Production Costing

The **production costing module** assists management in planning and controlling the production process by generating reports showing the status of work in process and the cost of all products. In addition to providing the cost of products being manufactured, this module tells management

1. If the production process is on schedule.
2. If there are cost efficiencies or cost overruns.
3. The current work load level for each defined work center.

Management can schedule additional work for underworked areas, and reschedule work away from overworked areas. The net effect is to increase cost efficiencies and adherence to schedules that satisfy customer demand.

Information Exchange. Production costing requires the implementation of the inventory management module within the sales and purchases subsystem. It also relies heavily on information provided by a number of other modules in the system. This exchange reinforces the use of the data base approach for accurate, efficient processing of information. The inventory management, accounts payable, payroll, and production monitoring modules provide up-to-date information on inventory levels, material costs, labor transactions and costs, released orders, and scheduling to the production costing module.

Inquiry and Response. To control the production process, a number of inquiry displays are available. Each display can be presented in either accounting format (dollars) or production format (hours and quantities). These displays answer questions about where an order is located in the manufacturing process, when it will arrive at each work center, when it will be completed, and its accumulated cost.

Production Monitoring

The **production monitoring module** assists management in controlling material and labor costs and provides data to update inventory, payroll, and production costing. Data may be entered as activities occur, or accumulated and entered in batch format from a workstation at a later time.

Information Exchange. As data are entered, the application categorizes each entry as labor data, transfer data, or inventory data. Employee time and attendance data records are sent to payroll for the processing of paychecks. The move (transfer) data and inventory data are checked for reasonableness, formatted into output reports, and used to update both the inventory management and production costing modules. Inventory management receives information on receipts and issues of goods. Production costing receives transfer data in order to control the production scheduling process and cost the products.

323

CHAPTER 9
Overview of
Computer-
Based
Accounting
Information
Systems

Inquiry and Response. In many manufacturing subsystems, the production monitoring module is combined with production costing to create a production costing and monitoring module (PCM), as these areas are closely related. Whether combined or not, we would expect the same inquiry and response capability discussed in product costing to be available to production monitoring.

SIMILARITIES AMONG COMPUTER-BASED INFORMATION SYSTEM COMPONENTS

The component subsystems we have discussed in this chapter have some important characteristics in common. Each subsystem and module presented has exhibited the following attributes:

1. Output reports of varying form, content, and frequency.
2. Interfaces (the exchange of information) with other modules.
3. Inquiry and response (interactive) capability.
4. Data organization into files.
5. Use of terminals (workstations) to input data, initiate processing, and receive output.

Chapters 10, 11, and 12 will examine in detail these attributes for each of the component subsystems and processing modules presented in Exhibit 9-1.

CHAPTER SUMMARY

Both manual and computer-based information systems must handle cash inflows and outflows, sales and purchases, financial accounting, and, in the case of a manufacturer, manufacturing or cost accounting. Therefore, most computer-based information systems will contain a subsystem to process cash receipts and disbursements, another to process sales and purchases, and a third to accomplish the financial accounting and reporting of the business. In addition, the system for a manufacturer might include a subsystem to process production data. Each subsystem is composed of several applications, or modules, that interact with other modules in the system. Within each module, new information in the form of transaction files is processed and is the data source for updating the area's master files.

The cash receipts and disbursements subsystem consists of the accounts receivable, accounts payable, and payroll modules. These modules interact, or interface, with modules in all of the other subsystems, but particularly those of the sales and purchases and financial accounting subsystems.

The sales and purchases subsystem consists of the order processing, inventory management, and sales analysis modules. These modules represent the point of original data entry for the majority of business events. They supply information directly to the cash receipts and disbursements and manufacturing subsystems, and through these, to the financial accounting subsystem.

CONCEPT SUMMARY

Information Flow and Transaction Flow in Systems

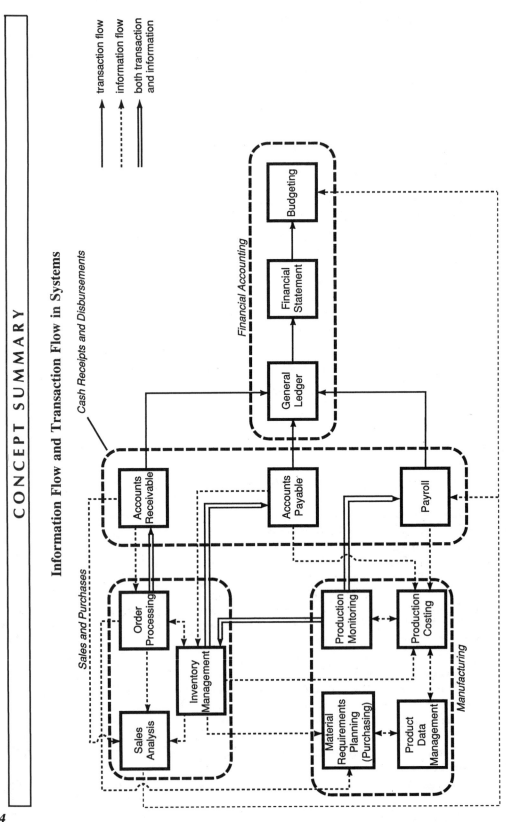

325

CHAPTER 9
*Overview of
Computer-
Based
Accounting
Information
Systems*

The financial accounting subsystem consists of the general ledger, financial statement, and budgeting modules. Transaction data flows from the other systems primarily into the general ledger module, which provides the basis for the financial statements and budgets. Budgeting helps managers plan and control business activities. The budgeting module produces a master budget consisting of a profit plan, a cash budget, and a budgeted balance sheet.

The manufacturing subsystem consists of the product data management, material requirements planning, and production costing and monitoring modules. This system obtains information from and supplies information to the sales and purchases and cash receipts and disbursement subsystems. The goals of the manufacturing subsystem are to reduce inventories, increase productivity, reduce late and incorrect shipments, and decrease indirect labor costs.

All modules within the information system produce output reports, interface with other modules, respond to user inquiries, organize data into files, and increasingly rely on terminals for data input, initiation of processing, and receipt of output. The concept summary on page 324 diagrams the information and transaction flows among the modules within a complete, computer-based information system.

KEY TERMS

Application modules (*p. 308*)
Budgeted balance sheet (*p. 318*)
Budgeting (*p. 316*)
Cash budget (*p. 318*)
Cash receipts and disbursements subsystem (*p. 313*)
Constant/report file (*p. 312*)
Financial accounting subsystem (*p. 315*)
Inquiry/response (*p. 311*)
Interface (*p. 311*)
Manufacturing subsystem (*p. 319*)
Master budget (*p. 317*)
Master files (*p. 312*)

Material requirements planning (MRP) module (*p. 321*)
Product data management (PDM) module (*p. 320*)
Production costing module (*p. 322*)
Production monitoring module (*p. 322*)
Profit plan (*p. 317*)
Pro forma statement (*p. 317*)
Sales and purchases subsystem (*p. 314*)
Terminals (*p. 311*)
Transaction files (*p. 312*)
Updating (*p. 312*)

QUESTIONS

9-1. Describe the four primary subsystems of a business information system and the nature of processing accomplished by each.

9-2. What is the major problem of maintaining a different computer program for each report to be printed? Give an alternative approach.

9-3. Discuss the interaction of the accounts receivable module with the order processing and sales analysis modules.

9-4. Discuss the interaction of the accounts payable module with the inventory management module.

9-5. What are the characteristics that make payroll somewhat different from other application modules?

326

PART III
Computer-
Based
Accounting
Applications

9-6. Discuss the interaction of the order processing module with the sales analysis and inventory management modules.

9-7. Describe the information flow that takes place between the manufacturing subsystem and the other subsystems of a business information system.

9-8. Discuss the primary functions of each of the four modules of a computer-based manufacturing subsystem.

9-9. Give the major information flows that take place among the four applications of a computer-based manufacturing subsystem.

9-10. What is a bill of materials? Give the types of data that would appear on a bill of materials and specify where in the manufacturing subsystem this data would be used.

9-11. Explain the difference between accounting information systems and transaction processing systems. Give two examples of data available from an information system that could not be produced by a transaction processing system.

PROBLEMS

9-12. A firm's total information system can be broken down into four component subsystems, each of which is represented in Exhibit 9-1 by a large curved shape. Give three examples of the major types of activity processed by each subsystem. In any information system, there must be information flow between application areas. For each of the arrows depicted in Exhibit 9-1, give a specific example of the information exchanged by these applications.

9-13. Each component subsystem depicted in Exhibit 9-1 can be broken down into application modules.

1. For each of the following application modules, give two specific examples of the activity processed by them:

   a. Order processing
   b. Inventory management
   c. Sales analysis
   d. Accounts receivable
   e. Accounts payable
   f. Payroll
   g. General ledger
   h. Product data management
   i. MRP (purchasing)
   j. Production costing
   k. Production monitoring

2. What are the purposes of the financial statement and budgeting application modules?

9-14. Give the five characteristics all processing modules have in common and provide an illustration of these characteristics for each of the modules given in Exhibit 9-1.

327

CHAPTER 9
*Overview of
Computer-
Based
Accounting
Information
Systems*

9-15. Some accounting events are not processed by the cash receipts and disbursements, sales and purchases, or manufacturing subsystems. These events enter the information system directly through the general ledger module of the financial accounting subsystem. Give five specific examples of events that might enter the system this way.

9-16. Most transactions enter the total information system through the sales and purchases subsystem. The information is then summarized and passed to the cash receipts and disbursements subsystem, which further summarizes the information and passes it to the financial accounting subsystem.

1. Assume that ten sales orders are received and processed and that sales invoices are then generated. What information would be required by the order processing, the accounts receivable, and the general ledger modules concerning these ten orders?

2. Assume that two purchase orders are created, the goods are shipped by the vendor and a purchase invoice is received. What information would be required by the inventory management, the accounts payable, and the general ledger modules concerning these orders?

9-17. (DeCoster and Schafer, *Management Accounting*, adapted) Two women who had been working in pottery as a hobby received so many requests for their stoneware dishes that they decided to produce the sets commercially. They formed a company, withdrew their savings, refinanced their homes, purchased equipment, rented an old barn, and started business as The Crockery Barn. However, they need additional financing from a bank and come to you for assistance in financial planning. Upon initial formation, the company has the following assets:

Cash	$ 2,000
Equipment	20,000

The women expect to sell 500 sets of dishes at $100 per set during the first six months. They believe an inventory of 20 finished sets is needed to fill rush orders. Because of drying time required, there will always be 20 half-finished sets in production. Costs (except depreciation and interest) for the first six months will be:

Production	$10,000 plus $50 per set *produced*
Selling and administration	$ 5,000 plus $10 per set *sold*

Purchases and sales will be on credit, with average balances of $20,000 for accounts receivable and $4,000 for accounts payable. Other payments will be made in the month the costs are incurred. A minimum cash balance of $2,000 is necessary.

The bank is willing to grant a two-year loan of up to $25,000 with 10 percent interest payable at maturity. Equipment is to be depreciated by the straight-line method over an estimated useful life of five years.

Prepare a master budget for the first six months of operations, including a profit plan, a cash budget, and a projected statement of financial position.

328

PART III
Computer-
Based
Accounting
Applications

9-18. (*CMA, adapted*) Springfield Corporation operates on a calendar year basis. It begins the annual budgeting process in late August when the president established targets for the total dollar sales and income before taxes for the next year.

The sales target is given to the marketing department, where the marketing manager formulates a sales budget by product line in both units and dollars. From this budget, sales quotas by product line in units and dollars are established for each of the corporation's sales districts. The marketing manager also estimates the cost of the marketing activities required to support the target sales volume and prepares a tentative marketing expense budget.

The executive vice president uses the sales and profit targets, the sales budget by product line, and the tentative marketing expense budget to determine the dollar amounts which can be devoted to manufacturing and corporate office expenses. The executive vice president prepares the budget for corporate expenses and then forwards to the production department the product line sales budget in units and the total dollar amount which can be devoted to manufacturing. The production manager meets with the factory managers to develop a manufacturing plan which will produce the required units when needed within the cost constraints set by the executive vice president. The budgeting process usually comes to a halt at this point because the production department does not consider the financial resources allocated to manufacturing to be adequate. When this standstill occurs, the vice president of finance, the executive vice president, the marketing manager, and the production manager meet to determine the final budgets for each of the areas. This normally results in a modest increase in the total amount available for manufacturing costs while the marketing expense and corporate office expense budgets are cut. The total sales and net income figures proposed by the president are rarely changed. Although the participants are seldom pleased with the compromise, these budgets are final. Each executive then develops a new detailed budget for the operations in his or her area.

None of the areas has achieved its budget in recent years. Sales often run below the target. When budgeted sales are not achieved, each area is expected to cut costs so that the president's profit target can still be met. However, the profit target is seldom met because costs are not cut enough. In fact, costs often run above the original budget in all functional areas. The president is disturbed that Springfield has not been able to meet its sales and profit targets and has hired a consultant with considerable experience in Springfield's industry. The consultant reviewed the budgets for the past four years and concluded that the product line sales budgets were reasonable and that the cost and expense budgets were adequate for the budgeted sales and production levels.

1. Discuss how the budgeting process as employed by Springfield Corporation may contribute to the failure to achieve the president's sales and profit targets.

2. Suggest how Springfield Corporation's budgeting process could be revised to correct the problems.

3. Should the functional areas be expected to cut their costs when sales volume falls below projections? Explain your answer.

9-19. (*CMA, adapted*) Tom Emory and Jim Morris strolled back to their plant from the administrative offices of Ferguson & Son Mfg. Company. Tom was manager of the machine shop in the company's factory. Jim was manager of the equipment maintenance department.

The men had just attended the monthly performance evaluation meeting

329

CHAPTER 9
*Overview of
Computer-
Based
Accounting
Information
Systems*

for plant department heads. These meetings had been held on the third Tuesday of each month since Robert Ferguson, Jr., the president's son, became plant manager a year earlier.

As they were walking, Tom Emory spoke. "Boy, I hate those meetings! I never know whether my department's accounting reports will show good or bad performance. I'm beginning to expect the worst. If the accountants say I saved the company a dollar, I'm called 'Sir,' but if I spend even a little too much—boy, do I get in trouble. I don't know if I can hold on until I retire."

Tom had just received his worst evaluation ever in his long career with Ferguson & Son. He was the most respected of the experienced machinists in the company. He had been with Ferguson & Son for many years and was promoted to supervisor of the machine shop when the company expanded and moved to its present location. The president (Robert Ferguson, Sr.) had often stated that the company's success was due to the high quality of the work of machinists like Emory. As supervisor, Tom stressed the importance of craftsmanship and told his workers that he wanted no sloppy work coming from his department.

When Robert Ferguson, Jr., became the plant manager, he directed that monthly performance comparisons be made between actual and budgeted costs for each department. The departmental budgets were intended to encourage the supervisors to reduce inefficiencies and to seek cost-reduction opportunities. The company controller was instructed to have his staff "tighten" the budget slightly whenever a department attained its budget in a given month; this was done to reinforce the plant manager's desire to reduce costs. The young plant manager often stressed the importance of continued progress toward attaining the budget; he also made it known that he kept a file of these performance reports for future reference when he succeeds his father as president. Tom Emory's conversation with Jim Morris continued as follows:

Emory: "I really don't understand. We've worked so hard to get up to budget, and the minute we make it they tighten the budget on us. We can't work any faster and still maintain quality. I think my men are ready to quit trying. Besides, those reports don't till the whole story. We always seem to be interrupting the big jobs for all those small rush orders. All that setup and machine adjustment time is killing us. And frankly, Jim, you were no help. When our hydraulic press broke down last month, your people were nowhere to be found. We had to take it apart ourselves and got stuck with all that idle time."

Morris: "I'm sorry about that, Tom, but you know my department has had trouble making budget, too. We were running well beyond at the time of that problem, and if we'd spent a day on that old machine, we would never have made it up. Instead, we made the scheduled inspections of the forklift trucks because we knew we could do those in less than the budgeted time."

Emory: "Well, Jim, at least you have some options. I'm locked into what the scheduling department assigns to me, and you know they're being harassed by sales for those special orders. Incidentally, why didn't your report show all the supplies you guys wasted last month when you were working in Bill's department?"

Morris: We're not out of the woods on that deal yet. We charged the maximum we could to our other work and haven't even reported some of it yet."

Emory: "Well, I'm glad you have a way of getting out of the pressure. The accountants seem to know everything that's happening in my department, sometimes even before I do. I thought all that budget and accounting stuff was supposed to help, but it just gets me into trouble. It's all a big pain. I'm trying to put out quality work; they're trying to save pennies."

330

PART III
Computer-
Based
Accounting
Applications

Tom Emory's performance report for the month in question is reproduced here. Actual production volume for the month was at the budgeted level.

MACHINE SHOP—OCTOBER
T. Emory, Supervisor

	Budget	Actual	Variances
Direct labor	$ 39,600	$ 39,850	$ 250 U
Direct materials	231,000	231,075	75 U
Depreciation, equipment	3,000	3,000	0
Depreciation, buildings	6,000	6,000	0
Power	900	860	40 F
Maintenance	400	410	10 U
Supervision	1,500	1,500	0
Idle time	0	1,800	1,800 U
Setup labor	680	2,432	1,752 U
Miscellaneous	2,900	3,300	400 U
	$285,980	$290,227	$4,247 U

U – Unfavorable   F – Favorable

1. Identify the problems that appear to exist in Ferguson & Son Mfg. Company's budgetary control system and explain how the problems are likely to reduce the effectiveness of the system.

2. Explain how Ferguson & Son Mfg. Company's budgetary control system could be revised to improve its effectiveness.

9-20. (*CMA, adapted*)   Kenbart Company has decided that increased emphasis is to be placed on profit planning and the analysis of results compared to its plans. A new computerized profit planning system has been implemented to achieve this objective.

The company employs the contribution margin approach for internal reporting purposes and applies the concept of flexible budgeting for estimating variable costs. The following items are used by Kenbart's executive management when reviewing and analyzing actual results and the profit plan.

- Original Plan: Profit plan approved and adopted by management at the beginning of the year.

- Revised Plan: Original plan modified as a consequence of action taken during the year (usually quarterly) by executive management.

- Flexed Revised Plan: The most current plan (i.e., either original plan or revised plan, if one has been prepared) adjusted for changes in volume and variable expense rates.

- Year-to-Date Actual Results: The actual results of operations for the year.

- Current Outlook: The combination of the actual year-to-date results of operations and the flexed revised plan for the remaining months of the year.

Executive management meets monthly to review actual results compared to the profit plan. Any assumptions or major changes in the profit plan usually are incorporated on a quarterly basis once the quarter is completed.

The following table gives an outline of the basic Profit Plan Report, which was designed by the data processing department. This report is prepared at the

331

CHAPTER 9
*Overview of
Computer-
Based
Accounting
Information
Systems*

end of each month. In addition, the report is generated whenever executive management initiates a change or modification in its plans. Consequently, many different versions of the company profit plan exist, which makes analysis difficult and confusing.

Several members of executive management have voiced disapproval of the Profit Plan Report because the columns are not well-defined and vary in meaning from one report to another. Furthermore, no current outlook column is included in the report. Therefore, the accounting department has been asked to work with the data processing department in modifying the report so that users can better understand the information being conveyed and the reference points for comparison of results.

Profit Plan Report
Month, Year

	Month			Year-to-Date		
	Actual	Over/(Under)		Actual	Over/(Under)	
	Plan	$	%	Plan	$	%
Sales						
Variable manufacturing costs						
Raw materials						
Direct labor						
Variable overhead						
Total						
Manufacturing margin						
Variable selling						
Contribution margin						
Fixed costs						
Manufacturing						
Sales						
General administration						
Income before taxes						
Income taxes						
Net income						

1. What advantages are there to Kenbart Company from having its profit plan system computerized?

2. Redesign the layout of the Profit Plan Report so that it will be more useful to Kenbart's executive management in reviewing results and planning operations. Explain the reason for each modification you make in the report.

3. What types of data would Kenbart Company be required to capture in its computer-based system in order to generate the plans and results that executive management needs for review and analysis?

9-21. (*CMA, adapted*) The following are two alternative narratives for a new computerized cash receipts system.

  a. The customer's payment and remittance advice are received in the treasurer's office. An accounts receivable clerk in the treasurer's office enters

332

*PART III
Computer-
Based
Accounting
Applications*

the amount of the cash receipt onto the remittance advice (if it is not already there) and forwards it to the EDP department. The payment amount is added to a control tape listing, and the receipts are filed for deposit later in the day. When the deposit slips are received from EDP (approximately 2:30 P.M. each day), the cash receipts are removed from the file and deposited with the original deposit slip. The second copy of the deposit slip and the control tape are compared for accuracy before the deposit is made and then filed together.

In the EDP department, the remittance advices received from the treasurer's office are held until 2:00 P.M. daily. At that time, the customer payments are processed to update the records on magnetic tape and to prepare a deposit slip in triplicate. During the update process, data are read from the master accounts receivable tape, processed, and then recorded on a new master file tape. The original and second copy of the deposit slip are forwarded to the treasurer's office. The old master file tape (former accounts receivable master file), the remittance advices (in customer number order), and the third copy of the deposit slip are filed in a secure place. The updated accounts receivable master file tape is maintained in the system for processing the next day.

b. The customer's payment and remittance advice are received in the treasurer's office as before. A terminal is located in the treasurer's office to enter the cash receipts. An operator keys in the customer's number and payment taken from the remittance advice and checks. The cash receipt is entered into the system once the operator has confirmed that the proper account and amount are displayed on the screen. The payment is then processed on-line against the accounts receivable master file maintained on disk. The cash receipts are filed for deposit later in the day. The remittance advice amount is added to a control tape and the remittance advices are then filed in the order processed.

The computer prints out a deposit slip in duplicate at 2:00 P.M. for all cash receipts since the last deposit. The deposit slips and the control tape are compared for accuracy before the deposit is made. The cash receipts are removed from the file and deposited with the original deposit slip; the duplicate deposit slip is filed for further reference along with the control tape. At the close of business hours (5:00 P.M.) each day, the EDP department prepares a record of the current day's cash receipts activity on magnetic tape. This tape is then stored in a secure place in the event of a systems malfunction; after ten working days the tape is released for other use.

1. For each narrative, draw a system flowchart.
2. Discuss the advantages and disadvantages of each approach.

DECISION CASE

(*CMA, adapted*) Allied Auto Parts is a wholly owned subsidiary of Total Merchandising, Inc. Total has examined Allied's operations and has placed pressure on Allied to integrate a computer into its operations. The top management of Allied has expressed some interest in introducing a computer system; however, they point out that the company has been operating profitably with the manual systems that were developed by current management.

333

CHAPTER 9
*Overview of
Computer-
Based
Accounting
Information
Systems*

Allied has annual sales of $90 million and operates under a franchise system through stores independently owned by individual businesspeople. Allied is considering providing advisory services to its dealers (store owners) in order to improve their chances of staying in business and earning the maximum possible profit, but currently Allied does not attempt to assess the profitability of each store.

Stores are supplied from a single, central warehouse. Orders are placed weekly by individual stores and shipped about three days after receipt of the order, if the item is in stock. Store owners fill out a 100-page order form based on the company's 8,500-item catalog by indicating alongside a printed item number the quantity of that item they wish to order. Each of the 75 stores usually places one order each week, and the orders are processed manually.

Orders are filled from inventory once they are approved by the credit manager. The inventory manager is well liked and respected by his employees, and Allied management is confident that the employees do not steal from inventory because they do not wish to lose the manager's friendship.

Inventory stock status is maintained by a totally manual system that uses separate ledger cards for each catalog item. The cards are coded with colored ink and are maintained by a member of the accounting department, who notes any change in stock status (receipt of an item, withdrawal of an item, ordering of an item, etc.) in an appropriate colored ink. The quantity on hand of each item is computed monthly. Allied takes an annual physical inventory and updates its ledger cards by write-offs of inventory based on the physical count. The company does not know when or why differences between quantities on hand and quantities recorded occur.

Purchasing is also a manual process. Purchasing agents review the stock ledger cards to determine when it is necessary to reorder. Each purchasing agent is assigned responsibility for particular products and uses judgment as to when to reorder. There have been some problems in the system because Allied relies solely on the product numbers assigned to individual items by vendors or manufacturers to identify the products. Since a wide diversity of product number systems exist among the many Allied suppliers, errors occur frequently in order writing and filing.

Required:

1. Identify problems in the ordering, inventory, and purchasing systems.
2. How might a computerized system help solve Allied's problems?
3. A computer-based information system should do more than automate clerical activities. Discuss how a computerized system might provide new information Allied could use in determining the profitability of its franchises.
4. Discuss the obstacles that might arise in the implementation of a computer system for Allied.

10 Cash Receipts and Disbursements Systems

Overview

The cash receipts and disbursements business cycles and the way computer-based information systems process these cycles through receivables, payables, and payroll.

Learning Objectives

Thorough study of this chapter will enable you to:

1. Relate the cash receipts and disbursements system to the information system as a whole.
2. Describe the capabilities of a typical accounts receivable module.
3. Describe the capabilities of a typical accounts payable module.
4. Explain why the payroll module differs from the other modules in the cash receipts and disbursements system.
5. Describe the capabilities of a typical payroll module.

Outline

SYSTEMS IN THE REAL WORLD

335

*CHAPTER 10
Cash
Receipts
and Dis-
bursements
Systems*

A Convert Confesses

Mike Patano, MIS director at Southern Steam, Inc., in Mobile, Alabama, wasn't in the market for an AS/400. Now, his company is something of a showcase for IBM's midrange machine. Southern Steam's system is featured in a video produced for Big Blue's sales staff.

The transportation company had $1.5 million invested in its existing system—two Digital Equipment Corporation VAX computers running a system via a network linking 25 offices across the nation. Converting to a different system didn't seem practical.

"We had serious problems in 1988," Patano says. The existing system was running at capacity. Although the company was ready to take on new customers, IS couldn't handle the additional work load. Digital was scheduled to make its pitch to Southern Steam's board members last October. Then, two weeks before the meeting, IBM wangled a change to make a rival presentation. "I don't know how they did it," Patano says, but IBM came to the meeting with a complete plan, including installation, training, and promises of ongoing support and maintenance. "Two weeks later, we were walking away from a $1.5 million investment."

By the first of the year, Southern Steam had converted to an AS/400 B60. Patano the skeptic is an evangelist now. "I no longer have to worry about whether I can deliver what I promised," he says. A ship delayed in port costs the company up to $15,000 a day, he says. So far, IBM's service and support have been able to meet the company's demand for full-time availability to prevent shipping delays caused by problems with the system.

One year after its much-publicized introduction, it can safely be said that IBM's Application System/400 is a winner. Some 32,000 units were shipped worldwide last year; as many as another 100,000 systems are forecast to ship this year. This demand has IBM's 3-million-square-foot manufacturing facility in Rochester, Minnesota, running at full tilt. Rumor has it that the AS/400 is the first IBM product since the System/360 to sell out completely.

So far, the vast majority of AS/400 systems have gone to replace IBM's aging System/36 and System/38 machines. No surprise there. A fair number of AS/400 systems are also showing up at IBM's large accounts as the middle tier in IBM's three-tier architecture. Again, no great surprise. The biggest surprise, it now turns out, is that the AS/400 is winning converts in mainframe quarters that IBM had not counted on at all. The very AS/400 features that were supposed to appeal to the small- to medium-sized user—a relational data base that is built into the operating system, a simple networking scheme, the machine's all-around user friendliness, its ability to be operated with a small programming staff—are attracting interest at large shops.

As a result, sales of the largest AS/400s have passed their lifetime projections in the first three months.

SOURCE: *Datamation*, May 1, 1989, p. 49 and July 15, 1990, p. 44.

336

Part III
Computer-
Based
Accounting
Applications

OVERVIEW OF A CASH RECEIPTS AND DISBURSEMENTS SYSTEM

An overview of the information flow in a cash receipts and disbursements subsystem is given in Chapter 9. Refer to Exhibits 9-1 and 9-2 to refresh your memory as to the place of the cash receipts and disbursements subsystem in the total information system and to review the interaction between this and other subsystems.

ACCOUNTS RECEIVABLE MODULE

Often the most decisive variable in the success of a business is its cash flow. Control of cash inflows and outflows is essential to the short- and long-term stability of any business. The primary sources of operating cash inflows are sales and collections of receivables. The **accounts receivable module** is designed to process these cash inflows and to provide information to help management minimize the amount of cash tied up in receivables or lost to uncollectibles. Ordinarily, this processing package should provide information on (1) who owes the business money, (2) how much, (3) for how long, and (4) past receivables collection experience. The focus of accounts receivable processing is on cash inflows from operations, and the goal is to provide information to help the business monitor, control, and accelerate these inflows. Exhibit 10-1 summarizes the information flow into and from the accounts receivable processing module. Because receivables necessarily interface with many other modules, the information flow is heavy. In the remainder of this section we will examine these information flows in detail.

The actual operation of accounts receivable begins with the main menu illustrated in Exhibit 10-2. Security and control provisions should limit access to the programs and data maintained by the module to authorized persons only.

Output Reports

Because each module achieves its goals through the output it generates, we will begin with the specific output reports that are generated by accounts receivable. Although the number and content of output reports from a computer-based receivables module can vary to meet a company's particular information needs, the printed reports outlined in Exhibit 10-1 are typical. The frequency of these reports can also vary from on demand to monthly or so.

Cash Receipts and Adjustments Journal (Exhibit 10-3). Unlike the cash receipts journal produced by manual accounting systems, a computerized **cash receipts and adjustments journal** records solely cash receipts from the collection of receivables, leaving other cash receipts (primarily cash sales) to be recorded elsewhere. This difference is by design and is not unusual in computer-based systems. The necessity to record all cash receipts in one journal, so important for control purposes in a manual accounting system, is not critical in a computer-based information system. The capabilities of a computer system allow

EXHIBIT 10-1 **Information Flow Through an Accounts Receivable Module**

337

CHAPTER 10
*Cash
Receipts
and Dis-
bursements
Systems*

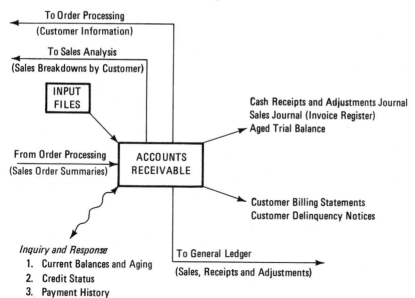

control over cash transactions to be exercised in a number of other ways that are discussed throughout this book. For example, notice that each entry in this journal contains a deposit number that connects the cash receipt entry to a deposit of cash in the bank, an important control and audit trail feature. Summaries and totals are provided in this computer-based journal.

EXHIBIT 10-2 **Accounts Receivable Main Menu**

```
**********                           *************           **
                        MENU: AMRM00

               A C C O U N T S   R E C E I V A B L E
                            Main Menu

                 1 Transaction Processing
                 2 Month End Closing
                 3 Statements
                 4 Delinquency Notices
                 5 Aged Trial Balance
                 6 Aged Receivables Report
                 7 Customer Inquiry
                 8 Master File Processing
                 9 Return to Application Selection Menu




     Enter number nn                   For another application or menu,
                                       enter program or menu name aaaaA6
```

Courtesy of IBM Corporation.

EXHIBIT 10-3 Cash Receipts and Adjustments Journal

				A/R CASH RECEIPT AND ADJUSTMENT TRANSACTION REGISTER					DATE 3/29/** TIME 14.16.40 PAGE 1 AMR401 BATCH 11			
DEPOSIT NO -REF-	CHECK/ ADJ NO -DATE-	CO/CUST NO -A/R-	NAME -DISC-	 -CASH-	SLSMN NO ADJUSTMENT	TRAN TYPE	A/R AMOUNT	DISCOUNT AMOUNT (ORIDE G/L)	CASH AMOUNT (ORIDE G/L)	ADJUSTMENT AMOUNT (ORIDE G/L)	CREDIT AMOUNT (ORIDE G/L)
98 	1126 3/29/**	1	POP MACHINE						13.35		13.35
98 SUMMARY	1542 3/29/**	100001400 375.00-	LAKESIDE IMPLEMENTS 20.00	 355.00	31702 .00	6	375.00-	20.00	355.00	.00	
84311	3/29/**	10.00-	.00	10.00	.00						
86672	3/29/**	355.00-	10.00	345.00	.00						
86686	3/29/**	10.00-	10.00	.00	.00						*
98 	226487 3/29/**	1	REBATE						25.00		25.00
98 SUMMARY	22568 3/29/**	100001700 625.00-	PHILLIPS & SONS .00	 625.00	31709 .00	6	625.00-	.00	625.00	.00	

		A/R CASH RECEIPT AND ADJUSTMENT TRANSACTION REGISTER		DATE 3/29/** TIME 14.16.40 PAGE 3 AMR401

FINAL TOTALS

TRANSACTION TOTALS   COUNT   * DISCOUNT EXCEEDED-   2

A/R RECEIPTS (1)	2,494.31-	11
DISCOUNTS	40.00	
WRITE-OFF ADJ (4)	.00	
CASH RECEIVED (5)	2,454.31	
APPLIED	2,454.31	
UNAPPLIED	.00	
A/R ADJUSTMENTS (2)	76.00	7
APPLIED	76.00	
UNAPPLIED	.00	
MISCELLANEOUS CASH (3)	38.35	2
TOTAL A/R AMOUNT (1+2)	2,418.31-	10
TOTAL ADJUSTMENTS (2+4)	76.00	
TOTAL CASH DEPOSIT (3+5)	2,492.66	

Courtesy of IBM Corporation.

Sales Journal or Invoice Register (Exhibit 10-4). The **sales journal** presents a record of all sales invoices, both cash and credit, created by the business during the current period. It is closely related to the cash receipts and adjustments journal, and together they present a whole picture of the general ledger effects of sales and collections of receivables. Since the accounts receivable module handles the recording of the sales invoices and the subsequent collections of accounts, the cash receipts and sales journals are produced by accounts receivable processing.

Since sales invoices are always sequentially numbered, journals that list

EXHIBIT 10-4   Sales Journal (Invoice Register)

INV/CM NO.	NAME CO-CUST NUMBER	SLSMAN NO.	INV. DATE SALES AMOUNT	AGING DATE SPECIAL CHG/CR	CLOSES CUR FREIGHT	SALES CD DISCOUNT	TOTAL TAXES	INVOICE TOTAL	INVOICE PROFITS	PROFIT PERCNT
				INVOICE REGISTER-ACCOUNTS RECEIVABLE DATE **/**/** TIME 15.00.29 PAGE 1 AMV451						
APPOLLO SUPPLY CO. 101	01-00000100	31701	4/12/** 1,060.00	4/12/** .00	0 .00	R .00	.00	1,060.00	1,060.00	100.0
APPOLLO SUPPLY CO. 102	01-00000100	31701	4/12/** 1,000.00	4/12/** .00	0 .00	R .00	.00	1,000.00	1,000.00	100.0
APPOLLO SUPPLY CO. 103	01-00000100	31701	4/12/** 1,025.00	4/12/** .00	0 .00	R .00	.00	1,025.00	1,025.00	100.0

Courtesy of IBM Corporation.

all invoices both cash and credit as this journal does, are a logical step given the way data are organized and transmitted in a computer-based system. A significant amount of data is provided by the journal on each sale, including the invoice number, customer number, and salesperson number, as well as information on the transaction amounts. In addition, because the data are input from the sales and purchases subsystem, the invoice register can provide the cost and profit associated with each invoice.

Aged Receivables Report or Aged Trial Balance (Exhibit 10-5).   Before it produces billing statements for customers, the accounts receivable module can print an **aged trial balance** for management analysis and audit purposes. This report provides a complete listing of amounts owed by each customer as of the statement date. Each amount is classified by the length of time the amount has been outstanding so that payment patterns and delinquent accounts are immediately apparent. Summaries at the bottom of the statement show the total amount due from customers and break down this total into amounts due in each of the aged categories chosen by the user. The percentage of total accounts receivable represented by each of these aged categories can be shown. The statement also summarizes the total charges to accounts receivable, total customer payments, and total returns and adjustments for the current period, which is the information needed for the general ledger and for financial statements. Although the format and information content of both reports is the same, this report is typically referred to as an aged receivables report when it is printed during an accounting period and an aged trial balance when printed at the end of a cycle (usually monthly). These reports can be printed in several levels of detail from an invoice-by-invoice level to a summary level providing only a single line for each customer.

Customer Billing Statements and Delinquency Notices (Exhibits 10-6 and 10-7).   The **customer billing statement** is a familiar document to anyone with a credit card or account. Almost all credit customers (certainly all at the retail level) now expect to be billed monthly for amounts owed. The billing statement is an important part of the control of cash inflows because it reminds customers of the amounts owed, and usually triggers payment. The statement must be

EXHIBIT 10-5 Aged Trial Balance

```
NORTHCREEK  STM  NO.  1                    AGED TRIAL BALANCE REPORT    DATE 12/18/**  TIME 15.56.09  PAGE    1 AMR821

          ALL CUSTOMERS                                           AGED AS OF CURRENT STATEMENT-DETAIL

NUMBERS, NAME,  CODES         CURRENT MONTH        TOTAL DUE   CURRENT    OVER 30     OVER 60     OVER 90    OVER 120

01       800  213-797-2202 FUT A/R:      .00      1,815.91
FOREMOST MACHINE COMPANY     PRBAL:  11,815.91
PO BOX 328                   CHGTD:        .00
ATLANTA
GA    30317-1903             CRDTD:  10,000.00
                             ADJTD:        .00
                             DLTPM:    8/27/**
BFOIC:0  SMTCD:1  CRLCD:   ILCAM:      .00
ILCAC:0  ILCCD:1  ILPCT:.015  ILCLS:     .00

  INVNR          AGECD   AMT RCVD   DISCOUNT   A/R AMOUNT

84323  INV   8/25/** 1                  .00   10,002.21
84323  PMT   8/27/** 1      9,500.00  500.00   10,000.00-
                                                      *         2.21
84566  INV   8/25/** 1                  .10        2.50
                                                      *                     2.50
84733  INV   8/29/** 1                72.45    1,811.20
                                                      *                              1,811.20
                             FUTURE A/R
                                    .00                     .00     1,815.91        .00        .00        .00
UNAPPLIED PMTS-        .00  UNAPPLIED ADJS-     .00
```

```
NORTHCREEK  STM  NO. 01 TOTALS             AGED TRIAL BALANCE REPORT    DATE 12/18/**  TIME 15.56.09  PAGE   14 AMR821

          ALL CUSTOMERS                                           AGED AS OF CURRENT STATEMENT-DETAIL

       PREV BAL          CURR CHGS           CURR PMTS          CURR ADJMNTS         TOTAL DUE    FUTURE A/R DUE
      76,684.51           1,292.30          11,371.63              33.51-           66,571.67         1,373.37

    CURRENT AMOUNT         OVER 30            OVER 60             OVER 90            OVER 120       SERVICE CHGS
        116.02           42,942.75          12,750.75           7,245.91           2,142.87           665.89

UNAPPLIED PAYMENTS-       482.16- UNAPPLIED ADJUSTMENTS-        19.40-

NOTE- P INDICATES RECORD MARKED FOR PURGE
```

Courtesy of IBM Corporation.

accurate if goodwill and customer confidence are to be maintained. Most computer-based systems are capable of producing billing statements as frequently as desired, or even on demand, something that is not practical with a manual system. The more often customers are billed (within some reasonable limit), the greater the likelihood that cash inflows will be accelerated. Exhibit 10-6 is a typical billing statement, and Exhibit 10-7 is a straightforward **delinquency notice** designed to prompt customer payment. Note that in both cases the system can automatically calculate periodic finance charges on past due amounts and add them to the statements.

Summary of Output Reports. These reports illustrate the most important printed output that can be generated by an accounts receivable module. Each of these computer-based reports provides information with an accuracy and timeliness not possible from a manual system. In addition to the regularly scheduled and recurring reports, a computerized receivables package can produce several special statements on demand as the need arises. This ability to use data available in the system in many different ways for different purposes is one of the major advantages of computer-based systems over manual systems.

EXHIBIT 10-6 Customer Billing Statement

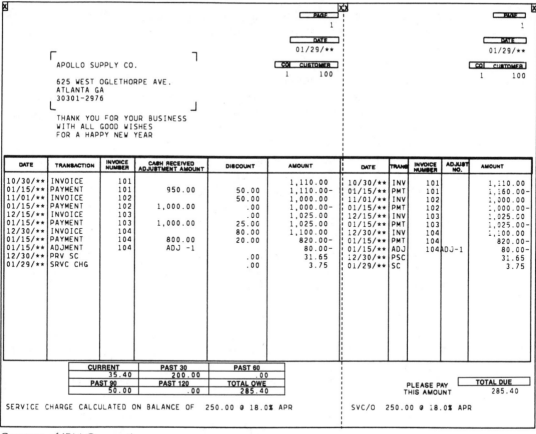

Courtesy of IBM Corporation.

EXHIBIT 10-7 Customer Delinquency Notice

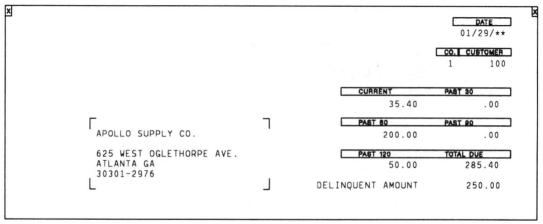

Courtesy of IBM Corporation.

342

PART III
Computer-
Based
Accounting
Applications

Information Exchange

The output generated by an accounts receivable module is not limited to printed reports. The information resulting from the transactions processed by the receivables module is often essential to the functioning of other modules. Several of the important inputs to the general ledger come from the credit sales and cash receipts transactions of the receivables module. This information may be passed from accounts receivable to the general ledger in the form of a file of processed transactions or as a series of summary totals resulting from the events already recorded in detail by receivables.

In addition, interaction takes place between receivables and the sales analysis and order processing modules of the sales and purchases subsystem. Accounts receivable provides information on customer sales breakdowns to sales analysis and provides important credit limit and history information to order processing. Order processing, in turn, passes summary information on all processed sales orders to accounts receivable. Hence, the flow is constantly two way, with each module producing information that is used by the other. Notice, however, that much of this flow is of information rather than accounting transactions. This routine flow of nontransaction information differentiates information systems from accounting systems.

Inquiry and Response. Notice in Exhibit 10-1 the wavy line leading to inquiry and response. This input/output line indicates an on-line connection between terminals (workstations) and the receivables module, so that questions concerning current customer account balances and age, credit status, and payment histories can be immediately answered by the computer. This capability is necessary for accounts receivable processing if credit-granting and other decisions are to be made based on up-to-date information. Exhibit 10-8 is an example of a typical response to a workstation inquiry concerning a customer account. Note that this on-line capability allows a user to inquire into customer data files at any time and receive immediate responses to questions about a specific customer or transaction based on information stored in the system.

Input Files

We can now discuss the direct system input necessary for accounts receivable processing to function. As the required files and their content are presented, keep in mind the basic data organization ideas discussed earlier in Part 2 of this book. Following are the major files necessary for the accounts receivable module to function.

Customer Master File. The **customer master file** contains one record for each credit customer. Each record consists of at least the following data-items:

1. Customer account number
2. Customer name
3. Customer address (including city, state, and zip code) and telephone number
4. Credit limit
5. Credit history code

EXHIBIT 10-8   **Display of Response Information from Accounts Receivable**   *343*

CHAPTER 10
*Cash
Receipts
and Dis-
bursements
Systems*

```
DATE 08/16/**          A/R INQUIRY - OPEN ITEM        SUMMARY    AMR902  V1

COMPANY  01            BICKERS & WHITE           PHONE 781-341-6658
CUSTOMER 00000400      8800 EAST 63RD ST.        STMT CD 0 SALESREP
LINE     N             LOS ANGELES               SVC CD 1  SVC PCT    015
                                                 LAST PAYMENT -  00/00/**
                       CA 64133-3820
SRVC CHGS -     41.24 CURRENT -       41.24 FUTURE DUE   -
CURR CHGS -           30 DAY -              CREDIT LIMIT -
CURR PMTS -           60 DAY -      172.50                 EXCEEDED
CURR ADJS -           90 DAY -    2,749.70 DETAIL TOTAL -
PREV BAL  -          120 DAY -              TOTAL DUE   -
                                 DR/CR   DISCOUNT     A/R     DATE LAST
LINE REF NO   DATE    TRAN AMT   TO DATE   TAKEN    AMT DUE   ACTIVITY
 1  084955 10/06/**    887.09      .00      .00     887.05 10/06/**
 2  085079 10/13/**  1,862.65      .00      .00   1,862.65 10/13/**
 3  084731 11/21/**    172.50      .00      .00     172.50 11/21/**
 4  SVCCHG 01/01/**     41.24      .00      .00      41.24 01/01/**
 5
 6
 7
 8
    ---END OF DETAIL---
                                            F24 END OF INQUIRY
```

Courtesy of IBM Corporation.

6. Current balance by age
7. Collections—year to date
8. Finance charges
9. Collections—previous year
10. Applicable taxes and discounts available

This file is updated with each processing cycle and is the accounts receivable data base for most system inquiries. Like most master files, the customer master file is input to, updated by, and output from each processing run of accounts receivable. The customer master file is the computer system counterpart of the accounts receivable subsidiary ledger and provides detailed information on sales to and collections from each customer, as well as current amounts owed by each customer.

New Sales Invoices File.   The **new sales invoices file** consists of all verified sales invoices created since the last processing of accounts receivable. Input data from this file are used to update the customer master file and is also the basis for the sales journal (invoice register) that can be produced as the summarized data is passed to the general ledger. The new sales invoices file is an input file only.

Cash Receipts and Adjustments File.   Like the new invoices file, the **cash receipts and adjustments file** is a transaction file that provides input data for the updating of the customer master file. This file shows the transactions that have reduced receivables balances since the last processing and is the basis for the cash receipts and adjustments journal discussed earlier. This is an input file only.

344

Part III
Computer-
Based
Accounting
Applications

Batch versus On-Line Processing

In an on-line system, transaction files are created and processed as the transactions are received by means of an on-line device, such as a terminal or workstation. The master file, then, is constantly updated by transactions as they occur. In a batch system, transactions can be stored on a disk as received and held until a sufficient file has been built. Then, a processing run can update the master file. This results in a master file that is not completely up to date at all times. The basic choice of an on-line approach or a batch approach to the processing of transactions balances considerations of cost and complexity against timeliness and responsiveness and must be made for each of the modules in a system. The on-line approach is obviously more desirable for some areas of processing than for others.

Exhibit 10-9 illustrates a display of customer data that a receivables module provides as a cash receipt or adjustment input transaction is entered by a user.

How the Accounts Receivable Module Works

The file structure and data organization of accounts receivable results in processing according to the following basic equation.

FOR EACH CREDIT CUSTOMER ACCOUNT	FILE PROVIDING OR STORING INFORMATION
Beginning amount owed by	Master
+ Credit sales to	New sales invoices
− Payments on account by	Receipts and adjustments
− Adjustments	Receipts and adjustments
= Ending amount owed by	Master

EXHIBIT 10-9   Display of Cash Receipt and Adjustment Input Transaction Entry

```
 DATE 08/31/**                                         ENTER     AMR203  04
                                CASH RECEIPT ENTRY


 COMPANY    1                   APPOLLO SUPPLY CO.        OPEN ITEM
 CUSTOMER      100              625 WEST OGLETHORPE AVE.
                                ATLANTA

                                          STATE GA  ZIP 30301-2976


 SERVICE CHGS -        47.57          CURRENT   -        47.57
    CURR CHGS -          .00          30 DAY    -          .00
    CURR PMTS -          .00          60 DAY    -          .00
    CURR ADJS -          .00          90 DAY    -          .00
      FUT DUE -          .00          120 DAY   -     3,171.54
        TOTAL DUE -   3,219.11        CREDIT LIMIT-        0    EXCEEDED

 CASH RECVD    DISCOUNT    GROSS RECVD    DATE  REF   CHECK    DEPOSIT  SLSMN
    151.29       25.00        176.29    0827**        16332       203 31701
                                             GL CASH ACCOUNT  GL DISC ACCOUNT
                                                    1050             7120




                                            F08 ENTRY CUSTOMER
```

Courtesy of IBM Corporation.

As accounts receivable processing occurs, this equation is carried out repeatedly.

345

CHAPTER 10
Cash
Receipts
and Dis-
bursements
Systems

CONCEPT SUMMARY

Accounts Receivable Module

	Input	*Information Exchange*	*Output*
Human/ Computer Interaction	1. New sales invoices file 2. Cash receipts and adjustments file	Inquiry/response on 1. Current customer account balances 2. Credit limits 3. Payment history	1. Special journals 2. Aged trial balance 3. Customer billing and delinquency statements
Computer Only	1. Customer master file	1. Sales and cash receipt transactions and summary totals *to* general ledger 2. Customer sales breakdowns *to* sales analysis 3. Credit limit and credit history *to* order processing 4. Sales orders processed *from* order processing	1. Customer master file

---

ACCOUNTS PAYABLE MODULE

The accounts receivable module just discussed is concerned with processing the transactions whose impact is on the operating cash inflows of a business. Equally important to the overall control of cash and cash flows are those transactions that affect operating cash outflows. These are primarily the purchase of merchandise and payment of amounts due suppliers (accounts payable). The **accounts payable module** is designed to monitor these cash outflows and provide information that will aid in the control of the costs and expenses associated with the flows. This module should provide information on (1) who the business owes money, (2) how much, (3) for how long, and (4) if outgoing checks are properly accounted for. The focus here is on cash outflows due to operations, and the goal is to process payables so that cash outflows will occur no sooner than necessary or later than prudent. Also, the package provides information that will direct attention to the control of the expenses associated with the purchase function. Exhibit 10-10 summarizes the information flow into and from an accounts payable processing module. The main menu to begin processing accounts payable is given in Exhibit 10-11.

346

PART III
Computer-
Based
Accounting
Applications

EXHIBIT 10-10   Information Flow Through an Accounts Payable Module

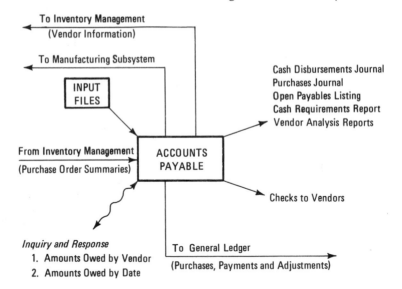

Output Reports

In order to relate the output to the goals of the module, our starting point will again be the output reports to be expected from accounts payable. The specific form, content, and frequency of reports may vary. We are presenting typical reports generated by this processing module.

Cash Disbursements Journal (Exhibit 10-12). The accounts payable module produces this journal; it is here that individual supplier accounts are updated

EXHIBIT 10-11   Accounts Payable Main Menu

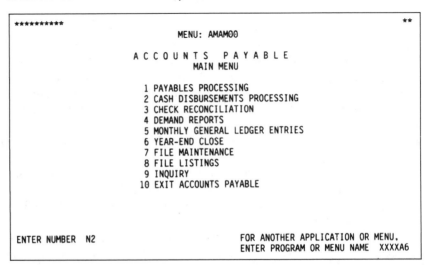

Courtesy of IBM Corporation.

EXHIBIT 10-12 Cash Disbursements Journal

■2 JOURNAL REFERENCE	VENDOR NAME	PAY SEL NUMBER	INVOICE NUMBER	PURCHASE JOURNAL	GROSS	DISCOUNT	NET	GL ACCOUNT	AMOUNT	CHECK NBR
CD03-0001	PARAMUS WH	2	4786A	PJ01-0007	103.00		103.00	2000	103.00	
CD03-0002			CHECK TOTAL		103.00		103.00	1050	103.00CR	126
CD03-0003	ALLRIGHT P	3	7621	PJ01-0009	200.00	10.00	190.00	2000	200.00	127
CD03-0004			CHECK TOTAL		200.00	10.00	190.00	1050	190.00CR	
CD03-0005			DISCOUNT TAKEN					8300	10.00CR	
CD03-0006	J & P CO	30	LT46	PJ01-0076	100.00		100.00	2000	100.00	
CD03-0007	J & P CO	31	LT46	PJ01-0078	45.00		45.00	2000	45.00	
CD03-0008	J & P CO	32	LT46	PJ01-0080	50.00		50.00	2000	50.00	
CD03-0009			CHECK TOTAL		195.00		195.00	1050	195.00CR	128
CD03-0010	BUTLER CO	8	QX4432A	PJ01-0024	771.60		771.60	2000	771.60	
CD03-0011			CHECK TOTAL		771.60		771.60	1050	771.60CR	129
CD03-0012	CITADEL CO	9	1111	PJ01-0026	17,734.20		17,734.20	2000	17,734.20	
CD03-0013			CHECK TOTAL		17,734.20		17,734.20	1050	17,734.20CR	130
CD03-0014	FULTON CO	11	777142A3	PJ01-0033	5,000.00	250.00	4,750.00	2000	5,000.00	
CD03-0015			CHECK TOTAL		5,000.00	250.00	4,750.00	1050	4,750.00CR	131
CD03-0016			DISCOUNT TAKEN					8300	250.00CR	
CD03-0017	KNEADS CO	34	0040	PJ01-0084	1,110.00	185.00	925.00	2000	1,110.00	
CD03-0018			CHECK TOTAL		1,110.00	185.00	925.00	1050	925.00CR	132
CD03-0019			DISCOUNT TAKEN					8300	185.00CR	

COMPANY TOTAL:	GROSS AMOUNT	53,169.80	■3
	PREPAID DISCOUNT	.00	
	PAYMENT DISCOUNT	455.00	
	PREPAID AMOUNT	.00	
	PAYMENT AMOUNT	52,724.80	
	JOURNAL AMOUNT	53,169.80	
	NUMBER OF CHECKS	10	

■1 You specify the check date.

■2 Application-assigned audit numbers.

■3 Open payables are reduced by this amount.

Courtesy of IBM Corporation.

(posted) as cash is disbursed. Just as the cash receipts journal is solely for receipts of cash collected on receivables, so the **cash disbursements journal** is solely for cash payments made on accounts payable. Other cash outflows typically appear in the general journal. Note that a journal reference number is assigned sequentially by the system and passed to the general ledger as a part of the transaction.

348

PART III
Computer-
Based
Accounting
Applications

Purchases Journal (Exhibit 10-13). This journal is closely related to the cash disbursements journal. The **purchases journal** records all incoming (purchase) invoices as they are received. As these invoices are later paid, they will appear in the cash disbursements journal. Both recording the invoice and subsequently paying it are accomplished in the accounts payable module. This information is then passed as input to the general ledger. The due date of each invoice (a necessary piece of information for scheduling payments) and a specific payment selection order based on criteria established by the user can be printed by the system. In addition, both prepaid invoices and cash purchases can be recorded in the purchases journal. The result is that all purchase invoices

EXHIBIT 10-13 Purchases Journal

```
NORTHCREEK IND.   NO. 01                 PURCHASE JOURNAL                    RUN DATE 12/01/** TIME 15.41.45  PAGE    1  AMA13
                                             AND                             BATCH DATE 12/01/**                  BATCH 002
                                         CHECK REVERSAL LISTING              ENTRY PERIOD  12

                                                              GROSS      GL             GL           GL           GL                 PAY
                                                              AMOUNT     DEBIT          DEBIT        CREDIT       CREDIT      DUE     SEL
 JOURNAL  VEND ASSIGNEE INVOICE  DESCRIPTION                             NO.            AMOUNT       NO.          AMOUNT      DATE    NO.
 REF NO.  NO.  NO.      NO.
 [1]                                                                                                                                [3]
 ----------------------------------------------------------
          000000   98642      TRASH REMOVAL                                                                              12/11/**    1
 PJ01-0001                    EMERGENCY P/U         150.00    6370           150.00
               [2]
 PJ01-0002    MHC TRASH          INVOICE TOTAL                                         2000         150.00


          000000   4786A      PACKING CARTONS                                                                           12/10/**    2
 PJ01-0003                    CARTONS 6x12           18.00    6170            18.00
 PJ01-0004                    CARTONS 8x15           22.00    6170            22.00
 PJ01-0005                    CARTONS 12x16          28.00    6170            28.00
 PJ01-0006                    CARTONS 20x28          35.00    6170            35.00

 PJ01-0007    PARAMUS WH         INVOICE TOTAL                                         2000         103.00


          000000   7621       JANITORIAL SUPPLIES                                                                         1/15/**    3
 PJ01-0008                    10 CASES CLEANR       200.00    6160           200.00

 PJ01-0009    ALLRIGHT P         INVOICE TOTAL                                         2000         200.00


          011011   M4698      NUTS & BOLTS        ** PREPAID CHECK NO.     120                                           12/12/**    4
 PJ01-0010                    NUT                  142.50     4100           142.50

 PJ01-0011    ABLE MFG.          INVOICE TOTAL                                         2000         142.50


          011011   M4698Z     NUTS & BOLTS        ** CREDIT MEMO                                                         12/01/**    5
 PJ01-0017                    NUT                  142.50                              4100         142.50
```

```
            NUMBER OF INVOICES/CR MEMOS     40

            OPEN PAYABLES            129,221.65

            PREPAID INVOICES            142.50    COSTS           129,221.65

            CHECK REVERSALS                .00    CONTROL         138,206.65

            DEBIT AMOUNT            138,206.65    CREDIT AMOUNT   138,206.65
```

[1] Purchase journal number is sequentially assigned by the application.

[2] The abbreviated vendor name.

[3] The number to use to select this item for later payment.

are listed together in one place, just as all sales invoices were listed in the sales journal.

349

CHAPTER 10
Cash
Receipts
and Dis-
bursements
Systems

Open Payables Listing (Exhibit 10-14). Purchase invoices should be paid in time to take advantage of discounts, but no sooner than necessary. Payment sequencing has a significant impact on a business' cash position, borrowing plans, and dealings with vendors (suppliers). The selection of which suppliers or specific invoices (if there are several from the same supplier) to pay is a matter of cash planning and should be based on complete information about the total amounts owed to each vendor, the discounts available from each, and the due dates of each amount. The **open payables listing** supplies this information for all vendors. The user may select particular accounts for immediate payment and assign a future payment sequence to the other amounts due. This report can be generated on demand or at predetermined times or intervals for analysis prior to the writing of checks and the disbursement of cash. Notice that incoming purchase invoices to be paid are numbered, but not necessarily sequentially or even on the same number scheme. These invoices originate with the suppliers of goods, and each of these firms maintains its own invoice numbering system. A purchaser of goods has no control over the numbering system of the purchase invoices received. (*See Exhibit, p. 350.*)

Cash Requirements Report (Exhibit 10-15). Once the payment selection process is complete, the impact of these planned disbursements on the cash position of the business can be immediately determined from the **cash requirements report.** This report can be sequenced by the due date of invoices selected for payment or by the vendors to be paid. Either way, the statement will show the cash required to cover the checks to be written to pay accounts for a particular date or dates. This report can also be used to answer questions from vendors on the current payment status of amounts owed. If for some reason a user reconsiders a payment selection and decides on a change, the cash requirements report can be updated and reprinted based on the new selections. The cash requirements report, then, is a complete listing of all invoices and vendors to be paid during a given period. As such, this statement represents critical cash control and audit trail backup to the bank statement, cash disbursements journal, and other cash-related documents. (*See Exhibit, p. 351.*)

Checks to Vendors (Exhibit 10-16). The computer-produced check is similar to the familiar handwritten version except for the very detailed check stub which is printed along with the check itself. Like all documents in a computer-based cash receipts and disbursements subsystem, this stub is designed to fit into a chain or trail through which all cash flows can be traced. Notice that all of the information on the check stub can be traced back to the cash requirements report, then to the open payables listing, and ultimately (as we will see in Chapter 11) to the creation of the data in the sales and purchases subsystem. This linkage or chain of entries and documents is essential to internal control with or without a computer-based system. (*See Exhibit, p. 352.*)

Vendor Analysis Reports (Exhibit 10-17). **Vendor analysis reports** of varying formats and emphasis can be generated on demand from the payables mod-

EXHIBIT 10-14 Open Payables Listing

1 You assign the current period date for this report (marker near AS OF DATE).

VENDOR NAME	INVOICE NUMBER	INVOICE DESCRIPTION	OPEN PAYABLES AMOUNT	DISCOUNT AMOUNT	PAID TO DATE	NET DUE	DUE DATE	DAYS	ASSIGN NO.	VEND NO.	SEL NO.	PAY YES
ALPHA CORP	110003	RM CYLINDERS	20,782.35	623.46		20,782.35	12/01/**	**		006592	5	Y
ABLE MFG.	M4698Z	NUTS AND BOLTS	142.50-	28.50		142.50	12/01/**	**		011011	7	HI
BUTLER CO	JX4432A	SCREWS / PINS	771.60			771.60	12/01/**	**		012893	8	Y
FULTON CO	876434A3	STEEL / IRON	16,955.09			16,955.00	12/01/**	**		024775	12	Y
NU-BAL CO	140063	COMPRESSORS	41,100.00	3,600.00		41,100.00	12/01/**	**		060421	35	PT
SATELLITE	976T	SHEET METAL	13,500.00			13,500.00	12/01/**	**		084385	38	PT
ZEBCOR INC	00643A	RUBBER / TIRES	1,200.00	128.75		1,200.00	12/03/**	**		096267	40	Y
ALLRIGHT P	7621	JANITORIAL SUPPLIES	200.00	10.00		200.00	12/05/**	**		000000	3	Y
J & P CO	LT43	PLATES / BRACKETS	3,437.50	341.60		3,437.50	12/05/**	**		036657	14	Y
FULTON CO	777142A3	STEEL / IRON	5,000.00	250.00		5,000.00	12/06/**	**		024775	11	Y
QUONSET CO	141733Z	WRENCHES	2,100.00-			2,100.00	12/08/**	**		072303	37	..
KNEADS CO	0040	CONTROL BOX	1,110.00	185.00		1,110.00	12/09/**	**		042598	34	Y
PARAMUS WH	4786A	PACKING CARTONS	103.00			103.00	12/10/**			000000	2	Y
CITADEL CO	1111	CASTING	17,734.20			17,734.20	12/10/**			015772	9	Y
J & P CO	LT44	35 MM CAMERA	200.00			200.00	12/10/**			036657	15	Y
J & P CO	LT44	8 X 10 CAMERA	575.00			575.00	12/10/**			036657	16	Y
J & P CO	LT44	2 1/4 CAMERA	324.00			324.00	12/10/**			036657	17	Y
J & P CO	LT44	55 MM LENS	85.00			85.00	12/10/**			036657	18	Y
J & P CO	LT44	28 MM LENS	115.00			115.00	12/10/**			036657	19	Y
QUONSET CO	141733	WRENCHES	2,100.00-			2,100.00	12/10/**			072303	36	H3
		** CURRENT TOTALS	118,850.15	5,110.31		118,850.15						
MHC TRASH	98642Z	TRASH REMOVAL	150.00-			150.00	12/11/**	01		000000	4	..
MHC TRASH	98642	TRASH REMOVAL	150.00			150.00	12/11/**	01	060421	000000	1	..
J & P CO	LT45	B & W ENLARGER	150.00			150.00	12/11/**	01		036657	20	Y
J & P CO	LT45	COLOR ENLARGER	375.00			375.00	12/11/**	01		036657	21	Y
J & P CO	LT45	CHEMICALS	65.00			65.00	12/11/**	01		036657	22	Y
J & P CO	LT45	TONERS	20.00			20.00	12/11/**	01		036657	23	Y
J & P CO	LT45	THERMOMETERS	35.00			35.00	12/11/**	01		036657	24	Y
ENGMAN INC	CR-456789	WASHERS	1,130.00			1,130.00	12/12/**	02		018834	10	..
HEAVY CO	9861743281	FERRULES / VALVES	3,198.00	50.00		3,148.00	12/12/**	02		030716	13	..
ULMAN CO	LT0467	WHEELS	3,749.00	14.99		3,734.01	12/12/**	02		090326	39	..
		** FUTURE TOTALS	10,229.00	64.99		10,164.01						
		*** COMPANY FINAL TOTALS	129,079.15	5,175.30		129,014.16						
		PREPAID TOTAL	.00									
		OPEN PAYABLES	129,079.15									

	OPEN PAYABLES AMOUNT	DISCOUNT AMOUNT	PAID TO DATE	NET DUE
** CURRENT TOTALS	118,850.15	5,110.31		118,850.15
** FUTURE TOTALS	10,229.00	64.99		10,164.01
*** FINAL TOTALS	129,079.15	5,175.30		129,014.16
PREPAID TOTALS	.00			
OPEN PAYABLES	129,079.15			

1 You assign the current period date for this report.

2 These items are overdue; discounts have been lost.

3 This item is in halt status.

4 Days remaining to take discounts.

Courtesy of IBM Corporation.

EXHIBIT 10-15 Cash Requirements Report

```
NORTHCREEK IND.  NO. 01          **** CASH REQUIREMENTS REPORT ****        RUN DATE 12/06/**  TIME 13.20.43  PAGE   1   AMA28
                                                                          PAY DATE 12/06/**

                                                                                                                        DO
VENDOR    INVOICE    INVOICE         OPEN       DISCOUNT     PAID      PAYMENT      ASSIGN    VEND  SEL   NOT
NAME      NUMBER     DESCRIPTION     PAYABLES   AMOUNT       TO DATE   AMOUNT       NO.       NO.   NO.   PAY

PARAMUS WH 4786A    PACKING CARTONS  103.00                           103.00                 000000       2 **
                    * VENDOR TOTAL   103.00        .00         .00    103.00

ALLRIGHT P 7621     JANITORIAL SUPPLIES 200.00    10.00              190.00   FORCED         000000       3 **
                    * VENDOR TOTAL   200.00       10.00        .00    190.00

ABLE MFG. LT46      FILTERS          100.00                           100.00         011011 036657       30 **
ABLE MFG. LT46      REFLECTORS        45.00                            45.00         011011 036657       31 **
ABLE MFG. LT46      UMBRELLA          50.00                            50.00         011011 036657       32 **
                    * VENDOR TOTAL   195.00        .00         .00    195.00

BUTLER CO QX4432A   SCREWS / PINS    771.60                           771.60                012893        8 **
                    * VENDOR TOTAL   771.60        .00         .00    771.60

CITADEL CO 1111     CASTING        17,734.20                       17,734.20                015772        9 ** [1]
                    * VENDOR TOTAL 17,734.20       .00         .00  17,734.20  EXCEEDS MAXIMUM AMT...

FULTON CO 777142A3  STEEL / IRON    5,000.00     250.00             4,750.00  FORCED         024775       11 **
                    * VENDOR TOTAL  5,000.00     250.00        .00   4,750.00

KNEADS CO 0040      CONTROL BOX     1,110.00     185.00              925.00   FORCED         042598       12 **
                    * VENDOR TOTAL  1,110.00     185.00        .00    925.00 [2]

NU-BAL CO 140063    COMPRESSORS    41,100.00                        15,000.00  PART          060421 [3]   13 **
                    * VENDOR TOTAL 41,000.00       .00         .00  15,000.00  EXCEEDS MAXIMUM AMT...

SATELLITE 976T      SHEET METAL    13,500.00                        10,000.00  PART          084385       14 **
                    * VENDOR TOTAL 13,500.00       .00         .00  10,000.00


                    ** COMPANY TOTAL 79,713.80   445.00        .00  49,668.80
```

```
                COMPANY BATCH TOTAL

                    TOTAL GROSS AMOUNT      53,169.80
                    PREPAID DISCOUNT             .00
                    PAYMENT DISCOUNT         445.00
                    PREPAID AMOUNT              .00
                    PAYMENT AMOUNT        52,724.80

                    NUMBER OF CHECKS          10
```

[1] Warning message.

[2] Current partial payment against this item.

[3] Space for you to negate selection.

Courtesy of IBM Corporation.

ule. Reports showing purchase activity from each supplier for the current period, the year to date, the previous year, or the overall historical total, as well as discounts taken and lost for the same periods, are available from the data base. Also, detailed vendor histories can be provided outlining all activity since the first purchase transaction with any one vendor. Thus, an overview of all purchases for a specified time period can be obtained, or the business' historical relationship with any one supplier can be examined. This information is passed along to the inventory management module discussed in Chapter 11 (where purchasing takes place) to aid in making purchasing decisions and vendor selections. (*See Exhibit, p. 353.*)

352

PART III
Computer-
Based
Accounting
Applications

EXHIBIT 10-16 Sample Printed Check

INVOICE NUMBER	INVOICE DATE	DESCRIPTION	GROSS AMOUNT	DISCOUNT	NET AMOUNT
		VENDOR JOHNSON & PARTNERS CO.		CHECK DATE	**/**/**
LT44	11/10/**	8 x 10 CAMERA	575.00		575.00
LT44	11/10/**	2 1/4 CAMERA	324.00		324.00
LT44	11/10/**	55 MM LENS	85.00		85.00
LT44	11/10/**	28 MM LENS	115.00		115.00
LT45	11/11/**	B & W ENLARGER	150.00		150.00
LT45	11/11/**	COLOR ENLARGER	375.00		375.00
LT45	11/11/**	CHEMICALS	65.00		65.00
LT45	11/11/**	TONERS	20.00		20.00
LT45	11/11/**	THERMOMETERS	35.00		35.00
LT46	11/12/**	BACKGROUNDS	320.00		320.00
LT46	11/12/**	STUDIO LIGHTS	650.00		650.00
LT46	11/12/**	LIGHT MOUNTS	70.00		70.00
		CONTINUED ON REMITTANCE ADVICE			
CHECK NO. 132		TOTALS	3,056.00		3,056.00

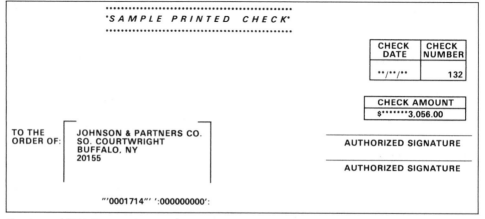

Courtesy of IBM Corporation.

Information Exchange

In addition to management reports, the accounts payable module also produces information used in other processing. Refer again to Exhibit 10-10 and notice the passage of information from accounts payable to the general ledger and between accounts payable and inventory management. There is also limited, one-way interaction of accounts payable and the manufacturing subsystem that will be discussed in Chapter 12. Specifically, the payables package passes summarized information on purchases, payments, and adjustments, to be included in the general ledger and in financial statements. The payables module also exchanges information with the inventory management module of the sales and purchases subsystem. Data on purchase orders created in inventory management serves as input to accounts payable, and vendor analysis information that results from the processing of payables is returned to inventory management to be used as a basis for future purchasing decisions. Notice again that there is information flow in addition to the flow of accounting transactions.

Inquiry and Response. As with accounts receivable, some inquiry and response capability is desirable in processing accounts payable. This interactive

EXHIBIT 10-17   Vendor Analysis Reports

```
                              VENDOR BUSINESS ANALYSIS REPORT              DATE 12/08/**  TIME 13.20.44  PAGE   1  AMA57

VENDOR  VENDOR     ----------  A M O U N T  ----------  ----- DISCOUNTS TAKEN -----  ---- DISCOUNTS LOST ------   LAST
NO.     NAME        TO-DATE       Y-T-D-     LAST YEAR    Y-T-D      LAST YEAR         Y-T-D     LAST YEAR     PAYMENT

054480 MIDGET IN   1,099,074.56  368,151.66  350,335.72   7,209.19    6,499.06         153.83     50.76  12/07/**
060421 NU-BAL CO     832,723.38  253,450.64  241,832.94   5,069.00    4,836.64            .00       .00  10/07/**
024775 FULTON CO   1,008,432.06  247,684.08  238,771.34  13,079.49   12,891.77        1,781.55    143.45  12/10/**
006592 ALPHA COR     43,697.08  181,051.32  166,979.08   1,012.77      896.16          204.13     31.36  11/09/**
084385 SATELLITE    330,423.55  161,557.50  149,799.41   3,119.86    2,498.77          111.28     49.72  11/07/**
042598 KNEADS CO    200,159.77   67,525.72   64,098.47   1,350.50    1,198.42            .00       8.35  10/10/**
078444 RANDY'S C     44,909.76   65,162.36   61,890.08   1,200.10    1,119.34          103.14     11.84  11/05/**
090326 ULMAN INC    152,061.31   54,748.99   52,008.77   1,006.33      898.07           88.63     14.20  12/10/**
096267 ZEBCOR IN     61,781.44   26,284.08   24,878.12     525.68      497.56            .00       .00  11/04/**
066362 P. GREGOR      7,307.32   25,911.72   24,717.11     518.22      402.18            .00       9.21   9/10/**
030716 HEAVY CO      91,746.45   25,559.98   24,225.52   1,489.22      127.55           44.38     17.80  11/04/**
036657 J & P CO      59,978.24   24,852.36   23,676.16   1,491.12    1,238.72            .00      18.18  11/04/**
011011 ABLE MFG.     47,645.78   18,880.09   17,645.78      31.20       28.60            6.40      7.10  10/08/**
018834 ENGMAN IN     60,549.82   18,721.97   17,559.23   1,087.08      987.08           36.24      6.64  11/04/**
072303 QUONSET C     29,117.08   12,774.88   12,098.77     255.48      241.96            .00       .00   8/04/**
012893 BUTLER CO     21,876.09    7,561.32    7,225.67     123.77      121.06           27.45      2.34  10/10/**
048539 KOPPERTEL     11,016.27    5,070.00    4,688.99     101.40       93.76            .00       .00  11/09/**
000000 MISC VEND          .00         .00         .00        .00         .00            .00       .00  11/09/**
015772 CITADEL C          .00         .00         .00        .00         .00            .00       .00
312404 HARPER PH          .00         .00         .00        .00         .00            .00       .00
452676 JEFF SERV          .00         .00         .00        .00         .00            .00       .00


   **  TOTAL      4,102,499.96  1,564,948.67  1,482,431.16  38,670.41   34,567.70      2,557.03    370.95
```

```
                                 VENDOR ANALYSIS REPORT                  DATE 12/08/**  TIME 17.05.04  PAGE   1  AMA55

VENDOR  VENDOR     ----------  A M O U N T  ----------  ----- DISCOUNTS TAKEN -----  ---- DISCOUNTS LOST ------   LAST
NO.     NAME        TO-DATE       Y-T-D      LAST YEAR    Y-T-D      LAST YEAR         Y-T-D     LAST YEAR     PAYMENT

000000 MISC VEND          .00         .00         .00        .00         .00            .00       .00
006592 ALPHA COR     43,697.08  181,051.32  166,979.08   1,012.77      896.16          204.13     31.36  11/09/**
011011 ABLE MFG.     47,645.78   18,880.09   17,645.78      31.20       28.60            6.40      7.10  10/08/**
012893 BUTLER CO     21,876.09    7,561.32    7,225.67     123.77      121.06           27.45      2.34  10/10/**
015772 CITADEL C          .00         .00         .00        .00         .00            .00       .00
018834 ENGMAN IN     60,549.82   18,721.97   17,559.23   1,087.08      987.08           36.24      6.64  11/04/**
024775 FULTON CO   1,008,432.06  247,684.08  238,771.34  13,079.49   12,891.77        1,781.55    143.45  12/10/**
030716 HEAVY CO      91,746.45   25,559.98   24,225.52   1,489.22      127.55           44.38     17.80  11/04/**
036657 J & P CO      59,978.24   24,852.36   23,676.16   1,491.12    1,238.72            .00      18.18  11/04/**
042598 KNEADS CO    200,159.77   67,525.72   64,098.47   1,350.50    1,198.42            .00       8.35  11/09/**
048539 KOPPERTEL     11,016.27    5,070.00    4,688.99     101.40       93.76            .00       .00  11/09/**
054480 MIDGET IN   1,099,074.56  368,151.66  350,335.72   7,209.19    6,499.06         153.83     50.76  12/07/**
060421 NU-BAL CO     832,723.38  253,450.64  241,832.94   5,069.00    4,836.64            .00       .00  10/07/**
066362 P. GREGOR      7,307.32   25,911.72   24,717.11     518.22      402.18            .00       9.21   9/10/**
072303 QUONSET C     29,117.08   12,774.88   12,098.77     255.48      241.96            .00       .00   8/04/**
078444 RANDY'S C     44,909.76   65,162.36   61,890.08   1,200.00    1,119.34          103.14     11.84  11/05/**
084385 SATELLITE    330,423.55  161,557.50  149,799.41   3,119.86    2,498.77          111.28     49.72  11/07/**
090326 ULMAN INC    152,061.31   54,748.99   52,008.77   1,006.33      898.07           88.63     14.20  12/10/**
096267 ZEBCOR IN     61,781.44   26,284.08   24,878.12     525.68      497.56            .00       .00  11/04/**
312404 HARPER PH          .00         .00         .00        .00         .00            .00       .00
452676 JEFF SERV          .00         .00         .00        .00         .00            .00       .00


   **  TOTAL      4,102,499.96  1,564,948.67  1,482,431.16  38,670.41   34,576.70      2,557.03    370.95
```

Courtesy of IBM Corporation.

capability allows the user to acquire immediate information such as the amounts owed to specific suppliers as of a certain date, or the total amounts owed to all suppliers now and as of future dates specified by the user. Information of the first type is necessary to answer vendor questions or provide information for purchasing decisions, while the second type is particularly useful for short-term cash disbursement planning. Exhibit 10-18 illustrates both types of information which could appear in response to inquiries by users. This inquiry and response capability is represented by the wavy line in Exhibit 10-10.

354

Part III
Computer-
Based
Accounting
Applications

EXHIBIT 10-18   Display of Response Information from Accounts Payable

Two inquiries are available in accounts payable. The first shows the open invoices for a vendor. You can page forward or backward through that vendor's invoices.

```
DATE 01/13/**          VENDOR OPEN INVOICES INQUIRY              AMA203  M1
COMPANY NO. 01         EXPECTED PAYMENT DATE 01/01/**


VENDOR NUMBER                   011011
VENDOR NAME    ABLE MANUFACTURING CO.
TELEPHONE NO.              605-555-4912


PAYMENT SELECTION NO.      130
INVOICE NUMBER             130      DESCRIPTION   TESTING MATERIALS
INVOICE DATE           09/15/**     DUE DATE                 10/05/**
GROSS AMOUNT            875.50      DISCOUNT AMOUNT               .00
PAID TO DATE            250.00      NET DUE                   625.50

HALT CODE <R/0-9>
PAY? <YES/NO>                   NO
PARTIAL PAYMENT AMT.           .00
FORCE DISCOUNT CODE <FD>

                                        CK02 PAGE FORWARD
                                        CK03 PAGE BACKWARD
                                        CK19 RETURN TO SELECT
                                        CK24 END OF JOB
```

The second inquiry ages the open payables file with five dates you supply. AP displays the total open payables due on each of the dates.

```
DATE 12/10/**        AGED OPEN PAYABLES INQUIRY        OPTIONS   AMA802  Q2



               COMPANY NO.   01

               AS OF DATE    12/10/**

               AGING DATE         NET AMOUNT DUE
               12/05/**               93,128.64
               12/10/**               19,312.20
               12/15/**                8,012.01
               12/31/**                     .00
               01/15/**                  103.00

               TOTAL DUE             120,349.00




                                        CK10 SELECT OPTIONS
                                        CK24 END OF JOB
```

Courtesy of IBM Corporation.

Input Files

355

CHAPTER 10
*Cash
Receipts
and Dis-
bursements
Systems*

As in all modules, certain input data is required that originates with the module rather than being passed from other modules. This direct input and the way it is organized rounds out our discussion of accounts payable. Following are the major files necessary for the payables module.

Vendor Master File. The **vendor master file** contains one record for each vendor. Each record consists of at least the following data-items:

1. Vendor number
2. Vendor name
3. Vendor address (including city, state, and zip code)
4. Vendor telephone number
5. Name of established contact at vendor
6. Discount provisions
7. Payments—current period
8. Payments—year to date
9. Payments—previous year
10. Discounts—current period
11. Discounts—year to date
12. Discounts—previous year
13. Historical total of payments and discounts
14. Current balance by invoice

Like all master files, the vendor master file is updated with each processing cycle and is the data base for most system inquiries. It is both input to and output from the accounts payable module. The vendor master file is also the accounts payable subsidiary ledger in a computer-based system and provides information on purchases and payments activity with each vendor, as well as amounts owed to each vendor at any time.

Open Purchase Invoices File. All open payables appear in this file, with one record for each unpaid invoice total and one record for each unpaid invoice detail amount. Each unpaid invoice is linked by vendor number to a vendor in the master file just discussed. The **open purchase invoices file** allows for retrieval of any or all open payables, and together with the vendor master file makes possible the determination of the total amount owed any specific vendor as well as the specific items purchased that led to the amount owed. It is updated with each processing and is therefore both input and output to the module. As such, it is a cumulative transaction file.

New Purchase Invoices File. The **new purchase invoice file**, like the similar one in accounts receivable, is made up of all verified purchase invoices created since the last processing of accounts payable. Input from this file, which represents transactions that increase accounts payable, is the basis for updating both the vendor master file and the open purchase invoices file. Also, this input file contains all necessary information for the production of the purchases journal discussed earlier.

356

PART III
Computer-
Based
Accounting
Applications

Cash Payments and Adjustments File. The **cash payments and adjustments file** contains transactions that decrease payables for a given period. Data from this file complete the updating of both the vendor master file and open purchase invoices file, and this file is the basis for the cash disbursements journal. This transaction file, like the new purchase invoices file, is input only.

How the Accounts Payable Module Works

The file structure and processing routine of the payables and receivables modules are basically the same. This should not be surprising since these areas represent the two sides of the operating cash flow coin. A fundamental difference between these two modules can be traced to the active role played by a business in the purchases and payments area versus the more passive role in the area of sales and receipts. A business may choose the exact timing, amount, and source of purchases and payments within broad constraints, while it must wait and respond to the choices of others in sales and receipts. The open purchase invoices file, which has no counterpart in the receivables module, provides the information for this active, ongoing, decision-making process in the purchases and payments area.

CONCEPT SUMMARY			
Accounts Payable Module			
	Input	*Information Exchange*	*Output*
Human/ Computer Interaction	1. New purchases invoices file 2. Cash payments and adjustments file	Inquiry/response on 1. Amounts owed to specific suppliers 2. Amounts due to all suppliers as of specific dates	1. Special journals 2. Open payables listing 3. Cash requirements report 4. Vendor checks 5. Vendor analysis reports
Computer Only	1. Vendor master file 2. Open purchase invoices file	1. Purchase and cash payment transactions and summary totals *to* general ledger 2. Vendor analysis information *to* inventory managment 3. Purchase order summaries *from* inventory management 4. Manufacturing subsystem	1. Vendor master file 2. Open purchase invoices file

Accounts payable processing occurs according to this basic equation:

357

CHAPTER 10
*Cash
Receipts
and Dis-
bursements
Systems*

FOR EACH VENDOR ACCOUNT	FILE PROVIDING OR STORING INFORMATION
Beginning amount owed to	Master and open purchase invoices
+ Credit purchases from	New purchase invoices
− Payments on account to	Payments and adjustments
− Adjustments	Payments and adjustments
= Ending amount owed to	Master and open purchase invoices

PAYROLL MODULE

Payroll is the final **module** of the cash receipts and disbursements subsystem. Like the other processing areas of this subsystem, payroll represents a large cash flow and is a significant component in the control of cash outflows. However, payroll differs from the other processing areas in two major respects—its relative independence from the rest of the information system and its relative dependence on the information requirements of interested external parties.

Relative Independence of the Module

The payroll module is probably the most ''stand-alone'' of all the processing areas of an information system. This is not to say that payroll is completely independent because that is usually not the case. However, you will notice from Chapter 9, in overview Exhibit 9-1, that there is no two-way interaction between payroll and the processing packages of other subsystems. Payroll also tends to be less complex to implement than other modules, although the information generated is important and the volume of data processed can be enormous.

External Demands on the Payroll Module

Governments, unions, insurance companies, and certain other entities have a legitimate interest in payroll processing. The payroll module must meet the information needs of these parties, and work within the various constraints that they impose. The payroll module should, therefore, be designed to provide the following information:

1. The amount that each employee has earned.
2. The types and amounts of taxes withheld from each employee's earnings.
3. The types and amounts of any other deductions withheld from each employee's earnings.
4. Evidence that paychecks have been properly accounted for.
5. Evidence that legal and reporting obligations have been met.

In addition, the payroll module should provide information that contributes to the management control of the expenses associated with salary and wage payments.

Exhibit 10-19 summarizes the information flow into and from a payroll module and Exhibit 10-20 gives the operating main menu for this package.

358

PART III
Computer-
Based
Accounting
Applications

EXHIBIT 10-19   Information Flow Through a Payroll Module

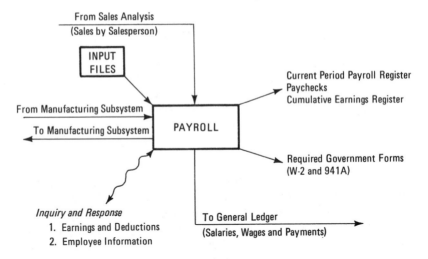

Output Reports

Typical output reports to be produced from payroll include at minimum the current payroll register, paychecks, the cumulative earnings register, and certain required government reports. The choice of possible additional reports is very broad and depends on the particular information needs and external reporting requirements that the business must meet.

Current Period Payroll Register (Exhibit 10-21).   The **current period payroll register** is a complete list of the current earnings of all employees paid this period and all the deductions taken (required and voluntary) from these earn-

EXHIBIT 10-20   Payroll Main Menu

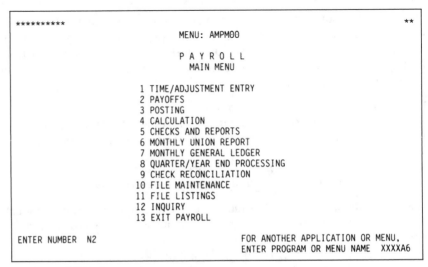

Courtesy of IBM Corporation.

EXHIBIT 10-21 Current Period Payroll Register

```
 NORTHCREEK IND. CO. NO. 01            ***** PAYROLL REGISTER *****          RUN DATE  4/09/**  TIME 14.36.03  PAGE   1   AMPDC
 DEPARTMENT - DP20                                                           W/E DATE  4/10/**

 EMP    EMPLOYEE NAME      HOURS  REG/OTH  TAXABLE/   TOTAL   TAXABLE  FEDERAL    FICA   STATE/   LOCAL/    MISC/      NET    CHECK
 NO.                              GROSS    *NON-TAX   GROSS   GROSS    TAX        TAX    *SDI     *COUNTY   *UNION     PAY     NO.
                                           ADJ                                          TAX      TAX       DED
   60 ADOR AGUILAR         41.00  1000.00             990.00  1000.00   263.23     .80   76.39    20.00     60.00     569.58    1
                                           *10.00-

  130 DANIEL MCNEILL       42.00   247.11   38.71    285.82   285.82    40.95    621.18-  9.01                         5.00     834.76    2
                                                                                                            *17.28

                                                            W AM-2203 MAXIMUM CHECK LIMIT HAS BEEN EXCEEDED

  140 TOM RYAN             43.00   145.80   37.19    182.99   182.99    30.27    384.35-  7.57     3.62     10.49     501.20    3
                                                                                                            *14.19

                                                            W AM-2203 MAXIMUM CHECK LIMIT HAS BEEN EXCEEDED

 * DEPT DP20 TOTALS       166.00            115.90           3,508.81          1,952.37-          63.82            3,982.78
                                           *10.00-
                                  3,392.91          3,498.81          1,002.81          219.96            75.49
```

```
 NORTHCREEK IND. CO. NO. 01            ***** PAYROLL REGISTER     *****  RUN DATE  4/09/**  TIME 14.36.03  PAGE   5   AMPDC
                                                                        W/E DATE  4/10/**
 ** COMPANY CONTROL TOTALS **

 ----------------- HOURS ------------------     ORDER      ---------- ADJUSTMENT ---------     --- DEDUCTION ----   -- UNION ADJUSTMENT--
   REG    OTH   VAC/HOL  SICK      TOTAL         HRS         TAXABLE    NON-TAX    SICK         ONE-TIME  PAY-ADV    TAXABLE  NON-TAXABLE
 212.50  11.00  44.00   16.50     284.00       101.50       120.00     10.00-     27.00          42.00    20.00      40.37     17.50

 ------- GROSS --------   SICK     ------------- TAXES ------------------      MISC      UNION     NET      REVERSE    --- NUMBER ---
 TOTAL   FIT TAXBL       GROSS      FIT       FICA      STATE/    LOCAL/    DEDUCTION   DED TOT    PAY      AMOUNT    EMP  TRAN  CHK
                                                        *SDI      *COUNTY
 4892.55  4902.55       585.00    1179.89   2909.03-    235.08     69.78     157.39     142.91   6016.23     .00      7    47    7
```

```
 *** FINAL CONTROL TOTALS ***          ***** PAYROLL REGISTER *****         RUN DATE  4/09/**  TIME 14.36.03  PAGE   6   AMPDC

 ----------------- HOURS ------------------     ORDER      ---------- ADJUSTMENT ---------     --- DEDUCTION ----   -- UNION ADJUSTMENT--
   REG    OTH   VAC/HOL  SICK      TOTAL         HRS         TAXABLE    NON-TAX    SICK         ONE-TIME  PAY-ADV    TAXABLE  NON-TAXABLE
 212.50  11.00  44.00   16.50     284.00       101.50       120.00     10.00-     27.00          42.00    20.00      40.37     17.50

 ------- GROSS --------   SICK     ------------- TAXES ------------------      MISC      UNION     NET      REVERSE    --- NUMBER ---
 TOTAL   FIT TAXBL       GROSS      FIT       FICA      STATE/    LOCAL/    DEDUCTION   DED TOT    PAY      AMOUNT    EMP  TRAN  CHK
                                                        *SDI      *COUNTY
 4892.55  4902.55       585.00    1179.89   2909.03-    235.08     69.78     157.39     142.91   6016.23     .00      7    47    7
                                                        *.30
```

Courtesy of IBM Corporation.

ings. The report reconciles gross earnings to net earnings for each employee by itemizing all deductions, and may also list total hours worked for the period. Each employee's paycheck number is printed with a cross-reference that helps in tracing payroll-related cash disbursements through the system and supports the bank reconciliation. If the business pays fringe benefits for employees, these payments can appear on the register and be classified as either taxable or nontaxable. The current payroll register provides a permanent record of employee pay activity by period and can be the basis for a series of other payroll-related reports.

Paychecks (Exhibit 10-22). Perhaps the most familiar of all payroll output documents is the paycheck. The only major decision consideration in producing this "report" is the type and amount of information to appear on the employee's check stub. The stub may include information on hours, pay rate, and year-

EXHIBIT 10-22 Sample Paycheck

CO.	EMPLOYEE NAME	EMP. NO.	HOME DEPT	DIST CODE	OCCUPATION	PERIOD ENDING	CHECK NO.	NET PAY
02	DENNIS KRUEGER	10200	SD02	MAIL	SALES REP	05/20/**	204	535.66

EARNINGS/ADJUSTMENTS/ADVANCES	CODE	HOURS	RATE	AMOUNT	TAXES/DEDUCTIONS/DEFERRAL/BENE	CODE	AMOUNT	YEAR-TO-DATE
REGULAR PAY	RG	30.00	20.000	600.00	UNITED FUND	02	2.00	40.00
REGULAR PAY	RG	10.00	24.000	240.00	MEDICAL PLAN	03	3.00	60.00
DOUBLE TIME	DT	4.00	40.000	160.00	LIFE INSURANCE	05	5.00	100.00
					GARNISHMENT	08	8.00	160.00
					STOCK PLAN	09	9.00	180.00
					TDD SUMMARY	10	50.00	1,000.00
					MISC DEDUCTIONS	MD	65.00	1,176.00
					IRA DEDUCTION	43	10.17	2,010.17
					KANSAS TAX	ST	15.00	300.93
					JO COUNTY TAX	KT	1.53	30.60
					EMPLOYEE UNION	EE	32.00	

CURRENT GROSS PAY	SUMMARY	FEDERAL	FICA	STATE	COUNTY	LOCAL	OTHER
1,000.00	TAXABLE CURRENT	950.00	1,000.00	950.00	950.00		
YEAR-TO-DATE / 20,033.00	TAXABLE Y-T-D	19,983.00	20,033.00	19,983.00	19,983.00		
	WITHHELD CURRENT	191.14	10.00	15.00	1.53		
	WITHHELD Y-T-D	3,791.14	1,044.12	1,500.93	30.60		

125

NORTHCREEK INDUSTRIES

CO.	DEPT.	EMPLOYEE NO.	CHECK DATE	CHECK NO.
02	SD02	10200	05/20/**	204

PAY THIS AMOUNT

TO THE ORDER OF: DENNIS KRUEGER $****598.16

FIVE HUNDRED NINETY-EIGHT AND 16/100**

DENNIS KRUEGER
14212 LONG STREET
LEAVENWORTH KA
60801-3416

NON-NEGOTIABLE

AUTHORIZED SIGNATURE

AUTHORIZED SIGNATURE

'''0001714''' ':000000000':

Courtesy of IBM Corporation.

to-date cumulative earnings, or it may reflect only the current period earnings and deduction information appearing in the current period payroll register. The illustrated sample printed check is comprehensive in that the stub shows cumulative information beyond that presented in the current period payroll register. This is a matter of user choice and can be accommodated easily within the payroll module.

Cumulative Earnings Register (Exhibit 10-23).   The **cumulative earnings register** is similar to the current period payroll register of Exhibit 10-21, except that cumulative year-to-date and quarter-to-date figures for earnings and deductions are given instead of current period figures. When printed in its final form at the end of each calendar year, this report becomes the permanent record of all payroll information that must be retained and periodically reported to federal taxing agencies (IRS and Social Security). In addition, separate cumulative state and local registers showing relevant earnings and tax information can be produced if desired, as well as separate cumulative deduction registers. The cumulative earnings register contains most of the employee earnings information needed for meeting external reporting requirements.

EXHIBIT 10-23 Cumulative Earnings Register

HOME EMP DEPT NO.	EMPLOYEE NAME	Y-T-D GROSS EARNINGS	Y-T-D FIT TAXABLE	Y-T-D FICA TAXABLE	Y-T-D FEDERAL TAX	Y-T-D FICA TAX	YTD WKS WRK	Q-T-D FIT TAXABLE	Q-T-D FEDERAL TAX	Q-T-D FICA TAX	QTD WKS WRK
DP90*90350	RICHARD QUAMMEN	817.83	817.83		74.92	49.48	4				
DP90*90400	DEAN RAU	838.38	838.38		156.52	50.73	4				
DP90*90450	JACK SANDERS	934.52	934.52		142.83	56.55	4				
DP90*90500	ED SCHNEIDER	705.21	705.21		120.95	42.67	3				
DP90*90550	MARCIA STAHL	105.44	105.44		9.14	6.38	2				
DP90*90600	RON STARKER	547.40	547.40		91.13	33.12	2				
DP99*92010	DON THOGERSON	55.00	55.00		4.37	3.33	1				
DP99*92011	RUSS TILLER	150.00	150.00		48.05	9.08	2				
DP99*92020	DORI WALLIN	500.00	500.00		98.36	30.25	2				
DP99*92021	WILL WARREN	2,000.00	2,000.00		530.48	121.00	4				
DP99*92022	BILL WHITE	2,564.00	2,564.00	264.00	808.04	16.18	2	264.00	46.08	122.97-	1
DP99*92023	JANICE WHITFIELD										
DP99*92030	RAYNOR MOORE	400.00	400.00		69.66	24.20	1				
DP99*92031	GENE ROBERTS	330.00	330.00		55.01	19.97	1				
DP99*92040	ROY BIRDSONG	40.00	40.00		4.08	2.42	1				
DP99*92041	MIKE KELLEY	41.00	41.00		4.24	2.48	1				
DP99*92042	RUTH LEE										
DP99*92044	LORI ZEMAN	400.00	400.00		73.04	24.20	2				
DP90*93000	TERMINATED EMPLOYEE	3,000.00	3,000.00		900.00	175.50	39	1,000.00	300.00	58.50	13

Courtesy of IBM Corporation.

Required Government Forms (Exhibit 10-24). Unique to payroll is the requirement that the module periodically produce reports that are exclusively for the use of external entities. Quarterly and annual government reports are mandatory for all businesses with a payroll. Primarily, the required reports have to do with the various taxes that have been withheld from employee paychecks (and in some cases matched by the employer) and periodically remitted to the appropriate governmental taxing authority. The two most common government forms, illustrated in Exhibit 10-24 on page 362, have to do with federal income and Social Security (FICA) taxes withheld and are called, respectively, Form W-2 and Form 941A. Typically these reports are printed by the payroll module directly on forms supplied by the government agencies responsible for collecting the taxes.

Information Exchange

Like other modules in cash receipts and disbursements, payroll may receive important input information from other subsystems and pass on information essential to different subsystems. Once data on the cash outflows and expenses associated with payroll have been processed, the transactions are transferred

EXHIBIT 10-24   Required Government Forms

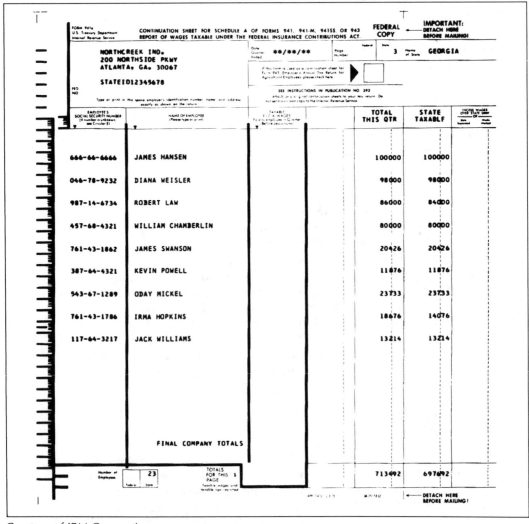

1 Control number		For Paperwork Reduction Act Notice, see back of Copy D. OMB No. 1545-0008	For Official Use Only ▶	

2 Employer's name, address, and ZIP code	3 Employer's identification number FEDID12345	4 Employer's state I.D. number STATEID100
RIVEREDGE PRODUCTS COMPANY 1500 RIVEREDGE PARKWAY ATLANTA, GA 30058-0331	5 Statutory employee ☐ Deceased ☐ Pension plan ☐ Legal rep. ☐ 942 emp. ☐ Subtotal ☐ Deferred compensation ☐ Void ☐	
	6 Allocated tips	7 Advance EIC payment

8 Employee's social security number 046-78-9232	9 Federal income tax withheld 3,791.14	10 Wages, tips, other compensation 19,983.00	11 Social security tax withheld 1,044.12
12 Employee's name (first, middle, last) DENNIS KRUEGER		13 Social security wages 19,983.00	14 Social security tips
14212 LONG ST.		16 (See Instr. for Forms W-2/W-2P)	16a Fringe benefits incl. in Box 10
LEAVENWORTH, KS 60801-3416		17 State income tax 1,500.93	18 State wages, tips, etc. 19,983.00	19 Name of State
15 Employee's address and ZIP code			
Form **W-2 Wage and Tax Statement** 1988 This information is being furnished to the Internal Revenue Service.		20 Local income tax 30.60	21 Local wages, tips, etc. 19,983.00	22 Name of locality

Copy B To be filed with employee's STATE tax return   Dept. of the Treasury – IRS

FORM 941a
U.S. Treasury Department
Internal Revenue Service

**CONTINUATION SHEET FOR SCHEDULE A OF FORMS 941, 941-M, 941SS, OR 943
REPORT OF WAGES TAXABLE UNDER THE FEDERAL INSURANCE CONTRIBUTIONS ACT.**

FEDERAL COPY

IMPORTANT:
DETACH HERE
BEFORE MAILING!

NORTHCREEK INC.
200 NORTHSIDE PKWY
ATLANTA, GA. 30067

STATEID12345678

FED NO

Date Quarter Ended **/**/**   Page Number   3   Name of State GEORGIA

If this form is used as a continuation sheet for Form 943, Employer's Annual Tax Return for Agricultural Employees please check box

SEE INSTRUCTIONS IN PUBLICATION NO. 393

Type or print in this space employer's identification number, name and address exactly as shown on the return

EMPLOYEE'S SOCIAL SECURITY NUMBER	NAME OF EMPLOYEE (Please type or print)	TAXABLE F.I.C.A. WAGES	TOTAL THIS QTR	STATE TAXABLE	EXCESS WAGES OVER STATE LIMIT
666-66-6666	JAMES HANSEN		100000	100000	
046-78-9232	DIANA WEISLER		98000	98000	
987-14-6734	ROBERT LAW		86000	84000	
457-68-4321	WILLIAM CHAMBERLIN		80000	80000	
761-43-1862	JAMES SWANSON		20426	20426	
387-64-4321	KEVIN POWELL		11876	11876	
543-67-1289	ODAY MICKEL		23733	23733	
761-43-1786	IRMA HOPKINS		18676	14076	
117-64-3217	JACK WILLIAMS		13214	13214	

FINAL COMPANY TOTALS

Number of Employees	23	TOTALS FOR THIS PAGE Taxable wages and taxable tips reported		713492	697492	

DETACH HERE BEFORE MAILING!

Courtesy of IBM Corporation.

in summary form to the general ledger for accounting and financial statement purposes. Input to payroll may come from the sales analysis package, particularly if employee compensation is based on some measure of sales activity. If salespeople are paid by commission, a breakdown of sales by salesperson is necessary to the calculation of payroll. The generation of this information is one of the goals of sales analysis processing. Payroll can accept as input this and additional information from other modules which may be needed to compute salaries, wages, and deductions.

363

CHAPTER 10
Cash
Receipts
and Dis-
bursements
Systems

The additional interface of the payroll module with the manufacturing subsystem will be discussed in Chapter 12.

Inquiry and Response.   All processing modules in the cash receipts and disbursements subsystem are improved by some type of on-line capability. Payroll is no exception to this; however, direct interaction and information on demand are not as critical here as in receivables and payables. Nonetheless, questions that require immediate answers may come up concerning earnings, deductions, or some personal information about an employee. If so, the type of inquiry and response capability discussed in connection with other modules will be useful here. Exhibit 10-25 is an example of a response to an inquiry into employee files for current information.

EXHIBIT 10-25   Display of Response Information from Payroll

Anyone who has the proper security clearance can inquire into the employee information retained by the payroll application. Such information as salary, wage rate, gross wages, taxes, and personnel information can be displayed.

The operator enters the number of the employee. If the operator has the first level of security clearance, only the top half of the display appears. The bottom half is not displayed unless the operator has a higher security clearance.

```
DATE 08/16/**                      PAYROLL                   INQUIRY      AMPTI2   Y2
                    EMPLOYEE NUMBER              300
COMPANY 01      NAME          JOHN SMITH                   HIRE DATE   09/16/**
                ADDRESS       123 COUNTRY CLUB RD.         TERM DATE
                CITY ST ZIP   ATLANTA, GA.       30301     MAIL CHK
                                                          PENSION
SHIFT 1   DEPT DP70   WRK CTR          OCCUPATION PRESIDENT   WRKMNS COMP CD

MARITAL     M     FIT APPLY    Y      STATE   100      REG HRS WORKED        0.00
MINORITY          FICA APPLY   Y      COUNTY 000       OVT HRS WORKED        0.00
PAY TYPE    S     FED EXEMP  03        LOCAL  000       HOL HRS PAID         0.00
PAY FREQ    MN    EXTRA %      0.00   UNION  000       VAC HRS PAID        40.00
PROTECT     P     EXTRA $    150.00                    SICK HR PAID         0.00

SALARY   6,000.00 REG RATE    .000 OVT RATE    .000 PREM RATE     .000

QTR        FIT         FICA    GROSS WAGES   FIT TAXABLE  FICA TAXABLE  WK WRK
 1       5,869.92    824.25     18,000.00     18,000.00          .00    18
 2       5,869.92       .00     18,000.00     18,000.00          .00    18
 3       5,869.92       .00     18,000.00     18,000.00          .00    18
 4       3,913.25       .00     12,000.00     12,000.00          .00     9
TOTAL   21,523.01    824.25     66,000.00     66,000.00          .00    48

                                           CK24  END OF INQUIRY
```

Courtesy of IBM Corporation.

364

PART III
Computer-
Based
Accounting
Applications

Input Files

Payroll processing requires direct input of its own in order to produce the required output reports. Following are the major files necessary for the payroll module to function.

Employee Master File. The **employee master file** contains one record for each employee. Each record consists of at least the following data-items:

1. Employee number
2. Employee name
3. Employee address (including city, state, and zip code) and telephone number
4. Employee Social Security number
5. Applicable pay rates
6. Marital status and exemptions
7. Deductions information code
8. Cumulative gross earnings
9. Cumulative taxable earnings
10. Cumulative federal and state withholding
11. Cumulative Social Security withholding
12. Cumulative other deductions by category
13. Cumulative hours worked

This file is updated with each processing run, and is the data base that supports most inquiries to the system. It is both input to and output from the payroll module, and both the cumulative earnings register and required government forms come directly from this file.

Tax Table and Deduction Table File. The **tax table and deduction table file** is composed of the tax and deduction rates, limits, values, and frequencies necessary to determine the amounts of tax withholdings and other deductions. When this file is combined with the earnings, exemptions, and deductions information for each employee from the employee master file, actual deductions can be computed and net pay determined. Since the data in this file is relatively constant, the file is not affected by the normal processing of payroll. Of course, the data may be changed as external conditions (withholding rates or deduction status or amounts) change, but otherwise the file remains unchanged and is input to each payroll run.

Current Hours and Activity File. The **current hours and activity file** supplies all of the current pay period hours and other data necessary to calculate current period gross pay. The number of regular and overtime hours worked for each employee, as well as applicable pay rates and special adjustments for certain hours, would be a part of this input file. Also, information on where (job, department, factory) the employee worked during the pay period could be provided for general ledger expense classification and posting. This file is used to update the employee master file and generate the current period payroll register.

365

CHAPTER 10
Cash
Receipts
and Dis-
bursements
Systems

CONCEPT SUMMARY

Payroll Module

	Input	Information Exchange	Output
Human/ Computer Interaction	1. Current hours file	Inquiry/response on 1. Employee earnings and deductions 2. Other employee information	1. Current payroll register 2. Paychecks 3. Cumulative earnings register 4. Government forms
Computer Only	1. Employee master file 2. Tax table and deduction table file	1. Expense and cash payment transactions and summary totals *to* general ledger 2. Sales by salesperson information *from* sales analysis 3. Manufacturing subsystem	1. Employee master file

CHAPTER SUMMARY

The cash receipts and disbursements system tracks operating cash flows and provides information that management can use to help control cash. Most such systems contain an accounts receivable module, an accounts payable module, and a payroll module.

The accounts receivable module processes cash inflows from collections of receivables. Using input from the customer master file and the transaction files for new sales invoices and cash receipts and adjustments, the module produces timely output reports. These reports include the cash receipts and adjustments journal, the sales journal or invoice register, an aged trial balance, customer billing statements, and customer delinquency notices. In addition, information passes from the accounts receivable module to the general ledger module, and between the accounts receivable and the sales analysis and order processing modules. An on-line connection for inquiry and response between terminals and the module provides up-to-date information on which to base credit-granting decisions and answer customer inquiries.

The accounts payable module processes cash outflows due primarily to purchases of merchandise and payments to suppliers. Using input from the vendor master file, the open purchase invoices file, and the transaction files for new purchase invoices and cash payments and adjustments, the module produces output reports that show how much money the business owes to whom and for how long, and whether outgoing checks are being properly ac-

366

PART III
Computer-
Based
Accounting
Applications

counted for. Output reports include the cash disbursements journal, the purchases journal, an open payables listing, a cash requirements report, various vendor analysis reports, and the checks to pay vendors. In addition, information passes from accounts payable to the general ledger and the manufacturing subsystem, and between accounts payable and inventory management. Inquiry and response capability provides up-to-date information for answering vendor queries, making purchasing decisions, and planning for short-term cash disbursement.

The payroll module processes cash outflows occasioned by salaries, wages, commissions, and related taxes and other withholdings. The payroll module differs from the others in that it is relatively free standing, but must conform to the demands of external entities such as governments, unions, and insurance companies. Using input from the employee master file, the tax table and deduction table constant file, and the transaction file for current hours and activity, the payroll module can produce a wide variety of reports. At a minimum, these reports include the current period payroll register, the cumulative earnings register, required government forms, and the checks to pay employees. In addition, information passes from payroll to the general ledger, and between payroll and the manufacturing subsystem. Inquiry and response capability may be desirable if immediate answers are routinely required for questions regarding earnings, deductions, or personal information about employees.

Output capabilities of the modules of the cash receipts and disbursements subsystem are not limited to the reports illustrated in this chapter. Rather, these reports represent only the minimum requirements of most businesses. Modules can be designed to produce virtually any additional related reports that the business requires. The ability to use data in different ways for different purposes is one of the major advantages of computer-based systems over manual systems.

KEY TERMS

Accounts payable module (p. 345)
Accounts receivable module (p. 336)
Aged trial balance (p. 339)
Cash disbursements journal (p. 347)
Cash payments and adjustments file
(p. 356)
Cash receipts and adjustments file
(p. 343)
Cash receipts and adjustments journal
(p. 336)
Cash requirements report (p. 349)
Cumulative earnings register (p. 360)
Current hours and activity file
(p. 364)
Current period payroll register
(p. 358)

Customer billing statement (p. 339)
Customer master file (p. 342)
Delinquency notice (p. 340)
Employee master file (p. 364)
New purchase invoices file (p. 355)
New sales invoices file (p. 343)
Open payables listing (p. 349)
Open purchase invoices file (p. 355)
Payroll module (p. 357)
Purchases journal (p. 348)
Sales journal (invoice register)
(p. 338)
Tax table and deduction table file
(p. 364)
Vendor analysis report (p. 349)
Vendor master file (p. 355)

QUESTIONS ━━━━━━━━━━━━━━━━━━━━━━━━━━━━━━━━━━━━━━━ *367*

Chapter 10
Cash
Receipts
and Dis-
bursements
Systems

10-1. List and briefly describe the output reports that should be produced by an accounts receivable module.

10-2. Name the files required by the accounts receivable module and generally describe the contents of each file.

10-3. List and briefly describe the output reports that should be produced by an accounts payable module.

10-4. Name the files required by the accounts payable module and generally describe the contents of each file.

10-5. The file structure and processing of accounts receivable and accounts payable are similar. Why, then, is there no counterpart in accounts receivable to the open invoices file of accounts payable?

10-6. List and briefly describe the output reports that should be produced by a payroll module.

10-7. Name the files required by payroll and generally describe the contents of each file.

10-8. Specify three items of interactive input/output for each of the three processing modules of the cash receipts and disbursements subsystem.

10-9. Specify the hardware devices that might be used for each of the files of an accounts receivable module, if processing is accomplished in a batch-oriented system. In an on-line system.

10-10. Specify the hardware devices that might be used for each of the files of an accounts payable module, if processing is accomplished in a batch-oriented system. In an on-line system.

10-11. Give the questions that information produced by an accounts receivable, accounts payable, and payroll module of a cash receipts and disbursements system should answer.

PROBLEMS ━━

10-12. The information flow into and from an accounts receivable module is depicted in Exhibit 10-1.

   1. Give a specific example of each type of input to this area.
   2. Explain how the examples you chose are actually processed by the module.

10-13. For each of the data-items stored in the customer master file, explain why such information is important in a computer-based system. Also, for each data-item, give the output report(s) in which the information is used. Which of these data-items would normally be updated with each processing run?

10-14. A critical output report generated by accounts receivable is the aged trial balance. Compare the aged trial balance presented in Exhibit 10-5 to the traditional accounts receivable subsidiary ledger. How do they differ? What do these differences indicate about the processing capabilities of computer-based versus manual systems?

10-15. The information flow into and from an accounts payable module is depicted in Exhibit 10-10.

368

Part III
Computer-
Based
Accounting
Applications

1. Give a specific example of each type of input to this area.

2. Explain how the examples you chose are actually processed by the module.

10-16. For each of the data-items stored in the vendor master file explain why such information is important in a computer-based system. Also, for each data-item, give the output report(s) in which the information is used. Which of these data-items would normally be updated with each processing run?

10-17. A critical output report generated by the accounts payable module is the open payables listing. Compare the open payables listing presented in Exhibit 10-14 to the traditional accounts payable subsidiary ledger. How do they differ? What do these differences indicate about the processing capabilities of computer-based versus manual systems?

10-18. The information flow into and from a payroll module is depicted in Exhibit 10-19.

1. Give a specific example of each type of input to this area.

2. Explain how the examples you chose are actually processed by the module.

10-19. For each of the data-items stored in the employee master file, explain why such information is important in a computer-based system. Also, for each data-item, give the output report(s) in which the information is used. Which of these data-items would normally be updated with each processing run?

10-20. Critical output reports generated by the payroll module include the current period payroll register, cumulative earnings register, and several required government forms.

1. Both the current period payroll register and the cumulative earnings register present earnings information by employee. How does this earnings information differ between reports?

2. What purposes are served by the required government forms presented in Exhibit 10-24 for the (a) government, (b) employer, and (c) employee?

10-21. At the bottom of both the cash receipts journal (Exhibit 10-3) and the cash disbursements journal (Exhibit 10-12) there are totals which summarize the effects of all the transactions listed in each report. For each total, explain its significance and where it might be used.

10-22. (*CIA, adapted*) In a large organization supplying goods and services, several departments may be involved in the processing of customer complaints and the issuance of any resulting credit memos for returned goods. Following is a list of such departments:

a. Receiving
b. Sales
c. Customer Service
d. Accounts Receivable

Explain briefly the control function each of the departments performs when processing complaints and issuing credit memos.

10-23. (*AICPA, adapted*) A CPA's audit working papers contain a narrative description of a segment of the Croyden Factory, Inc. payroll system (as follows) and an accompanying flowchart (Exhibit 10-26 on page 370).

Narrative

At the beginning of each workweek, payroll clerk no. 1 reviews the payroll department files to determine the employment status of factory employees and then prepares time cards and distributes them as each individual arrives at work. This payroll clerk, who is also responsible for custody of the signature stamp machine, verifies the identity of each payee before delivering signed checks to the foreman.

At the end of each workweek, the foreman distributes payroll checks for the preceding work week. Concurrent with this activity, the foreman reviews the current week's employee time cards, notes the regular and overtime hours worked on a summary form, and initials the time cards. The foreman then delivers all time cards and unclaimed payroll checks to payroll clerk no. 2.

The internal control system with respect to the personnel department is well functioning and is not included in the accompanying flowchart.

1. Based upon the narrative and accompanying flowchart, what are the apparent weaknesses in the current system of internal control for payroll?

2. Based upon the narrative and accompanying flowchart, what inquiries should be made with respect to clarifying the existence of possible additional weaknesses in the system of internal control?

10-24. (*AICPA, adapted*) The customer billing and collection functions of the Robinson Company, a small paint manufacturer, are attended to by a receptionist, an accounts receivable clerk, a general ledger clerk, and a cashier who also serves as a secretary. The company's paint products are sold to both wholesalers and retail stores.

The following list describes the procedures performed by the Robinson Company's employees pertaining to customer billings and collections.

a. The mail is opened by the receptionist, who gives the customers' orders to the accounts receivable clerk. Fifteen to twenty orders are received each day. Under instructions to expedite the shipment of orders, the accounts receivable clerk immediately prepares a five-part sales invoice form which is distributed as follows:

(1) Copy 1 is the customer billing copy and is held by the accounts receivable clerk until notice of shipment of the goods is received.

(2) Copy 2 is the accounts receivable department copy and is held for eventual posting of the individual accounts receivable records.

(3) Copies 3 and 4 are sent to the shipping department.

(4) Copy 5 is sent to the storeroom as authority for release of the goods to the shipping department.

b. After the paint ordered has been moved from the storeroom to the shipping department, the shipping department prepares the bills of lading and labels the cartons. Sales invoice copy 4 is inserted into one of the cartons as a packing slip. After the trucker has picked up the shipment, the customer's copy of the bill of lading and invoice copy 3, on which are noted any undershipments, are returned to the accounts receivable clerk. The trucker retains a copy of the bill of lading. The Robinson Company's copy of the bill of lading is filed by the shipping department. The company does not

EXHIBIT 10-26 Croyden Factory, Inc. Payroll System

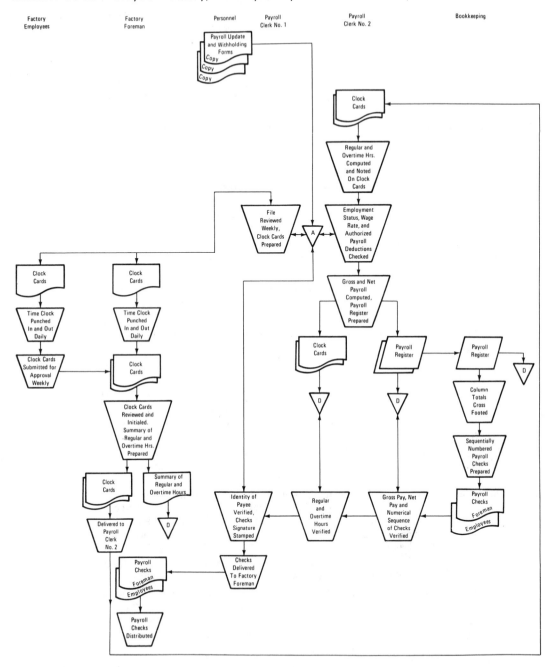

"back-order" in the event of undershipments; customers are expected to reorder the merchandise.

c. When invoice copy 3 and the customer's copy of the bill of lading are received by the accounts receivable clerk, sales invoice copies 1 and 2 are completed by numbering them and inserting quantities shipped, unit prices, extensions, discounts, and totals. The accounts receivable clerk then mails

371

CHAPTER *10*
*Cash
Receipts
and Dis-
bursements
Systems*

copy 1 and the copy of the bill of lading to the customer. Copies 2 and 3 of the invoice are stapled together.

    d.   The individual accounts receivable ledger cards are posted by the accounts receivable clerk using a bookkeeping machine procedure whereby a sales register is prepared as a carbon copy of the postings. Postings are made from invoice copy 2, which is then filed, along with staple-attached copy 3, in numerical order. Monthly, the general ledger clerk summarizes the sales registers for posting to the general ledger.

    e.   Since the Robinson Company is short of cash, the deposit of receipts is also expedited. The receptionist turns over all mail receipts and related correspondence to the accounts receivable clerk, who examines the checks and determines that the accompanying correspondence contains enough detail to permit posting of the accounts. The accounts receivable clerk then endorses the checks and gives them to the cashier, who prepares the daily deposit slip. No cash is received in the mail and no paint is sold over the counter at the factory.

    f.   The accounts receivable clerk uses the correspondence that accompanied the checks to post the individual accounts receivable ledger cards. The bookkeeping machine prepares a cash receipts register as a carbon copy of the postings. Monthly, the general ledger clerk summarizes the cash receipts registers for posting to the general ledger. The accounts receivable clerk also corresponds with customers about unauthorized deductions for discounts, freight, advertising allowances, returns, and so forth and prepares the appropriate adjustments. Disputed items of large amounts are turned over to the sales manager for settlement. Each month the accounts receivable clerk prepares a trial balance of open accounts receivable and compares the resulting total to the general ledger control account for accounts receivable.

    1.   Using a systems flowchart, diagram the customer billing and collection system for Robinson Company.

    2.   Discuss the internal control weaknesses in the procedures related to customer billings and collections and the accounting for these transactions. In your discussion, in addition to identifying the weaknesses, explain what could happen as a result of each weakness.

10-25.   *(CMA, adapted)* Metric Wrenches, Inc., produces metric tools for both commercial and industrial use. The firm consists of a factory, where the tools are made, and a warehouse, where the tools are stored before sale to wholesalers.

        Metric's payroll department accumulates the hours reported by the factory and warehouse, applies appropriate pay rates, and forwards the results to the EDP department, where pay is calculated and payroll checks are prepared together with a payroll register. Checks are signed and distributed to the departments by the general manager's secretary.

        Factory personnel are hired and terminated by the factory manager in coordination with the personnel department. The payroll department adds and removes personnel from the employee master file based on notices received from the personnel department. Changes in pay rates are similarly processed. Factory personnel submit their clock-punched time cards to their department heads at the end of each week for review, initialing and forwarding to the payroll department. Factory personnel are paid a week later.

        Warehouse personnel are hired and terminated by the warehouse manager in coordination with the personnel department. The warehouse personnel report their hours each day to their department head, who prepares a time summary report by individual and forwards it to the payroll department at the

372

*PART III
Computer-
Based
Accounting
Applications*

end of each week. The employees are paid every other week on an hourly basis for two standard 40-hour weeks plus or minus any adjustments from the previous two-week period for overtime, time off, and other special circumstances. The payments are staggered so that half the employees are paid at the end of each week.

Blank payroll checks stored in a vault by the payroll department are forwarded to the data processing department at the appropriate time for preparation of the payroll. The payroll system generates several incorrect reports because of an error in program logic. The payroll department must now manually check and recalculate or redetermine this information on a regular basis.

1. List the files required for the processing of payroll by Metric and specify the data-items necessary for each file.
2. Describe in detail the reports that the payroll module should generate for the Metric payroll department.
3. Summarize the internal control procedures Metric should have in place to support the payroll module.

DECISION CASE

(*CMA, adapted*) Value Clothing is a large distributor of all types of clothing acquired from buyouts, overstocks, and factory seconds. All sales are on account with terms of net 30 days from the date of the monthly statement. The number of delinquent and uncollectible accounts have increased significantly during the last twelve months. Management has determined that the information generated from the present accounts receivable system is inadequate and untimely. In addition, customers frequently complain of errors in their billing statements.

The current accounts receivable processing has not been changed since Value Clothing started its operations. A new computer was acquired 18 months ago, but no attempt has been made to revise accounts receivable because other processing areas were considered more important. The work schedule in the systems department has now slackened slightly enabling the staff to begin design of a new accounts receivable module. Top management has requested that the new module satisfy the following objectives.

1. Produce current and timely reports about customers that would provide useful information to
   a. aid in controlling bad debts (uncollectible accounts).
   b. notify the sales department of customer accounts that are delinquent (accounts that should lose current charge privileges).
   c. notify the sales department of customer accounts that are considered uncollectible (accounts that should be closed and written-off).
2. Produce time statements for customers regarding
   a. amounts owed to Value Clothing.
   b. a change in the status of their accounts (loss of charge privileges, account closed).
3. Incorporate the necessary procedures and controls to minimize the chance of errors in customers' accounts.

373

CHAPTER *10*
*Cash
Receipts
and Dis-
bursements
Systems*

Input data for the module would be taken from four source documents: credit applications, sales invoices, cash receipt remittances, and credit memoranda. The accounts receivable master file is to be organized by customer account number.

The preliminary design of the new accounts receivable module has been completed by the systems department. A brief description of the proposed reports and other output to be generated by the module follows.

1. *Accounts Receivable Register*—a daily alphabetical listing of all customers' accounts that shows the balance as of the last statement, activity since the last statement, and the current account balance.

2. *Customer Statements*—monthly statements for each customer showing activity since the last statement and current account balance; the top portion of the statement is returned with the payment and serves as the cash receipt remittance advice.

3. *Aging Schedule—All Customers*—a monthly schedule of all customers with outstanding account balances displaying the total amount owed classified into age groups—0–30 days, 31–60 days, 61–90 days, over 90 days; the schedule includes amounts and percentages for each age category.

4. *Aging Schedule—Past Due Customers*—a schedule prepared monthly that includes only those customers whose accounts are past due (i.e., over 30 days outstanding), classified by age. The credit manager uses this schedule to decide which customers will receive delinquent notices, temporary suspension of charge privileges, or have their accounts closed.

5. *Activity Reports*—monthly reports that show:
   a. customers who have not purchased any merchandise for 90 days.
   b. customers whose account balance exceeds their credit limit.
   c. customers whose accounts are delinquent even though they may have current sales on account.

6. *Delinquency and Write-off Register*—a monthly alphabetical listing of customers' accounts that are (a) delinquent or (b) closed. These listings show customer name, account number, and account balance. Related notices are then prepared and sent to notify these customers.

7. *Summary Journal Entries*—entries prepared monthly to record write-offs to the accounts receivable file.

Required:

1. Identify the data that should be captured and stored in the computer-based files for each customer in order for the new receivables module to function.

2. Review the proposed reports to be generated by the new accounts receivable module.
   a. Discuss whether the proposed reports will be adequate to satisfy the objectives outlined for the area.
   b. Recommend changes, if any, that should be made in the proposed reports to be generated by the new module.

11 Sales and Purchases Systems

Overview

The sales and purchases business cycle and the way computer-based accounting systems process these cycles through order processing, inventory management, and sales analysis.

Learning Objectives

Thorough study of this chapter will enable you to:

1. Relate the sales and purchases system to the information system as a whole.
2. Describe the capabilities of a typical order processing module.
3. Demonstrate how the order processing module utilizes a data base.
4. Describe the capabilities of a typical inventory management module.
5. Describe the capabilities of a typical sales analysis module.

Outline

SYSTEMS IN THE REAL WORLD

375

*CHAPTER 11
Sales and
Purchases
Systems*

The IS Engine Driving Infiniti

Unless you've been living in a cave, you've seen the ads for the Infiniti, Nissan Motor Co. Ltd's new entry into the luxury car market. Although those images of rocks and trees seem peaceful, the market would be better represented by a hurricane. Nissan is moving into an already crowded field at a time when automotive analysts are predicting slow sales for luxury cars. To gain an edge in that tough environment, Nissan and its suppliers spent 18 months developing an integrated network that links every dealer in the United States to the corporation's mainframe in Carson, California. Although Nissan officials won't say how much the company has invested in the system, they are more than willing to explain how Infinitinet works. An IBM AS/400 located at each dealership acts as a host for most functions and as a file server for parts of the application designed to aid the sales staff. A series of PS/2s link the dealer's sales and business staff to the AS/400, while mechanics and other service personnel are connected to the system through dumb terminals that can access either the local AS/400 or the mainframe host. What does all of this cost? Each dealer is required to buy a minimum system configuration for about $125,000, but can end up spending more to buy optional equipment.

The Total Systems Experience Behind Infiniti

Nissan sees Infinitinet as a way to catch every transaction in the process of buying and owning a car.

3090   AS/400   **Local Dealers**

Marketing

—Responses to an 800 number in an Infiniti ad are converted to sales prospects. Names of the callers are downloaded (at the end of the day or week) from Nissan's corporate mainframe to a local Infiniti dealer's system.

—A car salesman can search anywhere in the world for the particular Infiniti desired by the prospect. The system searches the dealer's own inventory, other dealers, a shipping port in California or the factory in Japan.

Operations

—Clerks can use their local systems to process bills and keep track of inventory and sales.

—A finance manager can automatically send a loan application to the corporate headquarters' finance division for quick approval.

Service

—A service manager downloads all records to the corporate mainframe every night, meaning that files on individual cars are updated every time the cars are serviced.

—A mechanic can use the corporate mainframe to diagnose problems with a car.

—A parts department manager can check his or her own inventory, inventories of other dealers or Nissan's warehouse to find the quickest way to find parts.

Source: Nissan Motor Co.

SOURCE: *Datamation*, February 15, 1990, pp. 89–90.

376

PART III
Computer-
Based
Accounting
Applications

OVERVIEW OF A SALES AND PURCHASES SYSTEM

An overview of the information flow in a sales and purchases subsystem is given in Chapter 9. Refer to Exhibits 9-1 and 9-3 to refresh your memory as to the place of the sales and purchases subsystem in the total information system and to review the interaction between this and other subsystems.

ORDER PROCESSING MODULE

The **order processing module** is where sales orders, returns, and adjustments from customers are first entered into the information system. The purpose of this package is to provide fast and accurate processing of orders from customers while minimizing both clerical costs and the costs associated with customer dissatisfaction. This processing package should tell the business

1. If sales orders have been properly filled.
2. If items sold have been properly priced.
3. The status of unfilled orders.

Exhibit 11-1 summarizes the information flow into and out of an order processing module. Notice the large amount of information flow between this module and others of the sales and purchases subsystem, as well as with the accounts receivable module of the cash receipts and disbursements subsystem.

EXHIBIT 11-1   Information Flow Through an Order Processing Module

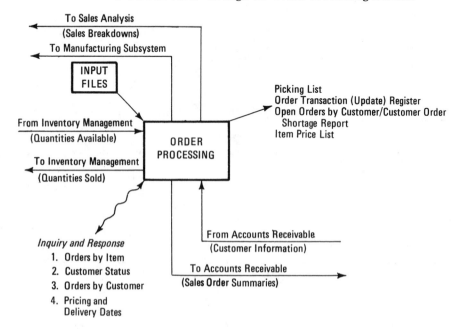

The operation of order processing starts with the main menu illustrated in Exhibit 11-2. Because the order processing module carries out so many different types of processing activities, second-level menus that expand the operations of the main menu are available. These second-level menus guide the user as processing activities are selected from the main menu. Exhibit 11-2 also illustrates a second-level menu for the order processing operation.

EXHIBIT 11-2   Order Processing Main and Supporting Menus

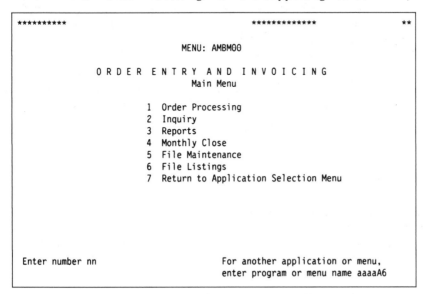

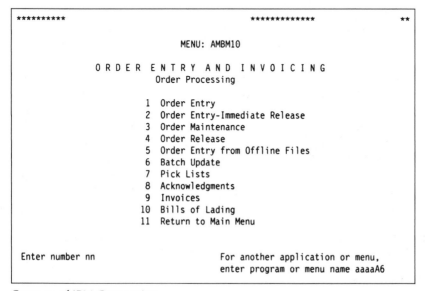

Courtesy of IBM Corporation.

378

PART III
Computer-
Based
Accounting
Applications

Output Reports

Some of the important printed output resulting from the processing of sales orders (invoice register and customer bills) is typically produced by the accounts receivable module. Other reports, however, are generated directly by order processing, and we will begin with this printed output. Typically, the following reports would be produced directly by the order processing module.

Picking List.   The idea here is to produce a list, based on a customer's order, that details the item ordered by name and number so that the order can be accurately filled from the warehouse or storeroom. This report can be quite detailed and may include the location of the items and packing codes, as well as shipping instructions and addresses. The list can also be cross-referenced to the original order and customer by order number and customer number. The **picking list** serves as a guide for employees in filling each order and then may double as a packing slip to be included in the shipment when the order is complete. One such list is printed for each order to be filled and shipped.

Order Transaction (Update) Register (Exhibit 11-3).   After a predetermined batch of orders has been checked for accuracy and accepted, the order processing module prints a list of all new orders since the last report as well as orders changed and orders released for immediate invoicing. This report, the **order transaction (update) register,** is part of the audit trail for orders processed that update the various master files. The sequencing of the report is usually by order number, and codes are used to denote the status of each order with regard to invoicing, special pricing, whether or not the order can be filled from current stock, and other pieces of information about the order. Listing all sales order activity for a given period of time in one report allows each order to be traced to a specific customer (by customer number) and to the order's point of entry into the system by a workstation identification (WSID).

Open Orders by Customer and Customer Order Shortage Report (Exhibit 11-4).   The **open orders by customer report** shows the orders that have been accepted but not yet filled, usually because quantities of the ordered item are not available in stock. Orders that can be filled from inventory, however, are included in this report if they are still outstanding as of the date of the printing. The open order report can be sequenced by customer, item, or due date and contains most of the same data found in a typical picking list, since both reports are generated from customer orders about to be filled. The only significant information that may appear in the open order report but would not be a part of the picking list is purchase or manufactured cost data on the items in each order. The reason is that a business would not want inventory cost information included on a document that will accompany items shipped to customers. The **customer order shortage report** shows all items of inventory unavailable or not in sufficient quantity to fill outstanding orders, so that management can immediately take action to purchase or manufacture the items.

Item Price List (Exhibit 11-5).   The **item price list** report serves as the source for quoting prices to customers or pricing received orders. The report lists each active item of inventory by number and gives the description, the

EXHIBIT 11-3 Update Register

ORDER NUMBER	BATCH TYPE	BATCH NUMBER	ORDER TYPE	CUST/CO NUMBER	WS ID	ITEM COUNT	SPEC CHG COUNT	PRICE OVERRIDE	BACKORDERS	**TYPE OF HDR		CMT	MAINTENANCE** ITEM	PICK SLIPS PRINTED
														UPDATE REGISTER DATE 8/08/** 14.08.51 PAGE 1 AMBEF
C003050	E	030	S	1135000-01	F1	·1	4	---	---	---	---	---		---
C003051	I	031	S	1444000-01	F1	3		---	YES	---	---	---		---
C007830	M	032	S	22315000-01	F1			---	---	---	---	---	YES	YES
C004010	R	033	S	8552000-01	F1	5		---	---	---	---	---		YES
C004050	R	033	S	11025000-01	F1			---	---	---	---	---		YES

```
                    TOTALS              BATCH        ITEM  SPEC CHG

NUMBER OF "E" BATCH TYPES -       1           1          4
NUMBER OF "I" BATCH TYPES -       1           3
NUMBER OF "M" BATCH TYPES -       1
NUMBER OF "R" BATCH TYPES -       1           5
```

Courtesy of IBM Corporation.

EXHIBIT 11-4 Open Orders by Customer and Customer Order Shortage Report

```
  COMPANY NO.2    NO. 02              OPEN ORDER BY CUSTOMER            DATE 8/16/**     14.10.01 PAGE   2  AMBGC
```

CO-CUSTOMER	SOLD-TO NAME	OUR ORDER	P.O. NUMBER	DUE DATE	WHSE NO.	WHSE LOC	ITEM NUMBER	DESCRIPTION	UM	QUANTITY	VALUE AT COST
02-00002800	CAN-DO ENG. CO.	C000154	MF00928	4/07/**			26006-22	TANK 12 BY 24	EA	8	167.97
							27000-02	COMPRESSOR	EA	20	137.00
							27003-20	PUMP ASSEMBLY	EA	1	27.33
							27003-20	PUMP ASSEMBLY	EA	5	136.97
							27006-10	TANK TOP SIZE 10	EA	10	32.10
							27006-20	TANK TOP -SIZE 12	EA	8	14.26
							27006-20	TANK TOP -SIZE 12	EA	25	118.13
							77683	SCREW	EA	30	.15
							98908	WASHER	EA	50	.26
							99001	SPRAY UNIT	EA	5	424.31

```
                                                          ORDERS    VALUE AT SALES   VALUE AT COST

                        XXX C000154  XXX       ORDER TOTALS      1         1,524.40        1,059.38

                        XXX 00002800 XXX    CUSTOMER TOTALS      1         1,524.40        1,059.38

                        XXX    02    XXX     COMPANY TOTALS      2         1,524.40        1,059.38

                        XXX          XXX       FINAL TOTALS      2         3,586.15        2,261.38
```

```
                              CUSTOMER ORDER SHORTAGE REPORT   DATE  8/08/**   TIME 16.08.05  PAGE   1  AMBMB
```

ITEM NUMBER	WHSE	ITEM DESCRIPTION	U/M	---ON ORDER STATUS--- PURCH	MFG	ON-HAND	------ALLOCATED TO----- MFG ORDERS	CUST ORDERS	AVAILABLE
03424	1	TREADLE ASSEMBLY	EA	100	0	133	0	150	17-
26006-20	1	TANK 8 BY 12 INCHES	EA	0	40	365	240	175	50-
26006-21	1	TANK 10 BY 18 INCHES	EA	0	200	185	0	500	315-
26006-22	1	TANK 12 BY 24 INCHES	EA	0	100	183	150	75	42-
27005-A	1	PUMPING UNIT	EA	0	10	19	0	80	61-

Courtesy of IBM Corporation.

EXHIBIT 11-5   Item Price List

ITEM NUMBER ---PRICE--- FACT CD DIV	DESCRIPTION STK PRI U/M U/M CLASS	TYPE	BASE PRICE		1	2	3	4	5	6
02892	LOCK CLIP EA EA 80	4	12.820	DISCOUNT % PRICE	10.000 11.538	20.000 10.256	30.000 8.974	40.000 7.692	40.000 7.692	40.000 7.692
03010	PLATE EA EA 70	4	8.975	MARKUP % PRICE	8.975	8.975	8.975	8.975	8.975	8.975
03011	THROW-OFF COLLAR EA EA 70	4	5.660	MARKUP % PRICE	5.660	5.660	5.660	5.660	5.660	5.660
03012	SPRING EA EA 84	4	6.500	DISCOUNT % PRICE	5.000 6.175	6.000 6.110	7.000 6.045	7.000 6.045	7.000 6.045	7.000 6.045
03021	VALVE EA EA 80	4	5.680	MARKUP % PRICE	5.680	5.680	5.680	5.680	5.680	5.680
03024	SHELL EA EA 50	2	80.000	MARKUP % PRICE	80.000	80.000	80.000	80.000	80.000	80.000
03025	PUMP HOUSING ASSEMBLY EA EA 20	1	68.700	MARKUP % PRICE	68.700	68.700	68.700	68.700	68.700	68.700
03370	MOTOR EA EA 70	4	14.950	MARKUP % PRICE	7.000 15.977	6.000 15.847	5.000 15.698	4.000 15.548	3.000 15.399	2.000 15.249
03385	WRENCH EA EA 80	4	.690	MARKUP % PRICE	7.000 .738	6.000 .731	5.000 .725	4.000 .718	3.000 .711	2.000 .704

ITEM PRICE LIST   DATE 4/09/** TIME 15.26.39 PAGE 1 AMV55

Courtesy of IBM Corporation.

base (unit) price, and the markup (increase) or discount (decrease) percentage for each of a series of different quantity breaks. In this way, quantity discounts or special markups can be built into the report for instant reference by those employees accepting orders and preparing them for the order processing module. The item price list may require frequent updating or may be quite stable, depending on how often prices change.

Information Exchange

Although the output reports of this module clearly are important, the most significant feature of order processing is its extensive information exchange with other modules. Notice in Exhibit 11-1 that order processing interfaces with both of the other modules of the sales and purchases subsystem. A strong tie exists between order processing and inventory management because each needs data from the other to perform its functions. Orders cannot be processed without information about the quantities of each item available and on order, and, in turn, each order processed and quantity shipped or committed affects the inventory on hand. The flow, then, must be constant and two way.

Similarly, the relationship between order processing and accounts receivable is very close. Orders that are created and enter the information system at order processing must be transferred in summary form to accounts receivable for billing and collection purposes, and then summarized again and passed on to the general ledger for financial statement purposes. Since all customer activity is processed in the receivables module and all permanent customer data are held there, customer status information from receivables must be available to order processing as necessary support for order acceptance decisions. Most of this same customer sales data is also necessary for the sales analysis module and can be transferred there from order processing. All of these interfaces can be accomplished with careful data base design.

The interface of order processing with the manufacturing subsystem will be discussed in Chapter 12.

Inquiry and Response. If sales order decisions are to be efficiently and effectively made, up-to-date, on-demand information about both products and customers must be available. Employees handling orders need immediate information on inventory item availability and customer credit status based on the best information the system can generate. The inquiry and response capability illustrated in Exhibit 11-1 gives the user constant access to this kind of information, something even the best designed manual system cannot do. This question-and-answer dialogue with the system is more important in order processing than in any of the other modules discussed so far. Exhibit 11-6 illustrates typical response information provided by order processing on all of the current orders for a particular customer, current customer status, and on all current orders for a particular inventory item. Other types of inquiries determined by the user are also possible.

How the Package Works

Interactive (immediate) processing is most useful in the area of sales orders. The need to meet customer demands in a competitive environment makes the interactive approach essential in order processing. Thus, an on-line input device such as a terminal or workstation would likely see greater use in the order processing module than in the other modules discussed so far.

EXHIBIT 11-6   Display of Response Information from Order Processing

```
                        CUSTOMER ORDERS INQUIRY                    AMB021  W2
   CUSTOMER 1135000    COMPANY  1
        NAME APPOLLO SUPPLY CO.           SALESREP 31701
                             ORDER      REQUEST     SCHEDULE    ORDER  PICK
   ORDER    CUSTOMER P.O.    DATE        DATE        DATE       TYPE   LIST
   C000022                   09/11/**    09/11/**    09/11/**    S     NO
   C000021                   09/11/**    09/11/**    09/11/**    S     NO
   C000020                   09/11/**    09/11/**    09/11/**    I     NO

                                                    F02 PAGE FORWARD
                                                    F24 END OF JOB
```

Exhibit continues on next page

382

PART III
Computer-
Based
Accounting
Applications

EXHIBIT 11-6 **Display of Response Information from Order Processing (continued)**

```
                       CUSTOMER STATUS INQUIRY                    AMB011  W4
CUSTOMER  1135000  COMPANY  1                STATUS    A    CLASS  10
   NAME APPOLLO SUPPLY CO.                   SALESREP 31701 TERRITORY  11
   ADDR ATLANTA                              BALANCE FORWARD/OPEN ITEM CODE 0
                                             STATEMENT CODE    N
                                             DATE LAST PAYMENT 07/15/**
        STATE GA      ZIP 30301-2976         SERVICE CHARGE CODE 0 PERCENT   .015
   PHONE 404-123-7654

   MEMO DUE                  30 DAY     2,311.25     TOTAL DUE        3,176.18
   CURR CHG        600.00    60 DAY                  CREDIT LIMIT     6,000.00
   CURR PMT      1,200.00    90 DAY       264.93
   CURR ADJ                 120 DAY                  CREDIT CODE
   CURR AMT        600.00


   BACKORDERS    YES                       TAX   TAX
   PARTIAL SHIP NO                         CLASS BODY
   UNIT PRICE DISC. CODE                     1    FE
   INVOICE DISCOUNT CODE    2                2    GA
   NO. OF OPEN ORDERS                        3    CT
   TERMS CODE    2                           4




                                               F24 END OF JOB
```

```
                    CUSTOMER REQUIREMENTS BY ITEM           AMB041  W2
   ITEM NUMBER 03011            WAREHOUSE 1
   DESCRIPTION COLLAR                            CLASS 71
               ON HAND      ON ORDER    ALLOC-MFG    ALLOC-PICK


                           ORDER     REQUEST   SCHEDULE  REL# /  ORDER  ALLO-
   CUSTOMER   ORDER   QUANTITY  DATE      DATE      DATE     CREDIT  TYPE   CATED
   12340000 C000045      30  09/11/**  11/25/**  11/25/**           S      NO
    1483000 C000044      75  09/11/**  12/06/**  12/06/**           S      NO
    1444000 C000043      25  09/11/**  11/07/**  11/07/**           S      NO
     123000 C000042      50  09/11/**  11/14/**  11/14/**           S      NO
    1670000 C000041     300  09/11/**  10/12/**  10/12/**           S      NO




             --- END OF ORDERS ---




                                           F02 PAGE FORWARD
                                           F24 END OF JOB
```

Courtesy of IBM Corporation.

Exhibit 11-7 shows a typical order entry sequence that would occur as orders are processed interactively. Note the give-and-take between the user and the system, with the terminal as the input/output vehicle. First, the user enters customer and order numbers, and the system responds with customer data from the customer master file. Then, the user enters data about the order and the item or items ordered, and the system responds with appropriate data

EXHIBIT 11-7   Display of Interactive Order Entry Sequence

383

CHAPTER 11
Sales and
Purchases
Systems

```
CUSTOMER ORDER DATA            E BATCH 026              ENTER    AMBS11  W2

ORDER  ORDER  CO/CUSTOMER  SALES  W  SHIP-TO --- OVERRIDE --- --- PREVIOUS ---
NUMBER TYPE   NUMBER       CODE   H  NUMBER SOLD-TO SHIP-TO ORDER   CUSTOMER
   18  S     01 00145400     1                        Y      17     78100

ORDER    REQUEST   MFG     ----- CREDIT MEMO ------  SHIPPING     SHIP
DATE     DATE      DATE    CODE   REFERENCE NUMBER   WEIGHT     LEAD TIME
1014**   1030**    1025**   A

-------- PURCHASE ORDER ---------                      CONTRACT
NUMBER               DATE     SHIPPING INSTRUCTIONS    NUMBER
  GZ987440          1010**    COMMON CARRIER

ADDITIONAL ORDER DATA <Y/N> Y

ORDER COMMENTS        <Y/N> Y

BASIC ITEM ENTRY      <Y/N> Y


                                           F01 END REVIEW
                                           F02 PAGE FORWARD
                                           F24 DISPLAY STATUS
```

```
BASIC ITEM ENTRY         E BATCH  026   ORDER   18  ENTER    AMBSA1  W2

COMPANY 01  CUSTOMER 145400   CHAMBLEE-TUCKER DIE CAST
LINE            A W                    QUANTITY    UNIT   - U/M -
NO.   ITEM NUMBER  L H      DESCRIPTION  ORDERED   PRICE  PRI STK
01   03010       Y 1 PLATE                    10   11.500 EA  EA
02   03011       Y 1 COLLAR                   10    5.000 EA  EA
03   03012       Y 1 SPRING                   20    3.180 DZ  EA
04   26006-20    Y 1 TANK 8 BY 12 INCHES      10   14.500 EA  EA
05   37855H      Y 1 7/8 x 16 UNF HEX BOLT    38   12.820 EA  EA


                    QUANTITY
LINE  ITEM NUMBER   ORDERED  UNIT PRICE    ALLOC  WH
06    27005-A          10      4.460         Y     1

                                           F06 ORDER COMMENT
                                           F07 ITEM ENTRY
                                           F10 SPECIAL CHARGE
                                           F19 UPDATE ITEMS
                                           F24 DISPLAY STATUS
```

Courtesy of IBM Corporation.

from the item master file (see the upcoming inventory management discussion) including prices. At this point order entry is complete, and the user has the option of releasing the order for immediate processing (printing of picking list, update register, and so on) or holding the order for a batch processing cycle at a later time.

Whether the module processes orders interactively or in batches, it still requires input from two master files and a permanent file:

384

*PART III
Computer-
Based
Accounting
Applications*

1. The customer master file, discussed in the receivables module in Chapter 10.
2. The item master file, to be discussed next in the inventory management section.
3. A permanent file (**quantity price file**) of more or less constant data on the prices of each item and appropriate price limits, breaks, markup, and discount percentages.

As the module receives new sales orders and changed or canceled orders for a period, it enters them into a current activity (transaction) file (the **new sales orders file**). As the new sales orders and changed or canceled orders are processed, they feed into the new invoices transaction file used in the receivables module. This file structure and design reflects the difference between

CONCEPT SUMMARY

Order Processing Module

	Input	Information Exchange	Output
Human/ Computer Interaction	1. New sales orders file	Inquiry/response on 1. Orders by item 2. Pricing and delivery dates 3. Customer status 4. Orders by customer	1. Picking list 2. Order transaction (update) register 3. Open orders by customer/ customer order shortage report 4. Item price list
Computer Only	1. Customer master file 2. Item master file 3. Quantity price file	1. Sales order transactions and summary totals *to* accounts receivable 2. Sales breakdowns *to* sales analysis 3. Customer status data *from* accounts receivable 4. Inventory items sold *to* inventory management 5. Inventory availability *from* inventory management 6. Manufacturing subsystem	1. Customer master file 2. Item master file 3. New sales invoices file

sales orders and sales invoices. Sales invoices represent accounting transactions, while sales orders are information, but do not yet represent completed transactions.

Data Base. With the introduction of the order processing module you should begin to see the concept of a data base at work. Order processing makes use of the same master data files (customer and item) used by other modules and creates a transaction file (new sales orders) that provides the basis for the transaction file (new sales invoices) of another package. The idea is that unique and separate master files are not needed for each module. Business data can be organized and stored flexibly enough to be readily accessible and usable by all modules within the system.

INVENTORY MANAGEMENT MODULE

As order processing is the point of original entry for sales orders, returns, and adjustments, so inventory management is the point of first processing for purchase orders and invoices, purchase returns, and purchase adjustments. The purpose of the **inventory management module** is to provide information that helps management control inventory and inventory costs and make sound purchasing decisions. An important goal is to minimize total costs and cash flows associated with the purchase function. The inventory management processing package should tell the business

1. If purchases have been properly timed.
2. If purchase orders have been properly filled and priced by vendors.
3. The status of unfilled purchase orders.
4. The status of inventory on hand and item availability.

The focus of this module is on maintaining the appropriate levels of inventory to meet customer demands, but no more than these necessary levels, and on safeguarding the items on hand.

Exhibit 11-8 summarizes the flow of information into and out of an inventory management module. Like order processing, there is extensive information flow between this package and others in the sales and purchases subsystem, and with the accounts payable module.

As with all modules in an interactive system, operation of inventory management begins with the main menu given in Exhibit 11-9. Secondary menus are also available for inventory management to aid in accomplishing the many functions of the package. For example, if a user selects the report option from the main menu, a second-level menu will appear so that the desired report can be selected.

Output Reports

The close relationship of inventory management and accounts payable results in two reports associated with the purchase function, the purchases journal and vendor checks, typically being generated by the payables module. The

386

*Part III
Computer-
Based
Accounting
Applications*

EXHIBIT 11-8   Information Flow Through an Inventory Management Module

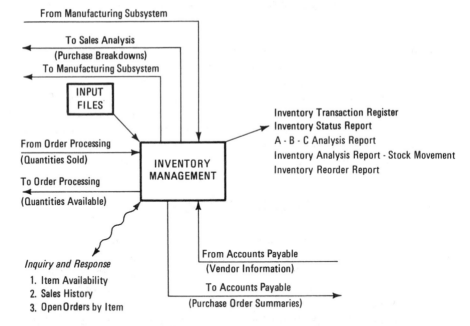

following output reports, however, are produced directly by inventory management because they are related to the goals of this module.

Inventory Transaction Register (Exhibit 11-10).   The **inventory transaction register** is a complete listing of all master file transactions in inventory for the period covered by the report. It includes orders, receipts, issues, and alloca-

EXHIBIT 11-9   Inventory Management Main Menu

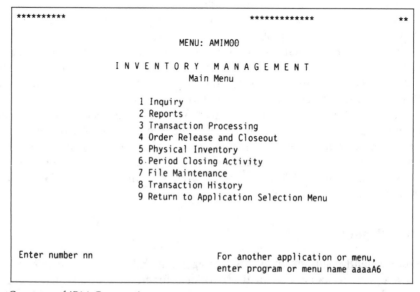

Courtesy of IBM Corporation.

EXHIBIT 11-10   Inventory Transaction Register

```
NORTHCREEK IND.              INVENTORY TRANSACTION REGISTER        DATE 6/01/**  TIME 16.06.16  PAGE   1  AMV3G
                                    PROCESSED ITEMS

ORDER        ITEM      -WHSE- OLD / NEW      DESCRIPTION              ---- TRANSACTION ----    REV  BCH   WS
NUMBER       NUMBER    NO  TR TRAN DATE                 * CALCULATED  TYPE          CODE            NO.   ID.

LOCATION     N/LOCATION    BATCH/LOT     GRN          FIFO DATE

BLKT VENDOR  SEQ. CMP. REASON          TRANS  U/  TRANS   *  OLD/NEW      VALUE CHNG/  -------- OLD/NEW BALANCE --------
REFERENCE    NO.  CD.                  QTY    /M  AMOUNT  *  STD COST     VARIANCE     ON-HAND  ON-ORDER  ALLOC    AVAIL
MJM7000      100100    1               BRIEFCASE              PRODUCTION RECEIPT *        RM         50      X6
MMMPCD                     BL507                   4/23/**
                      JM   4/16/**  10.000  EA     1.00                   53.49       35.000  145  0.000  180.000
TESTING                    4/23/**                                       53.49-      45.000  135  0.000  180.000

PJM5000      100145    1               PART FOR INSIDE POCKET  PURCHASE RECEIPT TO INSP    RI         50      X6
QQQQQR                     BL505                   4/23/**
                      JM          10.000  EA      .00                     .00        587.000  110  186.000  511.000
TESTING                    4/23/**                                       .00        587.000  110  186.000  511.000

PJM5010      200223    1               BROWN DYE              PURCHASE RECEIPT TO INSP    RI         50      X6
QQQQQS                     BL506                   4/23/**
                                  10.000  CS      .00                     .00         30.000  442  115.000  357.000
                           4/23/**                                       .00         30.000  442  115.000  357.000
```

Courtesy of IBM Corporation.

tions of inventory items, as well as adjustments to inventory. Transaction quantities and dollar amounts that account for changes in item balances are highlighted, as is the stage of completion of the inventory transaction. On-order amounts may be included in the availability calculation for each item if the user wishes. Since the register prints all transactions which update relevant master files, it provides an excellent cross-reference to all inventory-related source documents and contributes to the traceability of inventory transactions through the system. Certain conditions requiring management attention, such as reorder points, can be highlighted for management action.

Inventory Stock Status Report (Exhibit 11-11).   The focus of the **inventory stock status report** is on the quantities of each item available as of the end of a specified processing period. For each item, a unit cost is supplied and a total cost calculated. In this report standard cost is used, but any costing technique (average, FIFO, LIFO) can be applied to the items. Also, the report gives a base selling price for each unit to facilitate item-by-item profitability analysis. This is actually an activity as well as an availability report because it summarizes all inventory activity for the period as detailed in the inventory transaction register.

Remember, the focus of the inventory transaction register is on inventory activity, and the focus of the inventory stock status report is on inventory availability, although each report includes some information from the other.

Management Reports.   The inventory management module can provide decision-making and control-oriented reports of almost limitless variety. Management reports dealing with inventory analysis, stock movement, reorder quantity and point, and the status of purchase or manufacturing orders, as well as many other reports, can be produced routinely or on demand.

Inventory analysis reports highlight for management review such factors as the dollar sales volume, investment required, turnover, and profit and profit margin for each inventory item or class of inventory items. These reports can

EXHIBIT 11-11 Inventory Stock Status Report

```
GATEWAY MFG CO                 PERIOD END INVENTORY STOCK STATUS            DATE  4/09/**  TIME 15.25.50  PAGE   1  AMI6C


                                    SEQUENCE BY ITEM
                         ITEMS FROM 02892              TO 03385

ITEM     ITEM      ITEM      ITEM            STK PRI                                        STANDARD        BASE
CLASS    NUMBER    TYPE   DESCRIPTION        U/M U/M                                        UNIT COST       PRICE

WHSE     BEGIN     -------- PERIOD TO DATE-------      QTY        QTY.        QTY.        QTY           ON-HAND
NO.      BAL         ISS / SALE RECEIPTS    ADJ.     ON-HAND    ON-ORDER     ALLOC.      AVAIL.         COST

MX      01000      2   STRAWBERRY SHAMPOO       OZ  OZ                                          .0009         .000
 1        .000      64.000     10.000      .000     73000.000  384000.000  10445154.320  588154.320-      657.0000

SH      01008      1   STRAWBERRY SHAMPOO 8OZ  DZ  EA                                          .7604        1.500
 1        .000        .000       .000      .000       744.000   32920.000        .000     33664.000       565.7376

SH      01016      1   STRAWBERRY SHAMPOO 16OZ  EA  EA                                         .8418        2.900
 1        .000        .000       .000      .000       744.000   45600.000        .000     46334.000       626.2992

80      01405      4   WRENCH                   EA  EA                                          .3500         .690
 A      100.000-      .000       .000      .000        20.000    1123.000        .000      1143.000         7.0000
 1      100.000-      .000       .000      .000       100.000        .000        .000       100.000        35.0000
 1        0.000       .000       .000      .000       120.000    1123.000        .000      1243.000        42.0000


         * - UNIT COST DEFAULT TAKEN                          REPORT TOTAL             1,891.0368
```

Courtesy of IBM Corporation.

be sequenced in any manner so that items of high turnover, profit, profit margin, or investment can be listed first and the report given in descending order for any of the criteria. The purpose of inventory analysis reports is to provide information that will allow management to determine trends in the movement of inventory and pinpoint areas of success and difficulty for future planning purposes. A wealth of inventory activity data is stored in any computer-based information system; how it is channeled and used is at the discretion of the system user.

Exhibit 11-12 is an example of one type of inventory analysis report, called

EXHIBIT 11-12 A-B-C Analysis Report

```
NORTHCREEK IND.              A-B-C ANALYSIS REPORT            DATE  5/31/**  TIME 13.43.35  PAGE   1  AMI2H

WAREHOUSE- A                 ITEM TYPES 1,2,3,4,9


                                          ------------PRIMARY CALCULATION--------------------SEC CALC-----
WH    ITEM     ITEM      ITEM       STK PRI ITEM  CUM %  ESTIMATED STANDARD  ANNUAL   CUMULATIVE CUM % ANNUAL USE CUM %
NO   NUMBER    TYPE   DESCRIPTION   U/M U/M COUNT ITEMS ANNUAL USE UNIT COST USAGE AMT USAGE AMT USAGE  AT PRICE PRICE

                                          16  100.0                          5,117              8,223  100.0

A 99001      1 SPRAY UNIT             EA EA   1   6.3    37.33    100.2566    3743    3743  73.1   5600  68.0
A 03014      2 PUMP REBUILDING KIT    EA EA   2  12.5    39.14     20.0000     783    4526  88.5   2258  95.4
A 26006-20   1 TANK 8 BY 12 INCHES    EA EA   3  18.8    15.68     19.0840     299    4825  94.3    227  98.2
A 27006-00   2 TANK TOP 8 INCHES      EA EA   4  25.0    20.58      5.3284     110    4935  96.4      0  98.2
A 03426      2 TUBE 8 IN DIA          EA EA   5  31.3    20.58      3.4344      71    5006  97.8      0  98.2
A 27006-70   2 TANK BOTTOM 8 INCHES   EA EA   6  37.5    20.58      2.9424      61    5067  99.0      0  98.2
A 34250-A    1 TANK COVER ASSM        EA EA   7  43.8     7.49      4.6324      35    5102  99.7     82  99.2
A 03424      1 TREADLE ASSEMBLY       EA EA   8  50.0     3.14      4.7907      15    5117 100.0     66 100.0
A 03428      2 STAND                  EA EA  11  68.8      .00      2.4131       0    5117 100.0      0 100.0
A 03443      2 MOTOR SUPPORT          EA EA  12  75.0      .00      2.3655       0    5117 100.0      0 100.0
A 03594      2 LUG                    EA EA  13  81.3      .00      2.9301       0    5117 100.0      0 100.0
A 03595      1 LUG SUB-ASSEMBLY       EA EA  14  87.5      .00      3.5771       0    5117 100.0      0 100.0
A 27005-A    1 PUMPING UNIT           EA EA  15  93.8      .00     35.4507       0    5117 100.0      0 100.0
A 27007-A1   1 BASE ASSEMBLY          EA EA  16 100.0      .00     10.0287       0    5117 100.0      0 100.0

                              TOTAL        16                                      5,117              8,233
```

Courtesy of IBM Corporation.

an **A-B-C analysis report**. This report focuses on the dollar investment required in each type of inventory, which is defined as the number of units sold during the period multiplied by unit cost. For most businesses, only a few items of inventory account for most of the investment, sales, and profit activity of the business, so this report can be useful for management understanding of the products critical to business success.

    Inventory stock movement reports of the type illustrated in Exhibit 11-13 are also quite useful because decisions on when and how much to reorder are almost solely quantitatively based and can be easily programmed into the system. Unlike decisions on product emphasis or product elimination, which require judgment and insight by management, inventory reordering time and amount can be determined through the use of well-established standard formulas. Calculations for economical order quantity and order point can be made a part of the inventory management module, which can then produce reports

EXHIBIT 11-13   Inventory Analysis Report—Stock Movement

```
   GATEWAY MFG CO            INVENTORY ANALYSIS REPORT - STOCK MOVEMENT      DATE 12/11/**  TIME  8.39.49  PAGE   1  AMI2K2

                                      SEQUENCE BY ITEM NUMBER

                            ITEM NUMBERS     FROM 26006         TO 27006

            ITEM      WH  VENDOR    DATE OF  ESTIMATED  AVERAGE            ORDER      YTD                       YTD
   RANK    NUMBER     NO. NUMBER U/M LAST SALE ANNUAL USE  USE    E.O.Q.  POINT     ISSUES                    USED

        ITEM                      DATE OF  AVERAGE    AVERAGE          PTD        PTD         PTD           PTD
     DESCRIPTION                  LAST USE TURNOVER   LEVEL          ISSUES     RECEIPTS    ADJUSTS         USED

    1 26006-20     A    EA 10/11/**     .00        0      0        0            0                           0
      TANK 8 BY 12 INCHES          9/14/**       .0        0                   0          0          0      0

    2 26006-20     B    EA 12/02/**     .00        0      0        0            0                           0
      TANK 8 BY 12 INCHES         12/06/**       .0        0                   0          0          0      0

    3 26006-20     1    EA 11/01/**  2,268.00    174    456      402        1,800                       1,575
      TANK 8 BY 12 INCHES          9/20/**     24.5       92               1,500      1,589          0  18,900

    4 26006-21     1    EA  6/04/**  1,322.64    102    273      210       10,500                         919
      TANK 10 BY 18 INCHES         8/03/**     15.4       86                 875        905          0  11,022

    5 26006-22     1    EA 11/04/**    945.36     73    176      165        7,500                         656
      TANK 12 BY 24 INCHES        12/05/**     15.7       60                 625        716          0   7,878

    6 27000-02  1 060421 EA  9/23/**  4,500.00    346    283    1,119       36,500                       3,125
      COMPRESSOR                  10/22/**      6.2      725               3,042          0          0  37,500

    7 27001-01  1 036657 EA 10/21/**  4,380.00    337  5,192      556            0                       3,042
      ADAPTER GASKET              10/02/**      4.5      966                   0          0          0  36,500

    8 27002-01  1 036657 EA  9/22/**  4,380.00    337  1,478      608            0                       3,042
      ADAPTER PLATE                9/14/**      4.5      972                   0          0          0  36,500

    9 27003-20     1    EA 12/02/**  4,500.00    346    300      108            0                       3,125
      PUMP ASSEMBLY               12/04/**     12.4      363                   0      3,334          0  37,500

   10 27004-01     1    EA 10/27/**  4,368.00    336    935      575       36,000                       3,034
      HANDLE                       9/21/**      9.0      485               3,000      4,099          0  36,400

   11 27005-A     A    EA 11/16/**     .00        0      0        0            0                           0
      PUMPING UNIT                10/29/**       .0        0                   0          0          0      0

   12 27005-A     1    EA 12/01/**  4,380.00    337    117      108       36,000                       3,042
      PUMPING UNIT                11/17/**      9.0      488               3,000      4,105          0  36,500

   NOTE- * MANUALLY ENTERED

   TOTAL SUMMARY RECORDS      12

   PTD AND YTD USED INCLUDES SALES
```

Courtesy of IBM Corporation.

390

PART III
Computer-
Based
Accounting
Applications

listing the various reorder recommendations made by the module. Exhibit 11-14 illustrates such an **inventory reorder report**.

The key to all management-oriented reports is for the user to decide what information would be most useful, what form the information should take, and how often it should be supplied. Once these decisions are made, the system can deliver the data to support management action.

Information Exchange

The interfaces for inventory depicted in Exhibit 11-8 have been discussed earlier in the context of other processing modules. The strong relationship between inventory management and order processing has been established. An equally strong tie exists between inventory management and accounts payable, both of which are concerned with the processing of purchases and payments. Purchase orders created and entered into the system at inventory management lead to purchase invoices. Purchase invoices are processed in accounts payable, where payments are recorded, and then summarized and passed on to the general ledger for inclusion in financial statements. Since all vendor data are stored and processed in the payables module, payables must deliver vendor

EXHIBIT 11-14   Inventory Reorder Report

```
   NORTHCREEK IND.                    INVENTORY REORDER REPORT            DATE  7/19/**  TIME 11.12.09  PAGE    1  AMI2M
                                           SEQUENCE BY VENDOR

                                   VENDORS FROM 001011 TO 018834
   DESCRIPTION                                                           ORDER POLICY      LEAD    L/T
                                                                            CODE           TIME    ADJ

   VENDOR ITEM  ITEM       WH  U/   QTY        QTY        QTY        QTY    ORDER                          SAFETY     AVERAGE
   NUMBER CLASS NUMBER     NO  /M   ON-HAND    ON-ORDER   ALLOC      AVAIL  POINT     E.O.Q.               STOCK      PRD USE
   BOLT 1/4 BY 1                                                                G
   001011 80   03416        1  EA   11,096.000        0      0.000  11,096.000  10,000 *   1,299   15P    2       .000         5

   BOLT 1/2 BY 2                                                                G
   001011 80   03417        1  EA   10,502.000        0      0.000  10,502.000  10,000 *   1,027   15P    2       .000         5

   NUT                                                                          B
   001011 80   06014        1  EA    6,867.000        0    800.000   6,067.000   7,000 *   3,904   30P    2       .000        17

   NUT                                                                          C
   001011 80   07243        1  EA    4,945.000        0    800.000   4,145.000   7,000 *   4,001   30P    2       .000        17

   PLATED CYLINDER 12 IN                                                        G
   006592 23   99239-RM     1  EA    2,214.000      900  2,000.000   1,114.000   2,500 *     227    P             .000        55

   HINGE PIN                                                                    G
   012893 80   03419        1  EA    2,498.000        0    400.000   2,098.000   3,000 *   2,829   15P    2       .000         9

   SCREW                                                                        G
   012893 80   77683        1  EA    1,358.000        0  1,300.000      58.000   1,159     12,000 * 30P    2       .000        23

   CASTING                                                                      A
   015772 30   99990-RM     1  EA    1,447.000        0    275.000   1,172.000   5,000 *   1,003  150P   10       .000       349

   HINGE WASHER                                                                 G
   018834 80   03587        1  EA   12,489.000        0    800.000  11,689.000   2,000 *   2,735   15P    2       .000        17

   HINGE WASHER                                                                 G
   018834 80   03640        1  EA    4,729.000        0    800.000   3,929.000   6,000 *   12,000 * 15P    2       .000        17

   TOTAL NUMBER OF RECORDS SELECTED          12

   NOTE-   *   -MANUALLY ENTERED
           M   -LEAD TIME MANUFACTURING
           P   -LEAD TIME PURCHASING
           X   -OTHER LEAD TIME
```

Courtesy of IBM Corporation.

information to the inventory management module to aid in purchasing and vendor selection decisions. This inventory management and accounts payable relationship parallels that of order processing and accounts receivable. Also, in a manner similar to order processing, the inventory management module is capable of passing purchase analysis information (mostly cost breakdowns) on to sales analysis for the generation of various profit analysis reports.

The numerous interfaces of inventory management with the manufacturing subsystem will be discussed in Chapter 12.

Inquiry and Response. Recall that inquiry and response capability is important to the processing of sales orders because a business must react quickly and accurately to customer requests in the sales area. This need for immediate response information is not as critical in the purchase function, since actions by management in this area can be more planned and deliberate. Nonetheless, some question and answer capability on the current availability and activity patterns of inventory items as well as on items ordered can be useful in answering management questions related to short-term purchase and cash flow planning. Exhibit 11-15 illustrates typical response information about current quantities on hand, current outstanding orders by individual item of inventory, and historical sales activity, that can be retrieved on demand from an inventory management module. Many other types of inquiries as specified by the user can also be answered by inventory management.

**EXHIBIT 11-15 Display of Response Information
From Inventory Management**

```
 DATE 12/14/**                 ITEM AVAILABILITY                  AMI1E1 W5

  ITEM 27002-01        WHSE 1  ADAPTER PLATE                        MMDDYY
                               QTY ON HAND 2000.500        DATE 1 1214**
                               MFG ALLOCATIONS             DATE 2 0112**
                          PEND MFG ALLOCATIONS
           SCHEDULED RECEIPTS                    DATE 1    DATE 2      ALL
  ORDER NO  VEND/JOB  STAT  DUE DATE            12/14/**  01/12/**   OTHER
  P000031    072303    10   12/05/**             500.000

           CUSTOMER ORDERS
  ORDER NO  CUST NO    B/O  DUE DATE
  C000023   00000200        01/11/**                        5.000
  C000022   00001200        01/11/**                        5.000

                          NET AVAILABLE  2461.000  2461.000  2461.000




                                                  F02 PAGE FORWARD
       *** END ***                                F24 END OF JOB
```

Exhibit continues on next page

392

Part III
Computer-
Based
Accounting
Applications

EXHIBIT 11-15   Display of Response Information
From Inventory Management (continued)

```
DATE 01/06/**              OPEN ORDERS INQUIRY                   AMI1D1 W2

ITEM 33480-A        WHSE 1 CONTROL BOX              U/M EA TYPE 1 CLS 20
ENG DWG PXS04          WT  21.6  STND COST      312.0000 MAINT DATE 11/30/**
PEND ALLOC            MFG ALLOC      10      CUST ALLOC       5.000
NET AVAIL        135  QTY ON HAND  100.000  QTY ON ORDER    50.000
MRP FLAG  1  FLOOR STOCK CODE
                                                              CURRENT
ORDER NO VEND/JOB  STAT  ORD QTY    QTY OPEN  DUE DATE  HOURS REM OPER  W/C
M000020  C000152    40      55      50.000   01/10/**    32.50   0040   18




*** END ***                                      F02 PAGE FORWARD
                                                 F24 END OF JOB
```

```
DATE 01/12/**       ITEM BALANCE INQUIRY   - SALES HISTORY      AMI1C1  W7

ITEM 03590          WHSE 1  AUTO SWITCH               U/M EA  TYPE 1
CLASS 12  WHSE STOCK LOC G1260  PACKING CODE SK  PLANNER    901
DISC CODE D  PCTS  10.00  15.00    0      0      0      0

  BASE PRICE STND UNIT COST  TAX CODES  WEIGHT     D A T E   O F   L A S T
    14.500        6.0000     1 0 0 0     1.5  SALE 12/01/** USAGE 12/01/**

    ON HAND      PENDING     ALLOCATED    AVAILABLE    ON ORDER
    500.000       0.000       50.000      450.000      0.000

     SALES QTY    SALES AMT  AVG MONTHLY SALES  EST ANNUAL USAGE    QTY USED
M-T-D     20       290.00         1125.63                          DO 20
Y-T-D   1051     14561.26                        15523.66            1051

*----------- LEAD TIME -------------------*   ORD PT    SAFETY STK
               CODE  *                          80         20
       STD VAR ADJ  AVG  CUM  REV  VEN  SAF
MFG    20   5   1   24   70                    VENDOR    COST DEV CODE
PUR     0       0    0
MAT'L               119
                                              F02 PAGE FORWARD
                                              F24 END OF JOB
```

Courtesy of IBM Corporation.

Input Files

In order to keep track of the current availability of each item as well as the status of new orders to vendors for inventory items, the inventory management modules requires a master file of inventory items and a transaction file of new purchase orders.

Item Master File. The **item master file** contains one record for each individual item type in inventory. Each record consists of at least the following data-items:

1. Item number
2. Item description
3. Unit cost (standard, average, LIFO, FIFO)
4. Discount provisions
5. Markup provisions
6. Unit base selling price
7. Current quantity on hand
8. Current quantity on order
9. Receipts—current period
10. Receipts—year to date
11. Receipts—previous year
12. Issues—current period
13. Issues—year to date
14. Issues—previous year
15. Adjustments—current period
16. Vendor number(s) and name(s)

This file is updated by both inventory management and order processing runs and is the data base for most inquiries for these modules. Note that the file is input to and output from both the inventory management and order processing packages, since each uses data stored in the file and each provides information necessary to update the file. Thus, the item master file represents the interface between the inventory management and order processing modules. Note also that the file is linked to the vendor master file of accounts payable by vendor number(s) and name(s). This link is important because of the processing relationship between inventory management and accounts payable and the need for information from the vendor master file by the inventory management module.

New Purchase Orders File. The **new purchase orders file** is generated as new purchase orders are created in inventory processing. As the purchase orders are filled by vendors, this file becomes the basis for the new purchase invoices file discussed in connection with the accounts payable module in Chapter 10. The difference between purchase orders (information) and purchase invoices (accounting transactions) is highlighted in the file structure.

Important Relationships Among Modules

You can see from the relationships of accounts receivable to order processing, accounts payable to inventory management, and order processing to inventory management that these modules all make use of the same set of data. Careful organization of this data base increases efficiency by avoiding repetition and duplication and reducing errors, with the result that processing costs are lowered and better information flow is created.

394

*Part III
Computer-
Based
Accounting
Applications*

CONCEPT SUMMARY

Inventory Management Module

	Input	Information Exchange	Output
Human/ Computer Interaction	1. New purchase orders file	Inquiry/response on 1. Inventory item availability 2. Item history 3. Open orders by item	1. Inventory transaction register 2. Inventory stock status report 3. Inventory analysis report—stock movement 4. A-B-C analysis report 5. Inventory reorder report
Computer Only	1. Item master file 2. Vendor master file 3. Open purchase invoices file	1. Purchase order transactions and summary totals *to* accounts payable 2. Purchase analysis information *to* sales analysis 3. Vendor status data *from* accounts payable 4. Inventory availability *to* order processing 5. Inventory items sold *from* order processing 6. Manufacturing subsystem	1. Item master file 2. Vendor master file 3. New purchase invoices file 4. Open purchase invoices file

SALES ANALYSIS MODULE

The **sales analysis module** is interesting because it is wholly dependent upon output from other modules in order to function. The goal of sales analysis is to provide information that will help management

1. Forecast future sales activity and profitability for the business.

2. Evaluate the past profitability performance of salespersons, products, and customers.

This module can generate reports based on virtually any breakdown of sales and profits specified by management. The purpose of this module is to produce concise, understandable reports that present the most relevant information possible on past performance so that management may judge and analyze the data. With such data, management should be better able to anticipate the future and make appropriate decisions, spot potential difficulties while they are correctable, and create an evaluation and reward system that will contribute to achieving the objectives of the business.

Exhibit 11-16 summarizes the flow of information into and out of the sales analysis module. Note the significant flow of information from other processing modules, and note that sales analysis serves both payroll and budgeting by providing useful data that can be incorporated into their processing activities.

Output Reports

The most important contribution of sales analysis is the management reports which can be produced for planning, control and performance evaluation purposes. The most significant of these reports deal with sales and profits by salesperson, by item, and by customer.

Sales and Profits by Salesperson (Exhibit 11-17). A breakdown of sales by salesperson (and therefore by sales territory) is a significant aid to the budgeting process, which typically starts with the sales forecast. Those who are familiar with a territory and the people who work in it are more likely to make reliable

EXHIBIT 11-16   Information Flow Through a Sales Analysis Module

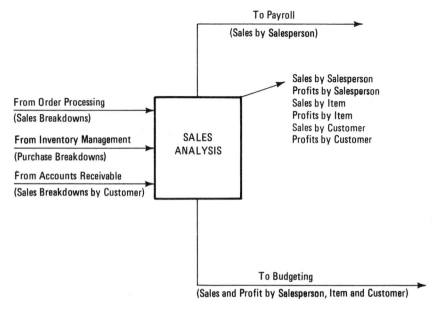

396

*PART III
Computer-
Based
Accounting
Applications*

sales predictions for that territory than a central manager forecasting for the firm as a whole. Territorial sales volume budgets can be summed up, and a sales forecast for the firm derived. A good starting point for this approach to sales forecasting is an accurate and detailed breakdown of past sales activity by salesperson and area. **Sales by salesperson** is one of the reports that provides this information. Notice that this report shows period-to-date sales and year-to-date sales for both the current and the previous year, together with the deviation from the preceding year's sales performance expressed as a percentage. The primary focus of this statement is on sales trends (in this case, by salesperson) that are the foundations of business budgets.

EXHIBIT 11-17 Sales and Profits by Salesperson

```
NORTHCREEK IND.    NO. 01           SALES ANALYSIS BY SALESREP        DATE 2/10/**  TIME 15.17.17  PAGE   1  AMS31
FIRST FISCAL PERIOD    07               FOR 09 PERIODS BY PTD/YTD

                         *-------PERIOD-TO-DATE SALES AMOUNTS -------* *------- YEAR-TO-DATE SALES AMOUNTS ---------*
SALESREP                                              PCT                                        PCT
NUMBER     NAME               THIS YEAR    LAST YEAR  DIFF      THIS YEAR     LAST YEAR           DIFF

  31701    ROBERT G. ARRON     17,542.45     5,498.70  219.0     65,661.35     959,184.45         93.2-
  31702    BOBBY JOE ADAMS     39,607.17     3,895.83  916.7     85,064.37     731,872.04         88.4-
  31705    WILLIAM E. ANDERSON 27,241.12     3,659.90  644.3     69,978.21     634,757.33         89.0-
  31706    CHARLES W. ARNOLD   27,142.43     4,136.89  556.1     75,410.52     738,850.06         89.8-
  31709    JOE DON BAKER       33,074.20    48,082.72   31.2-    89,174.01     846,511.89         89.5-
  31901    RAY PIERCE          32,340.12     4,116.45  685.6     80,355.38     128,917.17         37.7-

           COMPANY TOTALS     176,947.49    69,390.49  155.0    465,643.84   4,040,092.94         88.5-

           AM-4020 OFFSET BEYOND NEXT PERIOD TO CLOSE
```

```
NORTHCREEK IND.    NO. 01     PROFIT ANALYSIS BY SALESREP HOME COMPANY     DATE 2/10/**  TIME 15.17.22  PAGE  1  AMS322
FIRST FISCAL PERIOD   07              FOR 09 PERIODS BY PTD/YTD

                         *--------------- PERIOD-TO-DATE --------------* *--------------- YEAR-TO-DATE -------------*  LAST
SALESREP
NUMBER    NAME                                                                                                        LAST
             COMPANY    SALES AMOUNT                              SALES AMOUNT                                         YEAR
             NUMBER     COST AMOUNT    GROSS PROFIT     PCT       COST AMOUNT      GROSS PROFIT    PCT                 PCT

31701    ROBERT G. ARRON
             01         9,320.10                                 51,867.01
                        9,327.12           7.02-       .1-       51,485.96          381.05        .7                  .0
31702    BOBBY JOE ADAMS
             01        39,607.17                                 79,216.29
                       27,538.53          12,068.64    30.5      67,467.17        11,749.12       14.8                .3
31703    JOHN W. ENDSLEY
             01            .00                                      946.00
                           .00              .00        .0          830.00          116.00        12.3                .0
31705    WILLIAM E. ANDERSON
             01        27,241.12                                 65,469.13
                        9,879.45          17,361.67    63.7      47,921.69        17,547.44       26.8          1,116.0
31706    CAHRLES W. ARNOLD
             01        27,142.43                                 65,123.29
                       10,012.22          17,130.21-   63.1      86,532.10        21,378.81-      32.8-               24.7
31709    JOE DON BAKER
             01        33,074.20                                647,789.72
                       15,102.12          17,972.08-   54.3     629,032.97        18,756.75       2.9                 .8
31756    EDWARD (SAM) HOUSTON
             01            .00                                      800.00
                           .00              .00-       .0          800.00          .00           .0                  .0
31791    B. B. (LEROY) BROWN
             01            .00                                    1,800.00
                           .00              .00        .0        1,600.00          200.00        11.1                .0
31794    W. A. HARRY GREENBURG
             01            .00                                    7,202.00
                           .00              .00        .0        7,200.00          2.00           .0                 .0
31795    RAY PIERCE
             01        34,320.12                                 73,042.45
                        9,870.37          22,469.75    69.5-     49,824.35        23,218.19       31.8               5.6

         HOME COMPANY  168,725.14                               993,285.98
               TOTALS   81,729.81          86,995.33   51.6     942,694.24        50,591.74       5.1
         AM-4020 OFFSET BEYOND NEXT PERIOD TO CLOSE
```

Courtesy of IBM Corporation.

Evaluating the performance of salespersons and territories, however, requires more than just sales information. The **profit by salesperson report** is generally concerned with current profit activity (period and year), although the last column of this profitability statement does show the preceding year's gross profit percentages for comparison purposes. Since most businesses attempt to maximize profits (within certain broad constraints), a control system will be most effective if it encourages employees to maximize the same variable. The inclusion in the report of cost of sales, gross profit in dollars, and gross profit percentage for each salesperson allows management to structure an evaluation and reward system based on the quantitative measurement most likely to contribute to company goals. The focus of this report, then, is on evaluating performance and determining the areas meriting reward recognition or in need of corrective action. Like sales by salesperson, the profit by salesperson report also provides important information that can be used in the budgeting process.

Sales and Profits by Item (Exhibit 11-18). The breakdown of **sales by item** produces relevant budgeting information, as does the sales by salesperson report. Information on units and dollars sold for each item or class of inventory can be used as a verification of the sales forecast by salesperson and territory.

EXHIBIT 11-18 Sales and Profits by Item

```
NORTHCREEK IND.   NO. 01            SALES ANALYSIS BY ITEM            DATE 2/10/**  TIME 15.15.25  PAGE    1  AMS221
                                    FOR 09 PERIODS BY PTD/YTD

ITEM              *--- PTD QUANTITY ----* *---- PTD SALES AMOUNTS ----* *----- YTD QUANTITY -----* *---- YTD SALES AMOUNTS -----*
NUMBER/DESCRIPTION    THIS YEAR                THIS YEAR                      THIS YEAR                    THIS YEAR
                     LAST YEAR    PCT         LAST YEAR       PCT           LAST YEAR    PCT             LAST YEAR       PCT

03424             TREADLE ASSEMBLY
                        70                       705.00                         710                       16,660.36
                       499       14.0          1,550.25      45.5             4,098      17.3             14,424.89     115.5

03591-08          WHEEL 8 IN DIA
                        10                        15.00                          10                           15.00
                         0        .0                .00        .0               126       7.9                189.00       7.9

03591-10          WHEEL 12 IN DIA
                        35                        87.50                          35                           87.50
                         0        .0                .00        .0               304      11.5                760.00      11.5

03591-12          WHEEL 18 IN DIA
                        20                        50.00                          20                           50.00
                         0        .0                .00        .0               152      13.2                365.00      13.7

27005-A           PUMPING UNIT
                        35                     2,625.00                          35                        2,625.00
                         0        .0                .00        .0               305      11.5             22,875.00      11.5

33480-A           CONTROL BOX
                        17                        50.15                          17                           50.15
                         0        .0                .00        .0               154      11.0                454.30      11.0

32450-A           TANK COVER ASSM
                        83                       913.00                          83                          913.00
                         0        .0                .00        .0               549      15.1              6,105.00      15.0

99001             SPRAY UNIT
                        37                     5,735.00                          37                        5,735.00
                         0        .0                .00        .0               305      12.1             47,275.00      12.1

     COMPANY           307                    10,180.65                         947                       26,137.01
     TOTALS            499       61.5          1,550.25     656.7             5,993      15.8             92,448.19      28.3

     AM 4020 OFFSET BEYOND NEXT PERIOD TO CLOSE
```

Exhibit continues on next page

EXHIBIT 11-18 Sales and Profits by Item (continued)

```
NORTHCREEK IND.   NO. 01          PROFIT ANALYSIS BY ITEM           DATE  2/10/**  TIME 15.15.33  PAGE    1 AMS223
FIRST FISCAL PERIOD   07          FOR 09 PERIODS BY PTD/YTD


                  *-------- QUANTITIES --------* *----- PROFIT PTD ------* *---- YTD AMOUNT ---* *---------- PROFIT YTD -----------*
ITEM                  SOLD PTD    LOST PTD                                     SALES
NUMBER/DESCRIPTION    SOLD YTD    LOST YTD  GROSS AMOUNT     PCT               COST        GROSS AMOUNT    PCT   L.YR

03424          TREADLE ASSEMBLY
                      70          1                                        16,660.36
                      710         10            5.00         .7            24,346.50        7,686.14-    46.1-   .0

03591-08       WHEEL 8 IN DIA
                      10          1                                           15.00
                      10          1             7.50        50.0               7.50            7.50      50.0    .0

03591-10       WHEEL 12 IN DIA
                      35          10                                          87.50
                      35          10           43.75        50.0              43.75           43.75      50.0    .0

03591-12       WHEEL 18 IN DIA
                      20          0                                           50.00
                      20          0            25.00        50.0              25.00           25.00      50.0    .0

27005-A        PUMPING UNIT
                      35          0                                        2,625.00
                      35          0         1,3505.00       49.7           1,320.00        1,305.00      49.7    .0

33480-A        CONTROL BOX
                      17          0                                           50.15
                      17          0            18.70        37.3              31.45           18.70      37.3    .0

34250-A        TANK COVER ASSM
                      83          0                                          913.00
                      83          0           591.60        64.8             321.40          591.60      64.8    .0

99001          SPRAY UNIT
                      37          2                                        5,735.00
                      37          2         2,591.40        45.2           3,143.60        2,591.40      45.2    .0

     COMPANY           307        14                                      26.136.01
     TOTALS            947        23         4,587.95       45.1          29,239.20        3,103.19       6.6-

AM-4020 OFFSET BEYOND NEXT PERIOD TO CLOSE
```

Courtesy of IBM Corporation.

Using past data on unit and dollar sales by product for several time periods, management can spot shifting demand and changing trends and incorporate this information into sales forecasts. Also, sales by item provides information which helps in management decisions on sales emphasis and advertising, and on planning future inventory levels. As in the previous report, notice that period-to-date and year-to-date unit and dollar sales are given by item here.

This same type of breakdown is provided in the **profit by item report**. The major new information contained in the profitability report is the cost and gross profit figures (in dollars and percentage) for each item. The relative profitability of inventory items draws attention to the control of costs associated with acquiring and selling each item and (when associated with the contribution margin idea) supports product emphasis, product elimination, and new product decisions. These decisions are all an ongoing part of a business' planning process.

Sales and Profits by Customer (Exhibit 11-19).   The **sales by customer report** focuses on customer buying volumes and patterns and, to some extent, shifts in the composition of sales. Large decreases in sales to a customer disclosed by this report can be followed up with direct customer contact. Significant

EXHIBIT 11-19   Sales and Profits by Customer

```
NORTHCREEK IND.   NO. 01           SALES ANALYSIS BY CUSTOMER          DATE 2/10/** TIME 15.12.47 PAGE   1 AMS121
FIRST FISCAL PERIOD                FOR 09 PERIODS BY PTD/YTD
```

			------PERIOD-TO-DATE SALES AMOUNTS------			*------- YEAR-TO-DATE SALES AMOUNTS ------*		
CUSTOMER NUMBER	SLSRP NUMBER	CUSTOMER NAME	THIS YEAR	LAST YEAR	PCT DIFF	THIS YEAR	LAST YEAR	PCT DIFF
01135000	31701	APPOLLO SUPPLY CO.	4,372.17	588.63	642.8	11,239.60	10,524.59	6.8
01144000	31705	ALMON SAFETY EQUIPMENT	1,297.43	591.08	119.5	8,193.36	7,637.09	7.3
01154000	31706	AL'S CLEANING SERVICE	2,437.52	415.71	486.4	7,287.47	7,411.85	1.7-
01183000	31709	AMERICAN STEEL	6,732.41	732.01	819.7	15,272.56	13,092.03	16.7
02007000	31901	BICKERS & WHITE	4,316.41	595.95	624.3	11,269.23	11,060.47	1.9
03027000	31901	CAMERON COMPANY	1,796.83	717.70	150.4	10,170.09	12,671.95	19.7-
04015000	31705	DAY SUPPLIES, INC.	3,117.92	618.94	403.8	10,338.99	11,173.50	7.5-
07175000	31901	GOULD SUPPLY	4,782.37	784.32	509.7	13,932.80	14,131.42	1.4-
07181000	31702	GOLNER CONTROL CO.	6,312.41	6,792.58	7.1-	14,238.26	12,427.89	14.6
		COMPANY TOTALS	35,165.47	11,836.92	197.1	101,942.36	100,130.79	1.8

```
NORTHCREEK IND.   NO. 01           PROFIT ANALYSIS BY CUSTOMER        DATE 2/10/** TIME 15.12.53 PAGE   1 AMS123
FIRST FISCAL PERIOD   07           FOR 09 PERIODS BY PTD/YTD
```

CUSTOMER NAME CUSTOMER NUMBER	SALESREP NUMBER	*--------------PERIOD-TO-DATE--------------* SALES AMOUNT COST AMOUNT	GROSS PROFIT	PCT	*--------------YEAR-TO-DATE--------------* SALES AMOUNT COST AMOUNT	GROSS PROFIT	PCT	LAST YEAR PCT
DEKALB CHEMICAL CO. 00000800	31901	816.41 900.00	83.59-	10.2-	7,035.28 7,014.12	21.16	.3	4.1-
FOREMOST MACHINE SHOP 00001000	31702	700.00 705.00	5.00-	.7-	700.00 705.00	5.00-	.7-	3.8
QUAKER CITY FOUNDRY 00001200	31901	6,312.41 6,256.20	56.21-	.9	6,312.41 6,256.20	56.21	.9	37.8-
APOLLO SUPPLY CO. 01135000	31701	1,072.17 914.30	157.87-	14.7	1,072.17 914.302	157.87	14.7	.7-
ALMON SAFETY EQUIPMENT 01444000	31705	1,297.43 1,199.87	97.56-	7.5	1,297.43 1,199.87	97.56	.3	4.1-
AL'S CLEANING SERVICE 01454000	31706	437.52 430.80	6.72-	1.5	437.52 430.80	6.72	.3	4.1-
AMERICAN STEEL 01483000	31709	732.41 710.06	22.35-	3.1	732.41 710.06	22.35	.3	4.1-
AMERICAN WOOD PRESERVING 01487000	31709	1,796.83 1,987.41	190.58-	10.6-	1,796.83 1,987.41	190.58	10.6-	18.2
COMPANY TOTALS		13,165.18 13,103.64	61.54	.5	19,384.05 19,217.76	166.29	.9	

```
AM-4020 OFFSET BEYOND NEXT PERIOD TO CLOSE
```

Courtesy of IBM Corporation.

increases in sales activity to a customer can signal the necessity for increased attention to service levels for that customer. This report is helpful in planning sales strategy and allocating salesperson time.

The **profit by customer report** follows the general format of other profit breakdown reports with the highlighting of absolute and relative figures for profits resulting from sales activity with each major customer. This report draws management attention to those customers whose business generates substantial profit, as well as to those customers who contribute less to the business' profit picture. Customers that generate large profits deserve extra attention and consideration (terms, discounts, special ordering, and so on), and this statement presents the data on which decisions about these considerations can be made. Also, the reasons for a particularly small (or negative) absolute gross

400

PART III
Computer-
Based
Accounting
Applications

profit or gross profit percentage for a specific customer can be followed up so that management can discover and pursue unusual circumstances or unproductive relationships.

Flexibility of the Module

Remember that the reports illustrated here represent only a few of the possible management-oriented output that can be generated by a sales analysis module. The wealth of information available in an information system is enormous. A module like sales analysis can generate reports on demand about almost any area of company sales or profit activity, so that circumstances requiring immediate analysis and action can be pinpointed. The ability to draw from a base of data and provide tailor-made management reports quickly and accurately is one of the key advantages of computer-based information systems.

CONCEPT SUMMARY			
Sales Analysis Module			
	Input	*Information Exchange*	*Output*
Human/ Computer Interaction	None	Inquiry/response capability is not critical here	1. Sales and profits by salesperson 2. Sales and profits by item 3. Sales and profits by customer
Computer Only	No new files needed	1. Customer sales breakdowns *from* accounts receivable 2. Item and salesperson breakdowns *from* order processing 3. Purchase analysis breakdowns *from* inventory management 4. Sales by salesperson *to* payroll 5. Sales and profit analysis *to* budgeting	None

Information Exchange—No Separate Input Files

401

CHAPTER 11
*Sales and
Purchases
Systems*

In addition to producing management reports, sales analysis provides data that are useful to the processing activities of other modules. We have discussed the budgeting value of the various sales and profit breakdowns produced by sales analysis and the necessity for sales by salesperson data in payroll commission calculations. This type of interface between modules is not unusual. Unique to sales analysis, however, is the absence of both direct input files and the need for inquiry and response capability.

The information required for the reports generated by sales analysis is already stored in the system for use by other processing areas. It is only necessary for these other modules (primarily, accounts receivable, order processing, and inventory management) to transfer data on customers, sales, and purchases into sales analysis for further processing and the printing of reports. No new files are required in this module because of this information exchange within the system.

Instant response information in the area of sales analysis is not critical. The decisions resulting from sales and profit analysis information are generally predictable and recurring and can be programmed by management. The reports can then be generated when needed. As we have seen, this is not always possible in other modules where nonroutine or spontaneous decisions make the on-demand availability of up-to-date information highly desirable.

CHAPTER SUMMARY

The sales and purchases system tracks all activities related to these two important business functions. Most such systems contain an order processing module, an inventory management module, and a sales analysis module.

Sales orders, sales returns, and sales adjustments first enter the information system through the order processing module. In processing these activities, the module receives information from the customer and item master files and the quantity price file. By combining these inputs, the module produces output reports such as picking lists, order transaction (update) registers, open order reports, customer order shortage reports, and the item price list. In addition, the module exchanges information with the inventory management and accounts receivable module. The goals of the order processing module are to maximize customer satisfaction with order fulfillment while minimizing clerical costs and the costs associated with customer dissatisfaction. Order processing taps the information system data base by using the same master files used by other modules and contributes to the data base through a transaction file of new sales orders.

Purchase orders, purchase returns, and purchase adjustments first enter the information system through the inventory management module. The module also receives information from the item master file. By combining these inputs, inventory management produces the inventory transaction register, the inventory stock status report, and a variety of management reports including inventory analysis and inventory stock movement. In addition, this module exchanges information with order processing and accounts payable. The goals of

402

PART III
Computer-
Based
Accounting
Applications

the inventory management module are to control and protect inventory and to minimize the costs and cash flows associated with purchasing.

The sales analysis module requires no input of its own. Rather, it depends on input from order processing, inventory management, and accounts receivable to produce output reports and information regarding sales and profits breakdowns. Output reports include sales breakdowns and profit breakdowns by salesperson, item, and customer. Other sales and profit output reports needed for management analysis and decision making can be generated on demand. In addition, the module supplies information on sales and profit activity to payroll and to budgeting. The goals of the sales analysis module are to help management in forecasting future sales and profits and evaluating the past performance of salespersons, products, and customers.

KEY TERMS

A-B-C analysis report (p. 389)
Customer order shortage
  report (p. 378)
Inventory analysis report (p. 387)
Inventory management
  module (p. 385)
Inventory reorder report (p. 390)
Inventory stock movement
  report (p. 389)
Inventory stock status report (p. 387)
Inventory transaction register
  (p. 386)
Item master file (p. 393)
Item price list (p. 378)
New purchase orders file (p. 393)

New sales orders file (p. 384)
Open orders by customer
  report (p. 378)
Order processing module (p. 376)
Order transaction (update)
  register (p. 378)
Picking list (p. 378)
Quantity price file (p. 384)
Sales analysis module (p. 394)
Sales and profit by customer report
  (p. 398, 399)
Sales and profit by item report
  (p. 397, 398)
Sales and profit by salesperson report
  (p. 396, 397)

QUESTIONS

11-1. List and briefly describe the output reports that should be produced by an order processing module.

11-2. Why is the capability to give on-demand response to user inquiries so important in an order processing module? On which files are these responses based?

11-3. List and briefly describe the output reports that should be produced by an inventory management module.

11-4. What is an A-B-C analysis report? Why is it important?

11-5. Name the files required by the inventory management module and generally describe the contents of each file.

11-6. Give four questions an inventory management module should be able to answer.

11-7. List and briefly describe the output reports that should be produced by a sales analysis module.

11-8. Specify three items of interactive input/output for each of the three processing modules of the sales and purchases subsystem.

11-9. Specify the hardware devices that might be used for each of the files of an order processing module, if processing is accomplished in a batch-oriented system. In an on-line system.

11-10. Specify the hardware devices that might be used for each of the files of an inventory management module, if processing is accomplished in a batch-oriented system. In an on-line system.

11-11. Explain why the sales analysis module requires neither separate input files nor inquiry and response capability.

11-12. State the objectives of information processing by the order processing, inventory management, and sales analysis modules of a sales and purchases subsystem.

PROBLEMS

11-13. The information flow into and out of an order processing module is depicted in Exhibit 11-1.

1. Give a specific example of each type of input to this processing area.
2. Explain how the examples you chose are actually processed by the module.

11-14. For each of the data-items stored in the item master file, explain why such information is important in a computer-based system. Also, for each data-item, give the output report(s) that use the information. Which of these data-items would normally be updated with each processing run?

11-15. Two critical output reports generated by the order processing module are the order transaction (update) register and the customer open order report.

1. Both of these reports present order information. How does this information differ between reports? How is any common information presented differently in each report?
2. What is the difference between a sales order and a sales invoice? Explain the accounting treatment of each in a computer-based system.

11-16. In the interactive order entry sequence displayed in Exhibit 11-7, a dialogue occurs between the user and the information system. Specify the pieces of information from this dialogue that must be furnished by the user and the information that is furnished by the system from stored data.

11-17. The information flow into and out of an inventory management module is depicted in Exhibit 11-8.

1. Give a specific example of each type of input to this processing area.
2. Explain how the examples you chose are actually processed by the module.

11-18. The information flow into and out of a sales analysis module is depicted in Exhibit 11-16.

1. Give a specific example of each type of input to this processing area.
2. Explain how the examples you chose are actually processed by the module.

404

*PART III
Computer-
Based
Accounting
Applications*

11-19. The output reports of sales analysis are designed to be decision oriented and to assist management in the planning and control of the business. For each of the following fundamental management decisions, cite the output report(s) from sales analysis which would provide necessary information for the decision.

    a. Sales forecasting
    b. Production planning
    c. Product emphasis
    d. Bonuses to salespersons
    e. Pricing decisions
    f. Budgeted gross margin
    g. Sales quotas for next year
    h. Elimination of a product
    i. Hiring and firing of salespersons
    j. Advertising emphasis

11-20. Inquiry/response capability requires a dialogue between the user and the system. For each of the following processing modules, specify which inquiry information must be furnished by the user and which response information would be provided by the system from stored data.

    a. Accounts receivable
    b. Accounts payable
    c. Order processing
    d. Inventory management

11-21. Most transactions enter the information system through the sales and purchases subsystem. The information is then summarized and passed to the cash receipts and disbursements subsystem, which further summarizes the information and passes it to the financial accounting subsystem.

    1. Assume that ten sales orders are received and processed and that sales invoices are then generated. What information would be required by order processing, accounts receivable, and the general ledger module concerning these ten orders?
    2. Assume that two purchase orders are created, the goods are shipped by the vendor, and a purchase invoice is received. What information would be required by inventory management, accounts payable, and the general ledger module concerning these orders?

11-22. (*CIA, adapted*) When a shipment is ready, the shipping department prepares a shipping order form in three copies. The first copy is included with the goods shipped to the customer as a packing slip. The second copy is forwarded to the billing department. The third copy is sent to the accountant. When the billing department receives the second copy of the shipping order, it uses the information to prepare a two-part sales invoice. The second copy of the shipping order is then filed in the billing department. The first copy of the sales invoice is sent to the customer. The second copy of the sales invoice is forwarded to the accountant. Periodically, the accountant matches the copy of the shipping order with the copy of the sales invoice, attaches them, and files them alphabetically by customer name. However, before doing so the accountant uses the copy of the sales invoice to post the sales entry in the accounts receivable subsidiary ledger.

1. For use in evaluating internal control, prepare a flowchart covering the flow of documents described.

2. List the deficiencies and/or omissions revealed by the flowchart that would lead you to question the quality of internal control present.

11-23. (*CMA, adapted*) O'Brien Corporation is a medium-sized, privately owned instrument manufacturer supplying equipment manufacturers in the midwest. The corporation is ten years old and operates a centralized accounting and information system. Its administrative offices are located in a downtown building while the manufacturing, shipping, and receiving departments are housed in a renovated warehouse a few blocks away. The shipping and receiving areas share one end of the warehouse.

O'Brien Corporation has grown rapidly. Sales have increased by 25 percent each year for the last three years, and the company is now shipping approximately $80,000 of products each week. James Fox, O'Brien's controller, purchased and installed a computer last year to process payroll and inventory. Fox plans to fully implement and integrate other modules of the accounting information system within the next five years.

The marketing department consists of four salespersons. Upon obtaining an order, usually over the telephone, a salesperson manually prepares a pre-numbered, two-part sales order. One copy of the order is filed by date and the second copy is sent to the shipping department. All sales are on credit. Because of the recent increases in sales, the four salespersons have not had time to check credit histories. As a result, 15 percent of credit sales are either collected very late or never collected.

The shipping department receives the sales orders and assembles the goods from the warehouse, noting any items that are out of stock. The terminal in the shipping department is used to update the perpetual inventory record of each item as it is removed from the shelf. The packages of goods are placed near the loading dock door in alphabetical order by customer name. The sales order is signed by a shipping clerk indicating that the order is filled and ready to send. The sales order is then forwarded to the billing department where a two-part sales invoice is prepared. The sales invoice is prepared only after receipt of the sales order from the shipping department so that the customer is billed just for the items that were sent, not for back orders. Billing sends the customer's copy of the invoice back to shipping. The customer's copy of the invoice serves as the billing copy, and shipping inserts it into a special envelope on the package in order to save postage. The shipper is then contacted to pick up the goods. In the past, goods were shipped within two working days of the receipt of a customer's order; however, shipping dates now average six working days after receipt of the order. One reason is that two new shipping clerks are still undergoing training. Because the two shipping clerks have fallen behind, two experienced clerks in the receiving department have been assisting the shipping clerks in their tasks.

The receiving department is located adjacent to the shipping dock, and merchandise is received daily from many different sources. The clerks share the computer terminal with the shipping department. The date, vendor, and number of items received are entered on a receipt in order to keep the perpetual inventory records current.

406

PART III
Computer-
Based
Accounting
Applications

A hard copy of the changes in inventory (receipts and shipments) is printed once a month. The receiving supervisor makes sure the recorded receipts are reasonable and forwards the printout to the shipping supervisor who is responsible for checking the reasonableness of the shipments from inventory. The inventory printout is then stored in the shipping department by date. A complete inventory list is printed only once a year when the physical inventory is taken.

Exhibit 11-20 presents the document flows employed by O'Brien Corporation. O'Brien's marketing, shipping, billing, and receiving information system has some weaknesses. For each weakness in the system (1) identify the weakness and describe the potential problem(s) caused by the weakness, and (2) recommend controls or changes in the system to correct each weakness. Use the following format in preparing your answer.

Weaknesses and potential problem(s)	*Recommendation(s) to correct weaknesses*

11-24. (*AICPA, adapted*) The accounting and internal control procedures relating to purchases of materials by the Branden Company, a medium-sized company manufacturing special machinery to customer order, have been described by your junior accountant in the following terms:

"After approval by the manufacturing department foremen, material purchase requisitions are forwarded to the purchasing department supervisor who distributes such requisitions to the several employees under his control. The employees prepare prenumbered purchase orders in triplicate, account for all numbers, and send the original purchase orders to the vendor. One copy of the purchase order is sent to the receiving department where it is used as the basis for a receiving report. The other copy is filed in the purchasing department.

"When the materials are received, they are moved directly to the storeroom and issued to the foremen on informal requests. The receiving department sends a copy of the receiving report (with its copy of the purchase order attached) to the purchasing department and sends copies of the receiving report to the storeroom and to the accounting department.

"Vendors' invoices for material purchases, received in duplicate in the mailroom, are sent to the purchasing department and directed to the employee who placed the initial order. The employee then compares the invoice with the copy of the purchase order on file in the purchasing department for price and terms and compares the invoice quantity with the quantity received as reported by the receiving department on its copy of the purchase order. The purchasing department employee also checks discounts, footings, and extensions and initials the invoice to indicate approval for payment. The invoice is then sent to the voucher section of the accounting department where it is coded for account distribution, assigned a voucher number, entered in the voucher register, and filed according to payment due date.

"On payment dates, prenumbered checks are requisitioned by the voucher section from the cashier and prepared, except for signature. After the checks are prepared, they are returned to the cashier, who runs them through a check signing machine, accounts for the sequence of numbers, and passes them to the cash disbursements bookkeeper for entry in the cash disbursements journal. The cash disbursements bookkeeper then returns the checks to the voucher section which notes payment dates in the voucher register, places the checks in envelopes, and sends them to the mailroom. The vouchers are then

EXHIBIT 11-20   O'Brien Corporation Document Flowchart

407

CHAPTER 11
Sales and
Purchases
Systems

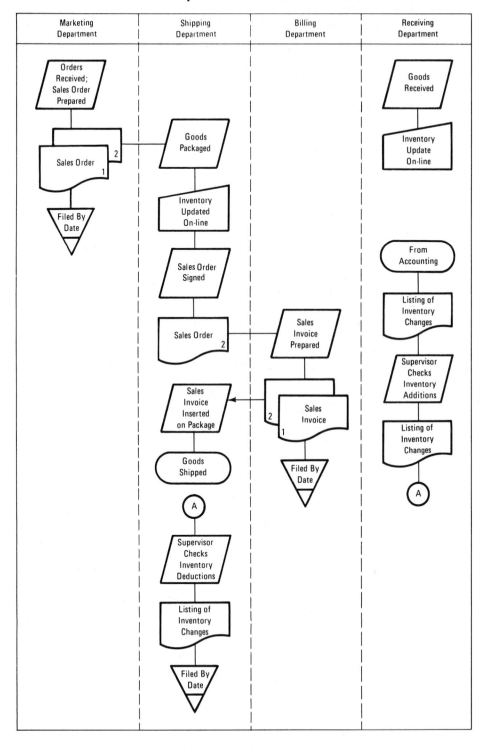

408

*PART III
Computer-
Based
Accounting
Applications*

filed in numerical sequence. At the end of each month, one of the voucher clerks prepares an adding machine tape of unpaid items in the voucher register, compares the total with the general ledger balance of payables, and investigates any differences disclosed by such comparison.''

Discuss the weaknesses, if any, in the internal control of Branden's purchasing and subsequent payments system, and suggest supplementary or revised procedures for remedying each weakness with regard to

a. Requisitions of materials.

b. Receipt and storage of materials.

c. Functions of the purchasing department.

d. Functions of the accounting department.

11-25. (*CMA, adapted*) Valpaige Company is a machinery and equipment manufacturer with several production departments. The company employs automated and heavy equipment in these production departments. Consequently, Valpaige has a large repair and maintenance department (R&M) for servicing this equipment.

The operating efficiency of the R&M department has deteriorated over the past two years. Further, repair and maintenance costs seem to be climbing more rapidly than other costs. The assistant controller has reviewed the operations of the R&M department and has concluded that the administrative procedures used since the early days of the department are outmoded due in part to the rapid growth of the company. The two major causes for the deterioration in efficiency, in the opinion of the assistant controller, are (1) an antiquated scheduling system for repair and maintenance work and (2) the system used to distribute the R&M department's costs to the production departments on the basis of the number of service calls made during each month.

The assistant controller has proposed that a formal work order system be implemented for the R&M department. The production departments would submit a service request to the R&M department for the repairs and/or maintenance to be completed, including a suggested time for having the work done. The supervisor of the R&M department would prepare a cost estimate on the service request for the work (labor and materials) and indicate a suggested time for completing the work on the service request. The R&M department supervisor would return the request to the production department initiating the request. Once the production department approves the work by returning a copy of the service request, the R&M supervisor would prepare a repair and maintenance work order and schedule the job. This work order provides the repair worker with the details of the work to be done and would be used to record the actual repair/maintenance hours worked and the materials and supplies used.

Production departments would be charged for the actual labor hours worked at predetermined standard rates for the type of work required. The materials and supplies used would be charged to the production departments at R&M cost.

The assistant controller believes that only two documents would be required in this new system—a Repair/Maintenance Service Request initiated by the production departments and the Repair/Maintenance Work Order initiated by the R&M department.

1. What data items (elements) would be important to both the repair and maintenance department and the production departments, and therefore should be incorporated into the Repair/Maintenance Work Order?

2. How many copies (parts) of the Repair/Maintenance Work Order would be required? How would each copy be distributed?

3. Prepare a flowchart to show how the Repair/Maintenance Service Request and the Repair/Maintenance Work Order would be coordinated and used to (a) request and complete the repair and maintenance work, (b) provide the basis for charging the production departments for the cost of the completed work, and (c) evaluate the performance of the R&M department?

DECISION CASE

(*CMA, adapted*)   Delmo, Inc., is a wholesale distributor of automotive parts serving customers in states east of the Mississippi River. The company has grown during the last 25 years from a small regional distributor to its present size.

The states served are divided into eight separate territories in order to facilitate service to Delmo customers. Delmo salespersons regularly call upon current and prospective customers in each of the territories. Delmo customers are of four general types:

a. Automotive parts stores
b. Hardware stores with an automotive parts section
c. Independent garage owners
d. Buying groups for garages and filling stations

Because Delmo, Inc., must keep in stock such a large variety and quantity of automotive parts in order to accommodate its customers, the company acquired its own computer system and implemented the inventory management module first. Other modules, including accounts receivable, accounts payable, payroll, and sales analysis, have since been added.

Delmo's inventory management module is comprised of an integrated purchase ordering and perpetual inventory system. Each item of inventory is identified by an inventory code number that identifies both the product line and the item itself. When the quantity on hand of an item falls below a specified level, a purchase order is automatically generated by the computer. The purchase order is sent to the vendor after approval by the purchasing manager. All receipts, issues, and returns of inventory are entered into the computer daily. A printout of all inventory items within each product line showing receipts, issues, returns, and current balances is prepared weekly. However, the up-to-date current status of any particular item of inventory can be obtained daily if desired.

Sales orders are filled within 48 hours of receipt. Sales invoices are prepared by the computer the same day the merchandise is shipped. At the end of each month, several reports are produced that summarize monthly sales. The current month and year-to-date sales by product line, territory, and customer category are compared with the same figures from the previous year. In addition, reports showing monthly figures for product lines within territories, and customers within territories are prepared. In all cases, the reports provide summarized data; detailed data, such as sales by individual customers or prod-

410

Part III
Computer-
Based
Accounting
Applications

ucts, are not presented. Terms of 2/10, net 30 are standard for all of Delmo's customers.

Customers' accounts receivable are updated daily for credit sales, sales returns, and receipts on account. Monthly customer statements are computer prepared and mailed following the completion of transactions as of the last day of the month. Each Friday, a schedule is prepared showing the total amount of accounts receivable outstanding by age—current accounts (0–30 days), slightly past due accounts (31–90 days), and long overdue accounts (over 90 days).

Delmo has also hired a new marketing manager. The new manager believes that more useful sales information should be provided for use by individual salespersons and the department as a whole. While the monthly sales reports currently prepared provide adequate summary data, the manager would like additional detailed data to support the sales effort.

The recent expansion of operations to a larger geographic area has created a cash strain on Delmo, particularly in the short run. Consequently, cash management has become much more important than was the case in prior years. A weekly report that presents a reliable estimate of daily cash receipts is needed. The treasurer discovered that a local company had improved its cash forecasting system by studying the timing of customers' receipts on account to see if a discernible pattern existed. The receipt pattern then became the model to be applied to outstanding invoices in order to estimate the daily cash receipts for the following week. The treasurer believes that this is a good approach and wonders if it can be done at Delmo.

Required:

1. Using only the data available from the current Delmo processing system, what additional reports could be prepared that would be useful to the marketing manager and individual salespersons? Briefly explain how each report would be useful to sales personnel and marketing.

2. If Delmo, Inc., were to implement a cash forecasting system similar to the one suggested by the treasurer, describe
   a. The data currently available in the system that could be used in preparing such a forecast.
   b. The additional data that must be generated.
   c. The modifications, if any, that would be required in the Delmo information system to carry out the forecasting.

12 Financial and Managerial Accounting Systems

Overview

How general accounting functions such as financial accounting, external reporting, and managerial and cost accounting are carried out in computer-based systems.

Learning Objectives

Thorough study of this chapter will enable you to:

1. Relate the financial accounting system to the information system as a whole.
2. Describe the capabilities of a typical general ledger module.
3. Relate the manufacturing system to the information system as a whole.
4. Describe the capabilities of a typical product data management module.
5. Describe the capabilities of a typical material requirements planning module.
6. Describe the capabilities of a typical production costing and monitoring module.

Outline

Financial Accounting System: Overview and Outputs

Financial Accounting System: Inputs

Overview of a Manufacturing System

Product Data Management Module

Material Requirements Planning Module

Production Costing and Monitoring Modules

412

*Part III
Computer-
Based
Accounting
Applications*

SYSTEMS IN THE REAL WORLD

Manufacturing in the Land of Perestroika

As the Iron Curtain rises, the world is getting a peek at aspects of life in Eastern Europe and the U.S.S.R. once closed to Western eyes. One such eye-opener is manufacturing. Due to security measures, few Americans had much knowledge of Soviet manufacturing techniques until recently, says Thomas C. Lavey, president and chief executive officer for Minx Software, Inc.

Recently, Lavey visited the Soviet Union to study that nation's manufacturing methods in pursuit of a possible business venture. Minx is a San Jose–based supplier of manufacturing planning software that runs on PC workstations, mini-computers, and mainframes.

Lavey's first contact with the Soviets was at the Saratov Aviation Plant, located in Saratov, a city on the Volga River south of Moscow, and once a closed Soviet city due to the manufacture of defense-related products.

Lavey spent a little over a week at the plant evaluating how to improve its management systems to increase production. "They very much wanted to improve the way they do things," says Lavey. The computers running the plant appeared to be of 1960s vintage, and Lavey believes they duplicate the IBM 360 and the Digital Equipment Corp. PDP/11 computer in function. The computers control material, routing, and job scheduling. As for the plant's machine shop, Lavey says that most of the 500 lathes, drill presses, and various numerically controlled devices appear old.

The plant's manufacturing process also differs sharply from typical Western manufacturing techniques, says Lavey. "Because there was no market economy, there was no place to buy standard parts. So this company is vertically integrated beyond anything found in the U.S. They manufacture their own rivets, screws, bolts, and washers. There's no concept of going down to a standard parts supplier and buying parts out of a catalog. It's stunning."

Minx may enter into a joint venture with the Soviets as a result of Lavey's visit. And Lavey thinks that other U.S. companies should do likewise. "Many U.S. companies think there's a big market for their products in the Soviet Union, but I think there's probably a better opportunity to find things for the Soviet Union to manufacture and export in joint ventures. They just don't have any hard currency."

Source: *Datamation*, August 15, 1990, p. 46.

FINANCIAL ACCOUNTING SYSTEM: OVERVIEW AND OUTPUTS

As was noted in Chapter 9, the financial accounting subsystem is the most basic of the processing subsystems. It must handle the ongoing recordkeeping and accounting cycle events of a business and is the final repository for all accounting transactions. This subsystem is responsible for the production of all

EXHIBIT 12-1 **Information Flow Through a General Ledger Module** *413*

CHAPTER 12
*Financial
and
Managerial
Accounting
Systems*

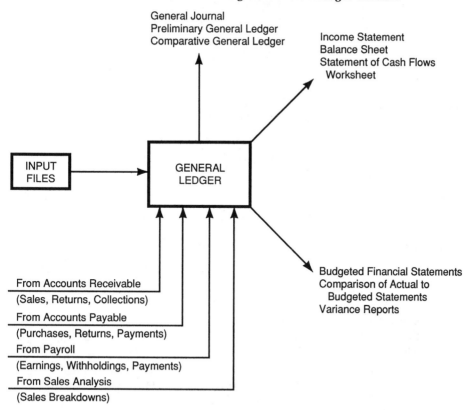

traditional financial accounting documents and reports, including journals, ledgers, trial balances, financial statements, and budgets. Exhibit 12-1 summarizes the information flow into and out of the **general ledger module** of the financial accounting subsystem. Since all transaction processing occurs here, this module is central to financial accounting activities of a business.

The actual operation of financial accounting processing begins with the main menu. A general ledger main menu is given in Exhibit 12-2. As is the case with other modules, users can move back and forth, to and from this main menu when performing general ledger processing.

The financial accounting subsystem must generate several output documents and reports as well as update master files of data to be stored for further processing. The production of useful and timely output to meet externally imposed reporting requirements is the primary goal of this system. As in other modules, the format, content, and frequency of output are a matter of user choice.

Journals

Following the information flow depicted in Exhibit 12-2, the first reports produced in a financial accounting subsystem are the company's journals. These journals are created by computer, but the principles (although not the me-

414

*PART III
Computer-
Based
Accounting
Applications*

EXHIBIT 12-2   General Ledger Main Menu

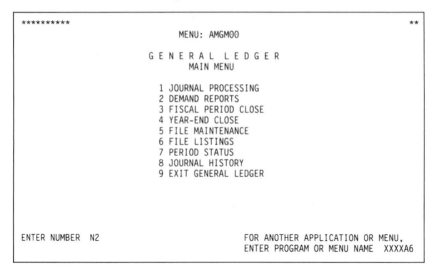

```
**********                                                              **
                              MENU: AMGM00

                    G E N E R A L   L E D G E R
                             MAIN MENU

                    1 JOURNAL PROCESSING
                    2 DEMAND REPORTS
                    3 FISCAL PERIOD CLOSE
                    4 YEAR-END CLOSE
                    5 FILE MAINTENANCE
                    6 FILE LISTINGS
                    7 PERIOD STATUS
                    8 JOURNAL HISTORY
                    9 EXIT GENERAL LEDGER




  ENTER NUMBER  N2                        FOR ANOTHER APPLICATION OR MENU,
                                          ENTER PROGRAM OR MENU NAME  XXXXA6
```

Courtesy of IBM Corporation.

chanics) underlying them are the same as in a manual system. This is an important idea; that is, the basic underlying concepts of business data processing do not change as computer-based systems replace manual accounting systems. The accountant must have a firm grounding in fundamental accounting concepts and procedures, no matter the nature of the processing system being used.

The **general journal** (Exhibit 12-3) is generated from data entered directly into the financial accounting subsystem from source documents. It is likely that a general journal proof would be printed before producing the final general journal, so that the accountant may ensure that the journal itself is error-free. Although the format of this computer-based journal is different from a manual system general journal, both contain the same information. Notice that most of the transactions are journalized using only one line (similar to the way special journals are used in a manual system). The format and content of this journal can be understood by examining any one of the entries.

The journal reference number of each transaction is assigned by the system as entries are made in order to preserve the sequence of events and provide an audit trail. Also assigned is the transaction source, which is the date of the event. A brief description of each transaction is followed by the general ledger debit account number and dollar amount, and credit account number and dollar amount. Account titles are not used in the journal because account numbers are more accurate (less ambiguous) and faster and easier for the computer to handle. This does mean, however, that a user must refer to the company's chart of accounts in order to read and understand each entry. In Exhibit 12-3, the first entry in the journal is an error correction of a previous period (November) entry requiring a debit to #1525 (from the chart of accounts not provided, Office Furniture and Fixtures) and a credit to #1300 (Raw Materials Inventory). The other entries follow this same basic format. Note also that all adjusting entries are entered as direct input to the general ledger module and have appeared as part of the general journal.

EXHIBIT 12-3 General Journal

```
NORTHCREEK IND.   [1] NO. 01              GENERAL JOURNAL                    DATE  6/16/**  TIME 19.17.16  PAGE   1  AMG14
                                          POSTING DATE 12/31/**
```

[2] JOURNAL REFERENCE	TRANSACTION SOURCE	TRANSACTION DESCRIPTION	-GENERAL LEDGER DEBIT- ACCOUNT	AMOUNT	-GENERAL LEDGER CREDIT- ACCOUNT	AMOUNT	BATCH-SEQUENCE
GJ02-0001	JE12-01	CORRECT NOV ERR	1525	7,500.00	1300	7,500.00	006-00001
GJ02-0002	JE12-02	NEW TRUCK	1530	5,837.98			006-00002
GJ02-0003	JE12-02	CHECK #1160			1050	875.70	006-00003
GJ02-0004	JE12-02	EST CITY TAX			2500	4,962.28	006-00004
GJ02-0005	JE12-03	A/R CORRECTION	4000	73.15	1200	73.15	006-00005
GJ02-0006	JE12-04	DEPR - BLDG	6020	2,500.00	1555	2,500.00	006-00006
GJ02-0007	JE12-04	DEPR - OFFICE	7510	850.00	1565	850.00	006-00007
GJ02-0008	JE12-04	DEPR - LAND IMP	6010	700.00	1550	700.00	006-00008
GJ02-0009	JE12-04	DEPR -AUTO/TRUCK	6040	1,200.00	1570	1,200.00	006-00009
GJ02-0010	JE12-07	INV THRU 12/8	1200	19,953.49			006-00010
GJ02-0011	JE12-07	12/1			4000	3,879.53	006-00011
GJ02-0012	JE12-07	12/5			4000	4,213.42	006-00012
GJ02-0013	JE12-07	12/6			4000	4,479.83	006-00013
GJ02-0014	JE12-07	12/7			4000	3,943.52	006-00014
GJ02-0015	JE12-07	12/8			4000	3.437.19	006-00015
GJ02-0016	JE12-11	A/P EXPENSE ADJ	4120	86.04	4100	422.59	006-00016
GJ02-0017	JE12-11	A/P EXPENSE ADJ	4130	336.55			006-00017
GJ02-0018	JE12-17	ALLOW BAD DEBTS	1290	350.00	7110	350.00	006-00018

```
                           JOURNAL TOTAL        39,387.21              39,387.21


                           COMPANY TOTAL        39,387.21              39,387.21
```

[1]   Company number 1 of a multicompany enterprise.

[2]   Application-assigned number identifying this general
      journal and transaction.

Courtesy of IBM Corporation.

Ledgers

Once the transactions of a period have been recorded and the journals printed (the general journal by the general ledger module and the other journals by other modules), the next major output from the financial accounting subsystem is the preliminary and comparative general ledgers.

Preliminary General Ledger (Exhibit 12-4). The **preliminary general ledger** is comprehensive in that it shows for each account (1) the balance at the beginning of the period, (2) the total of debits and credits for the period, (3) the balance at the end of the period, and (4) the net change in the account balance. Creating this ledger requires the transaction information contained in the journals plus input from a master file of data on the previous period balances in each general ledger account. The listing of this information in a report makes possible the extensive cross-checking of transactions for completeness and correctness before the permanent general ledger master file is updated for the period.

Comparative General Ledger (Exhibit 12-5). If the preliminary general ledger proves to be complete and correct, a **comparative general ledger** can be printed and the general ledger master file updated. This is an important report for managerial planning and control purposes, as well as for external reporting,

EXHIBIT 12-4   Preliminary General Ledger

```
NORTHCREEK IND.    NO. 01        PRELIMINARY GENERAL LEDGER           DATE  6/12/**  TIME 13.15.54  PAGE   1  AMG41A

                                      MONTH 12

ACCOUNT                    TRANSACTION TRANSACTION        JOURNAL          DEBIT          CREDIT              NET
NUMBER DESCRIPTION         SOURCE      DESCRIPTION        REFERENCE        AMOUNT          AMOUNT           CHANGE


0001000 PETTY CASH                                PREVIOUS BALANCE-       4,587.95           .00
                                                  ACCOUNT BALANCE         4,587.95           .00

0001050 CASH-IN-BANK - GENERAL                    PREVIOUS BALANCE-     227,548.14           .00
                           JE12-02     CHECK #1160        GJ01-0003                       875.70
                                                  MONTH 12 TOTAL              .00         875.70          875.70CR
                                                  ACCOUNT BALANCE       227,548.14        875.70

0001060 CASH-IN-BANK - PAYROLL                    PREVIOUS BALANCE-     195,789.70           .00
                                                  ACCOUNT BALANCE       195,789.70           .00

0001070 CASH-IN-BANK - OTHER                      PREVIOUS BALANCE-          .00             .00
                                                  ACCOUNT BALANCE            .00             .00

0001080 CREDIT UNION DEPOSITS                     PREVIOUS BALANCE-          .00             .00
                                                  ACCOUNT BALANCE            .00             .00

0001100 SHORT TERM INVESTMENTS                    PREVIOUS BALANCE-     408,739.59           .00
                                                  ACCOUNT BALANCE       408,739.59           .00

0001200 ACCTS REC - TRADE                         PREVIOUS BALANCE-     973,013.73           .00
                           JE12-03     A/R CORRECTION     GJ01-0005                        73.15
                           JE12-07     INVENTORY-12/8     GJ01-0010     19,953.49
                                                  MONTH  12 TOTAL       19,953.49         73.15        19,850.34
                                                  ACCOUNT BALANCE       992,967.22        73.15

0001220 ACCTS REC - EMPLOYEES                     PREVIOUS BALANCE-          .00             .00
                                                  ACCOUNT BALANCE            .00             .00

0001230 INTERCOMPANY PAYROLL REC                  PREVIOUS BALANCE-          .00             .00
                                                  ACCOUNT BALANCE            .00             .00

0001240 ACCTS REC - OTHER                         PREVIOUS BALANCE-     199,912.98           .00
                                                  ACCOUNT BALANCE       199,912.98           .00

0001260 NOTES RECEIVABLE                          PREVIOUS BALANCE-          .00             .00
                                                  ACCOUNT BALANCE            .00             .00

0001280 INTEREST RECEIVABLE                       PREVIOUS BALANCE-      40,142.16           .00
                                                  ACCOUNT BALANCE        40,142.16           .00

0001290 ALLOW FOR DOUBTFUL ACCTS                  PREVIOUS BALANCE-          .00        96,738.88
                           JE12-17     ALLOW BAD DEBTS    GJ01-0018       350.00
                                                  MONTH  12 TOTAL        350.00             .00          350.00
                                                  ACCOUNT BALANCE        350.00         96,738.88

0001300 RAW MATERIAL INVENTORY                    PREVIOUS BALANCE-     525,862.64           .00
                           JE12-01     CORRECT NOV ERR    GJ01-0001                     7,500.00
                                                  MONTH  12 TOTAL            .00        7,500.00        7,500.00CR
                                                  ACCOUNT BALANCE       525,862.64      7,500.00

0001320 WORK-IN-PROCESS INVENTORY                 PREVIOUS BALANCE-     755,316.10           .00
```

Courtesy of IBM Corporation.

because of the detailed comparisons made possible by the format of the statement. This report allows the user to

1. Compare the actual results for the reporting period (one month here) to the budgeted results for the period and to the actual results for the same period of the previous year.
2. Make the same comparisons for year-to-date results.

These comparisons highlight departures from planned results and/or past results and support analysis by management so that actions can be taken to correct these deviations when necessary. Also, future plans and budgets may be altered based on these actual results of current activities.

EXHIBIT 12-5   Comparative General Ledger

```
NORTHCREEK IND.    NO. 01          COMPARATIVE GENERAL LEDGER          DATE  6/16/**  TIME 19.51.16  PAGE   1  AMG42
                                        MONTH 12
```

ACCOUNT NUMBER DESCRIPTION	BUDGETED MONTH [1]	SAME MONTH LAST YEAR [1]	CURRENT MONTH	BUDGETED Y-T-D [1]	PREVIOUS Y-T-D [1]	CURRENT Y-T-D [2]
0001000 PETTY CASH	.00	.00	.00	.00	2,173.24	4,587.95
0001050 CASH-IN-BANK - GENERAL	.00	.00	875.70CR	.00	107,785.96	226,672.44
0001060 CASH-IN-BANK - PAYROLL	.00	.00	.00	.00	92,742.49	195,789.70
0001070 CASH-IN-BANK - OTHER	.00	.00	.00	.00	.00	.00
0001100 SHORT TERM INVESTMENTS	.00	.00	.00	.00	193,613.49	408,739.59
0001200 ACCTS REC - TRADE	.00	.00	19,880.34	.00	460,901.24	992,894.07
0001220 ACCTS REC - EMPLOYEES	.00	.00	.00	.00	.00	.00
0001240 ACCTS REC - OTHER	.00	.00	.00	.00	94,695.62	199,912.98
0001260 NOTES RECEIVABLE	.00	.00	.00	.00	.00	.00
0001280 INTEREST RECEIVABLE	.00	.00	.00	.00	19,014.71	40,142.16
0009050 DEFERRED TAX EXPENSE	.00	.00	.00	51,992.47	42,539.29	47,265.86
0009090 OTHER INCOME TAX	.00	.00	.00	.00	.00	.00
0009200 PROVISION FOR PROFIT/LOSS	.00	94,442.33	14,980.34	.00	94,442.33	255,476.34
COMPANY TOTALS	.00		.00 [3]		.00 [3]	
		.00		115,429.48CR		.00

[1]   Last year figures and budget figures are optional.

[2]   This column is similar to a trial balance.

[3]   Indicates the ledger is in balance.

Courtesy of IBM Corporation.

Financial Statements (Exhibits 12-6 and 12-7)

The computer-produced income statement and balance sheet are traditional in format and content. However, both statements contain significant information relevant for managerial decision making, planning, and performance evaluation not often found in financial statements produced by a manual accounting system. This information is particularly important in interim statements (monthly or quarterly) because management can use immediate feedback on the results of operations and activities to spot and correct negative situations and potential problems before it is too late. The most important additional features of these financial statements are

1. *Budgeted and Prior Period Results.* The income statement and the balance sheet can present the current period results of operations and financial position, as well as those of a previous period and/or budgeted figures for the period in both absolute and (for the income statement) percentage terms. Importantly, the variance between periods on each statement item is shown in percentage terms also.

2. *Profit Center Income Statements.* A complete income statement with all of the features just described can be produced for each profit center (department, store,

EXHIBIT 12-6   Income Statement

```
NORTHCREEK IND.   NO. 01          NORTHCREEK INDUSTRIES, INC.      DATE  6/12/**  TIME 11.22.37  PAGE    1    AMG43
                                        ATLANTA, GEORGIA

                                        INCOME STATEMENT
                                     FOR YEAR-TO-DATE 11/30/**
                                                                                                         ┌─┐
                                                                                                         │1│
                                                                                                         └─┘
                               --------C U R R E N T--------   %   --------B U D G E T --------   %   VAR-%

SALES - LESS RETURNS                      4,424,972.83  100.00       4,718,354.04  100.00    6.00-

COST OF GOODS SOLD
   COST OF SALES - MATERIAL           1,594,055.36DR     36.00   1,753,460.90DR     37.00    9.00-
   COST OF SALES - DIRECT LABOR         790,656.88DR     17.00     869,722.57DR     18.00    9.00-

COST OF SALES - MANUFACTURING OVERHEAD
   INDIRECT LABOR                       248,896.39DR      5.00     271,586.02DR      5.00    9.00-
   TOTAL COST OF GOODS SOLD --                      2,631,608.63DR  59.00          2,894,769.49DR  61.00    9.00-

   *** GROSS PROFIT/LOSS FROM SALES     1,793,364.20     40.00       1,823,584.55     38.00    2.00-

MANUFACTURING COSTS --
   PLANT & EQUIPMENT                    313,994.72DR      7.00     345,394.22DR      7.00    9.00-
   MISCELLANEOUS MANUFACTURING COSTS     89,059.99DR      2.00      97,965.99DR      2.00    9.00-
   TOTAL MANUFACTURING COSTS                      403,054.71DR   9.00           443,363.21DR   9.00    9.00-

   *** NET PROFIT/LOSS FROM SALES       1,390,309.49     31.00       1,380,224.34     29.00    1.00

GENERAL AND ADMINISTRATIVE EXPENSES
   SALARIES, COMMISSIONS & FEES         563,021.57DR     12.00     619,323.73DR     13.00    9.00-
   ADMINISTRATIVE EXPENSES               51,471.25DR      1.00      56,618.38DR      1.00    9.00-
   OFFICE EXPENSES                       77,227.98DR      1.00      84,950.78DR      1.00    9.00-
   GENERAL OFFICE EXPENSES               19,329.64DR       .00      21,262.61DR       .00    9.00-
   ADMINISTRATIVE DEPRECIATION EXPENSES   2,110.00DR       .00       2,321.00DR       .00    9.00-
   TOTAL GENERAL & ADMINISTRATIVE EXP             713,160.44DR  16.00           784,476.50DR  16.00    9.00-
   *** NET PROFIT/LOSS FROM OPERATIONS   677,149.05     15.00       595,747.84     12.00   14.00

OTHER INCOME                             40,517.45        .00      44,569.20         .00    9.00-
OTHER EXPENSES                           11,230.00DR      .00      12,353.00DR       .00    9.00-
DISPOSITION OF FIXED ASSETS               6,100.00        .00       6,710.00         .00    9.00-
   TOTAL OTHER INCOME/EXPENSES                      35,367.45   .00            38,926.20   .00    9.00-
   *** PRE-TAX INCOME/LOSS              712,536.50     16.00       634,674.04     13.00   12.00

INCOME TAXES --
   STATE INCOME TAX                     102,002.27DR      2.00     112,202.50DR      2.00    9.00-
   FEDERAL INCOME TAX                   322,772.35DR      7.00     355,049.59         7.00    9.00-
   OTHER INCOME TAX EXPENSES             47,265.88DR      1.00      51,992.47DR      1.00    9.00-
   TOTAL INCOME TAXES                             472,040.50DR  10.00           519,244.56DR  11.00    9.00-

   *** NET PROFIT AFTER TAXES           240,496.00      5.00       115,429.48      2.00  108.00

PROVISION FOR PROFIT/LOSS                     .00        .00             .00        .00
   *** NET PROFIT/LOSS ***              240,496.00      5.00       115,429.48      2.00  108.00
   ┌─┐                                          ┌─┐
   │2│                                          │3│
   └─┘                                          └─┘
```

1   The variance from last year is shown as a percent.

2   This account is used at year-end with the retained earnings account to transfer profit (loss) from the income statement to the balance sheet.

3   Net profit is 5.00% of total sales.

Courtesy of IBM Corporation.

product line) which helps trace companywide operating results to those responsible for producing the results by their decisions and actions.

3. *Tailored Statements.* Both the income statement and balance sheet can be presented in any format and detail specified by the user. Most accounting subsystems offer flexibility so that the income statement and balance sheet can be tailored to the information needs and particular circumstances of the user. Also, the format and detail can be different for different time periods.

4. *SCF Worksheet.* In addition to the income statement and balance sheet, a worksheet for the statement of cash flows can be produced by the financial accounting subsystem.

EXHIBIT 12-7   Partial Balance Sheet

```
NORTHCREEK IND.    NO. 01          NORTHCREEK INDUSTRIES, INC.        DATE  6/16/**  TIME 19.52.14  PAGE    1  AMG44
                                        ATLANTA, GEORGIA
                                    B A L A N C E   S H E E T
                                    AT DECEMBER 31, 19**

                              --------------C U R R E N T-------------- ---------- L A S T  Y E A R------------- VAR-%

ASSETS

CURRENT ASSETS

CASH AND SHORT TERM INVESTMENTS              835,789.68                           396,315.18                     111.00

ACCOUNTS RECEIVABLE
  ACCOUNTS RECEIVABLE             1,192,807.05                        555,596.86                                 115.00
  OTHER RECEIVABLES                  40,142.16                         19,014.71                                 111.00
  LESS ALLOWANCE FOR DOUBTFUL ACCOUNTS  96,388.88CR                    45,823.68CR                              110.00
  ACCOUNTS RECEIVABLE                        1,136,560.33                          528,787.89                   115.00

INVENTORY                                  1,829,651.15                           941,282.12                    94.00

PREPAID EXPENSES                              14,149.96                             6,702.62                    111.00

   TOTAL CURRENT ASSETS                                 3,816,151.12                        1,873,087.81        104.00

FIXED ASSETS -----

LAND & BUILDINGS                  1,454,355.00                        688,905.00                                111.00
  LESS - DEPRECIATION               118,628.33CR                       54,676.58CR                             117.00
  --- TOTAL LAND AND BUILDINGS              1,335,726.67                           634,728.42                   111.00
CAPITAL EQUIPMENT                 2,124,063.18                        999,817.20                               112.00
  LESS - DEPRECIATION               168,154.18CR                       78,680.93CR                             114.00
   TOTAL CAPITAL EQUIPMENT                  1,955,909.00                           921,136.27                   112.00
   TOTAL FIXED ASSETS                                   3,291,635.67                        1,555,364.59        112.00

INVESTMENTS                         421,853.20                        199,825.20                               111.00
OTHER ASSETS                          3,230.00                          1,530.00                               111.00
   INVESTMENTS AND OTHER ASSETS              425.083.20                            201,355.20                   111.00

   ***** TOTAL ASSETS *****                             7,532,869.99                        3,629,807.70        108.00
```

Courtesy of IBM Corporation.

It is clear from studying these output reports that there is no accounting mystery at work in computer-based systems. The output a user should expect from a computer-based accounting system is fundamentally no different from that provided by a manual accounting system. The advantages that these output reports offer (a variety of information readily available and improved frequency, accuracy, and timeliness) result from the computer characteristics of incredible speed and enormous memory. The section that follows will discuss the data organization and input necessary for a financial accounting subsystem to produce these output reports.

FINANCIAL ACCOUNTING SYSTEM: INPUTS

The number of files required for financial accounting processing and the content and design of each will vary according to the orientation and hardware configuration of the system, the sophistication of the processing, the kinds of output reports desired or needed, and the size of the business. Most important, file design will depend on what other processing modules are installed and the interfaces among these modules. A business' data base is its collection of stored

420

PART III
Computer-
Based
Accounting
Applications

CONCEPT SUMMARY

Output Reports from a Financial Accounting Subsystem

Report	When Produced	Information	Differences from Manual System
General journal	During accounting period as desired	Transactions which have occurred during the period that do not fit into one of the special journals	1. Uses one line for both debit and credit effect 2. Each transaction is assigned a unique reference number 3. Account titles are not used
Preliminary general ledger	End of accounting period	Shows for each account 1. Beginning balance 2. Total debits and credits 3. Ending balance	Manual system trial balance shows only the ending balance for each account
Comparative general ledger	End of accounting period	Comparison of actual results for the period to budgeted results for the period and to actual results from the previous period	Manual system trial balance shows only the actual results for the current period
Financial statements	End of accounting period	Income statement, statement of retained earnings (owners' capital), and balance sheet for current period and previous period in absolute and percentage terms for the whole company or by profit center	Financial statements produced by a manual system normally focus on the current period results of operations and financial position

data. This collection of stored data should be organized so that all processing modules requiring the same basic data input (although perhaps in different form) can access and use the same files of stored data.

421

CHAPTER 12
*Financial
and
Managerial
Accounting
Systems*

Input Files for the General Ledger Module

The financial accounting subsystem will require several files of data input in order to operate. Following are the major files necessary for the general ledger module.

General Ledger Master File.   The **general ledger master file** consists of one record for each general ledger account in the company's chart of accounts. Each record contains at least the following data elements:

1. Account number
2. Account description
3. Account classification (asset, liability, owners' equity, revenue, expense, contra or adjunct account)
4. Current year balances—by month
5. Current year total debits and total credits—by month
6. Previous year balances—by month
7. Budgeted balances—by month

This file is updated with each processing cycle, then stored, and used again as input to the following processing cycle. It is, therefore, both an input and an output file and is the data base for most of the financial accounting output reports and statements discussed earlier.

General Ledger Format File.   The **general ledger format file** consists of one record for each line of the income statement and balance sheet (and statement of cash flows worksheet). Each record contains at least the following components:

1. Account number
2. Account title
3. Account definition (heading, subtotal, total, column)
4. Other format information

Since this file defines and structures each financial statement, it is input to each processing run, unchanged by the processing, and used again as input to the next cycle.

Current Period Transaction File.   The **current period transaction file** consists of one record for each detailed and verified accounting transaction occurring during the current period. Input data from this file is used to update the general ledger master file and is also added to the permanent transaction file discussed next. The current transaction file is an input file only and is the data base for the current period general journal discussed earlier.

422

Part III
*Computer-
Based
Accounting
Applications*

CONCEPT SUMMARY

Files for a Financial Accounting Subsystem

Type of File	Input/Output	Contents	Batch System	Interactive System
General ledger master file	Input and output	One permanent record for each general ledger account with data-items for identification, description, classification, and account balances	Magnetic tape or disk	Disk
Current period transaction file	Input	One record for each accounting transaction for the current period with data-items to uniquely identify the transaction and its effect	Disk	Terminal
Cumulative transaction file	Input and output	One record for each accounting transaction for a specified period of time (such as 1, 2, or 5 years) with data-items to uniquely identify each transaction and its effect	Magnetic tape or disk	Disk
General ledger format file	Input—used repeatedly unchanged	One record for each line on a financial statement with data-items to identify format and content	Magnetic tape or disk	Disk

Cumulative Transaction File. The **cumulative transaction file** is a cumulative listing of all of the individual period transaction files. Unlike the current transaction file, this file is retained as a permanent file. It stores all the detailed and verified accounting transactions for a long period of time (perhaps a year or more) and is an important input and output file for legal, income tax, and audit trail purposes. The file is input to each processing cycle, added to, and then stored until the next processing run. The cumulative transaction file is the book of original entry and the chronological transaction history of the business that supports all reports, and to which all information in the system should ultimately be traceable. It is also important backup to other financial accounting subsystem files.

Other Files. In addition to the preceding files, summarized transaction files from the accounts receivable, accounts payable, and payroll modules are passed on to the financial accounting subsystem and added to the current month's transaction file. The general ledger master file and the permanent transaction file are updated for, and include the data processed by, these other modules.

Batch Versus On-Line System

In a sequential, batch-oriented system, the general ledger master file and permanent transaction file will likely be stored on magnetic tape, and the current transaction file will probably be input off-line to magnetic tape or disk for later use. A direct access, on-line system will use magnetic disks for the permanent files and will probably use an on-line terminal or workstation device to input current transactions. Exhibit 12-8 is an illustration of a terminal display of a typical accounting journal entry as it would appear in an on-line system after being entered by an operator.

EXHIBIT 12-8   Display of Accounting Journal Entry

```
DATE 08/16/**                    GENERAL LEDGER              ENTER      AMG021  Y2
                              JOURNAL TRANSACTION ENTRY

COMPANY NUMBER   01                                    POSTING DATE    12/12/**
                                                       POSTING PERIOD     08
SEQUENCE NUMBER 00002
                              DEBIT        DEBIT      CREDIT        CREDIT
SOURCE      DESCRIPTION     ACCOUNT     AMOUNT(2)    ACCOUNT      AMOUNT(2)

SEQ7-04     AUTO.TRUCK      0001555     00000120000   0006020     00000120000




                                                       CK03 PAGE BACKWARD
                                                       CK17 ACCEPT W/ERROR
                                                       CK24 DISPLAY STATUS
```

Courtesy of IBM Corporation.

423

CHAPTER 12
Financial
and
Managerial
Accounting
Systems

424

Part III
Computer-
Based
Accounting
Applications

To produce these journal entries, each area of the company collects the source documents (sales and purchase invoices, debit and credit memos, and so on) that support the transactions. The data from these documents are then entered on to a standard journal entry form. After accuracy checks and control-oriented verifications, the operator actually enters the transactions from the journal entry form into the system using a workstation terminal.

OVERVIEW OF A MANUFACTURING SYSTEM

Chapter 9 gives an overview of the information flow in a manufacturing subsystem. Refer to Exhibits 9-1 and 9-6 to refresh your memory as to the place of the manufacturing subsystem in the total information system and the interaction between this and other subsystems and modules. As the exhibit shows, the four primary modules in the subsystem are for product data management (PDM), material requirements planning (MRP), production costing (PC), and production monitoring (PM).

PRODUCT DATA MANAGEMENT MODULE

Exhibit 12-9 illustrates the information flow through a product data management module. This module maintains basic (and semipermanent) information about manufactured products, such as expected and historical costs, and the manufacturing process and production facilities required to make the product.

EXHIBIT 12-9   Information Flow Through a Product Data Management Module

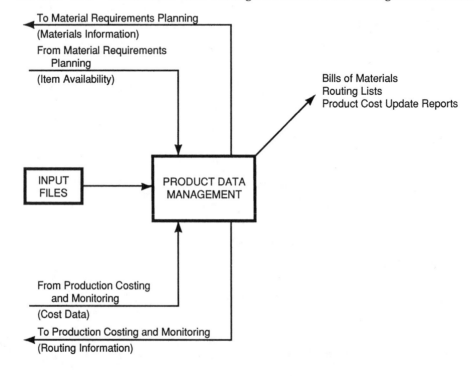

Specifically, this module is concerned with maintaining

425

CHAPTER 12
Financial
and
Managerial
Accounting
Systems

1. Bills of materials that describe the individual materials and components used in the manufacture of a product.
2. Manufacturing routings that describe the sequence of operations and departments required to produce the product.
3. Work center information that describes the physical facilities used to produce the product.
4. The manufactured cost of the product resulting from the bills of materials (components) and routings and work center information (labor and overhead).

Within the PDM module, the business can define standard and optional product features, cost each product feature, and simulate cost changes that may occur as design or other changes are implemented.

Like other modules, PDM operations start with the main menu given in Exhibit 12-10. Also given in Exhibit 12-10 for illustrative purposes are two widely used submenus (options 1 and 3) of the main menu.

PDM Output Reports

The PDM module produces several output reports used in controlling the manufacturing process. The most important of these are bills of materials, routing reports, and costing reports.

Bills of Materials. One of these reports is produced for each product or subassembly manufactured. The **bill of materials** lists each component going into a product, and the current or standard cost of that component. When the component is itself a subassembly, the bill of materials can list the components

EXHIBIT 12-10   Product Data Management Main and Submenus

```
**********                              *************           **


                         MENU: AMEM00

             P R O D U C T   D A T A   M A N A G E M E N T
                              Main Menu

                     1 Inquiry
                     2 Reports
                     3 Costing
                     4 File Maintenance
                     5 Yield Calculation
                     6 Return to Application Selection Menu








     Enter number nn                    For another application or menu,
                                        enter program or menu name aaaaA6
```

Exhibit continues on next page

426

Part III
Computer-
Based
Accounting
Applications

EXHIBIT 12-10   Product Data Management Main and Submenus (continued)

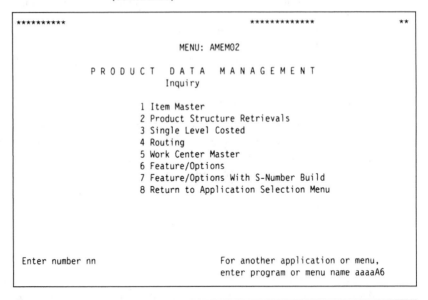

```
**********                    *************        **


                    MENU: AMEM02

         P R O D U C T   D A T A   M A N A G E M E N T
                       Inquiry

                  1 Item Master
                  2 Product Structure Retrievals
                  3 Single Level Costed
                  4 Routing
                  5 Work Center Master
                  6 Feature/Options
                  7 Feature/Options With S-Number Build
                  8 Return to Application Selection Menu




     Enter number nn               For another application or menu,
                                   enter program or menu name aaaaA6
```

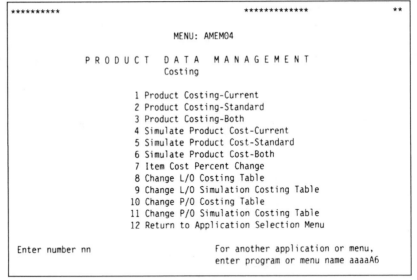

```
**********                    *************        **


                    MENU: AMEM04

         P R O D U C T   D A T A   M A N A G E M E N T
                       Costing

                  1 Product Costing-Current
                  2 Product Costing-Standard
                  3 Product Costing-Both
                  4 Simulate Product Cost-Current
                  5 Simulate Product Cost-Standard
                  6 Simulate Product Cost-Both
                  7 Item Cost Percent Change
                  8 Change L/O Costing Table
                  9 Change L/O Simulation Costing Table
                 10 Change P/O Costing Table
                 11 Change P/O Simulation Costing Table
                 12 Return to Application Selection Menu

     Enter number nn                 For another application or menu,
                                     enter program or menu name aaaaA6
```

Courtesy of IBM Corporation.

of that subassembly, if desired. In addition, when products have options the module can produce a bill of materials (detailed or summarized) for each available option. The module can also produce on-demand separate reports showing (1) all the options and features available for each product manufactured, and/or (2) all products requiring a specific material or component.

Routing Reports (Exhibit 12-11).   **Routing reports** give the exact paths through the manufacturing process (work center by work center) for each prod-

427

CHAPTER 12
Financial
and
Managerial
Accounting
Systems

uct being produced. The steps shown can be uncosted or costed at either current or standard costs. The **routing list** for strawberry shampoo illustrated in Exhibit 12-11 is uncosted, but the report gives a description of the steps of the process, where those steps occur, and the time expectations for machine, labor, and setup for each step. This report results from option 4 of the Inquiry submenu illustrated in Exhibit 12-10.

Costing Reports (Exhibit 12-12). **Costing reports** come in a variety of formats and can show either actual or simulated ("what if") costs. The **product cost update report** shown in Exhibit 12-12 (page 428) results from choosing option 1 of the Costing submenu illustrated in Exhibit 12-10. The report gives a wealth of cost data, including costs by product for two levels of activity broken into four cost categories, as well as total unit costs for past and present periods and the percentage variation between the two.

PDM Input Files

In addition to the item master file discussed in Chapter 11 in connection with the inventory management module, the PDM module requires at least two additional master files and a transaction file in order to operate.

Product Structure Master File. The **product structure master file** states the relationship between each raw material, component, or subassembly and the finished manufactured product. The quantity of each type of input required to produce a finished product is given; thus, this file is the basis for the bill of materials report discussed earlier.

Routing/Work Center Master File. The **routing/work center master file** provides information on each specific operation required for each different

EXHIBIT 12-11 Routing Report

```
THE PDM FIRM                    ROUTING LIST                    DATE 08/30/**  TIME 08.39.44  PAGE    1  AMEG11

ITEM NO. 19333        STRAWBERRY SHAMPOO                U/M OZ  I/T 2  ENGR DRAW

---OPERATION----    TIME -----RUN------  ---SETUP---  W/C ID       QUEUE  MOVE  OPERATION  --OPERATION YIELD--  DATE LAST
SEQ MS DESCRIPTION  BASIS MACHINE LABOR  TIME  CREW   DESCRIPTION  DAYS   DAYS  STATUS     STD   CUR   AVG      MAINTAINED
0010  MAKE PRODUCT BASE  4  .00  1.00   2.00   1      MIX40         .00   ACTIVE     1.000 1.000 1.000   2/25/**
              AVERAGE     .00   .00    .00            MIX SHAMPOO
0020  HEAT TO 150 DEGREES 4  .00  2.00   .00   1      MIX           .00   ACTIVE      .950  .950 1.000   2/25/**
              AVERAGE     .00   .00    .00            MIX SHAMPOO
0030  COOL TO 120 DEGREES 4  .00   .50   .00   1      MIX           .00   ACTIVE     1.000 1.000 1.000   2/25/**
              AVERAGE     .00   .00    .00            MIX SHAMPOO
      001  USE OVEN NO 237
0040  MIX FRAGRANCE & DYE 4  .00   .50   .00   1      MIX           .00   ACTIVE     1.000 1.000 1.000   2/25/**
              AVERAGE     .00   .00    .00            MIX SHAMPOO
0050  TEST COLOR          4  .00   .25   .00   1      TEST          .00   ACTIVE      .970  .970 1.000   2/25/**
              AVERAGE     .00   .00    .00            TEST SHAMPOO
0060  TEST VISCOSITY      4  .00   .25   .00   1      TEST          .00   ACTIVE      .970  .970 1.000   2/25/**
              AVERAGE     .00   .00    .00            TEST SHAMPOO
```

Courtesy of IBM Corporation.

EXHIBIT 12-12   Product Cost Update Report—Current Costs

```
    NORTHCREEK IND.            PRODUCT COST UPDATE REPORT          DATE 4/03/** TIME 11.09.18 PAGE 61  AMEJ10
   SELECT DATE  4/03/**             CURRENT COSTS
   LAST CURRENT 4/03/**            FOR MULTIPLE ITEMS
            RCST U/ I I/ COST                                                                               VAR
ITEM NUMBER  FLAG /M T /C TECH     -------THIS LEVEL-------  --------LOWER LEVELS--------  -----UNIT COSTS------ PCT
   DESCRIPTION


90034          EA 2 05   R             CURR OLD   CURR NEW    CURR OLD     CURR NEW    CURR OLD    CURR NEW
   FENDER, 90 DEGREE       PURCHASE      .0000      .0000     9.428800     9.428800
                           P-OVERHD      .0000      .0000      .000000      .000000
   CUR COST STATUS CD- L   LABOR      12.9572    12.9572     4.153800     4.153800     59.8846     63.0509   5.3
   STD BATCH QTY    1.000  L-OVERHD   18.0401    20.6634    15.304600    16.468300
                        W AM-4866 COST STATUS FOR A LL COMP IS NANK
                        W AM-4875 THIS-LEVEL LABOR IS ZERO OR NEE

98908          EA 4 80                 CURR OLD   CURR NEW    CURR OLD     CURR NEW    CURR OLD    CURR NEW
   WASHER                  PURCHASE      .0051      .0051      .000000      .000000
                           P-OVERHD      .0000      .0000      .000000      .000000
   CUR COST STATUS CD-L    LABOR         .0000      .0000      .000000      .000000      .0051       .0051   0.0
   STD BATCH QTY    1.000  L-OVERHD      .0000      .0000      .000000      .000000

99001          EA 1 10   R             CURR OLD   CURR NEW    CURR OLD     CURR NEW    CURR OLD    CURR NEW
   B SPRAY UNIT            PURCHASE    7.0314     7.0314    53.422900    56.785900
                           P-OVERHD      .0000      .0000      .000000     0.000000
   CUR COST STATUS CD-L    LABOR      12.7418    11.4366    61.487200    58.395100    246.1113    247.2705   0.5
   STD BATCH QTY    1.000  L-OVERHD   16.5391    18.7388    94.882900    94.882900
                        W AM-4866 COST STATUS FOR A LL COMP IS NANK

99001-1        EA 1 10   R             CURR OLD   CURR NEW    CURR OLD     CURR NEW    CURR OLD    CURR NEW
   B SPRAY UNIT            PURCHASE    7.0314     7.0314    53.422900    56.785700
                           P-OVERHD      .0000      .0000      .000000     0.000000
   CUR COST STATUS CD-L    LABOR      12.7478    11.4366    61.487200    58.395100    246.1113    247.2705   0.5
   STD BATCH QTY    1.000  L-OVERHD   16.5391    18.7388    94.882900    94.882900
                        W AM-4866 COST STATUS FOR A LL COMP IS NANK

99237-RM       EA 3 30                 CURR OLD   CURR NEW    CURR OLD     CURR NEW    CURR OLD    CURR NEW
   PLATED CYLINDER 8 IN    PURCHASE   10.4551    10.4551      .000000      .000000
                           P-OVERHD      .0000      .0000      .000000      .000000
   CUR COST STATUS CD-     LABOR         .0000      .0000      .000000      .000000     10.4551     10.4551   0.0
   STD BATCH QTY    5.000  L-OVERHD  725.9572      .0000      .000000      .000000

99238-RM       EA 3 30                 CURR OLD   CURR NEW    CURR OLD     CURR NEW    CURR OLD    CURR NEW
   PLATED CYLINDER 10 IN   PURCHASE   12.7786    12.7786      .000000      .000000
                           P-OVERHD      .0000      .0000      .000000      .000000
   CUR COST STATUS CD-L    LABOR         .0000      .0000      .000000      .000000     12.7786     12.7786   0.0
   STD BATCH QTY    5.000  L-OVERHD      .0000      .0000      .000000      .000000
```

Courtesy of IBM Corporation.

manufacturing routing. There may be fewer routings than products, however, since several different products may follow the same basic manufacturing routing. This file provides a description of each operation, the work center in which the operation occurs, the average and standard times for setup and run, and the machines/tools required to perform the operation.

Transaction File. A transaction file of changes (product design, engineering relationships, manufacturing process) to the product structure and routing/work station files is necessary to keep these files current and accurate.

PDM Interfaces

The product data management module provides critical information about required materials to the material requirements planning (purchasing) module. Based on the bills of materials generated in PDM, material requirements will be updated and orders placed when the quantity on hand of a particular item falls below a stated level. The bill of materials information also notifies material requirements planning of any changes in required materials, materials no longer needed, or new materials required. The material requirements planning module, in turn, provides information about item availability to product data management for routing and scheduling purposes. The production costing and monitoring module takes information from the routing reports of PDM as input in order to schedule production runs, and passes actual cost data back to the product data management module as products are manufactured.

429

CHAPTER 12
*Financial
and
Managerial
Accounting
Systems*

MATERIAL REQUIREMENTS PLANNING MODULE

The information flow through an MRP (purchasing) module is given in Exhibit 12-13. This module accomplishes in a manufacturing environment most of the complex purchasing functions that are carried out by the inventory management module (Chapter 11) in a nonmanufacturing environment. The MRP module controls all purchasing activities from the initiation of a purchase requisition (request for materials or components), to the creation of a purchase order, to the receipt of the goods and purchase invoice. Purchase orders can be generated automatically by this module at predetermined times or when specific prede-

EXHIBIT 12-13   Information Flow Through a Material Requirements Planning Module

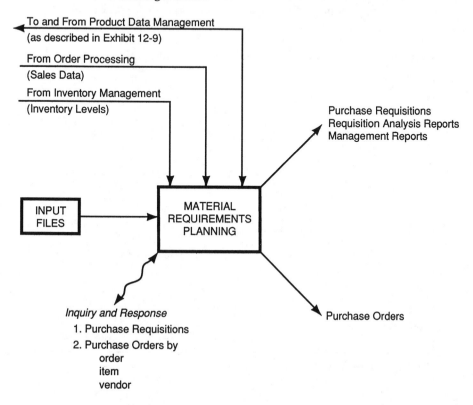

430

Part III
Computer-
Based
Accounting
Applications

termined conditions are met, or can be entered into the system from a work-station at any time.

MRP Output Reports

The MRP (purchasing) main menu is given in Exhibit 12-14. For illustrative purposes, we will focus on menu options 1 and 3 in our discussion of MRP processing. The most important reports processed by MRP are **purchase requisitions** and **purchase orders** and various requisition and order analysis reports.

Purchase Requisitions (Exhibit 12-15). The first step in the creation of a purchase order (other than those preplanned orders created automatically by the system) is a request by a department or workstation for the purchase of materials or components (a purchase requisition). The upper portion of Exhibit 12-15 shows a workstation purchase requisition entry display. Note that the requisition form layout can be the same as that of a purchase order, which saves time and improves document accuracy. At predetermined times or on demand, this module can generate several different purchase requisition analysis reports. The lower portion of Exhibit 12-15 illustrates one such report, a listing of purchase requisitions prioritized according to a formula specified by the user.

Purchase Orders (Exhibit 12-16). The MRP module can print purchase orders for a manufacturing firm in several formats. This allows for the possi-

EXHIBIT 12-14   Material Requirements Planning Main Menu

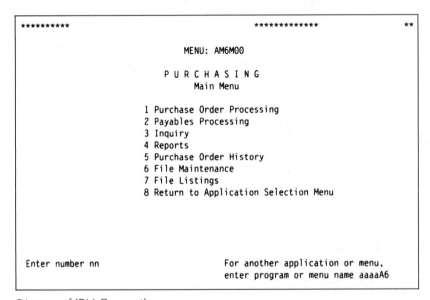

```
**********                          *************           **
                    MENU: AM6M00

                    P U R C H A S I N G
                         Main Menu

                1 Purchase Order Processing
                2 Payables Processing
                3 Inquiry
                4 Reports
                5 Purchase Order History
                6 File Maintenance
                7 File Listings
                8 Return to Application Selection Menu




    Enter number nn                For another application or menu,
                                   enter program or menu name aaaaA6
```

Courtesy of IBM Corporation.

EXHIBIT 12-15   Purchase Requisitions

```
DATE 11/30/**                   PURCHASING              ADD       AM64B2  WB
                         REQUISITION ENTRY AND EDIT

REQUISITION NUMBER R 000092     REQUISITION DATE   11/30/**  REVISION #

            ITEM  7362917       DESC  PLANNAR ASSY
--------------------------------------------------------------------------

EXT. DESCRIPTION

QUANTITY        25              DATES-
U/M       EA                    TO DOCK
WHSE      1                     TO STOCK     1215**
SHIP-TO ID                      FOLLOW-UP
ACCOUNT         1000            LAST MAINT
DEPT      656
CONTRACT
PRIORITY                        REQUISITIONER  CHUCK R.
JOB NUMBER  123450              PURCHASE ORDER P757100
REF NUMBER  L56122              PRICE          1550.0000
                                        F09 REQ COMMENTS
                                        F19 RETURN TO SELECT
                                        F24 DISPLAY STATUS
```

```
USER ID ALISON          ABC COMPANY        PURCHASING    DATE 2/07/**   TIME 11.38.31  AM62C1   PAGE   1

         REQUISITION ANALYSIS PRIORITIZED BY CRITICAL RATIO - LEAD TIME /  REQUESTED DUE DATE
                             BUYER RANGE FROM BEGINNING TO END

                         DEPARTMENT RANGE BEGINNING TO END
BUYER

REQ    PRITY    C/R   W   ITEM      REQN    DUE     DUE    QUANTITY  U/     VALUE    DEPT   ACCOUNT  REQ ID
NO.    MGT            H   NUMBER    DATE    DOCK    STOCK            /M
ITEM DESC                          EXTENDED DESCRIPTION
--------------------------------------------------------------------------------------------------------
R000080   109.90    1   2397045   4/23/**  5/26/**  5/27/**  1,000  EA    .0000                      AUTOREL
          LED,LIGHT

R000081   188.75    1   55901     3/30/**  4/13/**  4/15/**    149  EA    .0000                      AUTOREL
          WASHER,LOCK,EXT T,.172IDX.380D

   NUMBER OF RECORDS            2

   TOTAL VALUE            .0000
```

Courtesy of IBM Corporation.

bility of single or multiple items being ordered and one or several different delivery dates and ship-to addresses being requested. Exhibit 12-16 presents a purchase order for multiple items with several delivery dates and different ship-to addresses. This report would result from the use of option 1 of the main menu given in Exhibit 12-14.

MRP routinely produces numerous other management-oriented reports. The module can supply reports focusing on (1) the current status of purchase orders in the system, (2) the difference between standard and actual costs for purchased materials or components, and (3) the amounts of cash the business is committed to disburse in specified future periods for purchase orders placed, but not yet received or invoiced.

EXHIBIT 12-16   Purchase Order

```
YOUR FIRM NAME HERE
123 Main Street
YOUR TOWN,STATE and ZIP
Phone 123-4567
```
```
PO NBR-REV
P000135-00
```

VENDOR	SHIP TO	
P. GREGORY CORPORATION 1155 JEFFERSON ST ATLANTA, GA. 43455-1287	NORTHCREEK IND. RIVEREDGE PARKWAY BLDG R1 ATLANTA, GA. 30057-0331	PAGE 1

```
BILL TO
NORTHCREEK IND.
RIVEREDGE PARKWAY
BLDG R1
ATLANTA, GA. 30057-0331
```

PO DATE	VENDOR	SHIP VIA	FOB	TERMS	DELIV DATE
8/07/**	066362	AIR FREIGHT	YOUR DOCK	MAX 1-10 NET 60	SEE BODY

ORDER PLACED WITH	FREIGHT	BUYER	404-956-4444
RON LAMBERT			BUYER 4 MAX 4

	QUANTITY	UM	UNIT PRICE	AMOUNT
75219 22715 VALVE DATE 8/10/**	20	EA	8.0000	160.00

43602   F00010
   FASTENER
   LAST QTY RECD.   1000 ON 8/15/**
	BLANKET	EA	.0750	

** DROP SHIPMENT **   DELIVER BY 8/18/**
 	
   TO NORTHCREEK IND
   BLDG R2
   ATLANTA GA 30057-0331
	1000			75.00

** DROP SHIPMENT **   DELIVER BY 8/22/**
 	
   TO NORTHCREEK IND
   BLDG R3
   ATLANTA GA 30057-0331
	1000			75.00

354221 WH008 9 IN WHEEL DATE 8/10/**	40	EA	4.0000	160.00

** ORDER CONFIRMATION REQUIRED BY 8/27/** **	TOTAL	470.00

```
AUTHORIZED BY
```

Courtesy of IBM Corporation.

Inquiries (Exhibit 12-17 and Exhibit 12-18).   At any stage in the requisition-order-invoice process, the MRP module can provide information in response to user inquiries. Exhibit 12-17 illustrates workstation screens of responses to purchase requisition inquiries based on requisition number and item number. Exhibit 12-18 (page 434) gives displays of available system information on one specific purchase order and on all open purchase orders for a specific item cross-referenced to the appropriate purchase order. Also available are inquiries showing all open purchase orders for a given vendor.

EXHIBIT 12-17   **Requisition Inquiries**

433

CHAPTER 12
Financial
and
Managerial
Accounting
Systems

```
DATE    2/07/**         REQUISITION INQUIRY           INQUIRY    AM61E2   WB
                           BY REQUISITION


REQUISITION #  R 000102     STATUS  OPEN      ORDER           DATE   2/07/**

ITEM # 9486340            DESCRIPTION  PLASTIC PELLETS
EXT. DESCRIPTION


QUANTITY            75        LEAD TIMES          DATES
U/M        LB                 VENDOR        25    REQUISITION     12/09/**
WHAREHOUSE  1                 DOCK/STOCK     5    TO DOCK         12/19/**
SHIP-TO ID  000               REVIEW             TO STOCK        12/22/**
ACCOUNT                       SAFETY             FOLLOW-UP
DEPARTMENT                                       LAST MAINTENANCE 12/09/**
PRIORITY                      BUYER         00100
JOB NUMBER                    PLANNER       00100
REF NUMBER                    ITEM CLASS    RM
REQUISITIONER  BURNIE         PACKING CODE


UNIT PRICE(LB)           .0175           F09  DISPLAY COMMENTS
EXTENDED PRICE          1.3125           F19  RETURN TO SELECT
                                         F24  END OF JOB
```

```
DATE    2/07/**         REQUISITION INQUIRY           INQUIRY    AM61F2   WB
                           BY ITEM NUMBER

ITEM #      1940              WASHER,FLAT,#10X9/160DX3/64THK


                   ORD        DOCK         PRICE     STK
REQ #     QUANTITY  U/M  DATE  STOCK        VALUE      UM REQUISITIONER

RTEST       100.000  EA  4/29/** 12/30/**       .0150 EA    VAMBO
                                12/30/**       1.5000


R00123A 1,000,000.000 EA 4/29/**  5/23/**       .0150 EA    HL
                                 6/01/**    15,000.0000     ORDER P989178


R00123B      10.000  EA  4/29/**  5/23/**       .0150 EA    HL
                                 6/01/**        .1500       ORDER P989094


R00123C      10.000  EA  4/29/**  5/23/**       .0150 EA    HL
                                 6/01/**        .1500


                                         F02  PAGE FORWARD
                                         F19  RETURN TO SELECT
MORE REQUISITIONS TO DISPLAY             F24  END OF JOB
```

Courtesy of IBM Corporation.

MRP Input Files

The MRP module requires a combination of the files already discussed in connection with other modules in order to function. Specifically, the vendor master and item master files as well as the new purchase orders file (discussed in Chapters 10 and 11) would be needed. In addition, a quantity price file similar

434

PART III
Computer-
Based
Accounting
Applications

EXHIBIT 12-18 Purchase Order Inquiries

```
DATE  2/07/**                    PURCHASING          INQUIRY    AM61A3  Y2

                 PURCHASE ORDER INQUIRY - P.O. DETAIL

ORDER P989060  STATUS 20  CONTRACT        ITEM CLASS  5X   PACKING CODE

  ITEM 1940          WASHER,FLAT,#10X9/16ODX3/64THK WH 1      REQ# R000025

STOCK UM   EA      PURCH UM   OZ      CONV FACT    12.00    PLANNER 00300

WHOUSE LOCATION    J2111  DEPARTMENT  A715  BUY CODE
QUANTITY -                DATES -
ORDERED              150  ORDERED         4/29/**
DEVIATION           .000  DUE TO DOCK
AT DOCK             .000  DUE TO STOCK
INSPECT            .000  FIRST DELIVERY
SCRAPPED           .000                        F05 ITEM DETAIL
RETRN/VNDR         .000  LAST ACTIVITY          F06 MULTIPLE RELEASE
IN STOCK           .000  LAST MAINTAIN  4/29/** F07 OPERATIONS
                         COSTS -                F09 ITEM COMMENTS
                         UNIT COST       .0150  F10 ALTERNATE U/M
                         EXTND COST     1.5000  F13 ORDER SUMMARY
                                                F19 RETURN TO SELECT
                                                F24 END OF JOB
```

```
DATE 11/30/**                    PURCHASING         INQUIRY    AM61B2  WB

                 ALL OPEN ORDERS FOR AN ITEM
                                                      STOCK UM EA
  ITEM  7362917       WH  1   PLANNAR ASSY             PURCH UM EA

  ORDER     DUE      QUANTITY      QUANTITY ORDER  MULT RCVD ORDER REQN
            DATE     ORDERED         OPEN    UM  BL SHIP STAT STAT  NO.

P989149 12/15/**        30         30.C00  EA  N           10  R000090
P989150  1/04/**        30         30.000  EA  N           20  R000091




                                                F02 PAGE FORWARD
                                                F10 ALTERNATE U/M
                         CONV FACT 1.00         F19 RETURN TO SELECT
END OF DATA                                     F24 END OF JOB
```

Courtesy of IBM Corporation.

to the one discussed in connection with customer sales order processing (Chapter 11) could be used by MRP in the decision-making process on purchases and the creation of purchase orders.

MRP Interfaces

In order for MRP to operate, it must have access to up-to-date information from product data management in the form of bills of materials. The information on the bills of materials together with information from order processing on actual sales, from budgeting on expected sales, and from inventory management on inventory levels is used to calculate the quantity of materials, components, subassemblies, and other items needed to produce a particular product.

435

CHAPTER 12
Financial
and
Managerial
Accounting
Systems

PRODUCTION COSTING AND MONITORING MODULES

These are actually two separate processing modules (production costing and production monitoring), but they can be effectively discussed together because of the nature of their interaction and overlap. Also, in all but the most complex manufacturing environments, these modules might be collapsed into one, and their functions carried out by a single module. Together these modules

1. Track the detailed costs of production.
2. Report the status of manufacturing orders, work centers, and employees, showing departures (variances) from plans.
3. Monitor the work load at each work center and analyze work center efficiency.

Exhibit 12-19 gives the information flow through a PCM processing module.

EXHIBIT 12-19   Information Flow Through a Production Costing and Monitoring Module

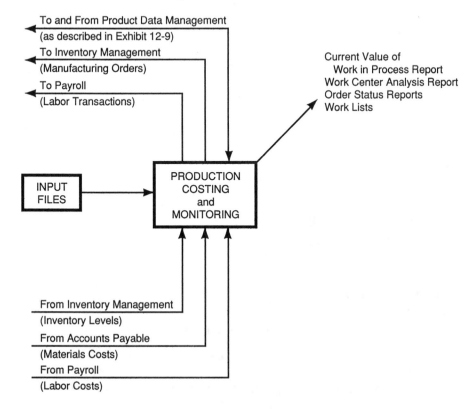

To and From Product Data Management
(as described in Exhibit 12-9)
To Inventory Management
(Manufacturing Orders)
To Payroll
(Labor Transactions)

Current Value of
  Work in Process Report
Work Center Analysis Report
Order Status Reports
Work Lists

INPUT FILES

PRODUCTION COSTING and MONITORING

From Inventory Management
(Inventory Levels)
From Accounts Payable
(Materials Costs)
From Payroll
(Labor Costs)

436

*PART III
Computer-
Based
Accounting
Applications*

EXHIBIT 12-20   Production Costing and Monitoring Main Menus

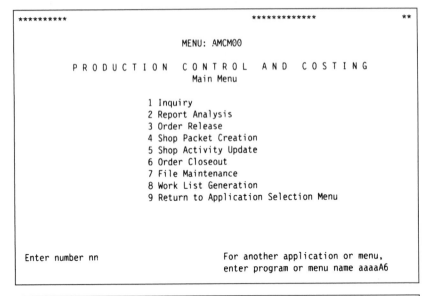

```
**********                      *************           **

                     MENU: AMCM00

       P R O D U C T I O N   C O N T R O L   A N D   C O S T I N G
                          Main Menu


                   1 Inquiry
                   2 Report Analysis
                   3 Order Release
                   4 Shop Packet Creation
                   5 Shop Activity Update
                   6 Order Closeout
                   7 File Maintenance
                   8 Work List Generation
                   9 Return to Application Selection Menu




   Enter number nn                For another application or menu,
                                  enter program or menu name aaaaA6
```

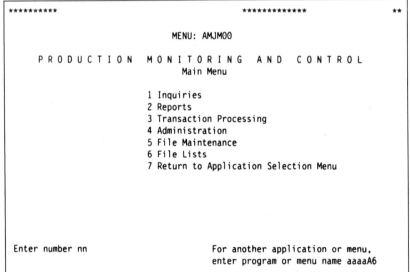

```
**********                      *************           **

                     MENU: AMJM00

       P R O D U C T I O N   M O N I T O R I N G   A N D   C O N T R O L
                          Main Menu


                   1 Inquiries
                   2 Reports
                   3 Transaction Processing
                   4 Administration
                   5 File Maintenance
                   6 File Lists
                   7 Return to Application Selection Menu





   Enter number nn                For another application or menu,
                                  enter program or menu name aaaaA6
```

Courtesy of IBM Corporation.

The main menus for production costing and monitoring are given in Exhibit 12-20.

PCM Output Reports

From these menus, the PCM module generates a range of output including work-in-process, work center, and order status reports.

Current Value of Work-in-Process Report.   The **current value of work-in-process report** shows the total dollar value to date of work-in-process and the movement (transfer) of work-in-process costs during the current period. Costs can be itemized into set-up, material, labor, overhead, miscellaneous, and scrap.

437

CHAPTER 12
*Financial
and
Managerial
Accounting
Systems*

Work Center Analysis Report. Information on the utilization, queue sizes, output, and efficiency for each work center can be printed for management analysis and action in a **work center analysis report.**

Order Status Reports (Exhibit 12-21). **Order status reports** help to point out situations in need of management attention by identifying important char-

EXHIBIT 12-21 Order Status Report Options

```
**********                            *************        **
                          MENU: AMCM21

      P R O D U C T I O N   C O N T R O L   A N D   C O S T I N G
                          Summary Reports

                  1 Order Number Sequence
                  2 WIP Totals Sheet
                  3 Order Due Date Limit Range
                  4 Overdue Orders
                  5 Specific Reference Code
                  6 Specific Customer Job Number
                  7 Order Due Date Sequence
                  8 Reference Code Sequence
                  9 Customer Job Number Sequence
                  10 Critical Orders List
                  11 Return to Report Analysis
                  12 Return to Application Selection Menu



  Enter number nn                    For another application or menu,
                                     enter program or menu name aaaaA6
```

```
  DATE 03/10/**      EXCEPTION ANALYSIS OPTIONS            AMC160  W2



        SELECT ONE OF THE FOLLOWING:

                  1 ACTUAL TIME OVER STANDARD TIME
                  2 ACTUAL COST OVER STANDARD COST
                  3 ACTUAL QUANTITY OVER STANDARD QUANTITY
                  4 ACTUAL QUANTITY UNDER STANDARD QUANTITY
                  5 TIME EFFECTIVITY OVER VALUE
                  6 TIME EFFECTIVITY UNDER VALUE
                  7 COST EFFECTIVITY OVER VALUE
                  8 COST EFFECTIVITY UNDER VALUE
                  9 ORDERS UNDER CRITICAL RATIO VALUE
                  10 ORDERS BY PRIORITY CODE AND VALUE



  ENTER NUMBER
  5
                                     F24 CANCEL THE JOB
```

Courtesy of IBM Corporation.

438

*PART III
Computer-
Based
Accounting
Applications*

acteristics of each manufacturing order, such as where the order is currently located, how long it will take to complete, its actual and standard costs, and other factors. The top portion of Exhibit 12-21 gives a submenu for order status and other summary reports, and the bottom portion illustrates a submenu of the array of exception analysis order status reporting options at the fingertips of management.

Work Lists (Exhibit 12-22). **Work lists by work center** show the center's orders running (currently being worked on), waiting (in the work center, but not currently being worked on), and arriving (not yet in the work center, but expected). The orders are given in priority sequence within each category.

PCM Input Files

Manufacturing Order Summary File. In addition to using the files of other modules, the PCM module requires one new file not previously discussed. The **manufacturing order summary file** brings together in one place all of the information pertaining to each manufacturing order. For each order, information on schedule dates, routings, standard and actual costs accumulated, pertinent purchase orders, and the customer for whom the order is intended would be collected in this file.

EXHIBIT 12-22 Work List by Work Center

Courtesy of IBM Corporation.

PCM Interfaces

439

CHAPTER 12
*Financial
and
Managerial
Accounting
Systems*

Production costing and monitoring requires the implementation of the inventory management module discussed in Chapter 11. In addition, it relies heavily on information from the accounts payable, payroll, and product data management modules. These modules supply up-to-date information on inventory levels, material costs, labor transactions and costs, routing, and scheduling for use by PCM.

CONCEPT SUMMARY

Output Reports from a Manufacturing Subsystem

Module	Output Reports
Product Data Management (PDM)	Bills of Materials Routing Lists Product Cost Update Reports
Materials Requirements Planning (MRP)	Purchase Requisitions Purchase Orders Requisition Analysis Reports Management Reports—Purchase Orders
Production Costing and Monitoring (PCM)	Current Value of Work-in-Process Reports Work Center Analysis Reports Order Status Reports Work Lists

CONCEPT SUMMARY

Files for a Manufacturing Subsystem

Type of File	File	Module
Master	Item Master Vendor Master Product Structure Master Routing/Work Center Master Manufacturing Order Summary Master	PDM, MRP, PCM MRP PDM, PCM PDM, PCM PCM
Current	Product Structure and Routing/Work Center Changes New Purchase Order	PDM MRP
Constant	Quantity Price	MRP

440

PART III
Computer-
Based
Accounting
Applications

CHAPTER SUMMARY

The financial accounting system processes all of the basic accounting activities of a business. Transaction analysis in this system produces the general journal, general ledger, trial balance, external financial statements, and budgets. Most financial accounting systems contain a general ledger module, financial statement module, and budgeting module.

The heart of the financial accounting system is the general ledger module. This module combines a general ledger master file and current period transaction file to produce a general journal, preliminary general ledger, and comparative general ledger and to update the general ledger master file and add to the cumulative transaction file. The financial statement module then uses a general ledger format file in order to produce an income statement, balance sheet, and statement of cash flows worksheet. The budgeting module integrates all of this information together with information from the sales analysis module to provide budgeted statements for the business.

The manufacturing system typically uses a product data management (PDM) module, material requirements planning (MRP) module, and production costing and monitoring (PCM) module to track the production-related activities of a manufacturing business.

PDM maintains semipermanent data about manufactured products through a product structure master file, a routing/work center master file, and a transaction file of product design and manufacturing process changes. The module produces three reports that aid in controlling the manufacturing process: bills of materials, routing reports, and product costing reports.

MRP accomplishes the materials, component, and subassembly purchasing function in a manufacturing environment. It requires the installation of the inventory management module discussed in Chapter 11 and uses information from that module and the vendor master file from Chapter 10 to process purchase requisitions and produce purchase orders, as well as various purchase requisition and order analysis reports for management use.

PCM is a combination of two separate modules that can be integrated in all but the most complex manufacturing environments. This module uses a manufacturing order summary file to keep track of the status of all orders (order status report), work centers (work center analysis report and work lists), and the accumulated costs of production (current value of work in process report).

The financial and managerial systems complete the presentation of the components of a computer-based information system.

KEY TERMS _____

Bill of materials (*p. 425*)
Comparative general ledger
  (*p. 415*)
Costing reports (*p. 427*)
Cumulative transaction file (*p. 423*)
Current period transaction
  file (*p. 421*)

Current value of work-in-process
  report (*p. 436*)
General journal (*p. 414*)
General ledger format file (*p. 421*)
General ledger master file
  (*p. 421*)
General ledger module (*p. 413*)

441

*Chapter 12
Financial
and
Managerial
Accounting
Systems*

QUESTIONS

12-1. What are the sources of input to the general ledger module? List the output which normally results from the general ledger module.

12-2. Discuss how the general journal and special journals in a computer-based system might differ from those of a manual system.

12-3. Identify information that might be included in a computer-based preliminary general ledger that would not be available from a manual system general ledger. How could this additional information be used?

12-4. Give the possible management control uses of the comparative general ledger.

12-5. What data-items should you expect to find included in the general ledger master file? For what purpose(s) would each be included?

12-6. Contrast the storage devices for the general ledger master file and the permanent transaction file in a batch-oriented system to that in an on-line system.

12-7. List the sources of input to the manufacturing subsystem? Which modules are the primary recipients of the output from the manufacturing subsystem?

12-8. Identify the four modules that make up the manufacturing subsystem. Describe the information flow among the four modules. Which two modules might be combined?

12-9. List and describe the output reports of the product data management module. Of the material requirements planning module.

12-10. Identify the input files necessary for the PDM and MRP modules. List the data-items you would expect to find in these files.

PROBLEMS

12-11. The series of steps a business goes through to process data in a manual accounting system is called the accounting cycle. The accounting cycle may be seen as having seven steps. Are these same seven steps accomplished in a computer-based financial accounting subsystem? Is the order of the steps the same? If not, explain why.

12-12. For each of the data-items stored in the general ledger master file, explain why such information is important in a computer-based system. Also, for each data-item, give the output report(s) in which the information is used. Which of these data-items would normally be updated with each processing run?

12-13. The preliminary general ledger and the comparative general ledger are both organized by general ledger account number and present similar information. There are, however, some significant differences in the information content of these reports.

442

PART III

*Computer-
Based
Accounting
Applications*

1. What information is contained in the preliminary general ledger that is not available in the comparative general ledger? Why is this information useful?

2. What information is contained in the comparative general ledger that is not available in the preliminary general ledger? Why is this information useful?

12-14. (*CMA, adapted*) The Argon Hospital is located in Argon County, a well-known summer resort area. The county population doubles during the vacation months (May to August), and hospital activity more than doubles during these months. The hospital is organized into several departments. Although it is a relatively small hospital, its desirable surroundings have attracted a well-trained and competent medical staff.

An administrator was hired a year ago to improve the business activities of the hospital. Among the new ideas he has introduced is responsibility accounting. This program was announced along with the introduction of new quarterly cost reports to be supplied to department heads. Previously, cost data were presented to department heads only infrequently. Excerpts from the responsibility accounting announcement and the cost report received by the laundry supervisor are presented below.

The hospital has recently adopted a "responsibility accounting system." From now on you will receive quarterly reports comparing the costs of operating your department to budgeted costs. The reports will highlight the differences (variations) so that you can zero in on the departure from budgeted costs (this is called "management by exception"). Responsibility accounting means you are accountable for keeping the costs in your department within the budget. The variations from the budget will help you identify which costs are out of line, and the size of the variation will indicate which ones are the most important. Your first such report accompanies this announcement.

ARGON COUNTY HOSPITAL PERFORMANCE REPORT
LAUNDRY DEPARTMENT
(July–September)

	Budget	Actual	Amount (Over) Under Budget	Percent (Over) Under Budget
Patient days	9,500	11,900	(2,400)	(25)
Pounds processed by laundry	125,000	156,000	(31,000)	(25)
Costs				
Laundry labor	$ 9,000	$12,500	$(3,500)	(39)
Supplies	1,100	1,875	(775)	(70)
Water, water heating, and softening	1,700	2,500	(800)	(47)
Maintenance	1,400	2,200	(800)	(57)
Supervisor's salary	3,150	3,750	(600)	(19)
Allocated administration costs	4,000	5,000	(1,000)	(25)
Equipment depreciation	1,200	1,250	(50)	(4)
Total	$ 21,550	$29,075	$(7,525)	(35)

Administrator's comments: Costs are significantly above budget for the quarter. Particular attention needs to be paid to labor, supplies, and maintenance.

The annual budget for 1992 was constructed by the new administrator. Quarterly budgets were computed as one-fourth of the annual budget. The administrator compiled the budget from an analysis of the prior three years' costs. This analysis showed that all costs increased each year, with the more rapid increases between the second and third year. The administrator considered establishing the budget at an average of the prior three years' costs, hoping that the installation of the new system would reduce costs to that level. However, in view of the recent rapid cost increases, he finally chose 1991 costs minus 3 percent for the 1992 budget. The activity level as measured by patient days and pounds of laundry processed was set at 1991 volume, which was approximately equal to the volume of each of the past three years.

443

CHAPTER 12
Financial
and
Managerial
Accounting
Systems

1. Comment on the approach used to construct the 1992 budget.
2. What information should be communicated by variations from budgets?
3. Does the report and budget system effectively communicate the level of efficiency of this department? Give reasons for your answer.

12-15. (*CMA, adapted*)   Bio-grade Products is a multiproduct company that manufactures animal feed and feed supplements. The need for a far-flung manufacturing and distribution system has led to a highly decentralized management structure. Each division manager is responsible for the production and distribution of all corporate products in one of eight geographical areas of the country.

Residual income is used to evaluate divisional managers. The residual income for each division equals that division's contribution to corporate profits before taxes less a 20 percent investment charge on the division's investment base. The investment base for each division is the sum of its year-end balances of accounts receivable, inventories, and net plant fixed assets (cost less accumulated depreciation). Corporate policies dictate that divisions minimize their investments in receivables and inventories. Investments in plant fixed assets are the result of a joint division/corporate decision based on proposals made by division managers, available corporate funds, and general corporate policy.

Alex Williams, division manager for the Southeastern Sector, prepared the 1992 and preliminary 1993 budgets in late 1991 for his division. Final approval of the 1993 budget took place in late 1992 after adjustments for trends and for the other information developed during 1992. Preliminary work on the 1994 budget also was done at that time. In early October 1993, Williams asked the divisional controller to prepare a report presenting the performance of his sector for the first nine months of 1993. The report is reproduced on the following page.

1. Evaluate the performance of division manager Alex Williams for the nine months ending September 1993. Support your evaluation with pertinent information.
2. Identify the features of the divisional performance measurement reporting and evaluating system which need to be revised if the system is to effectively reflect the responsibilities of the divisional managers.

(The divisional controller's report appears on page 444.)

444

Part III
Computer-
Based
Accounting
Applications

BIO-GRADE PRODUCTS—Southeastern Sector ($000) Omitted

	1993			1992	
	Annual Budget	*9-month Budget**	*9-month Actual*	*Annual Budget*	*Actual Results*
Sales	$2800	$2100	$2200	$2500	$2430
Divisional costs and expenses					
Direct materials and labor	$1064	$ 798	$ 995	$ 900	$ 890
Supplies	44	33	35	35	43
Maintenance and repairs	200	150	60	175	160
Plant depreciation	120	90	90	110	110
Administration	120	90	90	90	100
Total divisional costs and expenses	$1548	$1161	$1270	$1310	$1303
Divisional margin	$1252	$ 939	$ 930	$1190	$1127
Allocated corporate fixed costs	360	270	240	340	320
Divisional contribution to corporate profits	$ 892	$ 669	$ 690	$ 850	$ 807
Imputed interest on divisional investment (20%)	420	321†	300†	370	365
Divisional residual income	$ 472	$ 348	$ 390	$ 480	$ 442

	Budgeted Balance 12/31/93	*Budgeted Balance 9/30/93*	*Actual Balance 9/30/93*	*Budgeted Balance 12/31/92*	*Actual Balance 12/31/92*
Division investment:					
Accounts receivable	$ 280	$ 290	$ 250	$ 250	$ 250
Inventories	500	500	650	450	475
Plant fixed assets (net)	1320	1350	1100	1150	1100
Total	$2100	$2140	$2000	$1850	$1825
Imputed interest (20%)	$ 420	$ 321†	$ 300†	$ 370	$ 365

* Bio-grade's sales occur uniformly throughout the year.
† Imputed interest is calculated at only 15% to reflect that only nine months or three-fourths of the fiscal year has passed.

12-16. *(CIA, adapted)* Management has requested a review of internal control over manufacturing cash disbursements for parts and supplies purchased at manufacturing plants. Cash disbursements are centrally processed at corporate headquarters based on disbursement vouchers prepared and approved at the plants. Each manufacturing plant purchases parts and supplies for its own production needs.

445

CHAPTER 12
*Financial
and
Managerial
Accounting
Systems*

In response to management's request, a thorough evaluation of internal control over disbursements for manufacturing plant purchases of parts and supplies is being planned. As a preliminary step in planning the engagement, each plant manager has been requested to provide a written description of their plant's procedures for processing cash disbursement vouchers for parts and supplies. Here are some excerpts from one of the written descriptions.

a. The purchasing department acts on purchase requisitions issued by the stores department.

b. Orders are placed on prenumbered purchase order forms.

c. A completed purchase order copy is sent to the receiving department.

d. When goods are received, the receiving department logs the shipment in by stamping "order received" on their purchase order copy and forwards the stamped purchase order to accounts payable.

e. Purchase orders, receiving department–stamped purchase order copies, and vendor invoices are matched by accounts payable.

f. Clerical accuracy of vendor invoices is checked by accounts payable.

g. A prenumbered cash disbursement voucher is prepared and forwarded along with supporting documentation to the plant controller who reviews and approves the voucher.

h. Supporting documents are returned to accounts payable for filing, and approved disbursement vouchers are forwarded to corporate headquarters for payment.

i. A report listing checks issued by corporate headquarters is received and promptly filed by accounts payable.

For each of the manufacturing cash disbursement system procedures listed, state whether the procedure is consistent with good internal control and describe how each procedure strengthens or weakens the system of internal control.

Consistent/Inconsistent	*Strength or Weakness*
1. Consistent	Purchase requisitions provide the authorization for purchasing to place order.

12-17. The Bienville Company, Inc., sellers of fine antiques, opened for business on March 1. The following transactions occurred during the two weeks prior to opening and the two weeks following the opening.

a. February 15: The corporate charter was received from the state and the corporate books were opened with an investment of $25,000 in cash and $175,000 in antiques by the owner, Benny Bienville.

b. February 15: The corporation leased a building for one year and paid $9,000 to Cats Realty for the first six months' rent.

c. February 19: Paid $100 for a telephone deposit and $50 for a utility deposit, both of which will be returned after one year of satisfactory bill payments.

d. February 22: Paid $4,680 to Fat Harry Refinishers for cleaning and painting the building. This major overhaul was expected to last three years.

e. February 25: Paid $1,040 for a business sign and interior furnishings to Henry's Fine Signs, both of which were expected to last two years. Purchased at auction from Bids Unlimited $10,000 of antiques, to be paid for within 15 days.

446

*Part III
Computer-
Based
Accounting
Applications*

f. February 27: Paid $2,500 to Big Al's Movers for moving antiques into the store and laying out the selling floor.

g. March 2: Paid $1,500 to WINE-TV for one week's ad spots. Returned to Bids Unlimited $2,000 of antiques that were in unsatisfactory condition when received.

h. March 3: By the end of the first week, the company had sold antiques with a cost of $9,500 for $19,000 as follows—Tom, $10,000; Dick, $5,000; Harry, $4,000—all on credit.

i. March 6: Supplies costing $800 were delivered by the Lo-Ball Supply Company to be paid for within 30 days. One-fourth of these supplies were used up during the first two weeks of business. Tom changed his mind about $500 worth of antiques and returned them.

j. March 9: A deposit of $5,000 was received from the Duke of Prunes on a special order of antique Louis XIII furniture to be delivered in April. Paid amount due Bids Unlimited.

k. March 10: During the second week, the company sold antiques costing $15,000 for $32,000 as follows—Bertha, $17,000; Betty, $8,000; Beulah, $7,000—all for cash.

l. March 15: Paid $350 in wages to employees, Peter, Paul, and Mary for the first two weeks of operation. So far, in the third week, the company sold antiques costing $8,000 for $14,000 as follows—Tom, $4,000; Betty, $10,000—all on credit. Received checks from Tom for $3,000; Dick for $5,000; and Harry for $2,000.

1. Identify the data items necessary for the general ledger master file for Bienville and give an example of each data item using one or more of the transactions given above.

2. Identify the data items necessary for the current period transaction file and give an example of each data item using one or more of the transactions given.

3. For each transaction listed, identify the module where the data are originally captured and enter the system.

12-18. (*AICPA, adapted*) Tolliver Manufacturing Company uses a standard cost system in accounting for the cost of production of its only product, Product A. The following information flows through Tolliver's manufacturing subsystem:

Standards:

Direct materials: 10 feet of item 1 at $0.75 per foot and 3 feet of item 2 at $1.00 per foot
Direct labor: 4 hours at $15.00 per hour
Manufacturing overhead: applied at 150% of standard direct labor costs

There was no inventory on hand at July 1. Following is a summary of costs and related data for the production of Product A for the following year ended June 30.

10,000 feet of item 1 were purchased at $.78 per foot
30,000 feet of item 2 were purchased at $.90 per foot
8,000 unit of Product A were produced, which required 78,000 feet of item 1; 26,000 feet of item 2; and 31,000 hours of direct labor at $16.00 per hour
6,000 units of Product A were sold

447

CHAPTER 12
*Financial
and
Managerial
Accounting
Systems*

At June 30, there are 22,000 feet of item 1, 4,000 feet of item 2, and 2,000 completed units of Product A on hand. All purchases and transfers are "charged in" at standard.

Identify the originating source (module, file) of each of the pieces of information described and give the destination (module, file, report) of that information.

12-19. (*CMA, adapted*)   The LAR Chemical Company manufactures a wide variety of chemical compounds and liquids for industrial uses. The standard mix of raw materials for producing a single batch of 500 gallons of one chemical compound is as follows:

Material Input	Quantity (in gallons)	Cost (per gallon)	Total Cost
Maxan	100	$2.00	$200
Salex	300	0.75	225
Cralyn	225	1.00	225
	625		$650

There is a 20 percent loss in liquid volume during processing due to evaporation. The finished chemical compound is put into 10-gallon bottles for sale. The actual quantities of raw materials and the respective cost of the materials placed in production during November were as follows:

Material Input	Quantity (in gallons)	Total Cost
Maxan	8,480	$17,384
Salex	25,200	17,640
Cralyn	18,540	16,686
	52,220	$51,710

No inventories of raw materials are kept. Purchases are made as needed, and a total of 4,000 bottles (40,000 gallons) were produced during November.

1. Design a bill of materials for this product and discuss the use of the bill of materials.
2. Identify the data items necessary for the product structure master file.
3. Design a management report to analyze the raw materials variances. Identify the source of each data item on the report.

DECISION CASE

(*CIA, adapted*)   Virginia Utilities has just implemented a new computer-based system that is designed to process the billing of customers. A file contains a customer meter number and the customer name associated with the meter, as well as other data about that customer. The most recent reading from each meter together with the meter number are also input to the system each month. The meter numbers from the two files are matched, and the monthly bill is

448

PART III
Computer-
Based
Accounting
Applications

calculated by subtracting the prior meter reading from the current reading and multiplying the result by the appropriate billing rate.

The appropriate billing rate is input from a file that contains all currently applicable billing rates and is selected using a customer billing code. Billing codes of "1" through "5" are applicable to customers, and each billing code produces a different billing rate.

The customer's monthly bill is then printed out and mailed to the address which corresponds to the meter number in the file.

Required:

1. List and appropriately title all files required by this system and identify whether the file is master, transaction, or constant.
2. Specify the data-items to be included in each of the above files.
3. Design the customer billing statement in all specifics.
4. What other output should be produced in order to make this system complete?

13 Microcomputer-Based Accounting Information Systems

Overview

The implementation of microcomputer-based small business accounting systems and software packages, and how they differ from larger computer-based systems.

Learning Objectives

Thorough study of this chapter will enable you to:

1. Differentiate among the characteristics of the major integrated accounting software packages.
2. List the capabilities and limitations of a typical accounting software package.
3. Explain the procedures for using an integrated accounting package.
4. Use an integrated package to run the accounting system of a sample company.
5. Compare microcomputer accounting systems to the large-scale accounting systems.

Outline

Microcomputer Accounting Software

Introduction to a Microcomputer Integrated Accounting Package

A Microcomputer Accounting System Illustrated

Microcomputer Versus Large-Scale Accounting Information Systems

SYSTEMS IN THE REAL WORLD

450

*PART III
Computer-
Based
Accounting
Applications*

Where Business Buys Microcomputers

SMALL BUSINESS

Distribution channel

Local computer store
31%

Manufacturer's representative
16%

Distributor
16%

National computer chain
13%

Mail order
8%

Consultant/system integrator
6%

Office supply store
3%

Office supply warehouse club
3%

Other
4%

Local computer stores remain the most likely source for small businesses acquiring PCs, according to Business Research Group. While many PC vendors feel it's too expensive to sell direct to small businesses, that channel still ties for second place with distributors. BRG defines small businesses as those with less than 100 employees but with at least one employee other than the owner (thus excluding home offices).

BIG BUSINESS

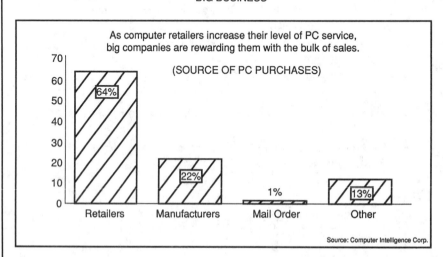

As computer retailers increase their level of PC service, big companies are rewarding them with the bulk of sales.

(SOURCE OF PC PURCHASES)

Retailers 64%
Manufacturers 22%
Mail Order 1%
Other 13%

Source: Computer Intelligence Corp.

SOURCE: *PC World*, November 1990, p. 92, and *Datamation*, November 1, 1990, p. 60.

There is a continuing revolution in small business accounting systems. The force in this revolution is the decreasing cost and increasing capabilities of small computers. We know from previous chapters that business data processing requires the storage of vast quantities of data and the repetitive processing of standard transactions. These needs are well suited to the filing, computing, and printing capabilities of the microcomputer. Microcomputers can now automate the accounting and bookkeeping tasks associated with virtually any business and prepare a variety of reports as desired. As a result, numerous microcomputer accounting programs have become available which automate accounting and bookkeeping tasks and provide support for analysis of the data that the computer generates.

451

CHAPTER 13
Micro-
computer-
Based
Accounting
Information
Systems

MICROCOMPUTER ACCOUNTING SOFTWARE

Microcomputer **accounting software** packages currently available span the range from simple software for automating a small business manual accounting system to sophisticated, integrated packages for larger, more complex businesses. Most of the available software uses a modular approach with the basic accounting program generally referred to as the general ledger package. A **general ledger package** usually provides for the automation of the accounting process from journalizing original transactions through preparing financial statements and closing entries. Some of these packages also handle subsidiary ledgers and/or special journals. However, many businesses need more than a basic general ledger program, perhaps because of a large customer list or the desire for more control over inventory items. Accounts receivable, accounts payable, payroll, inventory, and other modules are currently widely available to meet these extended needs. The current trend in microcomputer accounting is toward an **integrated general accounting package** that combines the general ledger and specialized modules into one program. The user then decides on the desired level of use and level of integration of these components and carries out steps within the one program to establish the interaction.

Controls

Control features offered by different accounting packages include password protection, control totals (such as batch totals), account prompts, forced balancing of transactions, required furnishing of certain information to complete processing, and required reviews of entered information. Some of these features may seem bothersome to someone first learning a program, but they are needed for effective internal control. Certain of the programs allow the user to turn off the controls while learning the program, but the controls must be turned back on for actual use of the program in a business environment.

452

*Part III
Computer-
Based
Accounting
Applications*

Output and Reports

All of the widely used accounting packages allow for the production of at least an income statement and balance sheet. Some programs contain a predetermined, standard format for these statements, while others allow the user the flexibility to define the financial statement format completely. This flexibility allows for the production of a more complete and tailored set of financial statements, but adds complexity to the program. When flexibility exists the user must specify the financial statement report formats when setting up the accounts. Although each program is unique, report formatting follows some general patterns and once you have gained experience with the logic behind this process it is not a difficult task. Other reporting features provided by some programs include comparative financial statements (historical and/or budget), consolidated statements, and departmental reports. There are also available numerous programs for specialized businesses, such as time and billing programs for attorneys and accountants, tax preparation programs for tax preparers, and special programs for not-for-profit businesses, such as churches and social organizations.

Vast possibilities exist for using a microcomputer as the basis of an accounting information system and for selecting the software for such a system. There is also a large margin for error in these decisions. The particular needs of the business should always be fully analyzed in order to find a "best fit" match from among the enormous selection of accounting software packages.

Overview of the Chapter

This chapter will discuss and illustrate one well-known general accounting program called **Bedford Integrated Accounting.** Bedford is a relatively simple, easy-to-use program for a small to moderate set of accounting records and is reasonably representative of the large universe of available accounting software. We chose Bedford over other well-known general accounting packages, such as Dac-Easy and Pacioli, because it possesses many of the same important features of these other programs (integrated modules, flexible financial statements) but is somewhat easier to use. Also, Bedford is available in an educational version with an accompanying book for a price that makes the package more accessible to students for individual purchase and classroom use.

The sections that follow will first introduce the use of Integrated Accounting by Bedford, a microcomputer general accounting package. Then the step-by-step application of this software package will be illustrated with a sample company accounting system example.

INTRODUCTION TO A MICROCOMPUTER INTEGRATED ACCOUNTING PACKAGE

The Bedford accounting software package records business transactions into one of several available accounting journals. The package then summarizes the transactions into ledger accounts, and produces on demand a variety of reports about the business, including a trial balance, income statement, and balance sheet. Journals, ledgers, invoices, statements, checks, and several customer and vendor schedules can also be produced as desired. The package is flexible and within limits will allow the user to customize the system to particular business needs.

453

CHAPTER 13
*Micro-
computer-
Based
Accounting
Information
Systems*

Features and Limits

The Bedford Integrated Accounting System offers a number of features that can be useful for keeping track of business activities. Some of the most important of these features are that the system

1. Creates accounts receivable and accounts payable subsidiary ledgers to record detailed information about individual customers and vendors.
2. Updates both the control (general) account and the appropriate individual (subsidiary) account automatically when a single receivable or payable transaction is entered.
3. Prints customer invoices or statements automatically (if desired) as credit sale transactions are entered.
4. Prints checks to vendors and others automatically (if desired) as cash disbursement transactions are entered.
5. Produces a single income statement for a company as a whole and/or multiple income statements for departments, stores, branches, or other defined units.
6. Does not require a hard disk in order to operate, so a company can permanently store all of its financial records on a single diskette.
7. Allows for the exporting of all standard reports to Lotus 1-2-3 files for further analysis.

The package has substantial capacity for handling the accounting activities of most businesses. However, some general limits do exist for the system. As a business automates its accounting records, one or more of these limits may become important. The Bedford system will

1. Limit a user to a maximum of 500 general ledger accounts numbered with a three-digit account code that falls within specified ranges depending on the type of account involved (asset, liability, equity, revenue, expense).
2. Not allow for standard, recurring, or reversing entries or for prior year comparisons or the maintenance of budgets.
3. Not track vendor invoice due dates and terms or customer credit limits. This must be done by the user.

Contents of the Integrated Accounting Package

The Bedford Integrated Accounting System Educational Version used in this chapter consists of a student manual and one disk. The disk contains the actual Bedford program, which is only one file. The educational version is exactly the same as the commercial version of Bedford except that (1) the educational version will not accept transaction dates after January 1, 1989 and (2) the educational version will print the phrase "For Instructional Use Only" on all reports.

454

*Part III
Computer-
Based
Accounting
Applications*

Overview of Bedford Integrated Accounting Software

Converting a company's accounting system from manual to microcomputer-based using Bedford requires four general steps:

1. Set up the company.
2. Establish the company's chart of accounts, vendors, and customers.
3. Enter and process company transactions.
4. Print desired statements, reports, and schedules.

A discussion of these steps follows, and the next section illustrates the process in detail using a sample company.

Set Up Company. Before creating your company with Bedford, you should create a subdirectory on your diskette named after your company. Then, you can load Bedford and access the company by entering the path to that subdirectory (for example, A:\name). At this point, your company will have no files and no data. You should access the SYSTEM module (the seven main modules of Bedford are given across the top of the screen), then the DEFAULT selection, then MODULE and, in turn, the GENERAL, SYSTEM, PAYABLE, and RECEIVABLE choices to create your default selections in each of these areas. In each case, the final default choice should be left in the *Not Ready* **status.**

Exhibit 13-1 provides a flowchart of the SYSTEM module menus that you should use when creating your company. Follow the paths through this flowchart to note the available selections and required information.

Establish Chart of Accounts, Vendors, and Customers. The most intricate part of this step is adjusting the chart of accounts provided by the program (called the **default chart**) to suit your own needs. Some accounts in the default chart of accounts are called **integration accounts** because they link the various modules of the Bedford program. You may not require many of these accounts to carry out your processing. If you want to delete an integration account, you must first delete it through the individual modules of the SYSTEM integrate function. First, access the **SYSTEM module,** then select INTEGRATE, then, in turn, the GENERAL, PAYABLE, RECEIVABLE, and PAYROLL selections to delete or modify the integration accounts in each of these areas as you choose. When the account number given for each integration account has been erased, the account has been deleted (even though the title remains on the screen). You should refer to Exhibit 13-1 for an illustration of this path.

Now it is possible to adjust the chart of accounts directly. Access the **GENERAL module** (across the top). Then choose LEDGER and, following the prompts, delete the accounts you will not use, modify the accounts as you wish (title, number, account type), and insert the new accounts you will require. When the chart of accounts is adjusted and complete, access the **PAYABLE module.** Then choose LEDGER and, following the prompts, add company vendors. Finally, access the **RECEIVABLE module.** Then choose LEDGER and add customers. Exhibit 13-2 on page 456 gives a summary of the *Not Ready*

EXHIBIT 13-1   Summary of SYSTEM Menu (*Not Ready*)

455

*CHAPTER 13
Micro-
computer-
Based
Accounting
Information
Systems*

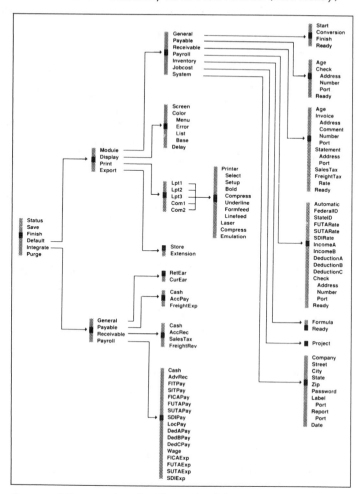

Courtesy of Computer Associates International, Inc.

GENERAL, PAYABLE, and RECEIVABLE menus and options that display the paths just discussed.

After all of this is done, you must convert each of the processing modules to the **Ready** status in order to begin processing transactions. Access the SYSTEM module, then DEFAULT, then MODULE, and, in turn, GENERAL, PAYABLE, and RECEIVABLE and change the module status (last default) from *Not Ready* to *Ready*. (We will not be using the PAYROLL, INVENTORY, or JOBCOST modules in this chapter, so leave them in the *Not Ready* status.) Refer again to Exhibit 13-1 to see the path to follow. The system is now ready to begin transaction processing.

Process Transactions. Transactions will typically be entered through three of the modules. Exhibit 13-3 on page 457 provides menu summaries for the PAYABLE and RECEIVABLE modules in the *Ready* status. Exhibit

EXHIBIT 13-2   Summary of GENERAL, PAYABLE, RECEIVABLE Menus (*Not Ready*)

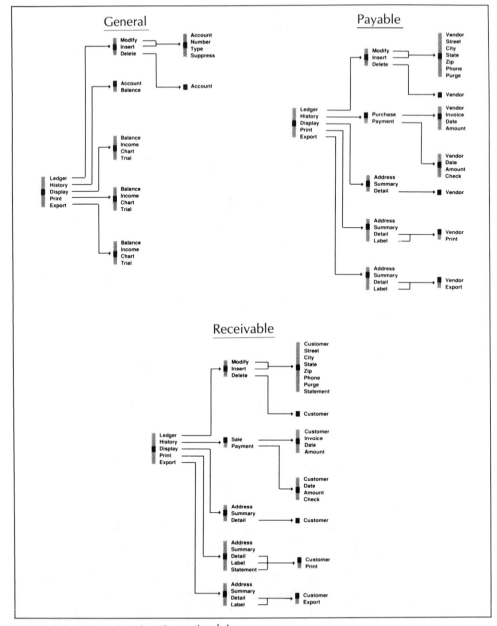

Courtesy of Computer Associates International, Inc.

13-4 on page 458 gives the menu summary for the GENERAL module in the *Ready* status.

All transactions involving vendors, including purchases, purchase returns, purchase discounts, and payments to vendors will be entered through the PAYABLE module. Access the PAYABLE module, then choose JOURNAL, then PURCHASE (for purchases, returns, and discounts) or PAYMENT, and enter the transaction information by following the prompts.

EXHIBIT 13-3 Summary of PAYABLE and RECEIVABLE Menus (*Ready*)

457

CHAPTER 13
*Micro-
computer-
Based
Accounting
Information
Systems*

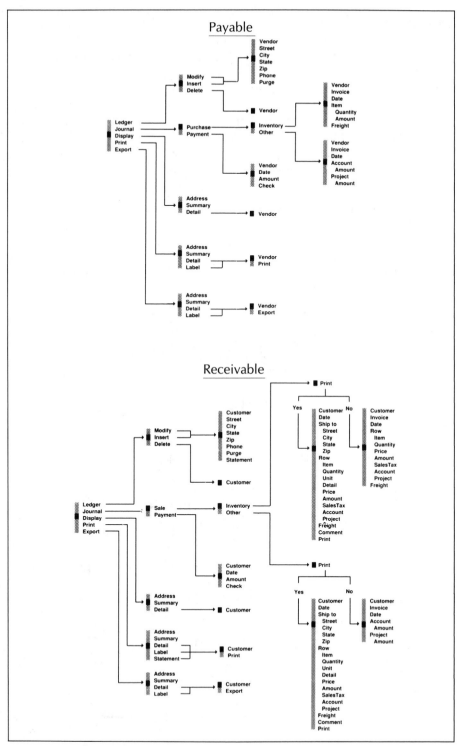

Courtesy of Computer Associates International, Inc.

458

*PART III
Computer-
Based
Accounting
Applications*

Transactions involving customers, including sales, sales returns, sales discounts, and collections from customers will be entered through the RECEIVABLE module. Access the RECEIVABLE module, then choose JOURNAL, then SALE (for sales, returns, and discounts) or PAYMENT (for collections), and enter the transaction information by following the prompts.

All other transactions will be entered through the GENERAL module. Access the GENERAL module, then choose JOURNAL and enter the transaction information by following the prompts.

You can review each transaction in each module on the screen after you enter the data but before you post by using the F2 function key. When you are satisfied that the transaction has been correctly entered, you can post (save it) by a combination of the Enter key and the Left Arrow key. Continue this

EXHIBIT 13-4   Summary of GENERAL Menu (*Ready*)

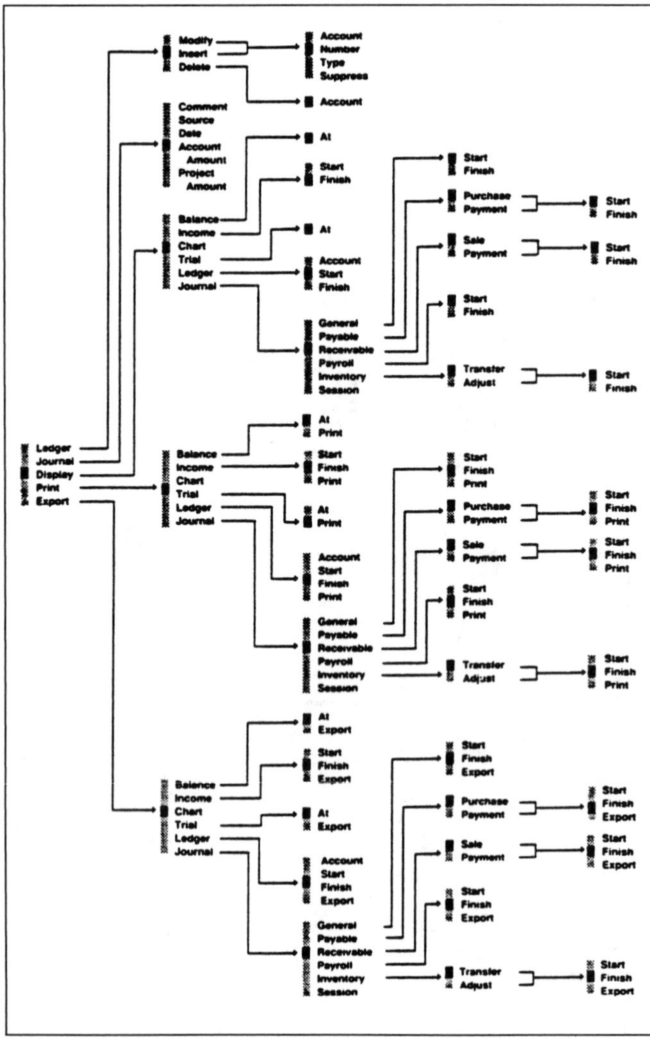

Courtesy of Computer Associates International, Inc.

process until you have correctly entered and posted all transactions for the period or for this session on the computer.

459

CHAPTER 13
Micro-
computer-
Based
Accounting
Information
Systems

Print Statements, Reports, and Schedules. The same three modules used to process transactions will also print all of the desired output. The chart of accounts, journal, ledger, trial balance, income statement, and balance sheet are all printed from the GENERAL module. The PAYABLE module prints vendor addresses in a list format or on labels, a **vendor summary report** (list of amounts owed to each vendor by age), and a **vendor detail report** (accounts payable subsidiary ledger). Vendor checks can also be printed, if desired. The RECEIVABLE module prints customer addresses in list form or on labels, a **customer summary report** (amounts owed by each customer by age), and a **customer detail report** (accounts receivable subsidiary ledger). This module will also print customer invoices or statements, if desired. These print paths can be followed in Exhibits 13-3 and 13-4.

CONCEPT SUMMARY

Overview of Bedford Accounting Software

Step	Activity	Bedford module
1.	Set Up Company	
	Establish company on diskette directory	DOS
	Access company	Bedford program
	Enter start, conversion, finish dates	SYSTEM
	Enter company information	SYSTEM
	Enter payable and receivable defaults	SYSTEM
2.	Establish Chart of Accounts, Vendors, Customers	
	Delete integration accounts	SYSTEM
	Adjust chart of accounts	GENERAL
	Reestablish needed integration accounts	SYSTEM
	Add vendors	PAYABLE
	Add customers	RECEIVABLE
	Convert to *Ready* status	SYSTEM
3.	Process Transactions	
	Purchases, returns, discounts, payments	PAYABLE
	Sales, returns, discounts, collections	RECEIVABLE
	All other transactions	GENERAL
4.	Print Output	
	Chart of accounts, journal, ledger, trial balance, income statement, balance sheet	GENERAL
	Vendor addresses, summary report, detail report, checks	PAYABLE
	Customer addresses, summary report, detail report, invoices, statements	RECEIVABLE

Note: The PAYROLL, INVENTORY, and JOBCOST modules of Bedford are not applied in this chapter.

460

*Part III
Computer-
Based
Accounting
Applications*

A MICROCOMPUTER ACCOUNTING SYSTEM ILLUSTRATED

This section will illustrate the step-by-step process of running the accounting system of a sample company using Bedford accounting software. First, however, you will want an overview of the important program keyboard functions and the keys that accomplish these functions. Exhibit 13-5 presents the important keys used in operating Bedford and the functions carried out by each key. You should keep this exhibit close at hand as a reference whenever using Bedford until you become familiar with the functions.

Company Information and Transactions

Two recent college graduates decide to open a sporting goods store devoted exclusively to selling ice hockey equipment. They feel that their chances of success are good since they will have the only ice hockey equipment store in Miami Beach, Florida. The store, called Puck & Stick, Inc., opened on June 1. Because the Educational Version of Bedford we are using in this chapter will not accept transaction dates beyond January 1, 1989, we have set this company's activities to take place during 1988. The following transactions occurred during June:

June 1	Each owner deposited $10,000 of personal funds into a business bank account and received 1,000 shares of company stock each in exchange.
4	Hockey merchandise was ordered and delivered from Puck & Sons. The invoice cost was $3,000, and a freight cost of $100 was added to that amount. The terms of the purchase are 2/10, n/30. Display equipment was purchased from A-1 Suppliers on 90-day credit terms for $2,400, and a company car was purchased for $4,500 with a $500 (Check No. 1) down payment and a bank loan for the remainder. Utilities were turned on and a deposit of $100 (Check No. 2) was paid. This deposit will be returned after one year if all bills are paid on time.
8	Hockey equipment in the amount of $500 was sold to the Bahama Flashers hockey team on credit. Invoice No. 1 was used.
12	Purchased $500 of hockey sticks from Crooked Stix, Inc., for cash with Check No. 3.
13	Returned $100 worth of defective pucks from the June 4 purchase from Puck & Sons, and was given credit against the amount owed.
14	Mailed Check No. 4 to Puck & Sons for the amount due less the appropriate discount.
15	Cash sales for the first half of the month were $2,500.
18	Additional purchases of merchandise from Crooked Stix, Inc. for $4,000 were made on credit terms of 2/15, n/30.
20	Sold to the Equator Eskimos $2,800 of merchandise on credit using Invoice No. 2.
21	Supplies costing $200 were purchased on credit from B-2 Suppliers.
25	Received a check from the Bahama Flashers settling their account in full.
28	Received a check from the Equator Eskimos for $2,300.
29	Paid salaries of $500 (Checks No. 5 and No. 6) to each of the owners. Amounts withheld for each were as follows: $50 for federal income taxes, $10 for state income taxes, and $30 for Social Security. In addition to matching Social Security, the company contributed $40 per month for each owner to an insurance plan (Check No. 7).
30	Cash sales for the last half of the month were $3,000.

EXHIBIT 13-5   Important Keys and Their Functions

461

CHAPTER 13
Micro-
computer-
Based
Accounting
Information
Systems

Arrow keys—These keys control movement within the menu structure and data entry screens.

Forward Arrow key—This key allows forward movement within the menu structure and clears data entry fields.

Backward Arrow key—This key allows backward movement within the menu structure, posts transactions, and records data changes.

Escape key—This key cancels data entry prior to posting and allows backward movement within the menu structure.

Return key—This key accepts a data entry field.

Function key—The F1 key will display general information.

Function key—The F2 key will display journal entries.

Function key—The F3 key will display documents.

Insert key—This key allows you to insert data into an invoice.

Delete key—This key allows you to delete data from an invoice.

Shift key—This key will override the automatic capitalization of the first letter in a word, and when used with the Ret key, will enter default information into a data field.

Backspace key—This key will remove data from a field one character at a time.

Alt and Ctrl keys—These keys will "boot" or load the operating system into RAM when pressed at the same time as the Del key.

Number Lock key—This key controls the definition of the ten-key pad. In the "on" position, the ten-key pad will enter numbers. In the "off" position the 8, 6, 2, and 4 keys are defined as the Arrow Keys.

Note: Enhanced keyboards separate the arrow and ten-key pads so that they may be used independently. If you do not have an enhanced keyboard, you must use the number keys at the top of your keyboard to enter numbers into the Bedford program because the ten-key pad will be used to operate the arrow keys.

SOURCE: Sylvia Hearing, *COMPUTERIZED ACCOUNTING: An Integrated Skills Approach,* © 1991, p. 8. Reprinted by permission of Prentice Hall, Englewood Cliffs, New Jersey.

The following additional information about the business is available:

1. The display equipment is expected to last ten years and the company car three years. Both are expected to be worthless at the end of their useful lives. Straight-line depreciation is used by the company.

2. Interest on the bank loan accrues at the rate of 1 percent of the unpaid loan balance at the end of each month.

3. An interest charge of 1 percent is added to all customer amounts owed to Puck & Stick, Inc., that remain unpaid as of the end of the month.

4. A physical count of inventory reveals that $350 of merchandise is still on hand at June 30.

462

PART III
Computer-
Based
Accounting
Applications

Chart of Accounts, Vendors, and Customers

Charts of accounts provide guidelines for the recording and classification of all events in the accounting system by giving the specific asset, liability, owners' equity, revenue, and expense account titles and numbers to be used by the business. All accounting software packages use **account numbering systems** in the chart of accounts to indicate the proper order, section, and financial statement placement of each individual account. In addition, Bedford employs an **account type classification** system to further refine the printing of amounts on financial statements (in the left or the right column of the statement) and to provide user-specified headings, subtotals, and totals on the statement. Exhibit 13-6 gives the account numbering system and account type classification codes used by the Bedford program.

The chart of accounts to be used in processing Puck & Stick with Bedford, including account numbers, titles, and type classifications, is given in Exhibit 13-7.

The vendor information to be used by Puck & Stick is given in the top portion in Exhibit 13-8 (page 464), and Puck & Stick customer information is listed in the bottom portion of that exhibit.

Setting Up the Company

To set up Puck & Stick on a microcomputer using Bedford, follow the steps given here (Remember throughout this process that (1) the *Escape* key will get you out of any unwanted circumstance, (2) you may accept the default data

EXHIBIT 13-6 Bedford Account Numbering System and Classification Codes

Asset accounts	100–199
Liability accounts	200–299
Equity accounts	300–399
Revenue accounts	400–499
Expense accounts	500–599

H	This is a nonpostable block **H**eading which will not show a balance.
R	This is a postable account printed to the **R**ight within a section.
L	This is a postable account printed to the **L**eft within a section and must be followed by a Subtotal account.
S	This is a nonpostable account that creates an automatically calculated **S**ubtotal of all **L**eft accounts which immediately precede it. **S**ubtotal amounts are printed to the right within a section.
X	There is only one **X** account—Current Earnings. This nonpostable account automatically lists the current earnings amount on the right within the EQUITY section of the balance sheet.
T	This is a nonpostable account that creates an automatically calculated **T**otal of all **R** and **S** account balances above it up to the preceding **H** account. The total is calculated automatically by the program and is printed to the right within a section.

SOURCE: Sylvia Hearing, *COMPUTERIZED ACCOUNTING: An Integrated Skills Approach*, © 1991, pp. 380–381. Reprinted by permission of Prentice Hall, Englewood Cliffs, New Jersey.

provided by using the *Shift* and *Enter* keys together, and (3) the only way to actually record any data on your disk is to post the new data entered by pressing the *Left Arrow* key):

463

Chapter 13
Micro-
computer-
Based
Accounting
Information
Systems

1. Install the Bedford program from the program diskette (now on drive A:) onto the hard disk. Then remove the Bedford program diskette and store it.
2. Create your company subdirectory on your data diskette by inserting your diskette in drive A: and typing *md puck* in response to the A drive prompt. Return to the hard drive and run the *Bedford* program by typing *bedford* in response to the prompt.
3. Now enter the company path, A:\Puck in response to the prompt and press *Enter*.

EXHIBIT 13-7   Chart of Accounts

Puck & Stick, Inc. FOR INSTRUCTIONAL USE ONLY
CHART OF ACCOUNTS

ASSETS		LIABILITIES	
100 CURRENT ASSETS	H	200 CURRENT LIABILITIES	H
101 Cash	R	210 Accounts Payable	R
110 Accounts Receivable	R	231 FIT Payable	R
115 Receivable From Utility	R	232 SIT Payable	R
120 Inventory	R	233 FICA Payable	R
130 Supplies	R	250 Bank Loan Payable	R
150 TOTAL CURRENT ASSETS	T	251 Interest Payable	R
		261 TOTAL CURRENT LIABILITIES	T
151 NONCURRENT ASSETS	H		
160 Equipment	L	EQUITY	
161 Acc Dep - Equip	L		
162 Net Equipment	S	300 OWNERS' EQUITY	H
170 Car	L	310 Capital Stock	R
171 Acc Dep - Car	L	350 Retained Earnings	R
172 Net Car	S	360 Current Earnings	X
199 TOTAL NONCURRENT ASSETS	T	365 Dividends	R
		370 TOTAL OWNERS' EQUITY	T
REVENUE		EXPENSE	
400 REVENUE	H	500 EXPENSES	H
405 Sales Revenue	R	509 Cost Of Goods Sold	R
415 Interest Revenue	R	510 Beg Inventory	L
450 TOTAL REVENUE	T	511 Purchases	L
		512 Freight-In	L
		513 Purchase Returns	L
		514 Purchase Discounts	L
		515 End Inventory	L
		516 TOTAL COST OF GOODS SOLD	S
		530 Salary Expense	R
		531 Payroll Taxes	R
		540 Insurance Expense	R
		550 Depreciation Expense	R
		560 Interest Expense	R
		599 TOTAL EXPENSES	T

464

Part III
Computer-
Based
Accounting
Applications

EXHIBIT 13-8   Vendor and Customer Information

VENDORS						
3	A-1	333 Three Street	Miami	Florida	12348	333-3333
4	B-2	444 Four Street	Miami	Florida	12349	444-4444
2	Crooked Stix, Inc.	222 Two Street	Miami	Florida	12347	222-2222
1	Puck & Sons	111 One Street	Miami	Florida	12346	111-1111

VENDORS on file: 4

CUSTOMERS						
1	Bahama Flashers	111 A Street	Miami	Florida	12222	555-5555
2	Equator Eskimos	222 B Street	Miami	Florida	13333	666-6666

CUSTOMERS on file: 2

4. Type in the **start, conversion,** and **finish dates** as follows:

Start	06/01/88
Conversion	06/01/88
Finish	01/01/89

5. On the main modules across the top of the screen, use the Right Arrow key to move to SYSTEM and the Down Arrow to DEFAULT and Right Arrow to accept. Another menu will appear, and you should select MODULE.

6. At MODULE, first select GENERAL and type in the dates you have already established, leaving the status as *Not Ready.* Next go to PAYABLE and then RECEIVABLE and accept the default information provided, always leaving the status as *Not Ready.* Finally, select SYSTEM and type in the company information requested (you should create any information requested that is not provided in the problem statement). The Password prompt should be skipped and the **default settings** for your printer changed only if necessary. The final prompt asks for the date format you prefer. Make your choice. Remember to post (Left Arrow) at the end of your work in each of these modules or your additions and changes will not be recorded.

Establishing the Chart of Accounts, Vendors, and Customers

First, delete the integration accounts you are not going to use, and modify those you will be using. Returning to the SYSTEM main module, you should select INTEGRATE, then GENERAL. Change the account number of Retained Earnings to 350 (as per the chart of accounts given in Exhibit 13-7), leave the Current Earnings number as given, and post this data. Now move to PAYABLE, RECEIVABLE, and PAYROLL, in turn, and delete the account numbers given for each of these integration accounts. We will return later and renumber some of these integration accounts, but deleting them now gives us more flexibility in adjusting the main chart of accounts to suit our needs. Always post the deletions for each module.

Next, return to the main modules across the top of the screen, move to the GENERAL module, and then choose LEDGER. Now, following the Puck & Stick chart of accounts given in Exhibit 13-7, adjust the default chart to the one given. First, by following the prompts, delete all accounts from the default chart that do not appear in Exhibit 13-7 (we can now delete the integration accounts because they have already been deleted in the individual modules). Then, modify (title, number, or account type) those requiring changes, and finally, add (insert) all new accounts (including headings, subtotals, and totals) required by Puck & Stick in Exhibit 13-7. In each case, the prompts for Delete, Modify, and Insert are easy to follow. The final prompt for each account will ask if you wish to suppress the account from appearing on financial statements if the account has a zero balance. Make your decision (Y or N) about each account as you go. Always remember to post each change as you complete it.

465

CHAPTER 13
Micro-
computer-
Based
Accounting
Information
Systems

When you have finished this process and your chart of accounts (you may view it on the screen or print it out for verification) looks exactly like the one in Exhibit 13-7, this step is completed. Now we will reestablish only those integration accounts that are needed with the new numbers from our new chart of accounts. Return to SYSTEM, then INTEGRATE, then PAYABLE, RE-CEIVABLE, and PAYROLL, in turn, to assign the numbers from the new chart of accounts to those integration accounts that remain in your new chart. Any integration accounts not included in your new chart of accounts should remain unnumbered and deleted. The chart of accounts is now established for Puck & Stick.

Now, move to the PAYABLE module and select LEDGER, then IN-SERT, and follow the prompts in order to add vendors to the company files using the vendor information given in Exhibit 13-8. You should create any information requested that has not been provided by the problem statement and press N at the Purge prompt to indicate that you want all vendor information retained. Each set of vendor information should be posted as you complete it (after the N response). Next, go to the RECEIVABLE module, then LEDGER and INSERT, and add customers to the files from the customer information given in Exhibit 13-8. Respond N at the Purge prompt, and then you may decide whether or not (Y or N) you wish to have a customer statement printed at the time that customer sales transaction data is entered. Post after each customer's information has been entered.

The company data, chart of accounts, vendors, and customers are now all established on the microcomputer. All that remains before you can process transactions is to change the ready status of each of the modules you will use from *Not Ready* to *Ready*. Return to the SYSTEM main module, then DE-FAULT, then MODULE, and, in turn, to GENERAL, PAYABLE, and RE-CEIVABLE, changing the final prompt of each to *Ready* and posting each change.

Processing Transactions

Exhibit 13-9 gives the entered transactions for Puck & Stick printed in a general journal format. Remember that transactions will be entered using three main modules: GENERAL, PAYABLE, and RECEIVABLE. All transactions involving vendors (purchases, returns, discounts, payments to vendors) are entered through the PAYABLE module, and all transactions with customers (sales, returns, discounts, payments by customers) are entered through the

466

Part III
Computer-
Based
Accounting
Applications

RECEIVABLE module. All other transactions enter the system using the GENERAL module.

In each case, the prompts for entering transactions are reasonably clear, and after you have entered a few transactions, any initial confusion will be cleared up. Some general comments will help get you on your way quickly, however. The Bedford program follows the normal debit/credit rules for accounts so that entering an amount will cause the account balance to *increase* (the computer will consider the amount a debit for accounts numbered as assets and expenses and a credit for accounts numbered as liabilities, equity, and revenues). If you wish for an account balance to *decrease* as a result of a transaction, the amount should be entered with a minus sign in front of it. The computer will record a negative amount as a credit if the account is an asset or an expense, and a debit if the account is a liability, equity, or revenue. Whenever a prompt asks for an account, vendor, or customer, the proper re-

EXHIBIT 13-9   General Journal

Puck & Stick, Inc. FOR INSTRUCTIONAL USE ONLY
GENERAL JOURNAL   Jun 1, 1988 TO Jun 30, 1988

PAGE 1					debits	credits
06-01-88 J1	Owner Investment	Stock	101	Cash	20,000.00	—
			310	Capital Stock	—	20,000.00
06-04-88 J2	Puck & Sons	210n30	210	Accounts Payable	—	3,100.00
			511	Purchases	3,000.00	—
			512	Freight-In	100.00	—
06-04-88 J3	A-1	90 Day	210	Accounts Payable	—	2,400.00
			160	Equipment	2,400.00	—
06-04-88 J4	Car Purchase	Loan	170	Car	4,500.00	—
			101	Cash	—	500.00
			250	Bank Loan Payable	—	4,000.00
06-04-88 J5	Utility Deposit	1 Year	115	Receivable From Utility	100.00	—
			101	Cash	—	100.00
06-08-88 J6	Bahama Flashers	1	110	Accounts Receivable	500.00	—
			405	Sales Revenue	—	500.00
06-12-88 J7	Cash Purchases	C Stix	511	Purchases	500.00	—
			101	Cash	—	500.00
06-13-88 J8	Puck & Sons	Return	210	Accounts Payable	100.00	—
			513	Purchase Returns	—	100.00
06-14-88 J9	Puck & Sons	Discoun	210	Accounts Payable	60.00	—
			514	Purchase Discounts	—	60.00
06-14-88 J10	Puck & Sons	1	210	Accounts Payable	2,940.00	—
			101	Cash	—	2,940.00
06-15-88 J11	Cash Sales	1 - 15	101	Cash	2,500.00	—
			405	Sales Revenue	—	2,500.00
06-18-88 J12	Crooked Stix, Inc.	215n30	210	Accounts Payable	—	4,000.00
			511	Purchases	4,000.00	—
06-20-88 J13	Equator Eskimos	2	110	Accounts Receivable	2,800.00	—
			405	Sales Revenue	—	2,800.00
06-21-88 J14	B-2	None	210	Accounts Payable	—	200.00
			130	Supplies	200.00	—
06-25-88 J15	Bahama Flashers	XXX	101	Cash	500.00	—
			110	Accounts Receivable	—	500.00

EXHIBIT 13-9   General Journal (continued)   **467**

CHAPTER 13
Micro-
computer-
Based
Accounting
Information
Systems

PAGE 2						debits	credits
06-28-88 J16	Equator Eskimos	YYY	101	Cash		2,300.00	—
			110	Accounts Receivable		—	2,300.00
06-29-88 J17	Monthly Payroll	Owners	530	Salary Expense		1,000.00	—
			531	Payroll Taxes		60.00	—
			540	Insurance Expense		80.00	—
			231	FIT Payable		—	100.00
			232	SIT Payable		—	20.00
			233	FICA Payable		—	120.00
			101	Cash		—	900.00
06-30-88 J18	Cash Sales	16 - 30	101	Cash		3,000.00	—
			405	Sales Revenue		—	3,000.00
06-30-88 J19	Monthly Depreciation	Eq/Car	550	Depreciation Expense		145.00	—
			161	Acc Dep - Equip		—	20.00
			171	Acc Dep - Car		—	125.00
06-30-88 J20	Interest On Loan	J4	560	Interest Expense		40.00	—
			251	Interest Payable		—	40.00
06-30-88 J21	Equator Eskimos	3	110	Accounts Receivable		5.00	—
			415	Interest Revenue		—	5.00
06-30-88 J22	Establish Inventory	Periodi	120	Inventory		350.00	—
			515	End Inventory		—	350.00
						51,180.00	51,180.00

sponse is the account number (from the chart of accounts) or the vendor or customer number assigned to each by the program. If, while you are entering a transaction, a prompt asks for information that is not a part of the problem statement, you should either create a response or attempt to skip past the request. In a few cases, you will have to provide the requested information before the transaction will be accepted.

Remember to

1. View each transaction (press the F2 function key) to verify that it has been correctly entered, and
2. Post the transaction (press the Enter key, then the Left Arrow key) before you move to the next event.

All transactions for Puck & Stick are reflected in the general journal illustrated in Exhibit 13-9, no matter which module was used to enter the transaction. Vendor and customer transactions will also be reflected in the specialized vendor and customer journals, if they are printed out. Vendor invoice and payment journals and customer invoice and payment focusing exclusively on purchase and sales activity can be printed, if desired.

Printing Reports

You can print a variety of reports using the PRINT menus of the GENERAL, PAYABLE, and RECEIVABLE modules. If a report covers a period of time (journals, ledgers, income statement), the prompt will ask you to specify a start and a finish date for the report. If the report is as of a point in time (trial

468

PART III
Computer-
Based
Accounting
Applications

balance, balance sheet, vendor, and customer reports) the prompt will ask for an "at" date. In general, the print prompts are straightforward and easy to follow.

Exhibit 13-10 provides the general ledger for Puck & Stick showing the results on accounts of all transactions for June. Exhibit 13-11 (page 471) gives the trial balance at June 30, 1988, Exhibit 13-12 (page 472) the income statement

EXHIBIT 13-10   General Ledger

Puck & Stick, Inc. FOR INSTRUCTIONAL USE ONLY
LEDGER   Jun 1, 1988 TO Jun 30, 1988

PAGE 1				debits	credits	debit balance	credit balance
101 Cash						0.00	—
06-01-88	Owner Investment	Stock	J1	20,000.00	—	20,000.00	—
06-04-88	Car Purchase	Loan	J4	—	500.00	19,500.00	—
06-04-88	Utility Deposit	1 Year	J5	—	100.00	19,400.00	—
06-12-88	Cash Purchases	C Stix	J7	—	500.00	18,900.00	—
06-14-88	Puck & Sons	1	J10	—	2,940.00	15,960.00	—
06-15-88	Cash Sales	1 - 15	J11	2,500.00	—	18,460.00	—
06-25-88	Bahama Flashers	XXX	J14	500.00	—	18,960.00	—
06-28-88	Equator Eskimos	YYY	J16	2,300.00	—	21,260.00	—
06-29-88	Monthly Payroll	Owners	J17	—	900.00	20,360.00	—
06-30-88	Cash Sales	16 - 30	J18	3,000.00	—	23,360.00	—
				28,300.00	4,940.00		
110 Accounts Receivable						0.00	—
06-08-88	Bahama Flashers	1	J6	500.00	—	500.00	—
06-25-88	Bahama Flashers	XXX	J14	—	500.00	0.00	—
06-20-88	Equator Eskimos	2	J15	2,800.00	—	2,800.00	—
06-28-88	Equator Eskimos	YYY	J16	—	2,300.00	500.00	—
06-30-88	Equator Eskimos	3	J21	5.00	—	505.00	—
				3,305.00	2,800.00		
115 Receivable From Utility						0.00	—
06-04-88	Utility Deposit	1 Year	J5	100.00	—	100.00	—
				100.00	0.00		
120 Inventory						0.00	—
06-30-88	Establish Inventory	Periodi	J22	350.00	—	350.00	—
				350.00	0.00		
130 Supplies						0.00	—
06-21-88	B-2	None	J13	200.00	—	200.00	—
				200.00	0.00		
160 Equipment						0.00	—
06-04-88	A-1	90 Day	J3	2,400.00	—	2,400.00	—
				2,400.00	0.00		
161 Acc Dep - Equip						0.00	—
06-30-88	Monthly Depreciation	Eq/Car	J19	—	20.00	—	20.00
				0.00	20.00		
170 Car						0.00	—
06-04-88	Car Purchase	Loan	J4	4,500.00	—	4,500.00	—
				4,500.00	0.00		
171 Acc Dep - Car						0.00	—
06-30-88	Monthly Depreciation	Eq/Car	J19	—	125.00	—	125.00
				0.00	125.00		

EXHIBIT 13-10   General Ledger (continued)

469

CHAPTER 13
*Micro-
computer-
Based
Accounting
Information
Systems*

PAGE 2				debits	credits	debit balance	credit balance
210	Accounts Payable					—	0.00
06-04-88	Puck & Sons	210n30	J2	—	3,100.00	—	3,100.00
06-04-88	A-1	90 Day	J3	—	2,400.00	—	5,500.00
06-13-88	Puck & Sons	Return	J8	100.00	—	—	5,400.00
06-14-88	Puck & Sons	Discoun	J9	60.00	—	—	5,340.00
06-14-88	Puck & Sons	1	J10	2,940.00	—	—	2,400.00
06-18-88	Crooked Stix, Inc.	215n30	J12	—	4,000.00	—	6,400.00
06-21-88	B-2	None	J13	—	200.00	—	6,600.00
				3,100.00	9,700.00		
231	FIT Payable					—	0.00
06-29-88	Monthly Payroll	Owners	J17	—	100.00	—	100.00
				0.00	100.00		
232	SIT Payable					—	0.00
06-29-88	Monthly Payroll	Owners	J17	—	20.00	—	20.00
				0.00	20.00		
233	FICA Payable					—	0.00
06-29-88	Monthly Payroll	Owners	J17	—	120.00	—	120.00
				0.00	120.00		
250	Bank Loan Payable					—	0.00
06-04-88	Car Purchase	Loan	J4	—	4,000.00	—	4,000.00
				0.00	4,000.00		
251	Interest Payable					—	0.00
06-30-88	Interest On Loan	J4	J20	—	40.00	—	40.00
				0.00	40.00		
310	Capital Stock					—	0.00
06-01-88	Owner Investment	Stock	J1	—	20,000.00	—	20,000.00
				0.00	20,000.00		
350	Retained Earnings					—	0.00
365	Dividends					—	0.00
405	Sales Revenue					—	0.00
06-08-88	Bahama Flashers	1	J6	—	500.00	—	500.00
06-15-88	Cash Sales	1 - 15	J11	—	2,500.00	—	3,000.00
06-20-88	Equator Eskimos	2	J15	—	2,800.00	—	5,800.00
06-30-88	Cash Sales	16 - 30	J18	—	3,000.00	—	8,800.00
				0.00	8,800.00		
415	Interest Revenue					—	0.00
06-30-88	Equator Eskimos	3	J21	—	5.00	—	5.00
				0.00	5.00		

for June, and Exhibit 13-13 (page 472) the balance sheet at June 30, 1988. These reports are all printed by the GENERAL module.

From the PAYABLE and RECEIVABLE modules, various vendor reports and customer reports can be printed at any time. Exhibit 13-14 (page 473) illustrates the vendor summary report (top) and vendor detail report (bottom) for Puck & Stick. The vendor detail report is the accounts payable subsidiary ledger showing all activity with each vendor during the month. Exhibit 13-15 (page 473) illustrates the customer summary (top) and customer detail (bottom) reports for Puck & Stick. The customer detail report represents the accounts

470

*Part III
Computer-
Based
Accounting
Applications*

EXHIBIT 13-10 General Ledger (continued)

PAGE 3			debits	credits	debit balance	credit balance
509 Cost Of Goods Sold					0.00	—
510 Beg Inventory					0.00	—
511 Purchases					0.00	—
06-04-88 Puck & Sons	210n30	J2	3,000.00	—	3,000.00	—
06-12-88 Cash Purchases	C Stix	J7	500.00	—	3,500.00	—
06-18-88 Crooked Stix, Inc.	215n30	J12	4,000.00	—	7,500.00	—
			7,500.00	0.00		
512 Freight-In					0.00	—
06-04-88 Puck & Sons	210n30	J2	100.00	—	100.00	—
			100.00	0.00		
513 Purchase Returns					0.00	—
06-13-88 Puck & Sons	Return	J8	—	100.00	—	100.00
			0.00	100.00		
514 Purchase Discounts					0.00	—
06-14-88 Puck & Sons	Discoun	J9	—	60.00	—	60.00
			0.00	60.00		
515 End Inventory					0.00	—
06-30-88 Establish Inventory	Periodi	J22	—	350.00	—	350.00
			0.00	350.00		
530 Salary Expense					0.00	—
06-29-88 Monthly Payroll	Owners	J17	1,000.00	—	1,000.00	—
			1,000.00	0.00		
531 Payroll Taxes					0.00	—
06-29-88 Monthly Payroll	Owners	J17	60.00	—	60.00	—
			60.00	0.00		
540 Insurance Expense					0.00	—
06-29-88 Monthly Payroll	Owners	J17	80.00	—	80.00	—
			80.00	0.00		
550 Depreciation Expense					0.00	—
06-30-88 Monthly Depreciation	Eq/Car	J19	145.00	—	145.00	—
			145.00	0.00		
560 Interest Expense					0.00	—
06-30-88 Interest On Loan	J4	J20	40.00	—	40.00	—
			40.00	0.00		

receivable subsidiary ledger showing all customer activity for the month. The
PRINT path of the *Ready* menus for the GENERAL, PAYABLE, and RE-
CEIVABLE modules displayed earlier in Exhibits 13-3 and 13-4 indicate the
other reports available on demand from Bedford.

Using Software Packages

We have just taken a whirlwind run through a microcomputer integrated accounting system. You should have developed a certain feel for the package
during this process, and you are probably now a bit more comfortable with it.

EXHIBIT 13-11   Trial Balance

471

CHAPTER 13
Micro-
computer-
Based
Accounting
Information
Systems

Puck & Stick, Inc. FOR INSTRUCTIONAL USE ONLY
TRIAL BALANCE Jun 30, 1988

		debits	credits
101	Cash	23,360.00	—
110	Accounts Receivable	505.00	—
115	Receivable From Utility	100.00	—
120	Inventory	350.00	—
130	Supplies	200.00	—
160	Equipment	2,400.00	—
161	Acc Dep - Equip	—	20.00
170	Car	4,500.00	—
171	Acc Dep - Car	—	125.00
210	Accounts Payable	—	6,600.00
231	FIT Payable	—	100.00
232	SIT Payable	—	20.00
233	FICA Payable	—	120.00
250	Bank Loan Payable	—	4,000.00
251	Interest Payable	—	40.00
310	Capital Stock	—	20,000.00
350	Retained Earnings	—	0.00
365	Dividends	—	0.00
405	Sales Revenue	—	8,800.00
415	Interest Revenue	—	5.00
509	Cost Of Goods Sold	0.00	—
510	Beg Inventory	0.00	—
511	Purchases	7,500.00	—
512	Freight-In	100.00	—
513	Purchase Returns	—	100.00
514	Purchase Discounts	—	60.00
515	End Inventory	—	350.00
530	Salary Expense	1,000.00	—
531	Payroll Taxes	60.00	—
540	Insurance Expense	80.00	—
550	Depreciation Expense	145.00	—
560	Interest Expense	40.00	—
		40,340.00	40,340.00

More importantly, you have tried out most of the basic features of the software. However, much detail and some sophistication have been omitted in this overview of the package. The *User's Manual* and *Accounting Manual* that accompany the commercial version of Bedford are valuable resources to help you develop further experience and expertise with this accounting package.

Remember, however, that Bedford is just one of many currently available microcomputer accounting system software packages. Although the actual keystrokes and options to operate other packages will differ somewhat, the fundamental ideas of setting up a company; establishing a chart of accounts, vendors, and customers; entering transactions and posting; and preparing reports will remain the same. The documentation accompanying these other packages

EXHIBIT 13-12   Income Statement

Puck & Stick, Inc. FOR INSTRUCTIONAL USE ONLY
INCOME Jun 1, 1988 TO Jun 30, 1988

REVENUE		EXPENSE	
REVENUE		EXPENSES	
Sales Revenue	8,800.00	Beg Inventory	0.00
Interest Revenue	5.00	Purchases	7,500.00
TOTAL REVENUE	8,805.00	Freight-In	100.00
		Purchase Returns	100.00 −
TOTAL REVENUE	8,805.00	Purchase Discounts	60.00 −
		End Inventory	350.00 −
		TOTAL COST OF	
		GOODS SOLD	7,090.00
		Salary Expense	1,000.00
		Payroll Taxes	60.00
		Insurance Expense	80.00
		Depreciation Expense	145.00
		Interest Expense	40.00
		TOTAL EXPENSES	8,415.00
		TOTAL EXPENSE	8,415.00
		INCOME	390.00

EXHIBIT 13-13   Balance Sheet

Puck & Stick, Inc. FOR INSTRUCTIONAL USE ONLY
BALANCE SHEET Jun 30, 1988

ASSETS			LIABILITIES	
CURRENT ASSETS			CURRENT LIABILITIES	
Cash		23,360.00	Accounts Payable	6,600.00
Accounts Receivable		505.00	FIT Payable	100.00
Receivable From Utility		100.00	SIT Payable	20.00
Inventory		350.00	FICA Payable	120.00
Supplies		200.00	Bank Loan Payable	4,000.00
TOTAL CURRENT ASSETS		24,515.00	Interest Payable	40.00
			TOTAL CURRENT LIABILITIES	10,880.00
NONCURRENT ASSETS				
Equipment	2,400.00		TOTAL LIABILITIES	10,880.00
Acc Dep - Equip	20.00 −			
Net Equipment		2,380.00	EQUITY	
Car	4,500.00		OWNERS' EQUITY	
Acc Dep - Car	125.00 −		Capital Stock	20,000.00
Net Car		4,375.00	Retained Earnings	0.00
TOTAL NONCURRENT ASSETS		6,755.00	Current Earnings	390.00
			Dividends	0.00
TOTAL ASSETS		31,270.00	TOTAL OWNERS' EQUITY	20,390.00
			TOTAL EQUITY	20,390.00
			LIABILITIES AND EQUITY	31,270.00

EXHIBIT 13-14 Vendor Summary and Vendor Detail Reports

Puck & Stick, Inc. FOR INSTRUCTIONAL USE ONLY
VENDOR Summary Jun 30, 1988

				total	current	31–60	61–90	91 +
3	A-1			2,400.00	2,400.00	—	—	—
4	B-2			200.00	200.00	—	—	—
2	Crooked Stix, Inc.			4,000.00	4,000.00	—	—	—
				6,600.00	6,600.00	—	—	—

Puck & Stick, Inc. FOR INSTRUCTIONAL USE ONLY
VENDOR Detail Jun 30, 1988

				total	current	31–60	61–90	91 +
3	A-1	90 Day	06-04-88 Invoice	2,400.00	2,400.00	—	—	—
4	B-2	None	06-21-88 Invoice	200.00	200.00	—	—	—
2	Crooked Stix, Inc.	215n30	06-18-88 Invoice	4,000.00	4,000.00	—	—	—
1	Puck & Sons	210n30	06-04-88 Invoice	3,100.00	3,100.00	—	—	—
		1	06-14-88 Payment	2,940.00 –	2,940.00 –	—	—	—
		Return	06-13-88 Invoice	100.00 –	100.00 –	—	—	—
		Discoun	06-14-88 Invoice	60.00 –	60.00 –	—	—	—
				—	—	—	—	—
				6,600.00	6,600.00	—	—	—

EXHIBIT 13-15 Customer Summary and Customer Detail Reports

Puck & Stick, Inc. FOR INSTRUCTIONAL USE ONLY
CUSTOMER Summary Jun 30, 1988

				total	current	31–60	61–90	91 +
2	Equator Eskimos			505.00	505.00	—	—	—
				505.00	505.00	—	—	—

Puck & Stick, Inc. FOR INSTRUCTIONAL USE ONLY
CUSTOMER Detail Jun 30, 1988

				total	current	31–60	61–90	91 +
1	Bahama Flashers	1	06-08-88 Invoice	500.00	500.00	—	—	—
		XXX	06-25-88 Payment	500.00 –	500.00 –	—	—	—
				—	—	—	—	—
2	Equator Eskimos	2	06-20-88 Invoice	2,800.00	2,800.00	—	—	—
		YYY	06-28-88 Payment	2,300.00 –	2,300.00 –	—	—	—
		3	06-30-88 Invoice	5.00	5.00	—	—	—
				505.00	505.00	—	—	—
				505.00	505.00	—	—	—

474

*Part III
Computer-
Based
Accounting
Applications*

CONCEPT SUMMARY

Manual System Versus Computerized System
Accounting Cycles

Step	Manual System	Computerized System
1.	Collect source documents underlying accounting activities.	Same step.
2.	Using the chart of accounts, code and classify transactions in terms of accounts to be debited and credited.	Same step.
3.	Record transactions into journals.	Enter transactions into computer.
4.	Post to accounts in general ledger.	Posting performed automatically.
5.	Prepare trial balance.	Trial balance prepared by computer.
6.	Gather adjustment data and record adjusting entries into general journal and post to accounts.	Gather adjustment data and enter adjusting entries into computer; posting performed automatically.
7.	Prepare adjusted trial balance.	Adjusted trial balance prepared by computer.
8.	Prepare financial statements.	Financial statements prepared by computer.
9.	Journalize and post closing entries.	Closing performed automatically.
10.	Prepare postclosing trial balance.	Postclosing trial balance prepared by computer.

will help you build on your experience with Bedford so that you can successfully use a range of integrated general accounting software.

MICROCOMPUTER VERSUS LARGE-SCALE ACCOUNTING INFORMATION SYSTEMS

We can now compare a microcomputer accounting system, such as Bedford, to the more sophisticated IBM AS/400–based system discussed and illustrated in Chapters 9–12. The similarities are striking. As you will remember, the AS/400 is a modular system with modules for cash receipts and disbursements (accounts receivable, accounts payable, payroll), sales and purchases (order processing, inventory management, sales analysis), manufacturing (product data management, material requirements planning, production costing and monitoring), and financial accounting (general ledger, financial statements, budgeting). Bedford and other integrated microcomputer accounting packages follow a similar format. Both systems handle the entire accounting process from journal entries to closing and produce a number of similar reports and statements. A close look at the reports from both systems illustrated in Chapters 9–13 reinforces the similarities.

When working the Bedford microcomputer-based accounting system example, you undoubtedly noticed some of the same controls available on large-scale accounting systems, such as account prompts for certain types of transactions and a complete audit trail of all entries through the system. You may also have recognized that microcomputer accounting packages use the same building blocks discussed in Chapters 9–12, and generally are not difficult to implement effectively. The repetitive process of entering transactions is perhaps the largest volume of work. However, the most difficult and creative part of the work is actually setting up the company on the computer, and that is generally done only once for each business. The more you use any accounting program, the more you will appreciate its many features. These features and the ease of data manipulation and information generation possibilities allowed by most packages account for the popularity and increasing use of both microcomputer and large-scale accounting systems.

The basic accounting process is the same whether you are working with a small, medium, or large business. The specific needs of the business with respect to types and sizes of accounts, complexity of transactions, and required reports may vary, but the overall processing approach of computerized accounting systems is the same. Whatever the needs and specifications of a business, there is probably a computer-based accounting system that will meet those needs. Businesses are no longer locked into investing in a substantial mainframe or even a minicomputer system in order to obtain a good accounting package. There is now available a vast selection of both hardware and compatible accounting software, ranging in price from less than one hundred to millions of dollars, to meet the varying needs of businesses from the small sole proprietor to the large multimillion-dollar corporation.

CHAPTER SUMMARY

Microcomputer-based accounting systems in the form of integrated general accounting software packages are now widely available for small businesses. These packages contain a general ledger module that performs most of the financial accounting functions of a business from journalizing transactions to producing financial statements. In addition, several specialized modules, such as accounts receivable, accounts payable, inventory, and payroll are usually part of these packages, and these modules can be integrated with the general ledger module to create an accounting system.

Bedford Integrated Accounting Educational Version is a typical general accounting software package. It offers modules for general, payable, receivable, payroll, inventory, and jobcost activities, as well as a system module for configuring the company and for overall control of the software package and its relationships to company data.

Converting a company's accounting records from a manual system to a microcomputer-based system using Bedford or any other general accounting package requires four steps.

1. Set up the company on the microcomputer.
2. Establish the company's chart of accounts, vendors, and customers on the microcomputer.

475

CHAPTER 13
Micro-
computer-
Based
Accounting
Information
Systems

476

*Part III
Computer-
Based
Accounting
Applications*

3. Enter and process company transactions.
4. Print desired statements, reports, and schedules.

Although the keystrokes and options may vary, most integrated general accounting software follows this same basic approach.

Microcomputer-based accounting systems such as Bedford and large-scale systems such as the AS/400 system illustrated in Chapters 9–12 use the same approach to the accounting process and the same overall processing building blocks. They also produce strikingly similar output reports. Differences between these systems have to do primarily with the amount of data that can be moved efficiently into and out of the system, the speed of processing, and the number of users and modules that can be supported.

KEY TERMS

Accounting software (p. 451)
Account numbering system (p. 462)
Account type classification (p. 462)
Bedford Integrated Accounting
  (p. 452)
Conversion date (p. 464)
Customer detail report (p. 459)
Customer summary report (p. 459)
Default chart (p. 454)
Default setting (p. 464)
Finish date (p. 464)
General ledger package (p. 451)

GENERAL module (p. 454)
Integrated general accounting
  package (p. 451)
Integration account (p. 454)
Not Ready status (p. 454)
PAYABLE module (p. 454)
Ready status (p. 455)
RECEIVABLE module (p. 454)
Start date (p. 464)
SYSTEM module (p. 454)
Vendor detail report (p. 459)
Vendor summary report (p. 459)

QUESTIONS

13-1. Distinguish between a general ledger software package and an integrated general accounting software package. How is the handling of modules different in each approach?

13-2. Which output reports from the Bedford Integrated Accounting program might be routinely exported to a spreadsheet program? What type of analysis might be carried out with this information by such a program?

13-3. Describe the steps to be followed in setting up a company on a microcomputer using Bedford.

13-4. What is the role of integration accounts in the Bedford program? Name two integration accounts from each of the GENERAL, PAYABLE, and RECEIVABLE modules.

13-5. Could Bedford accounting software function if all integration accounts were deleted? What might be the result?

13-6. Describe the six account classification types available in Bedford and the function of each in formatting financial statements.

13-7. Explain how the microcomputer and accounting software interpret the debit/credit and increase/decrease effect on accounts as transaction amounts are entered and processed.

13-8. Contrast the vendor invoices and vendor payments and customer invoices and customer payments journals produced by Bedford to the special journals typically produced by a manual accounting system.

13-9. Contrast the information provided in the general ledger produced by Bedford to that ordinarily found in a manual accounting system general ledger. Which seems more useful? Why?

13-10. Describe how the cost of goods sold section of the Puck & Stick income statement given in Exhibit 13-12 might be accomplished using the Bedford account numbering system and type classification scheme.

13-11. Give three areas of similarity and three areas of difference between large accounting systems, such as the AS/400, and microcomputer accounting systems, such as Bedford.

477

CHAPTER 13
Micro-
computer-
Based
Accounting
Information
Systems

PROBLEMS

13-12. Consider these transactions for the Conti Company (a sole proprietorship).

   a. Carl Conti invests $10,000 in the company.

   b. Inventory of $7,500 is purchased on credit from A-1 Corporation.

   c. A $15,000 loan is made from the Left Bank on a two-year note.

   d. Equipment is purchased for $5,000 on account from P-U Suppliers.

   e. Sales of inventory costing $2,600 are made to the following customers on credit: Leroy, $3,000; Mervin, $2,200.

   f. $2,500 of accounts payable is paid to A-1.

   g. $2,600 of accounts receivable is collected from Leroy.

   h. Salaries of $950 are paid to employees, Rob and Roy.

   i. Carl withdrew $1,500 for personal use.

Create the Conti Company on the microcomputer using the Bedford (or another) general accounting package. Journalize the transactions in appropriate journals and print the journals and the general ledger. You may assume dates for the transactions and create any other required information.

13-13. The Bienville Company, Inc., sellers of fine antiques, opened for business on March 1. The following transactions occurred during the two weeks prior to opening and the two weeks following the opening.

   a. February 15: The corporate charter was received from the state and the corporate books were opened with an investment of $25,000 in cash and $175,000 in antiques by the owner, Benny Bienville.

   b. February 15: The corporation leased a building for one year and paid $9,000 to Cats Realty for the first six months rent.

   c. February 19: Paid $100 for a telephone deposit and $50 for a utility deposit, both of which will be returned after one year of satisfactory bill payments.

   d. February 22: Paid $4,680 to Fat Harry Refinishers for cleaning and painting the building. This major overhaul was expected to last three years.

   e. February 25: Paid $1,040 for a business sign and interior furnishings to Henry's Fine Signs, both of which were expected to last two years. Purchased at auction from Bids Unlimited $10,000 of antiques, to be paid for within 15 days.

   f. February 27: Paid $2,500 to Big Al's Movers for moving antiques into the store and laying out the selling floor.

   g. March 2: Paid $1,500 to WINE-TV for one week's ad spots. Returned to

478

Part III
Computer-
Based
Accounting
Applications

Bids Unlimited $2,000 of antiques that were in unsatisfactory condition when received.

h. March 3: By the end of the first week, the company had sold antiques with a cost of $9,500 for $19,000 as follows—Tom, $10,000; Dick, $5,000; Harry, $4,000—all on credit.

i. March 6: Supplies costing $800 were delivered by the Lo-Ball Supply Company to be paid for within 30 days. One-fourth of these supplies were used up during the first two weeks of business. Tom changed his mind about $500 worth of antiques and returned them.

j. March 9: A deposit of $5,000 was received from the Duke of Prunes on a special order of antique Louis XIII furniture to be delivered in April. Paid amount due Bids Unlimited.

k. March 10: During the second week, the company sold antiques costing $15,000 for $32,000 as follows—Bertha, $17,000; Betty, $8,000; Beulah, $7,000—all for cash.

l. March 15: Paid $1,500 in wages to employees, Peter, Paul, and Mary, for the first two weeks of operation. So far, in the third week, the company sold antiques costing $8,000 for $14,000 as follows—Tom, $4,000; Betty, $10,000—all on credit. Received checks from Tom for $3,000, Dick for $5,000, and Harry for $2,000.

1. Create the Bienville Company, Inc., on the microcomputer with a general accounting package, providing any required information that is not given in the problem.

2. Enter all transactions for the period February 15 through March 15 using appropriate journals and post the entries.

3. Print the chart of accounts, trial balance, income statement, and balance sheet for Bienville.

4. Perform end-of-month activities for the company.

5. Print other journals, ledgers, reports, and schedules available from the general accounting system package as specified by your instructor.

13-14. Fly-Away, Inc., was organized June 1, 1992 for the purpose of transporting botanical expeditions to tropical islands. The following transactions took place in June:

June 1	Issued 7,000 shares of $6 par value common stock for $63,000. Purchased a small plane for $56,000 and parts for $2,000, paying $30,000 cash and issuing an 8 percent, two-year note for the balance owed.
2	Paid Safeguard Insurance for two months temporary coverage, cost—$1,500.
3	Paid $950 cash to rent a building for June and July.
8	Cash receipts from customers for a trip scheduled June 18 amounted to $4,500.
16	Employees earned $3,200 for the first half of June. (FICA tax rate is 6 percent, federal unemployment tax rate is 1 percent, state unemployment tax rate is 3 percent, income tax withheld, $420. Assume the full amount of wages is subject to tax.).
26	Paid $250 to Greasers, Inc., for repair work on plane.
28	Received a bill for gasoline from Fill-Ups amounting to $1,200, payable July 2.
30	Cash receipts from customers for a trip made on June 22 amounted to $7,300.

Employees are paid on the 1st and 16th and earn the same amount in each half of the month. The plane is estimated to have a useful life of six years and a residual value of $2,000. Straight-line depreciation is used. A check of spare parts revealed that $45 worth had been used in June. This is considered a repairs expense.

479

CHAPTER 13
*Micro-
computer-
Based
Accounting
Information
Systems*

Account titles used by the company are as follows:

Cash	Notes payable
Prepaid rent	Common stock
Prepaid insurance	Paid-in capital
Plane	Retained earnings
Acc dep—Plane	Flight revenue
Parts	Salaries expense
Accounts payable	Depreciation expense
Interest payable	Repairs expense
Advances from customers	Rent expense
FICA payable	Interest expense
Income tax withheld	Insurance expense
Unemployment taxes payable	Gasoline expense
Accrued payroll	Payroll tax expense

1. Determine the commands necessary to properly create Fly-Away, Inc., on the microcomputer using a general accounting package. Specify which steps (if any) would not be used in creating Fly-Away given the chart of accounts titles and transactions above.

2. Give the journals to be used in recording the Fly-Away transactions for June on the microcomputer.

3. Run the Fly-Away, Inc., using a general accounting package. You should create any required information that is not given in the problem.

4. Use the accounting package's export capacity to create a spreadsheet file of the income statement. Then use a spreadsheet program to read in the file and create a common size income statement where each item is given as a dollar figure and as a percentage of total revenue.

13-15. The following information pertains to Weston's Wares, Inc.

General Ledger Accounts

Cash	FICA taxes payable
Accounts receivable	Withholding taxes payable
Allow for bad debts	Income taxes payable
Notes receivable	Capital stock
Inventory	Retained earnings
Supplies	Income summary
Accrued receivable	Sales
Furniture and fixtures	Sales returns
Acc dep—F & F	Purchases
Building	Purchase returns
Acc dep—Building	Cost of goods sold
Land	Operating expenses
Accounts payable	Income tax expenses
Notes payable	Interest expense
Accrued payable	Interest income

480

*Part III
Computer-
Based
Accounting
Applications*

Accounts Receivable Subsidiary Ledger

Frank Churchill
H. Smith
Col. Campbell
J. Fairfax
Randall's Co.

Accounts Payable Subsidiary Ledger

Cox Furniture
Will Larkin's, Inc.
Elton's Elegancies
Bates' Bath Things
Highgate News

March transactions are as follows:

March	1	Capital stock sold for cash, $10,000. Capital stock issued for land and building, $30,000, of which one-fifth is allocable to land. A 30-day, 8 percent note in the amount of $12,000 is given for furniture and fixtures (the vendor, Cox Furniture).
	2	Supplies are bought from Woodhouse Co. for $275. Purchased merchandise on 2/10, n/30 terms from Will Larkin's, Inc., for $8,000.
	3	Sold merchandise on account to H. Smith, $600.
	4	Purchased merchandise on 2/10, n/30 terms from Elton's Elegancies, $7,000.
	5	Sold merchandise on account to Frank Churchill, $1,000.
	6	H. Smith is granted $40 sales return on the March 3 sale because of defective items.
	10	Summary of cash sales for the period March 1–10: $4,202.40. (Note: In practical situations, cash sales would be summarized and recorded more often.)
	11	Sold merchandise on account to Col. Campbell, $750, and received a 60-day, 6 percent note in settlement. Sold merchandise on account to Randall's Co., $750.
	12	Paid Will Larkin's, Inc., the balance due them.
	13	Collected balance due from H. Smith.
	14	Purchased merchandise on 2/10, n/30 terms from Will Larkin's, Inc., $3,200.
	15	Paid the payroll for the first half of March, $920.50, less income taxes withheld, $111.30, and FICA taxes withheld, $27.61.
	16	Sold merchandise on account to J. Fairfax, $4,200.
	17	Received $250 bill for advertising from *The Highgate News*.
	19	Purchased merchandise from Bates' Bath Things, $900, and gave a 30-day, 6 percent note in payment.
	20	Summary of cash sales for the period March 11–20: $3,799.50.
	21	Collected balance due from Randall's Co.
	24	Will Larkin's, Inc., granted a $150 return on the March 14 purchase because of defects in some of the merchandise.
	25	Received a bill from M. Dixon for repairs to adding machine, $30.

481

Chapter 13
Micro-
computer-
Based
Accounting
Information
Systems

27 Purchased merchandise on 2/10, n/30 terms from Elton's Elegancies, $1,225.

28 Sold merchandise on account to H. Smith, $712.

30 Bought additional fixtures on 30-day open account from Cox Furniture, $1,800.

31 Summary of cash sales for period March 21–31: $3,172.20. Paid note issued on March 1 together with interest. Paid the payroll for the last half of March, $987.30, less income taxes withheld, $115.50, and FICA taxes withheld, $29.61.

Use the following adjustment data to complete your work:

a. Unused supplies at March 31 are $120.

b. The month-end inventory of merchandise is $3,600.

c. Interest was accrued on the note received on March 11 (use a 360-day year as your base).

d. Bad debt loses are expected to amount to 1 percent of accounts receivable (round to the nearest dollar).

e. The annual rates of depreciation on the building and the furniture and fixtures are 2 percent and 12 percent, respectively. There is no residual value on these assets and straight-line depreciation is used.

f. Payroll taxes were accrued for the employer's matching contribution for FICA taxes.

g. Interest was accrued on the note given on March 19.

1. Create Weston's Wares, Inc., on the microcomputer using a general accounting package, providing any required information that is not given in the problem.

2. Enter all transactions for March into appropriate journals and post the entries.

3. Print the chart of accounts, trial balance, income statement, and balance sheet for Weston.

4. Perform end-of-month activities for the company.

5. Print other journals, ledgers, reports, and schedules available from the general accounting package as specified by your instructor.

6. Use the accounting package's export capacity to create spreadsheet files of the income statement and balance sheet. Then use a spreadsheet program to read in the files and create a common size income statement and balance sheet where each item is given as a dollar figure and as a percentage of total revenue or total assets.

13-16. A typical complete small computer system consists of a central processing unit, input device(s), output device(s), storage, and software. Microcomputers are being used extensively in business as small but complete data processing systems. Although these computers are used in businesses of all sizes, the largest number of applications have been in small businesses.

Some of the advantages of a microcomputer system are as follows:

a. The central processing unit is compact and can be conveniently located in a small area.

b. The system is simple to operate and relatively inexpensive.

482

*PART III
Computer-
Based
Accounting
Applications*

c. Users more closely control turnaround time, format of reports, and costs, rather than relying on a data processing or MIS staff. Turnaround time may actually be faster than with a larger computer system.

d. The system can be used as a stand-alone computer and/or as an input device to a larger system. Also, the system can be expanded as the need arises.

e. Standard software programs are readily available; therefore, programming expenses are minimized.

f. The system may be integrated with daily business activities so as to capture the data in computer-readable form on the spot as the events occur. Data conversion, entry, editing, and processing can all be done by one person.

The limitations of a microcomputer system include the following:

a. The amount of input and output that such a computer can process is much smaller than the amount processed by a large computer in the same amount of time.

b. Specialized forms of input, output, and processing may not be available.

1. Identify and explain the factors a business should consider before it decides to use a microcomputer-based system.

2. Give the advantages and disadvantages of using a minicomputer system with terminals versus a local area network with a number of microcomputers.

DECISION CASE

Total Systems, Inc. (which has been doing business as three subsidiary firms: Systems A, Systems I, and Systems Analyst), is interested in purchasing and installing a new microcomputer-based accounting system as soon as a suitable one can be found. The following is a description of the company and some of its specific requirements for an accounting system. It is likely that no single accounting package will accomplish all of its goals, so the company is prepared to compromise somewhat to get a working system. Total Systems does not want to do any programming for the new accounting package initially, but would consider programming special requirements at a later date after the system is completely operational.

Background

Total Systems is the name of an original computer program product developed by P. John and H. Paul to perform technical analyses on stock prices. This original product led to the three companies that exist today. Systems A sells the original product for an Apple computer; Systems I sells a modified version of the original product which runs on an IBM microcomputer; and Systems Analyst sells an on-line, real-time technical analysis package for both the Apple and the IBM. In addition, all three companies sell related hardware items and conduct seminars and conferences explaining the use of their products.

Systems Analyst is a separately owned partnership which must be accounted for separately. Systems A and Systems I are wholly owned subsidiaries of Total Systems, Inc. However, the two companies should be accounted for separately because existing agreements for the determination of management fees are different for the two firms.

483

CHAPTER 13
Micro-
computer-
Based
Accounting
Information
Systems

Status of the Current System

The individual in charge of the accounting system for Total Systems, Inc., recently left. He was in the process of developing a new computer-based accounting system for the companies to replace the system that had previously been used. The system in development was not completed when the individual abruptly departed taking the new system programs. As a result, the firm is interested in purchasing a software package to handle as many as possible of the important accounting functions.

The perceived deficiencies of the current accounting system that led to the original decision to develop a new system are the following:

1. There is available only a monthly printout of all transactions for each account; it is not possible to get a year-to-date printout of the transactions. This is felt to be a definite weakness since there are many transactions between the three firms, including corrections, chargebacks, co-payments, and so on. A year-to-date printout is considered very useful by the owners in detecting and correcting errors.
2. There is no way to combine the financial statements of the different companies. This is a problem since Systems A and Systems I are wholly owned subsidiaries and there needs to be a consolidated balance sheet and a consolidated income statement available.
3. There is only a limited general ledger account capacity. This does not allow the chart of accounts and financial statements to have the detail that management desires.

Ideally, any new system would not have the same deficiencies as the current one.

Billing and Accounts Receivable Requirements

The first problem in handling accounts receivable for these companies is the size of the files:

1. Systems A has approximately 2500 customers.
2. Systems I has approximately 500 customers.
3. Systems Analyst has approximately 500 customers.

These numbers are expected to grow by about 50 per month each.

For each company, the customer is assigned a member number which is used to personalize certain hardware and software sent to them. The same person can be a customer of more than one or even of all three companies. If so, the person has a different member number for each firm. Currently, no statements are sent to customers, but it would be desirable to be able to send such statements to all customers. If possible, one set of statements would combine all transactions with Systems A and Systems I. However, sending three different sets of statements would be acceptable.

484

*PART III
Computer-
Based
Accounting
Applications*

The accounts receivable system must also integrate with a dBase III file of names, addresses, and other information. This information is used for the personalization process of setting up computer programs specifically for an individual customer. Every six months, a new set of programs is sent to all customers who are current. As a result, Total Systems would like to retrieve the current/noncurrent status of each customer from the accounts receivable system and use that information to update the dBase III file, so that no new programs would be personalized and sent to customers who are not current on required payments.

Other desired features of a new billing/accounts receivable system include

1. An open item system showing individual invoices as well as payments attached to particular invoices.
2. A several line message on the invoice that is easily changed for different invoicing runs.
3. The ability to print an optional schedule of maintenance fees, as desired, on the face of the invoice.
4. The capacity to add 150 new customers per month with several new invoices for each new customer.
5. A miscellaneous account for all nonmembers who have small transactions with one of the businesses for such things as demo disks and conferences.
6. The automatic billing of an annual maintenance fee in January.
7. The ability to create the beginning accounts receivable file from a computer file rather than by typing in all 3,500 names, addresses, and other information, since the data are already in machine-readable form.
8. The ability to bill for services, such as the annual maintenance fee, that are not inventory items as well as bill for inventory items that are sold.

Financial Statement Requirements

Any general accounting package should

1. Combine the balance sheet and income statement of Systems A and Systems I. These income statements will be in different formats because of the difference in calculation of the management fee.
2. Provide departmental income statements for both Systems A and Systems I.
3. Identify revenue and expenses for each conference and seminar put on by each of the companies. This might be accomplished by some type of job or project costing system.
4. Provide subtotals for at least three levels on the income statements.
5. Generate a trial balance and allow transactions to be corrected before the final posting. In other words, after reviewing the trial balance it should not be necessary to enter correcting entries in order to correct an error.
6. Give a year-to-date listing of all transactions for a particular account or for all accounts.
7. Send output reports to the screen as well as to the printer.

Other System Possibilities

There are several other possibilities for new additions to the system, but these expansions do not have the priority of the system requirements just described.

485

CHAPTER 13
*Micro-
computer-
Based
Accounting
Information
Systems*

1. Currently, records of inventory are kept manually. A new computer-based inventory system could be updated as items are invoiced. Additionally, purchases of inventory could be linked to an accounts payable system.
2. Currently, payroll is being done using a stand-alone payroll system, and the related journal entries are made manually to the general ledger. This process could be integrated into the new system.

General System Requirements

Any new system should meet at least the following requirements:

1. Run on a hard disk which is hooked up to three IBM microcomputers. The company would like to be able to enter transactions at the same time from the different micros. However, these different micros would be using different specific modules. For example, perhaps accounts receivable would be updated at the same time as accounts payable, but there would never be a case where two micros would be updating accounts receivable simultaneously.
2. Allow extraction of data from the accounting records for use in a Lotus 1-2-3 worksheet.
3. Be easy to use and require a limited amount of time to enter transactions.
4. Allow Total Systems, Inc., to modify the package if necessary, in order to customize the system to its changing needs.

Required (Each requirement may be treated as a separate individual assignment):

1. Would the Bedford Integrated Accounting package discussed in this chapter be suitable as a solution to the processing problems of Total Systems, Inc.? If so, explain how it would work; if not, explain why the Bedford system would be inadequate.
2. Could Total Systems use a local area network (LAN) to connect its three IBM micros? Discuss the advantages and disadvantages of a LAN over the hard disk approach currently being used by Total Systems.
3. Describe in detail, including a list of steps to be taken, how Total Systems should go about the process of gathering information on which to base a decision about a new system to meet the requirements of the company. (What information is needed? From what source will the information come?)
4. What recommendation would you make to Total Systems about a minimum system to accomplish the processing objectives of the firm? Determine (or design) a system or package that would be acceptable to Total Systems. (Trade-offs and compromises in some of Total Systems' requirements will almost certainly be necessary in your recommendation.)

14 Overview of System Development

Overview

How information systems can benefit companies, how to manage those systems, and how to develop those systems

Learning Objectives

Thorough study of this chapter will enable you to:

1. Identify the areas of comparative advantage for a business using information technology.
2. Explain the advantages of the microcomputer and end-user computing.
3. Describe the goals of information systems.
4. Plan the development of information systems.
5. Incorporate the human considerations of information systems development into your plans.
6. Discuss the process of information systems development and the techniques useful in that process.
7. Give the unique characteristics of microcomputer-based system development.

Outline

Role and Value of Information Systems

Management of Information Systems

System Development

SYSTEMS IN THE REAL WORLD

487

*CHAPTER 14
Overview of
System
Development*

We Need Big Changes

At current rates, the United States' productivity will double in 120 years, Japan's in 20 years; its children's standard of living will double while our children's will stay about the same. W. Edwards Deming, Ph.D., Consultant in Statistical Studies, is the recipient of Japan's Second Order Medal of the Sacred Treasure from Emperor Hirohito. The citation says that the Japanese people attribute the rebirth of Japanese industry and its worldwide success to Ed Deming. He had met with the top management of Japan's leading companies in July of 1950, while he became a consultant to Ford only in 1981, and General Motors not until 1987. Why did his teachings catch on in Japan, but not here? The Japanese knew they were in an economic and industrial crisis and we don't.

Deming proposes ten basic concepts:

1. Create constancy of purpose. Identify the business you are in and how you can stay in that business.
2. Stay ahead of the customer. Do not only meet present needs, but plan for future needs as well.
3. Act on the fact that there is a new economic age with a single global market.
4. Make customers the most important people in your business.
5. Improve constantly and forever the system of production and service in order to improve quality and productivity, and thus constantly to decrease costs.
6. Build more quality into anything and it costs less because you design quality in rather than inspect it in. Improving quality automatically increases productivity. Continually improve, not in great leaps forward, but a little here, a little there, and it never gets any easier.
7. Develop an understanding of statistics and psychology, including how people learn, what makes them change, and their need to take pride and joy in their work. Use statistics to find out what any system might do, then design improvements to make that system yield the best results.
8. Buying from the lowest bidder is costly. Suppliers can no longer be played off one another for lower prices. They become your partners, and you have to help them improve so they can give you continually improving supplies for lower prices.
9. Start the commitment to quality in the boardroom, but everyone must have a part in changing. Management must lead, and not just give orders, but everyone has to understand where they're going. Do away with bonuses and incentive pay because they create competition.
10. If you and your employees don't work together in mutual respect toward the same goal, how good the supplies are won't matter. Job training alone is not enough; the company has to help with employee education in a more general way.

SOURCE: Lloyd Dobyns, "Ed Deming Wants Big Changes, and He Wants Them Fast," *Smithsonian*, August 1990, pp. 74–82. Reprinted by permission.

An executive is never dealing with the beginning of any event—the position from which we always contemplate it. The executive is always in the midst of a series of shifting events and so he never can at any moment consider the whole import of an event that is occurring. Moment by moment, the event is imperceptibly shaping itself and at every moment of this continuous shaping of events the executive is in the midst of a most complex play of intrigues, worries, contingencies, authorities, projects, counsels, threats, and deceptions and is continually obliged to reply to innumerable questions addressed to him, which constantly conflict with one another.

Tolstoy, *War and Peace*

ROLE AND VALUE
OF INFORMATION SYSTEMS

Earlier chapters have discussed computer hardware and software, data bases and data base management systems, data communications and networking, decision support systems, and the integration of accounting information systems. The term **information technology (IT)** is often used to refer to all of these different, but related, aspects of the computer and information systems.

Comparative Advantage of Information Technology

Information technology was once valued primarily for its ability to generate cost savings and raise productivity by automating routine transactions. Information technology now offers opportunities to open entirely new business areas and service established areas in new ways. There are three different stages of information technology:

> *Automation.* Information technology automates existing functions such as transaction processing and information filing.
>
> *Information.* Information technology is used to establish companywide telecommunications and computer access to a common data base and generate a flow of information to managers who need it.
>
> *Transformation.* Information technology is used to transform business units or entire businesses.

Examples of Transformations Generating
Comparative Advantage

Chapters 9–12 and Chapter 13 discussed the basic components of an accounting information system in a medium-scale and small-scale business, respectively. With these components, a company can achieve the automation and information stages, which are crucial to remaining competitive and increasing productivity. Although these stages should not be viewed as the final step toward optimal use of information technology, a company can use them as a base for important comparative advantages over its competitors.

External Advantage. Many firms have demonstrated the power of information technology to remake markets. One classic example is the airlines reservation system. United Airlines made a massive effort to bring its reservation system on-line and provide that information through terminals to travel agencies. American Airlines extended its SABRE system to offer travel agents not only its own flights but also those of other carriers, in an on-screen presentation that favored its own flights. Other airlines then got the government to require unbiased electronic reservation systems. Those systems today represent extremely lucrative businesses for the airlines that recognized the potential early and captured it. Implementing the systems was complex and costly, but the concept was obvious—once it had been found.

American Hospital Supply Company (AHSC) led its industry by instituting an on-line market called Analytic Systems Automatic Purchasing (ASAP) for its own products, which tied into hospital computers and purchasing departments. For the hospitals, ASAP made orders easier, reduced errors in orders and shipments, made shipments faster, and provided increased control over their inventory. For AHSC, the system allowed a tripling of sales without an increase in employees and tied the hospitals' purchasing to the company.

Notice that the SABRE system and the ASAP system are both, in essence, order entry applications, one of the Sales and Purchases system modules discussed in Chapters 9 and 11. Creative use of an accounting information system can have profitable competitive effects.

When the Internal Revenue Service recently authorized electronic filing of income tax returns, it created the opportunity for significant changes in operations, services, and marketing among tax preparers ranging from the Big Six accounting firms to individual consultants. Electronic filing may offer an opportunity to differentiate accounting services from those of competitors and to bundle add-on services with the basic function of tax preparation and filing. Already on the market, for example, is a Refund Anticipation Loan in which the tax preparer becomes a lender.

Internal Advantage. Opportunities for innovation based on information technology exist not only in markets but internally. A U.S. financial services firm relocated most of its back office to Ireland and achieved cost reductions without loss of productivity. Data communications and networks made it possible for this company to use the well-educated but less costly Irish labor pool for many tasks previously performed by the U.S. office.

Organizations that make themselves more cost-effective through new information technology may be able to sell their methodology as products and services. Or they may be able to develop information products for the marketplace as by-products of their own activities. Company data bases assembled for proprietary purposes may, in some instances, be rerouted into an information service for an industry, its customers, and/or investors and their advisors. Stock market quotation services of on-line, real-time information are marketed by publishers to supplement daily or weekly print.

Organizations that take advantage of new information technology have two characteristics in common. First, their managers feel that the technology will prove to be a worthwhile investment; they are ready to commit to it and see the process through. Second, the organizations are already efficient—they are among the low-cost producers. Such organizations find that information technology generates greater productivity and "bottom-up" innovations in products and processes. In slow-moving industries, information technology can yield longer-term competitive advantage. In faster-moving industries information technology may be more short term because competitors can copy successful innovations and, within a relatively short time, duplicate the gains achieved.

Information technology progresses so quickly that no one knows what strategic opportunities will arrive. However, they will arrive and those who move first tend to do well. Companies that see the potential and act are likely to control their market over the longer term.

The Promise of Integration

Internal Integration of Systems. A well-integrated organization is not necessarily a heavily centralized one. Decentralization has become a strategic goal for some companies that wish to encourage entrepreneurial energy. This strategy depends on information technology to bind the organization together through information and controls. However, many small companies undergoing rapid growth desire greater centralization and control through information technology. Whatever their size and pattern of organization, companies increasingly look to information technology to integrate activities from the factory floor or point of sale to the president's office.

For example, the manufacturer that can develop a new product in half the time of its competitors or the financial services firm that can develop new investments for changing market conditions will enjoy a competitive advantage. But this depends on teamwork, which in turn depends on sound organizational structures and easy access to relevant information. An engineer in Los Angeles may need to share and jointly analyze complex data with a cost accountant in New York this morning, not tomorrow. But the distances need not be that great for information technology to have real impact. The design team may be in one building, with the finance group in another. Similarly, external lines of communication with vendors, distributors, and other allies need to be convenient and capable of handling complex data.

When people throughout an organization can communicate via networked computers, horizontal links between peers in different locations begin to form that otherwise would not have formed. Not vertical, reporting relationships, peer links join people who can lend each other a hand, an item of information, a practical hint. Information technology, once feared as a force that would depersonalize the corporation, has begun to bind corporate employees together. However, as discussed in Chapters 4 and 7, while communications links create a more dynamic organization, they may also lay it open to electronic trespassers.

Integration with Other Companies. The acceptance of information technology has caused the companies producing and using this technology to cooperate with each other more than companies in the past would have found comfortable. Among producers, IBM broke new ground in the early 1980s by creating an "open architecture" for its microcomputers so that companies could design software for it, and competitors could build clones. In the later 1980s, corporate users' demand for connectivity among the products of competing manufacturers imposed a further degree of standardization and openness on the industry. Similarly, the banking industry created a number of jointly sponsored nationwide automated teller networks. This increased the overall market for such services, thereby benefiting all participating banks. Companies should look for the possibility of standardization and cooperation with competitors in industries that have become information technology intensive. Many companies, such as Sears and Procter & Gamble, require that their suppliers use electronic data interchange (EDI) to communicate order information. Chapter 7 discussed EDI in greater depth.

Electronic Markets.   When manufactured goods or components can be described in standard ways, electronic markets are possible. Suppliers can develop electronic markets to service their own customers and, for a fee, the customers of rival companies. Recall the airline reservation system and the hospital supply system discussed earlier. Purchasers, such as manufacturers, might array all possible sources, types, and prices of needed components on a computer screen and make purchase commitments electronically. Expert systems may be integrated into electronic markets to help buyers to specify the desired traits of the goods or services needed, especially when electronic markets become crowded with offerings.

A company can integrate vertically by purchasing its supplier or developing its own source of supply. Trade-offs between participating in a market and vertical integration involve production costs, coordination costs, and vulnerability costs. Production costs are those associated with manufacture. Coordination costs are those of managing the selection, purchase, and delivery of materials or services from outside vendors or, conversely, managing internal operations that result in the delivery of the same materials or services. Vulnerability costs refer to the greater potential for interruptions in the supply of components when they are purchased outside, such as the interruption of an external supply, a change in specifications that may cause a delay, negotiating difficulties, and other factors.

Production costs decline in an electronic market, and coordination costs decline even more. Electronic markets make management of purchase and delivery more efficient and less time consuming. In addition, price comparison on a broad scale becomes easier and thus reduces the desirability of making components in house when the components can be obtained at a lower cost from vendors in the electronic market. Managers need less time to scan suppliers, and delivery can be timed effectively through electronic control systems. The result may be to decrease the frequency of vertical integration as an organizing principle by replacing it with electronic markets in some industries.

A complementary trend toward close supplier relationships is also furthered by information technology. Just-in-time materials management can only be achieved by alliances between manufacturers and a reduced number of suppliers. In such virtual partnerships, sharing information, tracking inventory, and timing deliveries will depend on comprehensive electronic communication. The computer will not replace the telephone, but nothing can substitute for

CONCEPT SUMMARY	
Computer Systems for Comparative Advantage	
Possible Steps	*Potential Benefits*
Computer connection with customers	Make it easier for them to order (and make it harder to order from others).
	Allow them to track their orders and shipments.
Market research on customers, demographics, and competitors	Identify the best customer prospects so that effort can be directed to them.
	Identify market opportunities and niches.
Computer connection with sales representatives	Speed messages from the home office and customers.
	Allow direct entry of new orders, reducing delay of delivery to customers by up to a week.
	Reduce paperwork.
Computer connection with banks	Improve cash management.
Training via video disk	Cut training costs.
	Let employees learn at their own pace.
Use of computer system to provide services not previously available or possible	Enter a market early to capture the market and establish presence.

electronic networks that tie computers together, give them a common language, and allow them to query one another as well as respond to queries.

Executive Information Systems or Executive Support Systems

Chapter 8 discussed decision support systems (the use of accounting information systems data, management science techniques, and software support to make better decisions) and expert systems. Both DSS and ES are fairly structured and provide the user with the data and processing power to make a better decision.

Executives typically have too much data for their decision making and already have the necessary processing power. An **executive support system (ESS)** or an **executive information system (EIS)** extracts the type of information about their companies and the operating environment that executives need on a daily basis. An oil executive may rely on a daily estimate of the number of barrels in transit on the oceans as a leading price indicator. A retailer may need daily sales figures on a "basket" of dozens of selected items at hundreds of stores. The EIS then retrieves, formats, and presents the information at the executive's microcomputer. This information is often presented graphically as well as numerically.

In companies with well-structured data (see Chapter 6) and properly designed networks (see Chapter 7) an EIS can allow key employees to learn what they need to learn quickly, share information efficiently with others, ask unexpected but relevant questions, and receive comprehensive answers without delay—and move the company's business forward. The efficiency of an EIS can generate controversy about who should see company data first, and how much time line managers need to examine data before having to respond to senior management inquiries.

The data provided by an accounting information system are critical to the successful operation of any business and are the basis of an EIS. But these data can be made more useful by supplementing them with data from other sources. The data communications capabilities now available allow any business to access external data bases of all kinds for information that can then be incorporated into the reports and analysis used by management in the EIS.

There are three types of support technology for these EIS. **Status access** allows executives to call up preselected categories of data. **Query and analysis** allows "what if" analysis and other types of data manipulation. **Office automation** includes word processing, electronic mail, calendaring, and similar functions.

Exhibit 14-1 on page 494 gives examples of possible items in an executive support system.

Microcomputers and End User Computing

Office Automation. The first applications using microcomputers are usually office automation, such as word processing, budgeting spreadsheets, files used only by that user (such as personal mailing lists and employee evaluations), and electronic mail. At this stage, it seems that the microcomputer user is not part of the information system. But this quickly changes as microcomputer users become more experienced. The employee evaluations file kept in the personal files could tie to the corporate personnel file. The budgeting spreadsheets could take information off the corporate accounting records and those spreadsheets could then be incorporated into reports developed on and printed by the word processing program. In addition, these reports then are part of the information system and must be submitted to and processed by their recipients. Thus, the dividing line between office automation and information systems is fuzzy. The same microcomputer can be effective in both, and each can help support the other.

End User Computing. In the 1930s, telephone usage exploded in the United States. At that time, an operator was required to complete a call. Projections generated great consternation by estimating that by the 1950s, half of the women in the United States would have to be telephone operators in order

EXHIBIT 14-1   Possible Items in an Executive Support System

Source	Monthly	Weekly	Daily
Accounting information system	Financial statements	Product status Shipments Staffing summary Loan summary Construction progress Trial balances Expense exceptions Health insurance operations Auto loan operations Project tracking	Sales for key items Production output Quality summary Utility loads Cash balances Hospital admissions Bank asset summaries Overtime reports Energy consumption Customer service levels New account totals Rail operations report Utility meter readings Puchasing Utility operations report Brokerage sales
External data bases and data sources		Market summary Competitive summaries	Competitive pricing Load forecasting Exchange rates Stock performance Industry news Legislative action Government news

for the system to work. The primary reason this did not occur is that the telephone user became the operator and made the call directly. The computer industry in the 1990s is in a similar situation. There are huge backlogs of requests for additional information and systems. Half of the 560 European information services managers recently surveyed by Arthur Andersen reported that their departments were overwhelmed by requests for new or improved systems. Backlogs stretch up to three years. The situation in the United States is similar. The solution has to be similar to the telephone solution—the computer user must do more of the work of the computer specialist. That means the computer user must have

1. *Access*. The computer user must have access to needed information, but not unlimited access to all information in the file or the data base.
2. *Tools*. The computer user must have hardware and software tools that are powerful enough to get the job done, but not too difficult for nonprofessionals to use, and not too time consuming to set up.
3. *Training*. As the access and tools become available, the computer user must get training in both.

Management Approach to Microcomputers.   Management attitudes, training programs, and other elements of corporate culture significantly influence the productivity of microcomputer users. The following are the experiences of two companies that started on approximately equal footing. Their names are not used, but these are actual companies.

In Company 1, a production accounting group installed a number of microcomputers—far fewer than the number of accountants—in order to speed the completion of certain short-term, repetitive tasks. The group manager viewed microcomputers as fancy adding machines, provided minimal training in their use (largely on employees' own time), and strictly limited the tasks that could legitimately be accomplished on them. For example, word processing was not allowed because reports could be sent, as in years past, in handwritten form to the word processing pool. Under this set of expectations and rules, microcomputers had limited impact on productivity in the accounting group. While some employees reported that they were performing more efficiently, computers were viewed as a convenience rather than a necessity. Within 16 months, usage of the microcomputers dropped from its initial high. In sum, low expectations and limited encouragement yielded very modest results.

In Company 2, microcomputers were distributed throughout an accounting group and a management group as part of a program to put a computer on

CONCEPT SUMMARY		
Getting the Most Out of Information Systems		
Source of Improvement	*Objectives*	*Steps*
Information content	Approve IT investments that directly support business strategy.	Translate business vision into IT guidelines.
		Use information value analysis to ensure that IT expenditures produce net economic benefits.
Information technology	Reduce distance between information generators and users.	Decentralize IT capabilities to support frontline decision makers.
		Ensure that application development entails frequent interaction with users.
Delivery capabilities	Develop internal and external capabilities allowing IT to support business strategy.	Focus resources on pivotal IT jobs.
		Aggressively pursue outsourcing alternatives.
		Capture benefits by linking IT support to business change.

every desk. Planned uses included spreadsheet and data base work, word processing, and decision support. Employees had access to training on company time, and skilled users were put in both groups to help others and to develop customized applications. Expectations were high; the results were higher. Productivity in routine tasks increased, leaving time for better analytic work and "what if" scenarios, and useful new analyses and reports emerged. Some employees redesigned their jobs—for example, one person reduced 30 hours of routine work to 3 automated hours. Employees without computer literacy felt that they were stagnating, and computer literacy was soon defined as a job requirement. In sum, an established company shook itself up, trimmed down, educated for the future, encouraged job and organizational changes, and established a spirit of experimentation.

Company 1 viewed microcomputers as a tactial resource of limited importance, while Company 2 viewed them in a more open-ended, unstructured way that encouraged employees to make them their own. The second attitude allowed microcomputers to become an important resource. The equipment was the same; management support and training made the difference.

MANAGEMENT OF INFORMATION SYSTEMS

Information systems must be developed, equipment must be purchased and maintained, and the system must continue to operate over time. To do this well requires good management and a lot of hard work. The variety of tasks and steps required to create, operate, and update them is called the **management of information systems** (MOIS). Managers must consider what the system should accomplish in terms of the overall business strategy and develop a plan for delivering appropriate information where it is needed. If the company already has computer systems and networks, for the sake of efficiency managers should plan to integrate and consolidate systems. Finally, managers must evaluate the return on their investment in computer technology.

Because overall responsibility for MOIS crosses departmental and divisional boundaries, many organizations develop an **information systems steering committee**. This steering committee usually contains IS specialists as well as representatives of all line departments or divisions. Steering committee duties typically include:

1. Deciding upon the level of IS capability desired.
2. Setting IS long-range and short-range plans.
3. Determining project priorities.
4. Approving IS expenditures, including the annual budget and specific proposals for equipment.

Goals of Information Systems

Management starts with goals and objectives and the management of information systems is no exception. The goals of information systems are quite varied, as might be expected from an area which is at the same time visionary (examining leading edge technology for competitive advantage) and practical (processing the payroll checks for distribution every other Friday). These goals fall into three categories: strategic, end user, and operational.

Strategic Goals. A common misconception among management is that if information technology is not embedded in the product, it is not strategic. Yet, each company has the potential to invent its own equivalent of the SABRE reservations system in its industry. It is also important that the company not be surprised by a competitor. If management focuses on short-term financial goals, strategic use of computer systems becomes impossible. If strategic planning is adequate and goals are sufficiently long term, it is possible, though difficult, to plan for integration of information systems. Planning is especially critical for complex technology projects, which can run over several years and cost millions of dollars. Unfortunately, many times information systems projects have not delivered on competitive advantage promises. It is important for systems planners to be realistic and credible.

End User Computing Goals. If management does not support end user computing, the system is likely to be underutilized. One technique is to get top managers to use a personal computer. It is an experience they should no longer avoid, even if they cannot type.

Most companies need more interaction between information systems specialists and end users. Information systems specialists need to communicate with others in the company in business terms, not technology terms. A useful technique is to use simple analogies to work up to explaining the full complexity of technical decisions. One goal of the systems specialist should be the better understanding of business missions and projects. This may require training and then asking for additional responsibility to demonstrate business management skills. In addition to helping people become more productive, the information systems specialists can also help protect the user from the flood of conflicting information and advice from vendors. Unfortunately, information systems specialists and users usually each wait to be invited by the other.

The **information center** was originally conceived by IBM Canada in response to increasing demands by end users for programmers to provide them with mainframe solutions to their business problems. There was an enormous backlog of users' requests for applications development—a backlog involving a wait of months or years. As the backlog and user frustration grew, the need for a special department, the information center, that would exist specifically to provide end users with access to computer resources became more and more urgent. The information center staff was in charge of facilitating interactions with end users, and were valued more for their people skills than their technical skills. For the first time, end user tools for mainframes were brought in, and employees were given limited access to computer data and computers.

Microcomputers came into corporations as a way for employees to have control over their computer functions. Information centers often tried to control the microcomputer proliferation; they became the gatekeepers of the microcomputer environment, performing evaluations, purchasing equipment, and supporting users. End users are often more aware of how the technology could be used strategically in their particular jobs, business, or industry. As a result, more and more purchasing power is moved to functional departments, with the information center left in control of recommendations, training, and support. At this point, the information center is sometimes abolished as a cost-cutting move.

Some information centers have aligned themselves with end users and the strategic goals of the organization in order to provide real value. This means getting more involved in tactical and strategic business decisions (not only technical decisions) and working with end users to help them develop mission-critical applications. In essence, the information center becomes an internal consulting organization.

Operational Goals.   Day-to-day management of information systems is critical. The first goal should be to build credibility by delivering reliable IS services. This would include extensive backup of all information and the capability to quickly recover from physical disasters. The second goal should be to improve basic business processes. The third goal should be to control information systems costs. This is made more difficult and is often not properly rewarded if management does not understand information systems costs. Information systems costs must be explained in business terms.

Planning of Information Systems

Information systems planning requires that a company know what it wants. Companies must define how information technology fits in with their overall business strategy. From these broad goals, the company can derive an overall plan of what information is needed where in the company—and how it will be supplied by the system. The following questions should be answered as part of any information systems plan:

1. How should the company be using computers in the organization today and in the years to come? How should the company be spending its IS dollars?
2. What applications will remedy pressing problems? What applications will establish a basis for subsequent systems development?
3. What applications' successes are reasonably assured?
4. What applications will provide large, immediate savings? What applications will provide long-term return on investment?
5. What applications can be achieved with existing resources?
6. What applications will create visibility for the IS department? What applications will best demonstrate the IS department's contribution to the organization?
7. What applications will help the organization carry out its strategy and achieve its goals? What applications can help the organization create new strategy?

Information systems planning can be closely linked to strategic planning for an entire company and thus serve the company more effectively. It is critical to align the information technology efforts of a firm with its business objectives. Information technology addresses internal "markets"—different functions and levels of the company—and increasingly will be addressing external markets.

If it misses serving these markets early, it will harm rather than further the fulfillment of the firm's strategic plan.

Internal Consistency.   The plan must be internally consistent so that it makes sense from the highest level, the company mission, to the lowest level of operating detail. Because planning requires breaking down a complex company or information system into smaller, manageable units, the fully assembled plan can then be "reality checked" against the performance goals it should support.

External Validity.   The plan's external validity has to be verified. Establishing the external validity of even the most persuasive plan is difficult. The primary means of validating an information systems plan is through dialogue with the executives who have established the company's strategic plan. Planning at both levels—the company's strategic plan and its information technology strategic plan—accompanied by dialogue between the planning groups is the best approach in both areas. Top management's definitions can and should guide the formation of information systems strategy, and the knowledge of information technology professionals can serve as a "reality test" for management's overall strategic plan. Validation is a task of both management and information systems specialists.

Integration of Systems

If the next step in system development is a complex integration of existing systems and networks, it is often useful to use an outside firm. Martin Marietta had 15 independent business units, each of which developed independent and inconsistent information systems. Integration is now required because the company cannot start over. A typical problem will be to couple a materials requirements planning package on an IBM mainframe to a shop floor control system running on a Digital Equipment Corporation minicomputer. The two systems might cost $500,000, but it costs $5,000,000 to have Andersen Consulting integrate the two. The company must first develop a comprehensive requirements analysis. At that point, it is possible to enter into a contract with an outside firm, which lays out the responsibilities, liabilities, and risk. The contract should include

Performance specifications. There should be as many system performance specifications as possible.

Subcontracts. The contracts between the primary integrator and any secondary equipment suppliers being used should be included. Prices should be specified. Make sure the primary integrator has access to the source code of the application programs and a license that allows the modification and upgrade of software as required. Consider signing a separate agreement with each vendor on the job.

Liabilities. The contract should identify who is going to pay if something goes wrong or if the project turns out to require more, or more expensive, hardware.

Dispute resolution. Consider ways to expedite dispute resolution, such as out-of-court arbitration. These reduce legal expenses and allow work to continue while disputes are settled.

Plans for integrator's future. There should be a plan for what will happen if the integrator is acquired, merges with another firm, or goes out of business. Who becomes responsible for finishing the job? Can you get the source code of the application programs?

Confidentiality. Ensure that the integrator and the integrator's employees are prohibited from disclosing any confidential, competitive information they may pick up on the job.

Prohibition on raiding. Experienced systems analysts are a critical resource for consultants and integrators. Integrators and consultants usually get these experienced analysts from their clients. The contract should prohibit this.

Consolidation of Data Centers

Consolidation means bringing together two or more data centers into a coherent, compact, and uniform whole. AT&T went from 12 data centers to 7 supercenters, reassigning or retiring 1,000 of 7,400 workers and saving $70 million. U.S. Steel went from two data centers to one supercenter, chopping the work force by 25% and saving $5 million.

Technologies. A trend toward consolidation explains the emergence of a number of technologies that cater to this need in the most cost-effective manner possible. The development of these technologies points to further consolidations within the consolidated supercenter. Eventually, these facilities could become almost totally automated. Some of the key technologies are

1. *Data repositories.* These types of information/architecture banks gather essential knowledge for the development of key applications into a central warehouse of information.
2. *Network management software and systems.* Products such as Cincom Systems, Inc.'s NetMaster and Codex Corp.'s 9800 bring telephone and data management under one central point of control.
3. *Multipartitioned mainframe operating systems.* An operating system feature such as Amdahl Corp.'s Domain allows one machine to perform like six, and soon more. Users benefit because they only have to pay for one software license, not six as before.
4. *Automated storage.* Tape storage servers now allow Cray Research, Inc., Digital Equipment Corp., IBM, and other types of systems onto the same floor and share the same common tape storage repository. IBM is attempting to automate the management of its whole mainframe memory hierarchy via systems-managed storage.

If several of the following forces apply to a company, it may be time to start consolidating the organization's data centers.

Costs. There may be companywide and industrywide pressure to reduce costs, or a need to raise funds, perhaps by selling computer equipment, in order to repay leveraged buyout debt. Underutilization of capacity due to shrinking business needs is another possibility, or there may be a need to defer major jumps in fixed costs, such as hardware, space, and project teams.

Focus. Sometimes it is critical to focus on the core business, especially if information systems are nonstrategic and a diversion of top management's attention. For example, the data center or development areas may do commodity work, such as payroll processing, which is not strategic to business success or business competitive differentiation. Also, when systems have a high degree of technical complexity, such as different types of hardware and software, these can often be centralized and benefit from common environments. The company may need a common computer base for acquired companies or may need to implement common management practices and standards, such as consolidating other service bureaus and outsourcing contracts.

Technical Factors. Business operations may require a more robust level of information systems delivery than can be managed by the existing information systems equipment and staff. This could be because of chronic underfunding, a poor track record of service delivery, an organization too small to handle growing needs, an inability to attract and retain staff, or a need to improve IT responsiveness.

Evaluating Information Technology

Often information technology does not generate measurable productivity gains. The two dominant reasons that the measured returns are so low, despite the capabilities of information technology and businesses' voracious appetite for it, are inadequate organizational structures and the difficulty of measuring costs and benefits.

Organizational Structures. Often, management fails to align information technology investments with business strategy and organizational structures. Companies need to change the pattern of work when new information technology suggests the need to do so and to reward flexibility. Firms need to develop a top-down information technology strategy and decision-making process. Typically, information technology budgets are assembled by questions from below as to what equipment is needed; by an additive process, the budget is often assembled without senior management involvement in what should and needs to be accomplished on a companywide basis.

Measurement of Costs and Benefits. Companies anxious to have a strong competitive position may buy technologies before those technologies are evolved; hence they buy problems and are unlikely to enjoy the expected productivity gains until the technology has matured. Analyses based on financial measures alone may miss highly important factors such as quality and service improvements and shorter product life cycle. The burden is on management to assess the potential benefits of information technology and capture them through a more thorough organizational restructuring and through better informed management participation in decisions about information technology investments.

There are several common measurement systems that give the wrong incentives. Business managers are not measured on achieving true business value from IS investments. This year's IS costs are compared with last year's rather than against the demand being serviced. IS management is compensated according to the size of their budget and staff rather than the efficiency of their operations.

Evaluating the impact of information systems is quite difficult. To the extent that computer systems reduce the number of employees needed to perform specific functions and increase the productivity of those who operate the automated system, a standard cost/benefit analysis is appropriate. But measuring the bottom-line impact of a pervasive system is difficult. Stable benchmarks within the company against which costs and benefits can be measured may be lacking. When Columbus came to America, his cost/benefit analysis could be, at best, faulty. Successful approaches include the following:

CONCEPT SUMMARY

Management of Information Systems

Management Strategies	Develop a corporate information policy. Decide who needs what pieces of information, when, and in what form. Keep in mind that every time you alter the policy, you'll probably change the decision-making environment of the user. Establish priorities and stick to them until there's reason to rearrange them.
	Take a hard look at the issue of changing the business to take fuller advantage of computer capabilities—to put your "computer power" where it's most needed.
	Examine the use of outside services. Many companies find they can't do everything inside, and probably shouldn't try.
Questions for Long-Range Planning	Is the company's computing expansion weighted toward production or control?
	What are the long-range computer plans? How do they track with the company's overall objectives?
	How do they match the plans of users within the company?
	How are decisions on systems, needs, and priorities being made? How should they be made?
	Do we need a steering committee representing all major line departments?
	What is the basic role of information systems in our business?
	What is its present value?
	Can information systems be made a profit center? If so, how will we charge the users?
	What kind of information will we need in the future?
	To make what decisions?

1. A *user utility assessment* determines the degree to which the direct users of new information technology value it.
2. A *value chain assessment* attempts to quantify the impact of information technology on functional goals within the company.
3. An *assessment of competitive performance* compares the company's newly implemented information technology to that of competitors.
4. A *vision assessment* looks at what degree of management's vision of the result has been achieved.
5. A *chargeback system* bills intracompany customers for services received. The purpose is to provide a better grasp of how resources are used and a firmer handle on ways to cut back the associated costs. Chargeback systems are most successful when they send customers a fixed rate, usage-based bill and try to operate as a business within a business. These systems require a considerable, long-term resource commitment. Migration from one chargeback implementation to another occurs fairly frequently when the previous approach is no longer effective as the company's needs and technology changes.

The use of several different methods promises the best results.

SYSTEM DEVELOPMENT

Problems with System Development

System development is time consuming and difficult and requires that companies align their business objectives, organizational structures, and information technology efforts. Otherwise, executives may apply a good solution to the wrong problem or push state-of-the-art systems onto employees who need to be retrained. Top management must be well informed and active in order for the company to derive operational and strategic benefits from new information technology. Many firms have developed computer systems that

1. Did not meet users' needs.
2. Were not flexible enough to meet the business needs for which they were designed.
3. Overran their budget.
4. Overran their development schedule.
5. Did not have proper management approval.
6. Were difficult and costly to maintain.
7. Did not fit in with the company's long-term business, financial, and computerization plans.

Exhibit 14-2 provides some specific examples of problems in the development of different types of systems.

Design. System disasters often result when the system is designed either by accountants who know little about the computer or by computer people who know little about accounting. Accountants who know little about the computer usually use it to automate some mechanical, clerical tasks. Because the accountant knows little about the computer's capabilities, the computer is

EXHIBIT 14-2   Case Studies of Information Systems Development

Once the undisputed leader in data processing, government agencies are still using many of the same computer systems the government pioneered years ago. Many agencies are still in the Dark Ages in the uses of this technology.

1. The Treasury loses interest on millions of dollars because there isn't any integrated system to track the government's cash. If we ever had a balanced budget, it would be a miracle if you could tell when that moment came.

2. The system that serves the Maritime Administration is so creaky, according to the Grace Commission report on waste, that the "additional software fixes cannot be implemented for fear of causing total system failure."

3. At the Environmental Protection Agency, a computer system designed to keep track of thousands of legal cases and enforcement actions gathered dust for its first few years because nobody knew how to use it.

4. The tradition-bound Supreme Court insisted on a $2.2 million computer and word processing system as a solution to its burgeoning caseload. The backlog in the production of bound paperback volumes of court opinions, one of the system's main tasks, has grown to 18 months from one year since the system was installed.

5. After Iranian students clashed with police in the streets of Washington, the attorney general wanted to know how many Iranian students were in the United States. The Immigration and Naturalization Service (INS) did not know. The main information unit at the agency is an 8½-by-11-inch file folder. There are 20 million paper files, half in archives and the rest filed in offices. The 2.5 million active files in the New York City office are stacked so high on bookshelves and floors that workers can't reach most of them.

grossly underused. The major result is increased rigidity in the system because the computer must be served instead of a clerk. Additionally, because the accountant knows little of computer technicalities, the system usually takes far longer to develop and install than anticipated.

Systems specialists who know little about accounting try to use the computer's capabilities but wind up ignoring the legitimate needs of accounting. As a result, the developed system lacks adequate controls and possibly even an audit trail because the computer person ruthlessly eliminates checks and redundancies as inefficient. This inevitably leads to user dissatisfaction, excessive errors, and tremendous difficulty in backing up final figures from source documents.

Implementation.   Implementing information technology is not easy, changing the organization is not a trouble-free process, and good results are not guaranteed. Good management teams will achieve new levels of productivity and profitability through information technology, while mediocre management teams probably will not. Similarly, good technical teams are needed for complex tasks that will not yield to mediocre teams. A good management team can relate new technical possibilities to existing or potential markets and can foster top management interest in information technology. Project champions must emerge to defend initiatives and take a hands-on, optimistic approach to difficult and time-consuming implementations. The new system has to be thoroughly understood by many people, which means training. Work organization may have to change; new kinds of teams with a new mix of knowledge, and perhaps different reporting relationships, will probably be needed.

Also, management must be willing to scrap or supplement routine cost/benefit analyses where market changing information technology initiatives are concerned. There is always a way of measuring progress and impact, but it may not be the old way.

Setting Goals for System Development

The computer provides different types of assistance for different types of systems. The more structured the situation and the related decision making, the more the system can itself make the basic decisions. As an example, if a company has a policy to not sell to any firm that is over its credit limit, this decision can be programmed into the system. The more unstructured the decision, the more the system will function as support (with data and calculations) to a human decision maker. For example, if two production orders cannot be completed on time, the decision as to which should be delayed should be made by a manager, not a machine. The more operational the decision, the larger the computer's role in the decision making, while the more strategic the decision, the smaller the computer's role in the actual decision making. However, in all cases, the data accumulated and analyzed by the computer will be the critical basis for the decision. Exhibit 14-3 illustrates these concepts.

The cost of labor is increasing each year, the cost of electronic systems is decreasing each year, and almost 20 percent of this country's gross national product is yearly spent on office functions, much of which could be automated. The simple economics are clear. The computer has only begun to make its impact on American business.

In addition, the computer offers the chance for economic growth by more efficiently using the materials available. The potential for savings in production and distribution in the American economy is staggering. Furthermore, the computer represents an opportunity to use the capabilities of millions of people more effectively by relieving them of mechanical burdens that do not allow them to use their human capacity for creativity and judgment.

Exhibit 14-4 gives a brief chronology of the development of the ASAP system of American Hospital Supply Corp.,which was discussed near the beginning of the chapter. By providing an electronic connection between hospitals and its own order entry system, AHSC made it so easy for hospitals to order

EXHIBIT 14-3   Framework for an Information System

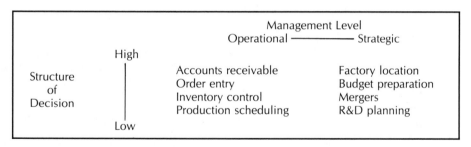

| | | Management Level |
| | | Operational ———————— Strategic |

		Operational	Strategic
Structure of Decision	High	Accounts receivable	Factory location
		Order entry	Budget preparation
		Inventory control	Mergers
		Production scheduling	R&D planning
	Low		

EXHIBIT 14-4   Development of the ASAP System of American Hospital Supply Corp.

Time	Functions
1957	Cards were keypunched at distribution centers for each order to produce a packing list, a summary for A/R, and item cards for sales analysis.
early 1960s	Card punch took place in distribution center connected to phone line. Hospitals received prepunched cards for every item ordered from AHSC and sent orders over the phone lines.
mid-1970s	Connection was made from hospital to mainframe computer rather than card punch. First use of name Analytic Systems Automatic Purchasing.
1977	ASAP 2 provided a printed, interactive response for verification and recommendation of substitutes for out-of-stock items.
1980	ASAP 3 allowed customization to the hospital's satisfaction; customer could also inquire on-line about the status of orders and prices.
early 1980s	ASAP 3 Plus added bar code scanning of shelf labels, requisition forms, and a catalog.
1983	ASAP 4 made first computer-to-computer connection, in which the hospital's computer produced orders that were sent to the AHSC mainframe. Confirmation was then sent back to the hospital's computer.
1984	ASAP 5 let the IBM PC act as the customer's input/output device to the system. The customer could use the microcomputer to build and edit order files rather than doing that on-line.
1988	ASAP*Express gave the customer the option of placing the order with another supplier.

its products that some virtually stopped ordering other suppliers' products. Later, ASAP became so popular that AHSC could use it to sell other suppliers' products. Initially, ASAP was limited to AHSC, but competitive pressure from the development of competing systems such as QuickLink from Abbott Laboratories and 3M Corp. broadened the system to allow purchase from any supplier. The following should be noted from this experience:

1. Creative use of information technology can provide a competitive advantage.
2. The development of sophisticated systems is a step-by-step process. Each step must provide a substantial improvement, but should not try to make too many changes at once. Later versions of the system can always make further improvements.
3. Even if the initial use of information technology provides a proprietary connection, it will eventually connect to other firms because of competitive pressure.

The potential of the computer has only barely been tapped. Even today, a majority of firms with sales under $25 million use essentially manual methods. Although all of the largest businesses, such as the firms in the *Fortune* 500, have their own computers, more than 90 percent of these firms have a backlog of applications they would like to develop that have not yet been completed. On average, these firms have three years of application backlog. The work involved in developing these systems can only be measured in person-centuries. Thus, even though large companies have their own computers, they are not even close to using the applications they presently conceive.

Management Assumptions About Information Technology

Management's attitudes toward information technology can have a decisive effect on the success or failure of technology in the workplace. Managers normally display one of three attitudes:

1. *Idealists* wholeheartedly favor the use of information technology and, where they perceive any difficulties, expect them to be positively resolved in due course.
2. *Skeptics* believe that information technology tends to undermine existing organizational strengths and believe their task is to minimize the disruptions imposed by the limited amount of information technology already in place.
3. *Realists* welcome information technology but consider that it has hidden costs and is likely to cause significant disruptions in the course of its implementation.

The major obstacle in the minds of key executives who are ambivalent or negative toward information technology is lack of communication and understanding between corporate management and information technology leaders. The obstacles can be overcome by efforts from both sides. Corporate managers need to become more familiar with information technology, while information technology specialists need to understand better the businesses to which they are contributing.

Overall System Development Process

Suppose a company is now convinced of the desirability of a computer-based system. How does the company go about developing this system? This **system development process** includes seven basic steps.

System Analysis.   In **system analysis**, the analyst becomes familiar with the process or task to be studied. Documentation in the form of written descriptions and flowcharts of the present system is needed in order to identify the information processing flow. Difficulties are identified and recommendations made.

Statement of Objectives.   The **statement of objectives** identifies the overall purpose and specific objectives of the proposed system; in other words, what the proposed system will try to accomplish. The analyst will have to determine the output necessary to accomplish these objectives and the data base necessary to generate this output.

System Design.   Once the system objectives have been approved, the **system design** must specify the system requirements more precisely, such as where data would be captured, the required processing, and where the output would be used. Then the analyst must define the basic modules that will satisfy these system requirements and arrange these modules into a functional design. The entire system must then be analyzed on a cost/benefit basis.

System Specification.   The **system specification** then details the system and how it will work. This includes the exact software and hardware environment, the exact appearance of input forms and output documents, the program flowcharts, and the complete details of the files to be maintained and their structure. The manual procedures are now totally spelled out.

Programming.   At this point, the specifications detail precisely what the individual programs are to do and the flowcharts of how the programs are to work. The **programming** tasks are then to

1. Write the computer programs in the chosen language.
2. Develop test data.
3. Test the programs to ensure that they are working.
4. Prepare documentation on the program and how to use it.

Implementation.   After the system is designed and the programs are working, the job is then the **implementation** of the new system in place of the old. This step consists of installing the new hardware (if any), writing detailed procedures orienting people to the new system (including any necessary training), converting files to the new format, and then operating the old and new systems in parallel.

Evaluation.   After the new system has been "shaken down" and has been in operation for a reasonable period of time (usually six months), an **evaluation** should assess the progress and status of the new system. This review should include the documentation, the general acceptance by users, and an analysis comparing the actual costs and benefits as opposed to the anticipated costs and benefits of the system.

Summary of Basic System Development

System development is a process of systematically refining the plans for the system, making them more and more specific until there is a completed implemented system. The process is similar to that of painting. The artist begins by sketching the overall conception of the painting, and gradually adds more and more detail until it is complete. It is impossible for a painter to start and completely finish one small segment of a painting, then start and finish another small segment, and continue in this fashion until the painting is complete. Each piece might be acceptable, but the work as a whole would not fit together. Similarly, it is impossible to jump directly to the programming of even a small section of a system until the entire system has been sketched in the system

CONCEPT SUMMARY

Basic Steps of System Development

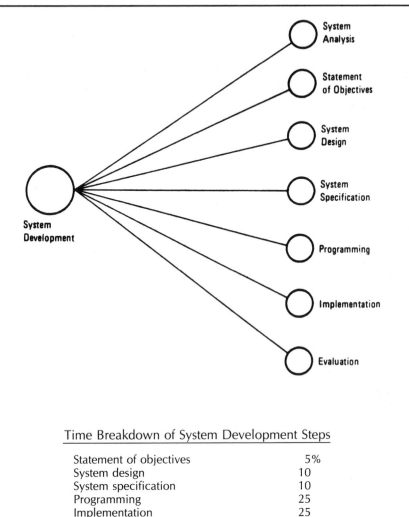

Time Breakdown of System Development Steps

Statement of objectives	5%
System design	10
System specification	10
Programming	25
Implementation	25
Evaluation	5
Contingency	20
	100%

Note: System Analysis will take little time for well-organized firms. For disorganized firms, however, it could take more time than the rest of system development combined. As a result, this step is omitted from this breakdown.

design and the system specification steps. However, the number of major preliminary sketches, so to speak, that must be made for any particular system development is a matter of judgment. In vast and complicated systems, the process must be more deliberate, with more intermediate stages. In extremely simple situations, the process might need only a rough sketch for an especially simple system. Although system development must go through the seven steps given in this chapter, it is not always necessary to go through them in seven completely separate steps. There can be more steps or fewer steps, as the occasion requires.

Feasibility Study

The first step in the development of a large-scale system is often a **feasibility study,** a preliminary review of the entire system development project. The system development process is very time consuming and expensive; the system analysis stage alone can easily cost tens of thousands of dollars, and the system development effort can take five years or more. For these reasons, management is understandably reluctant to start on a new system development effort—hence the feasibility study. The feasibility study reviews the potential of a new system development effort and tries to determine if the potential benefits make it worthwhile to proceed. The following five questions are the basic notions of feasibility:

1. Is it technically *possible* to get the system working with the available people and technology?
2. Do the *benefits* of this system justify its *costs* in time, money, and other resources?
3. Will the management and staff in the company *support* and *use* the system?
4. Does the system meet all *legal* and *regulatory requirements*?
5. Can the system be developed in the *time frame* given?

However, at the beginning of system development, the feasibility study must be very general, because without the detailed information of the system analysis, statement of objectives, and system design, it is impossible to have any degree of certainty about the costs and benefits. As a result, a separate feasibility study is not always necessary, especially in small systems. These five questions are answered during the system development process. Chapter 15 shows that these questions are answered in the statement of objectives and the system design, when more facts are available to better answer them.

Project Management

Chapters 14, 15, and 16 discuss the way system development should proceed. Unfortunately, there are many problems associated with actually getting these steps accomplished. There is the extensive time scale, since the entire system development process takes weeks, months, and even years. There is the large number of steps, all taking different amounts of time, done by different people at different locations, and some of which are dependent upon earlier steps. It is necessary to keep the entire process organized—with so many steps and so many people it is easy for the project to become confused. Because of this, techniques have been developed to help with this potential difficulty. The two primary techniques were discussed in Chapter 8—GANTT charts and PERT/CPM networks.

CASE Technology: The New Systems Engineering Environment

Virtually everyone involved in information technology agrees that:

1. The performance of systems design and implementation teams is a very real concern, with projects almost always taking longer than expected to complete.
2. The computer can be a tremendous tool for increased productivity.

As a result, there is a tremendous effort now underway to use the computer to assist in the development of computer-based systems. This effort is usually referred to as **computer-aided software engineering (CASE)**. CASE technology is a "toolbox" that helps build sophisticated systems more efficiently and more rigorously than previously possible. With CASE technology, a problem is defined and broken down into small units, and the units are distributed for solution to small teams responsible for only one unit at a time. Working in a parallel rather than in a linear fashion, teams solve their part of the problem. Those solutions are in turn synthesized into a whole system. Because the application program is efficiently written by a machine at each stage, more time can be invested at the design phase. Design errors must be identified because their impact will be magnified when the design is actually implemented.

Each CASE "toolbox" has strengths and weaknesses. The technology is new, powerful, and still unfamiliar to many potential users. For optimal quality and productivity, teams should be composed of (1) system designers and eventual users and (2) active team participants and boundary representatives. Boundary representatives are people in an organization who will be at least peripherally affected by a major new information system and will therefore need to be represented, to some degree, in the team that designs it.

Effect of Existing, Older Computer Systems

Markets change but often computer systems do not. When banks first began automating 20 or more years ago, they organized their data bases by account number because that is how transactions are recorded. Today, banks want to reorganize their data by customer name, which helps with marketing. Newer data bases have the flexibility that the banks need built in, but switching is difficult and costly. One British clearing bank estimates that its changeover will take five years and cost nearly $1.7 billion. The banks are not alone. In Europe, firms are rushing to revamp their old computer systems to cope with 1992's single market. Price Waterhouse found managers growing increasingly worried that they are getting less for each incremental information technology expenditure.

Even when the old systems become obsolete, their companies cannot run without them. Beset by increasing requests for modifications to existing systems, and tight budgets, many companies must fix the old systems. That reduces the backlog of requests, but at the cost of postponing still further a new, integrated system. As data processing matures in an organization, an increasing percentage of the total effort is spent on the maintenance of existing systems and a decreasing percentage is spent on the development of new systems. A programming staff may spend 80 to 90 percent of its time just maintaining current computer programs. A diagram of this relationship is shown in Exhibit 14-5.

Walling Off. One approach to old systems is to wall them off. Instead of constantly tinkering with them, use them as a platform on which to build the new, and build a "gateway" to link the old system with the new. But maintaining the discipline of not changing the old system is hard. Users are not happy to see their urgent request postponed until the new system can be built. Computer programmers find it hard to resist seemingly little changes. Nonetheless, the approach works, especially on big projects. Citibank used this method for "Operation Paradise," which during the 1970s moved much of the computing from mainframes to departmental minicomputers. In contrast, Bank of America's vacillation between renovating the old and building the new helped to create one of computing's biggest disasters, an $80 million project to improve administration of its trust department that never produced results.

Reengineering. Another approach to old systems is "reengineering." Software tools can convert old-style systems into almost new. Systems integrators—such as Cap Gemini Sogeti, Electronic Data Systems (EDS), Arthur

EXHIBIT 14-5   Breakdown of System Development Effort

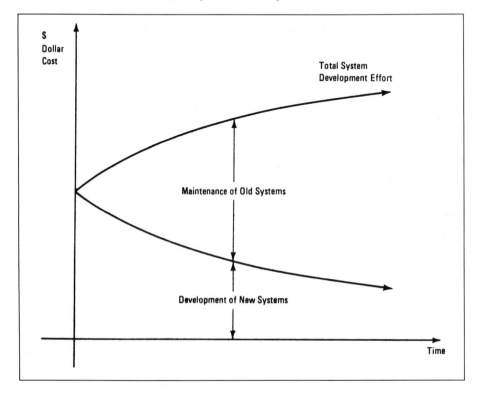

Andersen, and Price Waterhouse—offer help in building new computer systems from old. For example, a systems integrator may recommend that temporary programmers maintain the old system while the company's own people turn their attention to the new. Even when strong measures and consultants are not required to convert old systems into new, firms would still benefit from a stricter division between the old and new. Data processing departments that separate computer maintenance from new development are often more efficient than those that have the same staff do both.

Firms have trouble keeping up the morale of programmers doing maintenance work. The firm can replace the lack of a technical challenge with the business challenge to learn about the business functions that the systems are meant to support. Such a challenge breaks down the barriers between information systems specialists and management. Changing computer systems to fit changing business needs is the purpose of automation, and no one can do that better than someone who understands both.

Microcomputer-Based System Development

Chapter 13 discussed the microcomputer counterpart to the larger-scale system illustrated in Chapters 9 through 12. Microcomputers have many of the same characteristics as large-scale systems, but in a simplified way. Similarly, microcomputer-based system development has many of the same characteristics as large-scale system development but in a simplified way. However, microcomputers and large-scale systems were designed and developed from completely different perspectives. The larger systems emphasize control, security, accuracy, and privacy. The smaller (microcomputer) systems emphasize ease of use, low cost, user-friendliness, and simplicity. As a result, mainframe information systems tend to be controlled, accurate, and secure, but also expensive, difficult to use, and time consuming to develop. Similarly, microcomputer information systems tend to be easy to use, inexpensive, and relatively straightforward to develop, but also undocumented, insecure, relatively uncontrolled, and potentially inaccurate.

Downsizing. Some firms have no choice between mainframe-based systems and microcomputer-based systems. The very largest systems require a mainframe. Airline reservation systems, for example, need to be mainframe-based because of the huge volume of data to be stored and the huge number of transactions to be processed as millions of people make and change reservations, pay for tickets, get seat assignments, take flights, and so on. Small businesses only need and can only afford a microcomputer-based system. However, most large firms have to choose between developing their systems for the mainframe or for the microcomputer. The cost differences between mainframe and microcomputer systems are so dramatic that now virtually any system that can run effectively on a microcomputer is being developed for that "platform." Indeed, many firms spend much of their system development budgets on moving applications from mainframe systems to microcomputer systems. This process is called **downsizing.** The reason for this practice is that when the applications were originally developed, only a mainframe could process them. Recently, the capabilities of the microcomputer have increased so rapidly that many applications that required the use of a mainframe now no longer do so. Downsizing is certainly going to continue. Some analysts believe that it will soon mean the end of the mainframe. They liken the mainframe to a doomed dinosaur. Other analysts believe that the role of the mainframe, while shrinking as a percentage of computing, will remain. They liken the microcomputer to a pickup truck and the mainframe to an 18-wheel tractor-trailer.

Stand-alone. Before the development of microcomputer systems around 1980, virtually all accounting systems were either mainframe based or done by hand. These systems were often extremely difficult for most people to use or they did not generate needed information. As a result, many employees bought microcomputers for their own job needs, including budgeting, keeping track of clients, evaluating employees, and so on. These purchases of microcomputer systems were not controlled or coordinated. The result was a proliferation of individual microcomputer systems that could not communicate with each other or with the mainframe. Many centralized IS departments tried to ban the purchase of microcomputers, but were largely unsuccessful. Through tapping supplies budgets, and other remarkable examples of ingenuity, employees continued to purchase microcomputers. In many cases microcomputer users became their own small data processing managers. But these employees were not trained in or sensitive to the need for internal control. Often, they neglected to document their systems. As a result, a system would collapse when the employee responsible for it left or was promoted.

Even in the development of microcomputer-based systems, the basic seven steps of system development are important. This includes the necessity of documentation for the system and internal controls to detect and correct errors.

Movement to the Future

In large corporations, business units have often built independent information systems without anticipating the need to coordinate with other units' information systems. Thus, a company with multiple plants may be hampered in negotiating a new contract with a supplier because its purchasing officials cannot find out exactly what and how much overall the company buys from that supplier. Similarly, a company merging two divisions may discover that data definitions and systems in the divisions are incompatible. A company with an excellent transaction processing system may experience the need for management information—but the capability isn't there or it is primitive. Companies can simply outgrow their existing systems and face the need to rework them. Responding to such situations and many others, executives have a number of options, ranging from a ''patch'' that solves the problem for the present to a companywide system redesign.

Companies may consider implementing a strategic process that redefines the entire company data base. An integrated system is an ideal for which the conceptual and technological tools now exist, and some companies have tried to achieve it. However, such major projects can run into unexpected obstacles,

CONCEPT SUMMARY

Planning for Information System Change

Area	Questions
Information	What information flow is most effective to support the business system and strategy?
	How could this flow change over time?
	What changes does this imply both within the organization and for customers and suppliers?
	How are the information requirement priorities set?
Technology	What options exist and how will emerging technologies enhance those options?
	What technologies and configurations most effectively meet short and long-term requirements?
	For each technology choice, what standards must be established to meet long-term goals?
	What impact will these technology changes have on customers and suppliers?
Delivery	What requirements are needed to support the necessary technology and how will they be developed?
	What changes are needed in application development?
	Do the skills exist to convert to new technologies, and if not, how will they be acquired?
	Is any supplier or customer support required, and if so, what should it be?

including the impatience of line managers who find the time and money expenditures to be unnecessary burdens. Short of such overall efforts, 80/20 solutions have emerged as viable options—80 percent of the ideal achieved through 20 percent of the effort that the fully realized ideal would have required. Such solutions can generate many of the benefits without a major redesign and they serve as trial runs for larger projects.

Managers should develop business objectives to guide information technology efforts. These business objectives should include improved data coordination, flexibility, improved management information, and enhanced information systems effectiveness. Standard business disciplines are applicable, such as defining the project scope very tightly, and expecting some early evidence that the project is progressing well. Progress depends strictly on how well the system would serve business objectives.

REFERENCES

M. Earl, *Management Strategies for Information Technology* (Englewood Cliffs, NJ: Prentice Hall, 1989).

P. Gray, W. King, E. McLean, and H. Watson, eds., *The Management of Information Systems* (Chicago: Dryden Press, 1989).

K. Laudon and J. Turner, eds., *Information Technology and Management Strategy* (Englewood Cliffs, NJ: Prentice Hall, 1989).

B. Swanson and C. Beath, "Departmentalization in Software Development and Maintenance," *The Communications of the ACM*, Vol. 33, no. 6 (June 1990), pp. 658–667.

CHAPTER SUMMARY

Information technology can automate routine office work and deliver needed information. Taken a step farther, information technology can help a company achieve market advantage and cut internal costs. Integrating information systems within a company fosters communication among employees, which leads to increased productivity. Integrating systems among companies that do business together cuts coordination costs and encourages a more productive purchase-supplier relationship. From well-integrated systems, executive support systems can retrieve and process selected data needed for decision making.

Microcomputers typically are first used for office automation. As end users learn more about operating the computer, they link up with other end users and with the company data base. Companies that encourage microcomputer use tend to show increases in productivity and decreases in costs.

Managers should set goals for information systems, plan the system, integrate the new system with existing systems and evaluate the impact of the systems on the business. Computer consulting firms can help with complex integration of existing systems and networks. Companies can cut costs by consolidating data centers. Successful system development requires cooperation among management teams, technical teams, and other employees who will use the system. Systems are most useful and least costly when the accountant and the systems analyst cooperate in the development program.

System development entails system analysis, a statement of objectives, system specification, programming, implementation, and evaluation. The development process systematically refines the plans for the system until it is complete and implemented. Large-scale systems call for an initial feasibility study. CASE technology aids in system development and implementation by defining a problem and breaking it down into small units for solution. Obsolete systems can be either walled off or reengineered.

Mainframe systems provide control, accuracy, and security, but are expensive, difficult to use, and time consuming to develop. Microcomputers are relatively inexpensive, easy to use, and straightforward to develop, but they tend to be undocumented and relatively uncontrolled, potentially inaccurate, and insecure. Nevertheless, the dramatically lower cost of microcomputers has led many companies to downsize their applications from the mainframe.

Computer-aided software engineering (CASE) (p. 511)
Downsizing (p. 513)
Evaluation (p. 508)
Executive information system (EIS) (p. 492)
Executive support system (ESS) (p. 492)
Feasibility study (p. 510)
Implementation (p. 508)
Information center (p. 497)
Information systems steering committee (p. 496)
Information technology (p. 488)
Management of information systems (p. 496)
Office automation (p. 493)
Programming (p. 508)
Query and analysis (p. 493)
Statement of objectives (p. 507)
Status access (p. 493)
System analysis (p. 507)
System design (p. 508)
System development process (p. 507)
System specification (p. 508)

QUESTIONS ━━━

14-1. Briefly describe the three phases of information technology.

14-2. Briefly describe five different areas where computer systems can provide a company a differential advantage over its competitors.

14-3. List and briefly describe the three things that must be available for end users to do more of their own computer work.

14-4. Define management of information systems.

14-5. Distinguish between strategic goals, operational goals, and end user computing goals.

14-6. What are the basic questions that should be answered as part of any information systems plan?

14-7. Briefly describe the two dominant reasons why the returns on information technology are so low.

14-8. Contrast the philosophy of system development typically taken by accountants with that of computer professionals.

14-9. Distinguish between highly structured decisions and those with less structure. Distinguish between operational management decisions and strategic management decisions.

14-10. List the seven steps of system development and briefly describe what is accomplished in each.

14-11. What is a feasibility study? When might it be used? When might it not be used?

14-12. What does CASE stand for? What is it?

14-13. Compare walling-off and reengineering as solutions to the problems of older systems.

14-14. Explain the term downsizing and discuss its continuing importance in information systems development.

PROBLEMS ━━

14-15. Following is a list of important factors to be considered in the overall system development process. For each of these factors, state the phase of system development in which it would be considered and briefly mention how the factor affects that phase:

a. Privacy protection
b. Capacity for growth
c. Program flowcharting
d. Employee concern about change
e. Reliablity
f. Future problems
g. System flowcharting
h. Flexibility
i. Choice of programming language
j. Current problems
k. Cost

14-16. Following are ten background and personal characteristics of system development personnel. For each phase of system development, state the two characteristics that will most likely contribute to success in that phase:

a. Technical computer background
b. Extensive auditing experience
c. Familiarity with company operations
d. Effectiveness in written communication
e. Effectiveness in oral communication
f. Ability to focus on larger issues
g. Thoroughness
h. Systems point of view
i. Rigorous logical approach
j. Rapport with employees

14-17. Managers may become so accustomed to receiving only certain kinds of information that they fail to realize that additional information could be provided by a computer-based system. Give two specific examples of information that could easily be provided by a computer-based system but which is not normally available from a manual system for each of the following areas:

a. Accounts receivable
b. Accounts payable
c. Payroll
d. Financial statements
e. Sales

14-18. Computer-based information systems are capable of providing the data necessary for good performance evaluation of managers and employees. Give two specific examples of information that would be useful in the performance evaluation of each of the following positions:

a. Credit manager
b. Purchasing agent
c. Salesperson
d. Sales manager
e. President

14-19. (*CMA, adapted*) Curtis Company operates in a five-county industrial area. The company employs a manual system for all of its recordkeeping except payroll, which is processed by a local service bureau. Other applications have not been computerized because they could not be cost justified previously. The company's sales have grown over the past five years. With this substantial growth rate, a computer-based system seemed more practical. Consequently, Curtis Company engaged the management consulting department of its public accounting firm to conduct a feasibility study for converting its recordkeeping systems to a computer-based system. The accounting firm reported that a computer-based system would improve the company's recordkeeping system and still provide material cost savings. Therefore, Curtis Company decided to develop a computer-based system for its records. Curtis hired a person with experience in systems development as manager of system data processing. Her responsibilities are to oversee the systems operation, with special emphasis on the development of the new system. Describe the major steps that will be undertaken to develop and implement Curtis Company's new computer-based system.

14-20. (*CMA, adapted*) Business organizations are required to modify or replace a portion or all of their financial information system in order to keep pace with their growth and to take advantage of improved information technology. The process involved in modifying or replacing an information system, especially if computer equipment is involved, requires a substantial commitment of time and resources. When an organization undertakes a change in its information system, a series of steps is followed. The steps included in a system study are

a. Survey of the existing system
b. Analysis of information collected in the survey and development of recommendations for corrective action
c. Design of a new or modified system
d. Equipment study and acquisition
e. Implementation of a new or modified system

These steps tend to overlap rather than being separate and distinct. In addition, the effort required in each step varies from one systems change to another, depending on such factors as extent of the changes or the need for different equipment.

1. Explain the purpose and reasons for surveying an organization's existing system during a systems study.
2. Identify and explain the general activities and techniques that are commonly used during the systems survey and analysis of information steps of a systems study conducted for a financial information system.
3. In a financial information systems study, the systems survey and analysis of information steps are often carried out by a project team composed of a systems analyst, a management accountant, and other persons in the company who would be knowledgeable and helpful. What would the role of the management accountant be?

14-21. In a large organization, many different individuals might be associated with the system development process. In which steps of system development might each of the following people be involved, and what form would that involvement take?

a. Computer programmer
b. Data entry clerk
c. Systems analyst
d. Top management
e. Board of directors
f. Accountant
g. Bookkeeper
h. Outside consultant
i. Auditors
j. Data processing manager

14-22. In a small firm, only one person may be associated with the system development process. Suppose you are the accountant/bookkeeper for such a business and your employer wants to acquire a new computer-based system. In which steps of system development might you be involved, and what form would that involvement take?

14-23. Suppose a firm was considering the development of a new payroll system that would include the on-line collection of data on hours worked by each employee. A permanent identification card, unique to each employee, would be placed in a data collection terminal as employees entered and left each work area. This system would replace time cards, which were punched in and out as employees arrived and departed work; these time cards were collected and processed every two weeks.

1. What are the advantages for the company of the new on-line approach over the older system?

2. Why might employees react unfavorably to the new system? Give five actions you would take to overcome this negative attitude.

14-24. (*CMA, adapted*)   The headquarters of Gleicken Corporation, a private company with $3.5 million in annual sales, is located in California. Gleicken provides for its 150 clients an on-line legal software service that includes data storage and administrative activities for law offices. The company has grown rapidly since its inception three years ago, and its data processing department has mushroomed to accommodate this growth. Because Gleicken's president and sales personnel spend a great deal of time out of the office soliciting new clients, the planning of the EDP facilities has been left to the data processing professionals.

Gleicken recently moved its headquarters facility into a remodeled warehouse on the outskirts of the city. While remodeling the warehouse, the architects retained much of the original structure, including the wooden-shingled exterior and exposed wooden beams throughout the interior. The minicomputer distributed processing hardware is situated in a large open area with high ceilings and skylights. This openness makes the data processing area accessible to the rest of the staff and encourages a team approach to problem solving. Before occupying the new facility, city inspectors declared the building safe—adequate fire extinguishers, sufficient exits, and so on. In an effort to provide further protection for its large data base of client information, Gleicken has instituted a tape backup procedure that is on a time-delay mechanism and automatically backs up the data base weekly, every Sunday evening, avoiding interruption in the daily operations and procedures. All the tapes are then labeled and carefully stored on shelves reserved for this purpose in the data processing department. The departmental operator's manual has instructions on how to use these tapes to restore the data base should the need arise. In the event of an emergency, there is a home phone list of the individuals in the data processing department. Gleicken has recently increased its liability insurance for data loss from $50,000 to the current $100,000. This past Saturday, the Gleicken headquarters building was completely ruined by fire, and the company must now inform its clients that all their information has been destroyed.

1. Describe the computer security weaknesses present at Gleicken Corporation that made it possible for a disastrous data loss to occur.

2. List the components that should have been included in the disaster recovery plan at Gleicken Corporation in order to ensure computer recovery within 72 hours.

3. What factors, other than those included in the plan itself, should a company consider when formulating a disaster recovery plan?

14-25. (*CMA, adapted*) PWR Instruments is a manufacturer of precision nozzles for fire hoses. The company was started by Ronald Paige who has an engineering background and who serves as PWR's president. This closely held corporation has been very successful and has experienced steady growth. Reporting to Paige are six vice presidents representing the company's major functions—marketing, production, research and development, information services, finance, and personnel. The Information Services Department was established during the fiscal year just ended when PWR began developing a new computer-based information system. The new data base system employs a minicomputer with several terminals and microcomputers in each of the six departments connected to this main computer. The microcomputers are capable of both downloading data from and uploading data to the main computer. For example, analysts in the Finance Department are able to access the data stored on the main computer through the microcomputers and use the microcomputers on a stand-alone basis. PWR is still in the process of designing and developing new applications for its computer system.

Paige has recently received the management letter which was prepared by the company's external audit firm at the conclusion of the annual audit and has called a meeting with his vice presidents to review the recommendations. One of the major items that Paige wants to discuss with his management team is the recommendation that PWR form an information systems steering committee.

1. Explain why the external auditor would recommend that PWR Instruments establish an information systems steering committee and discuss the specific responsibilities of an information systems steering committee.

2. Identify the individuals at PWR Instruments who would most likely serve on the information systems steering committee.

3. Explain several advantages that PWR Instruments might realize from the establishment of an information systems steering committee.

4. An information systems steering committee must be familiar with the general system development cycle. Identify the steps in a system development cycle.

14-26. (*CMA, adapted*) The Internal Audit Department of Hastone Manufacturing Company recently concluded a routine examination of the company's computer facilities. The auditor's report identified as a weakness the fact that there had been no coordination by the Data Processing Service Department in the purchasing of microcomputer systems for the individual departments of Hastone. Of the 12 microcomputers in the organization, there now are three different hardware manufacturers. In addition, there are four or five different software vendors for spreadsheets, word processing, and data base applications, along with some networking applications for clusters of microcomputers. The reason for acquiring microcomputers in the operating departments was to allow employees in each department to conduct special analyses. Many of the departments also wanted the capability to download data from the mainframe. Therefore, each operating department had requested guidance and assistance from the Data Processing Services Department. However, Data Processing responded in a memorandum that it was understaffed and must devote full effort to its main priority, the mainframe computer system. There have been several complaints from managers of other operating departments regarding the memorandum. Apparently, before issuing this memorandum, the Data Processing Services Department had not consulted with any of the microcomputer users regarding their current and future software needs.

1. When acquiring microcomputers for various departments in an organization, describe the factors related to
   a. computer hardware that need to be considered during the initial design and setup phase of the microcomputer environment.
   b. operating procedures and system controls that need to be considered.
2. Discuss the benefits of having standardized hardware and software for microcomputers in an organization.
3. Discuss the concerns the memorandum is likely to create for the microcomputer users of Hastone Manufacturing.

14-27. (*IIA, adapted*) The Houseman Farms Company has decided to computerize its payroll, accounts payable, and general ledger operations. Houseman Farms consists of four separate farming companies owned and managed by the parent firm. All administrative and accounting functions are centralized at headquarters. Two people work full time in the accounting area. Payroll requires the most effort since labor comprises 35 percent of total operating expense. The size of the labor force varies, reaching a peak of several hundred workers from August through October. Weekly paychecks are prepared and records are kept for each worker. Payroll deductions include group hospitalization, Social Security taxes, and, if the employee desires, state and federal income taxes. Accounts payable are coded by company and crop as well as the account to which they apply. Some bills are allocated across several companies. About 300 checks are written each month. Some are delayed by the heavy payroll work load. The general ledger consists mostly of payroll and accounts payable entries. A separate set of books is kept for each company. These books provide the basis for financial statements and are used to prepare special reports, by crop, to respond to lender inquiries. Because Houseman Farms lacks the inhouse capability to perform the conversion to a computerized system, it plans to hire a consultant to analyze its needs and recommend equipment and software.

1. Prepare a schedule or list of activities which the consultant should be expected to perform for Houseman Farms.
2. Describe what data a consultant should gather and how the data should be collected.
3. Describe the techniques or methods a consultant should use to analyze the collected data.

14-28. (*IIA, adapted*)   A small manufacturer of automobile parts has just learned that its primary customer is requiring all of its suppliers to accept orders via electronic data interchange. The primary customer uses EDI instead of paper forms for transactions with its largest suppliers. The customer is expanding its use of EDI and intends to drop all suppliers who cannot participate in EDI within a year. Along with using EDI for orders, the customer also requires daily reports of the status of work-in-process for each of its orders so that it can modify orders by giving notice at least 48 hours before production begins. Currently, the manufacturer maintains manual records for receivables, payables, materials inventory, order entry, work-in-process, and finished goods inventory; it uses a service bureau for payroll. Finished goods inventory is very small as the manufacturer produces mostly "to order" for its larger customers and ships the parts immediately upon completion. The manufacturer wants to continue producing for its primary customer, even if it involves implementing EDI. Assume that the manufacturer has asked you to help it plan an automated system to respond to the primary customer's requirements. Specifically, you are to

1. Define the objectives of the new system.
2. Specify criteria for evaluating the system's effectiveness.
3. Describe the timing of systems analysis.
4. List the functions performed during systems analysis and relate each function to the new system.

DECISION CASE

(*CMA, adapted*)   Mickie Louderman is the new assistant controller of Pickens Publishers, a growing company with sales of $35 million. She was formerly the controller of a smaller company in a similar industry where she was in charge of accounting and data processing. She had considerable influence over the entire computer operations center, placing emphasis on decentralized data access, microcomputers with mainframe access, and on-line systems. The controller of Pickens, John Richards, has been with the company for 28 years and is near retirement. He has given Louderman managerial authority over both the implementation of the new system and the integration of the company's accounting information system (AIS). Louderman began to develop the new system at Pickens by using the same design characteristics and reporting formats that she had developed at her former company. She sent details of the new accounting information system to the departments that interfaced with accounting, including inventory control, purchasing, personnel, production control, and marketing. If they did not respond by a prescribed date, she would continue the development process. Louderman and Richards determined a new schedule for many of the reports, changing the frequency from weekly to monthly. After a meeting with the director of computer operations, she selected a programmer to help her with the details of the new reporting formats.

Most of the control features of the old system were maintained to decrease the initial installation time, while a few new ones were added for unusual situations; however, the procedures for maintaining the controls were substantially changed. Louderman appointed herself the decisive authority for all control changes and program testing that related to the AIS, including screening the control features that related to batch totals for payroll, inventory control, accounts receivable, cash deposits, and accounts payable. As each module was completed by the programmer, Louderman told the department to implement the change immediately, in order to incorporate immediate labor savings. There were incomplete instructions accompanying these changes, and specific implementation responsibility was not assigned to departmental personnel. Louderman believes that all operations people should "learn as they go," reporting errors as they occur. Accounts payable and inventory control were the initial areas of the AIS to be implemented; several problems arose in both of these areas. Louderman was disturbed that the semimonthly runs of payroll, which were weekly under the old system, had abundant errors and, consequently, required numerous manual paychecks. Frequently, the control totals of a payroll run would take hours to reconcile with the computer printout. To expedite matters, Louderman authorized the payroll clerk to prepare journal entries for payroll processing.

The new inventory control system failed to improve the carrying stock level of many items, causing several critical raw material stockouts that resulted in expensive rush orders. The primary control procedure under the new system was the availability of ordering and usage information to both inventory control personnel and purchasing personnel by direct access terminals so that both departments could issue purchase orders on a timely basis. The inventory levels were updated daily, so the previous weekly report was discontinued by Louderman. Because of these problems, system documentation is behind schedule and proper backup procedures have not been implemented in many areas. Louderman had requested budget approval to hire two systems analysts, an accountant, and an administrative assistant to help her implement the new system. Richards is disturbed by her request since her predecessor had only one part-time employee as his assistant.

Required:

1. List the steps Mickie Louderman should have taken during the design of the accounting information system to ensure that end user needs were satisfied.

2. Identify and describe three areas where Mickie Louderman has violated the basic principles of internal control during the implementation of the new accounting information system.

3. By referring to Mickie Louderman's approach to implementing the new accounting information system, identify and describe the weaknesses. Make recommendations that would help Louderman improve the situation and continue with the development of the remaining areas of the accounting information system at Pickens Publishers.

15 System Analysis and Design

Overview

The analysis of an existing system, identification of the objectives of the new system, and the logical design of the new system

Learning Objectives

Thorough study of this chapter will enable you to:

1. Recognize the different approaches to system development.
2. Describe the process of system analysis.
3. Give the components of a system analysis report.
4. Identify the purpose and elements of a statement of objectives.
5. Diagram a system using data flow diagrams and the entity-relationship model.
6. Explain the special system design considerations of distributed data processing.
7. Give the components of the system design report.

Outline

System Analysis

Statement of Objectives

System Design Considerations

The System Design Report

SYSTEMS IN THE REAL WORLD

Controlling Runaway Projects

A Sampling of "Runaway" Projects

Allstate Insurance. In 1982, with software from Electronic Data Systems, the insurer began to build an $8 million computer system that would automate it from top to bottom. Completion date: 1987. An assortment of problems developed, delaying completion until 1993. The new estimated price: $100 million.

City of Richmond. In 1984 it hired Arthur Young to develop a $1.2 million billing and information system for its water and gas utilities. Completion date: March 1987. After paying out close to $1 million, Richmond recently canceled the contract, saying no system had been delivered. Arthur Young has filed a $2 million breach of contract suit against the city.

State of Oklahoma. In 1983 it hired a Big Eight accounting firm to design a $500,000 system to handle explosive growth in workers' compensation claims. Two years and more than $2 million later, the system still didn't exist. It finally was finished last year at a price of nearly $4 million.

Blue Cross/Blue Shield United of Wisconsin. In late 1983 it hired Electronic Data Systems to build a $200 million computer system. It was ready 18 months later—on time. But it didn't work. The system spewed out some $60 million in overpayment and duplicate checks before it was harnessed last year. By then, Blue Cross says, it had lost 35,000 policyholders.

How to Keep a Project Under Control

1. Before designing the system, get suggestions from the people who will use it.
2. Put senior, nontechnical management in charge of the project to help ensure that it is finished on time and within budget.
3. Set up 12-month milestones—interim deadlines for various parts of the project.
4. Insist on performance clauses that hold suppliers and others legally responsible for meeting deadlines.
5. Don't try to update the system in midstream, before the original plan is finished.

Source: *Business Week*, 11/7/88, reprinted by permission.

This chapter goes through the system analysis and design phases of system development. The next chapter concludes the discussion of system development by presenting the implementation and evaluation phases.

System development can be done by many different people in many different ways. In all cases involving accounting information systems, accountants will be intimately connected with the system development. In some cases, an accountant, such as the controller, will direct the system development. In others, the accountant will be part of a system development team involving specialists from different areas of the business, including systems professionals. In small businesses, the accountant may do the entire system development with only clerical assistance. Some accountants specialize in this area and are called systems accountants. The chapter will refer to the system analyst as the one analyzing and developing the system. This system analyst may be a team that involves an accountant, or it may be an accountant alone.

System development has many purposes:

> *To undertake new accounting applications.* This would include, for example, the establishment and use of a perpetual inventory system in a firm which has only used a periodic system.

> *To expand the scope of existing accounting applications.* This might also include the extension of a perpetual inventory system to include a larger percentage of inventory or the addition of a new branch store.

> *To take advantage of technological changes.* The availability of a new type of cash register may make it possible for a retail store to utilize an entirely different method of checkout or price markings.

> *To correct mistakes in an existing system.* No system is perfect, and sometimes a major deficiency is identified which should be corrected. Often, systems have an excessive number of errors in the transactions, and the system must be revised to eliminate those errors or to detect them earlier.

> *To extend the accounting information system to provide competitive advantage.* Chapter 14 provided a number of examples of firms, such as American Hospital Supply Corp., that have achieved competitive advantage through the extension of their accounting information system.

Approaches to the Use of the Computer

There are three basic approaches to the use of the computer in the development of a new or revised system.

Implement a Standard Package. The first approach is to apply a standard package, or an approach that has been successful elsewhere, to the problem at hand. The advantages of this approach are clear:

1. The new or revised system can work, since it has already worked.
2. It is possible to become fairly familiar with the system either by observing it in operation or by studying its documentation.

The disadvantage is that it may not fit the present situation. Generally, this approach is the one taken by information systems specialists who know little about accounting.

Automate (or Reautomate) the Present System. The second approach is to use the computer to either automate or speed up the present system directly. Thus, if a clerk extends prices and adds up a column of figures, the new system will use the computer for the computations. If a computer is already used, the new system will use a faster computer. The advantage of this approach is that the present system is familiar and the new system will be essentially the same as the old. The disadvantages are that:

1. The new system underutilizes the capabilities of the computer.
2. The company loses the opportunity to rethink its mode of operation and to use the computer to operate more efficiently.

Generally speaking, accountants who know little about the computer take this approach.

Analyze and Develop. The third approach is to understand both the present system and the objectives it is to accomplish and then to use the computer to meet those objectives more efficiently and effectively. Rethinking the logic of the present system can lead to great savings. For example, one organization paid some employees daily, some weekly, some every two weeks, some semimonthly, and some monthly. The payroll system could easily be streamlined by paying all employees every two weeks. Apparently, the present system had just grown up, and no one had ever stopped to rethink it. The advantage of analysis and development is that potentially the organization will obtain the greatest benefits. The disadvantages of this approach are that:

1. It requires more time initially, although it will usually save time in the long run.
2. It requires more knowledge, discipline, and creative thought than the other approaches.

Exhibit 15-1 gives a parable of system design to show how this process should not be done. The rest of this chapter and the next will show how the process should be done.

SYSTEM ANALYSIS

In the system analysis, the analyst prepares documentation on the present system and how it works. This documentation will include both written descriptions and system flowcharts designed to picture the present information processing flow. A proper system analysis will include a brief description of the firm and its future prospects, a chart of the company's **organization structure**, samples of documents, forms, and flowcharts of procedures. The study should then identify any deficiencies and recommend improvements.

Process of System Analysis

To analyze a system successfully, the analyst needs to

1. Identify the system and its goals.
2. Understand and document how the system works.
3. Analyze the system for problems and deficiencies.
4. Develop cost-effective recommendations.

Congress passed legislation to encourage adequate student loan insurance programs. An Office of Education task force was established in the following year to support the Guaranteed Student Loan Program. The administration of the program had to establish the eligibility of schools and students to receive interest subsidies paid by the government. The staff could not catch up on the backlog and had to send interest subsidies relying only on lenders' statements.

An interim computer system was designed with the help of an outside contractor. Most of the personnel in the loan agency were new to the program and claimed that rigorous system specifications could not be developed. The computerized system used optical scanning and did not work satisfactorily, since the codes for schools had not been completed. Without the school coding, the guaranteed loan staff could not prepare a list of students to verify enrollment. Without the verification, interest payments could not be made automatically and had to be processed manually.

To overcome these difficulties, a contract to develop a system was awarded. The new system was supposed to streamline the loan history file and cover federal requirements. When this new system was introduced, a number of tapes containing essential data were lost in the conversion. The ten-reel master files had to be reconstructed many times. The system was run for the Office of Education, but the computer being used belonged to the Department of HEW, which did not give the system high priority.

Three years later, a contract to develop a successor system was awarded. A major accounting firm began to develop the second version of the system. The contractor claimed that the Guaranteed Student Loan Program staff was unclear in its requirements for the system. There were at least seven major amendments to the contract during implementation. Financial accounting requirements were not clearly specified. Major decisions took four to six weeks to be made. The contractor also underestimated the job. The slippage in implementation of the system created backlogs and contributed to an incomplete set of documentation for the system. Finally, the contractor was allowed to cancel the remaining part of the job before removing all of the errors in the system. The maintenance of this new system was awarded to yet another contractor and, as might be expected, the conversion was a rerun.

The General Accounting Office conducted a thorough study of the program four years later and identified a number of significant problems. The conclusion was that the system was poorly designed, poorly documented, and inadequately controlled.

5. Prepare a report to convince management that the analysis is correct and the recommendations are worth implementing. The report will also form the basis of further system development.

Components of the System Analysis Report

The **system analysis report** should present the seven components of a system analysis:

1. *General background.* The report should first describe the firm and its products, the competitive environment, and a statement of the firm's strategic plans. The firm's plans for acquisitions and growth should be included because they may indicate a need for increased system capacity.

2. *Organization structure*. The report should then describe where authority and responsibility lie in the company. This typically requires drafting organization charts.

3. *Job descriptions*. This section describes each position, its duties, areas of responsibility, and necessary qualifications. These descriptions would then tie to the organization charts. **Job descriptions** are critically important for later redefinitions of responsibility in a new system.

4. *Documents*. This section inventories all the documents, forms, and reports that the system uses or produces, both in blank and filled out. Typically, it becomes obvious that many documents can be eliminated. The document inventory indicates some of the types of information that a new system should generate.

5. *Procedures*. This section provides both a narrative description and system flowcharts of the important activities in the system. The documents described in the preceding section are a valuable reference. Keep in mind how the company makes its profit? Get in writing a complete discussion of all system procedures, and control techniques. This documentation is necessary for (a) communication with others, (b) assurance that the work is complete, and (c) backup for the later steps presented.

6. *Deficiencies*. This section pinpoints areas of difficulty or areas where important elements are missing. Use the knowledge of accounting theory, accounting systems, and internal control to identify weaknesses in the system under analysis. Weaknesses might include improper accounting treatment of transactions (such as not capitalizing assets appropriately), inefficient document or form design, lack of timeliness in report generation, inadequate internal control, and many others.

7. *Recommendations*. This final section specifies exactly what the company should do about the deficiencies. Develop cost-effective recommendations that the company can implement to correct any system deficiencies. The present system might be so unworkable that refining or modernizing it would not be worth the trouble. If so, the best recommendation might be to scrap the old system after developing a new one.

The report should begin with a title page and a table of contents. The title page names the report and identifies the system and company analyzed and the group preparing the report. The table of contents outlines the report. The report should be delivered with a **letter of transmittal** that provides an overall conception of the report, including the reason for its preparation and major results.

This is a general structure of a system analysis. It may not be entirely applicable to every case in exactly the same form. The analyst must use judgment in applying this structure to particular circumstances.

The analyst does not develop part one of the report, then part two, and so on until the report is complete. The first step is to sketch out the entire report, and develop the necessary material for each section. The second step is to make a final selection of recommendations. The third and final step is to write the report based on the chosen recommendations. The theme of the report is the need to adopt the proposed recommendations, and the report should build toward these recommendations. If someone reads the entire report, the recommendations should seem inevitable based on what has come before.

In addition to reading "forward," the report should also read "backward," so to speak. Most report users will read the letter of transmittal to understand the overall thrust of the report and will then skip directly to the recommendations. For these readers, the rest of the report must back up the recommendations. They should be able to turn to the deficiencies section for further discussion of the deficiencies that the recommendations are designed to correct. They should then be able to turn to the appropriate section—background, organization structure, job descriptions, documents, or procedures—to back up any claimed deficiency.

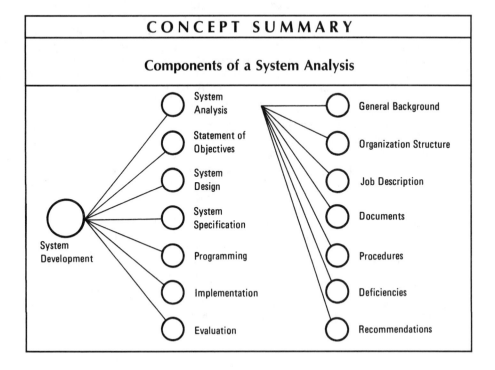

CONCEPT SUMMARY

Components of a System Analysis

- System Development
  - System Analysis
    - General Background
    - Organization Structure
    - Job Description
    - Documents
    - Procedures
    - Deficiencies
    - Recommendations
  - Statement of Objectives
  - System Design
  - System Specification
  - Programming
  - Implementation
  - Evaluation

STATEMENT OF OBJECTIVES

In his first letter to the Corinthians, Paul says, "For if the trumpet give an uncertain sound, who shall prepare himself to the battle." Our trumpet is the statement of objectives, and the battle is the system development. The statement of objectives must be clear about what the system should accomplish.

Guidelines for the Development of Objectives

A common mistake is simply to take what the present system provides, add a wish list put together by asking individual managers what they want, and then to collate this to obtain a statement of objectives.

> *Managers need useful information, not simply more and more information.* If anything, many managers have more information than they can process or understand. What they need is information that will help them to make better decisions.
> *Managers do not necessarily know what a new system could do for them.* The analyst must talk with managers about what they want. However, managers may not know what the computer could do for them. Also, the manager may

be too accustomed to the present system to think of other approaches. The analyst must sift through the information the present system provides and understand the manager's desires in order to help determine the information the manager needs. Thus, the need is for a creative partnership between the analyst and the manager. The analyst should not function simply as a clerk and write down what the manager says he needs. By the same token the analyst must not dictate to the manager how to run the business.

Even if the system provides the needed information, the manager's performance will not necessarily improve. A common assumption, though not always stated outright, is that a manager will use needed information and improve his or her decision making. This is not necessarily so. The analyst must determine how well the manager can use the information. If the manager cannot use the information well, one of the objectives must be to determine decision rules for proper use of the information. The system should also provide feedback to let managers know how well they are doing. Feedback helps managers to isolate areas of difficulty and improve their performance.

System goals follow from company goals. It is impossible to develop the goals for any particular system independently of the overall company goals. For example, in developing a general ledger system, the analyst must keep in mind the centralization or decentralization philosophy of management. The system must report budgeted and actual financial results by the organizational unit to which management has assigned the related authority and responsibility. Often, there are conflicting objectives, and real objectives are often masked. For example, when college presidents go to the legislature for increased funds, they usually talk about quality education, community service, and similar topics. Often the real objective of those same colleges is to grant the maximum number of degrees. Similarly, a corporation president will generally talk about the maximization of profits. The real objective often is the maximization of the company's size along with steady growth in, though not necessarily a maximization of, profits.

Overall Purpose

Statement of
Objectives

1. Overall
   Purpose
2. Specific
   Objectives
3. Required
   Output
4. Required
   Data
5. Necessary
   Controls
6. New Policies
   or Procedures
7. Signature of
   Management

As with system analysis, the statement of objectives is also broken down into seven components. The first component should state why the company is trying to develop the system at all. The overall purpose of an accounts payable system could be "to increase profitability by ensuring the obtaining of all discounts and the delaying, to the extent possible, of all payments." The company is interested in how much it owes only as a means to other ends. The overall purpose should not be merely to make the bookkeeping easier. The overall purpose of an accounts receivable system might be to encourage faster payment by customers of amounts due, to improve internal control over receivables and cash collections, to provide management with better information, or any combination of these goals. The overall purpose is the ultimate reason for creating the system.

Specific Objectives

The specific objectives component of the objectives statement shows how to achieve the overall purpose of the system. Specific objectives of the accounts payable system discussed might be

1. Preparation on demand of a printout detailing which invoices are due by their due date. This printout would tell management how much cash is needed on each day to pay suppliers and thus allow time to arrange financing as necessary.
2. Preparation of the checks to suppliers for all invoices due before a specific date. This would be a convenient way of paying all invoices due and would relieve the clerical staff of a huge burden of typing checks.

Statement of Objectives

1. Overall Purpose
2. **Specific Objectives**
3. Required Output
4. Required Data
5. Necessary Controls
6. New Policies or Procedures
7. Signature of Management

Consider a payroll system for a school board. Suppose the overall purpose is not merely to pay the employees but also to analyze payroll expense to determine the cost of each school activity. The school board may want to know costs by type of school (elementary, junior high, senior high), and that would become a specific objective: Determine costs by type of school. The board may want to know costs by discipline (math, French, and so on). This would be another objective. The board may want to know what the costs are by type of school and by discipline (the cost of math in junior high school, the cost of French in senior high school). This too would be a specific objective.

Other specific objectives might include the following:

Paper should not move. A paperless system is usually not a feasible goal. Reading things on computer screens is relatively inefficient, about 20 to 30 percent slower than print. The amount of information is not fixed, and the computer has captured a great deal more information. Keeping paper records is often required by law, such as licenses, insurance policies, contracts, and securities. There are more people wanting more information, and technology makes the information easier to transmit. However, on-line inquiry, remote printing, file downloading, and process redesign are all alternatives to delivering a printout in interoffice mail.

Numbers should be entered only once. A clerk or professional should not have to key data from a computer printout back into a computer.

Every change should be traceable to the source of the change. This is the audit trail. Responsibility for the data can sometimes be lost in a complex, networked information system. The user should always be able to find out how information has been changed and who changed it.

Every composite number should be analyzable. In essence, there should be an EXPLAIN key that allows users to trace their way through ledgers and sub-ledgers. This will typically require powerful hardware and a relational data base. This analysis capability should not be limited to auditors; it should be available also to end users.

Users should maintain their own systems. There must be a working partnership between information systems and the users so that users operate, maintain, and enhance their own systems to the extent possible.

The system should frequently check for errors. The system should often develop control totals, compare results from one area to another, and so on. It should be easy to identify errors, track them down, and correct them.

No person and no computer should do unnecessary things. Systems frequently contain steps that do not serve any useful purpose or are no longer needed because of changes elsewhere.

People should work smarter. At one time, computer main memory and mass storage were extraordinarily expensive. Today, they are cheap. Machines are no longer the scarce resource, we are.

The system development process depends on the specific objectives set for it. The more objectives there are and the more complicated they are, the more complex and more expensive the system will be.

Required Output

Once the specific objectives of the system are determined, the next step is to determine precisely what output the system should generate. If at all possible, the required output component should contain a sample or picture of the output exactly as it will be printed by the computer. The visual sample is extremely important for three reasons:

1. A picture helps the user to visualize the results of the system and develop a feel for what the system can do.
2. This picture will be a given goal for the system. Therefore, the user will have to focus on the proposed output and determine whether or not it is suitable. If the user wants something different later, it will be clear that there was a change of mind, and the responsibility for delays and increased costs will be pinpointed.
3. Small but significant changes can be identified early by the use of a picture. For example, the user might want to delete one column, or add one column, or perhaps switch the position of columns; these types of changes can be extremely important to the user, even though they are almost trivial from a systems or programming standpoint.

Required Data

This step will continue to move backward, so to speak. The components of the statement of objectives went from the overall purpose to the specific objectives to accomplish that purpose, to the required reports needed to meet those objectives. Now the analyst must determine the data necessary to develop those reports. If the system is to generate names on a report, these names must have come from some source that can be fed into the computer, stored in a file on the computer, and made available to a program for report generation. If the system is to generate an audit trail printout of all transactions that have affected an account balance, these transactions must have been captured at the time of file updating and stored for later recovery.

For the accounts payable system discussed earlier, one system objective was a report to give the amount needed to pay suppliers for any given day. To meet their objective, it will not be adequate to record an invoice when it arrives as a particular amount owed to a particular vendor. The system must also capture the total potential discount and the due date after which the discount is lost. If the system does not record and store this information, the computer will not be able to generate the required report. However, the net amount payable by the due date need not be stored in the computer system because it can easily be computed from the gross amount owed and the discount (net = gross − discount).

Determining the information necessary and the source of that information is absolutely essential for eliminating unpleasant surprises later in the system development process. Consider a general ledger system that can generate comparative financial statements (comparing this month's results to the results of the same month last year). This system must store an additional 12-data-items (one for each month of last year) in each general ledger account record. Storage is not the problem. The problem is the source of the data. If the chart of accounts is substantially changed, the data from last year will not be comparable to the data for this year. Short of reclassifying and reprocessing every transaction of the previous year, it may not be possible to generate last year's results to compare with this year's.

Necessary Controls

Chapters 2 and 4 discussed at length internal controls and their importance in all accounting systems. As detailed in those chapters, internal controls are absolutely necessary to ensure the accuracy and reliability of the accounting data and accounting reports. The importance of internal control is not reduced in a computer-based system; in many ways, internal control is even more important when using the computer. In an accounts payable system, one necessary control might be a separation of duties, whereby the person who enters an invoice for payment into the computer does not also authorize payment by the computer. Prenumbered documents, such as checks, are also necessary controls even for a computer-based system. For adequate physical control over the accounting records now on the computer, it may be necessary to limit access to the computer or computer terminal.

Statement of Objectives
1. Overall Purpose
2. Specific Objectives
3. Required Output
4. Required Data
5. **Necessary Controls**
6. New Policies or Procedures
7. Signature of Management

New Policies or Procedures

The next component of the statement of objectives discusses the impact of the new system on the organization. Often, to use fully the capabilities of the new system, changes must be made to long-standing policies or procedures of the company. These changes should be made apparent as soon as possible (1) to see if the proposed changes are acceptable to management, and (2) to give the organization enough time to get used to the changes if they are inevitable.

In one bank, a proposed system was to involve the cycling of bank statements. Instead of all customers receiving their statements at the end of the month, some customers would receive their statements as of the tenth, some customers as of the twentieth, and some at the end of the month. Management rejected this proposal, despite evidence that such cycling had worked well in other banks. Management insisted that their customers would not accept such a practice and that cycling was out of the question. In such a case, the systems analyst must defer to management and design as efficient a system as possible under the constraints.

Statement of Objectives
1. Overall Purpose
2. Specific Objectives
3. Required Output
4. Required Data
5. Necessary Controls
6. **New Policies or Procedures**
7. Signature of Management

Signature of Management

One of the major reasons for disasters in system development is the lack of top management involvement in the project. The statement of objectives helps to solve this problem by requiring the signature of top management on the report signifying approval. If top management is not interested enough to sign the report, it is possible to stop early and avoid potential disasters later.

No one in the organization will be as interested in new systems and their success as the system development people. An analyst may be developing a system for the controller, but the controller will not be as interested in the

1. Overall
   Purpose
2. Specific
   Objectives
3. Required
   Output
4. Required
   Data
5. Necessary
   Controls
6. New Policies
   or Procedures
7. **Signature of
   Management**

system as the analyst. The controller has other, pressing things to do and people to supervise. Even though the controller may work on or be interested in what he will consider to be the analyst's new system, the new system will tend to fall to the bottom of the controller's list of priorities. However, if the president is interested in the project, the controller will consider it to be the president's new system and make it a priority.

The basic problem is to get the president interested, and the best place to start is with the statement of objectives. The analyst should get the statement of objectives to the president, and ask for any necessary changes and a signature to indicate approval. If the president signs it, fine; there has been an excellent start in involving top management in the project. If the president does not sign it, this is also fine, since the analyst now knows the president will not back the project and it is best to move to another project. Top management's signature on the statement of objectives does not indicate approval of the project, only of the project's objectives. The analyst must continue to keep management deeply involved in the project until completion.

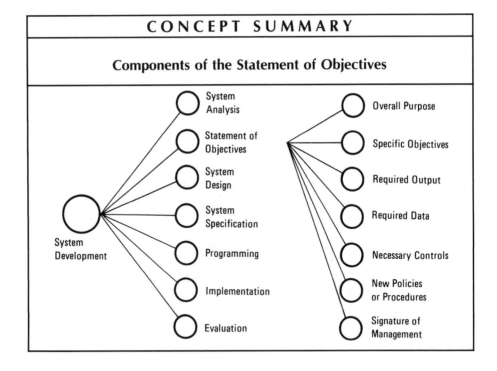

CONCEPT SUMMARY

Components of the Statement of Objectives

System Development → System Analysis, Statement of Objectives, System Design, System Specification, Programming, Implementation, Evaluation

Statement of Objectives → Overall Purpose, Specific Objectives, Required Output, Required Data, Necessary Controls, New Policies or Procedures, Signature of Management

Once the statement of objectives is developed, check to see that all of the following questions are answered:

1. So what? Newer isn't always better.
2. How will this improve our business?
3. Is the business purpose productivity or control?
4. What are the specific objectives?
5. How do those match the overall company objectives?

SYSTEM DESIGN CONSIDERATIONS

537

CHAPTER 15
*System
Analysis
and Design*

The system analysis details the design of the present system, and the statement of objectives details the objectives of the new system. The next step is to design a new system in place of the old. The task is not an easy one and is not even primarily technical. The task is primarily conceptual. The system design report evaluates the different approaches to take (interactive versus batch, multiple small computers versus one large computer, and so on). It shows where and how the system collects data, the flow of data, and the disposition of system outputs. It discusses the costs and benefits of each approach and then selects one approach to take. Exhibit 15-2 gives basic questions the system design report should answer.

Designing the new system is the most creative part of system development. The analyst must understand what the present status and future prospects of the company are, understand the goals of the new system, and then create a new system that is appropriate for that company. No one should worry about creating the perfect system. In a sense, "the best is the enemy of the good" because, in striving for the best, the company may not be satisfied with something that is perfectly adequate for its purposes.

One danger to avoid in system development is deviating too far from management's desires and having to throw out a great deal of work. It is better to check the design and get it approved prior to specifying the details of the system. For example, a consulting firm spent a great deal of time and effort designing a cost accounting system for a small manufacturer. The system was based on a central figure, a new cost accountant, the first cost accountant in the history of the company. The company president rejected the entire system without reviewing it. He insisted the company did not need a cost accountant, and he would not hire one. The consulting firm had to redesign the entire system from scratch. Fortunately, the writing of procedure manuals and other details had been deferred until the design was approved. Otherwise, all of the detail work would have been wasted.

Goals of System Design

There are several, often conflicting, goals to keep in mind in the development of a new system. How well the system balances these goals is a measure of how workable and cost-effective the system design is.

EXHIBIT 15-2   Questions for the System Design

1. Have we examined all the alternatives?
2. How do we know the evaluation data will be realistic?
3. Who is responsible for its validity?
4. What additional personnel will we need? (They are sometimes harder to find than hardware.)
5. What additional equipment will we need?
6. How does it compare to similar models, competitive systems?
7. What are the total costs—compared to benefits—in dollars, time, and operational effectiveness?

Simple. The system should be as simple as possible. Overly complicated system design has been the most common reason that systems exceeded their budgets and had innumerable operational problems. If the design starts to get too complicated, something has gone wrong somewhere. Stop and rethink the design.

Capable. The system should handle the present and the foreseeable future. If a system is developed in the off-season for a seasonal business, the designer should keep in mind the volumes that will be processed in the busy season. The firm's growth rate is also a consideration. Program flexibility and file sizes should be able to handle both the present volume of transactions and the future volume.

Modifiable. The system should be easily modified. No one can anticipate the future, and there is no way a system can be adequate forever. The system design must anticipate change, not by guessing what changes will occur, but by designing systems so they can be easily adapted to changing circumstances. For example, the Postal Service now wants a nine-digit zip code instead of the original five-digit zip code. The city of Los Angeles needs to modify over 1,000 programs. One U.S. senator estimated it will cost $51 billion to convert to the new zip code. Problems such as the zip code conversion are always arising in data processing, and they take resources away from new system development. Certain things are going to change, such as tax rates. Other changes that may or may not occur, such as future integration of separately developed systems, should also be provided for. A good system design at the time will save a great deal of work later.

Cost-Effective. The system should be cost-effective. It is important to always keep the cost of obtaining information in mind. For example, it may be possible to keep some information always current by using on-line transaction processing (OLTP). Other approaches may make that information available only on a daily, weekly, or monthly basis but for a much smaller cost. Only if the current information is worth its cost should the on-line approach be taken. Traditional data processing has been used for years, and its processes are well understood. The characteristics of traditional data processing are centralized data and processing, applications tied to proprietary (usually IBM) hardware and software, terminal/mainframe interfaces, and minimal connectivity. There is now a major shift toward distributed data processing. The characteristics of distributed data processing are distributed processing at individuals' microcomputers, distributed applications and data bases, applications portability, electronic data interchange (EDI), and a high degree of connectivity. Distributed data processing is difficult to achieve and is not always necessary. The questions to be answered to decide on whether it is a good idea are the following:

1. What is the pattern of communications?
2. What would be the relative costs of equipment?
3. What will be the relative costs of data entry?

4. Can recovery from error be guaranteed?
5. Can the necessary discipline be maintained? This includes using data dictionaries, updating records, entering data, and timely reporting.

Logical Modeling*

When an information system does not exist, our ideas about it are vague and general. The purpose of the system design is to take these necessarily vague ideas about requirements and convert them into precise definitions. For example, suppose the users say, "We need a system that integrates sales, inventory control, and purchasing." How would we start the design? The design should start with

1. Data flow diagram
2. Data model
3. Entity-relationship model
4. Normalized tables

Data Flow Diagram. A systemwide **data flow diagram (DFD)** describes the underlying nature of what occurs in the sales, inventory control, and purchasing areas of the business. The DFD uses only four symbols to produce a picture of the underlying logical nature of any information system, at any desired level of detail. They are

☐ The box for external entities
⊏ The open rectangle for data files
◯ The rounded box for a process
↑ The data flow arrow, which shows the direction of data movement

Exhibit 15-3 shows CUSTOMERS (an external entity, something outside the system) sending in a stream of sales orders along the data flow arrow. Process 1, Process Sales, handles those orders using product information from the data file called D1: PRODUCTS and puts information about sales into the data file named D3: SALES.

This figure also shows the whole of the business area, depicted using only the four symbols. For each sale, Process 1 updates the INVENTORY data file, D2, with the units sold. The data stored in D3 are used by Processes 2 and 3 to prepare bank deposit documents and send them to the bank and to prepare sales reports and send them to management. At some appropriate time—notice that time is not shown on the DFD—Process 4 extracts information about the inventory status of various products from D2 and combines it with information from D3 concerning their past sales, to determine whether a product needs to be reordered. If so, based on information in D4, which describes the prices and delivery times quoted by suppliers, Process 4 chooses the best supplier to

---

* This section on logical modeling is adapted from Chris Gane, *Rapid System Development* (Englewood Cliffs, NJ: Prentice Hall, 1988).

EXHIBIT 15-3   Dataflow Diagram for Sales, Inventory, and Purchasing

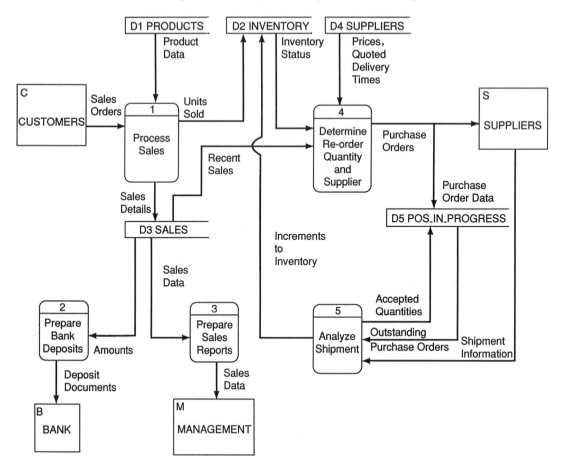

order from. Process 4 sends purchase orders to the external entity SUPPLIERS and stores information about each purchase order in D5: POS_IN_ PROGRESS. When a shipment is received from a supplier, Process 5 analyzes it by extracting data from POS_IN_PROGRESS to determine whether what has been received is what was ordered, increments D2: INVENTORY with the accepted amount, and stores the accepted quantities in POS_IN_ PROGRESS. This DFD achieves three things:

1. The DFD sets a boundary to the area of the system and of the business covered by the system. Things represented by the external-entity symbol (such as customers, the bank, management, and suppliers) are, by definition, outside the system. Processes not shown are not part of the project. For example, the diagram shows receiving shipments from suppliers but not handling the invoices received from them, implying that accounts payable is outside the scope of the project as well.

2. The DFD is nontechnical. The DFD is understood by people familiar with the business area depicted whether or not they know anything about computers.

3. The DFD shows both the data stored in the system and the processes that transform that data. It shows the relationships between the data and the processes in the system.

Data Model. A data model is a list of the data elements to be stored in each data file as defined on the DFD. You should draw up this list from your own knowledge and from the knowledge of users about what information you need to describe a product, a supplier, a sale, and so on. You can refine the list by examining the input and output. Look at each system input, such as sales orders or shipments in Exhibit 15-3, to determine what data elements each input represents. Look at each output in the same way. Then work from the outputs back to the data files or from the inputs forward to the data files.

Entity-Relationship Model. An **entity-relationship model** describes the structure of the data to be stored in the system. Exhibit 15-4 illustrates this process.

1. Identify the entities about which the system must store data. In this example, they would be CUSTOMERS, PRODUCTS, INVENTORY, SUPPLIERS, SALES, and PURCHASE ORDERS.
2. Create a diagram with a block for each entity. It is conventional in this diagram to state the entities as singular nouns, for example, CUSTOMER instead of CUSTOMERS.
3. Determine the relationships that exist between each pair of entities on the diagram. For example, one customer may be associated with many sales, but each sale can be for only one customer. This is shown by a line with an arrowhead against the "many" block and a plain line at the "one" block. Take, for instance, PRODUCT and SALE: One product may be associated with many sales, and one sale may be for many products—at least one, and possibly more. This relationship is shown by a line with an arrowhead on both ends. On the other hand, each product has only one inventory record, and each inventory record refers to only one product. Consequently, they are joined by a simple line.

EXHIBIT 15-4   Entity-Relationship Model for Sales, Purchasing, and Inventory

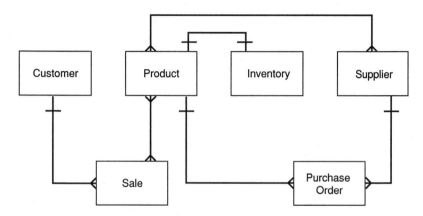

Normalized Tables.   Describe the data model as linked, two-dimensional tables using all the information now collected about the data. These tables should be normalized, that is, made as simple as possible. As discussed in Chapter 6, a normalized table has a column or combination of columns known as the key that uniquely identifies each row and all other columns depend only on the key.

Special Considerations for Distributed Data Processing

Successful distributed systems are likely to have the following four features:

Data Dictionary.   A complete, up-to-date data dictionary must be maintained for all data elements in the system. This rule, which applies regardless of file structure, must be followed to allow for communications between sites. In addition, many of the vendors' system programs that support distributed processing require data dictionaries.

Status Tags on Transactions.   All transactions should carry status tags. These are codes that say what has happened to transactions moving through the system. When a transaction has been successfully moved from one node in the network to another, the status code should be updated to indicate this. When the transaction has been modified, used to update a file record, decomposed into multiple transactions, or combined with others to form a larger transaction, the status record should also be updated accordingly. Delete the status code only when a transaction leaves the network. Status tags permit unambiguous recovery from any possible failure. Since all transactions are tagged, only those currently being altered can be lost. Using status tags carries a cost in terms of disk operations and processing time. Tags are nevertheless a good idea.

Accountability for Data Integrity.   The integrity of each data-item should be the responsibility of only one manager, though different data-items may be the responsibility of different managers. Any modification of a data-item should be performed only under the control of the responsible manager. This does not mean that a person must intervene before an update is performed, but rather that a master copy of each data-item should be accessible only through methods that incorporate enough edits and checks to satisfy the manager. The manager should also be available if the system gets confused. To prevent that from happening, the manager should check the data-item's status periodically.

Accountability for System Status.   Someone must be given responsibility for the status of the system at each site. This may or may not be the same person who oversees the data-items. The person certifies that all input is on schedule, alerts central management if not, certifies that only the current copy of a centrally provided file is used, and makes sure that end-of-the-day procedures are correctly followed.

Approaches to Distributed Processing

543

CHAPTER 15
*System
Analysis
and Design*

There are two primary approaches to distributed data processing, the geographical distribution method and the memo file method.

Geographic Distribution Method. This approach involves central maintenance of a data dictionary and geographical distribution of the data base. One copy of each data-item exists. That copy, which is situated in one of the local data bases, is identified in the central data dictionary. Modifying the local data-item can be done only with the approval of the local manager. One example of this approach is the parts repair system of some auto manufacturers. Each dealer has a parts inventory to manage and has a local computer system supplied by the auto manufacturer. The computer, which maintains the inventory, can also communicate with other dealers and the manufacturer's warehouses. The manufacturer maintains a central dictionary that contains all the part names and the locations of the dealers and warehouses that stock each part. When a dealer needs a part, the dealer sends a message to the central directory to discover the nearest location of the part. Then, the dealer contacts that location or another, if necessary, to order it. The geographic distribution method is inconvenient when maintaining a central data dictionary is onerous.

Memo File Method. In this approach, there is only one official copy of the master file. It is prepared centrally, usually on a daily basis, using batch processing controls. Unofficial copies of it are distributed to the local sites, generally early in the morning. The local users, who modify the files as needed, also send the individual transactions to the central site. At night, the master file is prepared again and distributed, and yesterday's local file is discarded. Local users can do anything to their files that they like without harming the integrity of corporate files. The disadvantage is that there is a cost for posting every transaction twice—once on-line locally and again at night centrally. While flexible and convenient for local people, the copy or memo file method involves duplicate data entry and redundant transmission of data. It may be impractical for data bases larger than a few tens of millions of characters.

Transaction Processing Benchmarks

Transaction processing systems can be developed in many ways, utilizing mainframes, minicomputers, and local area networks with file servers. How can these alternatives be compared? One approach is the benchmark, a test application that is run on all of the alternatives. Benchmarks to test distributed or OLTP performance are difficult to construct and execute. It is not sufficient to look at the capabilities of the central processor. An OLTP test must use virtually all significant hardware and software facilities, including the communications software, the operating system's scheduling mechanisms, the data base software, the transaction and data base logging capability, and the disk management software.

While a central processor test can be a routine, short-duration batch job that requires no special preparation, a meaningful OLTP test requires setting up a separate system to emulate the large number of terminals. The system needs to be configured with sufficient memory and a sufficient number of processors, disk controllers, and disks. Building the test data base can require many hours or even days. In many ways, a good OLTP benchmark is the ultimate system test. When the transaction rate is pushed to the limit, multiple bottlenecks may be discovered in the hardware and the software.

Results of OLTP tests are given in transactions per second (tps) or, for small systems, transactions per hour. Either figure is meaningless without a measure of the response time, such as the average response time for all transactions, or the percentage of all transactions meeting a specific response time (for example, 95 percent under 1 second). Results are often given in graphs of tps versus response time.

What is meant by a transaction varies widely from industry to industry, and even from application to application. A lottery transaction may mean the capture of wager information; hundreds of such transactions could be captured in one disk access. In the banking industry, each transaction may involve several data base accesses, usually requiring record locking and transaction recovery guarantees. In airline reservations systems, a transaction may consist of many messages, each of which may trigger multiple data base accesses. It is not meaningful to compare tps ratings from benchmarks that use different types of transactions.

THE SYSTEM DESIGN REPORT

There are seven components of the system design report. The following sections discuss them all.

Scope and Boundaries of the System

System Design

1. Scope & Boundaries
2. Specific Requirements
3. Conceptual Design
4. Resource Requirements
5. Tangible Benefits
6. Intangible Benefits
7. Cost/Benefit Analysis

The first component of system design is to lay out exactly what the system will and will not do. The system should be broad enough in scope to ensure that it will be a significant contribution to the business. However, the scope should be narrow enough to ensure that the system will be manageable. The worst possible approach is to try to develop all at once the total information system, one big system that handles everything. It is important to take bite-sized chunks and develop the overall information system one step at a time.

Consider an accounts receivable system. The system must keep track of customers and the balances they owe. To keep the the balances up to date, the system must process sales. But sales affect inventory and salespeople's commissions, so the temptation is then to include those aspects of the company's operations. Then sales could be analyzed by product, period, store, salesperson, and so on, so the system could be extended to include those elements. The system can thus grow until it processes everything because every aspect of the accounting system interrelates eventually with all other aspects. Therefore, it is essential to detail exactly where the system being designed stops, that is, what its boundaries are.

The company should not try to develop a perfect system or even the best possible system. The perfect system is constantly out of reach because new products are available essentially on a weekly basis. In an attempt to make the system "the best," it would have to be continually reworked to incorporate the latest equipment. This becomes a never-ending cycle that leads to countless delays. IBM worked for years on what it called the Future System, or FS. This system had such lofty goals it never worked and was ultimately abandoned.

More Specific System Requirements

The statement of objectives lays out the kind of information that the new system will require and will provide. The system design has to be more precise about these items.

Output. The design should include the outputs to be produced. It should consist of schematics of exactly what the reports will look like. Most users cannot conceptualize computer output. To get their useful cooperation, it is necessary to provide a specific output and ask, "Is this what you want?" The user can then respond and say, for example, "To drop the third column and interchange the fourth and fifth columns."

Files. The design should detail exactly what files the system will require. These files, such as a customer master file or a vendor master file, would always exist, though their contents would be constantly updated. At this point, the design should specify exactly what data will be kept in each file. For example, a customer master file for an accounts receivable system must contain at least the customer's name and address, but it may also contain a credit limit, a Dun & Bradstreet number, or any of a vast range of possible data-items.

Input. The design should specify the input to the system—exactly what source documents or sources of information will provide the raw data. The input section should detail the data volumes for the master files and transactions. It is important to the design whether there are 100 customers (such as a small store) or 100,000 customers (such as a major oil company). It is also important to the design whether there are 10 transactions to process each day or 10,000 transactions. The average transaction load is important, but the "peaks" are also critical; the system must not overload when the peak volumes occur. Additionally, the design should indicate system-timing considerations (how fast the system must respond). Exhibit 15-5 provides an illustration of a typical transaction volume for a business operating in three cities.

Conceptual Design

The next step is to define the **modules** that will satisfy the system requirements and then to arrange these modules into a functional design. In the context of a system design, a module is a self-contained process, including perhaps computer programs or manual processes. **Modularity** is an important design goal. Modularity in system design means that the overall system is broken down into smaller building blocks, called modules. Each module can then, if necessary,

EXHIBIT 15-5   Illustration of Transaction Volume

Item	Los Angeles	Seattle	Denver
Invoices per day	20	3	3
Lines per invoice	18	20	20
Total lines (1 × 2)	360	60	60
Credits per day	3	1	1
Lines per credit	7	9	9
Total lines (4 × 5)	21	9	9
Unpaid invoices at month end	3,850	630	630
Vendor purchase orders	10	5	5
Items per purchase order	360	200	200
Checks received per day	9	3	3
Number of customers	350	70	70
Number of inventory items	1,200	800	800
Number of vendors	2	2	2
Number of sales representatives	5	5	5

be further broken down into submodules. The goal is to make the modules fit together in a natural fashion. Each module can be developed independently and then fitted together to create the overall system. When future changes or modifications are made to the system (if all goes according to plan), only the affected module needs to be changed.

This is a **conceptual design**, not a detailed design. The conceptual design explains the way the system will fit together without detailing every step in the process. One approach to the conceptual design is the use of dataflow diagrams, as discussed earlier in the section on Logical Modeling. Once the logical model is complete, the next step is to identify the necessary processes of the system. These processes would depend on the nature of the business and the trade-off between cost and timeliness the company wishes to make. Exhibit 15-6 gives a general flow model, which outlines the processes that any information application should have.

The basic components of this model (coded to the number given in the exhibit) are

1. *Batch transaction updates.* These processes are responsible for batch posting formatted magnetic media transactions to the application. They produce extracts for all of the output data tables, files, and reports that result from this update. The end-of-day process, which is just one of the batch transaction updates, closes out processing for one processing day and sets up processing for the next processing day.

2. *On-line validation and update.* These processes handle direct input of on-line transactions to the application. They also facilitate real-time posting of transactions and resolution of exceptions from the batch transaction update runs.

3. *Sequential processing facilities.* These facilities sequentially process the account data base or item data base in order to perform periodic aging and condition-checking updates. They also generate extracts for account status reports. Like the batch transaction and on-line updates, the sequential processing runs produce extracts for the extract data base.

EXHIBIT 15-6   General Flow Model

547

CHAPTER 15
*System
Analysis
and Design*

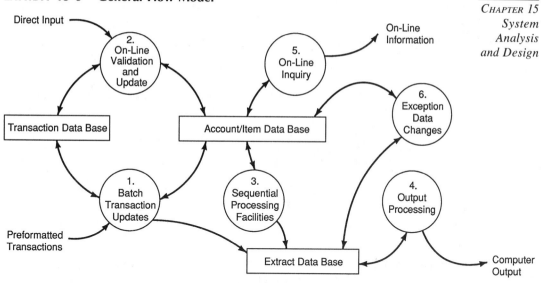

4. *Output processing.* This function takes extracts from the batch transaction update and sequential processing runs, removes them from the extract data base, and creates final-form reports, documents, and output data files.

5. *On-line inquiry.* This facility allows people needing information from the application data base to have on-line access to it.

6. *Exception data changes.* This facility permits emergency changes to data (subject to security controls) in order to ensure that processing can continue even in the face of unexpected data and programming problems.

Resource Requirements

The next step in system design is to estimate the resource requirements needed to implement, convert to, and operate every module. Implementation refers to the system design, system specification, and programming necessary to get the module working. Conversion refers to getting data from the present system into the new module and making the information available to the new system. Operation refers to the day-to-day running of the system. Exhibit 15-7 gives some guidelines for cost estimates.

Each of these steps of implementation, conversion, and operation will have its own resource requirements. These resource requirements will include

1. Manpower, the people needed to get each job done
2. Computer and other hardware, the equipment necessary for each step
3. Contracted services, such as outside consultants for programming services
4. Purchased or leased software

A possible trade-off often exists between these various resources. For example, it may be possible to hire fewer people and use more contracted

EXHIBIT 15-7   Questions For Cost Estimation

1. Is anything omitted? (e.g., the cost to debug)
2. Are there any small "price per" figures the computer will multiply by a million?
3. What about the things you can't see? (e.g., the cost of inadequate security)
4. What are good standards for this service?
5. Can we buy it for less?
6. How realistic are these estimates? (Careful. Murphy's law is strictly enforced.)
7. Can we modify it to make it cost less and still be effective?
8. What is the cost to install? to debug?
9. What proportion of the budget is for system development?
10. How much for maintenance?
11. Can we examine every part of this new operation against some meaningful standard?
12. What is the price per transaction compared to doing it the old way?
13. Will the operation be fully cost justified?

services. Similarly, it may be possible to spend more money on software and less money on manpower or contracted services.

Software Packages.   It is four to ten times more costly to develop a software program in-house than it is to buy one that is ready to use with very few changes. Payroll is an example of a system for which many large companies, such as General Electric, have purchased software. Such companies as GE could develop payroll systems themselves, but the cost of maintaining the systems would be too high. Almost every year, the tax rules of the federal government, virtually every state, and hundreds of cities change, and new taxes are often added. Maintenance alone can be the largest expense of the payroll system and make the purchase of software worthwhile.

But choosing suitable software is not easy. A frequent cause of system failure results from the inability of the software package to meet the unique requirements of a business. It is not uncommon after a computer has been purchased, programmed, and installed to have the billing clerk say, "But this invoicing procedure doesn't work because, after a customer purchases 1,000 units, we offer a 10 percent discount on any future purchases." Because all accounting systems are superficially alike, programs for these applications often appear to be able to meet a company's requirements when they are discussed at a general level or viewed in a demonstration. Ingenious use of a system may allow it to handle situations for which it was not specifically designed. In general, it is not advisable to accommodate exceptions that have a direct impact on accounting information, but exceptions that affect management information can often be worked around. Two examples of this principle follow:

1. The system can associate only one salesperson with an invoice, but occasionally, two salespersons make a single sale. The user can work around this limitation by having a code representing both salespersons.
2. Occasionally, the company adds a 15 percent surcharge to an invoice if the customer has not purchased in sufficient volume in the last month, but the computer system cannot handle this. A clerk could type the surcharge onto the invoice and

process a journal entry to account for the additional revenue, but the potential loss of control makes this an unacceptable alternative.

Tangible Benefits

These benefits include the reduction of direct operating expenses, the "hard dollar savings" many people prefer to see. Many years ago in the aerospace industry, enormous rooms were filled with clerks who performed endless volumes of mathematical computations. A computer was able to eliminate all of those clerical jobs—a dramatic, **tangible benefit**. Some examples of tangible benefits that might be achieved are

1. Replace a service bureau or timesharing service. Companies with a monthly service bureau bill may be able to achieve cost savings by using their own computer.
2. Eliminate clerical overtime.
3. Reduce the number of clerical workers.
4. Reduce the cost of supporting finance and accounting.
5. Cut the amount of paper printed in the data center by 80 percent.

However, the reduction of clerical costs is one of the most elusive of computer benefits. The computer eliminates some clerical jobs, but it usually generates such volumes of newly available information that new clerical positions are required to analyze and use the information. If the system must depend on clerical salary reduction for its justification, it is probably a good idea to rethink the entire system.

Intangible Benefits

Intangible benefits are the real justification and promise of computer systems. Unfortunately, these benefits are the most difficult to grasp and put a dollar value on. The primary intangible benefits are the following:

Capacity. This is the system's ability to handle increasing volumes of transactions with ease. Manual systems often require extensive hiring and training of new personnel to process an increased volume of transactions.

Timeliness. A well-designed computer system can often generate results faster, which can help improve decisions since better (more current) information is available. An example would be to shorten the month-end closing process, so that all managers have their financial reports by the fifth business day of the month or sooner.

Accuracy. A standard problem in manual systems is errors in computation such as incorrectly extending price times quantity for invoices. Such errors reflect poorly on the company and may lead customers to suspect they are being cheated. The computer can perform such tasks easily, without fear of error.

Improvement of Service. In a manual sales (or order entry) system for sales representative, time is spent filling out various forms, mailing them to the company, processing them, and so on. A computer system can eliminate such time-consuming activities and speed goods to customers days or even weeks earlier. Also, companies often need quick information about delivery status, availability, price, or credit and find that this information is not readily available from their system. They find that delivery problems are being discovered by chance because it is too cumbersome to use the current system. The right system can solve these problems.

Usability. Usability of a computer system can be identified in the following ways:

1. Time it takes to learn and to master. It is possible to set objectives for, and to measure, the time it takes for users to learn a system's basic operations or to reach a set level of mastery.
2. Errors. Specific objectives can be set for the rate and the kinds of errors, including all incomplete, inappropriate, or inefficient actions that users make.
3. Ability to recover from errors. No system can be perfect, and people will make some errors. In usable systems, people should be able to recover from errors quickly and with minimal difficulty. Recovery time can be a specific objective.
4. Warm-up time after being away. When a person learns to ride a bicycle or knit, those skills are seldom unlearned, even after time away from them. Unfortunately, that is not true of many systems. If systems are used infrequently, relearning time might be a separate objective.
5. Attitude. Usable systems have greater user acceptance, and that can translate into improved performance and better business results. It is possible to use general measures of user satisfaction or to construct instruments to measure how people feel about using particular systems regularly.

Improved Information. The task of digging out the significant nuggets of information from the data base can be overwhelming. For example, many companies want to find out which of their products or sales territories generate the most sales or profit. The computer is ideally suited to this laborious work.

Cost/Benefit Analysis

The final component of the system design report is to provide an economic analysis. Is this new system worth what it costs? This step should prevent extensive resources from being inappropriately directed. The goal is to have a workable system that satisfies the organization's objectives at a reasonable cost. Taking that perspective will not leave the haunting suspicion that "Well, if we waited just one more year, prices would be down 25 percent. . . ." The attitude should be: Costs will be down later, but this system project is worth what it costs, so it should be done.

Unfortunately, there are numerous examples of systems not meeting even the most simple tests of cost-effectiveness. For instance, one university decided to get a new computer costing several hundred thousand dollars, primarily because it could then buy extensive software for its admissions, student records, and alumni needs. The business manager then stated that the present clerk positions would have to be upgraded and their salaries raised because of the new computer system. However, the new system provided nothing that the old one did not. In other words, with the expenditure of several hundred thousand dollars for a computer, plus almost $100,000 for software, plus upgrading clerks, plus raising salaries, there was no advantage to the school. A sophisticated approach to **cost/benefit analysis** is to use the present value concepts of capital budgeting to determine whether the new computer system is worthwhile. Exhibit 15-8 illustrates such a cost/benefit analysis.

EXHIBIT 15-8   Illustration of a Cost/Benefit Analysis

A medium-sized manufacturing company is considering purchasing a small computer in order to reduce the cost of its data-processing operations. The manual bookkeeping system in use has the following direct cash expenses per month:

Salaries	$7,500
Payroll taxes and fringe benefits	1,700
Forms and supplies	600
	$9,800

Existing furniture and equipment are fully depreciated in the accounts and have no salvage value. The cost of the computer, including alterations, installation and accessory equipment, is $100,000. This entire amount is depreciable for income tax purposes on a double declining basis at the rate of 20% per annum.

The annual costs of computerized data processing after the first year of operation are projected to be:

Supervisory salaries	$20,000
Other salaries	19,000
Payroll taxes and fringe benefits	7,400
Forms and supplies	7,200
	$53,600

The computer is expected to be obsolete in three years, at which time its salvage value is expected to be $20,000. The company follows the practice of treating salvage value as inflow at the time that it is likely to be received. The firm's tax rate is 50%, and its required rate of return is 10%.

This complex situation can be dealt with by:
1. Computing the savings in annual cash flow after taxes
2. Computing the net present value of the investment

The calculations are as follows:

1. Annual cash expenses of the manual bookkeeping system,		
$9,800 × 12		$117,600
Annual cash expenses of computerized data processing		53,600
Annual cash savings		$ 64,000

	Year 1	Year 2	Year 3
Annual cash savings	$ 64,000	$ 64,000	$ 64,000
Depreciation	20,000	16,000	12,800
Increase in income before tax	44,000	48,000	51,200
Increase in income tax (50%)	22,000	24,000	25,600
Increase in income after tax	22,000	24,000	25,600
Add back depreciation (noncash expense)	20,000	16,000	12,800
Cash inflow after tax	$ 42,000	$ 40,000	$ 38,400

	Cash Flow		Present Value Factor		
2. Year 1	$42,000	×	.909	=	$ 38,178
Year 2	40,000	×	.826	=	33,040
Year 3	38,400	×	.750	=	28,800
Year 3	20,000	×	.750	=	15,000
					115,018
Investment					100,000
Net present value					$ 15,018

Subject to intangible factors, the computer is a sound investment because the rate of return exceeds the 10% after tax criteria.

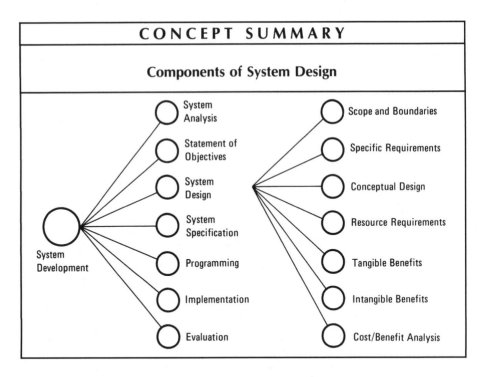

CONCEPT SUMMARY

Components of System Design

System Development
- System Analysis
- Statement of Objectives
- System Design
  - Scope and Boundaries
  - Specific Requirements
  - Conceptual Design
  - Resource Requirements
  - Tangible Benefits
  - Intangible Benefits
  - Cost/Benefit Analysis
- System Specification
- Programming
- Implementation
- Evaluation

REFERENCES

C. Gane, *Rapid System Development*. (Englewood Cliffs, NJ: Prentice Hall, 1988).

C. Gane, and T. Sarson, *Structured Systems Analysis* (Englewood Cliffs, NJ: Prentice Hall, 1979).

K. T. Orr, *Structured Systems Development* (New York: Yourdon Press, 1977).

E. Youdon, *Modern Structured Analysis* (New York: Yourdon Press/Prentice Hall, 1989).

J.-D. Warnier, *Logical Construction of Systems* (New York: Van Nostrand Reinhold, 1981).

CHAPTER SUMMARY

In all cases involving accounting information systems, accountants will be intimately connected with system development. In some cases, accountants, such as the controller, will direct the system development. In others, the accountant will be part of the system development team. In small businesses, the accountant will be responsible for the entire process.

The first major step in system development is system analysis. The systems analysis report includes general background about the company, its organization structure, job descriptions, documents, procedures, deficiencies, and recommendations for improvement.

The second major step in system development is the statement of objectives. The statement of objectives includes the system's overall purpose, its specific objectives, required output, required data, necessary internal controls, new policies the system will require, and signature of management showing approval.

The third major step in system development is system design. A useful technique for initially laying out a system is called data flow diagrams. The DFD uses four symbols to produce a picture of the underlying logical nature of the information system. These four symbols are the box for entities external to the system, the open rectangle for data files, the rounded box for a process, and a data flow arrow which shows the direction of data movement. A closely related technique is the entity-relationship model, which shows the structure of the data stored in the system.

Many companies are moving toward distributed data processing because of its responsiveness to local information needs. However, this requires special design considerations, including a data dictionary, status tags on transactions, and accountability for both data integrity and the system status. Two specific approaches to distributed data processing are the geographic distribution method and the memo file method.

The system design report will include the scope and boundaries of the system, the specific system requirements, a conceptual design of the new system, its resource requirements, tangible and intangible benefits, and an economic analysis comparing costs and benefits.

KEY TERMS

Conceptual design (*p. 546*)
Cost/benefit analysis (*p. 551*)
Data flow diagram (DFD) (*p. 539*)
Entity-relationship model (*p. 541*)
Intangible benefits (*p. 549*)
Job description (*p. 530*)

Letter of transmittal (*p. 530*)
Modularity (*p. 545*)
Module (*p. 545*)
Organization structure (*p. 528*)
System analysis report (*p. 529*)
Tangible benefits (*p. 549*)

QUESTIONS

15-1. Give four situations in which system analysis would be appropriate.

15-2. Discuss the three approaches to system development, citing the advantages and disadvantages of each.

15-3. List the five basic steps in the process of system analysis.

15-4. Is system analysis applicable only to a computer environment? Explain.

15-5. Describe the contents of a letter of transmittal. Why should this type of letter accompany a system analysis report?

15-6. List and briefly discuss the seven elements of a system analysis report.

15-7. Why are complete and detailed job descriptions for each position necessary in a system analysis report?

15-8. Distinguish between goals and objectives.

15-9. List the components of a statement of objectives, and briefly describe the purpose of each.

15-10. Management involvement in system development is a key element in the success of a project. In what ways can management become involved?

15-11. Why must management be made aware of proposed changes to company policy before proceeding to the system design stage?

15-12. List the seven components of system design, and briefly describe what is accomplished in each.

15-13. Identify three important goals of a system design and give examples of systems where the goals are achieved and three where they are not.

15-14. Contrast tangible and intangible benefits of computer systems, and give two examples of each.

15-15. How is cost/benefit analysis of the system design related to capital budgeting?

PROBLEMS

15-16. Following are components of a system analysis report. Arrange these components into the order in which they would appear.

   a. Detailed steps to be taken by management
   b. Examples of documents processed by the system
   c. Explanation of weaknesses
   d. Summary of report and conclusions
   e. Job description
   f. Description of procedures
   g. Place the system in its context
   h. Determine lines of authority and responsibility

15-17. In determining job descriptions and what tasks employees actually perform, the system analyst often does not get a clear picture from discussions with the particular employee involved. Discuss three approaches which might be used in addition to conversations with the affected employee to determine the real nature of the job.

15-18. Following is a list of deficiencies and omissions often discovered as a result of system analysis. Give one example of each of these deficiencies and omissions which might be found in an accounts receivable system.

   a. Wasted effort
   b. Duplication of effort
   c. Excessive cost
   d. Overstaffing
   e. Poor policies
   f. No clear policies
   g. Ineffective supervision
   h. Important information not available

15-19. Most computer-based systems are designed to process data in either an on-line interactive fashion or in discrete batches. Describe three processing applications that would be most appropriate for an on-line design and three applications that would be most appropriate for a batch design.

15-20. All data processed by a manual system can be traced back to properly authorized source documents, thus providing a built-in audit trail. However, in a computer system, data can be entered directly through terminals (eliminating many source documents), and this built-in audit trail no longer exists.

1. What specific control procedures can be built into the system design to ensure the proper authorization of all processed transactions?
2. How can an audit trail be established through a computer system in the absence of source documents?

15-21. A computer-based accounts payable system can provide both tangible and intangible benefits to a firm. These intangible benefits are often the most important advantages of the new system. List five specific intangible benefits that an accounts payable system should provide.

15-22. A computer-based general ledger and financial statements system can also provide tangible and intangible benefits. List five specific intangible benefits that a general ledger and financial statements system should provide.

15-23. Computer system design is based in part on the desired frequency of output reports. The following is a list of some typical output reports. For each of these reports, state whether it should be generated on demand, daily, weekly, once an accounting period, or never:

a. Trial balance
b. Income statement and balance sheet
c. Schedule of accounts receivable
d. Individual customer balance
e. Schedule of accounts payable
f. Amount owed particular supplier
g. Payroll register
h. W-2 forms
i. Inventory on-hand report
j. Breakdown of sales by salesperson

15-24. Proper system design entails performing numerous tasks, some of which depend on the prior completion of others. Arrange the following items in the order they would likely be performed in the system design and system specification. Note those that would be performed simultaneously:

a. Flowchart the programs
b. Flowchart the system
c. Estimate intangible benefits
d. Develop input forms
e. Specify output reports
f. Estimate resources required
g. Assign tasks to organizational units
h. Organize data files
(*continues on next page*)

i. Determine the limits of the system

j. Establish the framework for getting the system working

15-25. Accountants often view computer-based systems as simply extensions of the processing capabilities of manual systems. Computer technicians are often unaware of the recordkeeping and control needs of accounting. Distinguish between the use of the computer as a processing tool and as an analytical tool. Give three specific examples of the use of the computer as a processing tool and three examples of the use of the computer as an analytical tool. Your examples should be taken from a business information system.

15-26. Consider the development of a new payroll system for a retail firm.

1. Give the overall purpose of such a system and state five objectives necessary to accomplish this overall purpose.
2. Are any of these specific objectives conflicting? Discuss how trade-offs may be made between these objectives.
3. Might there be any unstated objectives that should be considered in the system development?

15-27. Consider the development of an inventory control system for a wholesale firm.

1. Give the overall purpose of such a system and state five objectives necessary to accomplish this overall purpose.
2. Are any of these objectives conflicting? Discuss how trade-offs may be made between these objectives.
3. Might there be any unstated objectives that should be considered in the system development?

15-28. Full use of the computer's capabilities may require changes in long-standing company policies and procedures. Consider the situation of a retail store developing a new billing system that is designed to bill customers every two weeks rather than once a month.

1. Summarize the potential advantages and disadvantages of this new approach.
2. Suppose the company wanted to measure customer reaction to this new billing system by a questionnaire. List five questions that should appear on the questionnaire.

15-29. (*CMA, adapted*) Robert Richards has been promoted recently to manager, Property Accounting Section of Deake Corporation. Richards has had difficulty in responding to some of the requests from individuals in other departments of Deake for information about the company's fixed assets. Some of the requests and problems Richards has had to cope with are as follows:

a. The controller has requested schedules of individual fixed assets to support the balances in the general ledger. Richards has furnished the necessary information, but he has always been late. The manner in which records are organized makes it difficult to obtain information easily.

b. The maintenance manager wished to verify the existence of a printing press, which he thinks was repaired twice. He has asked Richards to confirm the asset number and location of the press.

c. The Insurance Department wants data on the cost and book values of assets to include in its review of current insurance coverage.

d. The Tax Department has requested data that can be used to determine when Deake should switch depreciation methods for tax purposes.

e. The company's internal auditors have spent a significant amount of time in the Property Accounting Section recently, attempting to confirm the annual depreciation expense.

The property account records at Richards's disposal consist of a set of manual books. These records show the date the asset was acquired, the account number to which the asset applies, the dollar amount capitalized, and the estimated useful life of the asset for depreciation purposes. After many frustrations, Richards has realized that his records are inadequate, and he cannot supply the data easily when they are requested. He has decided that he should have a computerized system.

1. Identify and justify four major objectives Deake Corporation's automated property accounting system should possess in order to provide the data that are necessary to respond to information from company personnel.

2. Identify the data that should be included in the computer record for each asset included in the property account.

15-30. (*CMA, adapted*) Citizens' Gas Company is a medium-sized gas distribution company that provides natural gas service to approximately 200,000 customers. The customer base is divided into three revenue classes. Data by customer class are as follows:

Class	Customers	Gas Consumed (cubic feet)	Revenues
Residential	160,000	80 billion	$160 million
Commercial	38,000	15 billion	25 million
Industrial	2,000	50 billion	65 million
		145 billion	$250 million

Residential customer gas usage is primarily for residence heating purposes and, consequently, is highly correlated to the weather (i.e., temperature). Commercial and industrial customers, on the other hand, may or may not use gas for heating purposes, and therefore consumption is not necessarily correlated to the weather. The largest 25 industrial customers of the total 2,000 account for $30 million of the industrial revenues. Each of these 25 customers uses gas for both heating and industrial purposes and has a consumption pattern that is governed almost entirely by business factors.

The company obtains its gas supply from ten major pipeline companies. The pipeline companies provide gas in amounts specified in contracts that extend over periods ranging from 5 to 15 years. For some contracts the supply is in equal monthly increments, while for others the supply varies in accordance with the heating season. Supply over and above the contract amounts is not available, and some contracts contain take-or-pay clauses (i.e., the company must pay for the volumes specified in the contract, whether or not it can take the gas). To assist in matching customer demand with supply, the company maintains a gas storage field. Gas can be pumped into the storage field when supply exceeds customer demand, and likewise gas can be obtained when demand exceeds supply. There are no restrictions on the use of the gas storage field except that the field must be filled to capacity at the beginning of each gas year (September 1). Consequently, whenever the contractual supply for gas for the remainder of the gas year is less than that required to satisfy projected demand and to replenish the storage field, the company must curtail service to the industrial customers (except for quantities that are used for heating). The curtailments must be carefully controlled so that an oversupply does not occur at the end of the year. Similarly, care must be taken to ensure that curtailments are adequate during the year to protect against the need to curtail commercial or residential customers in order to replenish the storage field at the end of the year.

In recent years, the company's planning efforts have not provided a firm basis for the establishment of long-term contracts. The current year has been no different. Planning efforts have not been adequate to control the supply during the current gas year. Customer demand has been projected only as a function of the total number of customers. Commercial and industrial customers' demand for gas has been curtailed excessively. This has resulted in lost sales and has caused an excess of supply at the end of the gas year. In an attempt to correct the problems of Citizens' Gas, the president has hired a new director of corporate planning and has instructed the director to present him with a conceptual design of a system to assist in the analysis of the supply and demand of natural gas. The system should provide a monthly gas plan for each year of the next five years, with particular emphasis on the first year of the plan. The plan should provide reports that assist in the decision-making process and that contain all necessary supporting schedules. The system must provide for the use of actual data during the course of the first year to project demand for the rest of the year and for the entire year. The president has indicated to the director that he will base his decisions on the effect on operating income of alternative plans.

1. Discuss the criteria that must be considered in specifying the basic structure and features of Citizens' Gas Company's new system to assist in planning its natural gas needs.

2. Identify the major data-items that should be incorporated into Citizens' Gas Company's new system to provide adequate planning capability. For each item identified, explain why the data-item is important, and state the level of detail that would be necessary to be useful.

15-31. Draw a dataflow diagram for each of the following modules (discussed in Chapters 9, 10, 11, and 12):

a. Accounts receivable
b. Accounts payable
c. Payroll
d. Order processing
e. Inventory management
f. General ledger

g. Product data management

h. Material requirements planning

i. Production costing and monitoring

15-32. Combine the individual DFDs from the previous problem into DFDs that depict the four subsystems:

a. Cash Receipts and Disbursements

b. Sales and Purchases

c. Financial Accounting

d. Manufacturing

15-33. Draw an entity-relationship diagram for each of the following modules (discussed in Chapters 9, 10, 11, and 12):

a. Accounts receivable

b. Accounts payable

c. Payroll

d. Order processing

e. Inventory management

f. General ledger

g. Product data management

h. Material requirements planning

i. Production costing and monitoring

15-34. Combine the individual E-R diagrams into summary E-R diagrams that depict the four subsystems:

a. Cash Receipts and Disbursements

b. Sales and Purchases

c. Financial Accounting

d. Manufacturing

15-35. (*CMA, adapted*)   Jem Clothes, Inc., is a 25-store chain, concentrated in the Northeast, that sells ready-to-wear clothes for young men and women. Each store has a full-time manager and an assistant manager, both of whom are paid on a salary basis. The cashiers and sales personnel are typically young people working part time, who are paid an hourly wage plus a commission based on sales volume. The flowchart, in Exhibit 15-9, depicts the flow of a sales transaction through the organization of a typical store. The company uses unsophisticated cash registers with four-part sales invoices to record each transaction. These sales invoices are used regardless of the payment type (cash, check, or bank card).

On the sales floor, the salesperson manually records his or her employee number and the transaction (clothes class, description, quantity, and unit price), totals the sales invoice, calculates the discount when appropriate, calculates the sales tax, and prepares the grand total. The salesperson then gives the sales invoice to the cashier, retaining one copy in the sales book.

The cashier reviews the invoice and inputs the sale. The cash register mechanically validates the invoice by automatically assigning a consecutive

EXHIBIT 15-9 Sales Transaction Flowchart

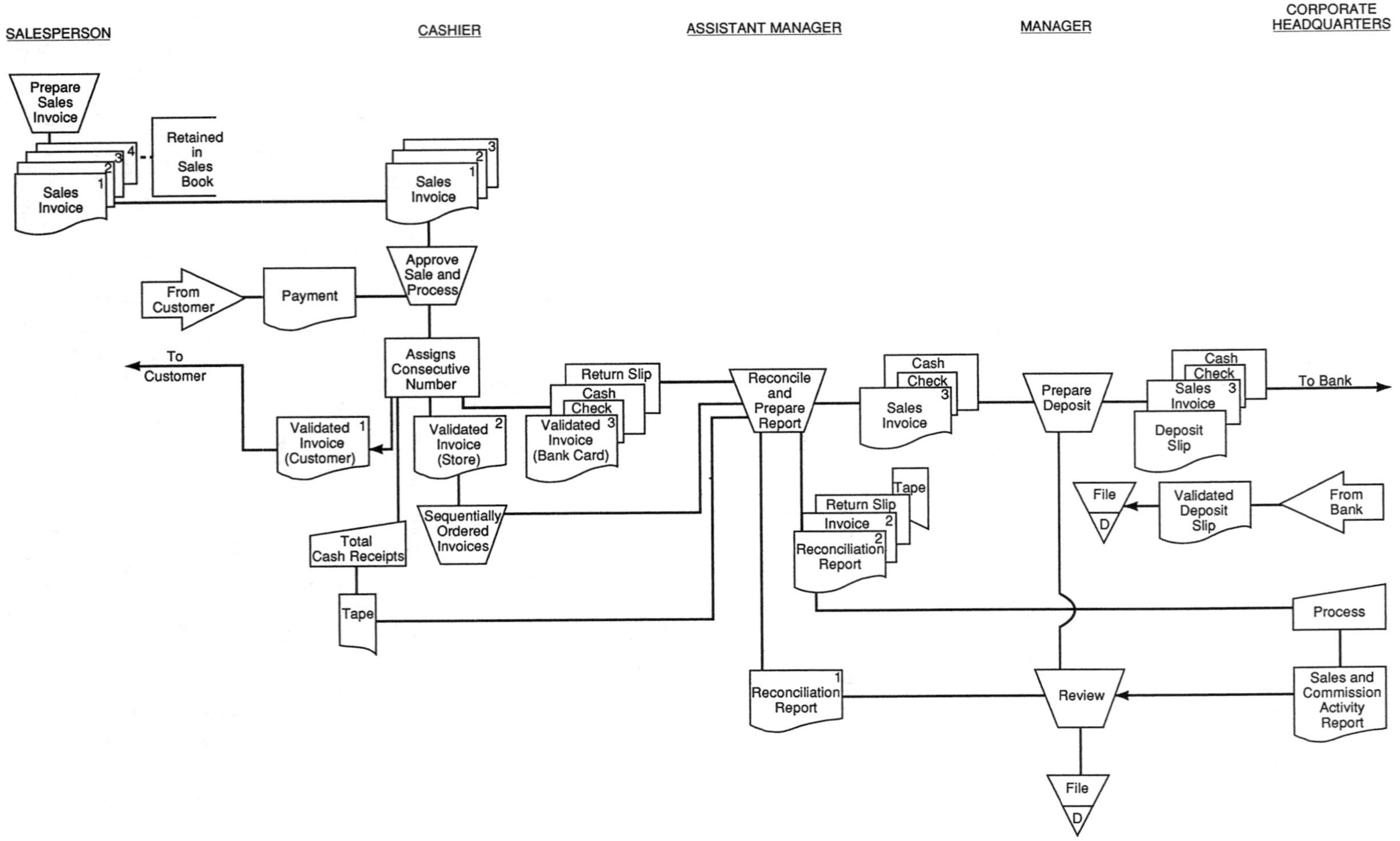

number to the transaction. The cashier is also responsible for getting credit approval on charge sales and approving sales paid by customer check. The cashier gives one copy of the invoice to the customer, retains the second copy as a store copy, and retains the third copy for a bank card deposit if needed. Returns are handled in exactly the reverse manner with the cashier issuing a return slip when necessary.

At the end of each day, the cashier sequentially orders the sales invoices and takes cash register totals for cash, bank card, and check sales and cash and bank card returns. These totals are reconciled by the assistant manager to the cash register tapes, the total of the consecutively numbered sales invoices, and the return slips. The assistant manager prepares a daily Reconciliation Report for the store manager's review.

Cash sales, check sales, and bank card sales are reviewed by the manager who then prepares the daily bank deposit (bank card sales invoices are included in the deposit). The manager makes the deposit at the bank and files the validated deposit slip. The cash register tapes, sales invoices, and return slips are then forwarded daily to the central data processing department at corporate headquarters for processing. The data processing department returns a weekly Sales Commission Activity Report to the manager for review. Each store in the Jem Clothes chain follows this sales and cash receipts system for control of sales transactions.

1. Identify six strengths in the Jem Clothes system for controlling sales transactions.

2. For each strength identified, explain what problem(s) Jem Clothes has avoided by incorporating the strength in the system for controlling sales transactions.

15-36. (*CMA, adapted*) You have been assigned to review the internal controls of the credit department of a recently acquired subsidiary. The subsidiary imports several lines of microcomputers and sells them to retail stores throughout the country. The department consists of the credit manager (who was hired only six months ago to replace the previous manager who retired), a clerk, and a part-time secretary. Sales are made through 15 sales representatives—5 at headquarters who handle large accounts with retail chains and the local area and 10 located throughout the country. Sales representatives visit the premises of current and prospective customers and, if a sale is made, prepare a customer order form which consists of the original and three copies. One copy is retained by the customer, one is retained by the sales representative, one is sent to headquarters. For new customers, if the order is for more than $5,000, a credit application is also completed and sent along with the order to headquarters. The credit application includes a bank reference and three credit references along with financial statements.

The purchase order sent to headquarters goes first to the credit department for approval. When the credit department receives the order, the clerk looks up the customer's name in a card file to determine if it is a new or old customer. Only customers with "good credit" are listed in the file. If the customer is found, the clerk examines a monthly report which lists all accounts which have not been paid in 60 days. If the customer's account is not listed in the report, the clerk initials the purchase order as approved and sends it to accounting for recording and billing. Orders from new customers or from customers listed on the "60-day" report are held for review by the credit manager.

For orders greater than $5,000 from new customers, the credit manager reviews the credit application along with the financial statements and calls at least one of the credit references. If approved, the manager initials the order and gives it to the secretary to prepare a card for the clerk's "card" file and to file the credit application. If denied, the manager adds the customer's name to a list of past rejected credit applications and canceled accounts. For new customers with orders for less than the $5,000 limit, the credit manager reviews the order and checks it against the list of past rejections. If not on this list, the order is initialed as approved and is sent to accounting. For orders from customers with accounts 60 days past due, the manager reviews the details of the accounts and the original credit application. If approved, the order is initialed and is sent to accounting.

If orders are not approved, the credit manager calls the warehouse to stop shipment. The order is marked "credit not approved" and is given to the secretary who notifies the sales representative and the customer that the order has been rejected. The order and the credit application are then thrown away. Once each quarter the credit manager requests that the accounting department provide a listing of all accounts over 90 days old with supporting detail of account activity for the last 12 months. The credit manager reviews this information and determines if action should be taken. Action consists of first calling the sales representative who handles the account and asking him or her to contact the client about payment. If payment is not received in three weeks, the credit manager calls the customer and requests payment. At this time, the credit manager also has the clerk pull the customer's card from the clerk's "customer card" file. If payment is not made in two weeks, the account is turned over to a collection agency. When an account has been with a collection agency for two months without receiving payment, the account is written off. The credit manager prepares the necessary adjusting entries.

List four internal control deficiencies associated with the credit function. Give the deficiency, its associated risk, and a control to eliminate the deficiency.

15-37. (CMA, adapted) Lexsteel Corporation is a leading manufacturer of steel furniture. While the company has manufacturing plants and distribution facilities throughout the United States, the purchasing, accounting, and treasury functions are centralized at corporate headquarters. While discussing the management letter with the external auditors, Ray Landsdown, controller of Lexsteel, became aware of potential problems with the accounts payable system. The auditors had to perform additional audit procedures in order to attest to the validity of accounts payable and cutoff procedures. The auditors have recommended that a detailed systems study be made of the current procedures. Such a study would not only assess the exposure of the company to potential embezzlement and fraud, but would also identify ways to improve management controls. Landsdown has assigned the study task to Dolores Smith, a relatively new accountant in the department. Because Smith could not find adequate documentation of the accounts payable procedures, she interviewed those employees involved and constructed a flowchart of the current system. This flowchart and descriptions of the current procedures are presented in the paragraphs that follow and in Exhibit 15-10.

Computer Resources Available. The host computer mainframe is located at corporate headquarters with interactive terminals at each branch location. In general, data entry occurs at the source and is transmitted to an integrated data base maintained on the host computer. Data transmission is made between the

EXHIBIT 15-10   Accounts Payable Procedures

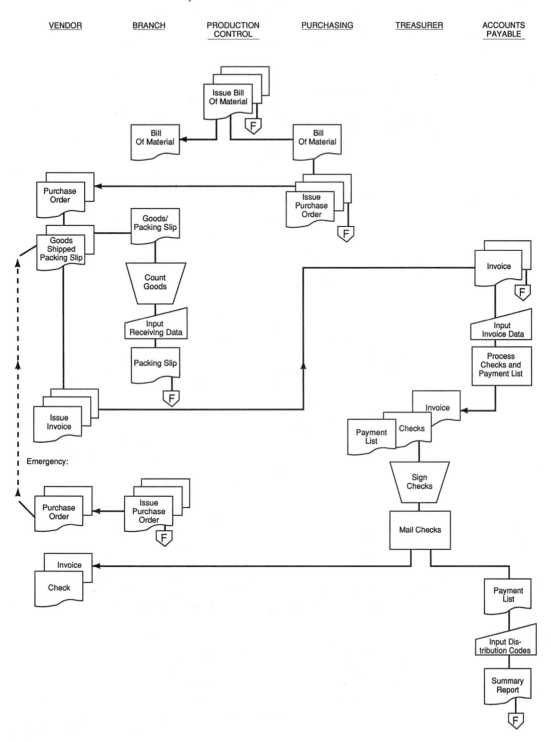

VENDOR   BRANCH   PRODUCTION CONTROL   PURCHASING   TREASURER   ACCOUNTS PAYABLE

branch offices and the host computer over leased telephone lines. The software allows flexibility for managing user access and editing data input.

Procedures for Purchasing Raw Materials. Production orders and appropriate bills of material are generated by the host computer at corporate headquarters. Based on these bills of material, purchase orders for raw materials are generated by the centralized purchasing function and are mailed directly to the vendors. Each purchase order instructs the vendor to ship the materials directly to the appropriate manufacturing plant. The manufacturing plants, assuming that the necessary purchase orders have been issued, proceed with the production orders received from corporate headquarters. When goods are received, the manufacturing plan examines and verifies the count to the packing slip and transmits the receiving data to accounts payable at corporate headquarters. In the event that raw material deliveries fall behind production, each branch manager is given the authority to order materials and issue emergency purchase orders directly to the vendors. Data about the emergency orders and verification of materials receipt are transmitted via computer to accounts payable at corporate headquarters. Since the company employs a computerized perpetual inventory system, physical counts of raw materials are deemed not to be cost effective and are not performed.

Accounts Payable Procedures. Vendor invoices are mailed directly to corporate headquarters and entered by accounts payable personnel when received; this often occurs before the receiving data are transmitted from the branch offices. The final day of the invoice term for payment is entered as the payment due date. This due date must often be calculated by the data entry person using information listed on the invoice. Once a week, invoices due the following week are printed in chronological entry order on a payment listing, and the corresponding checks are drawn. The checks and the payment listing are sent to the treasurer's office for signature and mailing to the payee. The check number is printed by the computer and displayed on the check and the payment listing and is validated as the checks are signed. After the checks are mailed, the payment listing is returned to accounts payable for filing. When there is insufficient cash to pay all the invoices, certain checks and the payment listing are retained by the treasurer until all checks can be paid. When the remaining checks are mailed, the listing is then returned to accounts payable. Often, weekly check mailings include a few checks from the previous week, but rarely are there more than two weekly listings involved. When accounts payable receives the payment listing back from the treasurer's office, the expenses are distributed, coded, and posted to the appropriate plant/cost center accounts. Weekly summary performance reports are processed by accounts payable for each cost center and branch location reflecting all data entry to that point.

1. Identify and discuss three areas where Lexsteel Corporation may be exposed to fraud or embezzlement due to weaknesses in the procedures described, and recommend improvements to correct these weaknesses.

2. Describe three areas where management information could be distorted due to weaknesses in the procedures described, and recommend improvements to correct these weaknesses.

3. Identify three strengths in the procedures described and explain why they are strengths.

DECISION CASE

565

CHAPTER 15
*System
Analysis
and Design*

Continental Fruits, Inc., is a small corporation canning fruits and vegetables for sale through wholesale and retail distribution. It supplies goods to its customers through a system of regional sales managers, and the company does not sell directly to the general public. Continental Fruits is having problems with accounts receivable and related credit operations. The company has over 850 customer accounts distributed over its five regional divisions. All customer orders are sent to the central credit department for approval before goods are shipped. After approval, two copies of the sales invoice are sent to the shipping department as the shipping order. The shipping department forwards one copy of the sales invoice as a billing notice to the accounts receivable department once the goods are shipped. Customer billing statements are prepared monthly from accounts receivable ledger cards. Continental Fruits does not maintain a listing of accounts by region.

Because of an increasing work load, billing statements have been delayed an average of 10 days. In addition to late billings, the average payment time is 55 days, although sales terms call for payment of the net amount within 30 days. The credit department does not receive copies of current customer statements promptly, and clerks must correlate current balances owed and credit limits manually. As a result, many accounts now have balances in excess of their credit limits, and a number of these accounts are also delinquent. The credit department also often lacks timely knowledge of customers' outstanding balances because payments are processed by the accounts receivable department. If a new order might cause an account to exceed its credit limit, a credit clerk searches the accounts receivable department's file of unprocessed payments and checks the accounts receivable ledger card.

There has recently been an increase in errors in customer billings, apparently caused by the increasing work load and management pressure to process monthly billings promptly. Continental Fruits anticipates a rapidly increasing sales volume, and management is very concerned about the ability of the manual accounts receivable system to handle any increase. You have been called in to design a computer-based accounts receivable system for Continental Fruits.

Required:

1. Prepare a statement of the system's overall purpose.
2. List the system's specific objectives.
3. Give the report requirements of the system together with a brief description of each report.

16 System Implementation and Evaluation

Overview

Translation of a logical system design into a physical design and the actual implementation of the system to get it into operation.

Learning Objectives

Thorough study of this chapter will enable you to:

1. Identify the components of a system specification.
2. Explain the role of programming in system development.
3. Create a programming report.
4. Discuss the process of implementation of a new system.
5. Evaluate a system once it is operational.

Outline

System Specification

Programming Considerations

The Programming Report

Planning for Implementation

The Implementation Process

System Evaluation

SYSTEMS IN THE REAL WORLD

567

CHAPTER 16
System
Implemen-
tation and
Evaluation

Bad News for Trees

Information technology was supposed to let us taper off paper. But we emphatically have not. The paperless office, the bookless library, the printless newspaper, the cashless, checkless society—all have gone the way of the Empire State Building's dirigible mooring, the backyard helipad, the nuclear-powered convertible and the vitamin-pill dinner.

The Micro Millennium is turning out to be the Cellulose Century. Computers have created more paper, lots more paper, rather than less.

Futurists have never liked paper, except in forms that nobody ever asked for, like disposable underwear. As early as 1895, a pair of French satirists were predicting that the record player would bring "the end of the book." Around the turn of the century Jules Verne doubted there would be novels or romances in 50 to 100 years.

The statistics speak for themselves. From 1959 to 1986, America's consumption of writing and printing paper increased from 6.83 million to 21.99 million tons, or 320 percent, while the real gross national product rose 280 percent. One magazine estimated that between 1981 and 1984 alone American business use of paper grew from 850 billion to 1.4 trillion pages, and printed material may rise again to 4 trillion pages in the nineties.

From 1936 to 1986, the volume of United States mail increased from 80 billion to 146 billion pieces a year, and the postal service estimates an annual volume of 170 billion pieces in the nineties. Meanwhile, none of the 10-odd public electronic-mail networks has more than 30,000 subscribers.

All these changes have something in common. Paper is flourishing, not in spite of but because of electronics. There is every reason to think electronics will drive, not drive out, print and paper as forcefully in the next decade as it has in the last. The computer, ironically, has turned us from pencil pushers to print pumpers.

SOURCE: *The Wall Street Journal*, 3/5/88, reprinted by permission.

It must be considered that there is nothing more difficult to carry out, nor more doubtful of success, nor more dangerous to handle, than to initiate a new order of things. For the reformer has enemies in all those who profit by the old order, and only lukewarm defenders in all those who would profit by the new order, this lukewarmness arising partly from fear of their adversaries, who have the laws in their favor; and partly from the incredulity of mankind, who do not truly believe in anything new until they have had actual experience of it.

Niccolo Machiavelli, *The Prince*

Chapter 15 went through the process of establishing the system objectives and discussed the system design to accomplish those objectives. At this point, the new system exists only on paper. The concern now must be with the process of getting the system design into operation.

All system development steps are critically important and must be done well. It is important to realize, however, that the balance between concepts and details changes as progress is made through this cycle. The system objectives step is primarily conceptual, with few required details; the focus is on the overall view and what the system is trying to accomplish. The system design and system specification steps are balanced between concepts and details; the new system must be structured; and the details of costs, files, and computer programs must be worked out. Implementing the system is primarily detail work. The concepts have been developed. The task is to put them into practice, and this will necessarily involve many details.

Implementing the system may be the hardest task because conceptual difficulties become apparent and have to be corrected. If system objectives are poorly chosen, this fact can often be obscured and the objectives approved without incident. If the system design or system specification is poorly done, this fact can often be lost in thick reports and flowcharts. During system implementation, however, these suppressed flaws come to light and must be dealt with. This is why some consulting firms prefer that their client not implement a system design they developed. The consultants get paid for a system design, but they do not have to risk failure by actually trying to get the system working in practice.

This balance between concepts and details is important for deciding who will do which tasks in the overall system development. The conceptual decisions are of critical importance but do not require many hours of work. Thus, the conceptual tasks of setting objectives and laying out the design of the system are those most suited to the capabilities (and fee structure) of outside consultants. The detail work of specifying the system and implementing it are more suited to permanent employees, since they will work with the system. As a result, consultants frequently help lay out the objectives and broad design of the system and then help monitor the progress of the permanent staff in specifying and implementing the system. However, the permanent staff must be capable of implementing the design. Otherwise, even a well-conceived and well-laid-out design will fail.

SYSTEM SPECIFICATION

Once the system design is developed and everyone agrees that this is the way for the system to operate, the next step is to specify the details of the system. System specification includes all the details of how the procedures and the programs will work and exactly what the files and output will look like. System details are worked out only for the one system selected in the system design. The system specification is the most important and difficult technical step in the entire system development process. Prior to this step, everything is somewhat conceptual, or even vague. After this step, the computer programming should be a fairly mechanical task if the specifications are done properly. There is no single way to translate a system design into specifications. However, the translation should be simple, modifiable, machine independent, and testable.

569

CHAPTER 16
*System
Implemen-
tation and
Evaluation*

Simple.   The programs and files should be as simple as possible. The programs should be easy to read, with clear logic paths. The file structure should be easy to understand.

Modifiable.   The programs and files should be easy to modify. Files will eventually have to accommodate more and different types of data. Programs will have to handle more and different types of situations. The specification should allow for business growth by providing room for the system to grow.

Machine Independent.   The programs and files should be machine independent. They should not become tied to one particular computer or computer company. Data storage should be done in a way that would work on a wide variety of computers. Do not choose a nonstandard storage technique, even if it is more efficient for a particular computer. A large investment in a nonstandard storage approach may make it impossible to switch when more attractive alternatives become available from other vendors. Similarly, programming languages should be used in their standard forms. Computer manufacturers often offer extensions of standard languages. Do not use them. Use standard languages in a standard way, and the task of converting to another computer will be much easier.

Testable.   The programs should be easy to test. This implies establishing separate programs to accomplish identifiable tasks so that the entire system is created from building blocks. Each building block is a program that does a reasonably small number of tasks. This technique makes it possible to test each program separately as it is written. If the system malfunctions, the faulty program can easily be identified. Giant programs that handle everything are hard to test because they present many more possibilities to test.

The amount of detail necessary in a system specification varies by project. Judgment, experience, and common sense are needed to keep the proper balance of detail in each particular situation. Suppose the people who are developing the specifications are also going to do the programming. In this case, it may not be necessary for every step in each program to be completely detailed. However, if another group, such as outside programmers, were to do the programming, the flowcharts must be more detailed in order to avoid both real and claimed misunderstandings.

Control Section

The control section helps to ensure proper approval and proper handling of revisions.

Approval.   The specifications must be approved in writing by the four major groups whose approval is necessary: management, the users, the system design group, and the programmers. Management and the users will approve the system if it will do the necessary job and satisfy their requirements. The system designers should approve their own work. Approval by the programmers shows that they believe the system has been sufficiently specified so that they can program directly from the information in the report; the flowcharts are acceptable and the files have been well laid out.

Revisions. Revisions must be properly recorded and authorized. In many system development projects, there may be five, ten, or more notebooks of system specifications. No matter who develops the specifications and no matter how good they are, there will inevitably be revisions and modifications during the programming and implementation process. It is then absolutely critical to ensure that all notebooks are updated consistently. The control section keeps a record of all modifications after initial approval and the authorization for each modification. Thus, the notebooks can be quickly checked to ensure that all necessary changes have been made.

System Description

This section of the system specification report should be in management terms and give an overt view of the system. Management must read and approve the system specifications, but they are simply not going to read (or understand if they do read) all the technical details. It is therefore essential that a discussion be provided which provides management with a reasonable basis for making a decision on the specifications. The overriding concern should be to provide the information a manager needs to determine if the system meets her requirements at a reasonable cost. This description should include

1. An overview of the entire system that places it in context and then details objectives and scope.
2. A discussion of alternative designs that were considered for adoption to accomplish those objectives.
3. A narrative describing the operation of the new system.
4. An economic analysis of the system design, including all tangible benefits, justifying the expense.
5. A description of the intangible benefits of the system and also its limitations since no system can do everything.
6. A discussion of how the system interfaces with other systems. No system stands alone, and the details of how this system will work with others should be developed in advance of programming and implementation.

System Flowchart

The next section of the report should show a flowchart of the entire system describing its document flow and operation. This flowchart can be taken from the system design, and modified to remedy any deficiencies that are revealed by system specification.

Computer System Requirements

This part of the system specification report should describe the requirements of the system design for both hardware and software. The hardware requirements would include the necessary computer and main memory for the system.

Focus here on exactly what the system needs, not simply what is available. If a company's computer has a huge amount of main memory available, but the new system requires only a small part of it, this should be specified. Thus, if the company were to get another computer, the demands of this system would be clear. Other hardware requirements include peripheral equipment (such as the number and capacity of any required printers, disks, or tapes), terminals, and other data communication devices. Specific points to consider are the printers, terminals, memory, and software.

Printer. The printer must be able to handle peak requirements. These peak demands typically occur at the end of the month when management and accounting reports must be produced.

Terminals. The number of terminals required is a function of how many transactions must be processed in a peak day and the time required for each transaction. The length of time required for each transaction can vary greatly depending on the application and whether transactions are entered in batch or interactive mode. It is usually very difficult to analyze time requirements. An estimate can be made, however, by assuming a maximum transaction rate of 200 transactions per day per terminal. A detailed analysis can be made based on an average typing keystroke rate for the operator.

Software. Software requirements include any required operating systems. There may also be requirements for software packages from outside vendors. Often there are requirements for a particular subroutine library or set of preprogrammed routines.

For systems involving data communications, additional requirements must be identified. Exhibit 16-1 on page 572 provides the basic specifications for a communications environment.

Data Management Summary

The next step in the system specification process is the technically tedious but necessary task of detailing the precise nature of the data the system will use. The contents of this **data management summary** can be separated into input data, files to be maintained, and output reports. As an example, an average application size on a mainframe is 6 master files, 13 million characters in the data base, and 26 predefined user reports.

Input. The input data summary should detail the source of all data and include an illustration of all new input forms. Then the name and the content of the input data should be given. Following this should be the data entry requirements and restrictions. Finally, there should be a projection of the volume of data that will need to be input. Exhibit 16-2 on page 573 gives an example of an input form.

Files. The file summary should discuss each file to be maintained by the system. This summary should begin with the type of file, either direct access

571

CHAPTER 16
*System
Implemen-
tation and
Evaluation*

EXHIBIT 16-1   Specifications for a Communications Environment

Area	Item
Capacity	1. Number of potential users, geographic sites, users at each site, and users supported simultaneously 2. Response times required for interactive users 3. Maximum resources required 4. All projected expansion in above areas for three years
Availability/reliability/flexibility	1. Percentage of time system must be available by site 2. Longest period of unavailability acceptable by site 3. Retransmissions acceptable because of distorted data 4. Importance of "soft" crash capability on warning that the system is about to fail 5. Modifications to be made to the network, such as terminals, sites, and users 6. Impact on current users acceptable during modifications
Security/accountability	1. Security requirements to log into the system, to access specific applications, and to modify system 2. Items to be recorded on a user basis: log-ins; log-outs; usage of resources, applications (when and how long), and data bases (modifications made, accesses) 3. Other recorded items: hardware failures, security violations, and percentage of time a device is actually used

or sequential. Following should be the contents of the file and the particular record layout to be used. There should be a discussion of retention cycles (namely, how long a copy of the file will be kept before it is scratched or replaced). The exact file name or label should be given. Next should be the file maintenance requirements: How often must the file be updated and how current must the file be kept? A projection of the volume of records in each file and the rate at which each will grow should be given. Finally, the report should detail the backup requirements, namely, how often a copy of the file should be made and where different copies of the file should be retained for protection.

Output.   The output summary should present the name of each report or other output of the system, discuss its content, and include a sample of the report to show its format and appearance. Next should be a discussion of the distribution of the report and the necessary control over each copy to prevent

EXHIBIT 16-2 Example of an Input Form

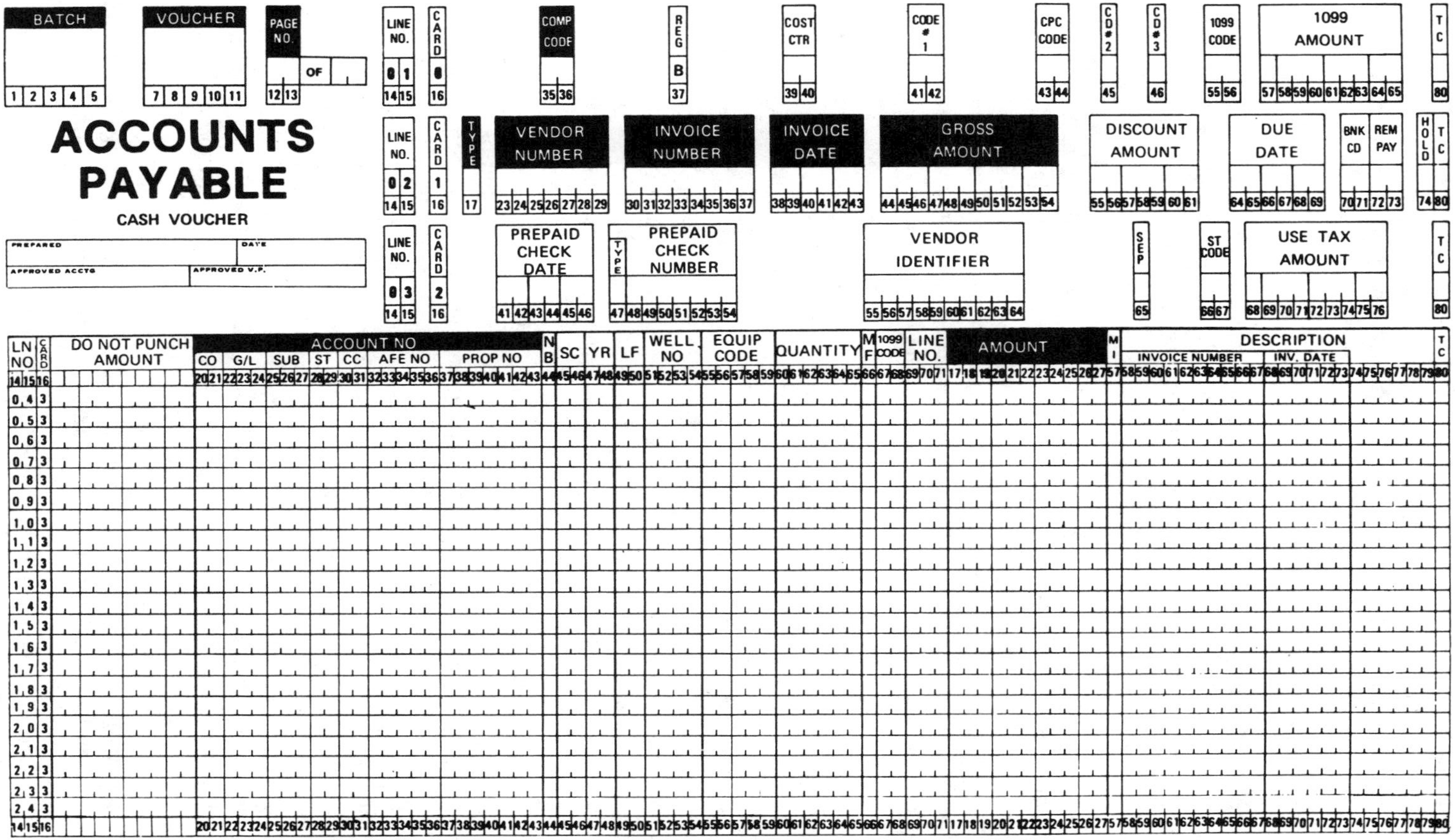

573

unauthorized access. Following this will be the frequency of the report or how often it will be generated (daily, monthly, on demand). Finally, there should be a projection of the report volume—how many pages will be printed.

Individual Module Design

The specification report should provide a detailed description of each individual system module. These modules will include manual procedures, electromechanical operations, and computer programs.

Manual Procedures. This section should have a narrative description of each manual procedure and assigned it to the organizational unit that will perform it. The staff designation and classification for employees who perform the procedure should be detailed. A description of tasks in the sequence to be performed should follow. Each source document, form, and report required for the procedure should be specified. Finally, the frequency and number of times the procedure will be performed should be projected.

Electromechanical Operations. Electromechanical operations are those that require the use of devices such as the burster (which separates pages), the decollator (which separates multiple-part output into individual copies), or off-line data input devices (such as key-to-tape or key-to-disk machines). This section should have a narrative description of the operation and mention the number and location of the devices. Next should be a description of the required tasks, in sequence. Each source document should be mentioned, and any messages or displays the device generates should be described. Finally, there should be a rate and volume projection of the usage of the device.

Computer Programs. An average application on a mainframe contains 55 programs and 23,000 source statements. This section should begin with a narrative description of each computer program. There should then be a flowchart of the program's basic structure. A summary of the input and output for the program and a list of file requirements should follow. Any necessary edit and validity checking features should be described. Additionally, any error conditions should be explained; the cause of the error and proper correction procedures should be given. Finally, there should be a discussion of checkpoint/ restart or other techniques to keep long programs that are interrupted from having to be rerun from the beginning. The program flowcharts must be done well in order to create reliable programs that are easy to modify as circumstances change and inexpensive to develop.

The programs should be specified so that they will be consistent. An example of how not to specify programs is IBM's Time Sharing Option (TSO). Among other problems, the system has inconsistent punctuation:

1. Sometimes parameters are enclosed in parentheses following the command, but other times parameters follow an equal sign.
2. "Fixed block" is (F B) in the Attribute command, but (FB) (without the space) for the Copy command.

These inconsistencies make using the system more difficult than necessary and lead to user frustration.

575

CHAPTER 16
*System
Implemen-
tation and
Evaluation*

Module Design Considerations. It is especially important for interactive systems to keep the user in mind when specifying the programs. The designer should always remember that users

1. Can make errors everywhere.
2. Do not know how they got where they are.
3. Do not know where to go next or how to get there.
4. Do not know why what they want to do will not work.
5. May know what they did wrong, but not how to fix it.
6. Begin today as a hesitant novice, but become tomorrow's impatient expert.

Exhibit 16-3 on page 576 provides guidelines for the specification of an interactive system.

Implementation Schedule

The final section of the specification report should detail the implementation schedule, that is, how to get from the system on paper in the system specification to the actual working system. This schedule should include the sequence of tasks to be performed and the interrelationships of those tasks. It is critical to know what tasks must be completed before other tasks can even begin. For each task, there should be a specific assignment of responsibility to ensure that it gets done or to determine why it does not. There should then be estimates

*System
Specification*

1. Control Section
2. System Description
3. System Flowchart
4. Computer System Requirements
5. Data Management Summary
6. Individual Module Design
7. **Implementation Schedule**

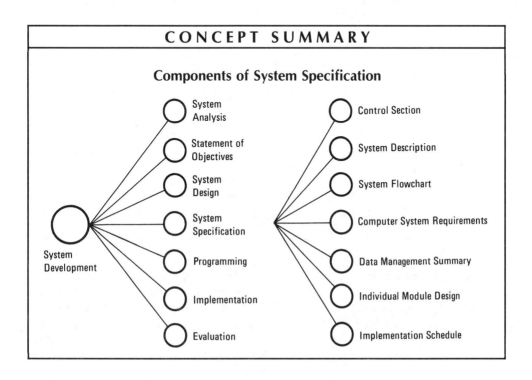

CONCEPT SUMMARY

Components of System Specification

System Development
- System Analysis
- Statement of Objectives
- System Design
- System Specification
- Programming
- Implementation
- Evaluation

System Specification
- Control Section
- System Description
- System Flowchart
- Computer System Requirements
- Data Management Summary
- Individual Module Design
- Implementation Schedule

EXHIBIT 16-3   Guidelines for the Specification of Interactive Systems

Do		
	1.	Keep it simple.
	2.	Always respond to the user; the screen should never be blank.
	3.	Keep user responses short, preferably a choice from a menu.
	4.	Keep important things under system control.
	5.	Clear error messages after handling corrections.
	6.	Use blank space (not special characters) to separate different parts of the screen.
	7.	Use a single, general layout with standardized data fields, such as dates or hours.
	8.	Justify alphabetic information on the left; numeric information on the right, aligned on a decimal point.
	9.	Use upper and lowercase, not just uppercase.
	10.	Ensure that all menu choices are valid, with a maximum of nine alternatives in each menu.
	11.	Put the most frequently chosen option first or alphabetize the options.
	12.	Allow backtracking in a nest of menus.
	13.	Start numbering with one; use numbers instead of letters.
	14.	Highlight items selected.
Do Not		
	1.	Tell users something they do not want to know.
	2.	Make attempts at humor or punishment.
	3.	Try to teach the person his or her job.
	4.	Exceed a two-second response time for an incomplete event— only at the end of a series of events.
	5.	Require transposing, computing, or translating into other units for information to be useful.
	6.	Exceed 55 characters on a line.
	7.	Use unnecessary punctuation, such as in an acronym.
	8.	Use color for its own sake; use it consistently for emphasis or differentiation.
	9.	Use evenly spaced parallel lines; they cause vibration and moiré patterns.
	10.	Use grids that compete with data they are supposed to be illuminating.
	11.	Draw attention to the style of a graph, where data measures become design elements.
	12.	Draw a graph with thin substance.
	13.	Use labels written in computer abbreviations.
	14.	Make the vertical scaling of a graph overly busy or include pointlessly ordered cross-hatching.

of both the time and the cost necessary for each of these tasks. Finally, these tasks should be arranged for clear comprehension. Chapter 8 presented two different ways of arranging the tasks necessary for implementation, the GANTT chart and the PERT/CPM network. The GANTT chart is easier to prepare and understand, while the PERT/CPM network directly reflects the interrelationships between tasks and provides more control.

PROGRAMMING CONSIDERATIONS

577

CHAPTER *16*
System
Implemen-
tation and
Evaluation

After the system specifications are made final and approved, the programming (that is, the writing of computer programs) necessary for system operation can begin. It may seem a waste of time to wait until the complete system specifications are finished in order to start programming. The temptation is to start programming even if all the details of the system specification are not completely spelled out. This is a mistake. One of the main reasons for delays in programming projects is the changing of system design or system objectives, thereby wasting large amounts of programming effort. The goal of the system specification step should be to provide enough detail so that the task of programming the system can be turned over to professional programmers. Ideally, programmers should not have to know anything about accounting or the system's application area. The system specifications should be complete and self-contained, and the programmers should be able to get everything they need from the specifications.

Programming is becoming both more difficult and easier. If the system involves networking, client/server applications, or distributed data processing, then the programming becomes enormously complex. Unfortunately, programming tools are not yet standardized for these applications in a way that provides acceptable performance. Programming difficulties include multiple simultaneous users who must be protected from each other, who need to refer to data on remote computers, and who could try to update the same information at the same time. An example would be two salespeople who might each try to sell the same item at the same time; only one should be allowed to do so.

However, if the system is designed for a single user, the programming tools which are now available often allow the programming to be done by the accountant. This programming is often referred to by different names. For example, a program written in a spreadsheet program like Lotus 1-2-3 or Quattro Pro is called a macro. A program written in the Paradox DBMS is called a script.

Structured Programming

Structured programming is a disciplined approach to program design that uses only the following three control structures in the program flowchart:

1. *Sequence.* This simplest control structure provides for sequential processing of statements (that is, commands).
2. *Condition.* This control structure tests a condition and executes one of two statements depending upon whether the condition is true or false.
3. *Loop.* This control structure executes a statement as long as a given condition is true.

Exhibit 16-4 provides a flowchart of these three different structures.

On the flowchart, it is important that (1) each control structure have only one entry point and only one exit point and (2) each of the statements in the structure can be extended to contain any of the three structures. If this design discipline is followed, the resulting programs can be easily written, easily tested, easily changed, and easily understood.

EXHIBIT 16-4   Flowchart of Programming Structures

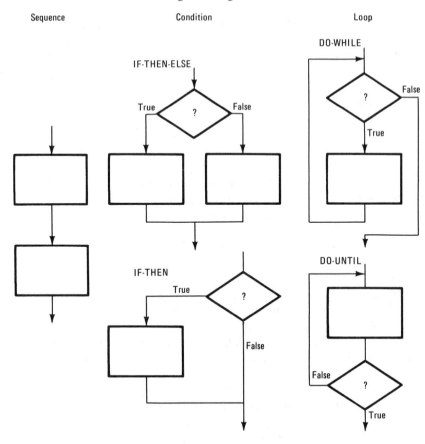

Sources of Programming

Some companies have a staff of permanent computer programmers to develop programs. This is probably the most common approach in medium- and large-scale computer installations. Other companies (even large ones) prefer to contract with software houses. For a fixed fee, the software contractor will deliver programs that meet the given system specification. Using software houses frees the company from the task of hiring, training, and retaining highly mobile computer programmers. Smaller companies sometimes use their information systems consultant to write the programs as well. This is wasteful in that the consultant is more qualified and demands a higher fee than does a programmer, but it can be less expensive in the long run because there is no need to write a full system specification in order to communicate with a separate programmer. Finally, many companies utilize software packages, which are generalized programs to handle a particular application area. Thus, the user company can buy the programs "off the shelf" to use in the system.

Programming and System Development

579

*CHAPTER 16
System
Implemen-
tation and
Evaluation*

Programming is more than just writing out statements in a programming language (which is called coding). For example, IBM's programming time is divided in the following way:

15 %	coding
35	documentation and testing
50	error correction
100 %	total programming time

Many people confuse program development with system development. **Program development** is the writing of computer programs to satisfy a set system specification. System development is the overall process which includes programming as only one of the seven steps. It is not uncommon for companies to advertise for and hire programmers when they need system developers. Not surprisingly, these companies have problems because the programmers do not have the necessary accounting and systems background to develop a complete system.

THE PROGRAMMING REPORT

The programming report developed as part of system development gives an overview of each program, shows what the input and output will look like, checks the program with test data, and provides operating instructions and a program listing. This documentation should be given for each of the programs needed for the system.

Narrative Description

The programming report should start with the purpose of the program and an overview of what the program does. The discussion should describe what the program can do for the user. The discussion need not go into where the program fits into the overall system design; this has already been covered in the system specification. Consider an accounts receivable file maintenance program as an example of the difference between the system-oriented approach and the user-oriented approach:

Programming
**1. Narrative
   Description**
2. User
   Instructions
3. Sample Input
4. Sample
   Output
5. Test Data
6. Operator
   Instructions
7. Program
   Listing

> System point of view—"This program maintains the master file, . . ."
> User point of view—"You would use this program to add customers, . . ."

The user ought to be able to read the description and know when and when not to use the program.

User Instructions

This discussion should explain to the user exactly how to operate and deal with the program. The **user instructions** should be laid out in detail—nothing should be left to the user's imagination. Always remember that the person using the program will not be a computer expert and will generally not have had any prior exposure to the computer. It is therefore not acceptable to say as part of the user instructions, "Answer the questions the program asks you." You must tell the user exactly what questions the computer will ask and exactly how to answer each one. These instructions must clearly indicate the difference between the number 0 and the letter O, between the number 5 and letter S, between the number 1 and the lowercase letter 1, and between the number 2 and the letter Z. The instructions should also indicate exactly what buttons to push: If the user needs to type in the letter A and then press the RETURN button, the instructions should say so:

> Type: A
> Press: RETURN

Sample Input

It is difficult for many people to conceptualize the input for the computer from pages of detailed instructions on program use. For all the basic types of input, there should be an example of what a complete set or package of input would look like.

Sample Output

Most people are primarily interested in the computer program output. Thus, the best way to explain the purpose of a program is to present a sample output. This sample output should be a selected printout representative of what the program generates. The sample should not include a huge stack of output that no one will be able to read or understand. A narrative description should accompany the sample output, including what each column of output or number means, because people who have had little exposure to the computer become baffled by a computer printout. In order to get all the information on one sheet of output, abbreviations must often be used. These abbreviations are clear to the programmer, but they are rarely clear to the user. Therefore, a list of abbreviations should be provided. Finally, guidance is necessary for the analysis of the computer output, namely, what this output means to the user.

Test Data

There are two distinct reasons for developing **test data**. First, the program has to be tested to make sure it is correct (that is, it processes the data in the manner anticipated by the system specification). Second, the program must be tested in the future when it is modified or extended in order to make sure that it still processes the old data in the same way. Test data are data for which the results are known. When the newly developed or recently modified program processes the test data, the results can be compared to what they should be. If the results are not correct, there is something wrong with the program.

Unfortunately, even if the results are correct, it is not possible to be absolutely positive that there are no errors in the program. An old saying in programming is that a working program is one with only undiscovered bugs.

Ideally, the test data should be chosen to test or exercise every major logic path of the program. Thus, if there are four types of transactions which can be processed, the test data should include at least one example of each transaction type. It is not sufficient for the test data to execute every statement at least once. For example, suppose a statement which should be $X = X + Y$ is written as $X = X - Y$. If Y has a value of 0, the testing will not indicate an error. Suppose a program should count the number of high-salaried employees and the number of all employees. If all employees in the test data are high-salaried, then every statement will be executed, but an error might not be detected. This example shows why every logic path should be executed, not just every statement. A program should be test run between 25 and 40 times. Most programs are tested approximately 10 times; they are usually off by a huge amount.

Operator Instructions

In large computer systems there is a distinction between the user and the operator. The user interacts with the program, develops necessary input, and uses any generated output. The operator is concerned with the care of the hardware. The operator will mount any necessary tapes on tape drives, will put paper as required into the printer, and perform related tasks. The **operator instructions** should detail exactly what tapes to use with the program and where to find those tapes, where to find any specific disks required, and where to distribute the generated output. In smaller systems, in which the user is also the operator, the user instructions should include any required discussions of physical tapes, disks, or paper.

Programming
1. Narrative Description
2. User Instructions
3. Sample Input
4. Sample Output
5. Test Data
6. **Operator Instructions**
7. Program Listing

Program Listing

The last component of programming is the actual listing of the program, that is, a printout of the statements written in the programming language. This listing has both a short-term and a long-term use. The short-term use is for the programmer's supervisor to review. The supervisor should go over the program to ensure that the program is written in the standard way, that all specifications are met, and that proper error-detecting code is included. Under pressure of deadlines, it is not uncommon for programmers to omit needed (but not immediately obvious) steps. These time savers will exact a high price later, so they should be prevented, if possible. The long-term use of the program listing is for later modifications to the program. Even after the program is written and working, it does not remain static. Future changes will be required, and a convenient listing of the latest version of the program will be extremely helpful for reference purposes.

The common theme of both long-term and short-term uses of the **program listing** is that people other than the programmer will look at the listing. Thus,

Programming
1. Narrative Description
2. User Instructions
3. Sample Input
4. Sample Output
5. Test Data
6. Operator Instructions
7. **Program Listing**

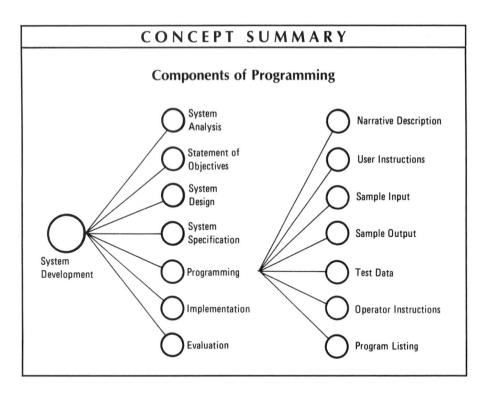

CONCEPT SUMMARY

Components of Programming

- System Analysis
- Statement of Objectives
- System Design
- System Specification
- Programming
- Implementation
- Evaluation

System Development

- Narrative Description
- User Instructions
- Sample Input
- Sample Output
- Test Data
- Operator Instructions
- Program Listing

the listing should be as easy to read as possible and should be self-documenting. In other words, the listing should explain itself with sufficient comments to make the program comprehensible. Exhibit 16-5 on page 583 presents a sample COBOL program listing.

Significant points about this sample program listing include (1) the four major divisions (identification, environment, data, and procedure) that make up the program and (2) the use of English-like data-names and syntax.

PLANNING FOR IMPLEMENTATION

System implementation is the difficult and time-consuming task of replacing the old system with the new one. The central problem is the people problem. People will be familiar with the old system and its operation and will be very likely to resent moving to a new computerized system and learning new procedures. In addition, most people will not comprehend a new system until it has been implemented and is operating. Once a system is operational, employees often like it and would not do without it, even though it might have been extremely difficult earlier to implement the system with those same people. A good sense of humor and an ability to get along well with others are invaluable to the system developer when implementing the system with the employees.

When planning for the implementation of a new computer-based system and in actually implementing the system, it is important to remember that there

EXHIBIT 16-5   Sample COBOL Program

583

CHAPTER 16
*System
Implemen-
tation and
Evaluation*

```
001010 IDENTIFICATION DIVISION.
001020 PROGRAM-ID. FORECAST.

001030 ENVIRONMENT DIVISION.
001040 CONFIGURATION SECTION.
001050 SOURCE-COMPUTER.
001060 OBJECT-COMPUTER.
001070 INPUT-OUTPUT SECTION.
001080 FILE-CONTROL.
001090     SELECT INPUT-DATA ASSIGN TO CARD-READER.
001100     SELECT OUTPUT-FILE ASSIGN TO PRINTER.

001110 DATA DIVISION.
001120 FILE SECTION.
001130 FD INPUT-DATA LABEL RECORD OMITTED DATA RECORD INCARD.
001140 01  INCARD.
001150     02 NEXT-MONTH       PICTURE 99.
001160     02 HOW-MANY-MONTHS PICTURE 99.
001170     02 BASE             PICTURE S9(8)V99.
001180     02 COEFFICIENT      PICTURE S9(8)V99.
001190     02 FILLER           PICTURE X(56).
002010 FD  OUTPUT-FILE  LABEL RECORD OMITTED DATA RECORD OUT-LINE.
002020 01  OUT-LINE PICTURE X(133).
002030 WORKING-STORAGE SECTION.
002050 77  WHICH-ONE          PICTURE S99        USAGE COMPUTATIONAL.
002055 77  MONTHS-FROM-NOW    PICTURE S99        USAGE COMPUTATIONAL.
002060 77  SALES              PICTURE S9(9)V99   USAGE COMPUTATIONAL.
002080 01  HEADER.
002090     02 FILLER           PICTURE X(15) VALUE SPACES.
002100     02 FILLER           PICTURE X(15) VALUE "PROJECTED SALES".
002110 01  PRINT-RECORD.
002125     02 FILLER           PICTURE X VALUE SPACE.
002120     02 MONTH-NAME       PICTURE X(12).
002130     02 FILLER           PICTURE X(5) VALUE SPACES.
002140     02 EDIT-SALES       PICTURE ZZZZZZZ99.99.
002150 01  MONTH-TABLE.
002160     02 JANUARY          PICTURE X(12) VALUE "JANUARY    ".
002170     02 FEBRUARY         PICTURE X(12) VALUE "FEBRUARY   ".
002180     02 MARCH            PICTURE X(12) VALUE "MARCH      ".
002190     02 APRIL            PICTURE X(12) VALUE "APRIL      ".
002200     02 MAY              PICTURE X(12) VALUE "MAY        ".
003010     02 JUNE             PICTURE X(12) VALUE "JUNE       ".
003020     02 JULY             PICTURE X(12) VALUE "JULY       ".
003030     02 AUGUST           PICTURE X(12) VALUE "AUGUST     ".
003040     02 SEPTEMBER        PICTURE X(12) VALUE "SEPTEMBER  ".
003050     02 OCTOBER          PICTURE X(12) VALUE "OCTOBER    ".
003060     02 NOVEMBER         PICTURE X(12) VALUE "NOVEMBER   ".
003070     02 DECEMBER         PICTURE X(12) VALUE "DECEMBER   ".
003080 01  MONTHS REDEFINES MONTH-TABLE.
003090     02 MONTH            PICTURE X(12) OCCURS 12 TIMES.

004010 PROCEDURE DIVISION.
004020 BEGIN.
004030     OPEN INPUT INPUT-DATA, OUTPUT OUTPUT-FILE.
004040     READ INPUT-DATA RECORD AT END GO TO JOB-END.
004050     WRITE OUT-LINE FROM HEADER AFTER ADVANCING TO TOP.
004060     MOVE ZERO TO MONTHS-FROM-NOW.
004070     MOVE NEXT-MONTH TO WHICH-ONE.
004080     PERFORM CALCULATION-ROUTINE
004100     HOW-MANY-MONTHS TIMES.
004110 JOB-END. CLOSE INPUT-DATA, OUTPUT-FILE, STOP RUN.
004120 CALCULATION-ROUTINE.
004130     ADD 1 TO MONTHS-FROM-NOW.
004140     IF WHICH-ONE IS GREATER THAN 12 SUBTRACT 12 FROM WHICH-ONE.
004150     MULTIPLY MONTHS-FROM-NOW BY COEFFICIENT GIVING SALES.
004160     ADD BASE TO SALES.
004170     MOVE MONTH (WHICH-ONE) TO MONTH-NAME.
004180     MOVE SALES TO EDIT-SALES.
004190     WRITE OUT-LINE FROM PRINT-RECORD AFTER ADVANCING 1 LINES.
004200     ADD 1 TO WHICH-ONE.
```

will be both reasonable and unreasonable opposition to the system. Any resistance based on specific problems with the new system design should have been mentioned and dealt with in the earlier stages of system development. Thus, at the implementation step, opposition will be primarily a generalized resistance to the computer and computer-based systems. There are a number of forms this resistance can take.

Employees may have had bad experiences with the computer in the past. Long-term employees may still remember an earlier ill-fated attempt to automate in the company. Also, employees may have worked at other companies with poor computer-based systems. The system developer must create a positive attitude about the computer; the employees must believe the computer can work and make a positive contribution.

Managers may subvert system implementation while trying to appear coopera-tive. Not all opposition will be verbal and clearly visible. Often, the major obstacles are managers who are opposed to the computer or the new system for personal reasons. One very real fear of managers is the future impact of computers on the manager's job. Even if the system to be implemented is not a direct threat, the manager may see a potential reduction in his prestige, power, or usefulness. Another major difficulty can be that managers do not understand the new system and will not identify with or commit to its suc-cessful implementation.

The person in charge of implementation should have a business orientation. As mentioned, the main problems of implementation will be people problems. The employees will want to know how the new system fulfills a business purpose and how the new system fits into the overall operation of the firm. They will be definitely less interested in the technical aspects of the system and how it works. Therefore, the implementation must be led by someone with the same orientation as that of the employees in order to motivate them to use the new system.

Top management must be involved in system implementation. One of the primary reasons to involve top management in the system development process from the beginning is to have management support in the implementation stage. Employees will take their attitude toward the new system from management. If management is enthusiastic and involved, the employees will be also. If management is not very interested and does not get involved, then the em-ployees will not be interested, and the implementation will fail.

THE IMPLEMENTATION PROCESS

Getting the new system up and running involves installing the hardware, making employees comfortable with the system, testing the system for bugs, converting files to the new system, and matching the new system against the old.

Hardware Installation

Implementation

1. **Hardware Installation**
2. Procedure Writing
3. Personnel Orientation
4. Training
5. Testing
6. File Conversion
7. Parallel Operation

If the new system uses the equipment available to the firm at the time, there is no need to install new hardware. However, a new system will sometimes require new equipment. In this case, the nature and timing of hardware in-stallation becomes extremely important. Many people purchase their first small computer and want it working for them in a month. However, delivery time on small computers can be about 3 months. Delivery on some equipment is 12 or even 18 months. All this has to be taken into consideration and properly planned for. Additionally, computer equipment is sometimes very sensitive to its environment, and you might then have to provide for special air-conditioning or humidity controls. Finally, raised floors, special wiring, and even special plumbing (some large IBM computers are water cooled!) are sometimes nec-essary, though less so now than in years past.

Procedure Writing

The system design outlines the manual procedures, and the system specification details how the new computer system will work. However, even this is not adequate in many situations because the procedures are

Implementation

1. Hardware
   Installation
2. **Procedure
   Writing**
3. Personnel
   Orientation
4. Training
5. Testing
6. File
   Conversion
7. Parallel
   Operation

1. Not segregated and specified by person or by job position. As a result, employees would have to read all the procedures in order to find out their tasks.
2. Not written in language appropriate to the actual employee who will do the job. Thus, the system reports may assume more knowledge than can reasonably be expected of the employee.
3. Not written in the organization's standard way and thus are not directly comparable to the procedures for other systems. This will make updating more difficult because employees will have to shift mental gears in going from one system to another.

As a result, the procedures have to be written down by job in a simple, easy-to-follow manner and in the organization's standard way. In short, a **policy and procedures manual** must be written that will fit together with the organization's other policies and procedures manuals. Exhibit 16-6 illustrates both an effective and an ineffective written procedure for requesting new facilities.

Personnel Orientation

As discussed, there are many possible employee attitudes toward the computer and new systems in general. It is impossible to assume that these attitudes will be positive. Often they will not be and will usually range from fearful to actively

EXHIBIT 16-6   Examples of Procedure Writing

INEFFECTIVE

Subject: Guide for Requesting New Facilities

The referenced procedure places the responsibility upon the requesting department to completely justify the necessity for additional equipment and/or facilities. In order to assist the requesting departments, a form, "Facilities Request," No. 347, has been made available to all departments, and if this form is completely filled out it will not only comply with Standard Practice Instruction #74 but will greatly facilitate the review and, in case of need, the acquisition of the required items. At the present time, many requests are coming to Facilities Engineering by memo, verbally, and on other forms that are either incomplete or inaccurate. A careful use of Form 347 will be beneficial for both the requester and the Company. As a further aid, if the requester will send two copies of Form 347 to Facilities Engineering, one copy will be returned to him or her with the assigned job number and preliminary action indicated, which will give the requester quickly a status of his or her request and will also serve as a ready reference file.

EFFECTIVE

Subject: Request for New Facilities

Action by	Action
Requester	1. Completes Form 347, "Facilities Request," in three copies.
	2. Sends 2 copies to Facilities Engineering.
Facilities engineering	3. Assigns job number to both copies of the request, indicating when preliminary action will be taken.
	4. Returns one copy of Form 347 to Requester.
Requester	5. In case of any inquiry, refers to job number of request.
Facilities engineering	6. Reviews all requests.
	7. Determines relative facility needs of various departments.
	8. Allocates available funds in accordance with such needs.

Source: Courtesy of Office Publications, Inc.

Implementation

1. Hardware
   Installation
2. Procedure
   Writing
3. **Personnel
   Orientation**
4. Training
5. Testing
6. File
   Conversion
7. Parallel
   Operation

hostile. The implementation therefore has to sell the system to the employees through personnel orientations. These orientations should stress the benefits of the new system and explain how it will make the employees' jobs easier by eliminating drudgery and mechanical burdens. The orientations should reassure employees that the computer will not make them obsolete or cost them their jobs. The orientations should also mention how the new system benefits the overall organization (but not mentioning any possible reduction in staff), though companywide benefits are not as important to most as how the system benefits them personally.

Training

Implementation

1. Hardware
   Installation
2. Procedure
   Writing
3. Personnel
   Orientation
4. **Training**
5. Testing
6. File
   Conversion
7. Parallel
   Operation

After the personnel understand the basic concepts of the new system, the next step is to train the people in the operation and use of the new system. Often, a company will weigh hiring outside people who have the necessary training but do not understand the company against using present employees who understand the company but need to be trained. In either case, training is often necessary and the kind of training varies. Training is often required in the use of terminals, data preparation, new procedures, or the analysis of system output. This training is generally done by one of three groups: in-house or permanent staff, the computer hardware vendor, or the outside consulting organization that designed the system. A great deal of work done by many of the large public accounting firms involves training client personnel in system operation and use.

Implementation

1. Hardware
   Installation
2. Procedure
   Writing
3. Personnel
   Orientation
4. Training
5. **Testing**
6. File
   Conversion
7. Parallel
   Operation

Testing

It is hardly possible to overstress the importance of testing in system development. Everything to this point has been conceptual. It has not been brought down to earth, so to speak, by actually using the new system on the company's data and seeing the result. A useful rule of thumb is that fully as much time should be spent on testing the programs once they have already been written as was taken for program design and coding combined. No matter how much thought and foresight goes into system development, not every aspect will have been considered, and unforeseen difficulties will arise. Unfortunately, program testing with even a wide range of actual data is not sufficient to determine every bug or error in the programs. However, such testing is necessary to have any confidence that the programs are adequate.

Implementation

1. Hardware
   Installation
2. Procedure
   Writing
3. Personnel
   Orientation
4. Training
5. Testing
6. **File
   Conversion**
7. Parallel
   Operation

File Conversion

Once the programs have been extensively tested, the next step is to convert the files from the old system to the new format. No one should convert any files prior to extensive program testing because subsequently discovered errors and modifications may require redoing a great deal of work. This file conversion often consists of going from manual records and files to computer records and files. As a result, there may be a huge one-time effort to convert all the present information to a machine-readable form. Since this conversion is so much greater an effort than normal operation, it does not make sense for the organization to use permanent staff for this work, and the work is often contracted to service bureaus. Huge conversions to a machine-readable form sometimes are airfreighted to Taiwan or other Southeast Asian countries because of the lower labor costs and greater accuracy for data entry work.

587

CHAPTER 16
*System
Implemen-
tation and
Evaluation*

Parallel Operation

Parallel operation is the process of using both the old system and the new system at the same time—and then comparing the results. The new system should generate the same results as the old system does. If the results are not the same, the new system is probably in error, though it is possible that the old system has been in error all along. Parallel operation is not as simple or easy as it may at first appear. The organization has to process everything twice: first with the old system and then again with the new system. Thus, in addition to the operation of the old system (which presumably kept everyone busy before), there is the added burden of another, completely new system. The double burden of parallel operation always tempts organizations to eliminate this step. Some succumb to this temptation and rationalize that the system has been sufficiently tested. This is a mistake! There are always unforeseen circumstances which only appear during parallel operation. Testing can never fully duplicate actual operation.

Implementation

1. Hardware Installation
2. Procedure Writing
3. Personnel Orientation
4. Training
5. Testing
6. File Conversion
7. **Parallel Operation**

CONCEPT SUMMARY

Components of Implementation

- System Development
  - System Analysis
  - Statement of Objectives
  - System Design
  - System Specification
  - Programming
  - Implementation
    - Hardware Installation
    - Procedure Writing
    - Personnel Orientation
    - Training
    - Testing
    - File Conversion
    - Parallel Operation
  - Evaluation

SYSTEM EVALUATION

After the new system has been in operation long enough for the initial difficulties to be overcome (usually, approximately six months), it is then necessary to evaluate the experience to date. The evaluation process should review how the system is operating, and compare the actual costs and benefits to the anticipated costs and benefits. The questions that an evaluation should answer include

1. How does management measure whether the system is performing well?
2. How are the evaluation data validated?
3. Who is responsible for the evaluation data?
4. What can be done to assure that the evaluation data are timely?
5. Would it cost less to perform the same functions another way?
6. Does a combination of small, scattered problems add up to gross inefficiencies?
7. Can the system generate interpretive data (projections, comparisons, and so on) in addition to raw numbers?

The reasons for this evaluation step are (1) to analyze the system in operation to determine whether the system can be improved and (2) to analyze the system development process to see if any lessons can be learned from the company's experience. The focus should be on both the individual system and the overall system process. If the focus is only on the one system in question, it is possible to miss lessons valuable in the development of future systems, such as a decision that the system development was rushed or that top management was not sufficiently involved in the system project. If the focus is only on the overall questions, it is possible to lose the chance to make significant changes to this specific system. The evaluation report should conclude with recommendations for improvement in operating efficiency and system design.

Evaluation is very difficult to do well, especially if it is done by the people who designed the system or the people who operate it. Writing some 4,000 years ago, Confucius said that he had "yet to meet a man who, on observing his own faults, blamed himself." As a result, the postimplementation evaluation should be done, if possible, by independent reviewers. However, even if the review is undertaken by people involved in the system, it will be a valuable exercise showing how the system concepts are applied in practice.

An independent audit is a form of evaluation and can substitute for an evaluation in some situations, especially in basic accounting systems. Auditors prepare a management letter, which should assess system operation and system design, and make recommendations for improvement.

Documentation Review

A manual system is visible and can thus be reviewed visually through the audit trail. In a sense, the manual system is self-documenting because one can see it. A computer-based system is largely electronic and hence invisible. Documentation is therefore critical to understanding, operating, and modifying a computer-based system.

Unfortunately, under the pressure of deadlines it is common for the persons responsible for documentation (especially programmers) to let it slide because the lack of documentation is not immediately obvious. This is such a standard problem that some companies have assigned a separate group solely to write system documentation. This approach does not work well, however, because the separate group is not in a position to know enough to write complete documentation. The people who develop the system must document their own work.

The **documentation review** is then an independent review of the work done to date on documentation of the system and the programs. The review first checks the completeness of the documentation and then reviews the quality of this work. Any necessary corrections and additional documentation can then be laid out.

Cost Analysis

As discussed in the preceding chapter, the system design details the costs of the new system. At the time of the system design, however, these costs are projections and estimates. The task here is to analyze the actual costs and compare them to the costs anticipated in the system design.

People sometimes protect a new system proposal by estimating costs at an unrealistically low figure. This approach can get a new system design accepted but at a great cost to the organization later on. The cost analysis can evaluate the process that was used to estimate future costs by checking the results of the estimate against actual results. Major differences may imply that the cost estimation process was seriously deficient. One of the most common deficiencies is not the determination of an inaccurate cost figure, but rather the complete omission of some major costs.

Evaluation
1. Documentation Review
2. **Cost Analysis**
3. Benefit Analysis
4. Acceptance by Users
5. Internal Controls
6. Deficiencies
7. Recommendations

Benefit Analysis

Along with the projected costs of the new system, the anticipated benefits were laid out in the system design. These anticipated benefits generally include reduction in clerical costs, improved service to customers, and faster and better information for management. However, as discussed earlier, some of these benefits (especially the reduction in clerical costs) often prove elusive. One important task of the evaluation process is to compare the actual benefits, if any, to those anticipated in the system design. It is common for the evaluation to turn up unanticipated benefits, which are more important than the anticipated benefits. For example, the system may unexpectedly point up some particular wasteful practice.

Evaluation
1. Documentation Review
2. Cost Analysis
3. **Benefit Analysis**
4. Acceptance by Users
5. Internal Controls
6. Deficiencies
7. Recommendations

Acceptance by Users

It cannot be stressed too strongly that the system does not consist solely of the computer programs. The system also consists of manual procedures and human use of the printed or displayed output. Thus, the system can only work through people. If the people do not like or will not use the system, then it

EXHIBIT 16-7   Causes of User Dissatisfaction to Look For

1. Autocratic, depersonalized management style of implementation
2. Lack of planning and communication before system implementation
3. No consultation with users in the design and implementation of the system
4. Fear that automation will cause job losses
5. Loss of opportunity to take pride in work
6. Lack of training before implementation
7. Inadequate cutover period when old and new systems run in parallel
8. Increasing work load
9. Increasing level of repetitive, boring work without human interaction
10. Disappointment with the actual system capabilities compared to those promised
11. Resentment of lower status than a machine
12. Resentment at discourteous software messages and the use of codes when words could have been used
13. Loss of individuality and decision-making power
14. Fear of appearing stupid by lack of knowledge of computing
15. Mistrust of data processing staff
16. No in-house support service to answer questions and solve problems with the new system

Evaluation

1. Documen-
   tation Review
2. Cost Analysis
3. Benefit
   Analysis
4. **Acceptance
   by Users**
5. Internal
   Controls
6. Deficiencies
7. Recommen-
   dations

cannot work. It is therefore an important task of the evaluation process to determine the level of user acceptance. There are many possible reasons for user dissatisfaction, but two of the most important and common are

> *Lack of confidence in the system.* It is common for the system to fail to provide adequate error-detecting and error-correcting techniques. If excessive errors creep into the system, and its output is not useful, the users then stop relying on the system and start keeping their own private system to help them in their work.
>
> *Excessive errors and rejected transactions.* If the system finds a large percentage of transactions in error and rejects them, it can collapse under the burden of correcting and reentering all those transactions in addition to the new transactions.

Exhibit 16-7 provides a summary of items contributing to user dissatisfaction.

Evaluation

1. Documen-
   tation Review
2. Cost Analysis
3. Benefit
   Analysis
4. Acceptance
   by Users
5. **Internal
   Controls**
6. Deficiencies
7. Recommen-
   dations

Internal Controls

As part of the evaluation process, there should be a specific review and evaluation of the system's internal controls. This review should include the adequacy of the design of the controls but should also stress how the controls are working in practice. The review should answer questions such as

1. Are the policies and procedures being followed? Are the controls effective?
2. What backup planning exists?

591

CHAPTER 16
*System
Implemen-
tation and
Evaluation*

3. How long would the backup plans take to implement?
4. What is the total loss potential in dollars? What is the total loss potential in business?
5. Can the facilities be better protected?
6. How does the system limit access to data from outsiders? How does it limit access from unauthorized insiders?
7. Can the data be stolen? Can the data be altered? Can they be destroyed accidentally? Intentionally?
8. How does the system protect employees' privacy? How does it protect the company's privacy?
9. Can the system be made more secure?

The internal control review cannot merely concern itself with the way things should be; it should also review the way things actually are. People are often content that certain internal controls are supposed to be in effect. This review should determine whether the controls are in effect. A useful means of determining the effectiveness of controls is to test them. For example, if access to computer terminals is supposed to be limited, an unauthorized person should attempt to use the terminals. If the computer is supposed to reject unreasonable transactions, an attempt should be made to process an unreasonable transaction, such as a payroll check for 100 hours of overtime or a credit sale of $1,000,000.

Deficiencies

The report documenting the work done for the preceding five steps in evaluation will doubtlessly be quite extensive. This material can form a basis for analyzing any deficiencies of either the specific system under evaluation or the entire system development process. There is a parallel discussion of deficiencies in Chapter 4 on the topic of system analysis. The thrust and emphasis is the same here: What are the weak points of the system? What areas should be looked at more closely? Exhibit 16-8 on page 592 provides the good and bad items to look for in assessing a new system.

Recommendations

The recommendations section is the goal of the evaluation process. If the organization did not change anything as a result of the evaluation, then the evaluation was of limited benefit. The recommendations should answer the following questions: What should the organization do now to improve performance? What should the organization do differently in the future to avoid some of the problems that have occurred? The emphasis here is the same as in the system analysis of Chapter 15—give the manager realistic and cost-effective guidance on what to do now.

EXHIBIT 16-8   Evaluation Items to Look For

Impact	Item
Good	1. Users are happy with the on-line response time and the on-time delivery of reports.
	2. System is easy to expand or modify as circumstances change.
	3. System costs less than expected to implement or to operate.
	4. Programs and data are compatible with existing systems.
	5. Any required new terminals and other peripherals are compatible with existing equipment, as promised.
	6. Errors are infrequent and easily caught.
	7. Productivity aids keep programming costs down.
	8. Language to access the data base is effective.
	9. Installation of new equipment occurred ahead of schedule.
	10. Development of new software occurred ahead of schedule.
Bad	1. System is too small.
	2. Delivery or installation of equipment was late.
	3. Development or implementation of software was late.
	4. System costs are in excess of expected total.
	5. All promised software or support was not provided.
	6. All promised program and data compatibility with existing systems was not attained.
	7. All promised terminal or other peripheral compatibility with existing equipment was not attained.
	8. Changes to hardware or software are hard to keep up with.
	9. Equipment is excessively noisy.
	10. Power or cooling requirements are excessive.

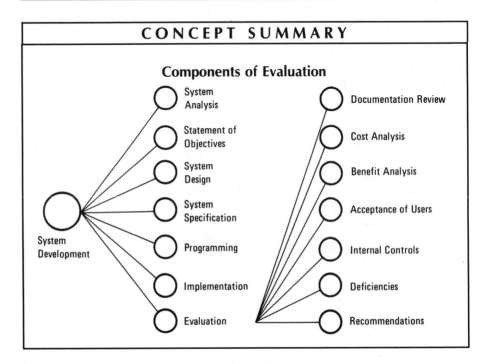

CONCEPT SUMMARY

Components of Evaluation

System Development

- System Analysis
- Statement of Objectives
- System Design
- System Specification
- Programming
- Implementation
- Evaluation
- Documentation Review
- Cost Analysis
- Benefit Analysis
- Acceptance of Users
- Internal Controls
- Deficiencies
- Recommendations

REFERENCES

593

CHAPTER 16
*System
Implemen-
tation and
Evaluation*

K. HANSEN, *Data Structured Program Design* 2nd ed. (Englewood Cliffs, NJ: Prentice Hall, 1986).

S. MARCH, ed. *Entity-Relationship Approach* (New York: North-Holland, 1988).

C. MCCLURE, *Software Automation* (Englewood Cliffs, NJ: Prentice Hall, 1988).

J.-D. WARNIER, *Logical Construction of Programs* (New York: Van Nostrand Reinhold, 1976).

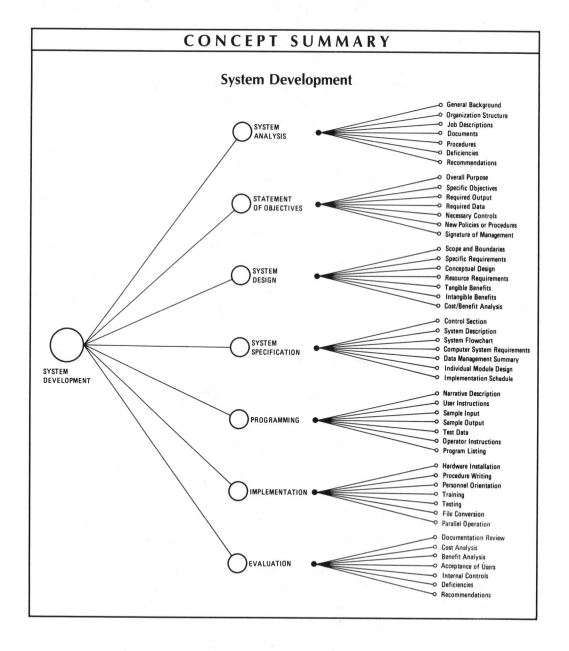

CONCEPT SUMMARY

System Development

CHAPTER SUMMARY

The system design exists only as a logical system, existing only in theory. System design must be translated into physical form and then implemented.

System specification takes the system design and identifies the hardware, software, input data, data files, output, and procedures necessary to get the system working. The specification should also give a detailed implementation schedule as a basis for planning. This specification and schedule will then be updated as implementation proceeds.

The software can be developed in-house, contracted for, or purchased as a package. If a suitable package is available, it will virtually always be the least expensive approach. However, many circumstances and organizations are sufficiently unusual that no appropriate package is available. In all cases, there should be sufficient documentation of the software to use it effectively and to test it sufficiently to be confident it is correct.

Implementation of the system then involves getting the new system to operate in place of the old. This involves the computer-related tasks of installing the hardware and testing the system. But, more important, it involves the orientation and training of the people who will operate the system. Implementation also involves file conversion from the old format to the new. The final step in implementation is parallel operation, where the new system and the old are operated at the same time with the same transactions. After the new system operates correctly through an entire accounting cycle, then the system can be deemed operational.

After the system has been implemented and operational for some months, there should be an evaluation which reviews the documentation, internal controls, and experience of users for the new system. Also, the evaluation should compare the actual costs and benefits of the system to those estimated in the system design. This evaluation can then be the basis for the system analysis of the next system or improvements in the system development process.

KEY TERMS

Data management summary (*p. 571*)
Documentation review (*p. 589*)
Operator instructions (*p. 581*)
Parallel operation (*p. 587*)
Policy and procedures manual
   (*p. 585*)

Program development (*p. 579*)
Program listing (*p. 581*)
Structured programming (*p. 577*)
Test data (*p. 580*)
User instructions (*p. 579*)

QUESTIONS

16-1. What is the relationship between conceptual design and specific system requirements?

16-2. List the seven components of system specification and briefly describe what is accomplished in each component.

16-3. How is the data management summary of the system specification related to the specific system requirements of the system design?

595

CHAPTER 16
System
Implemen-
tation and
Evaluation

16-4. What is an individual system module? Give examples of three individual system modules in an accounts receivable system.

16-5. Give five aspects of a system that should be detailed in a system specification in addition to the programs and files needed by the system.

16-6. List the seven components of programming, and briefly describe what is accomplished in each component.

16-7. Define structured programming, and give the three control structures used in a program flowchart.

16-8. Describe the techniques of computer program documentation.

16-9. Distinguish user instructions from operator instructions, and give an example of each.

16-10. Give four reasons for difficulty in system implementation, and recommend how each of these difficulties could be avoided.

16-11. List the seven components of implementation, and briefly describe what is accomplished in each component.

16-12. Why are personnel orientation and training important in implementation?

16-13. What is parallel operation? Why is it important?

16-14. List the seven components of evaluation, and briefly describe what is accomplished in each component.

16-15. Discuss two of the most common reasons for user dissatisfaction with a new system.

16-16. Why might actual costs of a new system differ from the costs estimated in the system design? Why might benefits of a new system differ from the benefits projected in the system design?

PROBLEMS

16-17. Proper system implementation entails performing numerous tasks, some of which depend upon the prior completion of others. Arrange the following items in the order they would likely be performed in system implementation. Note those which could be performed simultaneously.

    a. Reorganize data
    b. Determine actual system cost
    c. Hire data processing staff
    d. Review written descriptions of system
    e. "Sell" system to employees
    f. Determine actual system benefits
    g. Ensure programs work
    h. Run both old and new systems
    i. Explain how to use system
    j. Receive computer equipment

16-18. Once a system specification has been set, actual programs to meet that specification can be obtained in four basic ways. Discuss each of these sources of programs, and give the general advantages and disadvantages of each.

16-19. Listed here are several findings that might be turned up by a postimplementation evaluation. For each of these possible findings, give three different circumstances which could have brought about that result, and state generally how you would uncover the true reason for that result.

a. Continuing employee hostility
b. Errors in system output
c. Higher than anticipated costs
d. Inadequate program documentation
e. Tangible benefits not fully realized

16-20. The individual module design of the system specification contains a description of the programmed controls. Give three specific reasonableness tests for each of the following transactions:

a. Cash is disbursed in payment of an amount owed a vendor
b. Credit purchase of merchandise
c. Payroll check for a terminating employee

16-21. A firm's data base is a critically important resource that can be damaged or destroyed in a number of different ways. Explain what you would include in a system specification to safeguard a data base against each of the following occurrences:

a. Error by terminal operator
b. Error in application program
c. Conspiracy between programmer and chief accountant
d. Natural disaster, such as flood or fire
e. Power failure

16-22. (*CMA, adapted*)   Huron Co. manufactures and sells 8 major product lines with 15 to 25 items in each product line. All sales are on credit, and orders are received by mail or telephone. Huron Co. has a computer-based system. All sales orders received during regular working hours are typed on Huron's own sales order form immediately. This typed form is the source document for the keying of shipment or backorder data for each item ordered. These data are employed in the after-hours processing at night to complete all necessary recordkeeping for the current day and to facilitate the shipment of goods the following day. In summary, an order received one day is to be processed that day and night and shipped the next day. The daily processing that has to be accomplished at night includes the following activities:

a. Preparing the invoice to be sent to the customer at the time of shipment
b. Updating the accounts receivable file
c. Updating the finished goods inventory
d. Listing all items backordered and short

Each month the sales department would like to have a sales summary and analysis. At the end of each month, the monthly statements should be prepared and mailed to customers. Management also wants an aging of accounts receivable each month.

597

CHAPTER 16
System
Implemen-
tation and
Evaluation

1. Identify the master files that Huron Co. should maintain in this system to provide for the daily processing. Indicate the data content that should be included in each file and the order in which each file should be maintained.

2. Prepare a system flowchart of the daily processing required to update the finished goods inventory records and to produce the necessary inventory reports (assume that the necessary storage devices are available). Use the annotation symbol to describe or explain any facts that cannot be detailed in the individual symbols.

3. Describe the items that should appear in the monthly sales analysis report(s) that the sales department should have.

4. Describe the input data and master files that would have to be maintained to prepare these reports.

16-23. The following is a narrative description of a computer batch processing system. Sales invoices are created in the order department and sent to the billing department, where they are held awaiting shipment notification. When this notification is received, the pricing on the invoice is checked, extensions are made, and the original invoice is sent to the customer. For each day, a control total is derived, and copies of all invoices are given to the control group. Credit memos originate in the billing department after notification of credit approval is received from the credit department. The original is sent to the customer. A daily control total is calculated and copies are sent to the control group. Remittance advices are received by the mail clerk along with receipts on account. At the same time, money is given to the cashier, a control total is computed, and copies of the documents are given to the control group. The control group checks the documents and assigns batch numbers (a different number for each day).

At the same time data are entered, a count is made of the number of input records handled to provide assurance that data are not lost during computer processing. A program control is added by instructing the computer to tally the number of records read and processed. The control group checks the computer generated number with the record count number held in the data entry area. Two computer runs are made, one for editing the input data and the other for updating the customer ledger account balances and producing a transaction register and exception reports. The computer edit program produces a printed list and accompanying explanations of designated input errors detected by the edit program, as well as control totals of the sales invoices, credit memos, and remittance advices. The control group sees that any errors in the input data are corrected and also checks the computer generated control totals against the adding machine tapes kept by the billing department and the mail clerk. If the two sets of figures do not reconcile, the differences are checked and another computer run is made. No final updating of the master files can be done until the edit program clears the input data for errors and until the computer-generated control total agrees with batch totals produced by the adding machine tapes. After the data clear the first computer run, they are sorted according to customer number. Within the customer number, the data are arranged into sales invoices, credit memos, and remittance advices. The data are then transferred to magnetic tape, which is referred to as the transaction or detail tape. The transaction tape and master file tape are processed with a computer updating run.

1. Prepare a system flowchart.
2. List the files used by the system and specify the information to be contained in each.
3. List the system internal controls.

16-24. (*AICPA, adapted*) Kathy Centanni is examining the accounting system design of the Louisville Sales Corporation, which is planning to install an electronic computer. The following comments have been extracted from Ms. Centanni's notes on the plans for computer operations and the processing and control of shipping notices and customer invoices:

a. To minimize inconvenience, Louisville plans to convert without change its existing data processing system, which utilized tabulating equipment. The computer company will supervise the conversion and provide training to all computer department employees (except data entry operators) in systems design, operations, and programming.

b. Each computer run is assigned to a specific employee, who is responsible for making program changes, running the program, and answering questions. This procedure has the advantage of eliminating the need for records of computer operations because each employee is responsible for his own computer runs.

c. At least one computer department employee remains in the computer room during office hours, and only computer department employees have keys to the computer room.

d. System documentation consists of those materials furnished by the computer company—a set of record formats and program listings. These and the tape library are kept in a corner of the computer department.

e. The company considered the desirability of programmed controls but decided to retain the manual controls from its existing system.

f. Company products are shipped directly from public warehouses, which forwards shipping notices to general accounting. There, a billing clerk enters the price of the item and accounts for the numerical sequence of shipping notices from each warehouse. The billing clerk also prepares daily adding machine tapes ("control tapes") of the units shipped and the unit prices.

g. Shipping notices and control tapes are forwarded to the computer department for data entry and processing. Extensions are made on the computer. Output consists of invoices (in six copies) and a daily sales register. The daily sales register shows the aggregate totals of units shipped and unit prices which the computer operator compares to the control tapes.

Describe weaknesses in internal control over information and data flows and in the procedures for processing shipping notices and customer invoices. For each weakness, recommend improvements in these control and processing procedures.

16-25. (*CMA, adapted*) VBR Company has recently installed a new computer system which has on-line, real-time capability. Terminals are used for data entry and inquiry. A new cash receipts and accounts receivable file maintenance system been designed and implemented for use with this new equipment. All programs have been written and tested, and the new system is being run in parallel with the old system. After two weeks of parallel operation, no differences have been observed between the two systems other than data entry errors on the old system. Al Brand, data processing manager, is enthusiastic

599

Chapter 16
*System
Implemen-
tation and
Evaluation*

about the new equipment and system. He reveals that the system was designed, coded, compiled, debugged, and tested by programmers utilizing an on-line terminal installed specifically for around-the-clock use by the programming staff; he claimed that this access to the computer saved one-third in programming elapsed time. All files, including accounts receivable, are on-line at all times as the firm moves toward a full data base mode. All programs, new and old, are available at all times for maintenance. Program documentation and actual tests confirm that data entry edits in the new system include all conventional data error and validity checks appropriate to the system. Inquiries have confirmed that the new system conforms precisely to the flowcharts, a portion of which are shown in Exhibit 16-9 (pages 600–601).

Before authorizing the termination of the old system, Cal Darden, controller, has requested a review of the internal control features which have been designed for the new system. Security against unauthorized access and fraudulent actions, assurance of the integrity of the files, and protection of the firm's assets should be provided by the internal controls. Based upon the description of VBR Company's new system and the system flowchart that has been presented

1. Describe any defects that exist in the system.
2. Suggest how each defect you identified could be corrected.

16-26.   (*CMA, adapted*)   Lynn Duncan, controller of Lankar Company, has decided that the company needs to redesign its purchase order form and design a separate document to record the receipt of goods. Currently, a copy of Lankar's purchase order is serving as a receiving report, and the receiving clerk records the quantities received on the copy of the appropriate purchase order. Duncan has decided to implement these changes because there have been a number of inconsistencies and errors in ordering materials for inventory and in recording the receipt of goods. She believes these mistakes have resulted from the poor design of the current purchase order and the use of a copy of the purchase order as a receiving report. In addition to improved reporting, the introduction of these new forms will allow Duncan to reinforce the need for accuracy and thoroughness among the employees in the purchasing department. Presented in Exhibit 16-10 on page 602 is the revised purchase order; there will be multiple copies of the form with the original and one copy being mailed to the vendor. The form will be letter size for ease in filing. The clerical staff in the purchasing department will complete the form from the information provided on the purchase requisition, and the form will be signed by the purchasing manager before mailing to the vendor.

Presented in Exhibit 16-11 on page 602 is a condensed version of a draft of the new receiving report. This form will be approximately 5 inches in width and 8 inches long and will be prenumbered. There will be multiple copies so that all of the relevant departments will receive a copy. The new receiving report will be filled out in the receiving department by the receiving clerks.

1. Discuss several problems that can occur when a copy of a purchase order is used as a receiving report.
2. Review the forms that Duncan has designed for Lankar Company, and explain what should be added and/or deleted to improve the (a) purchase order and (b) receiving report.

(*continued on page 603*)

EXHIBIT 16-9 VBR Flowcharts

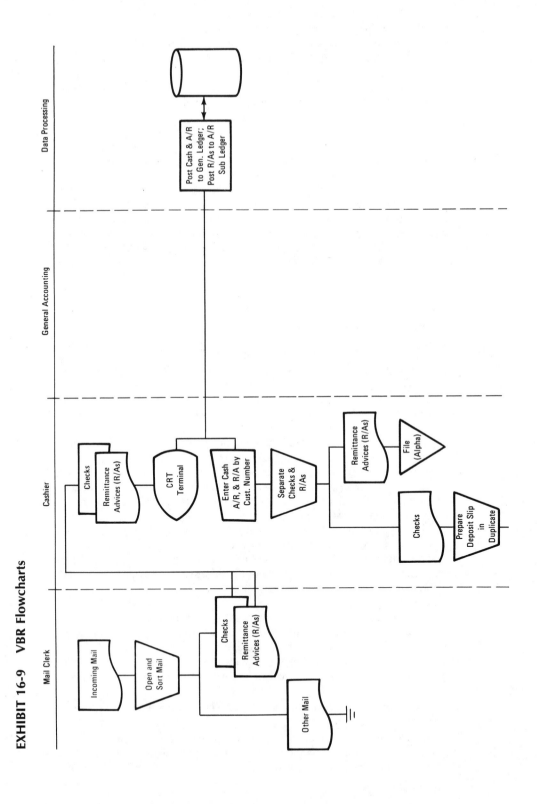

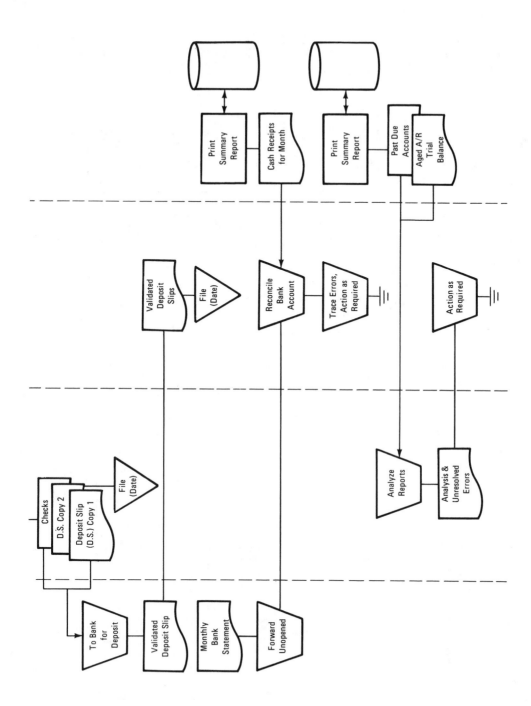

EXHIBIT 16-10 Revised Purchase Order

Lankar Company Purchase Order
One Fordwick Place
Arion, Indiana 36999

To: Ship to:

Delivery Date: P.O. Date

Shipping Instructions:

Item		Lankar	Vendor			Unit
No.	Quantity	Part #	Part #	Description		Cost

Special Instructions:

_____
Purchasing Manager

EXHIBIT 16-11 New Receiving Report

No. NNNNNN

Lankar Company
One Fordwick Place
Arion, Indiana 36999

Received From:
(Name/Address)

Quantity	Description	Unit Price	Amount
		Subtotal	
		Frt. Charges	
		Total	

Remarks/Conditions: Department Delivered to:

**BE SURE TO MAKE THIS RECORD
ACCURATE AND COMPLETE**

3. In order to provide good internal control and assure efficient document flow, identify the departments of Lankar Company that should receive a copy of the purchase order, and explain why each of the identified departments needs a copy of the purchase order.

4. Despite its apparent simplicity, a receiving department performs several vital control functions. Describe four of these functions.

603

CHAPTER 16
System
Implemen-
tation and
Evaluation

DECISION CASE

A system review is being conducted of Weststate Data Center. Weststate provides data processing services to four municipalities in the Denver area. It was created and is jointly owned by the four municipalities because none has sufficient need for data processing to justify the acquisition of a computer individually. Weststate Data offers the municipalities a billing and payroll application. The billing system is composed of about 20 programs, ranging from input validation to creation of billing address labels. Computer peripheral equipment includes two disk drives and a printer. Weststate uses disks to achieve processing efficiency at a low cost, even though the present system excludes the retention of extensive backup copies of files for recovery in case of disaster. Weststate has a staff of six people. Normal work loads require only a single operator, but during peak periods, vacation, emergencies, and so on, programmers and the company manager often operate the computer. When data errors are discovered, changes are telephoned to municipal clerks for corrections to billings. Corrections appear on the next transaction listing produced by Weststate.

The billing application was purchased as a software package designed to perform billing and statistical reporting for any type of municipality. Weststate has attempted to maintain a history of modifications to the system. The system documentation contains a system design overview with corresponding system flowcharts showing all existing programs and input/output files. There are also brief program narratives detailing the major functions of each program and the major logic decisions within the programs. Program flowcharts are included for all programs written in-house.

Programming changes are recorded on a program control form, which is used to update the program maintenance history. The changes and steps needed to incorporate the modifications are described on the form. The control forms are numbered in sequence, and changes within the computer program itself are tagged with this number. When the change is tested and placed in production, the program control form is filed so that changes in the system can be traced to the source. The system flowcharts are updated, but it has not been necessary to update the narrative descriptions.

Required:

1. Prepare a list of internal control deficiencies and provide recommendations for improvements to internal control.

(continued on next page)

2. Summarize deficiencies in the program modification system and documentation procedures and provide recommendations for improving modification and documentation procedures.

17 EDP Auditing

Overview

External review of controls, processing, and account balances of a computer-based accounting information system

Learning Objectives

Thorough study of this chapter will enable you to:

1. Explain the difference between auditing around and auditing through the computer.
2. Distinguish between compliance and substantive tests.
3. Describe the methods of evaluating internal control.
4. Compare and contrast general and application controls.
5. Give the most frequently used methods of compliance testing.
6. Discuss the most frequently used methods of substantive testing.
7. Identify the audit problems of advanced systems.

Outline

EDP Auditing Concepts

Internal Control Applied

Evaluation of Internal Control in a Computer Environment

Compliance Testing in a Computer Environment

Substantive Testing in a Computer Environment

Audit Problems of Advanced Systems

SYSTEMS IN THE REAL WORLD

S&L Backlash

The nation's accountants may soon feel a backlash from the savings and loan crisis.

In an effort to prevent another costly bailout like the one mounted on behalf of the savings and loan industry, Federal legislators are drafting a measure that would require independent auditors to alert regulators to any obvious illegal activities they discover in their audits. Under current law, accountants must only notify upper management and drop the account if they happen upon illegal acts and the client refuses to correct the problem.

Damages currently being sought by the Federal Deposit Insurance Corporation from major accounting firms that are accused of fraud, negligence or other professional misconduct in the audit of S&L's are listed below.

Accountant	Savings and Loan	Damages Sought
Coopers & Lybrand	First Federal Savings and Loan (Shawnee, Okla.)	$ 7,000,000
Arthur Young	Imperial Savings (San Diego)	26,000,000
Ernst & Young	Western Savings (Dallas)	500,000,000
Deloitte, Haskins & Sells	Sunrise Savings and Loan (Boynton Beach, Fla.)	250,000,000
	Commonwealth Federal (Fort Lauderdale, Fla.)	50,000,000
	Aspen Savings Bank (Aspen, Colo.)	Subject to compensatory damages
	Royal Palm Federal (West Palm Beach, Fla.)	None specified
Touche, Ross	Beverly Hills Savings and Loan (Beverly Hills, Calif.)	300,000,000
	Midwest Federal (Minneapolis)	100,000,000
	Westwood Savings and Loan (Los Angeles)	100,000,000
	Peoples Federal (Bartlesville, Okla.)	460,000
	Lee Savings and Loan (Giddings, Tex.)	38,500
Peat Marwick	Duval Federal (Jacksonville, Fla.)	16,500,000

Arthur Young has merged with Ernst & Whinney to become Ernst & Young. Deloitte, Haskins & Sells has merged with Touche, Ross.

Source: *The New York Times,* 7/31/90, reprinted by permission.

EDP AUDITING CONCEPTS

Chapters 14–16 presented the steps of the system development cycle for a business information system. This chapter introduces the auditing of electronic data processing (EDP) systems as a means of verifying the functioning of controls and the accuracy of accounting records once the system is operational. Chapter 2 included auditing as an important element of internal control. The audit provides an independent view of the system and determines (1) whether the system is functioning as it should and (2) whether the accounting records accurately reflect the company's financial condition. An independent audit is an excellent means of checking compliance with established standards and of identifying internal control deficiencies. An independent audit is of far less benefit as a means of detecting fraud.

Auditing Around Versus Through the Computer

A computer-based system can be audited around the computer or through the computer. **Auditing around the computer** involves examining the input to and output from the computer but not examining the computer's processing. This approach is most useful in unsophisticated stand-alone systems. For example, suppose a payroll system takes time card data and hourly rates as input and then generates payroll totals and deductions and has no connection to other systems. This payroll system could be audited by going around the computer to examine only the input and output. However, in more complicated systems, this approach is not possible. The input of the examined subsystem is often the output of other subsystems, and its output is the input to still other subsystems. Thus, it is not possible to treat any subsystem in isolation, and the audit must go through the computer.

   Auditing through the computer means using the computer to audit itself. Since both the data and the audit trail are in electronic form, they cannot be read or examined directly by the auditor, and the computer itself has to be used. This chapter will concentrate on auditing through the computer.

Compliance Versus Substantive Testing

The primary concern of the auditor is that there could be a significant undiscovered error. To perform the audit and help ensure there are no undisclosed errors, the auditor will use two different types of tests:

1. **Compliance testing** checks the internal controls to determine if they function properly.
2. **Substantive testing** checks the account balances to determine if they are properly stated.

   The better the internal controls, the less likelihood there is of an undiscovered error. Good internal controls make the auditor more confident that there is no such error. Therefore, the results of the compliance tests will affect the way the auditor designs the substantive tests. If the compliance tests indicate that the controls work properly, the auditor can deemphasize substantive tests. If the compliance tests indicate that the controls do not work properly, the auditor must expand the scope of the substantive tests.

Allowance for Bad Debts. An auditor would typically want to use the computer-generated aged accounts receivable listing as support for determining whether the allowance for bad debts is sufficient. If the auditor believes that internal controls are appropriate and functioning, then the auditor might use the listing without testing it further. Also, the auditor might perform some of the audit work at a preliminary time, such as in September or October for a calendar year firm, and only update the work at the end of the year. Preliminary testing of the aged listing would be appropriate because the auditor could rely on the internal controls to ensure that the aging is properly performed on a consistent basis during the period between the preliminary and year-end tests.

If the auditor cannot rely on the internal controls, the auditor will have to test the aged receivable listing in detail before performing the test of the allowance for bad debts. For example, the auditor will want to check agreement between the days past due on the listing against the actual days past due by reviewing the original sales invoices. The auditor would not use the report until satisfied with its accuracy. Further, the auditor would perform all testing of the allowance at year end because faulty internal controls could not ensure the reliability of the aging between the preliminary and year-end tests.

Inventory. An auditor would typically want to use a computer-generated inventory listing giving costs per unit, quantities, extensions, and totals as support for the client's inventory valuation. If the auditor can rely on the internal controls, the auditor can use the listing with only limited substantive testing of the report at year end. Further, adequate controls may also allow the auditor to perform more substantive testing at a preliminary date along with limited substantive testing at year end. This may prove to be more efficient and allow the auditor to concentrate on other audit issues at year end.

If the auditor cannot rely on the internal controls, there must be more extensive testing of the inventory listing. For example, the auditor may check that the invoice prices on the listing agree with the actual purchase invoices to ensure that the report is accurate and complete. Furthermore, substantive testing would likely be performed at year end.

INTERNAL CONTROL APPLIED

Since the evaluation of internal control is the first step and one of the most important in auditing computer systems, the auditor must understand how internal controls function in a computer environment. Chapter 4 discussed the basic concepts of internal control, but that discussion was necessarily very general. Chapters 9–12 presented a complete computer-based accounting system, so this provides the opportunity to see how internal control works in a complete system. This section illustrates how the basic concepts of internal control are used for the order processing application discussed in Chapter 11.

These basic procedures that will be presented here are applicable to the other components of the accounting system.

Ensuring Proper Authorization

One internal control difficulty with interactive processing is that, in the absence of special measures, anyone with access to a terminal can input data to the system, even without proper authorization. To combat this problem, an interactive system typically requires a user identification number (user ID) and a password. The user ID uniquely identifies a particular computer user, but the ID is public information and thus can be used for tasks such as identifying printouts. The password, however, is secret and ensures that only the proper person uses that user ID.

The system can limit the activities of specific users to only those transactions for which they are authorized. The system can then display, at the system console, any attempted security violations. Management can periodically change passwords for all employees and delete the user IDs and passwords for all employees who left the company.

Testing Input for Errors

When an operator enters a customer number, the computer displays the customer's name and address. The operator visually verifies that this is the correct customer. Similarly, when the operator inputs inventory item numbers for an order, the computer displays the appropriate description. This control, called descriptive feedback, ensures that the correct customer gets the exact items desired.

Because descriptive feedback is possible using interactive processing, two of the programmed controls used in batch processing—self-checking numbers and redundancy—are no longer needed. The self-checking number catches transposition errors, which may occur as clerks copy numbers onto forms, to ensure that the proper account gets updated. Redundancy also helps to ensure that the intended account gets updated. Because visually checking the customer name or inventory description is more effective, neither of these batch processing controls is used in interactive processing.

The computer validates all codes by matching them to tables of valid codes. If the computer finds an invalid code, it displays an error message and gives the operator the choice of correcting the error immediately or canceling the order. The system will not accept an order with invalid codes.

The system ensures that the sales representative number matches a valid salesperson. Additionally, the system verifies that the order number is not the duplicate of an order already on file. Again, if there are errors, the system displays an error message and gives the operator the choice of correcting or canceling the order.

The operator may key in a nonstandard price and thereby override the standard price on the inventory file. To detect a gross keying error, such as a misplaced decimal, the computer displays a warning message if the keyed price is not in the range of 20 percent to 200 percent of the standard price.

EXHIBIT 17-1   Credit Check Display

```
33200151   TOWNE OFFICE SUPPLY          ORDER 10248 - CREDIT CHECK
                                                        1   24
   PREVIOUSLY RECEIVABLE FROM CUSTOMER
      ACCOUNTS RECEIVABLE BALANCE                         720.84
      FUTURE CHARGES                                       75.20
      IN TRANSIT TO ACCOUNTS RECEIVABLE                    30.05
                                      TOTAL A/R           826.09
   ORDERS IN PROCESS
      ORDER 10248 - NOT YET INVOICED                      225.77
      ORDER 10131 - NOT YET INVOICED                      107.23
      ORDER  9980 - ALREADY INVOICED                       61.44

   CREDIT LIMIT                1,000.00   TOTAL DUE      1,220.53

   ORDER 10248 PLACED ON CREDIT HOLD     OVER LIMIT BY     220.53

   COMMAND KEYS
    1 RESUME ENTRY
   24 SIGN OFF
```

Credit Checking

The system automatically checks the customer's credit for every order. Exhibit 17-1 gives an example of such a credit check display. There are appropriate warning messages when the customer exceeds the credit limit. The system considers the accounts receivable balance, invoices that have not completed the billing process, and the invoice being processed in determining the customer's balance. If the balance exceeds the credit limit, the system places the order in hold status. To release the order from hold status, an operator must input a two-character authorization ID. This capability of the system reduces the work of the credit department, since the department will have to review only the orders for which the customer fails the credit limit tests.

Independent Verification
of Terminal Operators' Performance

The operator inputs transactions directly into the system without the backup of an authorized source document. Therefore, the system must verify the performance of the terminal operator independently. Exhibit 17-2 illustrates an Order Reconciliation report that can help perform this function. Because a terminal is often called a workstation, abbreviated W/S, the various terminals are identified as W1, W2, and so on.

The Order Reconciliation report shows all orders in the system, including the workstations where they were entered. The report further shows the action, if any, for that order that day. The report points out any orders on hold status

EXHIBIT 17-2   Order Reconciliation Report

ORDER RECONCILIATION
DMAS CORP.

ORDER NUMBER	CUSTOMER NUMBER	NEW TODAY	CONTROL TOTALS	ENTERED BY	ACTION TODAY	ITEMS	SPEC CHGS	CHANGED TODAY BY	PRICING OVERRIDE	PICK LIST	INVOICE PRINTED	ON FILE	ITEMS	SP/CHGS
5 O/ORDER	12780000	-		M1	CHANGED	1	0	SAME W/S	-	-	-	O/ORDER	1	0
9 O/ORDER	21000000	-		M1	RELEASED	1	0	SAME	-	-	-	ORDER	1	0
12510 O/ORDER	11430000	-		M4	RELEASED	1	0	SAME W/S	-	YES	-	ORDER	1	0
25111 O/ORDER	11750000	-		M3	-				-	-	-	O/ORDER	4	2
25137 O/ORDER	11111800	-		M2	CHANGED	3	1	SAME W/S	-	-	-	O/ORDER	3	1
75968 O/ORDER	17640000	-		M2	-				-	-	-	O/ORDER	1	0
75984 CR MEMO	20000020	NEW	BALANCED	M3	NEW	1	0	-	-	YES	YES	-		
77993 ORDER	11495000	NEW	BALANCED	M4	NEW	4	2	-	-	YES	YES	-		
77996 ORDER	28000000	NEW	BALANCED	M4	NEW	8	2	-	YES	YES	YES	O/ORDER	1	0
RBK 2970-1 BACKORDER CONVERTED TO OPEN ORDER														
77999 INVOICE	11800010	NEW	BALANCED	M4	NEW	3	3	-	-	-	YES	O/ORDER	1	0
RBK 2970-1 BACKORDER CONVERTED TO OPEN ORDER														
78186 ORDER	22400000	NEW	NO ENTRY	M2	NEW	3	0	-	-	YES	YES	-		
79211 ORDER	16300000	NEW	FORCED	M3	NEW	3	1	-	-	-	YES	-		
79212 INVOICE	21000000	NEW	BALANCED	M3	NEW	5	1	-	-	-	YES	-		
79250 ORDER	17600030	NEW	BALANCED	M3	NEW	1	0	-	-	-	-	-		
80342 ORDER	11750000	-		M1	-				-	-	-	ORDER	1	0
80345 INVOICE	11800020	NEW	BALANCED	M1	NEW	3	0	-	-	-	YES	ORDER	4	2
80347 ORDER	17600030	NEW	BALANCED	M1	NEW	2	1	-	-	-	YES	-		
80348 ORDER	25000020	NEW	FORCED	M1	NEW	6	2	-	YES	YES	YES	O/ORDER	1	0
RBK 2970-1 BACKORDER CONVERTED TO OPEN ORDER														
80349 O/ORDER	11610000	NEW	BALANCED	M1	NEW	4	1	-	-	-	-	O/ORDER	4	1
80350 ORDER	11111800	NEW	BALANCED	M1	NEW	1	0	-	-	YES	YES	-		
89000 INVOICE	10100000	NEW	NO ENTRY	M1	NEW	1	0	-	-	-	YES	-		
89001 ORDER	00000000	NEW	BALANCED	M1	CANCELED	0	0	-	-	-	-	-		
89020 ORDER	16005000	NEW	BALANCED	M1	NEW	2	0	-	-	YES	YES	-		
89021 ORDER	11380020	NEW	BALANCED	M2	NEW	1	0	-	-	YES	YES	-		
89025 ORDER	11380010	NEW	BALANCED	M2	NEW	1	0	-	-	-	-	ORDER	1	0
89026 INVOICE	11400000	NEW	BALANCED	M1	DELETED	0	0	DIFF W/S	-	-	-	-		
89028 O/ORDER	00000000	NEW	NO ENTRY	M1	CANCELED	0	0	-	-	-	-	-		
89029 CR MEMO	00000000	NEW	NO ENTRY	M1	CANCELED	0	0	-	-	-	-	-		
98541 ORDER	25000020	NEW	NO ENTRY	M1	NEW	1	0	-	-	-	-	ORDER	1	0
RBK 1600-1 ORDER IS ON CREDIT HOLD														
98542 ORDER	11630000	NEW	NO ENTRY	M1	NEW	2	0	-	-	-	-	ORDER	2	0
RBK 2530-1 CL AUTHORIZED RELEASE FROM CREDIT HOLD														

that an operator released by entering a two-character authorization ID and any orders for which the operator overrode the standard price.

The report also gives control totals at the end, as shown in Exhibit 17-3. These totals give the order volume by workstation, which (1) provides a method to measure operator performance and (2) helps ensure that orders were entered only from authorized workstations.

The totals from the Order Reconciliation report balance to a manually prepared **control log,** illustrated in Exhibit 17-4 on page 614. The operator will enter control totals for each order and then develop daily control totals. The information from this log should balance on a daily basis with the sum of the Orders Entered Today and New Open Orders Entered Today amounts, which appear in the Order Reconciliation report totals. This procedure assures that the system processed all orders that were logged as entered. It also ensures that the orders processed were received by the person maintaining the Order Entry Control Log.

It is possible to achieve additional control over unauthorized entry of transactions to the order files by comparing the Open Orders on File at End of Day (deferred orders) and the Orders on File at the End of Day (active orders) to the corresponding Start of Day totals on the Order Reconciliation report of the next day. This procedure assures that (1) the system processed the correct files and (2) there was no change in the number of orders since the run of the previous day.

EVALUATION OF INTERNAL CONTROL IN A COMPUTER ENVIRONMENT

Exhibit 17-5 on page 615 provides a flowchart of the study and evaluation of internal control in EDP systems. This flowchart will guide the discussion.

Preliminary Review

The first step in the evaluation process is to perform a preliminary review of the internal controls. The purpose of a preliminary review is to understand the accounting system, including both its computer and its manual components. In the preliminary review the following should be determined:

> _Information flow through the system._ The auditor must understand where the input data are generated, the type of processing that takes place, and the output that is developed.
>
> _Use of the output._ The auditor should determine how the results generated by the computer affect the rest of the system and, in particular, determine the significance of the output.
>
> _Extent of computer usage._ The auditor should determine how much the computer is used in accounting applications and the computer's significance in the overall system of the company.
>
> _Basic structure of internal controls._ The auditor should gain an overall view of the system's internal controls. He may examine these controls in more detail later, but an overview is sufficient at this point.

EXHIBIT 17-3 Order Reconciliation Totals

ORDER RECONCILIATION
DMAS CORP.

NEW ENTRIES TODAY --	----- NEW ORDERS -----			----- OPEN ORDERS -----		
	ORDERS	ITEMS	SP/CHGS	ORDERS	ITEMS	SP/CHGS
WORKSTATION W1	9	18	3	1	4	1
WORKSTATION W2	3	5	0	0	0	0
WORKSTATION W4	3	15	7	0	0	0
WORKSTATION W3	4	10	2	0	0	0
	---	---	---	---	---	---
	19	48	12	1	4	1

RECONCILIATION	ORDERS	ITEMS	SP/CHGS
OPEN ORDERS ON FILE AT START OF DAY	6	12	3
PLUS ... NEW OPEN ORDERS ENTERED TODAY	1	4	1
LESS ... OPEN ORDERS DELETED IN FULL	0	0	0
PLUS ... LINES ADDED/DELETED IN OPEN ORDERS ON FILE	0	1-	0
LESS ... OPEN ORDERS RELEASED TODAY	2	2	0
PLUS. ... PARTIAL RELEASES RETURNED TO FILE	0	0	0
PLUS ... BACKORDERS KEPT FOR LATER RELEASE	3	3	0
	---	---	---
OPEN ORDERS ON FILE AT END OF DAY	8	16	4

ORDERS ON FILE AT START OF DAY	ORDERS	ITEMS	SP/CHGS
	1	0	0
PLUS ... ORDERS ENTERED TODAY - EXCLUDES OPEN ORDERS	19	48	12
PLUS ... OPEN ORDERS RELEASED TODAY	2	2	0
PLUS ... STANDING ORDERS RELEASED TODAY	0	0	0
LESS ... ORDERS DELETED IN FULL	1	0	0
PLUS ... LINES ADDED/DELETED IN ORDERS ON FILE		4	2
LESS ... LINES HELD BACK IN PARTIAL RELEASES		0	0
LESS ... ORDERS RELEASED TODAY FOR INVOICING	14	43	12
	---	---	---
ORDERS ON FILE AT END OF DAY	7	11	2

```
15 ORDERS AND OPEN ORDERS ON FILE   ...   FILE CAPACITY-  190
68 RECORDS IN THE OPEN ORDER FILE   ...   FILE CAPACITY- 1700
34 RECORDS IN THE ORDER FILE        ...   FILE CAPACITY-  864
```

613

EXHIBIT 17-4 Example of a Control Log

Order Entry/Billing Control Log entries

1 Order number: The number assigned to the order.

2 Number of items: Count of line items entered for the order. This column total should balance to the corresponding total on the Order Reconciliation report.

3 Total quantity all items: A (hash) total of the quantity ordered of all transactions.

4 Number of special charges: Count of the special charges for the order.

5 Total of special charges: A total of the amounts of special charges.

Order Entry/Billing Control Log

Page No. _____
ID _____
W/S _____ Op. _____

Date	Order number **1**	Number of items **2**	Total qty. all items **3**	No. spec. charges **4**	Total of spec. chgs. **5**
1					
2					
3					
4					
5					
6					
7					
8					
9					
10					
11					
12					
13					
14					
15					
16					
17					
18					
19					
20					
21					
22					
23					
24					
25					
26					
27					
28					
29					
30					
31					
32					
33					
34					
35					
36					
37					
38					
39					
40					
Carry-forward Totals					
TOTALS *			*		

*Balance to Order Reconciliation

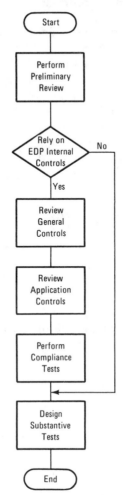

Methods

Four basic methods are employed to determine the information collected during a review.

Inquiry and observation. One of the auditor's most powerful tools is discussion with the employees who actually operate the system and the corporate officers to whom they report. The auditor should also watch the operations of the firm searching for deficiencies and omissions.

Review of documentation. As discussed in Chapter 4, documentation is critically important in a computer environment. At this point, the auditor should look over the documentation for the system.

Trace of transactions. Controls are worthless if they do not work properly. The auditor should trace selected transactions through operations to check the functioning of internal controls.

Internal control questionnaires and checklists. So as not to overlook important areas, the auditor will often use questionnaires and checklists that cover the basic topics relevant to all computer systems.

Decision: Rely on Internal Controls?

After the preliminary review, the auditor must decide whether or not the internal controls can be relied upon. An auditor might not rely on internal controls for several reasons. The accounting control procedures may be faulty. The effort to complete the review of controls might exceed the benefit of relying on the controls. Controls within data processing might be redundant if other controls exist. If the auditor decides not to rely on internal controls, the auditor can proceed directly to the design of the substantive tests.

If the auditor decides to rely on internal controls, the auditor must review them in depth. The auditor must feel that the accounting control procedures are good enough to warrant reducing the amount of substantive testing.

General Versus Application Controls

Chapter 4 presented internal control in a computer environment using the same six elements of internal controls as in the discussion of manual systems in Chapter 2. However, there is another breakdown that is more useful for the evaluation of EDP internal control: (1) **general controls,** such as the separation of duties within data processing, which apply to all application areas, and (2) **application controls,** such as the reasonableness tests built into accounts receivable, which apply to one particular application area.

Review of General Controls

General controls can be evaluated once for all applications. Weaknesses in any of the general controls would usually affect all EDP applications. There are five general controls:

Organization and Operation Controls.   These controls consist of the proper separation of duties between the EDP department and the users, as well as the separation of duties within EDP. If the organization structure is not adequate for good accounting control, the auditor should have serious reservations about the reliability of system results and substantive testing should expand significantly.

Systems Development and Documentation Controls.   These are controls over (1) review, testing, and approval of new systems; (2) changes to production programs; and (3) procedures for the development of documentation. If documentation is inadequate, it will be necessary to expend substantial effort to obtain an accurate description of the accounting applications. Weaknesses in control over new systems or changes to production programs are serious and should cause substantive testing to expand significantly.

Hardware and Operating System Controls.   These controls include periodic preventive maintenance on all hardware and the proper authorization of any changes to the operating system. If these controls are weak, the auditor might reduce the reliance he can put on the system output.

Access Controls. These are the controls that prevent unauthorized access to program documentation, data files, computer programs, and the computer hardware. If these controls are lacking, this decreases the integrity of the system and increases the chance of unauthorized modification of files and programs.

Data and Procedural Controls. These controls include (1) a control group separate from the operator; (2) written procedures manuals in support of the systems; and (3) the capability to reconstruct lost, damaged, or incorrect files. If these controls are weak, the auditor must reduce his reliance on the system's output. However, the audit consequences are less severe than some of the other possibilities mentioned.

For each of these basic general controls, the auditor will first determine how it operates. Next, the auditor reviews the controls to identify any that can be relied on. This involves consideration of possible compliance testing and the weighing of the effect of strengths and weaknesses in internal controls on compliance testing. The auditor will perform this review by (1) examining any appropriate documentation in detail; (2) interviewing internal auditors, members of the EDP department, and user department personnel; and (3) observing the operation of the internal controls.

Review of Application Controls

After completing the review of the general controls, the auditor will review controls that are related to significant accounting applications. The purposes and methods of reviewing application controls are the same as the purposes and methods of reviewing general controls as given.

Input Controls. Input controls ensure that data are correct and that the system will reject any incorrect data. Input controls include

1. Measures to see that the computer processes only properly authorized data.
2. Procedures to verify the data that are input, including all significant codes.
3. Techniques to control data entry, such as record counts, batch controls, and verification.
4. Controls to ensure the correction and resubmission of all errors detected by the application.

A lack of adequate input control may permit items to become lost, duplicated, or entered incorrectly, which could have a serious effect on the financial statements. A possible audit reaction is to expand the testing of transactions details.

Processing Controls. Processing controls ensure that all authorized transactions are processed, that no unauthorized transactions are processed, and that all processing is done correctly. Processing controls include

1. Control totals that can be reconciled with the input control totals.
2. Programs containing limit and reasonableness checks.
3. Cumulative totals and record counts for each printout to verify run-to-run controls.

A weakness in processing controls may have a serious effect on the data records and possibly cause errors in data that would be used in many applications.

Output Controls.   Output controls ensure that the output is accurate and that only authorized personnel receive it. Output controls include

1. Output control totals that reconcile to the input and processing control totals.
2. User scanning of the output and testing of it by comparison with source documents.
3. Output that is promptly delivered to only the authorized user(s).

If the control of output distribution is weak, there is a loss of power to detect errors and irregularities. The audit consequences of this loss depend on whether errors or irregularities have occurred, their variety, and the audit area they affect. A range of audit reactions is possible.

CONCEPT SUMMARY	
Evaluation of Internal Controls	
General Controls: Those that apply to all application areas	1. Organization and operation controls: Proper separation between EDP and user departments and separation of duties within EDP 2. Systems development and documentation controls: Controls over the development of new systems, including related documentation and modification of production programs 3. Hardware and operating system controls: Preventive maintenance and proper authorization for changes to the operating system 4. Access controls: Prevention of unauthorized access to documentation, files, programs, and equipment 5. Data and procedural controls: Separate control group, written procedures, and backup capability
Application Controls: Those that apply to only one application area, such as accounts receivable	1. Input controls: Ensure that data are correct and the system will reject any incorrect data 2. Processing controls: Ensure that all, and only, authorized transactions are processed 3. Output controls: Ensure that all output is accurate and that it is only received by authorized personnel

After completing the review of application controls, the auditor can test for compliance those controls he would like to rely on. The purposes of compliance testing are (1) to determine whether necessary controls are, in fact, in place; (2) to provide reasonable assurance that controls are functioning properly; and (3) to document when, how, and by whom the controls are performed. The methods of compliance testing would include examining records, testing the operation of internal controls, inquiring of client personnel, and observing client operations. The next section of this chapter discusses compliance testing in further depth.

After completing the compliance tests, the auditor can design the substantive tests. Every weakness pointed out by the compliance tests must be compensated for by the substantive tests. A later section will discuss substantive tests in further depth.

COMPLIANCE TESTING
IN A COMPUTER ENVIRONMENT

Test Deck

The fundamental tool for compliance testing in a computer environment is the **test deck,** a collection of transactions generated by the auditor. The auditor will know the correct results of processing the test transactions. The auditor will then process the test desk using the client's programs and compare the results generated by the client's programs to the previously determined correct results.

Exhibit 17-6 provides a schematic of test deck use. This schematic shows the usefulness of the test deck: The auditor can independently verify that the

EXHIBIT 17-6   Schematic of Test Deck Use

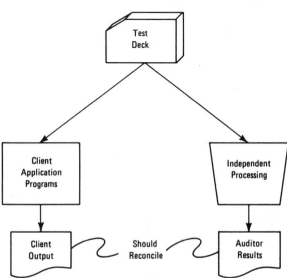

client application programs are functioning as they should. To function properly, the programs should both process correct data correctly as well as identify and reject incorrect data. Therefore, the test transactions should contain both correct and incorrect data for complete testing.

Suppose the auditor wished to perform a compliance test on the file maintenance program that adds, modifies, and deletes employees from the payroll master file. Exhibit 17-7 presents five test deck transactions the auditor might develop. The auditor would want to see the program reject the first four transactions and process the fifth transaction correctly. If the program does not reject all of the first four transactions, the programmed controls are not functioning as they should.

The test deck approach is most suitable in batch processing systems, because the auditor can make a copy of the client's master file for audit use at night or other low-demand time. Any changes to the auditor's copy of the file are of no consequence. Interactive processing systems, however, typically require all of the computer's resources to process the company's transactions. To process test transactions might destroy part of the client's files.

The test deck is most useful when the number of conditions to test is

EXHIBIT 17-7   Examples of Test Deck Transactions

Transaction Description	*Programmed Control*	*Desired Result*
Add an employee with an existing Social Security number.	Compare new Social Security number to those already on file.	Detect duplicate Social Security number; print error message; do not update file with new record.
Add a new employee omitting the required date employed.	Check input data for completeness of required data.	Detect incomplete data; print error message; do not update file with a new record.
Add a new employee with both an hourly rate of pay and a monthly salary.	Check input data for consistency.	Detect inconsistent data; print error message; do not update file with new record.
Increase the hourly rate of pay for an employee from $6 to $36, where the normal range of pay is $3.50 to $13.50 per hour.	Check input data for reasonableness.	Detect unreasonable data; print error message; do not change hourly rate for this employee.
Increase the hourly rate of pay for an employee from $6 to $7.	Print all data that have been changed.	Process the transaction; print the hourly rate both before and after the change; change the hourly rate in that one employee's record.

limited. In complex systems, it becomes almost impossible to describe a com-

621

CHAPTER *17*
EDP
Auditing

prehensive set of test data. For internal purposes, U.S. Steel developed a test deck for its payroll system. Because of the number of plants, the different types of jobs, the union contract, the overtime pay, and the different pay for different times of day, the test deck contained 10,000 transactions.

Integrated Test Facility

Because test transactions can destroy the client's live data, some companies had added dummy entities to their files. The auditor can process transactions against these dummy entities using the client's regular system. This is called an **integrated test facility (ITF)**. It is basically an adaptation of the test deck to an interactive processing environment.

The effect of the dummy entities must be removed for reporting purposes. This removal can be done (1) manually, (2) by reversing the effects of the test transactions, or (3) by special coding in the report program, which eliminates the dummy entities.

It is possible for the auditor to obtain a copy of the client's data files and process test transactions using the interactive processing system at night or at another off time. The difficulty is that the auditor cannot be sure that the system he is processing at an off time is the same one that the client uses for regular processing. If any unauthorized modifications had been made to the system, the auditor could easily be given an unmodified version. The integrated test facility approach assures the auditor that the system the auditor is using is the one the client uses for regular processing.

Program Tracing

In a manual system, the auditor can follow the flow of transactions from the source documents through the various processing steps. In a computer system, the auditor can follow the flow of transactions using program tracing. A program trace is a list of the steps a program follows in its processing of a transaction. The auditor can use this trace to identify exactly what happens to any given transaction.

The capability of generating a program trace may be built into the client's application program because it helps for both audit and debugging purposes. The trace may also be generated by special software, which generates tracings for other programs.

Review of Program Logic

In a manual system, the auditor can visually review the source documents, forms, accounting records, and reports. These will show the various processing steps involved and how the final results were generated. In a computer system, such a visual review of the process is impossible because many of the accounting records and the programs that process them are electronic and hence

CONCEPT SUMMARY

Techniques for Compliance Testing

Technique	Description	Advantages	Disadvantages
Test deck	Test transaction processed by both the client application programs and independently by the auditor	Requires little technical expertise; effective if the number of conditions is limited	Only tests preconceived conditions; almost impossible to design comprehensive test data for complex systems; time consuming; lacks objectivity
Integrated test facility	Dummy entities against which the auditor can process transactions using the client's regular system	Useful for interactive systems; tests system during regular processing; only moderate level of technical expertise required; other advantages parallel test deck	Removing test data from system may destroy client files; other disadvantages parallel test deck
Program tracing	List of program steps followed in the processing of a given transaction	Use of actual data; can be more effective when used in combination with ITF	May require special processing logic not normally used; no guarantee that all logic paths are traversed
Review of program logic	Review program documentation and the source listing of the subject program	Examines processing logic in detail; auditor is intimately aware of processing code	Very high level of technical expertise required; very time consuming; practical only in relatively simple systems

	Description	Advantages	Disadvantages
Program comparison	Compare a copy of a program that is under the auditor's control to the version currently used in processing	Compliance tests the general controls that all and only authorized changes are made to production programs; enhances auditor's understanding of the system	When discrepancies are found, it may be very time consuming to evaluate the results effectively, especially with object programs
Parallel simulation	Auditor develops program to perform same key functions as client application; compare results of client and auditor programs to ensure proper processing	Allow independence of auditor from client personnel; facilitates examination of a larger number of transactions; only moderate level of technical expertise required	No inference about unexamined data or processing; difficult to do in complex systems
Embedded audit modules	Section of program code to perform audit functions; can be used either periodically (e.g., confirmations) or continually (e.g., identification of overrides of controls)	Can detect exception conditions when they occur	Detects only anticipated exceptions
Job accounting data	Review activity record to determine production programs were run at the correct time and run the correct number of times	Can help determine that unauthorized applications were not processed and authorized applications were processed properly	Voluminous activity reports to review; may need special software to generate usable reports

cannot be looked at directly. However, the auditor can review the processing steps performed by the computer system by reviewing the program logic.

The auditor would review the program logic in two steps. The first step would be to collect and review the program documentation to get an overview of the program, its purpose, and its functions. The second step would be to examine the source listing of the program to see exactly how the program works. This process makes the auditor intimately aware of the system and how it functions. However, it requires extensive programming knowledge and would be extremely time consuming for complex systems.

Program Comparison

One of the auditor's primary concerns is to check that all authorized changes to production programs were made and that there were no unauthorized changes. This check can be accomplished using special software that compares one copy of a program to another and identifies any differences.

One approach is to compare an earlier version of a program to a later version. A second approach is to compare a library version of a program to the production version. The auditor should be able to explain any differences as approved, authorized, and tested changes. This comparison can be made for both the source programs written in the programming language and the machine language object programs. However, the interpretation of identified differences in object programs is quite difficult.

Parallel Simulation

In some situations, the processing in the client's application programs is so complex that the auditor cannot manually verify the results, as sketched in Exhibit 17-6. For these circumstances, the auditor can develop a program that performs the same key functions as the client's programs. The auditor can then use his own program to verify independently the results of the client's processing. The results of the auditor's processing should reconcile to the client's results. The auditor's program need not perform all the functions of the client's programs, only the key functions of audit interest.

Embedded Audit Modules

The client application programs can have audit functions built in by embedding audit modules into the programs. One approach is to build in audit modules that are used only periodically. An example would be confirmation capability built into the program that produces monthly billings. Another approach is to build in audit modules that are used continually. An example would be the ability to capture any transaction that tried to violate an established control. The transaction could then be written to a separate audit file for further examination. Embedded audit modules can, therefore, identify exception conditions as they occur. However, they can only identify anticipated exceptions.

Most sophisticated systems develop an activity record of all the programs processed by the computer. The auditor can review this activity record to determine exactly when production programs were run and how many times they were run. This review can help the auditor determine whether the programs were run correctly. For large systems, the activity record may be so vast that it requires special software to generate reports the auditor can interpret.

SUBSTANTIVE TESTING IN A COMPUTER ENVIRONMENT

Substantive tests involve checking account balances to ensure they are properly stated. If accounts receivable are an important asset, then the auditor would conduct substantive tests on accounts receivable to make sure they were properly stated. An important substantive test of accounts receivable is to send confirmations to selected customers, asking them to verify that the company's records accurately reflect what the customer owes.

The data files in computer applications often become extremely large. Sears, Roebuck has millions of customers, and the accounts receivable file will therefore have millions of records. To do all the necessary substantive auditing steps, such as confirmations, manually with a file this size would be extremely tedious and wasteful. The auditor must use the computer to audit the computer system.

Generalized Audit Software

In the case of accounts receivable, the auditor could write an application program which would select and print out the appropriate confirmations. This would avoid the task of selecting the accounts manually and typing the confirmations. However, even this would be time consuming if the auditor had to write a separate program for each audit client. In the early days of computer auditing, this was the only possibility. To do so required not only writing the program but also debugging it, testing it, documenting it, and running it. In actual cases, this process has taken 300 hours. At $50 per hour, this adds an additional $15,000 to the audit fee.

There is a better approach. The auditor can write one program to work for all of his audit clients. This program must work with all types of files, since each client is likely to set up the accounts receivable file differently. Because the program must be generalized in this way, it is harder to write. But the savings in writing the program only once make this approach worthwhile.

Such programs are called **generalized audit software (GAS).** They are useful in more situations than the one client/one application program would be because they are generalized. Exhibit 17-8 gives a schematic of generalized audit software use. This schematic shows that GAS can provide an independent processing of the client's application programs.

EXHIBIT 17-8   Schematic of Generalized Audit Software Use

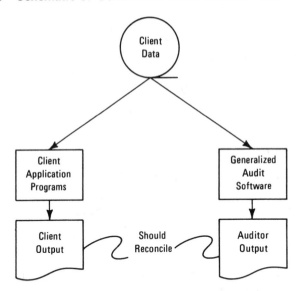

GAS programs can become quite sophisticated. Each of the major CPA firms and several independent software firms have developed such systems at the cost of millions of dollars for each system. The Concept Summary for this section gives the six basic capabilities of GAS and includes examples of their use in both accounts receivable and inventory applications.

Inventory Audit Case Study

The purpose of this case study is to demonstrate the use of generalized audit software in accomplishing an audit objective. This is not a complete application, but it does convey the basic concepts. The audit objective is to verify that the client's inventory as of December 31, 19X2 is stated at the lower of FIFO cost or market. The client took a physical inventory on December 31, 19X2 and created a magnetic tape file from the physical inventory count tickets. Exhibit 17-9 gives a description of this tape file and a flowchart of the audit procedures that will be followed:

1. Extend the 19X2 physical inventory counts at both the 19X1 standard cost and the 19X2 standard cost. Then, calculate the percentage change in standard costs during 19X2. See Exhibit 17-10 on page 628.
2. Identify any missing or duplicate tickets, and print an appropriate report. See Exhibit 17-11 on page 629.
3. Sort the file into part number order, and summarize records by part number.
4. Select items for a price test, including all items valued over $100,000 and a random sample of 10 percent of the items under $100,000.
5. Analyze inventory at 19X2 standard cost, and print a report of 19X2 inventory by part number. See Exhibit 17-12 on page 630.

EXHIBIT 17-9 **Tape File and Audit Procedures**

627

CHAPTER 17
EDP
Auditing

CLIENT DATA FILE

Field Description	Position on Record		Field Type	Number of Decimal Places
	Starting	Length		
Count ticket	1	6	Character	
Count team	7	3	Character	
Part number	10	5	Character	
Description	15	40	Character	
Quantity at 12-31-X2	55	8	Numeric	0
19X1 Standard unit cost	63	7	Numeric	3
19X2 Standard unit cost	70	7	Numeric	3
Filler	77	4	Character	

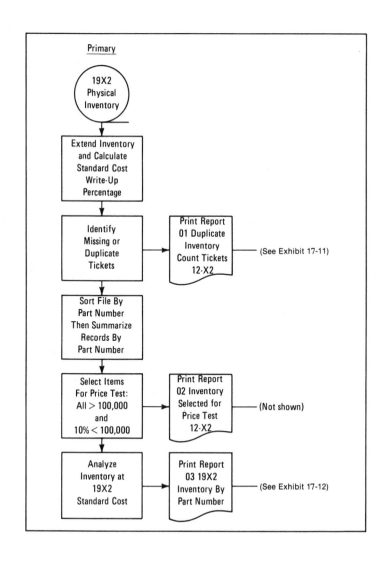

EXHIBIT 17-10 Calculate Percentage Change in Standard Cost

Input Function

FN	SEQUENCE NUMBER	INSTRUCTION	FIELD NAME	DESCRIPTION	TYPE	DEC	FIELD LENGTH	START POSITION	LENGTH	TYPE	DEC	OTHER	I/U FIELD
IP	00230	FIELD	TIKET	COUNT TICKET				1	6	N			SAMP
IP	00240	FIELD	TEAM	CNT TM				7	3	N			SAMP
IP	00250	FIELD	PAXNO	PART NUMBER				10	5	C			SAMP
IP	00260	FIELD	DESCB	DESCRIPTION				15	40	C			SAMP
IP	00270	FIELD	X2QTY	QUANTITY AT 12-31; X2				55	8	NO			SAMP
IP	00280	FIELD	X1CST	19X1 STANDARD COST				63	7	N3			SAMP
IP	00290	FIELD	X2CST	19X2 STANDARD COST				70	7	N3			SAMP
IP	00300	FIELD	X1VAL	INVENTORY AT X1 COST	N3								SAMP
IP	00310	FIELD	X2VAL	INVENTORY AT X2 COST	N3								SAMP
IP	00320	FIELD	WRTUP	AMOUNT OF WRITE-UP	N3								SAMP
IP	00330	FIELD	PERCT	PERCENTAGE WRITE-UP	N1								SAMP
IP	00340	FIELD	MSSG2	MESSAGE 2		C	20						SAMP

Processing Function

FN	SEQUENCE NUMBER	INSTRUCTIONS	FIELD NAME 1	OP CD 2	FIELD NAME 3	FIELD NAME 4	TO 5	CONSTANT AND OTHER	I/U FIELD
PR	04010	MUL	X1CST	BY	X2QTY	X1VAL			SAMP
PR	04020	MUL	X2CST	BY	X2QTY	X2VAL			SAMP
PR	04030	SUB	X1VAL	FRX	X2VAL	WRTUP			SAMP
PR	04040	DIV	WRTUP	BY	X1VAL	WKNO1			SAMP
PR	04050	MUL	WKNO1	BY	CONST	PERCT		100	SAMP
PR	04060	MISDUP	TIKET						SAMP
PR	04070	IF	ERDUP	EQ	CONST		04081	ON	SAMP
PR	04080	PRINT	01						SAMP
PR	04081	FOOT	X2VAL					INVENTORY AT 19— STANDARD COSTS	SAMP
PR	04090	SORT							

EXHIBIT 17-11   Identify Duplicate Count Tickets

Output Function—Report (System Formatted)

FN	SEQUENCE NUMBER	INSTRUCTION	RPT NO.	REPORT NAME	ID FIELD
OP	1,000,0	NAME	0,1	DUPLICATE INVENTORY COUNT TICKETS 12-X2	SAMP

FN	SEQUENCE NUMBER	INSTRUCTION	FIELD NAME	FIELD NAME	FIELD NAME	FIELD NAME	FIELD NAME		ID FIELD
OP	1,010,0	SORT	TIKET						SAMP

FN	SEQUENCE NUMBER	INSTRUCTION	FIELD NAME	S P A C E	FIELD NAME	S P A C E	FIELD NAME	S P A C E	FIELD NAME	S P A C E	FIELD NAME	S P DET AL		ID FIELD
OP	1,020,0	SUBTOT										2		SAMP

FN	SEQUENCE NUMBER	INSTRUCTION	FIELD NAME	F O U T	FIELD NAME	F O U T	FIELD NAME	F O U T	FIELD NAME	F O U T	FIELD NAME	F O U T	FIELD NAME	F O U T	FIELD NAME	F O U T	FIELD NAME	F O U T	FIELD NAME	F O U T	FIELD NAME	F		ID FIELD
OP	1,030,0	PRDATA	TIKET		TEAM		PARNO		DESCB		X2QTY		X2VAL											SAMP

Resulting Report (System Formatted)

```
SAMPLE COMPANY              CPA FIRM            12-31-X2      01-15-X3   AICPA COMPUTER AUDITOR        PAGE   1
COMPUTER COMMON AUDIT SOFTWARE - VENDOR        INVENTORY                REPORT 01      RUN  1         TIME 12:46

                                 DUPLICATE INVENTORY COUNT TICKETS 12-X2

   COUNT   CNT   PART                              QUANTITY AT          INVENTORY
   TICKET  TM   NUMBER  DESCRIPTION                 12-31-X2            AT X2 COST
 ...........................................................................................

       3   204   316   STARWHEELS                      70              70,300.000

       3   204   326   HOPPER                          75             187,500.000

      10   201   315   ACME PUNCH DIE                  75              48,750.000

      10   205   315   AJAX PUNCH DIE                  25              16,250.000

      17   202   313   WIRE                            40              15,000.000

      17   202   327   PUNCH KEYS                      80             280,000.000

      17   202   327   KEYS                            85             297,500.000

      23   203   304   DIRECT IMPULSE HUB             300              18,150.000

      23   205   328   FEED HOPPERS                    10              20,000.000

   COUNT    9                                                         953,150.000
```

EXHIBIT 17-12 Inventory by Part Number

Output Function—Report (Auditor Formatted)

OP	SEQUENCE NUMBER	INSTRUCTION	BY NO.	REPORT NAME			
OP	3,0,0,0,0	NAME		0,3,I,9,X,2, INVENTORY BY PART NUMBER			SAMP

OP	SEQUENCE NUMBER	INSTRUCTION	FIELD NAME	FIELD NAME	FIELD NAME	FIELD NAME	FIELD NAME		FIELD
OP	3,0,1,0,0	SORT	PARNO						SAMP

OP	SEQUENCE NUMBER	INSTRUCTION	FIELD NAME	FIELD NAME	FIELD NAME	FIELD NAME	FIELD NAME		
OP	3,0,1,1,0	SUBTOT					2		SAMP

FN	SEQUENCE NUMBER	INSTRUCTION	AUDIT FIELD	LINE NO.	PART	LENGTH		FINAL MAT	HEADING LINE 1	HEADING LINE 2	FIELD
OP	3,0,2,0,0	COLUMN	PARNO			5			PART	NUMBER	SAMP
OP	3,0,3,0,0	COLUMN	DESCB			40				DESCRIPTION	SAMP
OP	3,0,4,0,0	COLUMN	X1CST			8	N3QE		STANDARD	COST -- X1	SAMP
OP	3,0,5,0,0	COLUMN	X2CST			8	N3QE		STANDARD	COST -- X2	SAMP
OP	3,0,6,0,0	COLUMN	X2QTY			8	NOQE		19X2	QUANTITY	SAMP
OP	3,0,7,0,0	COLUMN	X1IVAL			12	2QE		INVENTORY AT	X1 STD COST	SAMP
OP	3,0,8,0,0	COLUMN	X2IVAL			12	2QE		INVENTORY AT	X2 STD COST	SAMP
OP	3,0,9,0,0	COLUMN	WRTUP			10	2QE		WRITE-UP	IN 19X2	SAMP
OP	3,1,0,0,0	COLUMN	PERCT			4	NOQE		PER	CENT	SAMP

Resulting Report (Auditor Formatted)

```
SAMPLE COMPANY                    CPA FIRM              12-31-X2    01-15-X3  AICPA COMPUTER AUDITOR        PAGE    1
COMPUTER COMMON AUDIT SOFTWARE - VENDOR                INVENTORY             REPORT 02      RUN   1        TIME 12:46

                                       19X2 INVENTORY BY PART NUMBER

   PART                             STANDARD    STANDARD      19X2     INVENTORY AT    INVENTORY AT    WRITE-UP    PER
 NUMBER  DESCRIPTION                COST--X1    COST--X2    QUANTITY   X1 STD COST     X2 STD COST     IN 19X2     CENT
 ************************************************************************************************************************

   301    ACCOUNTING MACHINES          .025        .035         0         0.00            0.00            0.00      0.0

   302    BOND FEED WHEELS            1.125       2.250      1000      1150.00         2250.00         1125.00    100.0

   303    CARD HOPPER                30.375      60.750       200      6075.00        12150.00         6075.00    100.0

   304    DIRECT IMPULSE HUB         40.500      60.500       300     12150.00        18150.00         6000.00     49.4

   305    FORM LIGHTS                50.525     101.000       400     20210.00        40400.00        20190.00     99.9

   306    GANGPUNCH SWITCH           60.594     112.675       250     15140.00        28168.75        13020.25     36.0

   307    HAND FEED WHEELS           70.596      90.250        10       705.96          902.50          196.54     27.8

   308    INTERPRETERS               81.000     100.000        15      1215.00         1500.00          285.00     23.5

   309    JACK PLUG                  92.000      98.000        20      1840.00         1960.00          120.00      6.5
```

CONCEPT SUMMARY

Capabilities of Generalized Audit Software

Capability	Examples	
	Accounts Receivable	Inventory
Select sample items	Customer balances for confirmation	Inventory items for observation
Examine records meeting specified criteria	Customer balances over credit limit	Negative or unreasonably large quantities
Test and make calculations	Recalculate interest charges	Recalculate inventory extensions
Compare data on separate files	Compared change in balance with details on transaction files	Compare current and prior period files to help identify obsolete items
Resequence and analyze data	Prepare accounts receivable aged trial balance	Resequence items by location to help observation
Compare data from audit procedures to company records	Compare customer responses to balances on file	Compare test counts with perpetual records

AUDIT PROBLEMS OF ADVANCED SYSTEMS

Data Base Management Systems

Chapters 5 and 6 introduced the basic concepts and uses of data base management systems (DBMS). DBMS are one of the most important developments in the history of data processing and will only increase in importance in the future. However, the DBMS present a difficult problem to the auditor. Generalized audit software cannot access the data maintained by the DBMS. GAS can deal only with data files maintained by conventional file systems. The data maintained by DBMS are stored in a very complex way, and each DBMS stores its data in a different way.

Therefore, the auditor cannot use GAS in a DBMS environment in the same way as in a traditional file environment. There are then two possibilities.

Transfer a copy of the data from the data base to tape and then use GAS. This is the most commonly used approach. However, it has three difficulties:

1. Special programs must reformat the data before GAS can use it.
2. The data are then stored in the conventional way and all interrelationships are lost.

3. The auditor has to rely on the client's system, which can be compromised, to transfer the data to the tape.

Use the inquiry capability of the DBMS to perform the audit functions. The selection, calculation, and analysis capabilities of GAS are often available as part of the DBMS to give the user maximum use of the data base. The auditor can then use these capabilities, but there are two major difficulties:

1. The auditor must rely on the client's personnel and system to access the data base, thus reducing independence.
2. Since the auditor often has to use the system during off-hours to avoid disruption, the auditor cannot be sure that the data and programs he tests are those used for daily processing.

There is now no perfect solution to the problem of auditing in a DBMS environment. Eventually, perhaps, DBMS vendors will build in audit "windows" so that the auditor's independent programs will be able to access the data base directly. Until then the auditor should be very conscious of the problem of independence with DBMS.

Distributed Processing

Distributed processing poses some unique and difficult control problems for the auditor. For example, if data are stored redundantly in the distributed system, a provision is needed for ensuring that a change of data in one location results in an identical change in the same data at all locations where they are stored. Also, distributed systems increase accessibility to the organization's data. While the ability to share data across the network is a desirable feature, data must also be protected from unauthorized user access. Moreover, with distributed processing networks there is the possibility that a failure in one component may shut down the entire system.

The auditor needs to further ensure that the software provides appropriate message accountability to ensure that no inputs or outputs are lost and that recovery from a system failure can be accomplished. This means that messages must be logged as they are received, their content checked for errors, and action initiated for correction of errors discovered. Software should also be tested to determine if it logs outgoing messages at the time of transmission.

Concurrent Auditing Techniques. Since distributed systems involve significant integration, the system needs continuous monitoring for immediate identification and correction of errors. With distributed systems, the auditor cannot directly observe security measures, management controls, and so on. In addition, it is frequently difficult for the auditor to complete the necessary data processing tests since files may need to be made available at several separate systems or the auditor's use of the system may unacceptably degrade system response time. Therefore, the auditor will often utilize concurrent auditing techniques which embed audit routines and records into application systems.

Traditional audit methods involve processing typical system transactions and observing their movement through the various logic branches of the system. In distributed processing systems, the number of logic paths makes this walk-through very complex and difficult. Concurrent auditing methods can help by capturing images of transactions as they move through the logic paths of the system and transferring that information to a file, which is available for audit inspection at a later time. The auditor can then examine the evidence at a later stage when time is available on the system for audit use.

The principal methods of concurrent auditing are integrated test facility, snapshot/extended record, and system control audit review file (SCARF). The ITF facilitates the processing of test data and real data during regular processing runs. Test transactions, known only to those who monitor the ITF, are created and allowed to enter the system along with regular, live transactions. As discussed earlier, the ITF allows the simultaneous processing of test data and live data during actual system operation. At a minimum, the ITF should include tests of network traffic statistics, processing of input/output requests from applications programs, logging of transactions, and error diagnosis.

Given the integration of distributed systems, tracing logic paths through the system is imperative. The snapshot technique embeds software routines at selected points in the application system to capture images of a transaction as it progresses through its processing. The SCARF techniques locate software modules within the operating system to gather information about events of audit interest, such as unauthorized attempts to access files, the frequency with which various types of errors occur, and the quality of system processing.

CONCEPT SUMMARY		
Techniques for Verifying Results of Processing		
Technique	*Advantages*	*Disadvantages*
Custom-designed or special-purpose computer programs	Aids in accessing data stored in machine-readable form; forces familiarity with the system	High cost; long lead times for program development; low degree of flexibility
Generalized audit software	Lower cost than special-purpose programs; uses business-oriented language; flexible	Designed for use with sequential file structures; typically written for ease of implementation rather than efficiency
Data base management systems	Can access more complex data structures; auditor not responsible for access of data	Auditor relies on client's system to generate data for audit; increased level of technical expertise needed

Certain tests can be accomplished by attempting to process erroneous data or to gain unauthorized access. For example, one test might check lockout procedures by attempting simultaneous updating of a master record. Similarly, it is possible to test access controls by checking a sample of passwords whose access limitations are known. Other areas, however, such as evaluating adequacy of crash recovery or line control procedures are in need of further study and development.

REFERENCES

Computer-Assisted Audit Techniques (New York: American Institute of Certified Public Accountants, 1979).

The Auditor's Study and Evaluation of Internal Control in EDP Systems (New York: American Institute of Certified Public Accountants, 1977.)

J. CASH, A. BAILEY, and A. WHINSTON, "A Survey of Techniques for Auditing EDP-Based Accounting Information Systems," *The Accounting Review* (October 1977), p. 813.

J. HANSEN, "Internal Control Considerations in Distributed Systems," *Communications of the ACM*, 1983.

CHAPTER SUMMARY

When auditing the simplest computer-based accounting systems, it is sometimes possible to audit around the computer by examining the input and the output documents and not examining the processing of the computer directly. In general, however, the computer is so important to the system that it is necessary to audit through the computer and examine the computer system and data directly. The examination will consist of both compliance tests of the adequacy of internal controls and substantive tests of the final account balances.

After a preliminary review of the system, the auditor must acquire evidence concerning the effectiveness of internal control. This evidence is usually acquired by observation, a review of the documents, traces of transactions, and internal control questionnaires. Using this evidence, the auditor must decide whether or not to rely on the internal controls to detect errors. If the internal controls can be relied upon, there is then a detailed review of both general controls and application controls. General controls apply to all systems, where the application controls only apply to one particular application, such as accounts receivable. Application controls are then grouped into input controls, processing controls, and output controls.

Compliance testing includes the use of a test deck, an integrated test facility, program tracing, a review of program logic, program comparison, parallel simulation, embedded audit modules, and job accounting data. Substantive testing will examine the account balances directly, usually with independent software under the control of the auditor called generalized audit software.

There is a trade-off between compliance and substantive testing. The greater the reliance that can be placed on the internal control of the system to detect errors, the less the need to analyze the balances directly.

Advanced computer-based systems provide additional difficulties. Particular difficulties are caused by data base management systems, on-line transaction processing, and distributed processing. These usually call for concurrent audit techniques that capture audit information on-line as the transactions are processed.

The Future

As a final note, we would like to make some summary comments and discuss the future impact of the computer on accounting and information systems.

1. Through the 1990s, the number of large- and medium-scale computer systems will continue to grow at a rate of approximately 5–10 percent per year. However, small systems should grow at a rate of over 25 percent per year.
2. The computer will affect all businesses strongly and therefore, all accountants must be familiar with the computer. Accountants for small businesses must know more about the computer than accountants for large businesses, since there will not be a separate data processing staff.
3. The development of good data base management systems, improved programming languages, and better software packages will make the use of the computer easier.
4. Improvements in data communications will allow the use of computers at widely dispersed sites, which will provide increased support for the operations of the business, in addition to accounting for these operations.
5. The impact of the computer on accounting and information systems has hardly begun. The uses of the computer now will be an insignificant percentage of the uses by the end of the 1990s.
6. When extensive data on the computer becomes available for analysis, the mathematical approach of management science or operations research will be much more applicable. The accountant of the late 1990s will then be much more quantitative and mathematical than most accountants are today.

The computer has the potential to free us from drudgery, expand our horizons, free our creative spirit, and expand our productive capacity. We must pursue this opportunity.

KEY TERMS ━━━━━━━━━━━━━━━━━━━━━━━━━━━━━

Application controls (p. 616)
Auditing around the computer (p. 607)
Auditing through the computer (p. 607)
Compliance testing (p. 607)
Control log (p. 612)

General controls (p. 616)
Generalized audit software (GAS) (p. 625)
Integrated test facility (ITF) (p. 621)
Substantive testing (p. 607)
Test deck (p. 619)

QUESTIONS

17-1. Contrast auditing "around the computer" with auditing "through the computer."

17-2. Distinguish between compliance testing and substantive testing.

17-3. How would you use the reports and log of Exhibits 17-1 through 17-4 to determine if transactions had been entered into the computer system after hours?

17-4. Give the basic steps involved in evaluating the internal control in a computer environment.

17-5. Identify the five basic general controls and give an example of each.

17-6. List the three types of application controls and give an example of each for an accounts receivable system.

17-7. What is a test deck? How is it useful in compliance testing? What are its limitations?

17-8. Describe each of the eight techniques for compliance testing besides the test deck, and give their advantages and disadvantages.

17-9. List the six capabilities of generalized audit software, and briefly explain how each might be useful in an audit situation.

17-10. Briefly narrate the objective of the inventory audit case study given in the chapter and the procedures followed to accomplish this objective.

17-11. Discuss the data base approach. Why is generalized audit software not directly useful with data base management systems?

17-12. Identify three special audit problems connected with distributed systems.

PROBLEMS

17-13. Generally, there are two approaches to the auditing of computer-based systems: auditing "through" the system and auditing "around" the system. State five specific techniques for each of these two basic approaches.

17-14. Distinguish between general controls and application controls. Give five basic types of general controls, the basic types of application controls, and five application controls useful in accounts receivable.

17-15. The book began with a discussion of manual accounting systems and ended with a discussion of computer-based information systems. The future of data processing lies in computer-based systems.

    1. What role should the accountant play as these new systems evolve?

    2. What skills will future accountants need to fulfill this role?

    3. What training will most likely foster the development of these skills?

17-16. An auditor is conducting an examination of the financial statements of a wholesale cosmetics distributor with an inventory consisting of thousands of individual items. The distributor keeps its inventory in its own distribution center and in two public warehouses. An inventory computer file is maintained on a computer disk, and at the end of each business day, the file is updated. Each record of the inventory file contains the following data:

a. Item number
b. Location of item
c. Description of item
d. Quantity on hand
e. Cost per item
f. Date of last purchase
g. Date of last sale
h. Quantity sold during year

The auditor is planning to observe the distributor's physical count of inventories as of a given date. The auditor will have available a computer tape of the data on the inventory file on the date of the physical count and generalized audit software.

The auditor is planning to perform basic inventory auditing procedures. Identify the basic inventory auditing procedures, and describe how the use of the generalized audit software and the tape of the inventory file data might be helpful to the auditor in performing such auditing procedures.

17-17. (*AICPA, adapted*) Johnson, CPA, was engaged to examine the financial statements of Horizon Incorporated, which has its own computer installation. During the preliminary review, Johnson found that Horizon lacked proper segregation of the programming and operating functions. As a result, Johnson intensified the study and evaluation of the system of internal control surrounding the computer and concluded that the existing compensating general controls provided reasonable assurance that the objectives of the system of internal control were being met.

1. In a properly functioning EDP environment, how is the separation of the programming and operating functions achieved?
2. What are the compensating general controls that Johnson most likely found? Do not discuss hardware and application controls.

17-18. When auditing an electronic data processing (EDP) accounting system, the independent auditor should have a general familiarity with the effects of the use of EDP on various characteristics of accounting control and on the auditor's study and evaluation of such control. The independent auditor must be aware of those control procedures that are commonly referred to as "general" controls and those that are commonly referred to as "application" controls. General controls relate to all EDP activities and application controls related to specific accounting tasks.

1. What are the general controls that should exist in EDP-based accounting systems?
2. What are the purposes of each of the following categories of application controls?
   a. Input controls
   b. Processing controls
   c. Output controls

17-19. In the past, the records to be evaluated in an audit have been printed reports, listings, documents, and written papers, all of which are visible output. However, in fully computerized systems which employ daily updating of transaction files, output and files are frequently in machine-readable forms such as tapes or disks. Thus, they often present the auditor with an opportunity to use the computer in performing an audit. Discuss how the computer can be used to aid the auditor in examining accounts receivable in such a fully computerized system.

17-20. After determining that computer controls are valid, Hastings is reviewing the sales system of Rosco Corporation in order to determine how a computerized audit program may be used to assist in performing tests of Rosco's sale records. Rosco sells crude oil from one central location. All orders are received by mail and indicate the preassigned customer identification number, desired quantity, proposed delivery date, method of payment, and shipping terms. Since price fluctuates daily, orders do not indicate a price. Price sheets are printed daily and details are stored in a permanent disk file. The details of orders are also maintained in a permanent disk file. Each morning the shipping clerk receives a computer printout which indicates details of customers' orders to be shipped that day. After the orders have been shipped, the shipping details are input to the computer, which simultaneously updates the sales journal, perpetual inventory records, accounts receivable, and sale accounts. The details of all transactions, as well as daily updates, are maintained on disks which are available for use by Hastings in the performance of the audit.

1. How may a computerized audit program be used by Hastings to perform substantive tests of Rosco's sales records in their machine-readable form?

2. After having performed these tests with the assistance of the computer, what other auditing procedures should Hastings perform in order to complete the examination of Rosco's sales records?

17-21. (*AICPA, adapted*) Linder Company is completing the implementation of its new computerized inventory control and purchase order system. Linder's controller wants the controls incorporated into the programs of the new system to be reviewed and evaluated. This is to ensure that all necessary computer controls are included and functioning properly. He respects and has confidence in the system department's work and evaluation procedures, but he would like a separate appraisal of the control procedures by the internal audit department. It is hoped that such a review would reveal any weaknesses or omissions in control procedures and lead to their immediate correction before the system becomes operational. The internal audit department carefully reviews the input, processing, and output controls when evaluating a new system. When assessing the processing controls incorporated into the programs of new systems applications, the internal auditors regularly employ the technique commonly referred to as "auditing through the computer."

1. Identify the types of controls that should be incorporated in the programs of the new system.

2. Explain how the existence of the computer controls and their proper functioning are verified by the "auditing through the computer" technique.

17-22. (*AICPA, adapted*) A CPA's client, Boos & Baumkirchner, Inc., is a medium-sized manufacturer of products for the leisure time activities market (camping equipment, scuba gear, bows and arrows, etc.). During the past year, a computer system was installed, and inventory records of finished goods and parts were converted to computer processing. The inventory master file is maintained on a disk. Each record of the file contains the following information:

a. Item or part number
b. Description
c. Size
d. Unit of measure code
e. Quantity on hand
f. Cost per unit
g. Total value of inventory on hand at cost
h. Date of last sale or usage
i. Quantity used or sold this year
j. Economic order quantity
k. Code number of major vendor
l. Code number of secondary vendor

In preparation for year-end inventory the client had two identical sets of preprinted inventory count cards. One set is for the client's inventory counts, and the other is for the CPA's use to make audit test counts. The following information has been printed onto the cards:

a. Item or part number
b. Description
c. Size
d. Unit of measure code

In taking the year-end inventory, the client's personnel will write the actual count quantity on the face of each card. When all counts are complete, the counted quantity will be input. The data will be processed against the disk file, and quantity-on-hand figures will be adjusted to reflect the actual count. A computer list will be prepared to show any missing inventory count cards and will identify quantity adjustments of more than $100 in value. These items will be investigated by client personnel and all required adjustments will be made. When adjustments have been completed, the final year-end balances will be computed and posted to the general ledger. The CPA has available a general-purpose computer audit software package that will run on the client computer.

1. In general and without regard to the facts given, discuss the nature of general-purpose computer audit software packages and list the various types and uses of such packages.
2. List and describe at least five ways a general-purpose computer audit software package can be used to assist in all aspects of the audit of the inventory of Boos & Baumkirchner, Inc. (For example, the package can be used to read the disk inventory master file and list items and parts with a high unit cost or total value. Such items can be included in the test counts to increase the dollar coverage of the audit verification.)

17-23. (*CMA, adapted*) Ristan Enterprises manufactures and sells colored plastic bottles. Ristan's financial and manufacturing control systems are completely automated. Christine Field, director of internal audit, is responsible for co-ordinating all the operational and financial audits conducted by Ristan's internal audit department. She has been reading and has observed how external auditors use computers in their audits. She believes that Ristan should acquire computer audit software to assist in the financial audits that her department conducts. For instance, a generalized computer audit program would assist in basic audit work such as data retrieval of computer files for review. It would also extract samples, conduct other tests, and generate balances, all of which would be printed out so that conventional audit investigation techniques could be used. She also could use an integrated test facility which uses, monitors, and controls dummy test data. These data would be processed with the regular data. The ITF and the test data would check the existence and adequacy of program data entry controls and processing controls. She has also read of computer-assisted audit software. While this software primarily is used to generate lead schedules, it is also useful in preparing analytical reviews, adjusting entries, and financial statements. However, for her department's basic function, she cannot identify applications that are not performed by the other two types of software. Field intends to prepare a proposal recommending that Ristan acquire generalized computer audit software and an ITF.

1. Without regard to any specific computer audit software, identify the advantages and disadvantages to the internal auditor of using computer audit software to assist with audits.

2. Describe the steps to be followed by the internal auditor to use

   a. generalized computer audit software.

   b. an integrated test facility, incorporating the use of dummy test data.

3. Would a computer-assisted audit software package provide any benefits to an internal audit department? Explain your answer.

17-24. *(IIA, adapted)* A company processes its payroll through a central EDP installation which features a large mainframe computer. Payroll data are processed in weekly batches which are input to the computer via magnetic tape. The auditor is considering performing compliance tests on internal controls over payroll by using the computer.

1. Identify three distinct approaches to auditing through the computer. Discuss the relative advantages of each.

2. Identify three situations which would lead an auditor to conclude that auditing through the computer is not appropriate.

DECISION CASE

One primary reason for the use of ITF is that the whole system can be tested, the manual procedures as well as EDP. The auditor can monitor test data from the point of its authorization and input into the system to its final disposition in output. The resulting transaction and file interactions caused by the test data can be reviewed, as can the manual procedures applied. This problem illustrates the use of ITF for compliance testing with an on-line savings deposit application. The objectives of this audit application are to

a. Determine whether missing, duplicated, or inaccurate data would be detected by the system by compliance testing the functioning of various controls within the system.

b. Determine whether data initiated internally by the system are accurate by comparing generated data to results of manual computations.

c. Determine whether errors are displayed on the terminal for teller review and correction.

d. Determine whether administrative policy and manual procedural controls are being carried out by employees.

e. Determine whether control totals on teller-terminal transaction amounts are generated for teller balancing and supervisory review.

f. Determine whether daily report totals produced off-line agree with teller cash reports and terminal transaction totals.

The data-items on the on-line savings master file are defined as follows:

Number	Description of Contents
1	Account Number
2	Customer Name
3	Customer Address
4	Social Security Number
5	Account Balance
6	Share Loan Balance
7	Uncollected Funds Hold
8	Miscellaneous Hold Code
9	Passbook Balance
10	Unposted Item Count
11	No/Book Withdrawal
12	Date Last Monetary Activity
13	Date Last Nonmonetary Activity

Required:

Develop three test transactions that would be appropriate in such an ITF application. For each transaction provide

1. A transaction description
2. The manual control or programmed control being tested
3. The desired result of the transaction

A Financial Statements

Overview

Review of the concepts and important relationships underlying external-reporting financial statements.

Learning Objectives

Thorough study of this appendix will enable you to:

1. Differentiate assets from resources.
2. Explain the basic accounting equation.
3. Arrange a business's assets, liabilities, and owners' equity on the balance sheet logically.
4. Relate revenue and expense to net income and owners' equity.
5. Distinguish between accrual-basis accounting and cash-basis accounting.
6. Connect the income statement and statement of retained earnings to the balance sheet.

Outline

Accounting System Measurements

Balance Sheet

Income Statement and Statement of Retained Earnings

The Origin of Accounting Jargon

Did you ever wonder where business and financial terms come from? Take a look at these etymological roots of some popular accounting words.

Account derives from the Latin *computare* (to count), which led to the French *a conter*.

Budget derives from the French *bougette*, meaning "a bag or wallet" (containing all income and expense items).

Capital stems from the Latin *caput* (head) and means "head of wealth."

Corporation stems from the Latin *corporare* (to shape into a body).

Credit comes from *creditus* (trusted).

Debit comes from the Latin *debitum* (something owed). Thus a debtor is someone who owes.

Depreciation comes from the Latin *de pretium* (to deprice), while *amortization* comes from the Latin *ad mors* (to put to death). Thus, in one case, you fully devalue the item, but you still have it. In the other, you put it gradually to death, and you end up with nothing.

Discount stems from the Latin *dis* (from) plus *computare* (to count).

Earning derives from the Anglo-Saxon *earnung* (to deserve).

Expense comes from the Latin *ex* (out) plus *pendere* (to weigh).

Invoice comes from the French *envoyer* (to send).

Journal comes from the Latin *diurnalis* (an account of daily transactions), which led to the Italian *giorno* (day) and from there to *giornale* (daily record book).

Profit comes from the Latin *profectus*, meaning advance or progress, while *loss* is from the Anglo-Saxon *los* (destruction), as in an "Advance and Destruction" statement.

Revenue stems from the Latin *revenire* (to come back).

Tax stems from the Latin *taxare*, meaning to touch sharply (It does!).

SOURCE: National Association of Accountants, *The Monthly Closing*, Vol. 19 No. 4, September 1990.

ACCOUNTING SYSTEM MEASUREMENTS

Every business, large or small, does essentially two major things. First, it acquires financial and productive resources from some source. Second, it uses these resources to create additional resources. The primary goal of business activity is to make total resources grow.

The Fundamental Accounting Equation

Accounting systems use the term **assets** to denote the resources that a business acquires from a source and uses to create additional resources. Every asset has a source, that is, it comes originally from some individual or organization. We use the term **equities** to indicate the sources of assets. Since every financial and productive resource in a business has either been acquired or created, the following is true for every business at all times in its life:

$$ASSETS = EQUITIES$$

This simple equation is the basis for all that is done in accounting, and is called the basic **accounting equation.**

Individuals or organizations that supply a business with assets would like those assets or others of equal or greater value returned to them someday. Similarly, if a business has created new assets by its successful activities, the owners of that business would like ultimately to enjoy the benefits of those assets. This means that equities not only indicate sources of assets, but also measure claims against the assets of the business. In effect, then, the basic accounting equation shows that all of the assets of a business have claims against them. These claims may have come about because assets were supplied to the business, or because the business has created its own assets and the owners may participate in this business success by receiving these assets.

Everything that accounting systems do is traceable directly to the basic accounting equation. The meaning of this equation is made clear by noting that the following three expressions are identical and may be used interchangeably:

$$ASSETS = EQUITIES$$
$$ASSETS = SOURCES\ OF\ ASSETS$$
$$ASSETS = CLAIMS\ AGAINST\ ASSETS$$

Resources Versus Assets

Assets are financial and productive resources; however, not all resources are assets. To be an asset and recorded in an accounting system for a particular business, a resource must meet three criteria:

1. The resource must possess future value for that business.
2. The resource must be under the effective control of that business.
3. The resource must have a dollar value resulting from an identifiable event(s) in the life of that business.

If any one of these criteria is not met, the resource is not an asset in accounting terms, regardless of its physical existence or presence. Let us examine each of these characteristics a little more closely.

Future Value. **Future value** simply means that there must be some benefit in the future to the business from holding the resource today. Resources may exhibit future value either by exchange value or by use value.

Exchange value means that the resource can be readily exchanged for other resources which a business may desire. The epitome of an exchange value asset is cash, which can be exchanged for just about anything. There are, however, other exchange value assets which may not be so obvious. For example, amounts of money owed to a business, often called accounts receivable, represent a resource with exchange value. The receivable is collected (exchanged) in cash, which is then exchangeable for any other resource. Inventory, which is the term used to indicate merchandise held by a business for resale to its customers, is also an exchange value resource because the inventory is sold (exchanged) either for cash or for an account receivable. Cash, accounts receivable, and inventory represent the primary exchange value assets. However, there may be many other exchange value assets in the life of an actual business.

Use value means that the resource is expected to contribute to a business by its physical use or by the use of the services that the resource represents. Resources that businesses actually use up, either physically or in terms of service capacities (usually a little at a time), are use-value assets. Buildings, equipment, machines, and vehicles are the most common use-value assets found. However, there may be other use-value assets in the life of a business.

Effective Control. Once we determine that a resource exhibits future value, we must then establish that the resource is under the control of the business. Effective control and legal ownership are not the same thing. Although it is possible for any business to possess ownership without control or vice versa, businesses will usually both own and control the resource or have effective control without legal ownership. This concept of effective control is an important factor in the determination of accounting assets. Air, sunshine, oceans, highways, and so on are resources of great value, but are under the control of no individual business; therefore, these resources could never be accounting assets to any business. However, a business may buy a truck or car on credit and have control over the vehicle even though legal ownership rests with the financing bank or credit company. Such a vehicle would meet the control criterion for inclusion as an asset of the business.

Dollar Value. When we are satisfied that the resource has future value and is controlled by the business, the final step in determining whether the resource is an asset is to determine whether it can be assigned an objective dollar value. The standard unit of measure in accounting systems is the dollar; hence, resources must be susceptible to dollar valuation if they are to be accounting assets. Since the accounting system prefers objectively determinable facts to subjective opinion, this dollar valuation must result from an identifiable event or series of events (usually an exchange between independent parties) in the life of the business. A firm's reputation for quality service or products, or the benefit of being in a favorable location, do not qualify as accounting assets. Though valuable, these resources are very difficult to measure in dollars. They do not usually result from an identifiable event or events, but rather are the outcome of many not specifically identifiable activities occurring over long periods of time.

To determine whether or not a resource is an accounting asset, simply apply the criteria given. If any one criterion is not met, a resource may exist, but it is not one with which the accounting system is concerned.

Liabilities

Recall that equities are sources of assets, and, at the same time, are claims against the assets of a business. A business can acquire assets from either (1) its owners or (2) nonowners, which includes all other individuals or businesses. When individuals or organizations other than owners supply a business with assets, the resulting claim against the assets usually takes the form of debt. That is, by accepting assets from outsiders (banks, suppliers, and the like), the business incurs a legal obligation to return to these outsiders an agreed-upon amount of assets at some time in the future. These sources of assets from nonowners and simultaneous claims on the assets of a business by nonowners are called **liabilities.** Liabilities represent the debts and other legal obligations of a business resulting from its acquisition of assets from individuals or organizations other than the owners. Keep in mind the following three characteristics of liabilities:

1. They represent the legal obligations of a business; that is, if these obligations are not satisfied, the business risks its very existence.
2. The amount of the obligation is generally known with certainty.
3. The future point in time at which the obligation must be satisfied is generally known with certainty.

Owners' Equity

Business assets may be secured from owners instead of from outsiders or in addition to outsiders. When the owners supply a business with assets, the resulting claim against these assets is called **owners' equity** (sometimes called **stockholders' equity** if the business is a corporation). As with liabilities, the business incurs an obligation by accepting assets from owners; however, owners' equity represents a different type of claim from that represented by liabilities. Note the following characteristics of owners' equity relative to those of liabilities:

1. Owners' claims against the business are not legally enforceable; that is, if the claims are not satisfied, the owners usually have no recourse but to attempt to change the board of directors and/or management or to sell their ownership interest.
2. The owners' claim is said to be residual because the owners claim all assets not specifically claimed by outsiders. They may claim whatever remains after other (liability) claims have been satisfied.
3. There is no specific time in the future when the owners' claim must be satisfied in total by the business. The claim is ongoing and open ended.

What we are saying about the owners' equity component of total equities is this: When owners of a business supply that business with assets, a claim against the business is created. However, the business makes no specific promise to return these or other assets to its owners, and the extent to which these claims are ever satisfied depends upon the company's success and upon decisions by those in control of the business. A certain amount of owners' claims against the assets of any business are more or less permanent and will not be satisfied as long as the business continues to operate.

Effect of Equity Types on the Accounting Equation

Since equities can be subdivided into two major groups, liabilities and owners' equity, it is possible to rewrite the basic accounting equation as follows:

$$\text{ASSETS} = \text{LIABILITIES} + \text{OWNERS' EQUITY}$$

This expanded version of the basic accounting equation is the basis for the **balance sheet,** one of the two primary reports produced by the financial accounting system (the other, the income statement, will be discussed later in this appendix).

For illustration purposes, Exhibit A-1 on page 648 presents the financial statements for Puck & Stick, Inc., the sample company whose transactions are given and processed in Appendix B. You may refer to these statements for examples as the following sections of this appendix discuss the balance sheet, income statement, and statement of retained earnings.

BALANCE SHEET

When a business reports its assets, usually in some specified order, and does the same with its liability claims and owners' equity claims against those assets, it has prepared a balance sheet. Notice that the title of this financial statement reflects the equality condition always present in the basic accounting equation. The balance sheet is much like a still photograph of the financial position (status) of the business as of the date it is prepared. For consistency and effectiveness of communication, assets are usually listed in a prescribed order on a balance sheet and classified so that similar assets are grouped together and dissimilar assets are kept separate from each other. The same is true for liabilities and owners' equity. The classification scheme used in balance sheet preparation conveys information about the nature of individual assets, liabilities, and owners' equities and the intentions of the business for their use.

Types of Assets

For reporting purposes, assets are classified into two major groups, current and noncurrent. **Current assets** are those resources expected to be converted to cash or used up within the next year. These are the business' most liquid assets and are listed on the balance sheet in order of their closeness to cash. **Noncurrent assets** (sometimes called fixed assets) are those resources that are

EXHIBIT A-1   Sample Financial Statements

PUCK & STICK, INC.
Balance Sheet
June 30, 199X

Current Assets		
Cash	$23,360	
Accounts receivable	505	
Receivable from utility	100	
Inventory	350	
Supplies	200	$24,515
Noncurrent Assets		
Equipment	2,400	
Accumulated depreciation—equipment	(20)	2,380
Car	4,500	
Accumulated depreciation—car	(125)	4,375
Total Assets		$31,270
Current Liabilities		
Accounts payable	$ 6,600	
Federal withholding payable	100	
State withholding payable	20	
Social security payable	120	
Bank loan payable	4,000	
Interest payable	40	$10,880
Owners' Equity		
Captial stock	20,000	
Retained earnings	390	20,390
Total Liabilities and Owners' Equity		$31,270

PUCK & STICK, INC.
Income Statement
for the Month of June, 199X

Revenues		
Sales revenue	$8,800	
Interest revenue	5	$8,805
Expenses		
Cost of goods sold	7,090	
Salary expense	1,000	
Payroll taxes	60	
Insurance expense	80	
Depreciation expense	145	
Interest expense	40	8,415
Net Income		$ 390

Statement of Retained Earnings

Retained earnings, June 1, 199X	$ 0
Net income for the month	390
Dividends	0
Retained earnings, June 30, 199X	$ 390

expected to be of use or benefit to the business for more than one year. These represent assets of long-term significance.

Current Assets. There are six primary current assets usually found on a business balance sheet. They are cash, receivables, and inventory, which we briefly discussed earlier, plus marketable securities, supplies, and prepaid expenses. Marketable securities represent short-term temporary investments of cash into some very liquid security such as U.S. government bonds. Supplies are items such as cleaning materials or office materials purchased to be used up during the upcoming accounting period. Prepaid expenses are slightly more complicated in that they represent claims to future services, such as insurance protection or advertising, that have already been paid for, but not yet received. In this case, the right to the future service is an asset.

Noncurrent Assets. Noncurrent assets may be grouped into categories called investments; property, plant, and equipment; and other assets. Investments represent the long-term commitment of cash by a business to securities, usually by the purchase of stocks and bonds of other businesses. Property, plant, and equipment indicates the business' holding of productive assets such as land, buildings, machines, and so on. Other assets is a catchall category for long-term assets that cannot be otherwise classified.

Current Liabilities and Long-Term Debt

Consider now the equities section of a balance sheet. First, note the major subdivision into liabilities and owners' equity. Remember that liabilities depict the legal obligations or debts of the business, which must be paid or satisfied at some known future date. It is the expected future date of satisfaction of the debt that is the most important factor in the balance sheet classification of liabilities. If the debt payment is expected to take place within the upcoming year and will require the use of current assets to make the payment, the obligation is reported on the balance sheet as a **current liability.** All other obligations that are expected to be repaid over many years make up **long-term debt,** the second major balance sheet category of liabilities.

Owners' Equity

The most difficult area of the balance sheet to understand is owners' equity. This is true for two reasons: First, because the nature of the owners' claim on assets is quite different from other claims, and second, because it is in the owners' equity section of the balance sheet that the two primary accounting financial statements (the balance sheet and the income statement) interact and come together.

Remember that owners' equity represents sources of assets from the owners and, at the same time, measures the owners' claims against the assets of a business. There are two ways in which an owner can supply a business with assets: By direct investment and through the creation and retention of income (called indirect investment).

**Capital Stock.** An owner may directly and voluntarily turn over assets (usually cash) to a business in exchange for ownership interest in that business. When the business is a corporation, this direct and voluntary investment takes the form of a purchase of shares of stock. Shares of stock represent ownership interest. As shares are sold, the business receives cash from its owners. Simultaneously, a claim is created against the total assets of the business in favor of those holding ownership interest. In a corporation, the sources of assets and claims against assets created by the sale of stock to owners is called **capital stock** or **common stock.**

**Income.** The second way in which owners may provide assets to a business is through the creation of new assets that are not distributed to the owners. Remember that successful business activity increases resources, which we now know to be assets. If successful operations create new assets, then who has a claim to them? Recall that with assets acquired by the business, the individuals or organizations supplying the assets hold a claim against the business for the return of similar assets. However, if assets have been created by successful operations rather than directly acquired, the source of the assets is the successful activities of the business itself, not an external entity. This increase in assets due to successful operations is called **income** in accounting. Because of the residual nature of the owners' claim, these new assets are claimed by the owners. The fruits of successful operations, which are the assets generated by a business in its profit-seeking activities, belong to the business owners. Business income then belongs to the business owners.

**Dividends.** Since the owners have a claim on created assets, from time to time the business may want to distribute these assets directly to them. That is, to keep its owners happy, a business will often distribute some portion of new internally generated assets (usually in the form of cash) to its owners. In a corporation, this distribution of assets to owners is called a **dividend.**

**Retained Earnings.** It is very unusual for corporations, large or small, to distribute to owners all of the assets the business has created in any one accounting period. For business growth and income tax, as well as other reasons, corporations usually retain (do not distribute) some of their internally generated assets. In practical terms, this means that for a successful business, income (assets created to which the owners have a claim) will be larger than dividends (assets distributed to satisfy owner claims). In each accounting period, owner investment in and claims against the business will grow by the difference between income and dividends. In effect, owners are reinvesting in the business by not receiving all of the new assets that belong to them. Since the owners do not receive these assets and then consciously decide to return them, this reinvestment is indirect. Since the decision as to how much the owners actually do receive (the amount of the dividend) is often not theirs to make, this reinvestment can be involuntary. Some owners may have preferred to receive all of the assets to which they are entitled and not reinvest at all.

The cumulative amount of new assets generated by business operations and not distributed to the owners from the inception of the business represents a source of assets to the business and an increased claim on the assets by all

CONCEPT SUMMARY

Balance Sheet
Classification and Valuation

Account	Type of Future Value or Claim	Basis of Valuation on Balance Sheet
Current Assets		
Cash	Exchange	Amount on hand
Marketable securities	Exchange	Purchase cost
Receivables	Exchange	Amount expected to be collected
Inventory	Exchange	Purchase cost
Supplies	Use	Purchase cost
Prepaid items	Use	Purchase cost of services not yet used
Noncurrent Assets		
Investments	Exchange or use	Purchase cost
Property, plant, and equipment	Use	Purchase cost minus amounts used up
Other assets	Use	Purchase cost minus amounts used up
Current Liabilities		
Accounts payable	Primary and legal	Amounts owed to suppliers of goods and services
Notes payable	Primary and legal	Amounts owed for which legal documents exist
Long-Term Liabilities		
Notes payable	Primary and legal	Amount owed over several future periods for which legal documents exist
Bonds payable	Primary and legal	Amounts owed over several future periods to creditors holding bonds
Owners' Equity		
Capital stock	Secondary and residual	Direct investment of all stockholders in the business—amounts received by the business from the sale of stock to owners
Retained earnings	Secondary and residual	Indirect investment of all stockholders in the business—assets generated by profit-seeking activities minus the amount of these assets withdrawn by stockholders (net income − dividends)

business owners. On corporate balance sheets, this source of assets is designated retained earnings. **Retained earnings,** then, is equal to income minus dividends over the entire life of the business.

Characteristics of Equities

The fundamental points to remember about the equities side of a balance sheet are:

1. Although all equities represent claims on assets, there is a definite hierarchy or priority of claims based mostly on the law. Claims held by nonowners have first priority; therefore, liabilities represent higher-order claims than do owners' claims. Liabilities are **primary claims** and owners' equity represents **residual claims.** The order in which these equities appear on the balance sheet reflects its priority.
2. Whether primary or residual, equities usually represent general claims against all of the assets of the business rather than specific claims on any specific assets. There is seldom a one-to-one relationship between a specific asset and a specific claim. Instead, the accounting system views the business as a collection of assets matched and balanced by a set of general claims which are assigned a priority listing in the balance sheet.

INCOME STATEMENT AND STATEMENT OF RETAINED EARNINGS

The second primary report that results from the accounting system is called the **income statement.** This report is a more dynamic statement than the balance sheet in that it summarizes the results of operations (profit-seeking activities) for a period of time, while the balance sheet presents the financial position of the business at a single point in time. The income statement shows the ultimate impact on the business of its profit-seeking activities for a specific accounting period and serves as a guide to understanding why that result came about. The bottom line of this statement shows net income, net profit, or net earnings (or net loss), the amount by which assets have been increased by successful operations (or decreased by unsuccessful operations). The income statement is directly related to the balance sheet, and the two statements interact and formally come together at retained earnings, as is demonstrated in the following section.

Expanded Accounting Equation

The following progression of equations illustrates the relationship of and interaction between the income statement and balance sheet.

The basic accounting equation is

$$A = L + OE$$

where A is assets, L is liabilities, and OE is owners' equity.

However, owners' equity can be divided into direct and indirect sources of and claims on assets by the owners, so we can rewrite the equation without changing its meaning as

$$A = L + CS + RE$$
where CS is capital or common stock and RE is retained earnings.

Remember that retained earnings measures net income minus dividends over the life of the business, so the equation can be further expanded as

$$A = L + CS + (NI - D) \text{ over the life of the business}$$
where NI is net income and D is dividends.

This equation can now be rewritten as

$$A = L + CS + \sum (NI - D)$$
where $\sum$ is a summation sign indicating the cumulative.

Net income is the difference between revenue and expense, so the completely expanded (for our purposes) version of the basic accounting equation becomes

$$A = L + CS + \sum [(R - E) - D]$$
where R is revenue and E is expense.

The expression within the parentheses $(R - E)$ measures net income for an accounting period, while the expression within the brackets $[(R - E) - D]$ represents the increase in indirect investment (increase in retained earnings) by the owners and, at the same time, the increase in claims against the assets of the business during this period because of this indirect investment. Stated another way, $(R - E) - D$ measures the amount of assets generated by successful operations during an accounting period, minus the amount of those assets distributed to the owners during that accounting period. If this increase in indirect investment is summed for each accounting period in the business' life, the result is the total indirect investment by owners since the inception of the business, which is retained earnings. If this figure is added to the total direct investment by owners (capital stock or common stock), the result is total owners' equity representing all the owners' claims on the assets of the business.

Revenue and Expense

Net income is the accounting system's measure of the success of a business. The determinants of net income are revenue and expense. These two measurement ideas are among the most difficult to grasp for two reasons: (1) the concepts underlying them are complex, and (2) we all have some lay notions derived from our general experience that tend to get in the way of precision in this area.

Both revenue and expense are measurement concepts. Both measure movements in assets and/or liabilities that result from the profit-seeking activities of a business within a given time period.

Aspects of Revenue. **Revenue** measures increases in or inflows of assets resulting from the profit-seeking activities of a business during an accounting period. Note the following important aspects of this definition of revenue:

1. Revenue is an abstraction that measures "real" movement in another area of the basic accounting equation. The actual movement takes place among assets, and revenue is the expression we use to measure the amount of that movement.
2. Assets may increase for many reasons in a typical business, but revenue measures only those specific increases resulting from profit-seeking activities.

Revenue Illustrated. To elaborate further on the second point, consider the following example: A business borrows money, with the result that assets (cash) increase. Since borrowing money is a financing rather than a profit-seeking activity, liabilities will increase (note payable), rather than revenue. Now consider the following example: A business sells some of its products to a customer for cash. Such a sale increases assets (cash). Because this transaction is profit seeking in nature, revenue (sales revenue) increases. Both borrowing money and selling products cause the business' assets to increase, but only the sale gives rise to revenue. The term revenue denotes asset increases caused by profit-seeking events, as opposed to asset increases caused by all other activities.

In terms of the basic accounting equation, acquiring assets (for example, borrowing money) causes assets (cash) to increase and liabilities (note payable to bank) to increase by the same amount; thus equality is maintained. Creating assets (for example, by selling products) causes assets (cash or accounts receivable) to increase and revenue (sales revenue) to increase. Referring to the progression of equations previously discussed, you will find that as revenue increases, so does retained earnings and, consequently, owners' equity. It should now be clear that the result of the sale of products is quite different from the result of the business' borrowing activity. The sale causes assets and owners' equity to increase by the same amount and thereby maintain equality in the accounting equation.

Aspects of Expense. Expense is conceptually the opposite of revenue. **Expense** measures decreases in or outflows of assets or increases in liabilities resulting from the profit-seeking activities of a business. In other words, when a business consumes or uses up its assets or incurs liabilities in the course of seeking a profit, it recognizes expenses. The two important points made earlier about revenue also apply to expense:

1. Expense is an abstraction that measures "real" movement in other area(s) of the basic accounting equation. Either a decrease takes place among the assets or an increase takes place among liabilities, and expense is the measurement of these changes.
2. Assets may decrease or liabilities may increase for many reasons in a typical business, but expense measures only those changes resulting from profit-seeking activities.

Expense Illustrated. Suppose, for example, a business pays off a bank loan and experiences a resulting decrease in cash. The act of repayment simply retires a legal obligation of the business, and therefore, its effect on the basic accounting equation would be a reduction of assets (cash) and an equal reduction of liabilities (note payable). In this event, an asset decreases but, importantly, no expense is created.

Now consider the previous sale of products to a customer. The sale caused an asset (cash) to increase and sales revenue was recognized, but at the same time another asset (inventory) was consumed. This asset decrease is measured and separated from other decreases in assets by the recognition of an expense. Again, referring to the progression of accounting equations, you will notice that as expense increases (it is a negative—or minus—factor in the equation), retained earnings and owners' equity decrease. Assets have decreased, and the balancing movement is a decrease in owners' equity.

Accrual-Basis and Cash-Basis Accounting

The guiding principle that a business should recognize accomplishment (revenue) and the related effort (expense) when any asset (not just cash) is created or consumed is the foundation of **accrual-basis accounting.** The principle that revenue and expense should be recognized only when cash is affected is the foundation for **cash-basis accounting.** Most businesses use an accrual-basis accounting system, while most individuals use a cash-basis accounting system. These different approaches are used for income tax reporting as well as for other purposes and result from the application of either legal or accounting principles. Throughout most of this book, we will focus on accrual-basis accounting systems for businesses.

Interaction of Income Statement and Balance Sheet

Recall that the balance sheet and income statement actually connect or come together at retained earnings (to reinforce this idea, review the progression of equations discussed earlier in this appendix). Net income (the bottom line of the income statement) minus the amount of assets distributed to the owners

CONCEPT SUMMARY		
Guidelines for the Recognition of Revenue and Expense		
System	*Revenue*	*Expense*
Cash-basis accounting	Cash is received from profit-seeking events.	Cash is paid for profit-seeking events.
Accrual-basis accounting	Any asset is received from profit-seeking events— usually when product is sold or services rendered.	Any asset is consumed or liability created from profit-seeking events— usually matched to revenue.

(dividends) represents the amount by which retained earnings (from the balance sheet) increases for the period. This interaction between the two major financial statements is so significant that most accounting systems produce a statement whose sole function is to emphasize this connection. The statement is called the **statement of retained earnings,** and its purpose is to make explicit the effect of income and dividends on the basic accounting equation and the balance sheet. The general format of this statement adds net income to and subtracts dividends from the beginning retained earnings amount to determine the ending retained earnings (balance sheet) amount.

KEY TERMS

Accounting equation (*p. 644*)
Accrual-basis accounting (*p. 655*)
Assets (*p. 644*)
Balance sheet (*p. 647*)
Capital stock (common stock) (*p. 650*)
Cash-basis accounting (*p. 655*)
Current assets (*p. 647*)
Current liabilities (*p. 649*)
Dividends (*p. 650*)
Equities (*p. 644*)
Expense (*p. 654*)
Future value (*p. 644*)
Income (*p. 650*)

Income statement (*p. 652*)
Liabilities (*p. 646*)
Long-term debt (*p. 649*)
Noncurrent assets (*p. 647*)
Owners' equity (*p. 646*)
Primary claims (*p. 652*)
Residual claims (*p. 652*)
Retained earnings (*p. 652*)
Revenue (*p. 654*)
Statement of retained earnings
(*p. 656*)
Stockholders' equity (*p. 646*)

QUESTIONS

A-1. Explain the three criteria used to determine whether a business resource is an asset?

A-2. Claims on the assets of a business may take the form of liabilities or owners' equity. Contrast the important characteristics of these two types of claims.

A-3. Describe the six current assets typically found on a balance sheet.

A-4. Describe the three major categories of noncurrent assets typically found on a balance sheet and give a specific example of each category.

A-5. Describe and contrast the two ways in which an owner may supply assets to a business.

A-6. What are the important characteristics of the equities side of the balance sheet?

A-7. Are all the resources of value to a business listed on its balance sheet? Why or why not? If not, give three examples of resources that would not appear on a balance sheet.

A-8. Present the expansion of the basic accounting equation from the $A = E$ form to its most expanded form.

A-9. Explain the relationship of the income statement and balance sheet in terms of the accounting equation $A = L + CS + \sum [(R - E) - D]$.

A-10. Discuss the difference between revenue and expense transactions and other transactions that result in movements in assets and/or liabilities.

A-11. What is the role of the statement of retained earnings? How does the statement fulfill this role?

A-12. Contrast the recognition of revenue and expense under the accrual basis of accounting to the recognition under the cash basis.

A-13. All changes in owners' equity are recorded in revenue and expense accounts. Is this statement correct? If not, give two examples of changes in owners' equity that do not involve revenue or expense.

PROBLEMS

A-14. *Requirement 1.* Which of the following are assets? For each item that is not an asset, explain why. For each asset, support your decision as to why it is an asset.

a. Copyright of a book
b. Highway next to the plant
c. A company's own capital stock not yet sold to stockholders
d. Amounts owed to the firm by customers
e. Amounts owed by the firm to suppliers
f. Amount paid to landlord for previous month's rent
g. Amount paid to landlord for next month's rent
h. Reputation of the firm based on years of quality service
i. Obsolete machine whose cost of removal would equal its proceeds

Requirement 2. Which of the following are liabilities? For each item that is not a liability, explain why. For each liability, support your decision as to why it is a liability.

a. A bank overdraft
b. A customer's account that was overpaid
c. The estimated amount you will pay to your employees in salaries next year
d. A 90-day note signed when $1,000 was borrowed from the local bank in order to finance the purchase of machinery
e. Amounts owed by customers

A-15. The operating activities of Kennedy Electrical Service for the month of March are as follows.

a.	Fees for jobs performed in March for which cash was collected at the time the job was performed	$15,000
b.	Collection of accounts receivable	4,500
c.	Fees for jobs performed in March to be collected later	7,000
d.	Cash purchase of supplies	350
e.	Payments to employees for salaries earned in February	2,000
f.	Supplies used in March	600
g.	Payments of March rents on office and trucks	2,500
h.	Salaries earned by employees in March and paid in March	12,000
i.	Salaries earned by employees in March to be paid in April	3,000

1. Prepare an accrual-basis income statement for the month of March.
2. Prepare a cash-basis income statement for the month of March.

A-16. The following account balances are taken from the books of the Iberville Corporation on June 30.

Accounts receivable	$17,000
Prepaid expenses	1,200
Inventory	20,000
Notes payable	15,000
Accounts payable	11,500
Investments	6,500
Plant and equipment (net of depreciation)	12,000
Cash	7,500
Wages payable	2,000

Owners' equity at the beginning of the year was $20,000. During the year, an owner, Isaac Iberville, made an additional investment of $15,000. He also received $13,000 in cash and $5,000 of inventory as salary. Dividends of $8,000 were paid to the owners, Isaac and his mother Ione, during the year.

1. Calculate net income for the year ending June 30.
2. Is it possible to prepare an income statement? If not, why not?

A-17.

The Royal Corporation
Balance Sheet
December 31, 199A

Cash	$ -0-	Accounts payable	$ 20,000
Accounts receivable	40,000	Notes payable	15,000
Inventory	60,000	Capital stock	40,000
Plant and equipment	75,000	Retained earnings	100,000
	$175,000		$175,000

Income Statement
For the Year Ended December 31, 199A

Sales revenue	$58,000
Expenses	43,000
Net income	$15,000

1. Could the Royal Corporation pay a cash dividend for the year to its stockholders? If so, how?
2. What do you think is meant by the phrase, "paying dividends from retained earnings"? How do these financial statements illustrate the misunderstandings contained in this phrase?
3. What is the relationship between retained earnings and the asset side of the balance sheet? What are the similarities between retained earnings and other equities?

Below are the transactions of the Chartes Company for the month of August.

a.	Cash sales	$10,000
b.	Collections of accounts receivable	5,000
c.	Credit sales	20,000
d.	Payments on accounts payable	7,000
e.	Credit purchases of merchandise	13,000
f.	Cash from bank loan	15,000
g.	Payment of dividends	2,000
h.	Cash purchases of merchandise	4,000
i.	Payment of salaries	6,000
j.	Payment of bank loan	5,000

Additionally, inventory at the beginning month was $14,000, and inventory at the end of the month was $8,000.

1. Determine total cash receipts, total cash disbursements, and the change in cash for the month.
2. Determine cash-basis revenue, cash-basis expense, and profit on a cash basis for the month.
3. Determine accrual-basis revenue, accrual-basis expense, and accounting net income (profit) for the month.
4. Explain the source of difference between these two profit figures.

A-19. John and Paul opened a bar in the French Quarter with an investment of $10,000 each on March 1. Rent for six months was paid on that date in the amount of $9,600. A complete line of bar equipment was purchased for $10,000, of which $5,000 was on account, and $3,000 worth of inventory (liquor, etc.) was purchased for cash. Sales for the first half of the month were $1,800 in cash. To increase sales, John and Paul embarked upon an advertising campaign and spent $3,000 of funds that had been borrowed from the bank on radio, television, and newspaper advertisements. In anticipation of increased business, they bought an additional $5,000 of inventory on account. Certain friends of the owners immediately established a tab which, at the end of the month, totaled $500.

    Salaries for the month (not including withdrawals of $750 each by the owners) were paid in cash in the amount of $1,000. Sales in the second half of the month totaled $3,600. The owners paid $2,000 on the amount owed for inventory and $1,500 to reduce the amount owed the bank. Inventory on hand on March 31 was $4,000. The owners estimated that $150 of the cost of the bar equipment was used up during the month.

1. Prepare a balance sheet as of March 31.
2. What was the amount of net income or loss for the month?

A-20. The following represent all of the information pertaining to the activities of the Decater Corporation as of December 31.

Cash on hand	$ 1,200
Amounts owed to suppliers	4,000
Amounts invested by owners	15,000
Expired insurance premiums	1,800

Unexpired insurance premiums	9,000
Inventory—January 1	3,000
Purchases of inventory	21,000
Cash in checking account	2,200
Amounts owed by customers	6,100
Investment in U.S. government bonds	3,800
Lease payment on a truck for next year	3,600
Unexpired cost of building and equipment	23,100
Unused supplies	200
Used supplies	300
Deposit from customers on future delivery of products	1,400
Retained earnings—January 1	9,800
Total sales during the year	30,900
Cash distributed to stockholders	2,000
Income taxes (unpaid as of year-end)	4,400
Inventory—December 31	4,000

1. Prepare an income statement and a statement of retained earnings for the year in good form suitable for external reporting.

2. Prepare a balance sheet as of December 31 in good form suitable for external reporting.

A-21. (AICPA, adapted) The Esplanade Company (a sole proprietorship) has not maintained its records on a double-entry basis since its inception. The following is all the information you could determine from the "books" of Esplanade.

a. The assets and equities as of December 31, 199A were:

	Debit	Credit
Cash	$ 5,175	
Accounts receivable	9,816	
Fixtures	3,130	
Accumulated depreciation		$ 1,110
Prepaid insurance	158	
Prepaid supplies	79	
Accounts payable		4,244
Accrued expenses		206
Accrued taxes		202
Merchandise inventory	19,243	
Notes payable		5,000
Owner's capital		26,839

b. A summary of the transactions for 199B, as recorded in the checkbook, showed:

Deposits for the year (including redeposit of $304)	$83,187
Checks written during the year	84,070
Customers' checks charged back by the bank	304
Bank service charges	22

c. The following information was available concerning accounts payable:

Purchases on account during the year	$57,789
Returns of merchandise allowed as credits against accounts by vendors	1,418
Payments of accounts by check	55,461

d. Information pertaining to accounts receivable showed the following:

Accounts collected	$43,083
Balance of accounts on December 31, 199B	11,221

e. Checks drawn during the year included the following items:

Salaries	$10,988
Rent	3,600
Heat, light, and telephone	394
Supplies	280
Insurance	341
Taxes and licenses	1,017
Withdrawals by owner	6,140
Miscellaneous expense	769
Merchandise purchases	2,080
Notes payable	3,000
	$28,609

f. Merchandise inventory on December 31, 199B, was $17,807. Prepaid insurance amounted to $122 and supplies on hand to $105 as of December 31, 199B. Accrued taxes were $216 and accrued expenses were $73 at the year end.

g. Cash sales for the year are assumed to account for all cash received other than that collected on accounts. Fixtures are to be depreciated at the rate of 10 percent per year.

1. Prepare a cash-basis income statement for the calendar year 199B.

2. Prepare an accrual-basis income statement for the calendar year 199B.

3. Prepare a balance sheet as of December 31, 199B.

A-22. Below is the income statement and statement of owners' capital of the Harvey Couch Company for the month ended January 31, 199B.

Income Statement and Statement of Owners' Capital
For the Month Ended January 31, 199B

Revenues		$26,000
Expenses		
Cost of goods sold	$17,000	
Rent expense	1,000	
Salaries expense	2,000	
Payroll tax expense	150	
Advertising expense	400	
Utilities expense	300	
Supplies expense	150	
Depreciation expense	200	21,200
Net income		$ 4,800
Couch, capital, December 31, 199A		49,600
Couch, capital, January 31, 199B		$54,400

The income statement was prepared on an accrual basis. Revenues were recognized when they were earned and expenses were recognized when they were incurred. Specific details about the nature and timing of the operating activities of the company are the following:

a. All revenues came from the sale of merchandise on hand at the beginning of the month. No inventory was purchased during the month. One-half of sales were cash sales and one-half were credit sales.

b. The rent for any given month is paid on the 15th of the preceding month.

c. Salaries for the month are paid on the 15th and 30th of that month.

d. Utility expenses are based on amounts billed for the month. Bills are received at the end of the month and are paid at a later date.

e. All supplies used during the month were on hand at the beginning of the month. No purchases of supplies were made during the month.

f. Depreciation expense pertains to the use of office equipment owned by the company.

g. All other expenses are paid for in cash at the time the expense is incurred.

h. No payments were made on liabilities during the month.

i. A balance sheet is prepared from the accounting records at the end of each month.

Based on the information provided, answer the following questions:

1. What changes in asset accounts do revenues for January measure? Indicate the specific asset account or accounts affected, the amount by which they changed, and whether the change was an increase or a decrease.

2. What changes in assets and liabilities do expenses for January measure? For each expense item, indicate the specific asset or liability account affected, the amount by which it changed, and whether the change was an increase or a decrease.

3. What is the dollar amount of the net change (increases less decreases) in assets as a result of profit-seeking activities for January? Indicate whether this net change was an increase or a decrease. Show your calculation.

4. What is the dollar amount of the net change in liabilities as a result of profit-seeking activities for January? Indicate whether this net change was an increase or a decrease. Show your calculation.

5. What portion (dollar amount) of the net increase in assets from profit-seeking activities in January (calculated in part 3) is associated with an increase in creditors' claims?

6. What portion (dollar amount) of the net increase in assets from profit-seeking activities in January is associated with an increase in the owner's claims? What is this amount called?

Listed in random order is information about B. A. Dictor Chemical Company. Unless otherwise specified, the values are those at December 31, 199B.

Capital stock (50,000 shares outstanding)	$ 454,000
Accounts and notes receivable	195,000
Accounts payable	136,000
Marketable securities	47,000
Notes payable	215,000
Allowance for uncollectible accounts receivable	3,000
Prepaid expenses	8,000
Inventory	304,000
Bonds payable	564,000
Supplies	3,000
Cash	70,000
Revenue for year ended December 31, 199B	1,929,000
Property, plant, and equipment, at cost	1,580,000
Accumulated depreciation, representing used portion of property, plant, and equipment	522,000
Trade name and trademarks	12,000
Retained earnings at December 31, 199A	308,000

Total expenses for year ended December 31, 199B, broken down as follows:		
Cost of sales	$1,425,000	
Selling, general, and administrative expense	165,000	
Depreciation expense	121,000	
Income tax expense	89,000	1,800,000
Deferred charges and other assets		28,000
Dividends paid during 199B		84,000

Additional information:

a. The B. A. Dictor Chemical Company has an operating cycle of three months.

b. All accounts and notes receivable are due by June 30, 199C.

c. Of the marketable securities, $25,000 are expected to be held indefinitely while $22,000 are temporary investments expected to be sold within a few months.

d. Notes payable of $90,000 are due March 15, 199C. The remainder of the notes payable are due October 15, 199D.

e. Bonds payable are due as follows:

Face Value	Maturity Date
$226,000	February 15, 199E
$121,000	September 30, 199F
$217,000	March 1, 200G

Prepare a balance sheet for the B. A. Dictor Chemical Company as of December 31, 199B, and an income statement (including earnings per share) and statement of retained earnings for the year ended December 31, 199B.

DECISION CASE

Fly-Away, Inc., was organized June 1, 1992 for the purpose of transporting botanical expeditions to tropical islands. The following transactions took place in June:

June 1   Issued 7,000 shares of $6 par value common stock for $63,000. Purchased a small plane for $56,000 and parts for $2,000, paying $30,000 cash and issuing an 8 percent, two-year note for the balance owed.

    2   Paid Safeguard Insurance for two months temporary coverage, cost—$1,500.

    3   Paid $950 cash to rent a building for June and July.

    8   Cash receipts from customers for a trip scheduled June 18 amounted to $4,500.

   16   Employees earned $3,200 for the first half of June. (FICA tax rate is 6 percent, federal unemployment tax rate is 1 percent, state unemployment tax rate is 3 percent, income tax withheld, $420. Assume the full amount of wages is subject to tax.).

   26   Paid $250 to Greasers, Inc., for repair work on plane.

   28   Received a bill for gasoline from Fill-Ups amounting to $1,200, payable July 2.

   30   Cash receipts from customers for a trip made on June 22 amounted to $7,300.

Employees are paid on the 1st and 16th and earn the same amount in each half of the month. The plane is estimated to have a useful life of six years and a residual value of $2,000. Straight-line depreciation is used. A check of spare parts revealed that $45 worth had been used in June. This is considered a repairs expense.

Account titles used by the company are as follows:

Cash	Notes payable
Prepaid rent	Common stock
Prepaid insurance	Paid-in capital
Plane	Retained earnings
Acc dep—Plane	Flight revenue
Parts	Salaries expense
Accounts payable	Depreciation expense
Interest payable	Repairs expense
Advances from customers	Rent expense
FICA payable	Interest expense
Income tax withheld	Insurance expense
Unemployment taxes payable	Gasoline expense
Accrued payroll	Payroll tax expense

Required:

1. Prepare an accrual-basis income statement in good form for the month of June.

2. Prepare a cash-basis income statement for the month of June.

3. Explain why the income figures are different under the two approaches and reconcile the two figures by listing the items of difference.

B Processing Transactions

Overview

Review of the processing steps used in noncomputerized accounting systems to record, classify, and summarize transactions.

Learning Objectives

Thorough study of this appendix will enable you to:

1. Explain the logic behind double-entry bookkeeping.
2. Enter transactions into a general journal, post them to ledger accounts, and prepare a trial balance.
3. Make adjusting entries and prepare an adjusted trial balance.
4. Close the revenue and expense accounts.
5. Use subsidiary ledgers for accounts receivable and accounts payable.
6. Use special journals for sales, purchases, cash receipts, and cash disbursements.
7. Use a voucher system and an invoice register.

Outline

Accounting Cycle and Double-Entry Bookkeeping

Subsidiary Ledgers and Special Journals

Comprehensive Accounting System Example

Voucher System

Fra Luca Pacioli

Fra Luca Pacioli, an Italian mathematician who is considered the Father of Accounting, lived from about 1445 to 1520 and was a close friend of Renaissance master Leonardo da Vinci. Pacioli published in 1494 De Computis et Scripturis ("Of Reckonings and Writings"), a work on double-entry recordkeeping for merchants. For the first time, he detailed the system of accounting which had been in wide use in the commercial center of Venice for many years.

Pacioli wrote that Italian merchants kept track of their business activities by making two entries, a debit and a credit. Additionally, each transaction was viewed separately. Further, Pacioli arranged his assets in much the same order as they are listed in a modern balance sheet, with cash and near-cash items listed first followed by others of a more fixed nature.

There is, however, a major difference between Pacioli's system and modern accounting: Profit was measured then not for a specified period such as a year, but only for specific ventures such as a ship voyage or for the entire life of a business.

The system described by Pacioli was not original with him. However, he was the first to bring the many diverse elements together in a way that has proved to be the foundation of modern double-entry bookkeeping. Indeed, Pacioli would feel right at home with the debits and credits of today.

Along with his ground-breaking description of the double-entry system, Pacioli dispensed a great deal of practical advice. Some of these comments still hold true today:

1. Books should be closed each year, especially in partnership, because frequent accounting makes for long friendship.
2. There are three things necessary to one who wishes to operate a business successfully. The most important is cash or some equivalent economic power. The second is to be a good accountant and a ready mathematician. The third is that all the business owner's affairs be arranged in a systematic way so that the owner may get the particulars at a glance.
3. If each thing is not in its right place, great trouble and confusion will arise. As the saying goes, "Where there is no order, there is chaos."
4. A credit balance in the Profit and Loss account represents a profit, and a debit balance represents a loss, from which latter may God preserve every man.
5. If the grand total of debits and credits are equal, you may conclude that the Ledger was well kept and closed. However, if one grand total exceeds the other, it would indicate an error in the Ledger. This error must be searched out diligently.

One of Pacioli's comments, however, is inappropriate in the modern world:

6. The servants of the household can make the daily entries in the book of original entry, or they can also be made by the master's women, if they know how to write.

Source: *Journal of Accountancy*, December 1977, "Pacioli Revisited," pp. 74–75. Copyright © 1977 by the American Institute of Certified Public Accountants, Inc. Opinions expressed in the *Journal of Accountancy* are those of the editors and contributors. Publication in the *Journal of Accountancy* does not constitute endorsement by the AICPA or its committees. *Woman CPA*, January 1977, "Luca Pacioli and the Summa," pp. 3–7.

ACCOUNTING CYCLE
AND
DOUBLE-ENTRY BOOKKEEPING

The accounting relationships discussed in Appendix A present a complete view of the concepts underlying accounting systems for businesses. The income statement, retained earnings statement, and balance sheet represent the output of the accounting system and are typically prepared only once each period. In this appendix, we turn our attention to the system that makes possible the preparation of these reports.

To take processing ideas from the textbook to the real world requires certain recording and classifying techniques as well as an understanding of several basic business procedures which are essential to the effective handling of the data processed by an accounting system. These devices, called journals and ledgers, are necessary refinements of the basic accounting cycle which allow the efficient processing of repetitive events. Additionally, journals and ledgers provide much of the information necessary for the management and control of a business.

The series of steps a business goes through to produce meaningful financial reports from the transactions that occur is called the **accounting cycle.** This cycle may be viewed as a seven-step process which has as its goal the recording, classifying, summarizing, and communicating of financial information. When this process is carried out by hand or with the aid of mechanical devices but without the use of computers, it is called a manual accounting system. The following is a typical accounting cycle:

1. Journalize accounting transactions.
2. Post accounting transactions.
3. Prepare a trial balance.
4. Journalize and post adjusting entries.
5. Prepare an adjusted trial balance.
6. Prepare financial statements.
7. Journalize and post closing entries.

Double-Entry Bookkeeping Concepts

Because financial statements are prepared only periodically, a technique is needed to keep track of the events that occur between one period's statements and the next. In order to record transactions in a way that facilitates financial statement preparation, we use a technique in accounting called double-entry bookkeeping. An appreciation of manual accounting systems requires a complete understanding of double-entry bookkeeping.

The two primary instruments used in double-entry bookkeeping are the journal and the ledger. The **journal** is a device that makes possible the recording of events as they occur in the life of a business. It provides a system for writing business events down in an orderly manner. The **ledger** is used to classify these events and determine their effect on the assets, liabilities, owners' equity, revenue, and expense of the business. In **double-entry bookkeeping,** each transaction is entered as both a debit and a credit in order to keep the accounting equation in balance. Exhibit B-1 summarizes the double-entry behavior patterns for each of the major financial statement account classifications.

Accounting Logic

Double-entry bookkeeping rules are simply mechanical reflections of the relationships described in Appendix A. For example, as expenses (a negative owners' equity item) increase, owners' equity decreases. The logical implementation of this connection in double-entry fashion is that debits reflect an increase in expenses and a decrease in owners' equity. By the same token, credits to expenses (unusual except for closing entries to be discussed later in this chapter) cause them to decrease.

As a business earns revenue, the ultimate effect on the accounting equation is an increase in owners' equity. Since this positive connection exists

EXHIBIT B-1   Double-Entry Behavior Patterns

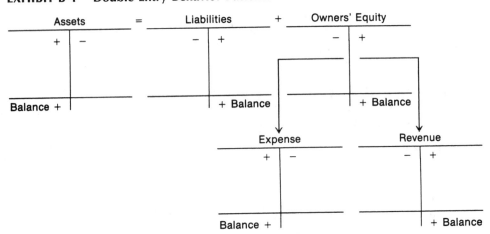

A **debit** is any entry made on the *left* side of an account.
A **credit** is any entry made on the *right* side of an account.

between revenue and owners' equity, it follows that the debit and credit rules should be the same for these accounts. In fact, the rules are exactly the same: Credits reflect increases in both revenues and owners' equity, and debits result in decreases in revenues (unusual except for closing entries) and owners' equity. Appendix A emphasized the interaction between these income statement and balance sheet accounts, and double-entry relationships are just a reflection of this tie-in. For a summary of the logic behind the debit and credit rules for revenues and expenses, refer to the definitions of these concepts presented in Appendix A.

The rules of double-entry bookkeeping make it a perfect internally logical system. There is no accounting event that cannot be recorded easily within these rules. As you apply these logical rules to business transactions and manual accounting systems, remember the following concepts:

Transactions. Accounting systems are not concerned with all of the events in which a business may engage, but only with a certain category called accounting transactions. To be considered a transaction by the accounting system (and therefore recorded, classified, summarized, and communicated), the event must immediately affect one or more parts of the basic accounting equation discussed in Appendix A. **Transactions,** then, are events which alter in some fashion the $A = L + OE$ equation (remembering the role of revenue and expense). Transactions provide the raw data of accounting systems.

Duality. Double-entry bookkeeping derives its name from its view of all accounting transactions as two-sided events. All transactions must have at least two different effects on the basic accounting equation; otherwise, equality of the equation could not possibly be maintained. For every transaction, there is at least one debit effect and at least one credit effect, and the total debits always equal the total credits for each transaction. This is called the duality idea in accounting. This idea of two effects for every transaction is one of the convenient self-checks built into the double-entry bookkeeping system. Knowing that every accounting transaction has a debit effect and a credit effect, and that these effects always equal, aids in achieving accuracy and the complete analysis of transactions.

Bookkeeping Equation. We now are able to state a version of the basic accounting equation in bookkeeping terms. The following two statements are equivalent; the first equation is the conceptually based basic accounting model of the firm, and the second is a mechanical bookkeeping model. Both equations are always true.

$$\text{ASSETS} = \text{LIABILITIES} + \text{OWNERS' EQUITY}$$
$$\text{DEBITS} = \text{CREDITS}$$

Exhibit B-2 summarizes the relationships between these two statements.

Beginning the Accounting Cycle—Journalizing Transactions

With the logic of double-entry bookkeeping clear, we can now examine the beginning of the accounting cycle. The first step in the cycle is the journalizing

EXHIBIT B-2   Debit/Credit Relationships

	Debit Balances	Credit Balances
Balance sheet	Assets	Liabilities and owners' equity
Income statement	Expense	Revenue

of accounting transactions. The journal should be thought of as the book of original entry for a business because all transactions are first written down in the journal. Most accounting systems use several different journals, and we will discuss all of the most common journal types in this appendix. In this section, however, we discuss only the **general journal.** Exhibit B-3 is a sample segment of a typical general journal from a manual accounting system.

The primary task of journals is to accomplish the recording function of the accounting process. Essentially, what we want is a diary that gives the chronological history of that business. We also want the transactions recorded in a way that makes it easy for us to determine their effect on the assets, liabilities, owners' equity, revenue, and expense of the business. A precise instrument like a journal with a well-known and widely used format is necessary if an accounting system is to analyze and record the results of a large number of transactions in a useful way.

Notice that the **posting reference (PR)** column in the journal gives the general ledger account number of the account to which the amount has been *posted* (transferred). This links the journal and the ledger and begins the process of tracing transactions within the accounting system. These posting references are part of what is called an **audit trail** of transactions through the financial records.

Posting Transactions to the Ledger   Recording the transactions of a business as they occur (so that they are not forgotten or overlooked) is critical to the accounting system because transactions are the raw data of the system. Recording, however, is only the beginning of the cycle. In order to produce

EXHIBIT B-3   General Journal Sample Page

Page 13

Date			Transaction Accounts	PR	Debit Amount	Credit Amount
199A Jan		5	Accounts payable	10	100	
			Cash	1		100
		20	Accounts receivable	3	450	
			Sales revenue	21		450
		20	Cost of inventory sold	25	300	
			Inventory	4		300
		25	Cash	1	200	
			Accounts receivable	3		200

useful reports about a business at the end of each accounting period, we must be able to determine the cumulative effect of all the period's transactions on the various accounts of the business. This process is called classification and it involves use of the second bookkeeping instrument, the ledger. The second step in the accounting cycle, **posting,** accomplishes the classification function. Exhibit B-4 shows a portion of a typical general ledger for a manual system.

EXHIBIT B-4   General Ledger Sample Accounts

Assets

CASH #1

Date	PR	Debit	Credit	PR	Date
12/31 199A	√	100			
1/25	J13	200	100	J13	199A 1/5
1/31	√	200			

ACCOUNTS RECEIVABLE #3

Date	PR	Debit	Credit	PR	Date
12/31 199A	√	500			
1/20	J13	450	200	J13	199A 1/25
1/31	√	750			

INVENTORY #4

Date	PR	Debit	Credit	PR	Date
12/31 199A	√	600			
			300	J13	199A 1/20
1/31	√	300			

Liabilities

ACCOUNTS PAYABLE #10

Date	PR	Debit	Credit	PR	Date
			400	√	12/31 199A
199A 1/5	J13	100			
			300	√	1/31

Owners' Equity

CAPITAL STOCK #15

Date	PR	Debit	Credit	PR	Date
199A			600	√	12/31 199A
			600	√	1/31

RETAINED EARNINGS #17

Date	PR	Debit	Credit	PR	Date
199A			200	√	12/31 199A
			200	√	1/31

Revenues

SALES #21

Date	PR	Debit	Credit	PR	Date
199A			450	J13	199A 1/20
			450	√	1/31

Expenses

COST OF INVENTORY SOLD #25

Date	PR	Debit	Credit	PR	Date
199A 1/20	J13	300			199A
1/31	√	300			

The primary task of the ledger is to classify the effect of the transactions recorded within the accounting system. The idea is to separate the components (debit and credit) of each transaction and then group together all of the components of the various transactions that affect each individual asset, liability, owners' equity, revenue, and expense account. In this manner we can show the cumulative effect of all the transactions on each individual account. Notice again the posting reference (PR) columns for each ledger account give the journal and page number from which the posted transaction has come, allowing the tracing of transaction either forward or backward through the accounting records.

CONCEPT SUMMARY		
Comparison and Contrast of the Journal and the Ledger		
	Journal	*Ledger*
Focus	Transaction	Account
Information Recorded	1. Date 2. Accounts affected 3. Posting reference 4. Debit amount 5. Credit amount	1. Date 2. Posting reference 3. Amount
When Updated	As transactions occur	As posting occurs
Dated	When transaction occurred	When transaction occurred
Posting Reference	Ledger account affected	Journal and page where recorded
Amount Recorded	Debit *and* credit effects of transaction	Debit *or* credit effect on individual account
Organization	In chronological order	In account number order

Trial Balance

You have probably noticed that certain numbers in each account in Exhibit B-4 display checkmarks rather than journal and page information in the Posting Reference column. These numbers bring up the third step in the accounting cycle, called the **trial balance**. Numbers with checkmarks in the PR column indicate the balance in the account at the specific date given in the Date column. It is important to distinguish between balances and transactions. A balance indicates the dollar value of an account at a specific point in time, after taking into account all of the transactions occurring up to that time. A transaction is a change in an account (debit or credit) from an individual event taking place since the last balance. The zero balances you may have noticed in revenue and expense at the start of the month will be discussed later in this chapter.

A business needs to know the dollar value of each of its accounts at various times for assurance that the basic accounting equation is still intact ($A = L + OE$) and for help in the detection of errors. However, it is not necessary that the new balance in each account be determined after each posting, although it is possible to do this particularly with the aid of a computer. As a result, most businesses calculate balances showing the cumulative effect of all prior transactions at various times, but not as frequently as posting of transactions takes place. An internal statement, called a trial balance, is usually created when these balances are determined. The trial balance is simply a list of all the accounts used by the business with the dollar balance in each account at a specified date. By periodically creating such a statement, we can get an overview of the accounts and their balances and can be sure that Debits = Credits and $A = L + OE$.

End-of-Period Procedures

Every business records transactions in its journal, usually as they occur. The business then classifies the effects these transactions have on its accounts by posting the transactions to the ledger. Periodically, the business determines the dollar balance of each account in the ledger and summarizes these balances in a trial balance. All these steps occur either constantly, frequently, or at least more than once during a typical accounting period. In addition to these ongoing steps, however, an important set of activities in the accounting cycle occurs only once each accounting period. These steps are carried out only at the end of each accounting period and are designated **end-of-period procedures.** To understand end-of-period procedures, it is necessary to distinguish two basic types of transactions in which most businesses engage—external and internal.

External Events

External events are transactions that take place between a business and outside individuals or organizations. These events are easy to identify because they occur at discrete points as a business interacts with its environment. Also, there are usually supporting documents (like checks or bills) created by one or both of the parties to the external transaction indicating that a transaction has occurred. Examples of external transactions include selling goods, purchasing inventory or other assets, borrowing money, selling stock, repaying loans, and paying dividends. External events are recorded as they occur in the first step of the accounting cycle because (1) they involve outsiders and (2) certain legal relationships are created as a result of the transaction that requires immediate documenting in the accounting system. In fact, external events are the only transactions that require recording in the accounting system as they occur and, therefore, steps 1 through 3 of the accounting cycle are concerned only with external transactions. In step 1, external events are journalized, and in step 2, these external events are posted. The trial balance of step 3 reflects only the cumulative effect of the external events recorded during the period and added to or subtracted from the account balances at the beginning of the period.

Internal Events

Internal events take place wholly within the firm; that is, no individual or other organization is directly involved. An example is the consumption of supplies. These events tend to occur continuously during the accounting period rather than at specific, identifiable points in time. Thus, there is rarely a **source document** supporting the internal transaction that would alert the system to its occurrence.

Because these internal events usually do not concern outsiders, there is no necessity to record them as they happen, and because they are constantly taking place in any business, it would be very cumbersome (and expensive) to record them in the way that we record external events. As a result, internal events are handled quite differently from external events in the accounting cycle.

Internal transactions occur but are not formally recorded during an accounting period. Instead, the cumulative effects of these continuous events are recorded at the end of the accounting period by a series of entries called **adjusting entries.** Although internal events need not be recorded as they occur, they must be properly recorded before financial statements are prepared at the end of the accounting cycle. Adjusting entries bring the books of a business up to date for the internal events not recorded during the accounting period. The adjustment process requires returning to the journal so that the internal events can be recorded, then to the ledger so that they can be posted.

Adjusting Entries and Their Types

The principles underlying adjusting entries, the internal events on which they are based, and the basic differences between these events and external events are summarized in Exhibit B-5.

The internal events recorded as adjusting entries can be categorized into four fundamental types. Exhibit B-6 gives these basic types of adjusting entries, all of which are recorded only at the end of the accounting period. Note that the need for adjusting entries arises from the use of accrual-basis accounting. If cash-basis accounting were used, adjusting entries of these types would not be necessary.

EXHIBIT B-5   External and Internal Events

	External	*Internal*
Who	Business and outsiders	Business only
When	Discrete occurrences Identified by source documents	Constantly occurring May be no source documents

Type	Debit	Credit	Example
Internal expiration of assets	Expense	Asset	Consume supplies
Accruing an expense	Expense	Liability	Accrue interest payable
Accruing a revenue	Asset	Revenue	Accrue interest receivable
Earning revenue received in advance	Liability	Revenue	Earn subscription revenue by delivering magazine

Adjusted Trial Balance

Step 4 of the accounting cycle (adjusting entries) represents the first in a series of end-of-period procedures that every business must go through. After all adjusting entries have been made, a second trial balance is usually prepared. This internal statement, called an **adjusted trial balance,** is more complete than the trial balance prepared earlier in the cycle because it includes all events (external and internal) that have occurred during the period. This adjusted trial balance concludes the summarization phase of activities.

Closing Entries

Financial statements, as discussed in Appendix A, are the output of the accounting system. They convey meaningful financial information about a business to external parties who may be interested. However, these statements are not the final step in the accounting cycle. When the communication function is fulfilled by preparation and dissemination of the income statement, retained earnings statement, and balance sheet, all that remains at the end of the accounting period is a housekeeping step called closing the books. This last step in the cycle is designed to prepare the accounts of the business for the new accounting period and to begin again the transaction processing cycle. To do this, it is necessary to return to the journal to record a series of special entries called **closing entries.** When these entries are posted to the ledger, the accounting cycle for a period is complete.

Closing entries are made only for the revenue and expense accounts and the dividends and retained earnings accounts. Remember that revenue and expense are **temporary accounts** created in order to measure movements in assets (and sometimes liabilities) that result from the profit-seeking activities of a business. In effect, at the beginning of each accounting period, we create revenue and expense accounts in order to keep track of the results of operations for that period. The balances in these accounts at the end of the period make up the income statement for the period, with retained earnings eventually increasing by the amount of net income and decreasing by the amount of dividends. When a new period starts, the revenue and expense accounts will have to start out again at a zero balance so that profit-seeking information for the new period can be collected. The accounting system must collect separate operating results each period because it cannot carry operating information from one period over to the next or the financial statements for each period would be useless. (Contrast this to the **permanent accounts** of the balance sheet which carry cumulative balances from period to period.) The closing process, then, is designed to accomplish two goals:

1. Closing entries result in the zeroing-out of the balances in all revenue and expense accounts of the period just completed. The accounting system will then begin again at zero to measure operations for the new period.
2. Closing entries transfer the difference between revenue and expense (net income) to retained earnings and transfer the balance in the dividends account to retained earnings as well.

You have now reviewed the basic ideas underlying a manual accounting system. The next section will add some necessary further practical refinements to the accounting system.

SUBSIDIARY LEDGERS AND SPECIAL JOURNALS

This section presents techniques designed specifically for the efficient mass manual processing of transactions and will complete your review of how manual accounting systems work. We will then illustrate a manual accounting system with a comprehensive example that will pull together Appendix A and this appendix.

Concept and Use of Subsidiary Ledgers

The accounting cycle may use T-accounts or some other account form in a ledger to represent (among other accounts) accounts receivable and accounts payable. That is, there will be one account for all amounts owed to the business and one account for all amounts owed by the business. For balance sheet purposes, this is adequate because all we need to know about receivables and payables is the total asset (receivable) and total liability (payable) existing at the balance sheet date. However, the managers of a business, its customers, and its suppliers require much more information about receivables and payables. Specifically, management must

1. Know the exact amount owed to the business by each customer.
2. Know when a specific customer has reached his limit of credit.
3. Be able to give specific customers credit for payments made.
4. For control purposes, have a general history of the purchase and payments patterns of each customer.

In addition, any business would need to know exact amounts owed to each individual supplier so that purchases can be monitored and payments made on time.

It is clearly not possible to get all this information from one account representing total receivables and another showing total payables. Even a business with only a few customers and suppliers needs some supplementary breakdown of aggregate amounts owed to (accounts receivable) and owed by (accounts payable) the business. This breakdown must be by individual customer and supplier. As a business gets larger, say, 100 or so customers and 15 or 20 suppliers, some mechanical technique for keeping track of the exact individual amounts owed to and owed by the business becomes necessary. The technique used by accounting systems for this purpose is the **subsidiary ledger.** Among other advantages, the use of subsidiary ledgers prevents the general ledger from becoming too cumbersome and unwieldy by placing detailed information on individual customers and vendors outside of the general ledger.

The General Ledger/Subsidiary Ledger Relationship

Subsidiary ledgers provide a detailed breakdown of the information that appears in certain general ledger accounts. The subsidiary ledger idea can be applied to any general ledger account; however, the need for this kind of detailed information is most critical in the area of receivables and payables.

Exhibit B-7 illustrates the general and subsidiary ledger relationship for accounts receivable using sample data. Notice that the sum of figures in the subsidiary ledger equals the total given in the general ledger account. Both the general ledger account and the subsidiary ledger accounts present the same accounts receivable information, but from a different point of view. It is always true that the information in the subsidiary ledger is simply a breakdown of the amounts in the general ledger account (in this case accounts receivable) and is based on the same transactions as the general ledger account. Because of this, general ledger accounts for which a business keeps this additional, detailed subsidiary information are called **control accounts.** Accounts receivable and accounts payable are usually control accounts for any business.

Exhibit B-8 presents this same type of general and subsidiary ledger relationship for accounts payable. Individual supplier balances have been assumed for illustrative purposes. The same process could be used if business management decided that additional subsidiary information on inventory, plant and equipment, or any other asset, liability, owners' equity, revenue, or expense would be useful for decision-making or control purposes. The basis for such subsidiary ledgers might be different items of inventory, types of plant and equipment, or any other categorization that could provide management with needed (or desired) information.

The subsidiary ledgers presented in Exhibits B-7 and B-8 are in the familiar T-account form for illustrative purposes. In most manual accounting systems these subsidiary ledgers might be of a running balance form (illustrated in the comprehensive example given in the next section) and could appear on a file card or a notebook sheet. Also, the subsidiary ledgers would contain much more detailed information about each customer or supplier.

EXHIBIT B-7   Accounts Receivable Subsidiary Ledger

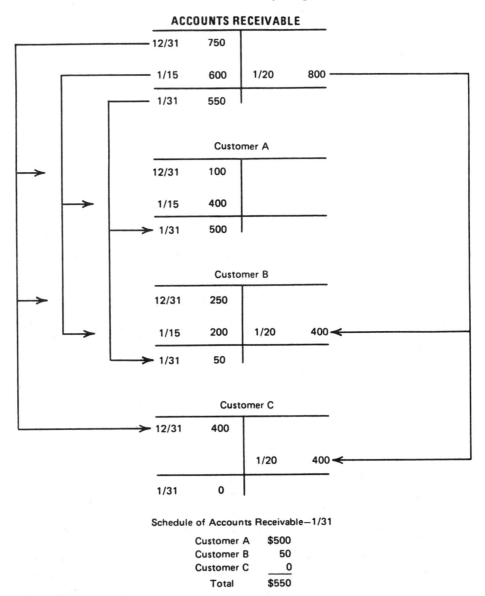

ACCOUNTS RECEIVABLE

12/31	750		
1/15	600	1/20	800
1/31	550		

Customer A

12/31	100	
1/15	400	
1/31	500	

Customer B

12/31	250		
1/15	200	1/20	400
1/31	50		

Customer C

12/31	400		
		1/20	400
1/31	0		

Schedule of Accounts Receivable—1/31

Customer A	$500
Customer B	50
Customer C	0
Total	$550

Purpose of Special Journals

Our discussions of the accounting cycle in the first section indicated that all accounting transactions are first journalized as a way of recording the event before it is forgotten or its supporting documents lost. At that time, the general journal was presented and its form illustrated. For the purpose of understanding the basic flow of data in a manual accounting system, the general journal is both necessary and sufficient. However, it is not the only journal used to record transactions in an accounting system and may actually be the least used journal in terms of the volume of transactions recorded.

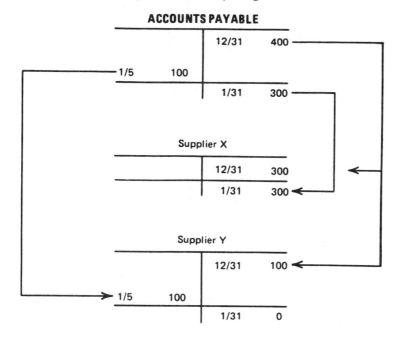

ACCOUNTS PAYABLE

	12/31	400
1/5	100	
	1/31	300

Supplier X

| | 12/31 | 300 |
| | 1/31 | 300 |

Supplier Y

	12/31	100
1/5	100	
	1/31	0

Schedule of Accounts Payable—1/31

Supplier X	$300
Supplier Y	0
Total	$300

Most businesses use a number of other journals that are called as a group, **special journals.** It would be usual to find four such special journals in an accounting system—**sales journal, purchases journal, cash receipts journal,** and **cash disbursements journal**—in addition to the general journal.

To understand why these special journals are necessary, consider the recording problems of a business. Although the actual number of events occurring each day might be quite large, most of these represent the same kinds of events happening over and over again. The possible different types of transactions in which businesses may engage is almost limitless, but, in fact, in most businesses only a few types of transactions account for most of the activities. A significant problem is how to process these repetitive transactions efficiently in a manner that makes posting and financial statement preparation easier. Special journals solve this problem.

Basically, businesses engage in four major types of transactions repeatedly.

1. Selling goods to customers. Sales may be made for cash or on credit, and this is usually the most frequent event for any business.
2. Purchasing goods from suppliers. Purchases may also be made for cash or on credit. However, most businesses purchase in larger quantities (and consequently less often) than they sell.

3. Receiving cash. Cash inflows frequently result from cash sales or collections of receivables, although other types of events may also give rise to the receipt of cash.

4. Disbursing cash. Cash outflows for the purchase of goods and payment of accounts payable are most frequent, although other types of payments may also occur.

Businesses do engage in other than the preceding types of transactions; however, if you think about normal business activity, it becomes apparent that the purchase-sell-collect-pay sequence accounts for most of the transactions. In recognition of this, manual accounting systems typically use one specialized journal for each of these constantly recurring transactions. Since each of these special journals is designed to record one basic type of transaction, each journal makes possible more efficient and accurate processing of that transaction than would be the case in the general journal. That is the idea behind special journals.

Types of Special Journals

Reflecting the four most frequently occurring types of transactions just described, a typical manual accounting system would usually include a sales, purchases, cash receipts, and cash disbursements journal in addition to the general journal.

Sales Journal. The sales journal records only one type of event—the credit sale of merchandise to customers—and that event affects only two different general ledger accounts (accounts receivable and sales revenue).

Purchases Journal. The purchases journal is usually reserved for the credit purchases of merchandise for resale (inventory) and supplies, although the journal could be designed to record the credit purchase of any asset. Since many different types of credit purchases may be recorded and several general ledger accounts are affected, this journal is somewhat more complex than the sales journal.

Cash Receipts Journal. All receipts of cash, no matter what the source, should be entered in the cash receipts journal. As a result, a number of general ledger accounts may be affected by the transactions recorded here. Although a cash sale represents both a sale and a cash receipt, cash sales are recorded in the cash receipts journal (rather than the sales journal) in most accounting systems. Reasons for this treatment have to do primarily with the control of cash by keeping all cash receipts recorded together in one place.

Cash Disbursements Journal. All disbursements of cash, no matter what the reason, should be recorded in the cash disbursements journal; thus, potentially, many general ledger accounts could be affected. Cash purchases of merchandise or supplies are recorded in the cash disbursements journal rather than the purchases journal, again for more effective control of cash by keeping all cash disbursements recorded together in one place.

CONCEPT SUMMARY

Special Journals and Subsidiary Ledgers

Special Journals and Their Use

Type of Journal	Transactions Recorded	Specific Account Columns	Other Account Columns	Organization
Sales	All credit sales	Customer account, amount	No	Date of transaction
Purchases	All credit purchases	Inventory, supplies, accounts payable	Yes	Date of transaction
Cash receipts	All receipts of cash	Cash, accounts receivable, sales	Yes	Date of transaction
Cash disbursements	All disbursements of cash	Accounts payable, wage expense, inventory, cash	Yes	Date of transaction
General	All events not recorded in special journals	No	No	Date of transaction

Typical General Ledger Control Accounts

Control Accounts	Information in Control Account	Basis of Organization of Subsidiary Ledger	Information in Subsidiary Ledger
Accounts receivable	Total amounts owed to the business	Customer	Amount owed by each individual customer
Accounts payable	Total amounts owed by the business	Supplier	Amount owed to each individual supplier
Inventory	Total cost of inventory on hand	Type of inventory item	Cost of each type of inventory item on hand
Furniture and fixtures	Total cost of furniture and fixtures on hand	Type of furniture and fixture	Cost of each type of furniture and fixture on hand
Capital stock	Total direct investment by stockholders	Stockholder	Direct investment by each individual stockholder

General Journal. Although the general journal design is capable of handling all types of transactions, its format is somewhat cumbersome. Therefore, most manual accounting systems use the general journal to record only those transactions which do not fit into one of the special journals described. Thus, you might think of the general journal as the "journal of last resort." If a transaction (or part of a transaction) is of the type covered by one of the special journals, it should be recorded in that journal in its entirety. Remember that every event is journalized only once in only one journal, and no event would ever be divided and entered into more than one journal.

The exact format and design of the journals discussed in this section depends on the particular accounts affected by the purchase-sell-collect-pay transactions of a given business; therefore, the actual journals may differ somewhat from business to business. Nevertheless, the concepts underlying these special journals are fairly constant and standard across businesses.

COMPREHENSIVE ACCOUNTING SYSTEM EXAMPLE

We have discussed the basic concepts and relationships underlying manual accounting systems, the series of steps necessary to make the accounting system operational, and certain recording refinements which must be understood and used if manual systems are to work in the real world. We will now solidify this material with an example illustrating the major concepts and mechanics discussed in Appendix A and this appendix.

Company Information and Transactions

Two recent college graduates decide to open a sporting goods store devoted exclusively to selling ice hockey equipment. They feel that their chances of success are good since they will have the only ice hockey equipment store in all of Miami Beach, Florida. The store, called Puck & Stick, Inc., opened on June 1, 199X. The following transactions occurred during June:

June 1	Each owner deposited $10,000 of personal funds into a business bank account and received 1,000 shares of company stock each in exchange.
4	Hockey merchandise was ordered and delivered from Puck & Sons. The invoice cost was $3,000, and a freight cost of $100 was added to that amount. The terms of the purchase are 2/10, n/30. Display equipment was purchased from A-1 Suppliers on 90-day credit terms for $2,400, and a company car was purchased for $4,500 with a $500 (Check No. 1) down payment and a bank loan for the remainder. Utilities were turned on and a deposit of $100 (Check No. 2) was paid. This deposit will be returned after one year if all bills are paid on time.
8	Hockey equipment in the amount of $500 was sold to the Bahama Flashers hockey team on credit. Invoice No. 1 was used.
12	Purchased $500 of hockey sticks from Crooked Stix, Inc., for cash with Check No. 3.
13	Returned $100 worth of defective pucks from the June 4 purchase from Puck & Sons and was given credit against the amount owed.

14	Mailed Check No. 4 to Puck & Sons for the amount due less the appropriate discount.
15	Cash sales for the first half of the month were $2,500.
18	Additional purchases of merchandise from Crooked Stix, Inc., for $4,000 were made on credit terms of 2/15, n/30.
20	Sold to the Equator Eskimos $2,800 of merchandise on credit using Invoice No. 2.
21	Supplies costing $200 were purchased on credit from B-2 Suppliers.
25	Received a check from the Bahama Flashers settling its account in full.
28	Received a check from the Equator Eskimos for $2,300.
29	Paid salaries of $500 (Checks No. 5 and No. 6) to each of the owners. Amounts withheld for each were as follows: $50 for federal income taxes, $10 for state income taxes, and $30 for social security. In addition to matching Social Security, the company contributed $40 per month for each owner to an insurance plan (Check No. 7).
30	Cash sales for the last half of the month were $3,000.

The following additional information about the business is available:

1. The display equipment is expected to last ten years and the company car three years. Both are expected to be worthless at the end of their useful lives. Straight-line depreciation is used by the company.

2. Interest on the bank loan accrues at the rate of 1 percent of the unpaid loan balance at the end of each month.

3. An interest charge of 1 percent is added to all customer amounts owed to Puck & Stick, Inc., that remain unpaid as of the end of the month.

4. A physical count of inventory reveals that $350 of merchandise is still on hand at June 30.

Puck & Stick, Inc., uses sales, purchases, cash receipts, and cash disbursements journals as well as a general journal in its manual accounting system. The business also maintains subsidiary ledgers for receivables and payables. It is the intention of the owners to adjust and close the accounts and to prepare financial statements on a monthly basis.

Chart of Accounts

The **chart of accounts** for Puck & Stick follows. The chart of accounts provides guidelines for the journalizing of all transactions in the accounting system by giving the specific asset, liability, owners' equity, revenue, and expense account titles and numbers to be used (debited and credited) in the recording of transactions.

Account Title	*Account Number*
Cash	1
Accounts receivable	5
Inventory	10
Purchases	11
Freight-in	12
Purchase returns	13
Purchase discounts	14

(continues)

Account Title	Account Number
Supplies	20
Equipment	25
Accumulated depreciation—equipment	26
Car	30
Accumulated depreciation—car	31
Accounts payable	51
Federal withholding payable	55
State withholding payable	56
Social Security payable	57
Bank loan payable	60
Interest payable	61
Capital stock	101
Retained earnings	105
Sales revenue	125
Interest revenue	130
Cost of goods sold	151
Salary expense	155
Payroll taxes	156
Insurance expense	157
Advertising expense	165
Depreciation expense	170
Interest expense	175
Income summary	199

You may add any new accounts you feel are necessary to properly reflect the month's transactions.

Requirements

You should accomplish the following for Puck & Stick, Inc., for the month of June 199X.

1. Journalize all transactions for the month in the proper special and general journals.
2. Post all journal amounts to the appropriate general and subsidiary ledgers at the end of the month.
3. Adjust the accounts (journalize and post adjusting entries).
4. Prepare financial statements.
5. Close the accounts.

It would be most beneficial for you to work through all of the month's transactions and actually complete the five requirements before looking at the solution that follows. Otherwise, you will not derive the maximum benefit from this example of a manual accounting system at work.

Solution

Exhibits B-9 through B-13 (pages 685–688) give the special and general journals for Puck & Stick, Inc., for the month. Exhibit B-14 (pages 689–690) gives the general ledger for the business with the ledger accounts in abbreviated form. Exhibits B-15 and B-16 (pages 691 and 692) are the subsidiary ledgers for re-

Puck & Stick, Inc., Sales Journal   Page 1

Date		Source Document #	Customer Account	PR	Amount
199X June	8	101	Bahama Flashers	√	500
	20	102	Equator Eskimos	√	2,800
	30		Balance	(5/125)	3,300

ceivables and payables. The accounts receivable and accounts payable subsidiary ledgers presented in this example are of the running balance form and are more realistic in information content than those discussed earlier in this appendix. Note also that the adjusting and closing entries for the month appear in the general journal and are posted to the general ledger.

Finally, the income statement, retained earnings statement, and balance sheet for Puck & Stick were presented as illustrations in Exhibit A-1 of Appendix A and can be reviewed there (page 648). The statement of cash flows has been omitted.

VOUCHER SYSTEM

An additional standard refinement to manual accounting systems sometimes used is the **voucher system.** This approach uses a voucher register and check register to replace the purchases journal, the cash disbursements journal, and the accounts payable subsidiary ledger. The approach is built around the **voucher,** which is a document that must be filled out and approved before any cash disbursement can be made.

Use of Vouchers

All vouchers are prenumbered to ensure that the documents are accounted for. When a purchase occurs and an amount is owed to a creditor or supplier, the next consecutive voucher is filled out. After the voucher has been completed, it is recorded in the **voucher register.** Exhibit B-17 on page 693 gives an example of a voucher register using the Puck & Stick example just completed. The voucher is then filed in the **unpaid vouchers file** by due date, so that it is immediately clear which bills are due, when, and in what order. When the voucher is approved for payment, a check is drawn and recorded in the **check register.** Exhibit B-18 on page 694 gives an example of a check register for Puck & Stick. Since the check is tied to a specific voucher, an entry is made in the voucher register payment columns to indicate that the voucher has now been paid. After the payment has been made, it is noted on the voucher, and the document is then filed by voucher number in the paid vouchers file.

EXHIBIT B-10 Purchases Journal

Puck & Stick, Inc., Purchases Journal

Date	Supplier Account	PR	Accounts Payable	DEBITS Purchases	DEBITS Freight-in	DEBITS Supplies	DEBITS Account	DEBITS PR	DEBITS Amount
199X June									
4	Puck & Sons	✓	3,100	3,000	100		Equipment	25	2,400
4	A-1	✓	2,400						
18	Crooked Stix	✓	4,000	4,000					
21	B-2	✓	200			200			
30	Balance	—	9,700 (51)	7,000 (11)	100 (12)	200 (20)	—	—	2,400

EXHIBIT B-11 Cash Receipts Journal

Puck & Stick, Inc., Cash Receipts Journal

Date	Explanation	Debit Cash	CREDITS Sales	Acc. Receivable PR	Acc. Receivable Amount	OTHER ACCOUNTS Account	OTHER ACCOUNTS PR	OTHER ACCOUNTS Debit	OTHER ACCOUNTS Credit
199X June									
1	Owner investment	20,000				Capital Stock	101		20,000
15	Cash sales 1–15	2,500	2,500						
25	Bahama Flashers	500		✓	500				
28	Equator Eskimos	2,300		✓	2,300				
30	Cash sales 16–30	3,000	3,000						
30	Balance	28,300 (1)	5,500 (125)	—	2,800 (5)	—	—	—	20,000

EXHIBIT B-12 Cash Disbursements Journal

Puck & Stick, Inc., Cash Disbursements Journal

Date	Check #	Explanation	Credit Cash	DEBITS Acc. Payable PR	DEBITS Acc. Payable Amount	DEBITS Salary Expense	DEBITS Purchase Discounts	CREDITS Fed. W/ Payable	CREDITS Soc Sec Payable	CREDITS St. W/ Payable	OTHER ACCOUNTS Account	OTHER ACCOUNTS PR	OTHER ACCOUNTS Debit	OTHER ACCOUNTS Credit
199X June														
4	1	Car Purchase	500								Car	30	4,500	
											Bank Loan Payable	60		4,000
4	2	Deposit	100								Rec. from			
12	3	Crooked Stix	500								Utilities	8	100	
14	4	Puck & Sons	2,940	✓	3,000		60				Purchases	11	500	
29	5	Payroll	410			500		50	30	10				
29	6	Payroll	410			500		50	30	10	Insurance Expense	157	80	
29	7	Insurance	80											
30		Balance	4,940 (1)	—	3,000 (51)	1,000 (155)	60 (14)	100 (55)	60 (57)	20 (56)	—		5,180	4,000

EXHIBIT B-13   General Journal

Puck & Stick, Inc., General Journal   Page 1

Date			Transaction Accounts	PR	Debit Amount	Credit Amount
199X June						
	13		Accounts Payable—			
			Puck & Sons	51/√	100	
			Purchase returns	13		100
	29		Payroll taxes	156	60	
			Social Security payable	57		60
			Adjusting entries			
	30		Depreciation expense	170	145	
			Accumulated depreciation— equipment	26		20
			Accumulated depreciation— car	31		125
	30		Interest expense	175	40	
			Interest payable	61		40
	30		Accounts receivable—			
			Equator Eskimos	5/√	5	
			Interest revenue	130		5

Puck & Stick, Inc., General Journal   Page 2

Date			Transaction Accounts	PR	Debit Amount	Credit Amount
	30		Cost of goods sold	151	7,090	
			Inventory	10	350	
			Purchase returns	13	100	
			Purchase discounts	14	60	
			Purchase	11		7,500
			Freight-in	12		100
			Closing entries			
	30		Sales revenue	125	8,800	
			Interest revenue	130	5	
			Income summary	199		8,805
	30		Income summary	199	8,415	
			Cost of goods sold	151		7,090
			Salary expense	155		1,000
			Payroll taxes	156		60
			Insurance expense	157		80
			Depreciation expense	170		145
			Interest expense	175		40
	30		Income summary	199	390	
			Retained earnings	105		390

CASH #1

6/30	CR1	28,300	4,940	CD1	6/30
6/30	√	23,360			

ACCOUNTS RECEIVABLE #5

6/30	S1	3,300	2,800	CR1	6/30
6/30	J1	5			
6/30	√	505			

RECEIVABLE FROM UTILITY #8

6/4	CD1	100			
6/30	√	100			

INVENTORY #10

6/30	J2	350			
6/30	√	350			

PURCHASES #11

6/30	P1	7,000	7,500	J2	6/30
6/30	CD1	500			

FREIGHT-IN #12

6/30	P1	100	100	J2	6/30

PURCHASE RETURNS #13

6/30	J2	100	100	J1	6/30

PURCHASE DISCOUNTS #14

6/30	J2	60	60	CD1	6/30

SUPPLIES #20

6/30	P1	200			
6/30	√	200			

EQUIPMENT #25

6/4	P1	2,400			
6/30	√	2,400			

CAR #30

6/4	CD1	4,500			
6/30	√	4,500			

ACCUMULATED DEPRECIATION— EQUIPMENT #26

			20	J1	6/30
			20	√	6/30

ACCUMULATED DEPRECIATION—CAR #31

			125	J1	6/30
			125	√	6/30

ACCOUNTS PAYABLE #51

6/13	J1	100	9,700	P1	6/30
6/30	CD1	3,000			
			6,600	√	6/30

FEDERAL WITHHOLDING PAYABLE #55

			100	CD1	6/30
			100	√	6/30

STATE WITHHOLDING PAYABLE #56

			20	CD1	6/30
			20	√	6/30

SOCIAL SECURITY PAYABLE # 57

			60	J1	6/29
			60	CD1	6/30
			120	√	6/30

BANK LOAN PAYABLE #60

			4,000	CD1	6/4
			4,000	√	6/30

INTEREST PAYABLE #61

			40	J1	6/30
			40	√	6/30

CAPITAL STOCK #101

			20,000	CR1	6/1
			20,000	√	6/30

EXHIBIT B-14   General Ledger (continued)

RETAINED EARNINGS #105					SALES REVENUE #125					
		390	J2	6/30	6/30	J2	8,800	3,300	S1	6/30
								5,500	CR1	6/30
		390	√	6/30						

INTEREST REVENUE #130						COST OF GOODS SOLD #151				
6/30	J2		5	5	J1	6/30	6/30	J2	7,090	7 090	J2	6/30

SALARY EXPENSE #155						PAYROLL TAXES #156				
6/30	CD1	1,000	1,000	J2	6/30	6/29	J1	60	60	J2	6/30

INSURANCE EXPENSE #157						ADVERTISING EXPENSE #165			
6/29	CD1	80	80	J2	6/30				

DEPRECIATION EXPENSE #170						INTEREST EXPENSE #175				
6/30	J1	145	145	J2	6/30	6/30	J1	40	40	J2	6/30

INCOME SUMMARY #199						
6/30	J2	8,415	8,805	J2	6/30
6/30	J2	390			

The voucher register identifies which vouchers are not yet paid, namely, those with blank payment columns. At the end of an accounting period a list can be prepared of all unpaid vouchers representing the total amount owed at that date. Exhibit B-19 on page 694 gives an example of such a listing for Puck & Stick. The voucher register and check register thus replace the purchases journal, the cash disbursements journal, and the accounts payable subsidiary ledger, when this approach is used.

Posting

The posting from the voucher register and the check register to the general ledger takes place in the same manner as posting from any special journal and the remainder of the accounting cycle occurs in the normal way. Adjusting entries and closing entries are unaffected by the addition of a voucher system, and financial statements are the same. For clarity, it is customary to use the title Accounts Payable instead of Vouchers Payable in published financial statements even if the voucher system is used.

Bahama Flashers #A/R-1

		Street Address City, State Zip Code		Credit Limit - $XXX		
Date		*Transactions*	*Debit*	*Credit*	*Balance*
199X					0
June	8	Credit sale - S1	500		500
	25	Cash receipt - CR1		500	0

Equator Eskimos #A/R - 2

		Street Address City, State Zip Code		Credit Limit - $XXX		
Date		*Transactions*	*Debit*	*Credit*	*Balance*
199X					0
June	20	Credit sale - S1	2,800		2,800
	28	Cash receipt - CR1		2,300	500
	30	Interest - J1	5		505

Replacement of Accounts Payable Subsidiary Ledger.   Notice that the accounts payable subsidiary ledger is completely eliminated under the voucher system. A detailed breakdown of the amounts due suppliers is given by the schedule of vouchers payable. Such a schedule for Puck & Stick is given in Exhibit B-19. Note that the following three amounts must be in agreement:

1. The total of the schedule of vouchers payable.
2. The balance of the vouchers payable account in the general ledger.
3. The total of the vouchers in the unpaid vouchers file.

The amount in this case, $6,600, is the balance for accounts payable.

It is important to realize that the voucher system may not communicate directly the total amount owed individual suppliers. A company may very well have more than one voucher for the same supplier, since purchases from that supplier could have occurred at various times and have different due dates. The total owed that supplier would then not be available directly from the voucher system.

Invoice Register

It is not always necessary to go to the formality of creating a complete voucher system. Purchase invoices from suppliers are generally physically large documents. It is possible to assign such invoices a consecutive number as they

EXHIBIT B-16   **Accounts Payable Subsidiary Ledger**

Puck & Sons #A/P - 1

	Street Address City, State Zip Code		Terms: 2/10, n/30		
Date		*Transactions*	*Debit*	*Credit*	*Balance*
199X					0
June	4	Credit purchase - P1		3,100	3,100
	13	Return goods - J1	100		3,000
	14	Cash payment - CD1	3,000		0

Crooked Stix, Inc. #A/P - 2

	Street Address City, State Zip Code		Terms: 2/15, n/30		
Date		*Transactions*	*Debit*	*Credit*	*Balance*
199X					0
June	18	Credit Purchase - P1		4,000	4,000

A-1 #A/P - 3

	Street Address City, State Zip Code		Terms: 90 day		
Date		*Transactions*	*Debit*	*Credit*	*Balance*
199X					0
June	4	Equipment - P1		2,400	2,400

B-2 #A/P - 4

	Street Address City, State Zip Code		Terms:		
Date		*Transactions*	*Debit*	*Credit*	*Balance*
199X					0
June	21	Supplies - P1		200	200

EXHIBIT B-17 Voucher Register

Voucher No.	Date	Payee	Payment Date	Payment Check Number	Vouchers Payable CR	Fed W/H Payable CR	Soc. Sec. Payable CR	St. W/H Payable CR	Salary Expense DR	Purchases DR	Freight-in DR	Supplies DR	Other Accounts Account	PR	DR	CR
101	199X June 4	Puck & Sons	199X see voucher 106		3100					3000	100					
102	4	A-1 Suppliers	June 4	1	2400								Equipment	25	2400	
103	4	Lemon Motors	4		500								Car	30	4500	
													Bank loan	60		4000
104	4	Miami Utility	4	2	100								Rec. Utility	8	100	
105	12	Crooked Stix, Inc.	12	3	500					500						
106	13	Puck & Sons	14	4	3000								Vouchers pay.	51	3100	
													Purchase ret.	13		100
107	18	Crooked Stix, Inc.			4000					4000						
108	21	B-2 Suppliers			200							200				
109	29	Joe Puck	29	5	410	50	30	10	500							
110	29	Ralph Stick	29	6	410	50	30	10	500							
111	29	Insurance Co.	29	7	80								Ins. expense	157	80	
					14700 (51)	100 (55)	60 (57)	20 (56)	1000 (155)	7500 (11)	100 (12)	200 (20)			10180	4100

EXHIBIT B-18   Check Register

Date	Check Number	Payee	Voucher Number	Vouchers Payable DR	Purchase Discounts CR	Cash CR
199X						
June 4	1	Lemon Motors	103	500		500
4	2	Miami Utility	104	100		100
12	3	Crooked Stix	105	500		500
14	4	Puck & Sons	106	3000	60	2940
29	5	Joe Puck	109	410		410
29	6	Ralph Stick	110	410		410
29	7	Insurance Co.	111	80		80
				5000	60	4940
				(51)	(14)	(1)

EXHIBIT B-19   Schedule of Vouchers Payable

Number	Payee	Amount
102	A-1 Suppliers	$2400
107	Crooked Stix, Inc.	4000
108	B-2 Suppliers	200
		$6600

CONCEPT SUMMARY

Comparison of Standard Journals and Voucher System

Type of Transaction	WHERE RECORDED	
	Standard Journals	Voucher System
Adjusting entry / Closing entry	General journal	General journal
Credit sale	Sales journal	Sales journal
Cash receipt	Cash receipts journal	Cash receipts journal
Credit purchase	Purchases journal	Voucher register
Cash payment of amount owed	Cash disbursements journal	Voucher register and check register
Cash purchase	Cash disbursements journal	Voucher register and check register

arrive from suppliers and to make all necessary notations on the invoice itself. The assigned invoice number would necessarily be different from the vendor's own invoice number printed on the document. This approach eliminates the need for a separate complete voucher system. The voucher register is then called an **invoice register,** and the voucher number column is then replaced by an invoice number column, when this variation is used.

KEY TERMS

Accounting cycle (*p. 667*)
Adjusted trial balance (*p. 675*)
Adjusting entries (*p. 674*)
Audit trail (*p. 670*)
Cash disbursements journal (*p. 679*)
Cash receipts journal (*p. 679*)
Chart of accounts (*p. 683*)
Check register (*p. 685*)
Closing entries (*p. 675*)
Control account (*p. 677*)
Credit (*p. 668*)
Debit (*p. 668*)
Double-entry bookkeeping (*p. 668*)
End-of-period procedures (*p. 673*)
External events (*p. 673*)
General journal (*p. 670*)
Internal events (*p. 674*)
Invoice register (*p. 695*)

Journal (*p. 668*)
Ledger (*p. 668*)
Permanent accounts (*p. 676*)
Posting (*p. 671*)
Posting reference (*p. 670*)
Purchases journal (*p. 679*)
Sales journal (*p. 679*)
Source document (*p. 674*)
Special journals (*p. 679*)
Subsidiary ledger (*p. 677*)
Temporary accounts (*p. 675*)
Transaction (*p. 669*)
Trial balance (*p. 672*)
Unpaid vouchers file (*p. 685*)
Voucher (*p. 685*)
Voucher register (*p. 685*)
Voucher system (*p. 685*)

QUESTIONS

B-1. What is the difference in focus between the journal and the ledger? How does this difference affect the organization of the journal and the ledger?

B-2. Distinguish external and internal events. When and how are internal events recorded for an accounting period?

B-3. Specify the four types of adjusting entries and give an example of each.

B-4. Describe the closing entry process. Which types of accounts are always closed? Which types are never closed?

B-5. What information might the management of a company need about its receivables and payables? What accounting device is used to help provide this information?

B-6. Do the general ledger and the subsidiary ledgers present the same information for a particular account? Explain.

B-7. What is the purpose of special journals in a manual accounting system?

B-8. Identify the four major types of transactions businesses engage in and specify the special journal used to record each type of transaction.

B-9. The sales journal provides a special column for a source document number. Why is this information important? What forms might the source document take?

B-10. Why is the format of the purchases journal more elaborate than that of the sales journal?

B-11. List the primary sources of cash inflow for a business. List the primary reasons for cash outflow.

B-12. Which figures from a cash receipts journal would be posted as totals? Would any figures be posted individually from a cash receipts journal?

B-13. Which figures from a cash disbursements journal would be posted as totals? Would any figures be posted individually from a cash disbursements journal?

B-14. When are posting references recorded in manual accounting systems? Why are posting references necessary?

B-15. Which special journals and which subsidiary ledgers are replaced by a voucher system? How are credit purchases of and subsequent payments for inventory processed under the voucher approach?

B-16. What is an invoice register? What is its relationship to a voucher system?

PROBLEMS

B-17. The following accounts (which have normal balances) were taken from the records of a certain company. For each account, give the adjusting journal entry that was probably responsible for the observed change in that account balance.

Account	Trial Balance	Adjusted Trial Balance
Advances from customers	$19,000	$13,000
Prepaid insurance	6,000	4,000
Wages payable	2,000	3,500
Interest revenue	600	1,000
Accumulated depreciation	12,000	14,200
Supplies	–0–	500

B-18. The following occurred during the calendar year for the Toulouse Corporation.

a. Inventory of $72,000 was purchased and freight of $720 was paid on the purchases. Of these purchases, $1,500 of goods were returned to suppliers and discounts of 2 percent were taken as $50,000 of the amount owed to suppliers was paid. Inventory on hand at the beginning of the period was $17,000 and at the end, $32,000.

b. Supplies on hand at January 1 were $1,000. Additional supplies of $1,200 were purchased during the year for cash, and a count showed $400 of supplies left at December 31. (Note: Two assumptions are possible with respect to the original treatment of the supplies when purchased.)

c. The company borrowed $40,000 from the bank on April 1 on a 10 percent one-year note. Principal and interest are to be repaid at the due date of the note.

d. At the end of each month, a carrying charge of 1½ percent is added to all amounts owed to Toulouse by its customers. Accounts receivable at December 31 were $50,000.

e. On December 1, a major customer made a payment of $30,000 on products to be delivered over the next two months. By December 31, 40 percent of these products had been delivered and accepted.

1. Journalize the external transactions included in the descriptions given.
2. Journalize all adjusting entries that would be necessary at December 31. You should state any assumptions necessary for the determination of these adjusting entries.

B-19. Explain the term double-entry as it is used in double-entry bookkeeping. Would a single-entry system be possible? If so, give an example of a single-entry record-keeping system and explain how it might work.

B-20. Distinguish the relationship of a special journal to a general journal from the relationship of a subsidiary ledger to a general ledger. What functions do special journals and subsidiary ledgers serve in manual accounting systems? Are these devices absolutely necessary?

B-21. The concept of special journals and subsidiary ledgers can be applied to many areas in accounting other than those specifically reviewed in this appendix. Name three areas where the idea of special journals could be applied, and name three areas where the idea of subsidiary ledgers could be applied beyond those already discussed.

B-22. Appendix B presents subsidiary ledgers as T-accounts which contain detailed breakdowns of the receivables and payables general ledger control accounts to which they pertain. In fact, subsidiary ledgers may take any one of a number of possible other forms depending on the information needs of the business.

1. Describe in detail the information that should be kept on each credit customer of a small department store.
2. Describe in detail the information that should be kept on each supplier of a small department store.
3. Design and illustrate a sample accounts receivable subsidiary ledger account for one customer and a sample accounts payable subsidiary ledger account for one supplier, as they might actually appear in the records of this department store.

B-23. For the following types of businesses, name the journals that each would likely use in recording its accounting events and specify the transactions that would be recorded in each journal.

a. Doctor's office where patients pay upon leaving
b. Department store
c. Hot dog vendor
d. Doctor's office with customer billing
e. Gift shop with cash and major credit card sales only

B-24. For each of the following accounting transactions, indicate whether the transaction should be recorded in the sales journal (SJ), purchases journal (PJ), cash receipts journal (CRJ), cash disbursements journal (CDJ), or general journal (GJ). If the recording of any transaction would depend upon the design of the special journals or upon an assumption to be made, give two alternative treatments of that transaction and/or state the appropriate assumption.

   a. Cash sale
   b. Credit purchase of inventory
   c. Purchase of truck with cash down payment and note
   d. Sales return by customer
   e. Correction of incorrect posting of customer payment
   f. Credit sale
   g. Sale—25 percent cash down and balance in one month
   h. Withdrawal of cash by owner
   i. Depreciation
   j. Transfer of net income figure to retained earnings
   k. Purchase of equipment on account
   l. Purchase discount taken

B-25. The following are transactions for the Conti Company (a sole proprietorship).

   a. Carl Conti invests $10,000 in the company.
   b. Inventory of $7,500 is purchased on credit from A-1 Corporation.
   c. A $15,000 loan is made from the Left Bank on a two-year note.
   d. Equipment is purchased for $5,000 on account from P-U Suppliers.
   e. Sales of inventory costing $2,600 are made to the following customers on credit: Leroy, $3,000; Mervin, $2,200
   f. $2,500 of accounts payable is paid to A-1.
   g. $2,600 of accounts receivable is collected from Leroy.
   h. Salaries of $950 are paid to employees, Rob and Roy.
   i. Carl withdrew $1,500 for personal use.

Journalize the transactions in good general journal form.

B-26. Refer to the transactions for the Conti Company given in B-25. Journalize those transactions in good form, using a sales journal, purchases journal, cash receipts journal, cash disbursements journal, and general journal. Post these transactions to the appropriate general and subsidiary ledger accounts.

B-27. The Bienville Company, Inc., sellers of fine antiques, opened for business on March 1. The following transactions occurred during the two weeks prior to opening and the two weeks following the opening.

   a. February 15: The corporate charter was received from the state and the corporate books were opened with an investment of $25,000 in cash and $175,000 in antiques by the owner, Benny Bienville.
   b. February 15: The corporation leased a building for one year and paid $9,000 to Cats Realty for the first six months rent.
   c. February 19: Paid $100 for a telephone deposit and $50 for a utility deposit, both of which will be returned after one year of satisfactory bill payments.
   d. February 22: Paid $4,680 to Fat Harry Refinishers for cleaning and painting the building. This major overhaul was expected to last three years.

e. February 25: Paid $1,040 for a business sign and interior furnishings to Henry's Fine Signs, both of which were expected to last two years. Purchased at auction from Bids Unlimited $10,000 of antiques, to be paid for within 15 days.

f. February 27: Paid $2,500 to Big Al's Movers for moving antiques into the store and laying out the selling floor.

g. March 2: Paid $1,500 to WINE-TV for one week's ad spots. Returned to Bids Unlimited $2,000 of antiques that were in unsatisfactory condition when received.

h. March 3: By the end of the first week, the company had sold antiques with a cost of $9,500 for $19,000 as follows—Tom, $10,000; Dick, $5,000; Harry, $4,000—all on credit.

i. March 6: Supplies costing $800 were delivered by the Lo-Ball Supply Company to be paid for within 30 days. One-fourth of these supplies were used up during the first two weeks of business. Tom changed his mind about $500 worth of antiques and returned them.

j. March 9: A deposit of $5,000 was received from the Duke of Prunes on a special order of antique Louis XIII furniture to be delivered in April. Paid amount due Bids Unlimited.

k. March 10: During the second week, the company sold antiques costing $15,000 for $32,000 as follows—Bertha, $17,000; Betty, $8,000; Beulah, $7,000—all for cash.

l. March 15: Paid $1,500 in wages to employees, Peter, Paul, and Mary, for the first two weeks of operation. So far, in the third week, the company sold antiques costing $8,000 for $14,000 as follows—Tom, $4,000; Betty, $10,000—all on credit. Received checks from Tom for $3,000, Dick for $5,000, and Harry for $2,000.

1. Develop a general journal for Bienville and journalize the external transactions.

2. Post the transactions to the proper general ledger accounts.

3. Journalize and post all appropriate adjusting entries as of March 15.

4. Prepare an income statement, statement of retained earnings, and balance sheet.

5. Close the books as of March 15.

B-28. Refer to the transactions for the Bienville Corporation given in B-27. Journalize those transactions in good form using a sales journal, purchases journal, cash receipts journal, cash disbursements journal, and general journal. Post these transactions to the appropriate general and subsidiary ledger accounts. Would any changes in adjusting entries, financial statements, and closing entries result from the use of these special journals and subsidiary ledgers? If so, make any necessary changes in these steps.

B-29. Refer to the transactions for the Bienville Corporation given in B-27. Assume now that Bienville uses a voucher system. To the chart of accounts, add Vouchers Payable No. 203 and delete Accounts Payable No. 201. Set up a voucher register (begin with Voucher No. 101), a check register (number checks consecutively beginning with No. 1), a sales journal, a cash receipts journal, and a general journal. Journalize the transactions into these journals. Set up the ledger and post to the appropriate general and subsidiary ledger accounts. Journalize and post the necessary adjusting entries and prepare an adjusted trial balance. Journalize and post the closing entries. Prepare a schedule of vouchers payable. If financial statements were prepared while Bienville used the voucher system, would they differ from the financial statements in B-27?

DECISION CASE

The following information pertains to Weston's Wares, Inc.

General Ledger Account Numbers and Titles

100	Cash	230	FICA taxes payable
110	Accounts receivable (control)	240	Withholding taxes payable
111	Allow for bad debts	250	Income taxes payable
115	Accrued receivable	300	Capital stock
120	Notes receivable	350	Retained earnings
130	Inventory	399	Income summary
140	Supplies	400	Sales
160	Furniture and fixtures	405	Sales returns
161	Acc dep—F & F	410	Interest income
170	Building	500	Purchases
171	Acc dep—Building	505	Purchase returns
180	Land	510	Cost of goods sold
200	Accounts payable (control)	520	Operating expenses
210	Notes payable	530	Income tax expense
220	Accrued payable	540	Interest expense

Accounts Receivable Subsidiary Ledger

11001	Frank Churchill
11002	H. Smith
11003	Col. Campbell
11004	J. Fairfax
11005	Randall's Co.

Accounts Payable Subsidiary Ledger

20001	Cox Furniture
20002	Will Larkin's, Inc.
20003	Elton's Elegancies
20004	Bates' Bath Things
20005	*Highgate News*

March transactions are as follows:

March 1	Capital stock sold for cash, $10,000. Capital stock issued for land and building, $30,000, of which one-fifth is allocable to land. A 30-day, 8 percent note in the amount of $12,000 is given for furniture and fixtures (the vendor, Cox Furniture).
2	Supplies are bought from Woodhouse Co. for $275. Purchased merchandise on 2/10, n/30 terms from Will Larkin's, Inc., for $8,000.
3	Sold merchandise on account to H. Smith, $600.
4	Purchased merchandise on 2/10, n/30 terms from Elton's Elegancies, $7,000.

5	Sold merchandise on account to Frank Churchill, $1,000.
6	H. Smith is granted $40 sales return on the March 3 sale because of defective items.
10	Summary of cash sales for the period March 1–10: $4,202.40. (Note: In practical situations, cash sales would be summarized and recorded more often.)
11	Sold merchandise on account to Col. Campbell, $750, and received a 60-day, 6 percent note in settlement. Sold merchandise on account to Randall's Co., $750.
12	Paid Will Larkin's, Inc., the balance due them.
13	Collected balance due from H. Smith.
14	Purchased merchandise on 2/10, n/30 terms from Will Larkin's, Inc., $3,200.
15	Paid the payroll for the first half of March, $920.50, less income taxes withheld, $111.30, and FICA taxes withheld, $27.61.
16	Sold merchandise on account to J. Fairfax, $4,200.
17	Received $250 bill for advertising from *The Highgate News*.
19	Purchased merchandise from Bates' Bath Things, $900 and gave a 30-day, 6 percent note in payment.
20	Summary of cash sales for the period March 11–20: $3,799.50.
21	Collected balance due from Randall's Co.
24	Will Larkin's, Inc., granted us a $150 return on the March 14 purchase because of defects in some of the merchandise.
25	Received a bill from M. Dixon for repairs to adding machine, $30.
27	Purchased merchandise on 2/10, n/30 terms from Elton's Elegancies, $1,225.
28	Sold merchandise on account to H. Smith, $712.
30	Bought additional fixtures on 30-day open account from Cox Furniture, $1,800.
31	Summary of cash sales for period March 21–31: $3,172.20. Paid note issued on March 1 together with interest. Paid the payroll for the last half of March, $987.30, less income taxes withheld, $115.50, and FICA taxes withheld, $29.61.

Use the following adjustment data to complete your work:

a. Unused supplies at March 31 are $120.

b. The month-end inventory of merchandise is $3,600.

c. Interest was accrued on the note received on March 11 (use a 360-day year as your base).

d. Bad debt losses are expected to amount to 1 percent of accounts receivable (round to the nearest dollar).

e. The annual rates of depreciation on the building and the furniture and fixtures are 2 percent and 12 percent respectively. There is no residual value on these assets and straight-line depreciation is used.

f. Payroll taxes were accrued for the employer's matching contribution for FICA taxes.

g. Interest was accrued on the note given on March 19.

Required:

1. Design and illustrate appropriate special journals that would be used by Weston's Wares, Inc., to record its transactions.

2. Journalize the transactions for March using the general journal and the

special journals you created in part (1). Include all adjusting entries except income tax expense, but no closing entries. Balance all journals.

3. For receivables and payables, create the general ledger account and design subsidiary ledgers. Post the appropriate transactions to the general ledger control accounts and to the subsidiary ledger accounts.

4. Which other general ledger accounts might also function as control accounts? What would be the basis of organization of the subsidiary ledgers for each of these possible control accounts?

C Systems Case and Applications

Overview

Description of a business and application of the system development process to that business to make the discussion of the text more concrete.

Learning Objectives

Thorough study of this appendix will enable you to:

1. Analyze an accounting system.
2. Develop a statement of objectives.
3. Acquire a computer system appropriate for a company's needs.
4. Design a new accounting system.
5. Apply the basic techniques of project management to system development.

Outline

Systems Case

System Analysis

Statement of Objectives

Computer Acquisition

System Design

Project Management of System Development

How to Write Clearly

Clear Writing: Some Do's

DO: 1. Tell your audience what you are going to talk about; 2. Talk about it, and 3. Tell them what you talked about. This old saying is as valid as ever. Not observing it is a common failing of much technical writing today.

DO: Include a *theme sentence* near the beginning of your writing that concisely sums up what you want to say in the piece.

DO: Tell your story in miniature in the figures, photos, tables, listings, and other illustrations. Your readers may not have time to read all of your report; give them a quick summary and they will thank you for it.

DO: Spell out acronyms and abbreviations when they first appear in text. How many times have you been stopped cold by an unfamiliar abbreviation in the middle of an interesting article?

DO: Use verbs. Avoid adjectives and adverbs. A verb in a title can add a lot of spice. Adjectives and adverbs are the spinach of technical prose. Everybody says they are vital, but few of us would miss them if the majority of them suddenly disappeared tomorrow.

DO: Break up your text into digestible chunks with subheadings.

DO: Remember the questions you had when you were first learning a subject.

DO: Look for the most common word wasters: *windy phrases*.

Windy phrases	Cut to
At the present time	Now
In the event of	If
In the majority of instances	Usually

Clear Writing: Some Don'ts

DON'T: Use the passive voice as your primary voice. Many of us were taught to use the passive voice when writing technical reports and the like. But the passive voice lends an air of coldness and formality to writing—the sort of thing you would expect in technical transactions, but not in an article that is designed to be *read*. For example, "I ran the program" is more personal than "The program was run."

DON'T: Make your reader search for information in an article. If you have a list of items in text, perhaps they could be set off in a table. If you have a glossary in your article, tell the reader at the beginning.

DON'T: Use big words when small words will do. A good example is *utilize*, a word that can almost always be replaced with *use*. Another popular word that should be avoided is *implement*. Don't implement when you can *install, design,* or *operate*; your readers will have a better idea of what you are doing.

DON'T: Use a clever title if it fails to convey the content. Imagine that your title is all that the reader has to go on in deciding whether or not to read your work.

DON'T: Use *it* or other pronouns if the meaning is obscured. Vague pronoun references in an article slow the reader down. What does the *it* mean?

DON'T: Use positive/negative sections from which you can cut the negative: *See how we did it here: "The answer ~~does not rest with carelessness or incompetence. It lies largely in~~* [is] *having enough people to do the job."*

SOURCE: Reprinted with permission from the December 1980 issue of *Byte* magazine. Copyright © by McGraw-Hill, Inc., New York 10020. All rights reserved.

This appendix introduces a sample company to illustrate the basic accounting system and to serve as an application for many of the discussions throughout the book. This sample company illustrates the many business functions (such as ordering, shipping, billing, handling of cash receipts, approval of vendor invoices, preparation of checks, and so on) that necessarily precede formal accounting activity. This appendix also reviews system analysis and demonstrates a complete system analysis report for the sample company. Learning how to document and analyze a system will also help you understand computer-based information systems since these activities must be performed in such systems as well. Computer-based system development extends naturally from this grounding in the accounting system.

SYSTEMS CASE

In November 1976, John Paul Pagoo and his wife Pamela opened the Pagoo Audio Center in New Orleans, Louisiana. The company was organized as a corporation with 2,000 shares of no-par common stock ($20 stated value), 1,200 shares of which were owned jointly by John Paul and Pamela Pagoo. The remainder of the shares were unissued. Pagoo Audio Center (hereafter PAC-1) is a retail store selling a complete line of audio equipment ranging from small and inexpensive radios to professional-level components and systems. In addition, supporting equipment such as stereo headphones, albums, compact discs (CDs), and cassettes account for a major share of PAC-1 sales volume.

So successful was PAC-1, that in June 1979, J.P. and Pamela opened a second store to sell audio equipment plus a full complement of home appliances. This new store, called Pagoo Appliance Center (hereafter PAC-2), also proved to be an immediate success primarily because of the substantial sales volume generated by sales of stoves, refrigerators and freezers, washing machines and dryers, dishwashers, air conditioners, and televisions. The Pagoos believe that the success of their stores is due to their courteous and knowledgeable staff and the friendly and efficient service for which the Pagoo Centers are known. Prices at both stores on all merchandise are competitive, but not lower than those of competing stores.

Sales and Profits

For the fiscal year ended June 30, 1992, the company showed net sales of $5,400,000 and net income of $276,000. Although audio and appliance retail trade became fiercely competitive in the past few years, both stores continued to increase sales volume at a remarkable rate. Sales per month for the remainder of this fiscal year are expected to be $180,000 to $210,000 for PAC-1 and $390,000 to $420,000 for PAC-2, with projected net income of $300,000 to $330,000 for the fiscal year. PAC-1 sales have steadily been 75 percent cash and 25 percent credit, while sales at PAC-2 have been consistently 75 percent credit and 25 percent cash. The firm has carried between 50 and 100 accounts receivable representing credit granted directly by the stores and regularly uses 15 to 20 different major suppliers of inventory items.

Company Organization

Pagoo Centers, Inc., employs 21 people including Mr. Pagoo, who acts as president and general manager of the firm. Each store is supervised by a manager and, because both stores are open from 10:00 A.M. to 10:00 P.M. six days a week, there are two shifts of employees at each location. A shift at PAC-1 consists of two salespeople, with the more senior salesperson on each shift acting as assistant manager. At PAC-2, where sales volume is greater and customers expect more attention and time, a shift requires four salespeople. Here, also, the most senior salesperson doubles as assistant manager. At both stores, the assistant manager supervises the store in the absence of the manager.

All of Pagoo's purchasing, accounting, and inventory control are centralized. A full-time buyer and a full-time accountant handle these functions. The accountant supervises a bookkeeper and an inventory stock clerk. A janitor cleans and straightens both stores from 11:00 P.M. to 7:00 A.M. on Sunday through Friday evenings.

Mr. Pagoo, the managers of PAC-1 and PAC-2, the buyer, and the accountant form what J.P. likes to call his management group. This group seems to get along quite well together and at Pagoo's insistence meet once a week, usually at lunch on Friday afternoons, to discuss company activities and plans. These meetings are very important to J.P. as a vehicle for making his feelings known to his key people and as a feedback mechanism that keeps him in touch with what is going on in the stores on a day-to-day basis. They also serve as a social event for the group. Other employees of the Pagoo Centers show great interest in what happens at these weekly meetings.

Company Operations

Pagoo Centers, Inc., maintains a manual accounting system and information flow. In addition to a general journal, the company keeps a sales journal, a purchases journal, a cash receipts journal, and a cash disbursements journal. The company uses a subsidiary ledger system for receivables and payables. The accountant's office records transactions as the various supporting documents are received, usually the day after the event occurs. Posting takes place at the end of each week. Company books are adjusted and closed and financial statements prepared for J.P. and Pamela Pagoo monthly.

Documents typically used by the firm include checks (incoming and outgoing), cash register tapes, sales slips, purchase orders, shipping reports, and debit and credit memos. The creation and flow of these documents and the roles of each of the employees in this flow is described in the paragraphs that follow.

J. P. Pagoo

J. P. Pagoo prefers assigning himself a minimum of specific duties in the firm. Since beginning his organization, he has enjoyed becoming involved in all aspects of company activities as the mood strikes him and that continues today. J.P. has always been an audio buff, however, and still feels more comfortable in this end of the business, particularly when dealing with people. He is 38 years old, and Pagoo Centers, Inc., which he started with a trust fund that he received upon graduation from college, has been his only business venture of any consequence. John Paul Pagoo delegates authority easily, expects responsible performance by his employees, and is generally well liked by those who work for him.

Because of his love for the audio and people end of the business, J.P. is probably personally closest to the firm's buyer and to the manager of PAC-1. Both are young and enjoy the complete confidence of the owner, but often accept large amounts of advice from him on how best to do their jobs.

The Buyer

The buyer is responsible for all merchandise purchases made by both stores and makes all decisions about which vendor or supplier to use. What to purchase, the timing of purchases, and reorder points are established by frequent informal discussions among the buyer, the PAC-1 manager, the PAC-2 manager, the accountant, and sometimes Pagoo. The buyer's decisions prevail on all purchasing matters. To purchase merchandise, the buyer prepares a purchase order of the type illustrated in Exhibit C-1 (page 708). The form consists of an original and three copies. The vendor gets the original, the buyer keeps one copy, and the accountant gets the other two. The buyer forwards all major purchase orders to J.P. for his approval before they are sent out.

The buyer spends a good deal of time in each store checking inventory quantities and discussing sales patterns with store managers. He makes it a practice to be present, along with the inventory stock clerk, when major shipments of merchandise arrive and often personally checks the goods and compares the shipping report accompanying the goods to his purchase order. The buyer is known around the firm and among vendors to be very careful (some even say picky) about the goods he accepts. When merchandise is deemed unacceptable for one reason or another, it is physically separated, and the buyer prepares a four-copy debit memorandum as shown in Exhibit C-2 (page 709).

The buyer retains one copy, which is forwarded to the accountant after verification by the supplier. The original is immediately forwarded to the vendor, one copy stays with the goods to be returned, and the accountant receives one copy. Some travel is required of the buyer, but he makes most purchases through catalogs and personal contacts in the industry.

The Store Managers

The two store managers have approximately the same duties, although their personal styles and approach to their jobs are quite different. The PAC-2 manager is much the elder. He was the appliance manager of a major department store and has substantial experience in appliance sales. He is much less interested in the audio equipment component of PAC-2 merchandise and feels that the people at PAC-1 are better equipped to handle this kind of product. He is also more autocratic in style than the PAC-1 manager and is considerably less

EXHIBIT C-1   Sample Company Purchase Order

PURCHASE ORDER
PAGOO CENTERS, INC.

No. _____

To: _____   Date: _____

_____

_____

_____   Shipping Instructions: _____

_____

Ship To:

_____

_____   Terms: _____

_____

Quantity	Description	Unit Price	Total

Ordered By: _____

---

close to his salespeople. Of the people in the management group, the PAC-2 manager gets along best with the accountant.

Each manager supervises his store in his own way, evaluates the performance of his salespeople, approves all customer checks and returns of merchandise, is responsible for the layout and display of merchandise, oversees the movement of goods from the stockroom to the sales floor, and occasionally waits on special customers or helps out if the store is particularly busy. Each manager must also see that all documents generated in his store are forwarded to the accountant by the day following their creation and that cash sales receipts are deposited intact in the bank twice each workday.

EXHIBIT C-2   Sample Company Debit Memorandum

```
                        DEBIT MEMORANDUM
                        PAGOO CENTERS, INC.



   Date: _____


   To:  _____

        _____

        _____

        _____

   Purchase Order No. _____
```

Quantity	Description	Unit Price	Total

```
   Returned By: _____
```

Store Documents

Documents originating in the stores include cash register tapes, some customer checks, sales slips, and credit memos. While on duty, all sales employees have access to all store cash registers. Cash registers have special keys which all salespeople press to record the quantity sold, the stock number of the item, the unit price and total price of the items, and the total amount of the sale. In addition, the salespeople must key in a code to identify the person entering the transaction for each cash sale and each cash refund made. One copy of the register tape goes to the customer as a receipt, and a second, internally stored copy automatically keeps a cumulative total of cash sales and cash refunds. Twice a day, first thing in the morning and again late in the afternoon, store managers remove these internally stored tapes from all registers, together with all cash and checks except for $300 in small bills and change. The store managers prepare bank deposit slips from the tapes and deposit intact the cash and checks from the registers into the bank. One copy of the deposit slip, together with the cash register tapes, is brought to the accountant's office twice daily.

Sales slips in three copies, as illustrated in Exhibit C-3, are prepared only for credit sales. Credit sales made on charge accounts already opened and in good standing are handled by the salesperson if the total amount of the sale is under $75. If a credit sale amounts to $75 or more, the salesperson must receive approval from the accountant's office or, if that is not possible, from the store

EXHIBIT C-3   Sample Company Sales Slip

SALES SLIP		
PAGOO CENTERS, INC.		

No. _____

Salesperson	Date / /	Store
Account No.		Approval Code
Name		Telephone No.
Address		
City	State	Zip
Delivery Instructions:		

Quantity	Stock No.	Description	Unit Price	Total

X _____

Customer Signature

manager. Lists of accounts not in good standing or over their credit limit are prepared each week by the bookkeeper and are sent to each store.

The initial credit application for all new accounts must be approved by the accountant, who also sets a credit limit set. Credit sales slips and supporting information on new account customers are collected at the store and forwarded to the accountant for credit approval before merchandise is released to the customer. All copies of approved credit sales slips are returned to the store manager, usually within one week. All copies of disapproved credit sales slips are retained by the accountant. One copy of each sales slip is given to the credit customer. The original and one copy of the sales slips are delivered to the accountant twice daily.

Pagoo Centers also accepts a major credit card for sales in both stores. For all credit card sales, the salesperson must get telephone approval from the credit card agency. The credit card customer gets one copy of the Pagoo sales slip and one copy of the credit card sales slip. The originals of both are stapled together and forwarded to the accountant. The third copies of both are sent to the credit card agency. The credit card agency charges a fee of 5 percent of the total gross credit card sales. Pagoo Centers always receives 95 percent of its credit card sales in cash from the credit card agency within four weeks of reporting the sales to the agency. Pagoo records credit card sales each week.

Credit memos must be prepared for all goods returned, either for cash or to reduce an account balance, and all returns must be approved by the store manager. If the return is for cash, the transaction appears on the cash register tape, and copies of the credit memo go to the accountant. When the return involves a reduction in the customer's account balance, one copy of the credit memo goes to the customer and one copy to the accountant. Exhibit C-4 on page 712 shows the form of a credit memo for Pagoo Centers, Inc.

The Accountant

The firm's information flow and all supporting documents eventually converge on the office of the accountant. There, each type of document is filed separately by the date of the transaction, and by customer or supplier as well if the accountant has received another copy. The accountant is very experienced in small businesses and manual accounting systems and took this job with Pagoo Centers, Inc., at the time PAC-2 was opened. He is a hard worker, but sees his current position as low pressure compared to earlier jobs. Both he and the PAC-2 manager joined the firm at the same time and are considerably older than the other three members of the management team, and they have become very close within the company and socially.

The accountant handles on a continuing basis sales slips that require initial credit approval and incoming and outgoing checks. For credit purposes, he analyzes supporting information on the customer, follows up on the information where necessary, and uses standard credit rating agencies for additional information. If credit is approved, the accountant's office notifies the store manager and returns the sales slips to the store. The sale then goes through the normal sales slip processing cycle. The accountant personally processes the monthly billings to customers and incoming checks from customers, so that the chance of an error in a customer's account is minimized.

EXHIBIT C-4   Sample Company Credit Memorandum

CREDIT MEMORANDUM
PAGOO CENTERS, INC.

No._____

Salesperson	Date / /	Store

Account No.	Approval Code
Name	Telephone No.

Address		
City	State	Zip

Quantity	Stock No.	Description	Unit Price	Total

Approved By _____

It is the policy of the accountant, with total support from J. P. Pagoo, that the firm take all available discounts on purchases. Since this had not been a common practice prior to the opening of PAC-2, the accountant views this policy as a major contribution to the company's financial health. All outgoing Pagoo Centers checks, no matter the purpose or amount, must be signed by both the accountant and J. P. Pagoo. The accountant supervises the bookkeeper, the inventory clerk, and the janitor.

The Bookkeeper

The bookkeeper records all transactions and events from the source documents that reach the accountant's office. From the buyer come purchase orders and debit memos; from the store managers come cash register tapes, sales slips, and credit memos. The bookkeeper holds one copy of each purchase order and gives one copy to the inventory stock clerk so he can match it against the shipping report when the goods arrive.

The bookkeeper records all transactions under the guidance and supervision of the accountant. She feels overworked and believes that she could do the entire accounting job alone for less money than the accountant is currently being paid. Some support has been given these feelings by the manager of PAC-1, with whom the bookkeeper has formed a relationship. At any rate, most incoming documents physically go to the bookkeeper for checking and recording. She records bank deposit slips and cash register tapes, holds them for comparison to the bank statement received each month, and then discards them if there are no discrepancies in the bank reconciliation. She reports discrepancies immediately to the accountant and holds the deposit slips and cash register tapes until the discrepancies are cleared. She also records debit memos, sales slips representing completed sales, and credit memos as received and files them by day.

The Inventory Stock Clerk

The inventory stock clerk has become something of a protégé of the buyer. The clerk carefully observes the buyer's style and technique in evaluating merchandise and, at the suggestion of the buyer, studies catalogs, product comparisons, and pricing structures. The clerk obviously admires the buyer's skill, is ambitious, and wants to learn as much as possible from his job. A primary duty of the stock clerk is to be present when all shipments of goods arrive (there is usually one shipment per week) to help the buyer check the shipment. If the shipment is accurate and merchandise is in good shape, the shipping report accompanying the goods is attached to the clerk's copy of the purchase order, and both are returned to the accountant. If inaccuracies or damaged goods materialize, the buyer prepares debit memos.

The clerk also keeps order in the stockrooms, which are located in the rear of each store, and helps move inventory onto the sales floor at the direction of the store managers. Occasionally, the clerk moves goods from one store location to the other, or picks up specially shipped goods from nearby locations. The buyer has come to appreciate the clerk's energy and abilities and makes considerable informal use of his familiarity with the inventory of both stores.

Payroll

The work force at Pagoo Centers, Inc., has been very stable over the years primarily because the employees feel that they are well paid and that J.P. and the other management people are fair and evenhanded. J. P. Pagoo in the past fiscal year took a salary of $150,000 for himself; the buyer, managers, and accountant are paid $60,000 each per year; and the bookkeeper, stock clerk, and janitor earn $2,400, $1,800, and $1,500 per month, respectively, for 40-, 40-, and 48-hour workweeks. Salespeople at each store average $3,600 per month, and assistant managers average $4,200 per month on a compensation plan that includes a small base salary ($600 for salespeople and $1,200 for assistant managers) and a commission on sales. The accountant and the book-keeper manually calculate amounts due to salespeople by analyzing their individual sales totals. The accountant handles the entire payroll and issues paychecks to all employees.

The Secretary

The newest employee in the firm is a secretary hired by J. P. Pagoo to handle the typing of all company correspondence including company checks, purchase orders, and debit memos. In addition, she files all company documents, opens mail, and tends to various other office duties. It is clear to everyone in the firm that the secretary works directly for J.P. and she will do no typing for anyone else. She earns $1,800 per month for 40 hours' work each week.

Future Outlook

Pagoo Centers, Inc., has grown so rapidly during the past several years that J.P. has become concerned about the ability of the firm's current organizational structure and manual accounting system to serve the needs of the company. As of July 1992, certain operational and control problems began to surface which seemed to threaten the success of the company. An overall review of the basic structure, information and document flow, and accounting system used by the firm appears to be in order.

SYSTEM ANALYSIS

This discussion will apply the general concepts of system analysis to Pagoo Centers, Inc. Many people believe that system analysis is necessarily related to the computer and computer systems, but this is a misconception. System analysis is a necessary first step in the development of computer-based systems. However, system analysis can also be used effectively in any system. Therefore, in this section we will present a system analysis for a manual system so that we can focus our understanding on the basic system analysis concepts. Later, we will use system analysis in the context of the computer and computer-based systems.

Before you read the system analysis for Pagoo Centers, Inc., sketch out the material that you would include in each section of the report if you were preparing it. You can then compare your thoughts to the system analysis that follows on pages 715–738.

System Analysis

Pagoo Centers, Inc.

Friendly & Wise
Certified Public Accountants
September, 1992

FRIENDLY & WISE
CERTIFIED PUBLIC ACCOUNTANTS
1000 Bourbon Street
New Orleans, Louisiana 70100

September 14, 1992

Mr. John Paul Pagoo, President
Pagoo Centers, Inc.
1000 Canal Street
New Orleans, Louisiana 70100

Dear John Paul:

We have completed our engagement to prepare an analysis of your firm's accounting system. The results of our work are included in the attached report.

The primary objective of our engagement was to determine whether your accounting system should be improved to deal with your recent problems and to handle your expected future growth. We have made a number of recommendations that we believe are realistic and will meet the information and control needs of management.

The secondary objective was to involve management more deeply in the operation of the accounting system. We feel that this objective has been accomplished. There is now a general appreciation of the importance of good accounting controls and the assistance accounting reports can provide management.

Thank you for the opportunity to conduct this study. We believe our analysis has provided your company with a means of improving its operating efficiency. Thanks also to each employee of your company who participated in this study.

Very truly yours,

FRIENDLY & WISE

Jack R. Friendly

Jack R. Friendly

JRF/ms

CONTENTS

System Analysis
Pagoo Centers, Inc.

SYSTEM ANALYSIS—PAGOO CENTERS, INC.

General Background

Pagoo Centers, Inc., began as an audio equipment store in November 1976. John Paul and Pamela Pagoo opened this store on their own and continue to be the sole shareholders. The success of the company led the Pagoos to open a second store in June 1979. Both stores have proven successful, but recent concerns about profitability and cash flow have called for an analysis of their accounting systems.

The original store continues to specialize in retail audio sales. It sells equipment ranging from small and inexpensive radios to professional-level components and systems. Also sold are audio accessories and related equipment, such as stereo headphones, needles, albums, compact discs, and cassettes. This original store is called the Pagoo Audio Center and is referred to as PAC-1.

The second store also carries audio equipment, but concentrates on the sale of appliances. These appliances include stoves, refrigerators, freezers, washing machines, dryers, dishwashers, air conditioners, and televisions. The second store is called Pagoo Appliance Center and is referred to as PAC-2.

Until early 1992, both stores enjoyed increasing sales and profits. Despite intense competition, the Pagoo Centers stores have done well because of an excellent reputation based on their efficient, courteous staff. However, the company has recently experienced some operational and control problems. Specifically, continually increasing sales have not resulted in the expected profitability. Also, a cash flow problem has developed, which necessitated increased borrowing from the bank to make payments to suppliers and employees. Pagoo Centers has requested an analysis of its accounting system with a view toward correcting the problems.

Organization Structure

The organization structure at Pagoo Centers is not a rigidly defined hierarchy. The people are closely knit and get along at all levels and between levels. Exhibit C-5 charts this structure.

John Paul and Pamela Pagoo are the sole stockholders. John Paul is also the president of the firm. A management group meets weekly to set policies for the company and guide its growth. The management group consists of the president, the accountant, the buyer, the manager of Pagoo Audio Center, and the manager of Pagoo Appliance Center. The last four report to the president.

The accountant supervises the bookkeeper, the stock clerk, and the janitor. The buyer supervises no one directly, but does use the stock clerk informally. Each manager has two assistant managers reporting to him, one for each shift. PAC-1 has one additional salesperson in each shift, and PAC-2 has three.

Job Descriptions

There are ten separate job positions at Pagoo Centers. In this section we give a description of each of these positions as they now exist. The Recommendations section then suggests a number of changes to these positions.

EXHIBIT C-5   Organization Chart

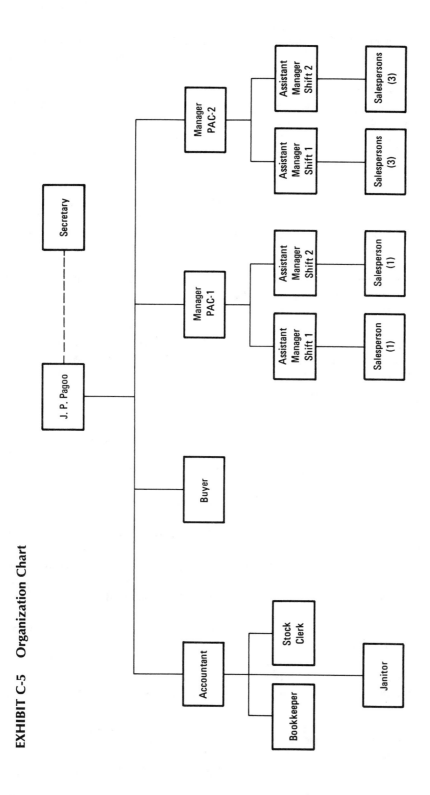

President. The president is also the general manager and hence supervises all aspects of the company's activities. He also provides guidance and long-range planning for the company and arranges financing and planning investments. He attends and chairs weekly meetings of the management group. He keeps up with the activities in both stores by personal visits and informal meetings with employees. He approves all major purchase orders before they are mailed and signs all checks.

Supervises:	The president supervises the accountant, the buyer, and the managers of each store.
Qualifications:	The president needs detailed knowledge of the audio equipment and appliance business; he also needs experience with the full range of business activities, including bank financing, advertising, merchandising, and dealing with employees.
Salary:	The president receives $150,000 annually.

Accountant. The accountant is in charge of the recordkeeping of the business and is responsible for the design and operation of the accounting system. Specifically, the accountant

1. Approves credit applications for potential customers on account.
2. Prepares monthly statements of accounts for credit customers.
3. Processes all incoming checks.
4. Signs all outgoing checks.
5. Issues payroll checks to employees.
6. Prepares monthly financial statements.
7. Assists bookkeeper with bank reconciliation as necessary.
8. Assists bookkeeper with calculation of commissions due salespeople.
9. Attends weekly meetings of the management group.

Supervises:	The accountant supervises the bookkeeper, the stock clerk, and the janitor.
Supervised by:	The accountant is supervised by the president.
Qualifications:	The accountant needs a college degree in accounting, experience supervising a complete accounting system, and experience in small business and manual accounting systems.
Salary:	The accountant receives $60,000 annually.

Buyer. The buyer purchases all products for sale by the company. Specifically, the buyer

1. Monitors inventory quantities.
2. Confers with the members of the management group concerning purchases.
3. Decides on suppliers to use.
4. Prepares purchase orders, with review by the president for major purchase orders.
5. Receives goods when they arrive and checks both their quantity and quality.

6. Prepares debit memos for rejected goods which are returned to the vendor.
7. Attends weekly meetings of the management group.

Supervised by: The buyer is supervised by the president.

Qualifications: The buyer should have a detailed knowledge of both audio equipment and appliances; he should also have an eye for details because the reputation of the firm depends on the quality of product. An engineering background is desirable.

Salary: The buyer receives $60,000 annually.

Manager. The manager is the day-to-day supervisor of the store. There is a separate manager for each of the two stores. As members of the president's management group, the managers report to the president weekly on sales trends, employee relations, and other activities of their store. Specifically, the manager

1. Meets informally with the buyer about needed inventory, the timing of purchases, and the establishment of reorder points; he also assists the buyer in checking inventory quantities and determining sales patterns.
2. Evaluates performance of assistant managers and salespeople.
3. Approves returns of merchandise.
4. Sets up the layout and display of merchandise.
5. Oversees the movement of inventory from the stockroom to the sales floor.
6. Waits on special customers or helps out when the store is busy.
7. Makes sure that all documents generated in his store are forwarded to the accountant by the day following the transaction.
8. Sees that cash sales receipts are deposited intact in the bank twice each workday.
9. Approves checks of cash sales customers.

Supervises: The manager of PAC-1 supervises two shifts of employees consisting of one assistant manager and one salesperson per shift. The manager of PAC-2 supervises two shifts of employees consisting of one assistant manager and three salespeople per shift.

Supervised by: The managers are supervised by the president.

Qualifications: The manager should have as much knowledge about either audio equipment or major appliances (depending on which store) to be able to make a sale effectively to any customer. Some experience in management with good recommendations from former employers would also be necessary.

Salary: The managers each receive $60,000 annually.

Assistant Manager. The assistant manager serves in the place of the manager when the manager is not in the store and assumes the manager's duties, such as approving checks. Otherwise the assistant manager serves as a salesperson. (Detailed duties are listed under Salesperson.)

Supervises:	In the absence of the manager, the assistant manager supervises the other salespeople in the store.
Supervised by:	The assistant manager is supervised by the store manager.
Qualifications:	The assistant manager is the senior salesperson of the store and should have the same qualifications as the other salespeople.
Salary:	The assistant managers receive a base salary of $1,200 per month plus commissions. The average annual salary has been $50,400.

Salesperson. The task of the salesperson is to make sales. PAC-1 salespeople sell audio equipment. PAC-2 salespeople sell audio equipment and major appliances. Specifically, the salesperson sells the goods available in the store, fills out the proper forms for credit sales, and puts information properly into the cash register for cash sales.

Supervised by:	All sales personnel are supervised by the store manager or by the assistant manager in the absence of the manager.
Qualifications:	The salesperson should have enough knowledge about either audio equipment or major appliances (depending on the store) to make a sale effectively to any customer.
Salary:	Each salesperson receives a $600 base salary per month plus commission. The average annual salary has been $43,200.

Bookkeeper. The bookkeeper helps the accountant maintain the books of the manual accounting system. The bookkeeper also

1. Records all transactions from source documents which reach the accountant's office.
2. Reconciles the bank statement received monthly.
3. Helps the accountant calculate commissions due to store personnel from an analysis of sales.
4. Posts general ledger, accounts receivable, and accounts payable ledgers.

Supervised by:	The bookkeeper is supervised by the accountant.
Qualifications:	Either business school training or sufficient experience is required.
Salary:	The bookkeeper receives $2,400 per month or $28,800 annually.

Stock Clerk. The stock clerk is responsible for the stockrooms and manually handles the storage and moving of inventory for the two stores. Specifically, the stock clerk

1. Is present when all shipments of merchandise arrive.
2. Moves goods from the stockroom to the sales floor of each store.
3. Helps the buyer check goods received from vendors and sends his copy of the purchase order with the shipping report to the accountant.
4. Keeps order in the stockrooms located in the rear of each store.

5. Moves goods from one store location to the other or picks up specially shipped goods from nearby locations.

Supervised by: The stock clerk is supervised by the accountant; however, he also follows the directions of the buyer and store managers when he is helping them.

Qualifications: The stock clerk should have a driver's license and be in good health. No formal education is required.

Salary: The stock clerk receives a monthly salary of $1,800 or an annual salary of $21,600.

Secretary. The secretary types and performs general office duties. Specifically, the secretary

1. Types all of the company's correspondence, including company checks, purchase orders, and debit memos.
2. Files all of the company's documents.
3. Opens all mail.
4. Answers the phone.

Supervised by: The secretary is supervised by the president.

Qualifications: The secretary should be able to type, file, and handle ordinary office procedures. Either business school training or practical experience is necessary.

Salary: The secretary receives a monthly salary of $1,800 or an annual salary of $21,600.

Janitor. The janitor is responsible for keeping the stores clean. He removes the dirt and trash that accumulate during the day. The janitor cleans and straightens both stores between 11 P.M. and 7 A.M., Sunday through Friday.

Supervised by: The janitor is supervised by the accountant.

Qualifications: The janitor does not require a formal education, but must be stable, honest, and reliable.

Salary: The janitor receives a monthly salary of $1,500 or an annual salary of $18,000.

Documents

This section details the documents, forms, and reports used or generated by the Pagoo Centers accounting system.

Sales Slip. Sales slips are prepared for all credit sales. If the sale is on a major credit card, the salesperson secures telephone approval for the charge from the credit card agency. For all credit sales, whether on a credit card or a company account, the salesperson gives one copy of the sales slip to the customer and puts the original and one copy in a folder near the cash register. These credit sales slips are delivered to the accountant twice daily. If the sale is for a new account to be carried by Pagoo Centers, Inc., the credit sales slip and supporting information on the customers are forwarded to the accountant for credit approval. One copy of each approved credit sales slip is normally returned to the store manager within a week and the merchandise is then given to the customer.

The bookkeeper records sales slips representing completed sales as received at the accountant's office and files them by day. The salesperson fills out the sales slip with the following information:

1. The sales slip number
2. The name of or code identifying the salesperson making the sale
3. The date of the sale
4. The store where the sale was made
5. The customer's account number
6. The approval code
7. The customer's name, address, city, state, zip code, and telephone number
8. The delivery instruction specified by the customer
9. A detailed description of the items sold:
    a. the quantity of each item
    b. the stock number of each item
    c. the description of each item
    d. the unit price of each item
    e. the extension of each item (unit price $\times$ quantity)
    f. the total price of all items

The customer signs the sales slip in the space provided at the bottom of the sales slip.

Credit Memorandum. Credit memoranda are prepared in duplicate for all sales returns by customers, either for cash or for credit. All returns must be approved by the store manager. If the return is for cash, the transaction appears on the cash register tape, and the copies of the credit memorandum go to the accountant. Where the return reduces the customer's account balance, one copy of the credit memorandum goes to the customer and one to the accountant.

When received by the accountant's office, the credit memorandums are recorded as received and filed by day. The salesperson fills out the credit memorandum with the following information:

1. The credit memorandum number
2. The name of or code identifying the salesperson handling the transaction
3. The date and the store where the transaction took place
4. The customer's account number
5. The customer's name, address, city, state, zip code, and telephone number
6. A detailed description of the items returned:
    a. the quantity of each item
    b. the stock number of each item
    c. the description of each item
    d. the unit price of each item
    e. the extension of each item (unit price $\times$ quantity)
    f. the total price of all items

The person who approves the merchandise return (usually the store manager) signs the form at the space provided at the bottom of the form.

Purchase Order. The buyer prepares a purchase order to purchase merchandise. The original goes to the vendor, the buyer keeps one copy, and the accountant receives the other two. All major purchase orders are forwarded to the president for approval before they are mailed.

The accountant gives one copy of the purchase order to the stock clerk to compare with the shipping report when the goods are received.

When the goods arrive, the shipping report accompanying the goods is compared to the stock clerk's copy of the purchase order. The purchase order is then sent to the accountant if all is in order. The bookkeeper records the transaction in the purchases journal.

The buyer fills out the following information:

1. The purchase order number
2. The vendor and his address
3. The date of the purchase order
4. Where the goods are to be shipped
5. The shipping instructions on how the goods are to be shipped
6. The terms of the purchase
7. A detailed description of the items ordered:
   a. the quantity of each item
   b. the description of each item
   c. the unit price of each item
   d. the extension of each item (unit price × quantity)
   e. the total price of all items

The buyer then signs the bottom of the purchase order.

Debit Memorandum. The buyer prepares a debit memorandum when he receives unacceptable merchandise from a vendor. There are four copies of the debit memorandum: The buyer retains one copy, the original is sent to the vendor, one copy is shipped with the returned goods, and one copy goes to the accountant. Debit memorandums are recorded when received at the accountant's office but are held to be matched against confirmations from suppliers that the goods have been returned and appropriate adjustments have been made. The buyer fills out the debit memorandum with the following information:

1. The date the debit memo is prepared
2. The purchase order number to which the debit memo relates
3. The vendor to whom goods are being returned
4. A detailed description of the items returned:
   a. the quantity of each item
   b. the description of each item
   c. the unit price of each item
   d. the extension of each item (unit price × quantity)
   e. the total price of all items

The buyer then signs the bottom of the debit memorandum.

Cash Register Tapes and Bank Deposit Slips. Cash registers have special keys which all salespeople use to record

1. the quantity sold
2. the stock number of the item
3. the unit price
4. the total price of the items
5. the total amount of the sale
6. a code to identify the person making the cash sale

Each cash refund is similarly recorded. The total amount of the transaction is computed by the register and entered on the tape. One copy of the tape goes to the customer as a receipt while a second, internally stored tape automatically keeps a cumulative total of cash sales and cash refunds. Twice a day, first thing each morning and late in the afternoon, store managers remove these internally stored tapes from all registers together with cash and checks except for $300 in small bills and change. The store managers prepare bank deposit slips from the tapes and deposit intact the cash and checks from the register into the bank. One copy of the deposit slip together with the cash register tapes goes to the accountant's office twice daily. Bank deposit slips and cash register tapes are recorded and held to be compared by the bookkeeper to the monthly bank statement. Discrepancies are immediately reported to the accountant.

Shipping Report. The shipping report is the request for payment that the vendor sends us for the goods we receive. A shipping report arrives with ordered goods, and the buyer and stock clerk compare it to its related purchase order. The shipping report is sent to the accountant's office with the clerk's copy of the purchase order if all merchandise is acceptable. When unacceptable merchandise is received, a debit memorandum is attached to the shipping report and the purchase order for returned goods before being sent to the accountant's office.

Financial Statements. Monthly, the accountant prepares a set of financial statements. These financial statements include the standard income statement and balance sheet. The statements also include schedules of accounts payable and accounts receivable. The schedule of accounts payable is a listing of all amounts owed to vendors; the total of this list then balances to the control total of accounts payable in the balance sheet. The schedule of accounts receivable is a listing of all amounts owed by customers; the total of this list then balances to the control total of accounts receivable in the balance sheet.

Procedures

This section provides narrative descriptions and flowcharts for the company's accounting system procedures.

Credit Sales. The salesperson prepares a three-copy sales slip. If it is a major credit card purchase, the salesperson must call the credit card agency for approval. If the sale is based on an account to be carried by Pagoo, the salesperson must determine if the customer has an already established account or if it is an initial credit purchase. If it is an initial credit purchase, all credit sales slips are sent to the accountant with supporting information on the customer. The accountant uses standard credit-rating agencies to assist him in making his decision. The merchandise is not released to the customer until credit is approved. Upon giving his approval, the accountant sends one copy of the sales slip back to the store manager, within one week, which is given to the customer when the merchandise is released. The other two copies are sent to the bookkeeper. If the purchase is on an already established account or a major credit card purchase, one copy of the sales slip is given to the customer, and the original and one copy are put into a folder near the cash register. Twice daily, the store manager sends the sales slips to the accounting office. In the accounting office, the bookkeeper checks the sales slips and records the transaction in the sales journal. From the journal, the bookkeeper posts weekly to the general ledger and the accounts receivable subsidiary ledger. The secretary files the sales slips by day in a temporary file. They will later be used by the bookkeeper and accountant to determine commissions for the salespeople. (See Exhibit C-6 on page 728.)

Cash Sales. The salesperson rings the transaction into the cash register. The register is equipped with special keys to record

1. quantity sold
2. the stock number of the item
3. unit price
4. total price
5. salesperson number on the tape

One copy of the tape is given to the customer as a receipt, while the other is internally stored in the cash register. The machine keeps a cumulative total of cash sales and cash refunds. Twice daily, the store manager prepares a two-copy deposit slip. He sends one copy with the cash to the bank, while the other copy is sent to the accounting office with the tape. In the accountant's office, the bookkeeper checks over the documents and the tape and compares the tape with the deposit slip. The bookkeeper records the transaction in the cash receipts journal and posts weekly to the general ledger. The deposit slip and tape are filed temporarily and are compared with the bank statement when it arrives. The cash register tape is temporarily filed by day, to be used later to determine commissions. If any discrepancies appear in the bank reconciliation, they are reported to the accountant. (See Exhibit C-7 on page 729.)

Sales Returns and Allowances. The salesperson prepares a two-copy credit memo, which is sent to the store manager for his approval. If the return is for cash, the transaction is entered into the cash register and appears on the cash register tape. The customer is given the cash and a copy of the tape, while both copies of the credit memo are sent to the accountant's office. If the return

EXHIBIT C-6 Pagoo Centers, Inc., Credit Sales Flowchart

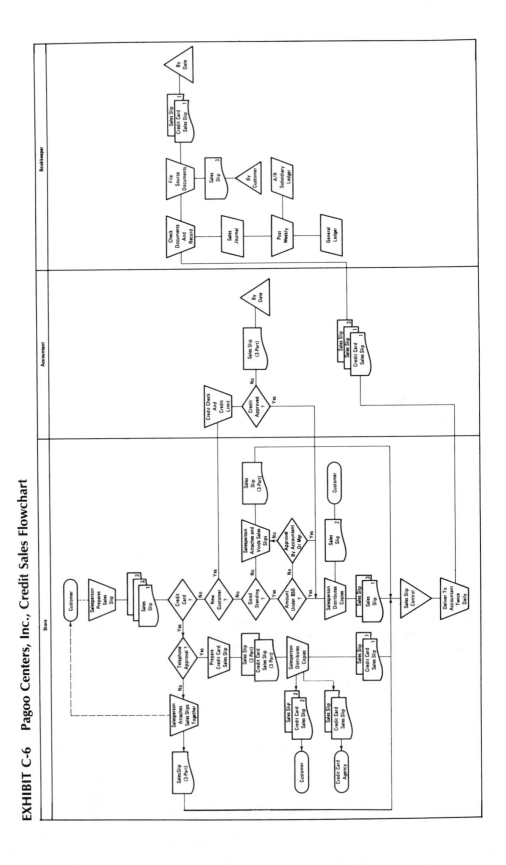

EXHIBIT C-7 Pagoo Centers, Inc., Cash Sales Flowchart

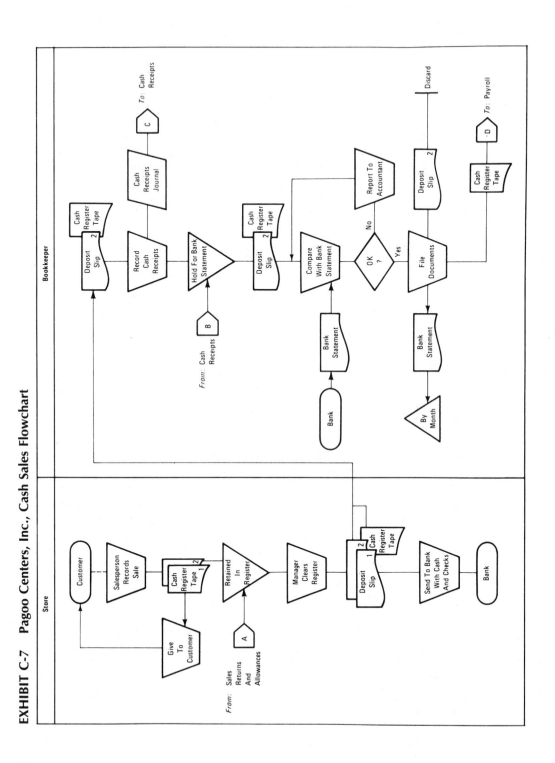

is for credit on the customer's account, one copy of the credit memo goes to the customer and the other is sent to the accountant's office. When received, the bookkeeper checks the credit memo and records the transaction in the general journal and then posts weekly to the general ledger. The secretary files the credit memo permanently by day. (See Exhibit C-8.)

Cash Receipts. The secretary opens the mail and sends all customer checks to the accountant, who records all customer payments in the cash receipts journal and prepares a two-part deposit slip. One copy goes to the bank with the checks, and the other is held to compare with the bank statement when it arrives. This comparison with the bank statement is discussed in the section on Cash Sales. The bookkeeper posts weekly from the cash receipts journal to both the general ledger and the accounts receivable subsidiary ledger. (See Exhibit C-9 on page 732.)

Purchasing. The buyer, with suggestions from the managers of both PAC-1 and PAC-2, the accountant, and J. P. Pagoo, decides what and when to purchase and prepares a four-part purchase order. If it is a major purchase, it goes to J. P. Pagoo for his approval. The original purchase order is sent to the vendor. One copy is held by the buyer and the other two go to the accountant's office. One copy of the purchase order is filed by the bookkeeper in a temporary file to be matched later with the shipping report. The second copy goes to the stock clerk. The stock clerk uses this purchase order to help the buyer check over the shipment when it arrives. The buyer makes the decision whether or not to accept the shipment. If the shipment is acceptable, the purchase order and shipping report are sent back to the accountant's office. The bookkeeper matches the shipping report and the purchase order and records the transaction in the purchases journal; weekly, she posts to the general ledger and accounts payable subsidiary ledger. The buyer compares his copy of the purchase order to the shipment with the help of the stock clerk. Then the buyer refiles the purchase order. If the shipment is not acceptable, the buyer prepares a four-copy debit memo. One copy is sent to the vendor, one to the bookkeeper, one to the stock clerk to be put with the goods, and one is kept by the buyer. The bookkeeper records this return transaction in the general journal and posts weekly to the general ledger. The secretary temporarily files the debit memo, which is held to be matched against the vendor's confirmation. The stock clerk keeps his copy of the purchase order for the next shipment. (See Exhibit C-10 on page 733.)

Cash Disbursements. The accountant prepares all outgoing checks and gathers all support for the checks. This support includes purchase orders and shipping reports for payments to vendors, invoices from the utility company and so on. The accountant believes in taking all available discounts. The secretary types the checks and both J. P. Pagoo and the accountant sign them. The accountant mails the checks to vendors and creditors. The check support is given to the bookkeeper who records the transactions in the cash disbursements journal and posts weekly to the general ledger and the accounts payable subsidiary ledger. The secretary files the supporting documents. (See Exhibit C-11 on page 734.)

EXHIBIT C-8 Pagoo Centers, Inc., Sales Returns and Allowances Flowchart

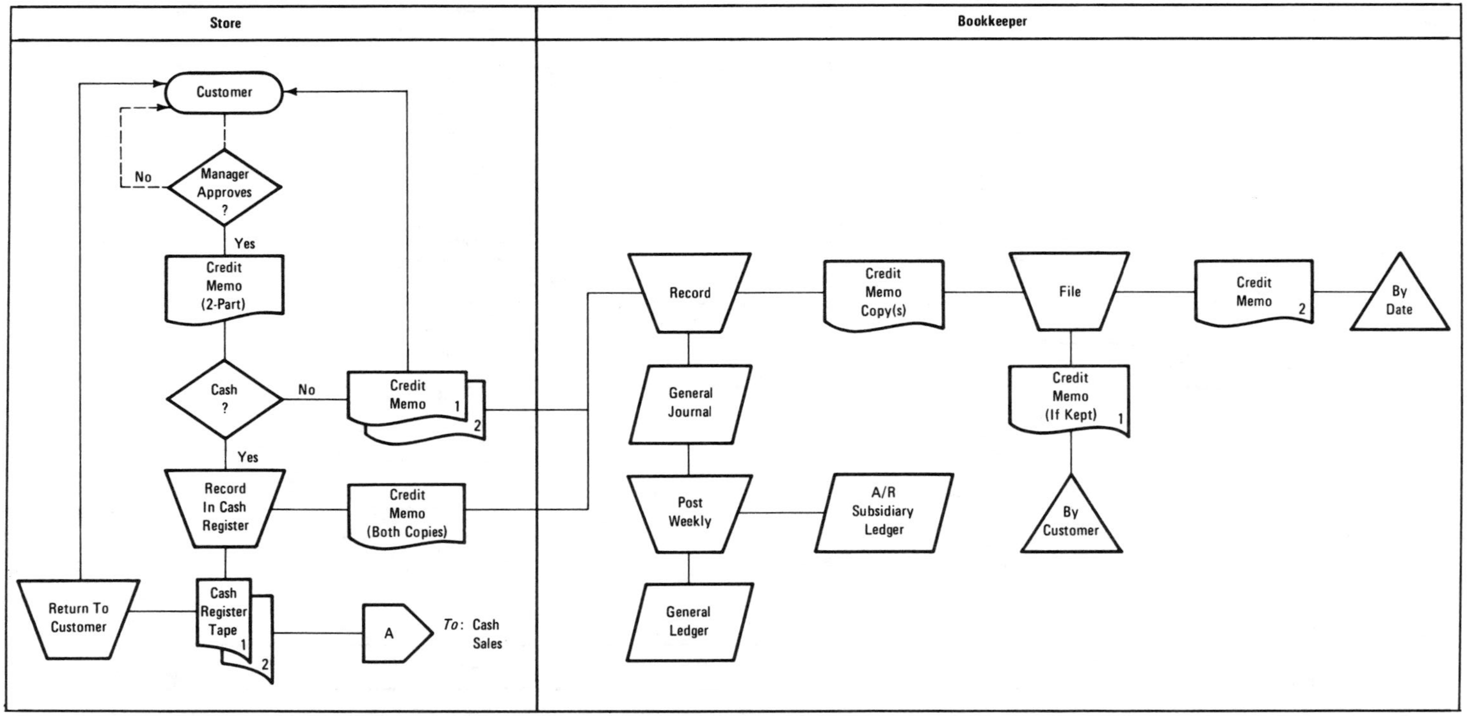

EXHIBIT C-9 Pagoo Centers, Inc., Cash Receipts Flowchart

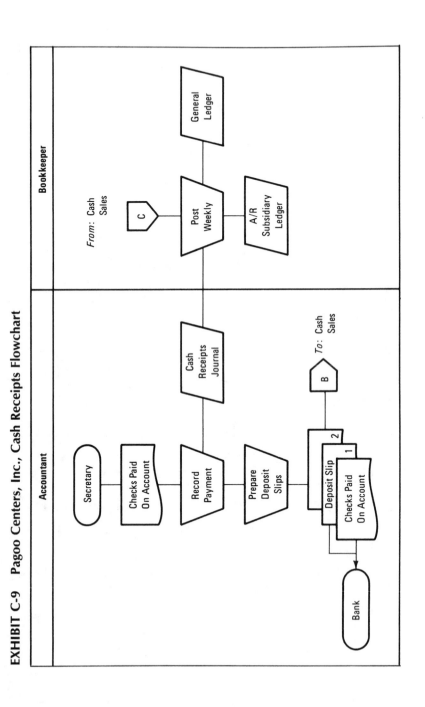

EXHIBIT C-10 Pagoo Centers, Inc., Purchasing Flowchart

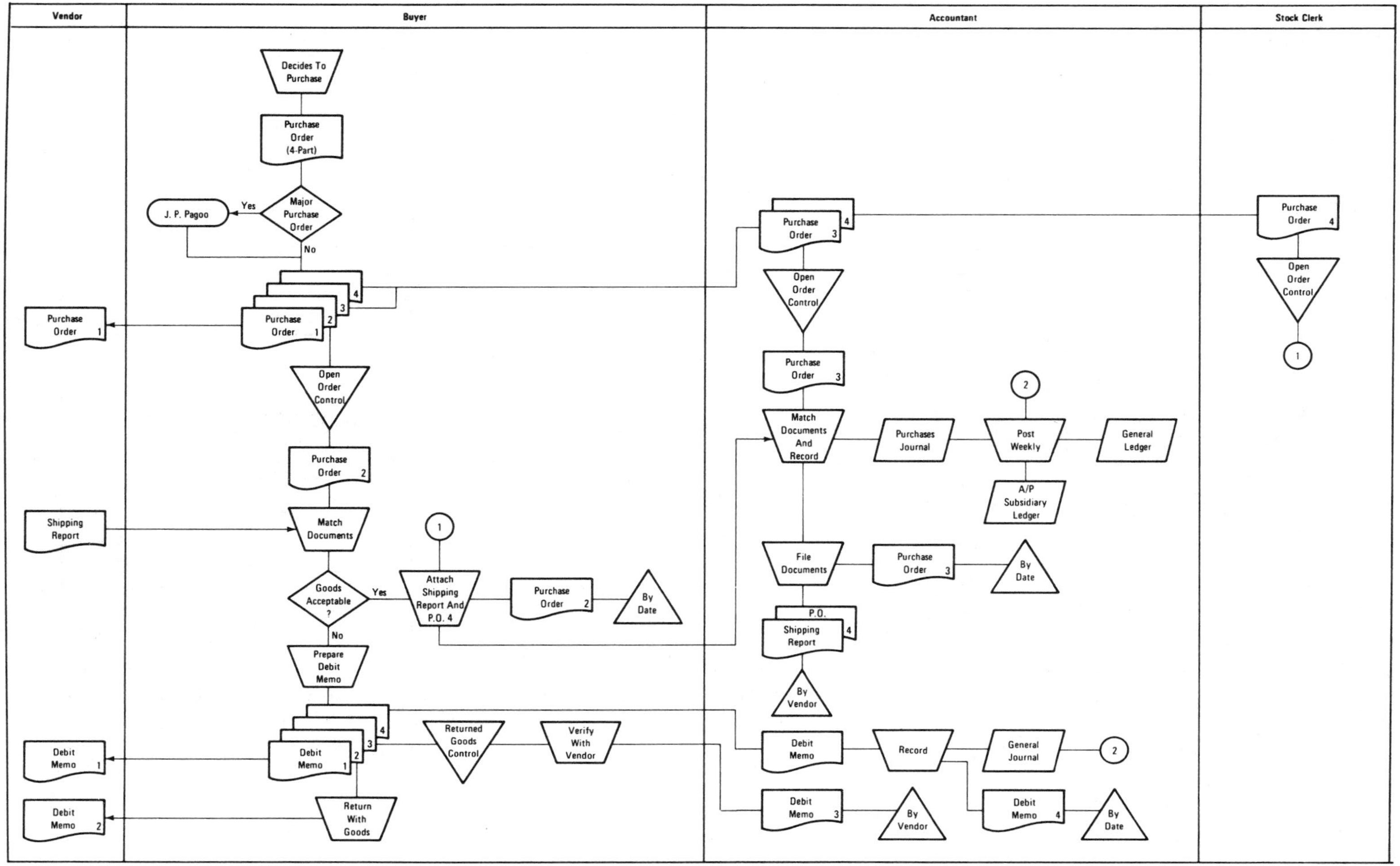

EXHIBIT C-11   Pagoo Centers, Inc., Cash Disbursements Flowchart

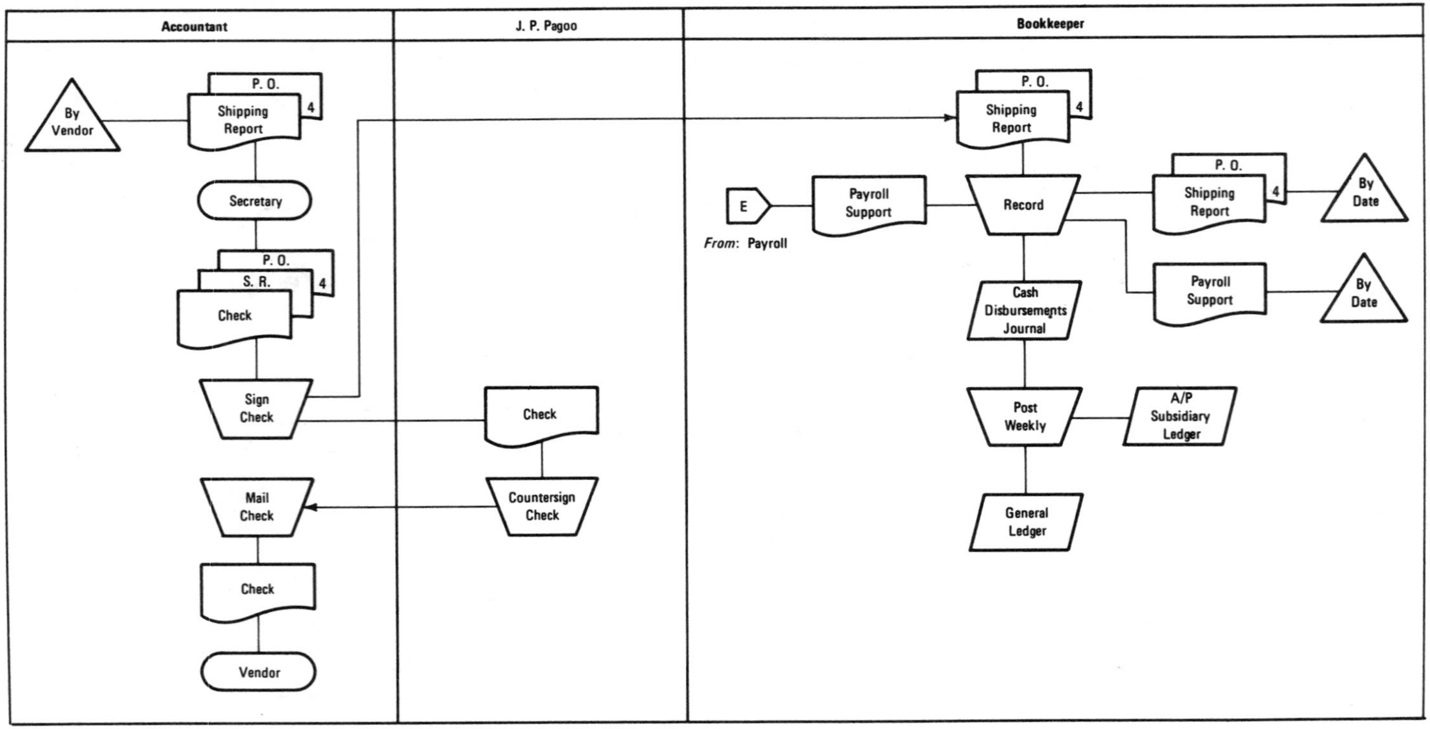

Payroll. The accountant, with the assistance of the bookkeeper, calculates the amount of commission due to each salesperson from sales slips and the cash register tapes. The bookkeeper, stock clerk, secretary, and janitor are paid semimonthly. All other employees are paid monthly. The other payroll items computed include federal withholding, FICA, and federal and state unemployment. The company share of FICA is computed and recorded at each payroll. Unemployment tax is recorded once a month. The secretary types the payroll checks from the supporting information given to her by the accountant. Then, both J. P. Pagoo and the accountant sign the checks. The accountant then distributes the checks to the employees. The supporting payroll documents, from which the checks are typed, are sent to the bookkeeper to be recorded in the cash disbursements journal and posted weekly to the general ledger. The supporting documents are filed by the secretary. (See Exhibit C-12.)

EXHIBIT C-12   Pagoo Centers, Inc., Payroll Flowchart

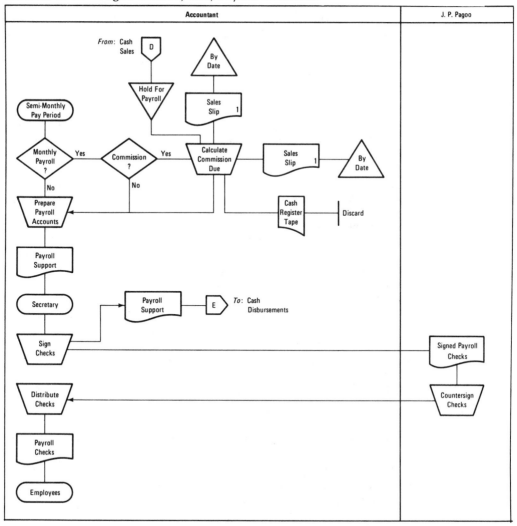

Deficiencies

This analysis uncovered a number of deficiencies and omissions in Pagoo Centers' accounting system. This section will discuss each of these deficiencies and briefly indicate why the area might be a problem. The next section of this report will lay out recommendations for improvement.

No Bonding of Employees. Pagoo Center employees, including those who handle large amounts of cash and inventory, are not bonded. This exposes the company to a substantial risk.

Vague Policies. There are a number of areas where the company policy is left unnecessarily vague. These areas include

1. Conflicts of interest or dealing with related firms by, for example, salespeople of PAC-1 and PAC-2 or the buyer.
2. The definition of a major purchase order which the president must approve.
3. A chart of accounts to detail precisely which accounts to use in specific cases.
4. A basis of comparison to judge good or bad performance (as it is, there is no budget with which to compare actual performance, nor do the monthly financial statements provide any comparative figures).
5. The procedure for determining uncollectible accounts (those accounts from which the company will never receive payment, either due to bankruptcy or some other reason).

Division of Duties. There are a number of points where employees' duties are not consistent with accepted practice and thus present internal control problems. These areas include

1. The concentration of both custody of inventory (which is handled by the stock clerk) and the related record keeping (which is handled by the bookkeeper) under one person, the accountant.
2. The concentration of duties whereby the bookkeeper both records transactions in the journals and posts them to the ledgers.
3. The concentration of duties whereby the accountant approves credit for customers, sends out customer statements, and receives payments on account.
4. The lack of a record of cash received in the mail which is independent of those processing the receipts.
5. A (perhaps) excessive closeness of the PAC-1 manager and the bookkeeper.
6. The concentration of duties whereby the bookkeeper both records cash disbursements and reconciles the bank statement.
7. The lack of an independent record of the sales slips sent to the bookkeeper for credit sales.
8. The lack of an independent record, such as a perpetual inventory system, of the inventory moved and controlled by the stock clerk.

Weak Procedures. There are a number of areas where procedures are weak and leave the company open to excessive risk. Paid invoices are not perforated or canceled and thus, potentially, could be used more than once. The invoice does not seem to accompany the check for signing, and thus there may be inadequate support for the checks. The documents—purchase order, debit memorandum, sales slip, and credit memorandum—are not prenumbered; this practice allows the possibility that documents could be lost or misplaced without that fact becoming apparent. Important accounting records, such as the accounts receivable subsidiary ledger, are not kept in a safe and could be lost in a fire or other accident. Too many people have access to cash in the stores' cash registers; since all salespeople have equal access to the registers, it would be impossible to assign specific responsibility for any discrepancies in the cash figure. The cash is left in the cash registers overnight; this leaves the firm open to considerable risk of loss, especially since the janitor has access to both stores overnight.

No Independent Audit. There is no audit of the financial statements by an independent CPA firm. There is, therefore, no independent check that the company's financial statements are fairly presented and that generally accepted accounting principles are applied and proper procedures followed. Without an audit, financing would be more diffcult to obtain.

Recommendations

This section details the recommendations the company should implement in order to have a more controlled, more efficient and effective accounting system. These recommendations are as follows.

Bonding of Employees. The company should obtain a fidelity bond for each employee who handles cash and inventory. Experience has shown that bonding provides a psychological deterrent and an additional independent check on backgrounds in addition to protection in case of loss.

Policies and Procedures Manual. The company should develop a policies and procedures manual to provide guidance and direction to employees in their duties. The manual would additionally have the benefit of assisting in the training of new employees. This manual should detail company policy concerning conflicts of interest, amount of paid vacation, sick leave, maternity leave, hiring and firing of employees, the length of time to keep records, issuing credit, accepting personal checks, and writing off uncollectible accounts. It should also detail company procedures, as well as guidelines for transaction processing and should include a chart of accounts which will give the appropriate use of each account. Finally, the manual should spell out the duties and responsibilities of employees and the procedures which should be followed in a variety of circumstances. (The sections of this report on Job Descriptions, Documents, and Procedures could provide a start for this manual.)

Division of Duties. The company should divide the duties of the employees differently, to promote efficiency and provide more effective internal control.

1. The secretary should continue to open all mail (except the bank statement), but should also make a list of cash received. This list should then be compared to the entry in the cash receipts journal and the bank statement.

2. The bank statement should go unopened to Mr. Pagoo, who should prepare the bank reconciliation.

3. The bookkeeper should continue to record the transactions in the journals, but the accountant should post the transactions to the ledgers.

4. The bookkeeper should prepare the customer statements of account.

5. Mr. Pagoo should receive the checks for signing together with the supporting invoice or shipping report. After signing the check, he should perforate or otherwise cancel the supporting documents.

6. All duties concerning custody of inventory should be assigned to the buyer and separated from the accountant's recordkeeping function.

Improved Procedures. The company procedures should be changed in a number of areas. These changes will provide increased efficiency and improved internal control.

1. The financial statements should include a comparison of this month's and this year's performance to the same period last year. Also, there should be a separate profit and loss statement for each store. When the company becomes more stable, budgets for each store should be developed.

2. The monthly financial statements should include an aged trial balance of accounts receivable instead of a simple schedule. This would help indicate the collectibility of these accounts.

3. The documents—purchase order, sales slip, credit and debit memorandums—should all be prenumbered to allow better physical control.

4. Important documents should be kept in a safe for better physical control.

5. Cash deposits should be made nightly upon closing rather than being left in the store overnight.

6. There should be one cashier at each store who would not function also as a salesperson. The cashier would have sole responsibility for the cash register and the handling of cash in the store.

7. All credit sales should be recorded on the cash register tape to provide an independent record of the credit sales slip sent to the bookkeeper.

8. The company should implement a perpetual inventory system to keep better track of the location and quantity of the inventory.

Independent Audit. The company should have an audit by an independent CPA firm at least every two or three years.

STATEMENT OF OBJECTIVES

FRIENDLY & WISE
CERTIFIED PUBLIC ACCOUNTANTS
1000 Bourbon Street
New Orleans, Louisiana 70100

November 2, 1992

Mr. John Paul Pagoo, President
Pagoo Centers, Inc.
1000 Canal Street
New Orleans, Louisiana 70100

Dear John Paul:

We have completed our engagement to lay out a statement of objectives for your new accounts receivable system. This letter gives the results of our study.

Overall Purpose

The overall purpose of the new system is to improve profitability and speed up cash flow by

1. Improving internal control over credit sales, receivables, and cash collections,
2. Providing better information to management concerning credit sales, and
3. Encouraging timely collection of accounts.

Specific Objectives

Specifically, the objectives identified to accomplish the above goals are

1. To ensure that all transactions relating to the creation of and collection of receivables are recorded correctly and in a prompt and timely manner.
2. To eliminate extension of credit to customers when their balance exceeds an established credit limit or when their payment on account is past due.
3. To spotlight accounts that are past due and prompt management attention.
4. To separate, to the extent feasible, the duties of receiving payments on account, recording payments, authorizing credit sales, recording credit sales, authorizing credit memos, recording credit memos, and preparing statements of account.
5. To produce monthly statements on a balance-forward basis, which will be sent to customers to solicit payment.

Required Output

To accomplish these objectives, the system needs two basic reports:

1. *Aged Trial Balance.* This report will extend the material in the schedule of accounts receivable and will replace that report. The aged trial balance will generate one line of output for each customer. Each line will contain the customer's name and balance due. In addition, the balance due will be broken down into the

portion that is current, the portion that is over 30 days old, and the portion that is over 60 days old. Finally, the report will total the amount due and the amounts that are current, over 30 days, and over 60 days. This report will be invaluable in identifying accounts that are past due and must be acted upon. It will also prevent extension of credit to those who are already past due.

2. *Statement of Account.* This report will appear on a monthly basis for every customer. The statement will give the customer's name, address, and the balance due at the beginning of the period. Then the report will detail each transaction (credit sale, cash payment, or adjustment) of the period and conclude with the balance due at the end of the period. This report is essential because it provides an audit trail backing up the balance due for each customer. The report also will encourage timely payments on account.

Required Data

To generate these reports, the system needs two data files:

1. *Customer Master File.* This file will contain the basic data on each customer. This information will include the customer's name, address, credit limit, and balance due.

2. *Accounts Receivable Transaction File.* This file will contain the necessary audit trail information backing up each transaction. For each transaction, the file will contain the type of transaction (whether credit sale, cash payment, or adjustment), the customer number, the date, and the amount.

The data for creation of the customer master file is available from the accountant when the credit is initially granted. There are three types of transactions.

1. Credit sale information is available from the sales slip.
2. Cash payment information is available from the checks received in the mail.
3. Adjustments by credit memo are available from the credit memo the salesperson fills out.

Necessary Controls

The following internal control techniques and procedures are recommended to ensure the accuracy and reliability of the accounting data.

1. All sales slips and credit memos will be prenumbered to maintain physical control of the forms and to pinpoint any lost or mislaid forms.
2. The secretary will make an independent record of all incoming checks. This record will be compared to the accounts receivable postings, the bank deposit, and the cash receipts journal to ensure that no amounts have been recorded in error.
3. Credit sales, in addition to cash sales, will have to be rung up on the cash register. This independent record will be compared by the accountant to the totals generated by the bookkeeper from the sales slips.
4. The company will continue to prepare and use the sales journal and the cash receipts journal as before. The balance in the accounts receivable control account will therefore be an excellent check on the accuracy of the computer files and reports, since they should balance.

New Policies or Procedures

The following new policies and procedures will be necessary for the proper functioning of the new systems.

1. The accountant will establish credit limits for each customer when he initially grants credit to that individual or company. This will help ensure that no customer exceeds his ability to pay.
2. Salesclerks will verify the credit status of each customer before processing a credit sale. This will be accomplished by a phone call to the bookkeeper and will ensure that credit is not granted when the customer has already exceeded his credit limit or when his account is past due.
3. Salesclerks will total sales slips and attach an adding machine tape before transmitting them to the bookkeeper for processing. This total should be compared with the cash register total of credit sales to ensure that all credit sales have been recorded.
4. The accountant will use the aged trial balance on a monthly basis to contact customers whose payments are slipping. This will help speed up cash flow and encourage timely payment by customers.

If this statement of objectives is acceptable to you, please sign below and date your signature.

Very truly yours,

FRIENDLY & WISE

Jack R. Friendly

Jack R. Friendly

JRF/ms

Approved: _____ Date: _____
              John Paul Pagoo, President

Approved: _____ Date: _____
                    Accountant

Approved: _____ Date: _____
                 Manager PAC-1

Approved: _____ Date: _____
                 Manager PAC-2

COMPUTER ACQUISITION

FRIENDLY & WISE
CERTIFIED PUBLIC ACCOUNTANTS
1000 Bourbon Street
New Orleans, Louisiana 70100

September 30, 1992

Computer Systems Vendor

Dear Ladies and Gentlemen:

This letter is an invitation for proposals concerning a computer system for Pagoo Centers, Inc. This request for proposals has been submitted to computer service bureaus, timesharing services, and small-scale computer system equipment vendors. We recognize that the basic approach to the various application areas will vary by vendor and request that each company submit specifications for each application that best uses the capabilities of its equipment and/or services. The rest of this letter consists of three parts. First is the background, which is a brief description of the company. Second are the automated applications that are the areas of potential automation. Third is the proposal format, which is the material that must be covered in your proposal.

Background

In August 1992, the CPA firm of Friendly & Wise initiated a study of the accounting system of Pagoo Centers. As a result of that study, Pagoo Centers decided to investigate the feasibility of converting the existing manual systems in order to use current EDP technology. Pagoo Centers, Inc., operates two stores: the Pagoo Audio Center (PAC-1) and the Pagoo Appliance Center (PAC-2). PAC 1 sells a complete line of audio equipment and related accessories, while PAC 2 stresses home appliances but also sells audio equipment. Both stores have been successful, but there are no immediate plans for expansion. The company now employs 21 people, including the owner, Mr. Pagoo, who serves as president. Sales for the company now approach $4 million annually. Based on the study, the following areas are potential candidates for automation:

1. Accounts receivable
2. Inventory
3. Payroll
4. Accounts payable
5. General accounting

Automated Applications

As a result of the study, the following functions were selected as practical and economically feasible areas for the application of automated data processing. All proposed systems must provide detailed listings of all master file update transactions, including file maintenance transactions; an adequate audit trail is essential.

Accounts Receivable. Accounts receivable would include the application of cash on a balance-forward basis. All necessary billing information will be contained on the sales slip. All charges are currently being manually priced. This pricing function could be automated if the recommended equipment has the capacity to do so; however, this is not an absolute requirement of any system to be proposed. There are up to 50 open accounts at any given time, but this should grow to several hundred as the stores continue to grow. The system should be capable of producing a complete, detailed aged trial balance listing, a report describing the current status of delinquent accounts, and monthly detailed customer statements. These reports will generally be issued on a scheduled basis; however, capability must be provided to issue these reports on a request basis.

Inventory. The current inventory system is on a periodic basis and is based on a monthly physical inventory for both stores. This information is sufficient for the preparation of the present financial statements; however, there are no reports to assist inventory management for the several hundred items the stores sell. The new system must be capable of issuing inventory status reports, reorder reports by item for all products that get too low, and usage reports. The system should be able to produce a monthly cost usage report by store, using the cash register tapes and sales slips as input.

Payroll. The payroll is paid on a bimonthly and a monthly basis. The monthly payroll consists of five salaried management people. The bimonthly payroll includes 4 salaried employees and 12 salespeople who work on a base salary plus commission basis. The information for commission computations is available from the sales slips. The payroll system must be capable of producing all required government reports, the information necessary for the preparation of payroll checks, and the required expense distribution for the general accounting system.

Accounts Payable. The accounts payable system must be capable of providing the information necessary for check preparation as well as expense distribution data that would be used in the general accounting system. The system should provide a schedule of all invoices and a cash requirements report that details the invoice due by a specific date, in order to ensure the taking of all discounts. The company processes approximately 50 invoices per month, representing 40 expense account entries. Each month the company issues approximately 35 checks, and the company has approximately 50 active vendors and suppliers.

General Accounting. The present general accounting system only provides one income statement for the entire company. The proposed system must provide a separate income statement for each store, along with an overall income statement. The system should provide for posting all journal entries (approximately 100 per month) to the approximately 200 various general ledger accounts. This information will be used in the preparation of trial balances and will also be used in preparation of audit trail printouts on demand.

Proposal Format

Send the original copy of the proposal to:

> Mr. Israel H. Wise
> Friendly & Wise
> Certified Public Accountants
> 1000 Bourbon Street
> New Orleans, Louisiana 70100

Any questions regarding the specifications should be directed to Mr. Wise at the above address. If necessary, he can be reached at (504) 561-0000. If Mr. Wise is not in the office, leave word and he will contact you directly. All proposals are due in New Orleans no later than October 22, 1992. Mr. Wise will pick up a second copy of the proposal when he meets with each company the week of

October 26, 1992. Under no circumstances should the vendor contact Pagoo Centers directly. Failure to comply with this request will automatically eliminate that vendor from further consideration.

The proposal must include the following specifications:

1. A detailed description of the recommended equipment and any peripheral equipment. Where alternatives are indicated, the relative order of these alternatives should be indicated. Where other than on-site facilities are recommended, a detailed description of the remote facility should be made.
2. A breakdown of costs for each item of hardware. Where applicable, maintenance or service charges should be listed. Terms of all purchase or lease agreements (including alternative costs) should be presented in detail.
3. A statement on physical planning considerations, such as space requirements, temperature and humidity limitations, and electrical outlets. The reliability of the equipment (percent downtime), the recommended preventive maintenance schedule, and the availability of backup facilities will be stated.
4. A statement giving the location of service facilities and the availability of maintenance, including the maximum time between notification of a problem and arrival of service technician.
5. A detailed description (such as a systems manual) of any relevant applied systems and program packages available through the proposing firm.
6. An explicit statement of what, if any, systems or programming assistance the proposing firm will furnish. Where applicable, each separate application should have its own separate cost for systems and programming assistance.
7. A list of facilities available for education, testing, and preinstallation operation.
8. The name, address, and telephone number of the representative responsible for the preparation and submission of the proposal.

All proposals and correspondence submitted to Friendly & Wise will be retained; however, these proposals will be disclosed only to Pagoo Centers' management. We look forward to receiving your proposal.

Very truly yours,

FRIENDLY & WISE

Israel H. Wise

Israel H. Wise

IHW/ms

SYSTEM DESIGN

Following on pages 745–759 is a sample system design of an accounts receivable system for Pagoo Centers. Remember that there is far more to system design than simply buying a suitable program package. Much of the material appears technical. Nevertheless, managers must remain deeply involved in the system development process to ensure that their wishes are carried out and that the system is effectively pushed to operation.

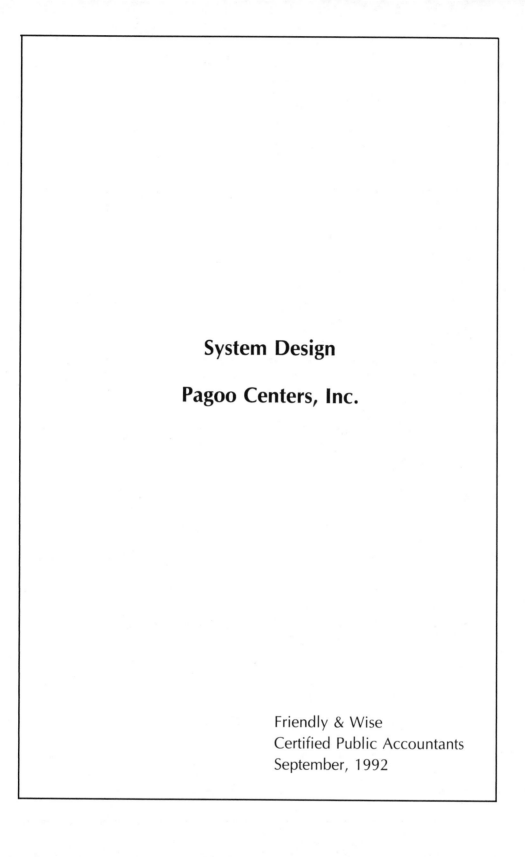

System Design

Pagoo Centers, Inc.

Friendly & Wise
Certified Public Accountants
September, 1992

November 16, 1992

Mr. John Paul Pagoo, President
Pagoo Centers, Inc.
1000 Canal Street
New Orleans, Louisiana 70100

Dear John Paul:

We have completed our engagement to design your new accounts receivable system. This system is based upon the objectives for the system which we presented in our report of November 2, 1992, and which you approved. After careful analysis of your present and future information needs, we have designed a simple but efficient system to meet those needs.

Since this is your and your firm's first experience with a computer-based system, we have deliberately designed the system to be as simple to use as possible. Importantly, however, the system can be expanded and extended when you become comfortable with this system and wish to expand into other application areas. Please indicate your approval of this design by signing this letter below.

Thank you for the opportunity to work on this engagement. We stand ready to assist you in the implementation process in any manner you desire. Please call us if we can be of further assistance.

Very truly yours,

FRIENDLY & WISE

Jack R. Friendly

Jack R. Friendly

JRF/ms

Approved: _____ Date: _____
John Paul Pagoo, President

Approved: _____ Date: _____
Accountant

Approved: _____ Date: _____
Manager, PAC-1

Approved: _____ Date: _____
Manager, PAC-2

CONTENTS

Accounts Receivable Design
Pagoo Centers, Inc.

Scope and Boundaries

This computerized accounts receivable system will perform the bookkeeping tasks of

1. Recording credit sales
2. Recording payments received
3. Recording returns and adjustments
4. Producing billing statements

In addition, information on customer account status will be available through on-line access for credit checks. Further, a periodic summary of account status (an aged trial balance report) will be printed to spotlight accounts that are past due.

This accounts receivable system is a balance-forward system. Because this type of system keeps track of the total amount each customer owes the business, it is ideal for retail businesses. The system accumulates charges, credits, and payments for each customer during the month. At the end of the month, the system generates a billing statement showing these accumulated charges. The monthly statement of account is, thus, also a bill. The billing statement begins with the ending balance of the previous period (the previous balance is brought forward; hence, the term balance forward). The statement then lists all transactions of the period in date order and ends with the cumulative balance owed at the end of the period.

The Pagoo Centers system does not provide open-item capability. An open-item system keeps track of the amount each customer owes by invoice. Credit and payments must apply to specific invoices rather than to a customer account. In an open-item system, the invoice is the bill and the customer pays by invoice. Any monthly statement is issued only to speed payment and to identify errors in the customer records. More sophisticated than the balance-forward system, the open-item system is suited primarily to wholesalers and manufacturers.

As is typical of balance-forward systems, the Pagoo Centers system has no provision for discounts to encourage timely payments since the system does not keep track of payments by invoice. Instead, the system can assess finance charges for those customers who do not pay on time. The system does not compute interest (financing) charges automatically, but it does allow the user to enter finance charges as transactions.

In essence, this new system replaces the accounts receivable subsidiary ledger with computer files. The system processes sales and cash receipts, but only to the extent necessary for updating accounts in the accounts receivable subsidiary ledger. The new system will not do any analysis of sales. The sales journal and cash receipts journal will continue to be prepared manually and used as before. While the accounts receivable system is only a part of the total accounting system, the design is such that it will easily be integrated with the rest of the current manual system. The proposed system can be expanded in the future, and other accounting applications can easily be added to the present system.

749

Systems Case and Applications

Specific Requirements

This section of the report will detail

1. The output to be generated by the system
2. The files to be maintained by the system
3. The input data needed by the system

Output

The system will generate three basic outputs: the aged trial balance, the statement of account, and the file status report.

Aged Trial Balance. This report replaces and extends the present schedule of accounts receivable. Like the schedule of accounts receivable, this report lists every credit customer, the balance that each owes, and the total balance owed by all customers. This total then balances to the control total in the general ledger. In addition, the aged trial balance determines the portion of each customer's balance that is current, the portion that is over 30 days old, and the portion that is over 60 days old. These amounts are then totaled. This information indicates which customers have old and potentially uncollectible accounts.

Statement of Account. One statement of account is issued for each customer. The statement of account includes the name and address of the customer, the amount due, and a detailed analysis of the transactions that generated the amount due. The analysis first lists the balance due at the beginning of the period, and then provides a separate line for each transaction giving the transaction date, the type of transaction, the amount of the transaction, whether it was a debit or credit, and finally a running balance. After the last transaction is printed, the running balance should equal the amount due. This statement of account goes to each customer at the end of every month to request payment.

File Status Report. The file maintenance program generates a report that details the current file status for each customer. The report gives, for each customer, the name, address, credit limit, beginning balance, total debits, total credits, ending balance, and amount of credit available. The bookkeeper uses this report to determine whether credit should be extended on a potential credit sale.

Files

The system will require two files, the customer master file and the transaction file.

Customer Master File.   The customer master file contains one record for each customer. Each customer record contains information about the customer, including

1. Name
2. Address
3. Credit limit
4. Beginning balance
5. Total debits for the period
6. Total credits for the period
7. Ending balance for the period
8. Current balance
9. Over 30-day balance
10. Over 60-day balance

Transaction File.   The transaction file contains one record for each transaction that has updated any customer record. Each transaction record contains the pertinent information for one transaction for one customer, including

1. Customer number
2. Transaction type
3. Date of transaction
4. Amount of transaction

Every time the system processes a transaction, it accomplishes two separate steps:

1. The system goes to the appropriate customer's record in the master file and updates the ending balance and either the total debits or total credits as necessary. For each customer, the following equation should always hold true:

$$\text{ending balance} = \text{beginning balance} + \text{total debits} - \text{total credits}$$

2. After updating the customer's record, the system adds a transaction record to the transaction file. There is, therefore, an audit trail kept in the transaction file—every transaction that has updated any customer record will be kept in the transaction file.

Input

Sales Slip.   The sales slip form will be retained but the sales slips will now be prenumbered. This will allow better physical control and ensure that no sales slips have been lost or misplaced. The bookkeeper uses the sales slip to input all credit sales.

Checks.   The bookkeeper uses the payment checks received from customers to input all cash payments.

Credit Memo.   The credit memo form will be retained, but the credit memos will now be prenumbered. The prenumbering will allow better physical control and will indicate all lost or misplaced credit memos. The bookkeeper uses the credit memo as input for all merchandise returns.

Cash Payments Log. See Exhibit C-13. The bookkeeper uses the log for bank reconciliation.

Conceptual Design

The accounts receivable system has five modules.

Credit Purchase on Account

Credit customers may purchase merchandise in either of the Pagoo stores. The salesperson prepares a prenumbered sales slip in duplicate. The slip contains

EXHIBIT C-13   Cash Payments Log

PAGOO CENTERS, INC.
Cash Payments Log

Month of _____

Date	Recorded By	Amount

Total Cash Payments

the date; the customer's name and address; the salesperson's name; the description, quantity, unit price, and extension of each item purchased; and the total price of the sale. The salesperson then phones the bookkeeper for credit approval. The bookkeeper compares the proposed sale to the credit available for the customer which is printed on the bookkeeper's copy of the file status report. If the sale is acceptable. the bookkeeper makes a memo note of the

EXHIBIT C-14   Credit Purchase on Account

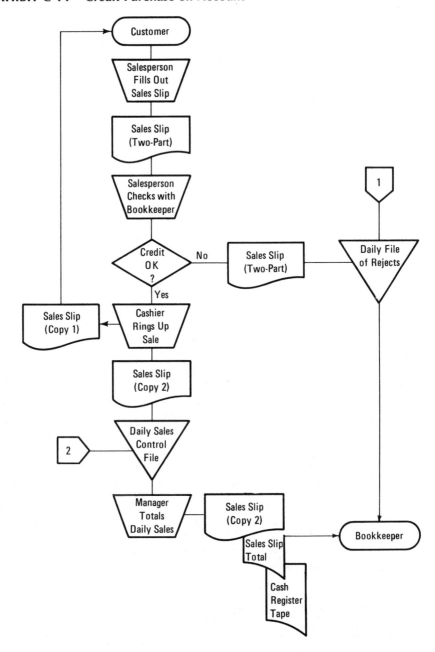

sale to prevent another purchase before the file gets updated and informs the salesperson of the decision. The customer signs the sales slip and receives the original as a merchandise receipt. The salesperson then rings up on the cash register for totaling purposes, despite the fact that no cash was received. If the sale is rejected, the salesperson marks the sales slip void and informs the customer. In either case, the sales slips are filed numerically by sales slip number. At the end of the day, the manager assembles the sales slips and runs a calculator tape on them. The manager compares this total to the cash register total from the cash register tape. The sales slips and attached calculator tape, along with the cash register tape, are sent to the bookkeeper (see Exhibit C-14 on page 752).

Credit Purchase with Credit Card

For major credit card sales, the salesperson will fill out the sales slip in the same fashion as for a purchase on account. Then, using the customer's card, the salesperson will fill out the credit card sales slip. If the amount exceeds that credit card company's threshold, the salesperson must then phone the credit card company for approval. If approved, the salesperson enters the approval code onto the credit card sales slip and gives the customer a copy of both the Pagoo Centers sales slip and the credit card sales slip. The salesperson then rings up the credit sales on the cash register, files the Pagoo Centers sales slip numerically, and files the remaining two copies of the slip next to the cash register for delivery to the bookkeeper at the end of the day. If credit is not approved by the credit card company, both the credit card and Pagoo Centers sales slips are marked void and filed (see Exhibit C-15 on page 754).

Payments on Account

All payments on account are made through the mail by check. The secretary opens all mail (except the bank statement) and sorts it. The secretary assembles all payments and runs a calculator tape on them. The bookkeeper records this information in the cash payments log by entering the date, initials, and total amount of payments (see Input). John Paul Pagoo will use this log as a check against the bank reconciliation. The checks and attached tape are then sent to the bookkeeper. The bookkeeper prepares a bank deposit slip and sends the checks and bank deposit slip to the bank for deposit into the firm's checking account (see Exhibit C-16 on page 755).

Credit Memos

When a customer returns merchandise, the salesperson records the customer name, customer address, date, and merchandise description on a prenumbered credit memo form. The credit memo must then be approved by the store manager. One copy goes to the customer; the second copy is kept next to the cash register and is sent to the bookkeeper at the end of the day (see Exhibit C-17 on page 756).

EXHIBIT C-15   Credit Purchase with a Credit Card

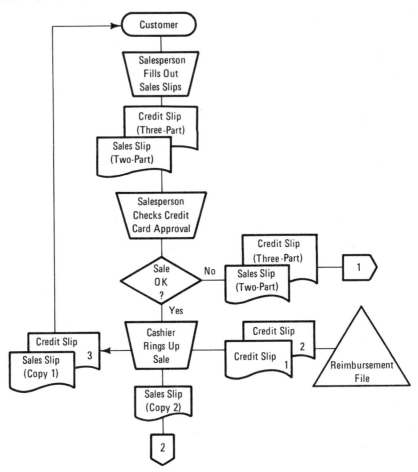

Recordkeeping

The sales slips, checks, and credit memos are input documents for the computer system. The bookkeeper enters the data into the system using a terminal. The computer system will keep updated all balances owed by Pagoo Centers' customers. The total of cash payments is used for an entry in the cash receipts journal. The total of the sales slips is used for an entry in the sales journal. The credit memos are used for individual entries in the general journal. The total of the interest charges is used for a general journal entry (see Exhibit C-18 on page 757).

At month end, the accountant foots and rules all journals and posts entries to the general ledger. At that time, a balance will be struck in the accounts receivable control account in the general ledger. The bookkeeper will use the computer system to generate an aged trial balance, and this will be compared to the total in the control account. When the subsidiary ledger and control account balance, the bookkeeper uses the system to generate the statements of account, which are mailed directly to the customers.

EXHIBIT C-16   Payments on Account

755

Systems
Case and
Applications

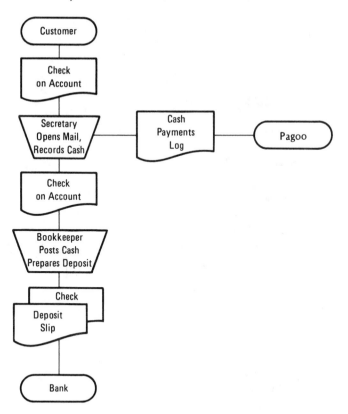

Computer Programs

The new system will include computer programs that

1. Maintain the customer file with additions, deletions, and modifications.
2. Update the data files with transactions.
3. Print the aged trial balance.
4. Print the statements of account.

There are literally hundreds of available accounting systems. Regardless of the system you choose, it should provide for file maintenance, transaction processing, an aged trial balance, and statements of accounts.

File Maintenance.   The system must be able to continually update the information in the customer master file. There are three types of changes to the file: additions, deletions, and modifications. For all types of changes, the program should check the input customer number to make sure it is valid. If it is not valid, the program should print an error message and ask for another customer number.

Additions add new customers to the file after their credit is approved by the accountant. The user must input the customer number, the name, the ad-

EXHIBIT C-17   Credit Memos

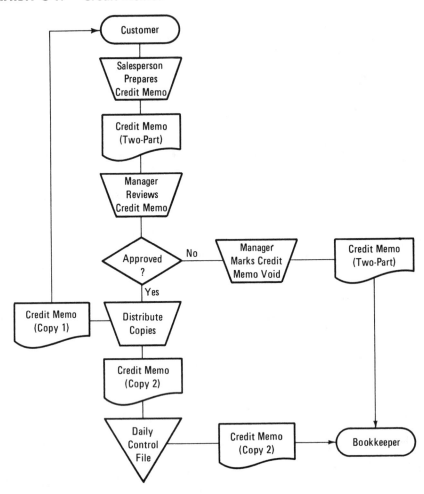

dress, and the credit limit. The program then should initially create that customer record and make the beginning balance, debits, credits, and ending balance all zero.

Deletions remove customers from the file. This would be necessary if the
customer declared bankruptcy or moved out of town. The program should not
let the user delete a customer with a nonzero balance; the account should first
have to be written off. Even if a valid customer number with a zero balance
is selected for deletion, the program should first print out the status of that
customer's account to help ensure that only the correct customers are deleted.

Modifications are changes to the customer's name, address, or credit
limit. The program should first print out the current status of the customer's
account. The program should then ask what data-items the user would like to
change. The user should not be able to change the balances with this program.
Balances should be changed only by a transaction processing program. The
file maintenance program could also generate the file status report.

EXHIBIT C-18   Recordkeeping

757

*Systems
Case and
Applications*

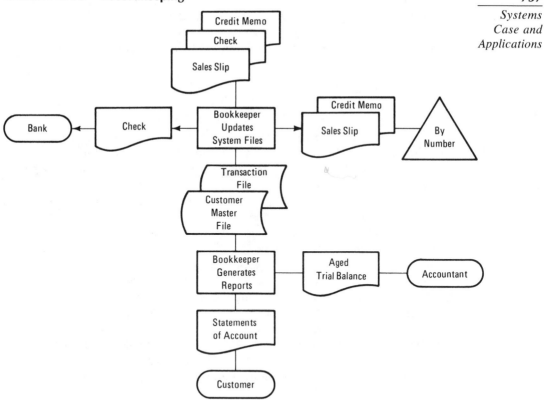

Transaction Processing.   The system should process the four basic types of transactions—credit sales, cash payments, credit memos, and debit memos. The input will be directly from the documents described earlier (see section on Specific Requirements). This input will consist of the type of transaction, the customer number, the date of the transaction, and the dollar amount of the transaction. The program should accept individual transactions and update the appropriate record on the customer master file. The program should then add the transaction at the end of the transaction file to act as an audit trail.

Aged Trial Balance.   The system should generate the aged trial balance, previously described in detail (see section on Specific Requirements). The only input by the user to the program is the date the program is run. Using the customer master file, the program prints the total amount owed, the amount that is current, the amount that is over 30 days old, and the amount that is over 60 days old for each customer. When all customer balances have been printed, the program prints a final total for all customers.

Statements of Account.   The system should generate a statement of account for each customer. The statement of account is described in detail in the section on Specific Requirements. For each customer, the program reads the name, address, and current balance due from the customer master file. This information is printed out. The program then reads every transaction off the transaction file that matches this customer, and a line is printed for that transaction. Also, for each line (and hence each transaction) a running balance is kept. Totals of each type of transaction are then printed for that customer.

Resource Requirements

Implementation, conversion, and operation of this new system will not require any additional personnel. Because of the simplicity of the proposed equipment and programs, the bookkeeper can easily be trained to use the system. The hardware necessary for this system is a microcomputer with some peripheral equipment, primarily a printer. A microcomputer was chosen because it is specifically designed to be a personal computer, in this case to assist the bookkeeper. This computer is relatively inexpensive, can be as portable as a typewriter, fits on a desk or table with no special electrical or environmental control requirements, and does not require a data processing professional to operate it. There is a series of programs available from numerous companies for a wide range of accounting functions. These programs have an accounts receivable capability and may be suitable for your needs. The programs are available with documentation for approximately $500. If suitable, this would be less than the cost of having the programs specified, programmed, and documented by an outside professional. We would particularly recommend the systems of DacEasy, Pacioli, CYMA, SBT, and Great Plains. The system will also require certain materials that are different from ordinary office supplies:

1. *Stock paper.* The aged trial balance and customer billing statements will be printed on this paper. Standard 11″ × 14″ computer paper, which has holes along the edges of the paper, can be purchased. These holes are used by the printer tractor to keep the paper aligned. Your vendor can supply the paper in many different formats and colors. If you need more than one copy of a report, it may be more efficient to order some multipart paper rather than to rerun the report.
2. *Binders.* To hold reports neatly, you may want to order top-bound binders that are especially made for computer printouts. Top binding will save you from having to separate the pages.
3. *Diskettes.* Diskettes contain machine-readable information. You will want to have enough to hold your backup information and programs. Twenty diskettes will be sufficient for the accounts receivable system.
4. *Ribbon.* You will need ribbons for your printer. These ribbons will need to be replaced approximately once a month.

Tangible Benefits

The purchase of equipment and related material will total approximately $4,500. This will lead to additional depreciation expense of $4,500, since it qualifies as Section 179 property and can therefore be written off in the first year. At the 3 percent marginal tax rate, this will yield a $1,530 tax saving. There will be no direct clerical reduction with this new system. However, when the firm is familiar with the computer, there is the potential for use of the computer in other areas of the business. As the company expands, there may be no need for additional personnel because the computer can ease the paperwork and bookkeeping burden. Thus, the computer system may lead to future tangible benefits when more employees need not be hired. The new computer system may also lead to tangible benefits in reducing bad debt expense. By checking credit status, the salesperson should sell less frequently to delinquent customers. With the aged trial balance, the company should follow up more quickly when customers do not pay on time. Both of these aspects of the new system should reduce the loss from uncollectible accounts, but it would be impossible to identify a specific number.

Intangible Benefits

The new computer system will introduce the employees of Pagoo Centers to electronic data processing. After they become familiar with the use of the computer, additional applications, such as accounts payable, payroll, general ledger, and inventory, will be natural extensions. In addition, the system

1. Shortens bookkeeping time required to maintain accurate records. This may generate tangible benefits if there are overtime costs for bookkeeping.
2. Reduces bookkeeping errors by eliminating redundant writing, calculating, and typing.
3. Eliminates the need for the monthly, manual preparation of customer billing statements.
4. Assists in maintaining complete, accurate, and consistent records because it encourages the use of standard bookkeeping practices.
5. Makes information available when needed.
6. Protects the firm from losing important business information by allowing backup copies of all data to be made.

Cost/Benefit Analysis

The benefits of the new system cannot be sufficiently quantified to perform a fully numerical cost/benefit analysis. However, the balance between the costs and benefits of this new system is clear. The cost of the new system is relatively modest. The immediate benefit is the improvement of the bookkeeping system. The future benefits lie in introducing employees to the computer. As Pagoo Centers, Inc., continues to grow, the eventual companywide use of the computer is inevitable. Therefore, we believe that the benefits are overwhelming, and we urge the system's adoption.

PROJECT MANAGEMENT OF SYSTEM DEVELOPMENT

Exhibit C-19 gives an installation and progress chart for Pagoo Centers, Inc., that applies the basic systems case to the systems material illustrated in Chapters 8 and 16.

EXHIBIT C-19 Accounts Receivable Installation Schedule for Pagoo Centers, Inc.

Step	Activity	Weeks (−12 to +8)	Scheduled Start	Actual Start
1	Make Key Decisions	(bar −12 to −11)	_/_/_	_/_/_
2	Complete Training	(bar −12 to −6)	_/_/_	_/_/_
3	Order Supplies	(bar −12 to −10)	_/_/_	_/_ _
4	Gather Business Information	(bar −11 to −9, dashed to +2)	_/_/_	_/_/_
5	Receive System	(bar at 0)		_/_/_
6	Start-up System	(bar at 0)		_/_/_
7	Install A/R	(bar at 0)		_/_/_
8	Load Master Files	(bar 0 to +3)	_/_/_	_/_/_
9	Apply Controls	(bar 0 to +6)	_/_/_	_/_/_
10	Load Past Due	(bar 0 to +4)	_/_/_	_/_/_
11	Load Current Transactions	(bar +2 to +4)	_/_/_	_/_/_
12	Begin Daily Operations	(bar +4 to +6)		

Column headers across Weeks: −12 −11 −10 −9 −8 −7 −6 −5 −4 −3 −2 −1 | 0 | +1 +2 +3 +4 +5 +6 +7 +8

QUESTIONS

C-1. Describe the processing of a purchase order by Pagoo Centers, Inc., including an explanation of how each copy is used.

C-2. Describe the processing of a debit memo by Pagoo Centers, Inc., including an explanation of how each copy is used.

C-3. Describe the processing of a sales slip by Pagoo Centers, Inc., including an explanation of how each copy is used.

C-4. Describe the processing of a credit memo by Pagoo Centers, Inc., including an explanation of how each copy is used.

C-5. Explain how cash sales and cash receipts on account are processed by Pagoo Centers, Inc.

C-6. Explain how cash payments on account are processed by Pagoo Centers, Inc.

C-7. Outline the functioning of the payroll system, including the disposition of all supporting payroll information.

C-8. What element of internal control is violated in each of the following areas:

a. Bookkeeper records transactions in journal and posts them to the ledger

b. No separate list is maintained of cash received in the mail

c. Freedom of stock clerk to move goods between stores

C-9. Suggest how company policy might be improved in the following areas:

    a. Definition of what is a major purchase order

    b. Procedure for determining uncollectible accounts

    c. Judging the profit performance of the company

C-10. Suggest how control procedures might be improved in the following areas:

    a. Safeguarding accounting records

    b. Access to cash registers

    c. Proper support for checks

C-11. Identify the major problem areas of Pagoo Centers, Inc., which have led to the need for a system analysis.

C-12. The organization chart depicted in Exhibit C-5 shows three major lines of authority. Describe each of these lines of authority. Who else reports directly to John Paul Pagoo?

C-13. Discuss why each piece of information recorded on the sales slip is necessary and how it is used.

C-14. List the steps which take place in the procedure for sales returns and allowances.

C-15. Give the five most critical deficiencies present in the Pagoo Centers accounting system in descending order of importance.

C-16. List the first five steps which should be taken by Pagoo Centers to deal with their problems and the order in which the steps should be taken.

C-17. Outline the Statement of Objectives presented in this appendix and give the purpose of each section and sub-section.

C-18. Outline the System Design presented in this appendix and give the purpose of each section and sub-section.

C-19. Distinguish between "balance-forward" and "open-item" accounts receivable systems. Give the situations in which each would be most appropriate.

C-20. Identify the type of diagram in Exhibit C-19 and explain its usefulness in system development.

PROBLEMS

C-21. Using your knowledge of the organization structure, personalities, and accounting system at Pagoo Centers, discuss five specific internal control problems which currently exist in the firm. For each of these areas of internal control difficulty make a recommendation as to how the problem might be solved.

C-22. Some of the most critical internal control deficiencies for Pagoo Centers, Inc., exist in the areas of purchasing, custody, and recordkeeping for inventory. Specify how purchasing could be better controlled. What changes would you suggest in the responsibility for physical custody and movement of inventory? How might recordkeeping for inventory be improved?

C-23. System analysis is the first step in correcting systems which are not working properly, as well as in the creation of new systems. This is true no matter the nature of the system. Give three specific examples of systems you have come into contact with which should be analyzed with the purpose of improving the system or determining what is preventing effective operation.

C-24. The recommendations at the end of the system analysis report are the goal of the entire system analysis process. However, these recommendations must consider the political environment of the firm and must be acceptable to management.

1. In the sample report for Pagoo Centers, items were mentioned in the section on deficiencies which were not followed by specific recommendations. Identify these deficiencies and state why recommendations might not have been made for each of them.

2. Give three examples of recommendations which may seem called for in Pagoo Centers but which would probably not be made because they are impractical or unrealistic.

C-25. The system analysis report for Pagoo Centers given in the chapter included a recommendation that a policies and procedures manual be developed. Such a manual would include a chart of accounts consisting of the number, name, and guideline for use for each asset, liability, owners' equity, revenue, and expense account. Develop a chart of balance sheet accounts for Pagoo Centers providing the number, name, and guideline for use for each account. Develop a chart of income statement accounts for Pagoo Centers providing the number, name, and guideline for use for each account.

C-26. Prepare a credit application form that Pagoo Centers could use when customers desired to purchase on account. The form should contain all detailed information Pagoo Centers would need to make sound credit-granting decisions.

C-27. The system analysis report for Pagoo Centers given in the chapter included a recommendation that a perpetual inventory system be implemented. Explain how a perpetual inventory system would work for Pagoo Centers.

C-28. The system analysis report for Pagoo Centers given in the chapter included a recommendation that the duties and responsibilities of several positions be altered. Rewrite job descriptions for the accountant, bookkeeper, and buyer consistent with the findings of the report.

C-29. The system analysis report for Pagoo Centers given in the chapter included a recommendation that separate profit and loss figures be developed for each store. Develop a new chart of accounts which would make possible the generation of profit and loss figures by store. This chart of accounts should include only account number and account name (guidelines for use may be omitted). How would you handle the salaries of those employees who work for both stores?

C-30. The system analysis report for Pagoo Centers given in the chapter included a recommendation that a policies and procedures manual be developed. Such a manual would give the basic policies of the firm concerning conflicts of interest, vacation, leave, hiring, firing, record retention, credit granting, personal checks and uncollectible accounts. Develop a summary of appropriate policies for Pagoo Centers.

C-31. Using the data base software available to you, create the master file and transaction file for the Accounts Receivable subsystem for Pagoo Centers.

C-32. Design the output reports for the Accounts Receivable subsystem for Pagoo Centers using the available data base software.

C-33. Design the input screens for the Accounts Receivable subsystem for Pagoo Centers using the available data base software.

DECISION CASE

Refer back to the Well-Body Drug Co. data given in the Decision Case for Chapter 2.

Required:

Prepare a system analysis report for the Well-Body Drug Co. Your report should contain all seven elements of system analysis plus a title page, letter of transmittal, and table of contents. Where data are incomplete (job descriptions and content of documents), you should supply logical information of your own.

GLOSSARY

A-B-C analysis report. An inventory analysis report that separates inventory items into classes based on the dollar investment required and shows the investment in each inventory item for the period compared to its usage (*p. 389*).

Account numbering system. A Bedford-specific system that indicates the proper order, section and financial statement placement of individual titles, totals, and accounts and balances (*p. 462*).

Account type classification. An expansion of the Bedford account numbering system that further refines the formatting of financial statements (*p. 462*).

Accounting. A system for keeping track of the financial events in the life of any individual or organization in a manner that makes it possible for that individual or organization to report on its financial position and activities to anyone who may be interested (*p. 2*).

Accounting controls. Accounting techniques aimed at protecting assets from being lost or stolen and at ensuring that accounting records are accurate and complete (*p. 44*).

Accounting cycle. The process a business goes through in order to record, classify, summarize, and communicate financial information on a regular basis (*p. 667*).

Accounting equation. A representation of the financial relationships within a business showing that the resources equal the sources and claims on those resources: *Assets = Liabilities + Owners' Equity*. For the corporate form of business, the equation may be expanded: *Assets = Liabilities + Common Stock +* $\sum$ *[(Revenue − Expenses) − Dividends]* (*p. 644*).

Accounting software. Computer software packages, such as Bedford, used to automate the accounting process and to provide support for analysis of the financial data that the computer generates (*p. 451*).

Accounts payable module. Application designed to monitor cash outflows resulting from payments of amounts due suppliers and to provide information that will aid in the control of the costs and expenses associated with the purchase and payment function (*p. 345*).

Accounts receivable module. Application designed to monitor cash inflows from the collections of receivables and to provide information that will aid in reducing the amount of cash tied up in receivables (*p. 336*).

Accrual-basis accounting. A system of accounting in which revenues are recognized when earned and expenses are recognized when a legal liability is incurred without regard for the receipt or payment of cash (*p. 655*).

Adjusted trial balance. Trial balance prepared after all adjusting entries have been made and posted. It summarizes the effect of both internal and external transactions on the accounts of a business (*p. 675*).

Adjusting entries. Journal entries made at the end of an accounting period to record the cumulative effects of internal events. These entries bring the books of a business up-to-date (*p. 674*).

Administrative controls. Accounting techniques designed (1) to promote efficient operations by reducing waste and duplication of effort, and (2) to encourage compliance with company policies and procedures (*p. 44*).

Aged trial balance. Output report that provides a complete listing of amounts owed by each customer for each outstanding invoice and in total as of the statement date. Each amount is classified by its length of time outstanding (*p. 339*).

AIS (Accounting Information System). A system that combines transaction processing and the production of external financial statements and reports with the generation of other accounting information for management decision making and control of the business (*p. 7*).

Algorithm. A fixed procedure or set of steps to follow to solve a particular problem (*p. 257*).

Application controls. Internal controls that are involved with one specific application area, such as the programmed controls for accounts receivable (*p. 616*).

Application module. Building blocks of a system that accomplish a specific area of processing and can be developed or altered independently of the other areas in a system (*p. 308*).

Application program. A computer program designed to solve a specific problem or answer a specific set of questions for the end user (*p. 83*).

Application programmer. Person who develops effective, efficient, well-documented programs meeting the specifications of the systems analyst (*p. 130*).

Artificial intelligence (AI). The use of computer systems to either mimic the decision-making process of humans or to solve problems mechanically that would otherwise require human intelligence to solve (*p. 281*).

ASCII (American Standard Code for Information Interchange). The coding standard (that is, how letters, numbers, etc. are represented by the 0s and 1s of the computer system) for all computer equipment except IBM mainframes (*p. 225*).

Assets. Financial and productive resources which are controlled by a business, result from specific transactions, and are expected to possess future value for the business (*p. 644*).

Attributes. Specific identifying characteristics of a record such as name, address, or current balance. Data-items store specific values of the attributes for each entity (*p. 156*).

Audit. Systematic examination of accounting records to ensure their accuracy and completeness. An audit may be conducted internally by company personnel or by an independent certified public accountant (*p. 48*).

Audit trail. References in the accounting records that make it possible to trace source documents through the journal and ledger to their appearance on financial statements and to track numbers on financial statements back to their original source (*p. 7, p. 49*).

Auditing around the computer. Approach to auditing where the auditor only examines input to and output from the computer, treating the computer processing as a "black box" (*p. 607*).

Auditing through the computer. Approach to auditing where the auditor examines the flow of information within the computer and uses the computer in the audit of the system (*p. 607*).

Authorization. Approval of a transaction by a responsible official (*p. 46*).

Balance sheet. A primary external reporting financial statement that gives the financial position of a business at a point in time by listing its assets, liabilities, and owners' equity (*p. 647*).

Bank reconciliation. Process of explaining any differences between the cash balance as shown on the company records and the cash balance as shown on the monthly bank statement (*p. 49*).

Base table. The tables created in a relational data base management system that contain data. Logical tables, called views, can then be created from the base tables (*p. 190*).

Batch processing systems. Computer-based systems in which items to be processed are collected into groups (batched) for processing at predetermined times (*p. 88*).

BEDFORD Integrated Accounting. A microcomputer general accounting software package that combines the general ledger and specialized modules into one program (*p. 452*).

Bill of materials. Listings of the components going into a manufactured product or subassembly (*p. 425*).

Budgeted balance sheet. A projected/pro forma balance sheet (*p. 318*).

Budgeting. Process of integrating the planning and control functions to produce a master budget of projected (budgeted) financial statements (*p. 316*).

Bus network. A network configuration where all computers are connected to a central line, called a bus, rather than to each other. Communication between computers then occurs through this bus (*p. 236*).

Business cycle. The set of activities making up an important recurring business activity, such as the sales cycle, cash receipts cycle, purchases cycle, and cash disbursements cycle (*p. 8*).

Capital stock (common stock). The sources of assets and claims against assets created by the sale of stock to owners (*p. 650*).

Cash budget. A projected statement of cash flows; a component of the master budget (*p. 318*).

Cash disbursements cycle. The set of activities involved in disbursing cash, including authorization and placement of the purchase, receipt of the product, invoicing from the supplier, and subsequent payment (*p. 12*).

Cash disbursements journal. A special journal for recording all outflows (disbursements) of cash (*p. 347*).

Cash payments and adjustments file. Input file consisting of transactions which decrease payables for a given period; data from this file completes the updating of the vendor master and open invoices files and is the basis for the cash disbursements journal in a computer system (*p. 356*).

Cash receipts and adjustments file. Input file consisting of transactions which provide data for the updating of the customer master file; transactions are those that have reduced receivables balances since the last processing (*p. 343*).

Cash receipts and adjustments journal. A record of all cash receipts from the collection of receivables (*p. 336*).

Cash receipts and disbursements subsystem. A subsystem consisting of the accounts receivable, accounts payable, and payroll modules (*p. 313*).

Cash receipts cycle. The set of procedures for receiving cash, including billing, receipt, the control and deposit of cash, and the updating of the customer records (*p. 12*).

Cash receipts journal. A special journal for recording all inflows (receipts) of cash (*p. 679*).

Cash requirements report. Report which shows the effect of planned disbursements on the cash position of the business. It includes a complete listing of all invoices and vendors to be paid during a period (*p. 349*).

Cash-basis accounting. A system of accounting in which revenues and expenses are recognized only when cash is received or paid (*p. 655*).

Central processing unit (CPU). The computer in a computer system. The CPU directs the activities of the entire system. Often called the processor (*p. 84*).

Chart of accounts. A listing of all accounts in the general ledger in numerical order, indicating their sequence in the ledger. It could also contain a description of each account and guidance on when each should be used (*p. 46*).

Check register. A journal used to record checks issued; it is used with a voucher register in a voucher system (*p. 685*).

CIS (Computer Information System). Any information system that is computerized or computer-based as opposed to manually-based (*p. 7*).

Client/server approach. Approach to local area networks where the client, usually a user's microcomputer, requests data from the server, usually a much larger micro-computer or minicomputer. The data base access and processing occurs on the server, and only the result is passed back to the client (*p. 235*).

Closing entries. Journal entries made at the end of an accounting period (1) to reduce the balance in all temporary accounts to zero, (2) to transfer the difference between revenue and expense to owners' equity, and (3) to transfer the effect of dividends or withdrawals to owners' equity (*p. 675*).

Coding. Assigning unique numbers to entities in a file so that the identification numbers convey information about the entity, such as having all general ledger accounts beginning with the number 1 be assets (*p. 155*).

Column. A column in a relational data base corresponds to a field or data-item. All data in a relational data base are stored in the row and column format of a table (*p. 192*).

Comparative general ledger. Report which allows the user to (1) compare actual results for the reporting period to budgeted results for the period, and to the actual results for the same period of the previous year; and (2) make the same comparisons for year-to-date results (*p. 415*).

Compiler. A computer program whose purpose is to translate higher level language statements into a form that can directly activate the computer hardware (*p. 84*).

Compliance testing. Testing the internal controls to determine if they function properly (*p. 607*).

Computer maintenance. The process of keeping computer equipment in operating condition, stocking the necessary spare parts, and keeping repair technicians available (*p. 100*).

Computer operations. The physical steps necessary to use a computer system, such as changing paper in the printer and mounting tapes (*p. 101*).

Computer operator. Person who runs the programs using specified instructions and physically operates the computer system, such as by mounting tapes (*p. 130*).

Computer system. Combination of hardware and software that can then be used for some desired end, such as business data processing (*p. 81*).

Computer system acquisition. Process of selecting the most appropriate computer system from the alternatives available from vendors (*p. 100*).

Computer-aided software engineering (CASE). Use of computers and programs in the development of computer-based systems by automating steps in the process, such as the computer generation of source language statements for a new system rather than requiring the programmer to generate all of the statements by hand (*p. 511*).

Conceptual design. A general overview of the system, achieved by defining the basic modules of the system and their interrelationships (*p. 546*).

Constant file/report file. Files of relatively permanent data which are used over and over as input to processing applications, but are not altered by the processing and are infrequently changed externally, such as the permanent input file that specifies the constant data to be used or the headings for each output report (*p. 312*).

Control accounts. General ledger accounts for which a detailed subsidiary ledger is maintained. Accounts payable and accounts receivable are always control accounts (*p. 677*).

Control log. A manually prepared listing of control totals of computer input to be reconciled with computer-generated control totals (*p. 612*).

Control total. Sum of a meaningful item, such as a dollar value, for a batch of transactions; used to compare manual and computer processing totals (*p. 133*).

Conversion date. A Bedford-specific term indicating the date of conversion from a manual to a computerized accounting system (*p. 464*).

Cost/benefit analysis. Comparison of the costs versus the benefits of a proposed new system to ensure that the new system has economic value to the organization (*p. 551*).

Costing report. A report summarizing product manufacturing costs (actual, standard, simulated) by cost categories for past and present periods (*p. 427*).

CREATE statement. Command in the Structured Query Language to create the structure (including the component data-items) of a base table (*p. 204*).

Credit. The right-hand side of any account (*p. 668*).

Credit memorandum. A document prepared when a customer returns goods originally sold on credit which verifies that the goods have been returned and that the amount owed by the customer should be decreased (account credited) (*p. 9*).

Critical path. Longest path in a PERT/CPM network; if any activity along the critical path is delayed, completion of the entire project will be delayed (*p. 271*).

Cumulative earnings register. A report of cumulative year-to-date and quarter-to-date earnings and deductions for all employees (*p. 360*).

Cumulative transaction file. Transaction file which accumulates all of the individual prior and current transaction files for a given period of time (*p. 423*).

Current assets. Assets which are expected to be converted to cash or used up within one accounting period or operating cycle (whichever is longer) from the balance sheet date (*p. 647*).

Current hours and activity file. Transaction file which supplies all of the current pay period data necessary to calculate gross pay; used to update the employee master file and generate the payroll register (*p. 364*).

Current liabilities. Liabilities whose payment or satisfaction is expected to occur within the upcoming accounting period and will require the use of current assets (*p. 649*).

Current period payroll register. Report listing the current earnings of all employees to be paid in the current period and all deductions from those earnings (*p. 358*).

Current period transaction file. An input file consisting of one record for each detailed and verified accounting transaction which occurred during the current period (*p. 421*).

Current value of work in process report. This report shows the dollar value to date of work in process inventory and the movement of work in process during the current period (*p. 436*).

Customer billing statement. Output report of the accounts receivable application area. Billing statement sent to customers who purchase on credit (*p. 339*).

Customer detail report. A Bedford-specific report giving the accounts receivable subsidiary ledger (*p. 459*).

Customer master file. Master file which serves as the accounts receivable subsidiary ledger in a computer-based system and stores detailed information on sales to and collections from each customer, as well as amounts owed by each customer at any time (*p. 342*).

Customer order shortage report. A report giving all inventory items currently unavailable or in insufficient quantity to fill outstanding customer orders for that product (*p. 378*).

Customer summary report. A Bedford-specific report giving a listing of amounts owed by each customer by age (*p. 459*).

Data base. A collection of interrelated information stored independently of the programs and applications which use it (*p. 166*).

Data base management system (DBMS). Generalized software that handles the necessary programming after allowing the user to specify file structures. The system also handles the task of managing the data base (*p. 174*).

Data control clerk. Person who identifies and corrects errors in transactions or in the computer processing of data by comparing control totals from the computer with manually prepared control figures (*p. 130*).

Data dictionary. Identification of all data-items stored in a data base along with their definitions (*p. 158*).

Data entry clerk. Person who enters information into a computer through a terminal or by otherwise keying it into machine-readable form (*p. 130*).

Data flow diagram (DFD). Schematic representation of the files, processing, and relationships of a computer-based system (*p. 539*).

Data management summary. System specification detailing the precise nature of the input, data files, and output used by the system (*p. 571*).

Data processing (DP) manager. The top executive in the data processing department, who directs long- and short-range plans and supervises the data processing staff (*p. 130*).

Data-item. The smallest unit of information that has meaning to users, such as a customer name or a price for an inventory item (*p. 154*).

Debit. The left-hand side of any account (*p. 668*).

Debit memorandum. A document prepared when goods purchased on credit are returned to the supplier; the debit memo supports the decrease in accounts payable and notifies the supplier that goods are being returned (*p. 9*).

Decision support systems (DSS). Computerized systems that help managers make structured and semistructured decisions by accumulating and presenting relevant data and performing required calculations (*p. 258*).

Defalcation. Fraudulent appropriation of assets; defalcation is the term commonly used in accounting for embezzlement (*p. 51*).

Default chart (of accounts). A chart of accounts that is a part of Bedford accounting software and can be used as is or adjusted by the user (*p. 454*).

Default setting. A Bedford-specific status selection that controls in the absence of any action by the user (*p. 464*).

DELETE statement. Command in the Structured Query Language to remove a row from a table in a relational data base (*p. 207*).

Delinquency notice. Letters which can be automatically generated by an accounts receivable package to notify customers of seriously overdue accounts (*p. 340*).

Direct access. Process of storing data in, or getting data from, a storage device in such a manner that preceding data need not be scanned to locate the desired data (*p. 86*).

Direct organization. File organization in which the primary key for the record is the storage address on the disk drive where the file is stored (*p. 162*).

Distributed data processing. A network of computers, with local machines processing local information, while sending only summary information to the central, host computer system. This places computing power in the organization at the appropriate levels so that data entry, inquiry, and initial processing occur where the data originate and where the data are used (*p. 96*).

Dividends. Assets resulting from successful operations that are disbursed to the owners of a corporation (*p. 650*).

Document flowchart. A diagram depicting the number of copies of individual documents and the flow of each document. The flowchart shows only the flow of documents in a system and omits all the processing steps (*p. 29, 30*).

Documentation. Flowcharts and textual material that provide an overview of an entire system, describe the sources and disposition of system inputs and outputs, aid in program modification, or instruct the user on how to operate a given program (*p. 135*).

Documentation review. Independent review of systems documentation to check for completeness and to review the quality of the work done (*p. 589*).

Double-entry bookkeeping. A technique for the orderly recording and classification of business transactions in which the dollar amount of debits equals the dollar amount of credits for each transaction. Each entry affects at least two ledger accounts because all transactions have at least two different (offsetting) effects on the basic accounting equation (*p. 668*).

Downloading. Moving data from the mainframe to the microcomputer (*p. 99*).

Downsizing. Moving applications from mainframe systems to microcomputer systems (*p. 513*).

EBCDIC (Extended Binary Coded Decimal Interchange Code). The coding standard (that is, how letters, numbers, etc. are represented by the 0s and 1s of the computer system) for IBM mainframes (*p. 225*).

EDI (Electronic Data Interchange). An exchange in which data on intercompany transactions, such as sales and purchases, are sent to and from the company's computers electronically, without printout or reentry (*p. 240*).

EFT (Electronic Funds Transfer). A transaction in which funds are transferred electronically without the use of printed checks; the organization authorizes its bank to electronically transfer funds to the accounts of its suppliers or employees (*p. 241*).

Embezzlement. Fraudulent appropriation of assets; also called defalcation (*p. 51*).

Employee master file. File which contains one record for each employee; each record consists of data-items such as employee name, number, address, pay rate, deductions, and cumulative earnings (*p. 364*).

End-of-period procedures. A series of steps in the accounting cycle from adjusting entries to closing entries that are performed only once each accounting period at the end of the period (*p. 673*).

Entity. The type of person or object about which the master file has data. In an accounts receivable master file, the entity is a customer. Other entities might be employee, general ledger account, inventory item, or vendor (*p. 155*).

Entity-relationship model. Schematic representation of the logical relationships between the entities in different files (*p. 541*).

Equities. The sources of and claims on assets; individuals or groups (either owners or nonowners) from which a business has acquired its resources and the obligations that resulted (*p. 644*).

Ethernet. The most widely used method of communication on local area networks (LANs) that use a bus configuration. The primary LAN approach of all firms except IBM (*p. 236*).

Evaluation. Analysis of a previously developed system to determine if the system is adequately controlled and that the costs and benefits are as had been planned in the system design (*p. 508*).

Executive information system (EIS). Computer-based system which provides top management with needed summary and strategic information, as opposed to the detailed information needed at the operational level of the firm (*p. 492*).

Executive support system (ESS). Another name for an executive information system (*p. 492*).

Expense. Measures decreases in, or outflows of, assets or increases in liabilities caused by the profit-seeking activities of a business during an accounting period (*p. 654*).

Expert system. Computerized programs that use a defined set of rules and a related data base to help solve problems typically requiring the knowledge, experience, and judgment of an expert in a specific area (*p. 281*).

External controls. A series of controls on business activities or their reporting that originate outside of the business, such as from outside auditors, regulatory agencies, or police (*p. 44*).

External events. Transactions which take place between a business and persons or other businesses. They occur at discrete points in time when a business interacts with its environment (*p. 673*).

External/secondary/peripheral storage. The storage capacity outside of the processor, usually tapes or disks (*p. 86*).

Facilities management. The business of operating (for a fee) a client's computer and providing the necessary support services, including programming (*p. 103*).

Feasibility study. A preliminary review of the entire system development project, often carried out as the first step of the development of a large scale system; includes a cost/benefit analysis for the project (*p. 510*).

Fifth normal form. A table with a data-item that is associated with multiple but not a fixed number of values of another data-item is split into three tables so there are no join dependencies (*p. 196*).

File. A collection of related records treated as a unit and stored on a secondary storage device (*p. 154*).

File creation program. A program which initially loads information onto the file so it can be used by other programs (*p. 158*).

File device. Input/output device with storage capacity which makes possible the retention and use of large files of data within the system (*p. 85*).

File maintenance program. A program which keeps the master file current by processing all changes to the information on the file (such as changed names and addresses) except for transactions (*p. 158*).

File organization. The sequence in which records are stored in a file and how those records are later accessed (*p. 162*).

File server approach. Approach to local area networks where the disks and files on the file server (a larger microcomputer or minicomputer not used for other purposes) appear to each user on the network to be disks and files on the user's microcomputer. The data processing occurs on the user's microcomputer (*p. 235*).

Financial accounting. The process of accumulation of financial information about an organization to be supplied primarily to outside individuals and groups through financial statements (*p. 3*).

Financial accounting subsystem. A subsystem consisting of the general ledger, financial statement, and budgeting modules (*p. 315*).

Finish date. A Bedford-specific term indicating the last day of business activity covered by the current accounting period (*p. 464*).

First normal form. Data are stored in the row and column format of a table; repeating groups are eliminated in the representation of the data (*p. 194*).

Flow line. A solid line in a flowchart showing a document flow, or a broken line showing an information flow (*p. 14*).

Footing. Adding a column. Underfooting is the misadding of a column to get too small a total, while overfooting is the misadding of a column to get too large a total (*p. 53*).

Fourth normal form. A table with a data-item that is associated with multiple values of another data-item is split into two tables so there are no multiple value dependencies (*p. 196*).

Front-end processor. A processor attached to the host computer that calls (or polls) each terminal to determine if there are any messages to be transmitted. It can also be used to terminate and initiate calls for internal control purposes (*p. 139*).

Future value. Criterion for a resource to be an asset: The company must be able to exchange or use the resource in the future (*p. 644*).

GANTT chart. A semistructured decision model. Chart showing different tasks to be performed in carrying out a complex project and the time frames for their accomplishment (*p. 267*).

General controls. Internal controls in a computer system which apply to all applications, such as the proper separation of duties (*p. 616*).

General journal. An accounting instrument for recording transactions not recorded in one of the special journals (*p. 414*).

General ledger format file. This file consists of one record for each line of the income statement and balance sheet (*p. 421*).

General ledger master file. File which contains one record for each general ledger account in the chart of accounts; each record consists of data-items such as account number, account description, account classification, and current and previous year balances, as well as budgeted balances by month (*p. 421*).

General ledger module. Component of the financial accounting subsystem which updates the general ledger and produces journals and ledgers (*p. 413*).

General ledger package. A package that provides the automation of the general financial accounting process (*p. 451*).

GENERAL module. The Bedford module that accomplishes the general ledger accounting functions (*p. 454*).

Generalized audit software (GAS). Software designed to work with a variety of file structures and data formats in performing a computer-based audit (*p. 625*).

Generally accepted accounting principles (GAAP). A set of principles that govern the collection and reporting of financial information to external users (*p. 3*).

Group decision support system (GDSS). A decision support system that is available to numerous users (*p. 264*).

Hard copy. A physical record such as a check copy or invoice (*p. 132*).

Hardware. The physical equipment of a computer system, such as mechanical, magnetic, electric or electronic devices (*p. 84*).

Hash total. Meaningless sum, such as a sum of part numbers, for a batch of transactions; used to compare manual and computer processing totals (*p. 133*).

Heuristics. Methods of solving problems which are based on rules of thumb; the result is usually a good solution, but there is no proof the optimal solution has been reached (*p. 282*).

Host computer. One stand-alone computer that processes every transaction and maintains all data files for the system (*p. 95*).

Implementation. The process of getting a new system working, including the operation of the old and new systems in parallel (*p. 508*).

Imprest petty cash system. An internal control system for the petty cash fund in which the total of all vouchers plus the cash on hand is always equal to the established amount (*p. 53*).

Income. Increase in a business's assets due to successful operations; income of an accounting period is the difference between revenue and expense (*p. 650*).

Income statement. A primary external reporting financial statement that summarizes the results of the profit-seeking activities of the business for a period of time by listing revenues and expenses (*p. 652*).

Indexed sequential organization. File organization in which records are stored sequentially by primary key, but there is also a separate index file containing the location on the file for the record matching the primary key. Data can be accessed randomly by using the index file (*p. 163*).

Inference engine. The component of an expert system that contains the logic and reasoning necessary to apply the decision rules (*p. 284*).

Information center. Group within the information systems department to provide computer-oriented assistance to end users, either with mainframe access or microcomputer skills (*p. 497*).

Information system. A comprehensive collection of information available to facilitate external reporting and communication and enhance management decision-making and control of the business (*p. 5*).

Information systems steering committee. Group composed of information systems specialists and representatives of line departments or divisions that provides guidance and sets priorities for information systems in the organization (*p. 496*).

Information technology. All of the different but related aspects of computers and information systems (*p. 488*).

Inquiry/response. On-line interaction with the computer for questions and answers (*p. 93*).

Intangible benefits. System benefits, such as increased capacity and timeliness, for which it is difficult to determine a dollar value (*p. 549*).

Integrated general accounting package. Computerized accounting software (usually microcomputer based) that brings together general ledger functions and specialized modules (such as receivables, payables, and inventory functions) in one program (*p. 451*).

Integrated test facility (ITF). Separate records built into all files of an on-line system so that test transactions can be processed without affecting "live" data (*p. 621*).

Integration account. An account that links modules of the Bedford accounting program (*p. 454*).

Interactive processing systems. Computer systems where data are processed individually and continuously as transactions take place and output is generated instantly (*p. 92*).

Interface (information exchange). The ability to transfer data between modules (*p. 311*).

Internal control. Organizational plan and other measures designed to safeguard assets, check the accuracy and reliability of accounting data, promote operational efficiency, and encourage adherence to managerial policies (*p. 43*).

Internal events. Transactions which take place wholly within the firm without the direct involvement of other persons or businesses; these events tend to be continuous in nature, like depreciation (*p. 674*).

Inventory analysis report. Inventory control management report highlighting turnover, profit, profit margin, and investment required for each item (*p. 387*).

Inventory management module. Point of original entry of purchase requisitions and purchase orders, purchase returns, and purchase adjustments into the AIS; intended to provide information aiding in controlling inventory and making purchase decisions (*p. 385*).

Inventory reorder report. A report providing product reorder recommendations based on standard formulas and past inventory stock movement data from the business (*p. 390*).

Inventory stock movement report. A report summarizing individual product sales patterns and trends to aid in inventory reorder decisions (*p. 389*).

Inventory stock status report. Inventory control output report showing the quantity of each inventory item available as of the end of a processing period, the unit cost per item, and the total cost extended (*p. 387*).

Inventory transaction register. Inventory control output report listing all transactions in inventory for the period covered by the report, including orders, receipts, and issues of inventory items as well as adjustments to inventory (*p. 386*).

Invoice. A billing statement for goods purchased or sold on credit (*p. 10*).

Invoice register. Journal where purchase invoices are recorded as approved; the invoices are assigned a sequential number and treated in essentially the same way as vouchers in the voucher system (*p. 695*).

Item master file. Input-output file for the order processing and inventory control applications providing one record for each individual item number in inventory (*p. 393*).

Item price list. This report lists each active item in inventory and gives price information including base price, markup, or discounts (*p. 378*).

JIT (Just-in-time). An inventory system where long-term arrangements are made with suppliers to deliver items only as necessary for production (*p. 241*).

Job description. Narrative description including job title, the position which supervises this one, the positions which this one supervises, a narrative of the duties, the salary, and a list of the educational and experience requirements (*p. 530*).

Joins. Operations that put relational tables together to form new tables. A common data-item is used to tie the tables together (*p. 192*).

Journal. A device for recording events as they occur in the life of a business (*p. 668*).

Knowledge acquisition mechanism. A tool used in the development of expert systems by the experts and knowledge engineers to capture the rules, heuristics and knowledge of the expert (*p. 284*).

Knowledge base. The component of an expert system that is the combination of the data base and the collection of decision rules that an expert would use to solve the problem (*p. 283*).

LAN (Local Area Network). A communications network for microcomputers used to allow them to send mail to each other, to share expensive peripherals, and to access centralized data bases (*p. 222*).

Lapping. Theft of cash collections on accounts receivable; the theft from the first customer is concealed by using cash received from a second customer, the theft from the second customer is concealed by cash received from a third customer, and so on (*p. 54*).

Ledger. A collection of the individual accounts of a business used to classify transactions and determine their cumulative effect on the accounts (*p. 668*).

Letter of transmittal. Part of a system analysis report which provides an overall conception of the report, including the reason for its preparation and major findings (*p. 530*).

Liabilities. Debts or legal obligations of a business which result from the acquisition of assets from a person or group other than the owners of the business (*p. 646*).

Lists. A vector or one-dimensional array; data may be stored in a list in the computer's main memory during the operation of a program (*p. 152*).

Long-term debt. Amounts owed to creditors from borrowings which are expected to be repaid over many years (*p. 649*).

Main memory/primary storage. The storage capacity of the processor. The storage is usually reserved for the operating system and the particular application program and related data currently being processed (*p. 84*).

Management of information systems (MOIS). Direction and control of computer-based systems for business advantage, as opposed to the technical details of information technology (*p. 496*).

Managerial accounting. The creation of information for the management group of the organization concerned with decision making and performance evaluation (*p. 4*).

Manufacturing order summary file. This file contains all of the information pertaining to each manufacturing order (*p. 438*).

Manufacturing subsystem. A subsystem consisting of the product data management, material requirements planning, production costing and production monitoring modules (*p. 319*).

Master budget. Projected income statement, statement of projected cash needs, and a projected balance sheet (*p. 317*).

Master file. A relatively permanent file that contains the information occurring once per entity. The file contains relatively permanent information which is used as a source of reference and may be periodically updated (*p. 159, p. 312*).

Material requirements planning (MRP) module. A manufacturing module for carrying out complex purchasing decisions to maximize production efficiency while minimizing inventory levels (*p. 321*).

MIS (Management Information System). The total system providing information for management needs (accounting, production, personnel, marketing); it may be computer-based or manual but is usually built around a computer system (*p. 7*).

Model base. A collection of independent decision models (*p. 259*).

Modularity. A system design concept which requires that a system be constructed solely of independent but interrelated components called modules (*p. 545*).

Module. A part of a larger system with defined input, processing, and output. Ideally, the module could be developed separately from other modules and can be modified without affecting the rest of the system (*p. 545*).

MVS (Multiple Virtual System). The primary IBM mainframe operating system (*p. 227*).

Network. The physical and logical connections between computers needed for communications to take place (*p. 222*).

Network interface card. The card in a microcomputer that provides the connection to the network, usually either an Ethernet or a Token Ring card (*p. 235*).

New purchase invoices file. Transaction file containing all verified purchase invoices since the last processing date (*p. 355*).

New purchase orders file. Transaction file generated as new purchase orders are created in the processing of inventory (*p. 393*).

New sales invoices file. Transaction file containing all verified sales invoices created since the last processing of accounts receivable (*p. 343*).

New sales orders file. Transaction file containing all sales orders received since the last processing date (*p. 384*).

Node. A device on a network that receives or generates messages (*p. 244*).

Noncurrent assets. Those assets whose future benefit is expected to extend beyond the next accounting period (*p. 647*).

Not ready status. A Bedford-specific module status that does not allow transactions to be entered in that module (*p. 454*).

Object program. The original set of instructions (source program) translated (compiled) into machine language. It is the object program that is understood by the processor (*p. 84*).

Off-line. Hardware devices and data which are not directly accessible to the processor and require some human action to make them available to the processor (*p. 85*).

Off-page connector. A symbol used to show where and how flowcharts on separate pages fit together (*p. 17*).

Office automation. Use of computer systems to assist normal office functions, such as word processing to help generate documents, and electronic mail to help communicate between employees (*p. 493*).

On-line. Computer hardware devices which have direct communication access to the processor; data which are always available to the processor (*p. 85*).

On-line transaction processing (OLTP). Direct interaction with the computer is possible for questions and answers and for the processing of data. Files are always current (*p. 93*).

On-page connector. A circle containing a number on a flowchart indicating the point where the flow is being interrupted and another keyed with the same number indicating where the flow is picked up (*p. 17*).

Open orders by customer report. This report lists all the sales orders that have been accepted from customers, but not filled (*p. 378*).

Open payables listing. Output report of the accounts payable module showing total amounts owed to each vendor, discounts available from each, and the due dates of each amount (*p. 349*).

Open purchase invoices file. File of all purchase invoices not yet paid with one record for each unpaid invoice (*p. 355*).

Operating system. A set of internally stored general instructions which control and coordinate the activities of the various hardware devices (*p. 83*).

Operator instructions. Element of programming which details what tasks a system operator must do, such as mount tapes and distribute output (*p. 135, p. 581*).

Order processing module. Point of original entry of sales orders, returns, and adjustments from customers; intended to provide fast and accurate processing of orders from customers (*p. 376*).

Order status report. This report is used to point out situations in need of management attention by identifying important characteristics of each manufacturing order (*p. 437*).

Order transaction (update) register. Order processing output report which lists all new orders accepted; provides an audit trail for all orders that will ultimately update the various master files (*p. 378*).

Organization chart. Chart designed to portray the structure of responsibility and authority in the company; provides a pictorial representation of the way in which the firm is structured (*p. 19*).

Organization structure. A description of where authority and responsibility lie in the company (*p. 528*).

OSI (Open Systems Interconnect). A multilayered protocol reference model put forward by the International Standards Organization for use with wide area networks (*p. 242*).

Owners' equity. Owners' claims against the assets of a business resulting from owners' investment in the business; it is a residual claim on all assets not claimed by outsiders (*p. 646*).

Packet switching. Technique for breaking computer messages down into smaller blocks called packets. The packets are sent separately from the origin of the message and are reassembled at the destination (*p. 234*).

Padding. A means of issuing checks to others and then appropriating them by either (1) issuing checks to employees who have quit or been fired, or (2) adding fake employees to the payroll (*p. 52*).

Parallel operation. Process of using both the old system and the new system at the same time and then comparing the results (*p. 587*).

PAYABLE module. The Bedford module that processes all transactions with vendors (*p. 454*).

Payroll module. Application for processing and reporting all payroll-related expense and cash flow transactions. Also, a Bedford module (*p. 357*).

Peripheral. External hardware controlled by the processor, including input/output devices and storage devices such as tape drives, disk drives, and printers (*p. 85*).

Permanent accounts. Balance sheet accounts (for example, assets, liabilities, and owners' equity); unlike revenue, expense, dividend, and withdrawal accounts, permanent accounts are not closed at the end of the accounting period (*p. 676*).

Permanent file. The permanent repository for documents (*p. 16*).

PERT/CPM network (Project Evaluation Review Technique/Critical Path Method network). A semistructured decision model characterized by networks which show a sequence of tasks to be performed in carrying out a project and the interrelationships between activities (*p. 268*).

Petty cash. Cash kept on hand to pay for small expenses, such as postage due, which cannot be handled conveniently by check (*p. 53*).

Physical inventory. An actual count of inventory items on hand at a specific point in time (*p. 60*).

Picking list. A list based on the customer order, which details the items ordered by name and number so that the order can be filled in the warehouse (*p. 378*).

Plex structure. A multi-level file structure where an element can have more than one parent (*p. 170*).

Policy and procedures manual. Documentation of overall company policies and the methods by which the company processes transactions (*p. 585*).

Polling. Method of controlling terminals, usually by minicomputers, where the host computer cycles from one terminal to the next checking to see if there is a message from that terminal (*p. 231*).

Posting. Transferring debit and credit amounts and audit trail information from the journal to individual accounts in the ledger (*p. 671*).

Posting reference. In a journal, the account number which indicates that the transaction has been posted to the ledger; in a ledger, the journal and page from which the amount has been posted (*p. 670*).

Preliminary general ledger. A comprehensive ledger showing each account with its beginning balance, total debits and credits for the period, the ending balance, and net change (*p. 415*).

Primary claims. The nature of outsiders' (liability-holders) claims on assets; their claims must be satisfied before those of the owners (*p. 652*).

Primary key. A unique identifier that allows the computer to unmistakably pick out one and only one record (*p. 155*).

Pro forma statements. Projected/budgeted financial statements against which actual results can be compared as a control device (*p. 317*).

Procedures manual. Written manual detailing company policies and procedures; used to train new employees in the operation of a system and to ensure that the same types of transactions will always be handled in the same way (*p. 46*).

Processor. The computer in a computer system. The processor directs the activities of the entire system. Sometimes called the central processing unit or CPU (*p. 84*).

Product cost update report. This report gives current cost data for products (*p. 427*).

Product data management (PDM) module. A manufacturing module which contains permanent and semipermanent data about a product and the manufacturing process (*p. 320*).

Product structure master file. This file states the relationship between each type of raw material, component, or sub-assembly and the finished product (*p. 427*).

Production costing module. A manufacturing module which tracks detailed costs of production and deviations (variances) from budgets and standards (*p. 322*).

Production monitoring module. A manufacturing module which monitors the production flow and workload and analyzes work center efficiency (*p. 322*).

Profit plan. A projected/budgeted/pro forma income statement (*p. 317*).

Program development. Writing of computer programs to satisfy a set system specification or applications need (*p. 579*).

Program documentation. Flowcharts and narrative which explain (1) how to operate the program and (2) how the program works, to aid in future modification (*p. 135*).

Program listing. A list of the source language statements of a computer program (*p. 581*).

Programmed controls. Internal controls built into applications programs, such as reasonableness tests or terminal dialogue that are designed to make incorrect data entry, whether accidental or deliberate, impossible (*p. 132*).

Programmer. Person who converts program specifications into a programming language, including writing, documenting, and maintaining the computer programs (*p. 83*).

Programming. Writing the computer programs, developing test data, testing the programs, and preparing documentation (*p. 508*).

Projections. Operations that use one table to create another by identifying the name of the desired table and selecting the data-items that should be in the table (*p. 192*).

Purchase order. An order for materials, supplies, or components from a specific vendor under specifically requested terms (*p. 9*).

Purchase requisition. A request by a department or work station for the acquisition of materials, supplies, or components (*p. 430*).

Purchases cycle. The set of activities concerned with the purchase of merchandise from vendors, from the creation of purchase requisitions to the receipt of goods (*p. 11*).

Purchases journal. A special journal typically used to record all credit purchases of assets (*p. 348*).

Quantity price file. Permanent file of constant data on the prices of each item and appropriate price limits, breaks, markup and discount percentages (*p. 384*).

Queries. Questions asked about the contents of a data base, such as which are the five best customers in a particular region (*p. 188*).

Query and analysis. Use of the computer to respond to a question (query) and to perform desired calculations and processing (analysis) (*p. 493*).

Query-by-example (QBE). A method of accessing a data base by using a schematic diagram of the data files and their contents to show which data-items are desired (*p. 188*).

Random access. Process of storing data in, or getting data from, a storage device in such a manner that the desired data location can be gone to directly, as opposed to sequentially scanning the data (*p. 86*).

***Ready* status.** A Bedford-specific module status that allows the entry of transactions in that module (*p. 455*).

Real-time processing. On-line processing where the appropriate files are updated immediately as transactions occur, as opposed to batch processing (*p. 92*).

RECEIVABLE module. The Bedford module that processes all transactions with customers (*p. 454*).

Record. A set or collection of related data-items. The file is then a collection of related records (*p. 155*).

Record count. Count of transactions by a program which is compared to a manual count to identify any loss of transactions (*p. 133*).

Relational data base. A data base that is based on tables (flat files) and relations between them. All data are stored and accessed in the row and column format of a table (*p. 173*).

Relational DBMS (RDBMS). A data base management system that uses the relational data base approach. They are characterized by ease of use but can be slow in processing transactions (*p. 189*).

Report writing program. A program that reads information from data files and generates a printout analyzing the information (*p. 158*).

Residual claims. Nature of owners' claim on assets; owners can claim all assets which are not claimed by outsiders (*p. 652*).

Retained earnings. The portion of owners' equity which measures assets created by the successful operation of a business and retained in the business rather than distributed to owners (*p. 652*).

Revenue. Measures increases in, or inflows of, assets resulting from the profit-seeking activities of a business during an accounting period (*p. 654*).

Ring network. A network configuration that connects computers in a circle (*p. 236*).

RJE (Remote job entry). Batch processing with remote data transmission (*p. 89*).

Routing list/routing report. Document which gives the exact paths through the manufacturing process for each product (*p. 426–27*).

Routing/work center master file. Provides information on each specific operation required for each different manufacturing routing (*p. 427*).

Row. A row in a relational data base corresponds to a record (*p. 192*).

SAA (Systems Application Architecture). The IBM plan to ensure consistency in use between different types of computers and to facilitate disparate computers working together in cooperative processing (*p. 241*).

Sales analysis module. Application designed to generate reports to aid management in predicting future sales activity and profitability for the business, as well as evaluating the past performance of salespeople, products, and customers (*p. 394*).

Sales and profit by customer report. Sales analysis output report focusing on customer buying volumes as well as absolute and relative figures for profits resulting from each customer (*p. 398–99*).

Sales and profit by item report. Sales analysis output report showing a breakdown of sales by item and providing information on individual and relative item profitability (*p. 397–98*).

Sales and profit by salesperson report. Sales analysis output report showing a breakdown of sales by salesperson and sales territory and profit by salesperson and sales territory (*p. 396–97*).

Sales and purchases subsystem. A subsystem consisting of the order processing, inventory management, and sales analysis modules (*p. 314*).

Sales cycle. The set of activities concerned with selling goods or services to customers, from the receipt of a customer order to the filling of the order and the shipment of goods (*p. 10*).

Sales journal. A special journal used to record the credit sales of goods to customers. Sometimes called an invoice register (*p. 338*).

Sales slip. A document made out to verify the goods and terms of a sale (*p. 8*).

Schema. A diagram giving a representation of a file structure and the relationship of data between files (*p. 167*).

Second normal form. Data are split into tables so that data depending on components of the primary key are not repeated (*p. 194*).

Secondary key. Data-items that identify a record, but do not provide a unique identification, such as a zip code (*p. 156*).

Self-checking number. A number with a final digit added to identify transposition errors (*p. 133*).

Semistructured decision. A partially structured decision, where the final decision requires the judgment of the decision maker (*p. 257*).

Sequential access. Process of storing data in, or getting data from, a storage device in such a manner that data must be scanned in the same order as it physically resides in the file, usually organized in numerical order (*p. 86*).

Sequential organization. File organization in which records in the file are sequenced by the primary key. Access is provided by reading through a file until a match is found for the primary key (*p. 162*).

Serial organization. File organization in which records are placed in the file in no particular order. Access to a particular record is provided by reading through the file until the value on a record matches the given primary key (*p. 162*).

Service bureau. Computer services companies that receive input from their customers, process the data, and then return the results (*p. 102*).

Slack time. In a PERT/CPM network, the difference between the earliest time and the latest time; the amount of time an activity could be delayed without delaying completion of the entire project (*p. 272*).

SNA (System Network Architecture). A network and communications design by IBM (*p. 228*).

Software. The instructions which direct a computer system, including the operating system, compiler, utility, and applications programs (*p. 83*).

Source document. An original document created when a transaction occurs which supports and authorizes the transaction (*p. 7*).

Source language. A high-level programming language like BASIC, COBOL, or FORTRAN which must be translated by a compiler into a form that can instruct the machine directly; the problem solution can be expressed in the source language more easily than in the machine language (*p. 84*).

Source program. An application program written in a programming language (*p. 84*).

Special journal. A journal used to record repetitive transactions in a manner that facilitates classification and internal control (*p. 679*).

Star network. A network configuration where a central or host computer is connected to terminals or other computers (*p. 231*).

Start date. A Bedford-specific term indicating the first day of business activity covered by the accounting period (*p. 464*).

Statement of objectives. Identification of the overall purpose and specific objectives of the proposed system (*p. 507*).

Statement of retained earnings. Financial statement which represents the interrelationship of the balance sheet and the income statement; net income is added and dividends subtracted from beginning retained earnings to determine ending retained earnings (*p. 656*).

Status access. Use of the computer to check the current condition and progress of some aspect of the organization's operations, such as a particular customer's order in process (*p. 493*).

Stockholders' equity. Owners' claims against the assets of a corporation resulting from their direct investment (purchase of stock) and indirect investment (net income − dividends) in the corporation (*p. 646*).

Store-and-forward system. Method of data communication which stores incoming messages by copying them to a storage medium and later transmitting them to their destinations only after the entire message is received (*p. 134*).

Structured decision. Decisions that are repetitive and use a predetermined series of steps to reach a conclusion (*p. 257*).

Structured programming. Disciplined approach to program design which uses only three control structures in the program flowchart: (1) sequence, (2) condition, and (3) loop; usually includes thorough documentation (*p. 577*).

Structured query language (SQL). A language for interacting with relational data bases. SQL is not a full application development language (*p. 188*).

Subschema. A representation that extracts a part of the overall data and file structure needed in one particular application program (*p. 167*).

Subsidiary ledger. A ledger which provides a detailed breakdown of summary information appearing in a general ledger control account; subsidiary ledgers are most commonly used for payables and receivables (*p. 677*).

Substantive testing. Auditor examination of general ledger balances, such as accounts receivable or inventory, to ensure they are properly stated (*p. 607*).

System analysis. The process of determining how well a system accomplishes its objectives, pointing out deficiencies or omissions, and making recommendations for improvements. Documentation in the form of written descriptions and flowcharts of the present system are done to identify the information processing flow (*p. 507*).

System analysis report. A report which documents and supports all work done in the system analysis and all recommendations made to improve the system (*p. 529*).

System analyst. The person or group analyzing the system and developing the system analysis report. Also, one who works with users to define data processing projects, formulate programs, define solutions and develop specifications for programmers (*p. 130*).

System design. System requirements needed to attain the system objectives as well as an analysis of the costs and benefits of the proposed design (*p. 508*).

System development process. The overall process of developing a system including (1) system analysis, (2) statement of objectives, (3) system design, (4) system specification, (5) programming, (6) implementation, and (7) evaluation (*p. 507*).

System documentation. An overall view of the system, including flowcharts and narrative which explain how a system works, the input needed, the control features, and the output produced (*p. 135*).

System flowchart. A flowchart of an entire system, including processing steps and document flows (*p. 13*).

SYSTEM module. The Bedford module that establishes the company on the computer and configures the accounting package to receive and process company data and print reports (*p. 454*).

System programmer. Person who maintains the operating system and adapts its capabilities to the particular company needs (*p. 130*).

System specification. Detailing of a proposed system and how it will work, including the exact hardware and software environment, input and output documents, program flowcharts, and complete details of files to be maintained (*p. 508*).

Table. A representation of data in a row and column format. All data in a relational DBMS are stored in and accessed through tables (*p. 171*).

Tangible benefits. The system benefits that can be expressed in dollars, such as a reduction of direct operating expenses (*p. 549*).

Tax table and deduction table file. Permanent constant file composed of the tax and deduction amounts or percentages necessary to determine the amounts of payroll tax withholdings (*p. 364*).

TCP/IP (Transmission Control Protocol/Internet Protocol). A method developed for the Department of Defense computers for communication between computers and between different types of networks (*p. 234*).

Temporary accounts. Non-balance-sheet accounts, such as revenue, expense, dividends, and withdrawals, which are closed out at the end of an accounting period (*p. 675*).

Temporary file. A file where documents reside only for an interim period, or until a specific event occurs (*p. 16*).

Terminal. The beginning or end in a system flowchart. The terminal generally shows something coming in from outside the system or going from the inside of the system to the outside (*p. 14*). Also, a hardware device (*p. 311*).

Terminal dialogue. The "conversation" between the computer program and the user, as the system prompts for information and the operator gives a response (*p. 132*).

Test data. An element of programming. Data for which the results are known and which can, therefore, be used to check the accuracy of a specific program's processing (*p. 580*).

Test deck. Test transaction data, usually used by an auditor, which can be processed to see whether the computer system processes information correctly (*p. 619*).

Third normal form. Tabular structure of data where data redundancies not involving the primary key are eliminated (*p. 196*).

Token ring. The most widely used method of communication on local area networks (LANs) that use a ring configuration. The primary LAN method of IBM (*p. 236*).

Transaction. Events or activities that impact the basic accounting equation of $A = L + OE$ in some fashion and are recorded in transaction processing systems (*p. 669*).

Transaction file. A file containing transaction data which were processed to update master file account balances (*p. 159, p. 312*).

Transaction processing. Updating of all appropriate components of the accounting system as transactions occur. This can be done manually or with a computer-based system (*p. 81*).

Transaction processing accounting system. A system that records the details and effects of accounting transactions, updates the appropriate documents and files, and produces external reporting financial statements and reports (*p. 5*).

Transaction processing program. A program which updates the master file balances as required by the transactions that occur and which then stores the transaction information in a transaction file (*p. 158*).

Tree structure. A hierarchical file structure. A tree is composed of a hierarchy of elements, where each element can have only one parent (*p. 169*).

Trial balance. A summary listing of the debit or credit balances of all accounts in the ledger; this listing provides an overview of the accounts and ensures the equality of debits and credits (*p. 672*).

UNIX. An operating system for minicomputers designed by Bell Laboratories. It is the dominant operating system for minicomputers (*p. 232*).

Unnormalized. Data that is not arranged in the form of a table with rows and columns. Repeating groups may appear in the data (*p. 201*).

Unpaid vouchers file. A list of open and not yet paid vouchers filed by their due date (*p. 685*).

Unstructured decision. Complex decisions for which no established method of solution exists and/or decisions that have not previously been addressed (*p. 257*).

Updating. A process of inputting a file and then changing one or more of the data-items in the file by the addition of new current period activity and outputting the file for future processing (*p. 312*).

User instructions. Element of programming that explains to the user how to operate the program (*p. 579*).

User interface. A user friendly mechanism, such as menus, for the manager to interact with the decision support system (*p. 259*).

VAN (Value Added Network). Public network based on packet switching that allows remote use of a host computer with a local telephone call (*p. 234*).

Vendor analysis report. Report provided on demand by the accounts payable application area showing purchase activity, discounts taken, and discounts lost with each supplier for the current period, year-to-date, or previous year (*p. 349*).

Vendor detail report. A Bedford-specific report giving the accounts payable subsidiary ledger (*p. 459*).

Vendor master file. Master file which serves as the accounts payable subsidiary ledger in a computer-based system; provides information on purchases from and payments to each vendor as well as amounts owed to each vendor at any time (*p. 355*).

Vendor summary report. A Bedford-specific report giving a list of amounts owed to each vendor by age (*p. 459*).

Views. Logical tables of data created using a relational data base management system that can be queried by the user (*p. 190*).

Voucher. Document used to authorize cash disbursements which describes the purpose of the cash disbursement and the person who authorized it (*p. 685*).

Voucher register. A record of vouchers issued, listing the vouchers in numerical order (*p. 685*).

Voucher system. A method of controlling cash which uses vouchers to authorize each cash disbursement. The voucher register and check register replace the purchases journal, cash disbursements journal, and accounts payable subsidiary ledger (*p. 685*).

WAN (Wide Area Network). A computer network that spreads over a large geographic area (*p. 241*).

Work center analysis report. Includes information on the utilization, queue sizes, output, and efficiency for each work center (*p. 437*).

Work lists by work center. A list showing the orders running, waiting, and arriving for each work center (*p. 438*).

INDEX

An entry in **bold** can be referenced in the Glossary or in the text (bold numbers) for its precise definition.